How to Prepare for the Advanced Placement Examination

Physics B

JONATHAN S. WOLF

PHYSICS TEACHER - SCARSDALE HIGH SCHOOL
SCARSDALE, NEW YORK

BARRON'S

All inquiries should be addressed to:
Barron's Educational Series, Inc.
250 Wireless Boulevard
Hauppauge, New York 11788

Library of Congress Catalog Card No. 95-12040
International Standard Book No. 0-8120-9031-4

Library of Congress Cataloging-in-Publication Data

Wolf, Jonathan S.
How to prepare for the advanced placement examination : AP physics B / Jonathan S. Wolf.
p. cm.
Includes index.
ISBN 0-8120-9031-4
1. Physics—Examinations—Study guides. 2. Universities and colleges—United States—Entrance examinations—Study guides. 3. Advanced placement programs (Education)—Study guides. [1. Physics–Examinations—Study guides. 2. Universities and colleges—Entrance examinations—Study guides. 3. Advanced placement programs (Education)—Study guides.] I. Title.
QC32.W73 1995 95-12040
530'.0076—dc20 CIP
AC

PRINTED IN THE UNITED STATES OF AMERICA
6789 100 987654321

Contents

Preface

In this review book, you will be taught several strategies for making your learning and studying more efficient. These are skills that will always be useful and that you can apply across the curriculum for many different subjects.

Each topical review chapter contains ten multiple-choice questions that differ in variety, style, and level of difficulty. Their purpose is to provide you with a balanced set of questions that test your level of understanding of the review material. Some questions may be easier or more difficult than the actual AP Physics B exam questions because, unlike the actual test, which covers a broad range of subjects, each chapter in this book deals with a specific topic. In addition to the multiple-choice questions there are three free-response problems that also vary in difficulty. Full solutions and explanations follow the questions. Additional solving strategies are also provided.

In Chapter 2, there is a diagnostic examination designed to measure your initial level of understanding or to use for practice. At the end of the book, two additional sample examinations are provided. Each examination is fully explained with solutions and guidelines.

Many people contributed to this effort. I am grateful to Pat Wilson, Project Editor at Barron's Educational Series, for all of her ideas and suggestions; to Todd Gordon, for helping to facilitate the early stages of this project; and to my wife Karen and my daughters Marissa and Ilana for their understanding, love, and support.

Scarsdale, New York
June 1995

Jonathan S. Wolf

CHAPTER 1

The Structure of the Advanced Placement Examination

1.1 Introduction

When you enter an advanced placement physics course, you are preparing for a great adventure in exploration. If this is your first physics course in high school, then the wonders of the mechanical universe are about to be unfolded before you. If this is your second course in physics, then what you previously learned was only the tip of a vast iceberg of knowledge.

This book is designed to prepare you for the Advanced Placement Examination in Physics B. This examination is administered by the Educational Testing Service in Princeton, New Jersey. The designation "Physics B" indicates that this is a non-calculus based survey course in college level physics.

1.2 The Structure of the Advanced Placement Examination in Physics

The Advanced Placement Examination in Physics B consists of two parts. Part I contains seventy multiple choice questions while Part II contains six free response problems. Both parts are weighted at fifty percent of your reported score (on a scale of 1–5; a "5" being the best score). The entire exam takes three hours to complete.

Answer Sheet: Diagnostic Test

1. Ⓐ Ⓑ Ⓒ Ⓓ Ⓔ
2. Ⓐ Ⓑ Ⓒ Ⓓ Ⓔ
3. Ⓐ Ⓑ Ⓒ Ⓓ Ⓔ
4. Ⓐ Ⓑ Ⓒ Ⓓ Ⓔ
5. Ⓐ Ⓑ Ⓒ Ⓓ Ⓔ
6. Ⓐ Ⓑ Ⓒ Ⓓ Ⓔ
7. Ⓐ Ⓑ Ⓒ Ⓓ Ⓔ
8. Ⓐ Ⓑ Ⓒ Ⓓ Ⓔ
9. Ⓐ Ⓑ Ⓒ Ⓓ Ⓔ
10. Ⓐ Ⓑ Ⓒ Ⓓ Ⓔ
11. Ⓐ Ⓑ Ⓒ Ⓓ Ⓔ
12. Ⓐ Ⓑ Ⓒ Ⓓ Ⓔ
13. Ⓐ Ⓑ Ⓒ Ⓓ Ⓔ
14. Ⓐ Ⓑ Ⓒ Ⓓ Ⓔ
15. Ⓐ Ⓑ Ⓒ Ⓓ Ⓔ
16. Ⓐ Ⓑ Ⓒ Ⓓ Ⓔ
17. Ⓐ Ⓑ Ⓒ Ⓓ Ⓔ
18. Ⓐ Ⓑ Ⓒ Ⓓ Ⓔ
19. Ⓐ Ⓑ Ⓒ Ⓓ Ⓔ
20. Ⓐ Ⓑ Ⓒ Ⓓ Ⓔ
21. Ⓐ Ⓑ Ⓒ Ⓓ Ⓔ
22. Ⓐ Ⓑ Ⓒ Ⓓ Ⓔ
23. Ⓐ Ⓑ Ⓒ Ⓓ Ⓔ
24. Ⓐ Ⓑ Ⓒ Ⓓ Ⓔ
25. Ⓐ Ⓑ Ⓒ Ⓓ Ⓔ
26. Ⓐ Ⓑ Ⓒ Ⓓ Ⓔ
27. Ⓐ Ⓑ Ⓒ Ⓓ Ⓔ
28. Ⓐ Ⓑ Ⓒ Ⓓ Ⓔ
29. Ⓐ Ⓑ Ⓒ Ⓓ Ⓔ
30. Ⓐ Ⓑ Ⓒ Ⓓ Ⓔ
31. Ⓐ Ⓑ Ⓒ Ⓓ Ⓔ
32. Ⓐ Ⓑ Ⓒ Ⓓ Ⓔ
33. Ⓐ Ⓑ Ⓒ Ⓓ Ⓔ
34. Ⓐ Ⓑ Ⓒ Ⓓ Ⓔ
35. Ⓐ Ⓑ Ⓒ Ⓓ Ⓔ
36. Ⓐ Ⓑ Ⓒ Ⓓ Ⓔ
37. Ⓐ Ⓑ Ⓒ Ⓓ Ⓔ
38. Ⓐ Ⓑ Ⓒ Ⓓ Ⓔ
39. Ⓐ Ⓑ Ⓒ Ⓓ Ⓔ
40. Ⓐ Ⓑ Ⓒ Ⓓ Ⓔ
41. Ⓐ Ⓑ Ⓒ Ⓓ Ⓔ
42. Ⓐ Ⓑ Ⓒ Ⓓ Ⓔ
43. Ⓐ Ⓑ Ⓒ Ⓓ Ⓔ
44. Ⓐ Ⓑ Ⓒ Ⓓ Ⓔ
45. Ⓐ Ⓑ Ⓒ Ⓓ Ⓔ
46. Ⓐ Ⓑ Ⓒ Ⓓ Ⓔ
47. Ⓐ Ⓑ Ⓒ Ⓓ Ⓔ
48. Ⓐ Ⓑ Ⓒ Ⓓ Ⓔ
49. Ⓐ Ⓑ Ⓒ Ⓓ Ⓔ
50. Ⓐ Ⓑ Ⓒ Ⓓ Ⓔ
51. Ⓐ Ⓑ Ⓒ Ⓓ Ⓔ
52. Ⓐ Ⓑ Ⓒ Ⓓ Ⓔ
53. Ⓐ Ⓑ Ⓒ Ⓓ Ⓔ
54. Ⓐ Ⓑ Ⓒ Ⓓ Ⓔ
55. Ⓐ Ⓑ Ⓒ Ⓓ Ⓔ
56. Ⓐ Ⓑ Ⓒ Ⓓ Ⓔ
57. Ⓐ Ⓑ Ⓒ Ⓓ Ⓔ
58. Ⓐ Ⓑ Ⓒ Ⓓ Ⓔ
59. Ⓐ Ⓑ Ⓒ Ⓓ Ⓔ
60. Ⓐ Ⓑ Ⓒ Ⓓ Ⓔ
61. Ⓐ Ⓑ Ⓒ Ⓓ Ⓔ
62. Ⓐ Ⓑ Ⓒ Ⓓ Ⓔ
63. Ⓐ Ⓑ Ⓒ Ⓓ Ⓔ
64. Ⓐ Ⓑ Ⓒ Ⓓ Ⓔ
65. Ⓐ Ⓑ Ⓒ Ⓓ Ⓔ
66. Ⓐ Ⓑ Ⓒ Ⓓ Ⓔ
67. Ⓐ Ⓑ Ⓒ Ⓓ Ⓔ
68. Ⓐ Ⓑ Ⓒ Ⓓ Ⓔ
69. Ⓐ Ⓑ Ⓒ Ⓓ Ⓔ
70. Ⓐ Ⓑ Ⓒ Ⓓ Ⓔ

CHAPTER 2

Diagnostic Examination

The purpose of a diagnostic examination is to assess your beginning level of understanding before reviewing the topical material. Since ETS prohibits use of its examinations in review books, practice examinations are necessarily simulated. In some cases, the questions may be slightly more difficult or easier than those on an actual exam. Additionally, since the awarding of points for Section II—Free Response varies from year to year, as do the cutoffs for the various AP grades, it is difficult to predict what your grade on the actual exam would be from your performance on a practice test. However, as the saying goes, "Practice makes perfect," and taking the practice examinations will almost certainly improve your performance on the actual examination. After taking the Diagnostic Test, go over the solutions and explanations that follow and then plan your further studies accordingly.

Chapters 3, 4, and 5 present an introduction to concept identification and problem-solving skills that are integral parts of any successful learning experience. Topical review of material from the AP Physics B curriculum begins with Chapter 7 and continues through Chapter 28. Following the topical review chapters are two more practice examinations, also with fully explained solutions, a glossary, and a mathematical appendix. A cumulative index of material appears at the end of the book. Note: Vectors are represented in boldface type.

Good luck!

TABLE 2.1 Useful Constants

1 atomic mass unit	$1\ \mu = 1.66 \times 10^{-27}$ kg
Rest mass of the proton	$m_p = 1.67 \times 10^{-27}$ kg
Rest mass of the neutron	$m_n = 1.67 \times 10^{-27}$ kg
Rest mass of the electron	$m_e = 9.11 \times 10^{-31}$ kg
Magnitude of the electron charge	$e = 1.60 \times 10^{-19}$ C
Avogadro's number	$N_0 = 6.02 \times 10^{23}$ per mole
Universal gas constant	$R = 8.32$ J/(mole · K)
Boltzmann's constant	$k_B = 1.38 \times 10^{-23}$ J/K
Speed of light	$c = 3 \times 10^8$ m/s
Planck's constant	$h = 6.63 \times 10^{-34}$ J · s $= 4.14 \times 10^{-15}$ eV · s
1 electron volt	1 eV $= 1.6 \times 10^{-19}$ J
Vacuum permittivity	$\epsilon_0 = 8.85 \times 10^{-12}$ C²/Nm²
Coulomb's law constant	$k = 1/4\pi\epsilon_0 = 9 \times 10^9$ N · m²/C²
Vacuum permeability	$\mu_0 = 4\pi \times 10^{-7}$ Wb/(A · m)
Magnetic constant	$k' = k/c^2 = \mu_0/4\pi = 10^{-7}$ Wb/(A · m)
Acceleration due to gravity at Earth's surface	$g = 9.8$ m/s²
Universal gravitational constant	$G = 6.67 \times 10^{-11}$ m³/(kg · s²)
1 atmosphere pressure	1 atm $= 1.0 \times 10^5$ N/m² $= 1.0 \times 10^5$ Pa
1 nanometer	1 nm $= 1.0 \times 10^{-9}$m

For this examination the following conventions hold:

I. All frames of reference are assumed to be inertial unless otherwise indicated.

II. Electrical current will follow the direction of a positive charge (conventional current).

III. For any isolated charge, the potential at infinity is taken to be equal to zero.

DIAGNOSTIC TEST

Section I

Multiple-Choice Questions

70 questions
90 minutes
50 percent of total grade

Directions: For each of the questions or incomplete statements below there are five choices. In each case select the best answer or completion and fill in the corresponding oval on the answer sheet.

1. Which of the following quantities is *not* a vector?
   (A) Momentum
   (B) Displacement
   (C) Acceleration
   (D) Work
   (E) Impulse

2. A 5-gram ball is thrown upward with an initial velocity of 30 meters per second. If air resistance is neglected, how long will the ball take to reach its maximum height?
   (A) 3.06 s
   (B) 39.80 s
   (C) 6.90 s
   (D) 1.75 s
   (E) 19.6 s

3. A projectile is launched at an angle θ to the horizontal with an initial velocity **v**. In the absence of any air resistance, which of the following statements is correct?
   (A) The horizontal velocity increases and then decreases during the flight.
   (B) The horizontal velocity remains constant.
   (C) The vertical velocity remains constant.
   (D) The horizontal velocity decreases and then increases during the flight.
   (E) At the projectile's maximum height, the acceleration vector is zero.

GO ON TO THE NEXT PAGE ➤

4. Which pair of graphs represents one-dimensional uniformly accelerated motion?

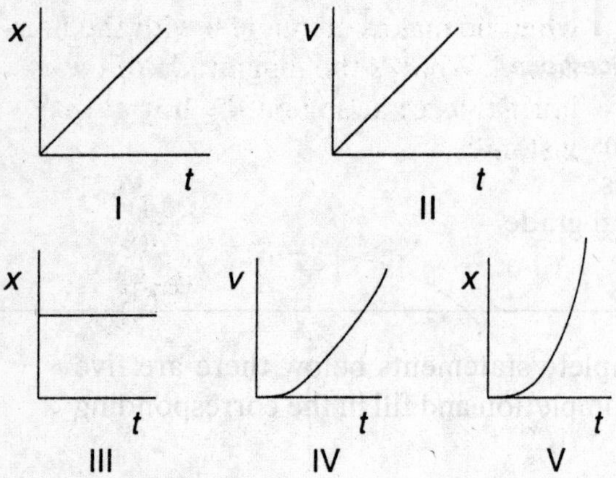

(A) I and IV
(B) II and III
(C) II and V
(D) IV and V
(E) II and V

5. A rock is thrown horizontally off the top of a building that is 7.5 meters above the ground. It is observed that the rock lands 22 meters away from the base of the building. With what velocity was the rock thrown?
(A) 1.24 m/s
(B) 2.77 m/s
(C) 6.35 m/s
(D) 14.67 m/s
(E) 17.74 m/s

6. A student swings a 3.5-gram rubber stopper in a horizontal circle over her head. The length of the string is 0.6 meter. The stopper is observed to complete 10 revolutions in 11.7 seconds. What is the tangential velocity of the stopper at any time *t*?
(A) 1.17 m/s
(B) 3.22 m/s
(C) 4.5 m/s
(D) 6.27 m/s
(E) 8.63 m/s

7. A projectile launched at a 25-degree angle to the ground lands 1650 meters away along a flat plane. What was the initial velocity of the projectile?
(A) 145 m/s
(B) 125 m/s
(C) 130 m/s
(D) 150 m/s
(E) 115 m/s

8. Which of the following statements is correct about a projectile in flight?
(A) Its acceleration increases during its flight.
(B) Its acceleration decreases during its flight.
(C) Its acceleration decreases, then increases, during its flight.
(D) Its acceleration increases, then decreases, during its flight.
(E) Its acceleration remains constant.

9. A 15-newton force is applied to a mass *M* that is adjacent to a wall, as shown below. If the mass is 2 kilograms, the force that the wall exerts on the mass is equal to

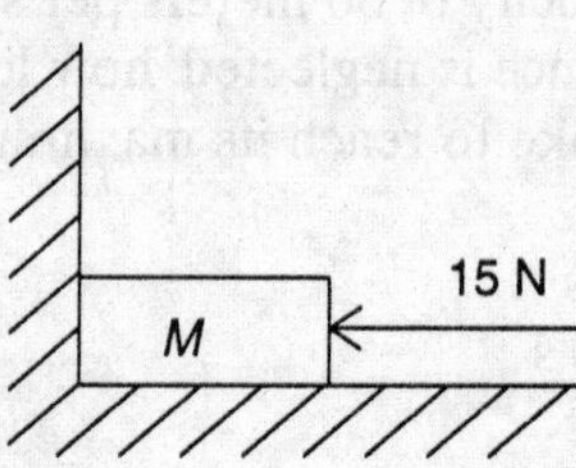

(A) 0 N
(B) 2 N
(C) 15 N
(D) 19.6 N
(E) 30 N

GO ON TO THE NEXT PAGE ➤

10. In the diagram below, a force **F** is applied to a mass M at an angle θ to the horizontal. The mass is moving along a flat, smooth horizontal surface. What is the magnitude of the normal force?

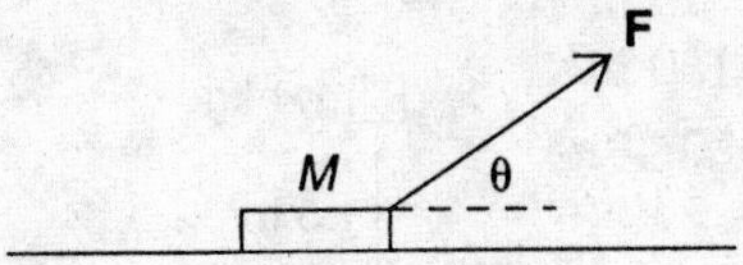

(A) $M\mathbf{g} - \mathbf{F}\sin\theta$
(B) $M\mathbf{g} + \mathbf{F}\sin\theta$
(C) $M\mathbf{g} / \mathbf{F}\sin\theta$
(D) $\mathbf{F}\sin\theta / M\mathbf{g}$
(E) $M\mathbf{g}$

11. In the situation shown below, a 2-kilogram mass is attached by a light string over a frictionless pulley to a 5-kilogram mass hanging below. The 2-kilogram mass rests on a frictionless surface. If the system is released, what will be the acceleration of both masses?

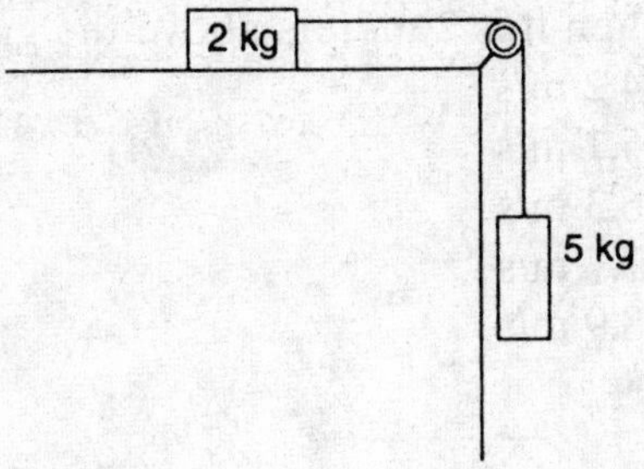

(A) 7 m/s^2
(B) 9.8 m/s^2
(C) 12.2 m/s^2
(D) 15 m/s^2
(E) 18.5 m/s^2

12. A mass M rests on top of a frictionless inclined plane. Which of the following statements is correct about the normal force acting on the mass as the angle of elevation increases?
(A) The normal force increases.
(B) The normal force decreases.
(C) The normal force increases, then decreases.
(D) The normal force decreases, then increases.
(E) The normal force remains constant.

13. A 45-kilogram boy is sliding down a frictionless hemispherical surface with a radius R as shown in the diagram below. The boy loses contact with the surface when he makes an angle θ with the horizontal. What is the magnitude of the normal force acting on the boy at that instant?

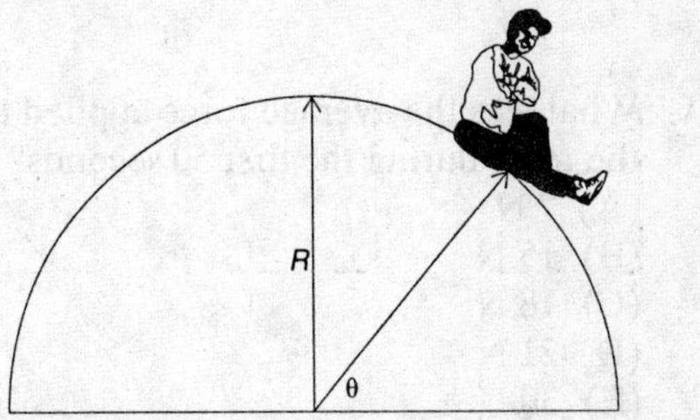

(A) Mg
(B) $Mg\,R\cos\theta$
(C) $Mg(\cos\theta - R)$
(D) $Mg\cos\theta$
(E) 0

14. A crate weighing 15 newtons is moving along a horizontal rough surface with a constant velocity **v**. The coefficient of kinetic friction between the crate and the surface is 0.17. What is the magnitude of the force maintaining the constant velocity?
(A) 15 N
(B) 17.55 N
(C) 12.45 N
(D) 2.55 N
(E) 0 N

Questions 15–17 are based on the graph of force versus time shown below for a 15-kilogram mass.

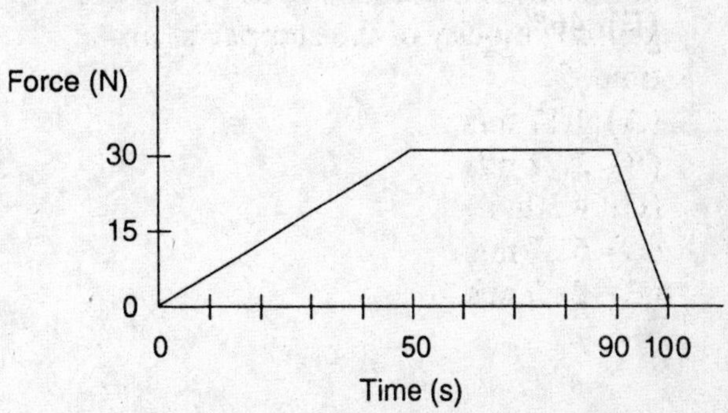

GO ON TO THE NEXT PAGE ➤

15. What was the total impulse applied to the mass for the entire 100-second interval?
(A) 1750 N · s
(B) 1800 N · s
(C) 1900 N · s
(D) 2100 N · s
(E) 2500 N · s

16. What was the average force applied to the mass during the first 50 seconds?
(A) 7 N
(B) 15 N
(C) 18 N
(D) 21 N
(E) 30 N

17. If the mass had an initial velocity of 4 meters per second, what was its velocity at the end of 50 seconds?
(A) 46 m/s
(B) 50 m/s
(C) 54 m/s
(D) 60 m/s
(E) 66 m/s

18. A 10-kilogram object has a velocity of 2 meters per second to the right. It is struck by a 0.05-kilogram wad of putty moving to the left at 10 meters per second. The putty sticks to the object. What percentage of initial kinetic energy is lost in this inelastic collision?
(A) 15%
(B) 84%
(C) 24%
(D) 76%
(E) 46%

19. A 1.4-kilogram mass is dropped onto a spring from a height of 1.5 meters, as shown below. The force constant, *k*, of the spring is 350 newtons per meter. How much will the spring be compressed?

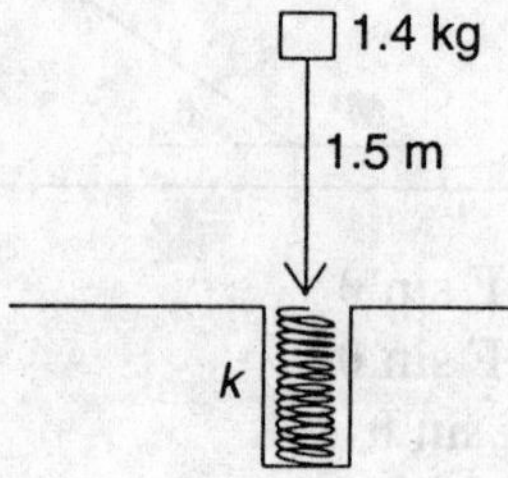

(A) 0.11 m
(B) 0.34 m
(C) 0.47 m
(D) 0.95 m
(E) 1.23 m

20. A 5-kilogram block is dropped from a height of 5 meters. What will be its velocity when it is 2 meters above the ground?
(A) 4.2 m/s
(B) 5.1 m/s
(C) 6.3 m/s
(D) 7.7 m/s
(E) 8.9 m/s

21. A pulley is used to lift a 10-kilogram mass to a height of 2 meters. If 150 newtons of effort was used, the work done to overcome friction was equal to
(A) 14 J
(B) 52 J
(C) 104 J
(D) 196 J
(E) 300 J

22. Power is to work as force is to
(A) impulse
(B) momentum
(C) velocity
(D) acceleration
(E) displacement

GO ON TO THE NEXT PAGE ➤

23. Which pair of forces could produce a resultant force of 7 newtons?
(A) 2 N, 6 N
(B) 3 N, 11 N
(C) 1 N, 5 N
(D) 4 N, 2 N
(E) 3 N, 3 N

24. A radio tower is supported by two guy wires as shown below. Each of the wires makes an angle of 15 degrees to the ground. What is the magnitude of tension, **T**, in each wire?
(A) 5000 N
(B) 14,625 N
(C) 19,319 N

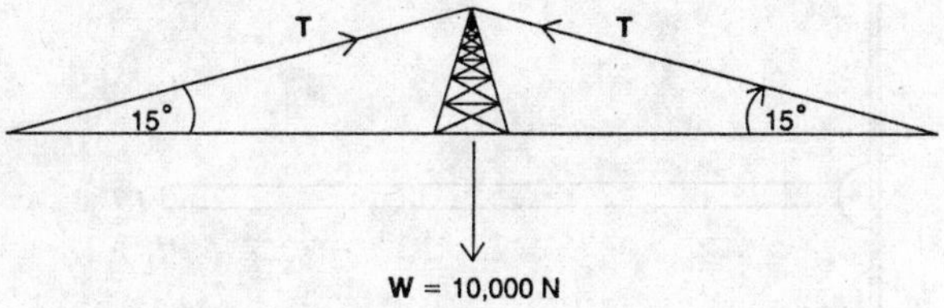

(D) 38,637 N
(E) 43,678 N

25. A 20-newton force and a 10-newton force act concurrently at a point, making an angle of 37 degrees. What is the magnitude of the equilibrant for these forces?
(A) 28.6 N
(B) 17.5 N
(C) 13.4 N
(D) 11.6 N
(E) 9.2 N

26. Which of the following expressions represents the kinetic energy of a mass M that has a mometum **p**?
(A) $2m/\mathbf{p}^2$
(B) $2m\mathbf{p}^2$
(C) $2\mathbf{p}/m$
(D) $\mathbf{p}^2/2m$
(E) $2\mathbf{p}m^2$

27. Kepler's second law of planetary motion states that a planet sweeps out equal areas in equal time. Which of the following statements is *not* an implication (are *not* implications) of that law?
I. The angular momentum of the planet is conserved.
II. There are no external torques acting on the planets at any time.
III. For any planet, $R^3/T^2 = k$ is valid and a constant.
(A) I
(B) II
(C) III
(D) I and II
(E) II and III

28. A spring with a force constant of $k = 500$ newtons per meter is compressed horizontally by a 10-kilogram mass along a rough surface, as shown below. The spring is compressed 0.3 meter, and the coefficient of kinetic friction, μ, between the mass and the surface is 0.15. If the system is released, what will be the velocity of the mass when the spring is no longer compressed?

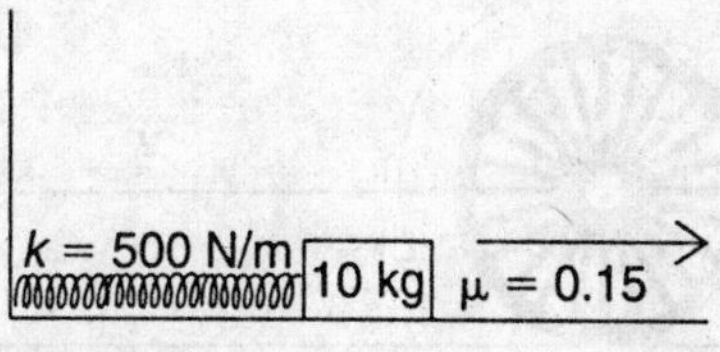

(A) 0 m/s
(B) 1.25 m/s
(C) 1.38 m/s
(D) 1.56 m/s
(E) 1.9 m/s

29. Which of the following expressions is equivalent to 1 watt?
(A) kg · m²/s³
(B) kg · m/s
(C) kg · m²/s
(D) kg · m²/s²
(E) kg · m/s²

GO ON TO THE NEXT PAGE ➤

30. A meter stick is balanced at the 50-centimeter mark as shown below. Four masses are suspended at the positions shown. What is the magnitude, m, of the missing mass?

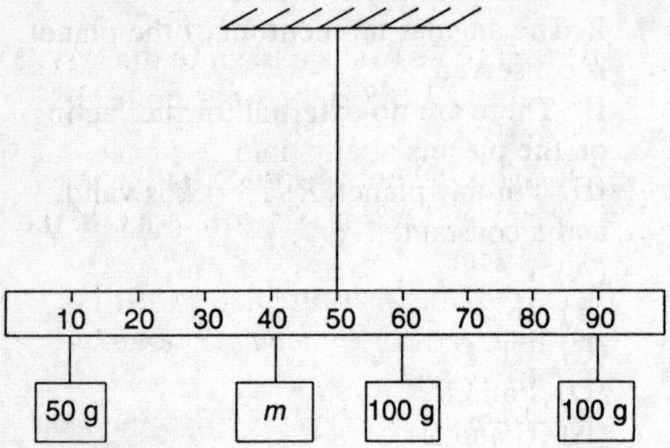

(A) 100 g
(B) 200 g
(C) 300 g
(D) 400 g
(E) 500 g

Questions 31 and 32 are based on the following information:

A wheel is rolling to the right with a constant velocity **v**.

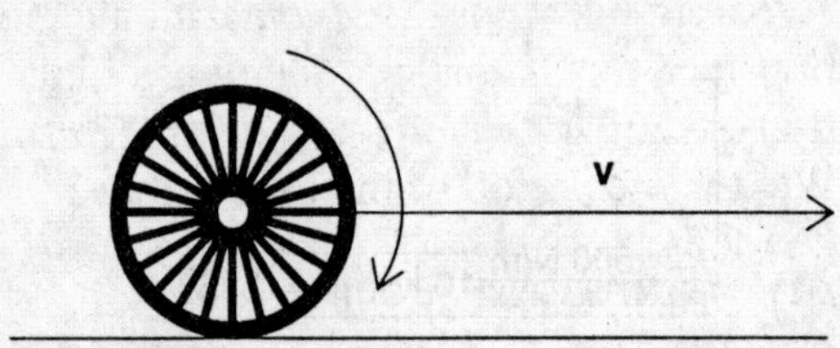

31. What is the direction of the angular velocity vector **ω**?
(A) Up the page
(B) Down the page
(C) Out of the page
(D) Into the page
(E) To the right

32. If the radius of the wheel is 0.45 meter and the velocity is 5 meters per second, then the magnitude of the angular velocity ω is
(A) 5 rad /s
(B) 11 rad /s
(C) 2.25 rad /s
(D) 0.45 rad /s
(E) 5.45 rad /s

33. In the diagram below, a meter stick is attached to the wall with a pivot that it is free to rotate. If the meter stick is initially horizontal and at rest and is then released, the magnitude of the angular acceleration of the edge of the meter stick is equal to

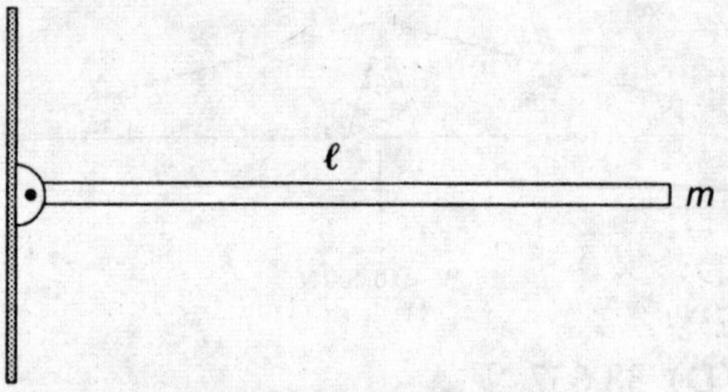

(The moment of inertia for the stick about this axis is equal to $(1/3)mL^2$.)
(A) **g**
(B) (2/3)**g**
(C) (3/2)**g**
(D) (1/2)**g**
(E) 2**g**

34. Two insulated containers are filled with water. The amounts of water in the two containers are given by m_1 and m_2, respectively ($m_1 \neq m_2$). The initial temperatures of the two masses of water are T_1 and T_2, respectively ($T_2 > T_1$). The contents of the two containers are mixed together with no loss of heat to the surroundings. Which expression represents the final equilibrium temperature?
(A) $(m_1m_2 / m_1 + m_2)\ (T_1 + T_2)$
(B) $(m_1T_1 + m_2T_2) / (m_1 + m_2)$
(C) $(m_1T_1 + m_2T_2) / (m_1m_2)$
(D) $(m_1T_1 + m_2T_2)(m_1 + m_2)$
(E) $(T_1 + T_2) / (m_1 + m_2)$

GO ON TO THE NEXT PAGE ➤

35. An insulated tank contains 2.5 cubic meters of an ideal gas under a pressure of 0.5 atmosphere. If the pressure is raised to 3 atmospheres, while the temperature remains constant, the new volume of the gas will be
(A) 2.5 m^3
(B) 5 m^3
(C) 1.25 m^3
(D) 0.42 m^3
(E) 0.37 m^3

36. An insulated tank contains carbon dioxide gas (CO_2 = 28 grams per mole) and nitrogen gas (N_2 = 14 grams per mole). What is the ratio of the root mean square velocity of the nitrogen molecules to the carbon dioxide molecules?
(A) 2
(B) $\sqrt{2}$
(C) 14
(D) 28
(E) $2\sqrt{7}$

37. An ideal gas experiences an adiabatic change. Which of the following statements is correct?
(A) The temperature of the gas remains the same.
(B) No work is done to the gas.
(C) The internal energy of the gas remains the same.
(D) The entropy of the gas decreases.
(E) None of the preceding statements is correct.

38. An ideal gas is kept under constant pressure. What change in Celsius temperature must occur in order to double the volume of the gas?
(A) 100°C
(B) 373°C
(C) 273°C
(D) The required change depends on the starting temperature.
(E) The required change depends on the starting volume.

39. The first law of thermodynamics states that $\Delta Q = \Delta U + \Delta W$. Which of the following statements is correct?
(A) ΔQ is the heat supplied to the system, and ΔW is the work done to the system.
(B) ΔQ is the heat supplied to the system, and ΔW is the work done by the system.
(C) ΔQ is the heat supplied by the system, and ΔW is the work done to the system.
(D) ΔQ is the heat supplied by the system, and ΔW is the work done by the system.
(E) None of the preceding statements is correct.

40. An insulated container has 50 grams of ice at 0°C. Water is added at 20°C. If all of the ice is to melt, the minimum amount of water necessary is
(A) 50 g
(B) 100 g
(C) 200 g
(D) 300 g
(E) 400 g

41. A system undergoes simple harmonic motion such that its displacement as a function of time is given by $\mathbf{x} = 2.5 \sin (3\pi t)$. What is the period of the oscillations?
(A) 2.5s
(B) 3πs
(C) $\frac{2}{3}$s
(D) $\frac{3}{2}$s
(E) 3s

Questions 42 and 43 are based on the following information:

A mass attached to a horizontal spring with a force constant k oscillates with simple harmonic motion. The amplitude of the motion is 0.2 meter, and the period is 0.5 second.

GO ON TO THE NEXT PAGE ➤

42. Which of the following expressions represents the displacement of the mass as a function of time?
(A) $\mathbf{x} = 0.2 \sin (0.5\, t)$
(B) $\mathbf{x} = 0.2 \sin (4\pi t)$
(C) $\mathbf{x} = 0.5 \sin (0.2t)$
(D) $\mathbf{x} = 0.2 \sin (2\pi t)$
(E) $\mathbf{x} = 0.5 \sin (2\pi t)$

43. What is the magnitude of the force constant *k* if a 0.4-kilogram mass is used?
(A) 63 N/m
(B) 5 N/m
(C) 17 N/m
(D) 35 N/m
(E) 27 N/m

44. A taut string is vibrating in its fundamental resonance mode. If the length of the string is ℓ and the velocity of wave propagation is **v**, the frequency of the fundamental mode is
(A) $2\mathbf{v}/\ell$
(B) $2\,\ell\mathbf{v}$
(C) $\ell/\mathbf{v}$
(D) $2\,\ell/\mathbf{v}$
(E) $\mathbf{v}/2\,\ell$

45. If the tension of a taut string is increased, the frequency of its fundamental mode of vibration will
(A) increase
(B) decrease
(C) remain the same
(D) increase, then decrease
(E) The result depends on the type of material in the string.

Questions 46–48 are based on the circuit shown below:

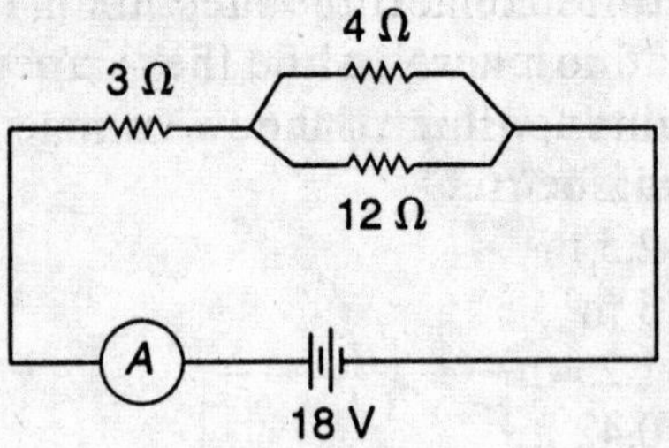

46. What is the equivalent resistance of the circuit?
(A) 3 Ω
(B) 6 Ω
(C) 9 Ω
(D) 12 Ω
(E) 16 Ω

47. What is the current measured in ammeter *A*?
(A) 1.125 A
(B) 3 A
(C) 4 A
(D) 5.2 A
(E) 6 A

48. Compared with the potential difference across the 3-Ω resistor, the potential difference across the 4-Ω resistor is
(A) greater
(B) less
(C) the same
(D) sometimes greater, sometimes less
(E) Not enough information is given to make the comparison.

GO ON TO THE NEXT PAGE ➤

49. An electric circuit consists of two parallel plates separated by a distance *d*. The plates are connected to a potential difference *V* as shown below. If the plates are separated, which of the following statements is correct?

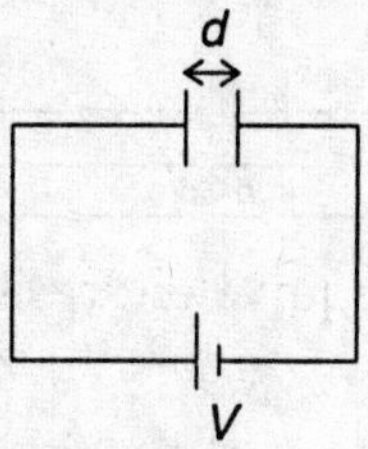

(A) The charge on the plates remains the same, while the electric field decreases.
(B) The charge on the plates decreases, while the electric field remains the same.
(C) The charge on the plates decreases, while the electric field decreases.
(D) The charge on the plates increases, while the electric field decreases.
(E) The charge on the plates increases, while the electric field remains the same.

50. Which two of the following electric circuits have the same equivalent capacitance?

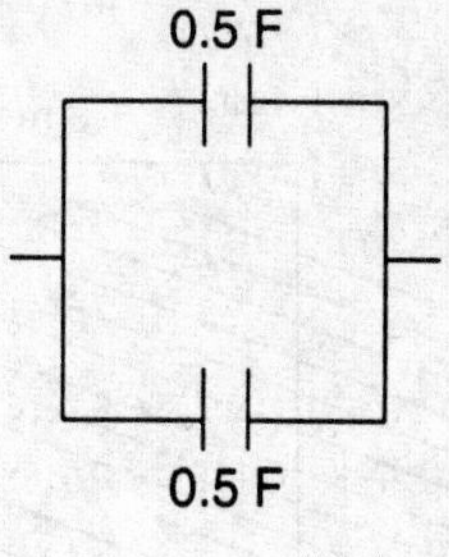

I

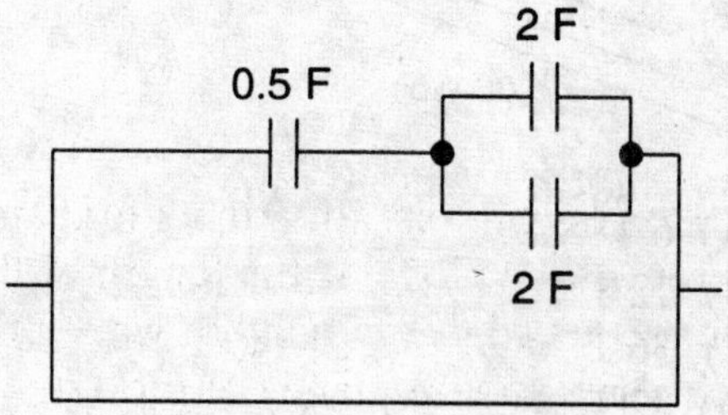

II

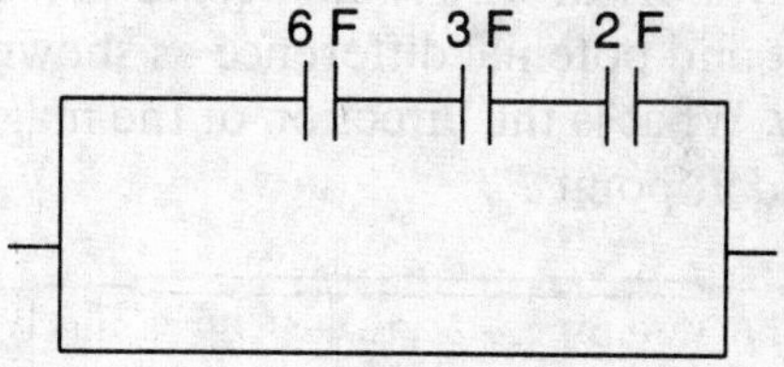

III

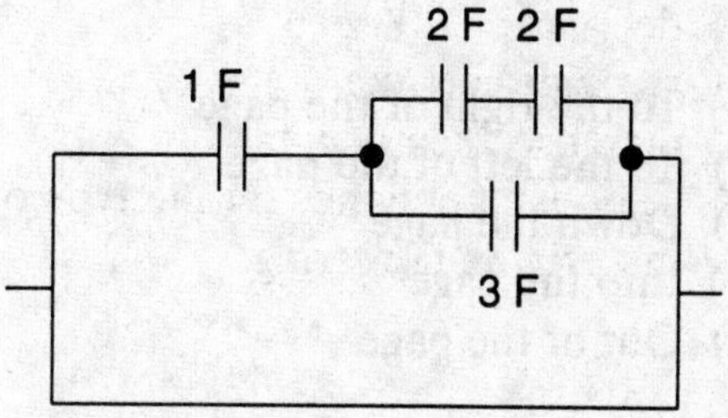

IV

(A) I and III
(B) I and IV
(C) II and III
(D) III and IV
(E) II and IV

GO ON TO THE NEXT PAGE ➤

51. The diagram below shows a magnetic flux of 36 webers crossing a region at right angles. What is the magnitude of the average flux density across the region?

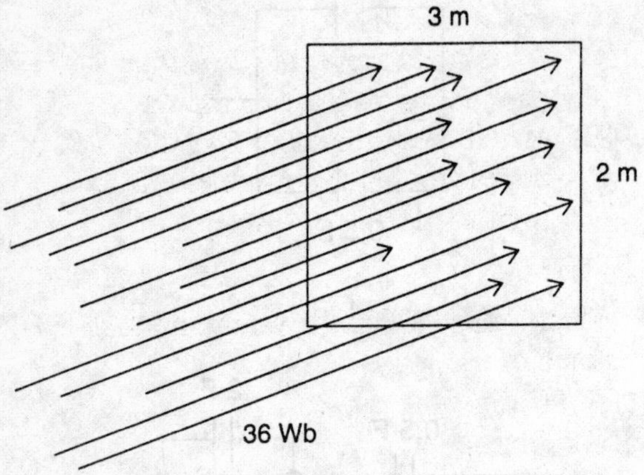

(A) 6 T
(B) 12 T
(C) 36 T
(D) 42 T
(E) 216 T

52. A cylindrical wire is connected to a circuit and potenial difference as shown below. What is the direction of the magnetic field at point *P*?

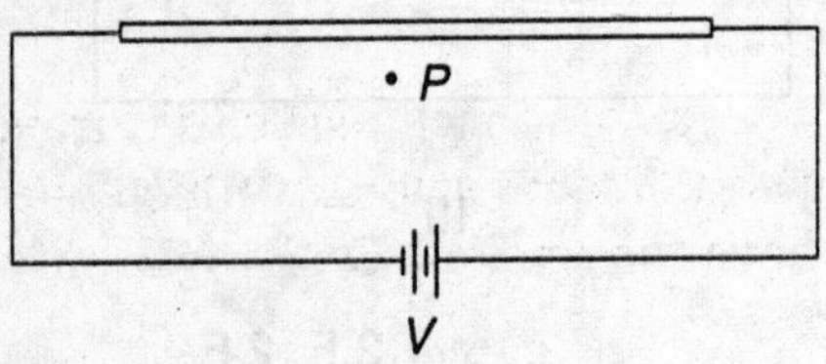

(A) To the right of the page
(B) To the left of the page
(C) Down the page
(D) Into the page
(E) Out of the page

Questions 53 and 54 are based on the ideal transfomer shown below.

A-3000 turn primary is connected to a 120-volt (AC) source. Through an iron core, there is a 150-turn secondary coil.

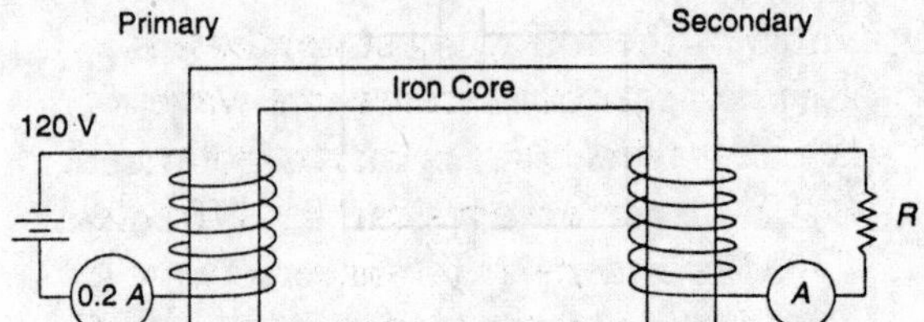

53. What is the magnitude of the induced EMF in the secondary coil?
(A) 6 V
(B) 25 V
(C) 120 V
(D) 1200 V
(E) 2400 V

54. If the current in the primary coil is 0.2 ampere, the current in the secondary coil is
(A) 0.2 A
(B) 2 A
(C) 4 A
(D) 6 A
(E) 100 A

55. A wire loop is rotated at a constant rate in a uniform magnetic field. The axis of rotation is perpendicular to the magnetic field. The current induced in the loop reverses direction every
(A) quarter revolution
(B) half revolution
(C) full revolution
(D) two revolutions
(E) The current never reverses direction.

GO ON TO THE NEXT PAGE ➤

56. Which of the following electromagnetic waves have the shortest wavelength?
(A) Light rays
(B) Radio waves
(C) X rays
(D) Ultraviolet rays
(E) Infrared rays

57. Which of the following statements is (are) correct about transverse waves?
(A) Transverse waves can be polarized.
(B) Transverse waves can be diffracted.
(C) Microwaves are transverse waves.
(D) Vibrations are perpendicular to the propagation.
(E) All of the preceding statements are correct.

58. A light ray is incident on the boundary between two transparent media. If the velocity of light is less in medium 2 (the light is going from medium 1 to medium 2), the relative index of refraction for the two media is
(A) less than 1.0
(B) equal to 1.0
(C) greater than 1.0
(D) greater than or equal to 1.0
(E) sometimes more or less than 1.0, depending on the surface

59. A ray of monochromatic light is incident, from air, on a converging lens of focal length *f*. If the lens is replaced by one having a greater absolute index of refraction, the focal length will
(A) increase
(B) decrease
(C) remain the same
(D) increase or decrease, depending on the material in the lens
(E) increase or decrease, depending on the wavelength of light used

60. Total internal reflection can occur between two transparent media if their relative index of refraction is
(A) less than 1.0
(B) greater than 1.0
(C) equal to 1.0
(D) sometimes greater or less than 1.0, depending on the two media
(E) sometimes greater or less than 1.0, depending on the wavelength of light used

61. Which of the following phenomena is evidence of the wave nature of light?
(A) Reflection
(B) Refraction
(C) Diffraction
(D) Photoelectric effect
(E) Shadows

62. What is the momentum of a photon that has a wavelength of 100 nanometers?
(A) 6.63×10^{-34}/kg · m/s
(B) 6.63×10^{-27}/kg · m/s
(C) 6.63×10^{-41}/kg · m/s
(D) 6.63×10^{-29}/kg · m/s
(E) 6.63×10^{-24}/kg · m/s

63. Each of the following particles is traveling with the same velocity. Which one will have the smallest De Broglie wavelength?
(A) An electron
(B) A proton
(C) A positron
(D) A neutron
(E) An alpha particle

64. In the Rutherford scattering experiment, the paths of alpha-particle deflections were
(A) hyperbolas
(B) parabolas
(C) circular
(D) elliptical
(E) straight lines

GO ON TO THE NEXT PAGE ➤

65. Which particle *cannot* be accelerated by a magnetic field?
(A) A neutron
(B) A proton
(C) A positron
(D) An electron
(E) An alpha particle

66. In the Bohr model of the atom, the angular momentum of an electron is proportional to
(A) Kepler's constant
(B) Planck's constant
(C) Avogadro's number
(D) the universal gravitation constant
(E) Boltzmann's constant

67. When a radioactive nucleus emits a beta particle, the
(A) atomic number remains the same and the mass number increases
(B) atomic number decreases and the mass number decreases
(C) atomic number increases and the mass number remains the same
(D) atomic number increases and the mass number decreases
(E) atomic number and the mass number both remain the same

68. Relativistic momentum can be expressed in units of
(A) c / MeV
(B) MeV / c
(C) c (MeV)
(D) mc^2
(E) $(MeV)c^2$

69. How many neutrons are in the isotope $^{191}_{77}Ir$?
(A) 77
(B) 100
(C) 114
(D) 191
(E) 268

70. In the hydrogen atom, ultraviolet spectral lines can be emitted when electrons make transitions from higher levels to level
(A) 1
(B) 2
(C) 3
(D) 4
(E) 5

STOP

THIS IS THE END OF SECTION I.

YOU MAY USE ANY REMAINING TIME TO CHECK YOUR WORK IN THIS SECTION.

Section II

Free-Response Questions

6 questions
90 minutes
50 percent of total grade

Directions: Solve the following problems. Be sure to show all work, including substitutions with units, and to explain clearly.

1. In the arrangement shown below, a spring with a force constant k is attached to a vertical wall. The other end of the spring is attached to a mass m that rests on a rough horizontal surface. The coefficient of kinetic friction for the mass and the surface is μ. A light string is attached to m and passed over a frictionless pulley to an overhanging mass M. The system is initially at rest. If mass M is released, it will fall a distance h until coming to rest.

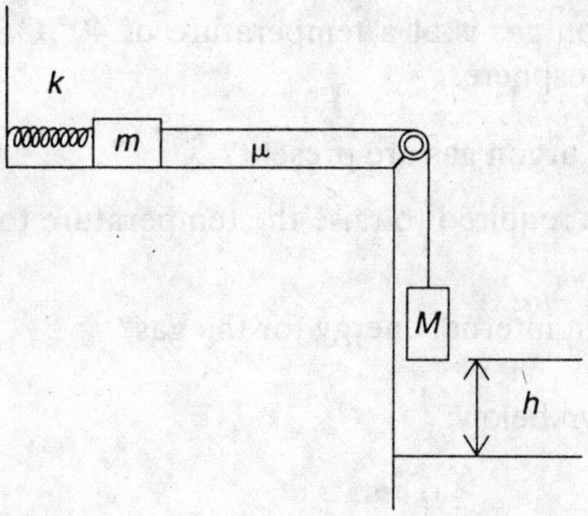

(a) Write an expression for the conservation of energy as it applies to this situation.

(b) In terms of m, M, g, h, and k, derive an expression for the coefficient of kinetic friction μ.

(c) If k = 1000 newtons per meter, m = 0.5 kilogram, M = 1.5 kilograms, and h = 0.04 meter, calculate the value of μ.

GO ON TO THE NEXT PAGE ➤

2. A rigid rod with a mass of 20 kilograms and a length ℓ is attached to a wall by means of a frictionless pivot as shown below. A mass of 5 kilograms is hung from the middle of the rod, and a light string is attached to the free end. The string is attached to the wall, making an angle of 25° to the horizontal. The system is in equilibrium.

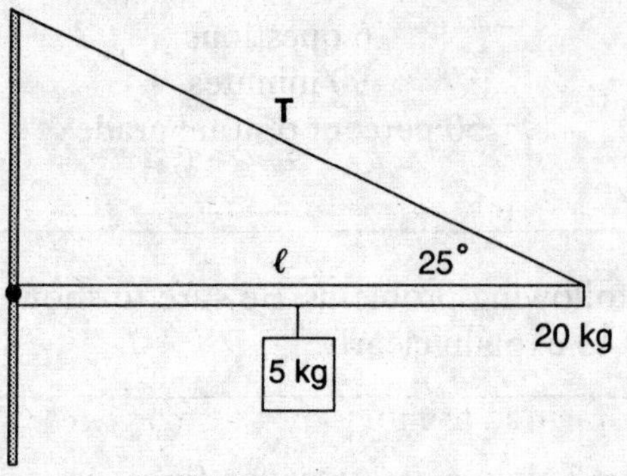

(a) Draw a free-body diagram for this situation, and label all forces involved.

(b) Determine the magnitude of the tension **T**.

(c) Determine the magnitude and direction of the reaction force **R** acting at the pivot.

3. Three cubic meters of argon gas is at a temperature of 40° C in an insulated container. The pressure of the gas is 2 atmospheres.

(a) How many moles of argon gas are present?

(b) How much energy is required to raise the temperature to 60° C if no work is to be done by the gas?

(c) What is the change in internal energy for the gas?

4. For the electric circuit drawn below:

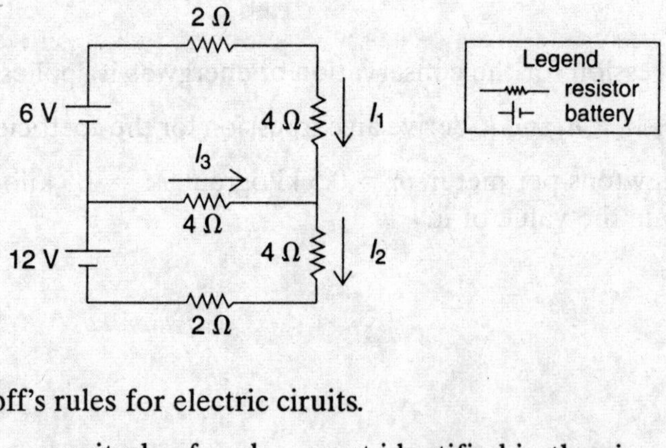

(a) State Kirchhoff's rules for electric ciruits.

(b) Determine the magnitude of each current identified in the circuit.

5. An electron is accelerated across a 1200-volt potential difference, as shown in the diagram below. Upon reaching the other side, the electron enters a downward electric field of uniform strength **E** = 1000 newtons per coulomb. The length of the second region, containing the electric field, is 1.2 meters.

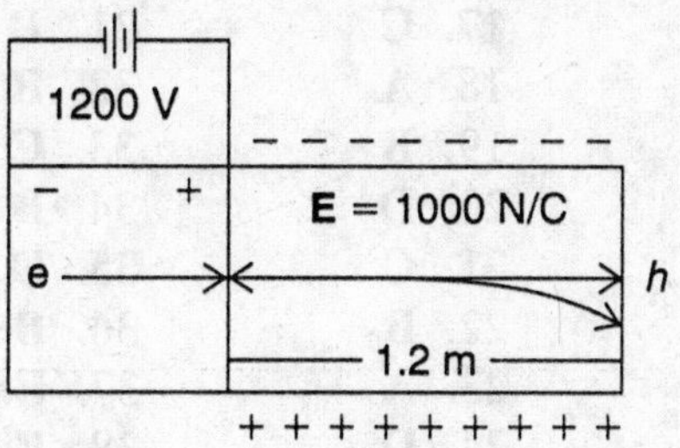

(a) How much work is done to move the electron across the potential difference region?

(b) What is the velocity of the electron as it enters the electric field region?

(c) Neglecting any gravitational effects, the electron is deflected away from its straight path. Derive an expression for the deflected distance h in terms of the mass of the electron, its charge, the length of the region ℓ, and its entrance velocity **v**. Assume constant horizontal velocity.

(d) Using the known value of each quantity, calculate the magnitude of the deflected distance h.

6. The threshold frequency for a photoelectric metal is 2.5×10^{15} hertz. Electromagnetic radiation with a wavelength of 50 nanometers is incident on the surface of the metal.

(a) What is the frequency of the radiation?

(b) If the total energy of the radiation is equal to 9.945×10^{-16} joules, how many photons are associated with this radiation?

(c) What is the work function for this metal?

(d) What is the maximum kinetic energy, in joules and electron volts, for the emitted electrons?

(e) What is the stopping potential for the emitted electrons?

STOP

THIS IS THE END OF SECTION II.

YOU MAY USE ANY REMAINING TIME TO CHECK YOUR WORK IN THIS SECTION.

Answer Key for Section I

1. **D**	15. **D**	29. **A**	43. **A**	57. **E**
2. **A**	16. **B**	30. **C**	44. **E**	58. **C**
3. **B**	17. **C**	31. **D**	45. **A**	59. **B**
4. **E**	18. **A**	32. **B**	46. **B**	60. **A**
5. **E**	19. **B**	33. **C**	47. **B**	61. **C**
6. **B**	20. **D**	34. **B**	48. **C**	62. **B**
7. **A**	21. **C**	35. **D**	49. **C**	63. **E**
8. **E**	22. **B**	36. **B**	50. **A**	64. **A**
9. **C**	23. **A**	37. **E**	51. **A**	65. **A**
10. **A**	24. **D**	38. **B**	52. **E**	66. **B**
11. **A**	25. **A**	39. **B**	53. **A**	67. **C**
12. **B**	26. **D**	40. **C**	54. **C**	68. **B**
13. **E**	27. **C**	41. **C**	55. **B**	69. **C**
14. **D**	28. **E**	42. **B**	56. **C**	70. **A**

Answer Explanations for Section I

1. **D** Work and energy are scalar quantities. The other choices are all vectors.

2. **A** The time for the ball to rise to its maximum height is given by

$$\frac{\mathbf{v}}{\mathbf{g}} = \frac{30}{9.8} = 3.06 \text{ s}$$

3. **B** In the absence of any air resistance, the horizontal velocity remains constant.

4. **E** Graphs II and V both represent one-dimensional uniformly accelerated motion.

5. **E** First, we must determine the time to fall 7.5 m. This will be the same time that is needed to go out the 22-m distance. The time is given by

$$t = \sqrt{2y/g} = \sqrt{15/9.8} = 1.24\ s$$

The horizontal velocity **v** is therefore equal to 22 m / 1.24 s = 17.74 m/s.

6. **B** The tangential velocity **v** is given by

$$\mathbf{v} = \omega r = 2\pi\, f\, r = (6.28)(10 / 11.7)\,(0.6) = 3.22 \text{ m / s}$$

7. **A** The formula for the range of the projectile is

$$R = \frac{\mathbf{V_0}^2 \sin 2\theta}{\mathbf{g}}$$

Substituting the given values yields 145 m / s for the initial velocity.

8. **E** The acceleration of the projectile, given by gravity, remains constant during its flight.

9. **C** Newton's third law of motion states that for every action there is an equal but opposite reaction. The reaction force by the wall is therefore equal to 15 N.

10. **A** If no string was attached to the mass, the normal force would be equal in magnitude to the weight, $M\mathbf{g}$. However, the upward component of the string opposes the force of gravity, and therefore we have

$$\mathbf{N} = M\mathbf{g} - \mathbf{F} \sin \theta$$

11. **A** To find the acceleration of both masses (since they are coupled), we set up Newton's second law of motion in both directions. The tension $\mathbf{T}$ in the string caused by the weight of the hanging mass is the same mass that accelerates the 2-kg mass to the right. In the y-direction we can write

$$\mathbf{T} - (5)(9.8) = -5\,\mathbf{a}$$

In the x-direction we can write

$$\mathbf{T} = 2\,\mathbf{a}$$

Thus, eliminating $\mathbf{T}$ from both equations, we get $\mathbf{a} = 7\ \text{m/s}^2$.

12. **B** On an inclined plane, the normal force is given by $M\mathbf{g} \cos \theta$. Thus, as the angle of elevation increases, the magnitude of the normal force acting on the mass will decrease.

13. **E** At the instant the boy loses contact with the surface, the normal force acting on the boy is zero.

14. **D** The force necessary to maintain a constant velocity is equal to the force of kinetic friction. This force is given by

$$\mathbf{f} = \mu\mathbf{N} = (0.17)(15) = 2.55\ \mathbf{N}$$

15. **D** The total impulse applied to the mass for the entire 100-s interval is given by the total area, which equals 2100 N · s.

16. **B** For the first 50 s, the impulse applied was equal to 750 N · s, determined by finding the area of that triangular segment. The average force is equal to the impulse divided by the time, 50 s, or 15 N.

17. **C** During the 50-s interval, the impulse was equal to 750 N · s. This is equal to the change in momentum, given by $\mathbf{m}\,\Delta\mathbf{v}$. Since the mass is equal to 15 kg, the velocity changed by 50 m /s. Since the force was directed to accelerate the mass, the new velocity is 54 m / s.

18. **A** The initial kinetic energy of the object is equal to 20 J . The initial kinetic energy of the putty is 2.5 J. The total initial kinetic energy is therefore equal to 22.5 J. To find the kinetic energy after the collision, we need to know the final velocity. This is an inelastic collision, but momentum is still conserved. Therefore:

$$(10)\,(2) - (0.05\,)(10) = (10 + 0.05)\,\mathbf{v}$$

$$\mathbf{v} = 1.94\ \text{m/s}$$

The final kinetic energy of the combined 10.05-kg mass (object and putty) is therefore 18.9 J. The percentage of energy lost is 15%, since 18.9 / 22.5 = 0.85.

19. **B** The change in PE for the falling mass must equal the gain in elastic potential energy for the spring.

$$(1.4)(9.8)(1.5) = \frac{1}{2}(350)x^2 \qquad \text{so} \qquad x = 0.34\text{m}$$

20. **D** The change in potential energy is equal to the change in kinetic energy:

$$mg\,\Delta h = \frac{1}{2}mv^2$$

$$\mathbf{v} = \sqrt{2\mathbf{g}\,\Delta h} = 7.7 \text{ m/s}$$

21. **C** The work needed to raise the 10-kg mass 2 m is equal to 196 J ($W = mgh$). The actual work done is equal to 300 J. Thus, the work to overcome friction is equal to the difference between these two values: 300 J − 196 J = 104 J.

22. **B** Power is equal to the rate of change of work. Force is equal to the rate of change of momentum.

23. **A** Only the pair 2 N, 6 N could produce a resultant force of 7 N. The maximum resultant is 8 N, and the minimum resultant is 4 N. Thus, there does exist an angle at which the resultant force could equal 7 N.

24. **D** To maintain equilibrium, the upward vertical components of the wires must be equal in magnitude to the weight of the tower. Thus,

$$2\mathbf{T}\sin\theta = \mathbf{W}$$

and, using the given values, we find that **T** = 38, 637 N.

25. **A** The magnitude of the equilibrant is equal to the magnitude of the resultant. The resultant's magnitude is given by the law of cosines:

$$\text{Resultant} = \sqrt{(20)^2 + (10)^2 - 2(20)(10)\cos 143} = 28.6 \text{ N}$$

26. **D** The momentum $\mathbf{p} = m\mathbf{v}$. The kinetic energy $KE = (1/2)m\mathbf{v}^2$. Thus,

$$KE = \frac{\mathbf{p}^2}{2m}$$

27. **C** Kepler's second law of planetary motion implies that the angular momentum is conserved (I) and that no external torques are acting on the planets at any time (II).

28. **E** The law of conservation of energy states that the potential energy stored in the spring will be converted into kinetic energy and the work done by friction:

$$\frac{1}{2}kx^2 = \frac{1}{2}mv^2 + W_f = \frac{1}{2}mv^2 + \mu mgx$$

Substituting the given values yields **v** = 1.9 m/s.

29. **A** One watt is equal to 1 J/s. Thus, since 1 J = 1 kg · m²/s², we have 1 W = 1 kg · m²/s³.
30. **C** We need to show that the torques on both sides of the balance point are equal. Since all masses would be multiplied by **g**, we can leave **g** out without any loss of generality:

$$(50)(40) + m(10) = (100)(10) + (100)(40)$$

This implies that m = 300 g.
31. **D** According to the right-hand rule for rotation, the direction of the angular velocity vector **ω** is into the page.
32. **B** We use this formula:

$$\omega = \frac{\mathbf{v}}{r} = \frac{5}{0.45} = 11\frac{rad}{s}$$

33. **C** Torque $\boldsymbol{\tau} = I\boldsymbol{\alpha}$, where I is equal to the moment of inertia for the given axis and $\boldsymbol{\alpha}$ is the angular acceleration. Thus:

$$\frac{M\mathbf{g}\ell}{2} = \frac{1}{3}M\ell^2\alpha$$

$$\alpha = \frac{3}{2}\mathbf{g}\ell$$

where ℓ = 1 m.
34. **B** From the laws of heat conservation we know that, for a water-water mixture,

$$M_1(T - T_1) = M_2(T_2 - T)$$

Solving for T, we get

$$T = \frac{M_1T_1 + M_2T_2}{M_1 + M_2}$$

35. **D** At constant temperature, we use Boyle's law for an ideal gas:

$$P_1V_1 = P_2V_2$$

$$(0.5)(2.5) = (3)V_2$$

$$V_2 = 0.42\ \text{m}^3$$

36. **B** The ratio of the root mean square velocities is equal to the square root of the inverse ratio of molecular masses:

$$\mathbf{v}_{\text{ratio}} = \sqrt{\frac{28}{14}} = \sqrt{2}$$

37. **E** None of the given statements is correct about an adiabatic change.
38. **D** We need to know the starting temperature in order to answer this question.
39. **B** In the first law of thermodynamics, ΔQ is the heat supplied to the system while ΔW is the work done by the system.
40. **C** To melt ice at 0°C, we must add 80 cal / g. Thus, 4000 cal of heat must be supplied by the water. Since the water is at 20°C, we must have 200 g of water (the specific heat of water is 1 cal / g · °C).
41. **C** In the expression for simple harmonic motion, we have

$$\mathbf{x} = A \sin \omega t$$

where the angular frequency $\omega = 2\pi / T$. Thus, $T = \frac{2}{3}$ s.

42. **B** As in question 41, we have as a general expression

$$\mathbf{x} = A \sin \omega t$$

where A is the amplitude in meters and $\omega = 2\pi / T$. Thus, in this case $\omega = 4\pi$, A = 0.2 m, and $\mathbf{x} = 0.2 \sin (4\pi t)$.

43. **A** In simple harmonic motion, $\omega^2 = k/m$. Substituting the known values yields $k = 63$ N / m.
44. **E** Since $\mathbf{v} = f\lambda$, then $f = \mathbf{v} / \lambda$. For a string vibrating in its fundamental mode, $\lambda = 2\ \ell$, so $f = \mathbf{v} / 2\ \ell$.
45. **A** In a taut string, the velocity of wave propagation increases with tension. Therefore, the frequency increases as well.
46. **B** We first reduce the resistance in the parallel branch:

$$\frac{1}{R} = \frac{1}{4} + \frac{1}{1_2} \quad \text{and} \quad R = 3\ \Omega$$

This resistance gets added, in series, to the other 3-Ω resistor, making a total of 6 Ω in the circuit.

47. **B** Using Ohm's law, we have

$$I = \frac{V}{R} = \frac{18}{6} = 3\text{A}$$

48. **C** Since the equivalent resistance of the parallel branch is also 3 Ω, the two resistors share the same potential difference—9 V.
49. **C** As the plates are separated, both the charge on the plates and the strength of the electric field between them will decrease.
50. **A** The equivalent capacitance of circuits I and III is the same—1 F.
51. **A** The average magnetic flux density across the region is equal to the flux divided by the area: 36 / 6 = 6 T.
52. **E** According to the right-hand rule for conventional current, the magnetic field is out of the page at point P.
53. **A** In an ideal transformer, the ratio of the emf in the primary to the number of turns in the primary is equal to the ratio of the emf in the secondary to the number of turns in the secondary. Using this relationship, we find that the secondary emf is equal to 6 V.

54. **C** In an ideal transformer, the power in the primary equals the power in the secondary:

$$(120)(0.2) = 6I,$$

which implies that the secondary current equals 4 A.

55. **B** In an electromagnetic generator, the current reverses every half revolution.

56. **C** In the electromagnetic spectrum, X rays have the shortest wavelength.

57. **E** All of the given statements about transverse waves are correct.

58. **C** If light is slowing down, the relative index of refraction for the two media is greater than 1.0.

59. **B** If a lens having a greater index of refraction is used, the angle of refraction will be larger, resulting in a shorter focal length.

60. **A** Total internal reflection can occur only if light speeds up as it goes from one medium to another. This implies that the relative index of refraction is less than 1.0.

61. **C** Interference and diffraction are typical wave phenomena.

62. **B** We use the formula

$$p = \frac{h}{\lambda}$$

Thus,

$$p = \frac{6.63 \times 10^{-34}}{1 \times 10^{-7}} = 6.63 \times 10^{-27}\ \text{kg} \cdot \text{m/s}$$

63. **E** Since the alpha particle has the greatest mass, it will have the shortest De Broglie wavelength.

64. **A** In the Rutherford scattering experiment, alpha particles were deflected in hyperbolic trajectories.

65. **A** Since a neutron is electrically neutral, it cannot be accelerated by a magnetic field.

66. **B** In the Bohr theory, the angular momentum of an electron is proportional (and quantized) to Planck's constant, *h*.

67. **C** In a beta decay process, a neutron transforms into a proton and an electron. Therefore, the total number of nucleons (mass number) remains the same, but the number of protons (atomic number) increases by 1.

68. **B** We can write the relativistic momentum as $\mathbf{p} = E / \mathbf{c}$. Thus, the units can be MeV / **c**.

69. **C** The number of neutrons in the isotope $^{191}_{77}\text{Ir}$ is equal to $A - Z = 191 - 77 = 114$.

70. **A** In the Bohr theory, electron transitions to the ground state (level 1) form UV spectral lines.

Solutions to Section II

1. (a) In this situation the potential energy lost by falling mass M is converted into stretching the spring and moving mass m horizontally by doing work against friction. Thus,

$$\Delta GPE = \Delta EPE + W\,(\text{friction})$$

where GPE = gravitational potential energy, and EPE = elastic potential energy.

(b) We write out each of the specified terms in part (a):

$$\frac{1}{2}kh^2 = Mgh + \mu mgh$$

$$\mu = \frac{(1/2)kh - Mg}{mg}$$

Notice that the elongation of the spring x is equal to the downward displacement h.

(c) We substitute the given values to get :

$$\mu = \frac{(0.5)(1000\text{ N/m})(0.04\text{ m}) - (1.5\text{ kg})(9.8\text{ m/s}^2)}{(0.5\text{ kg})(9.8\text{ m/s}^2)} = 1.08$$

2. (a) The free-body diagram is shown below:

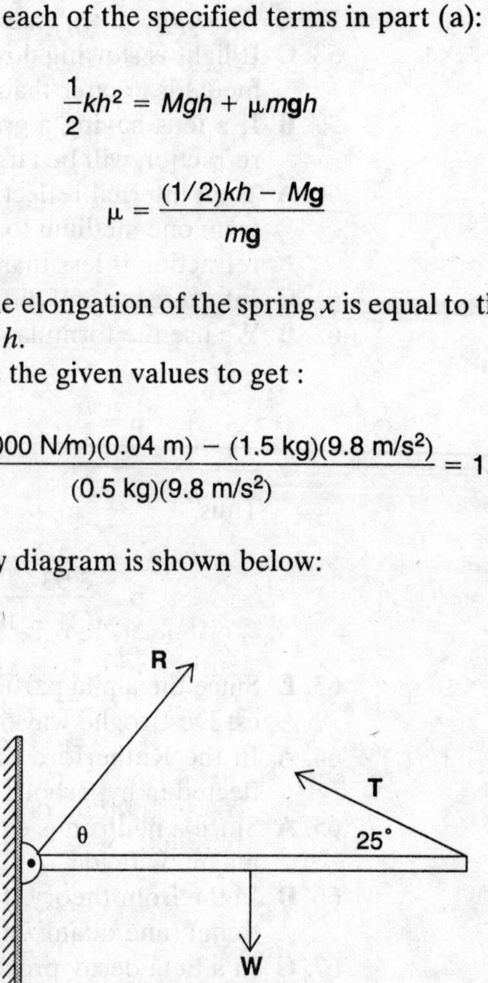

We take the action of the weight of the rod to be at its center of mass ($\ell/2$). The weight of the 5-kg mass is acting at the center of the rod as well. This makes for a combined weight **W**.

(b) To find the tension **T**, we choose the equilibrium point to be about the pivot. The reaction force **R** does not contribute to any torques about this point. The upward component of the tension, **T** sin θ, is a counterclockwise torque acting at length ℓ. The total weight

$$\mathbf{W} = (25\text{ kg})(9.8\text{ m/s}^2) = 245\text{ N}$$

acts at distance $\ell / 2$ and is a clockwise torque. Thus:

$$\Sigma\tau = 0$$

$$(\mathbf{T} \sin \theta)\, \ell = \frac{W\ell}{2}$$

$$\mathbf{T} \sin 25 = \frac{245 \text{ N}}{2}$$

$$\mathbf{T} = 290 \text{ N}$$

(c) To find the reaction force, note that **R** has perpendicular components R_x and R_y. Now, consider the torques about the far right edge of the rod. The tension **T** and $\mathbf{R}_x$ do not contribute to any torques about this axis. However, the total weight **W** acts at a distance of $\ell / 2$ from the right edge, and component force $\mathbf{R}_y$ acts at a distance ℓ. In equilibrium, the sum of these torques must be equal to zero:

$$\Sigma\tau = 0$$

$$\mathbf{R}_y \ell = \mathbf{W}\frac{\ell}{2}$$

$$\mathbf{R}_y = \frac{245 \text{ N}}{2} = 122.5 \text{ N}$$

To find $\mathbf{R}_x$, we note that, in equilibrium, the sum of all forces must equal zero as well:

$$\Sigma\, \mathbf{F} = 0$$

This means that $\mathbf{R}_x$ must balance the horizontal component of the tension, which equals $\mathbf{T} \cos \theta$.

$$\mathbf{R}_x = (290 \text{ N}) \cos 25 = 262.83 \text{ N}$$

The magnitude of the reaction force is given by the Pythagorean theorem:

$$\mathbf{R} = \sqrt{(122.5 \text{ N})^2 + (262.83 \text{ N})^2} = 290 \text{ N}$$

The direction of **R** is given by:

$$\tan \theta = \frac{\mathbf{R}_y}{\mathbf{R}_x} = \frac{122.5 \text{ N}}{262.83 \text{ N}} = 0.466$$

$$\theta = 25°$$

3. (a) The number n of moles is given by:

$$n = \frac{(12.2)(2 \text{ atm})(3 \text{ m}^3)(1000 \text{ L}/\text{m}^3)}{313 \text{ K}} = 233.87 \text{ mol}$$

(b) From the first law of thermodynamics,

$$\Delta Q = \Delta U + \Delta W.$$

If no work is done by the gas, $\Delta W = 0$ and $\Delta Q = (3/2)nR\,\Delta T$ ($\Delta T = 20$ K in this case). Thus:

$$\Delta Q = (1.5)(233.87 \text{ mol})(8.31 \text{ J / mol} \cdot \text{K})(20 \text{ K}) = 58{,}303.79 \text{ J}$$

(c) Since no work is done by the gas, $\Delta U = \Delta Q = 58{,}303.79$ J.

4. (a) (i) The sum of any currents entering a junction in an electric circuit must equal the sum of the currents leaving that junction.
(ii) The algebraic sum of the changes in potential across any element in a closed loop must equal zero.

(b) Applying Kirchhoff's rules to the circuit in the question, we take the two given loops and move clockwise around them, using the conventions discussed in the text:

$$I_2 = I_1 + I_3$$

$$6 - 6I_1 + 4I_3 = 0$$

$$I_2 - 4I_3 - 6I_2 = 0$$

Now, we substitute for I_2 in the third equation to get

$$6 - 6I_1 + 4I_3 = 0$$

$$I_2 - 6(I_1 + I_3) - 4I_3 = 0$$

Eliminating I_1 from the two equations yields $I_3 = 0.429$ A. We substitute back into either equation to get $I_1 = 1.286$ A. Finally, substitution back into the first equation yield $I_2 = 1.714$ A.

5. (a) The work done is equal to the product of the electron's charge and the potential difference:

$$W = eV = (1.6 \times 10^{-19} \text{ C})(1200 \text{ J/C}) = 1.92 \times 10^{-16} \text{ J}$$

(b) The work done is equal to the change in the kinetic energy. Thus:

$$\mathbf{v} = \sqrt{\frac{2KE}{m}} = \sqrt{\frac{(2)(1.92 \times 10^{-19} \text{ J}}{(9.1 \times 10^{-31} \text{ kg})}} = 2.05 \times 10^{7} \text{ m/s}$$

(c) Since the electron enters the electric field with an assumed constant horizontal velocity, the downward acceleration will cause a parabolic projectile path. Thus, since the electric field is uniform, we know that $\mathbf{F} = e\mathbf{E}$ (where e is the magnitude of the electron charge). Also, we know that $\mathbf{F} = m\mathbf{a}$; thus $\mathbf{a} = e\mathbf{E} / m$. Now, with a constant horizontal velocity $\mathbf{v}$ and a distance ℓ, the time within the electric field is given by $\ell / \mathbf{v}$. This is the same time needed to fall the deflected distance h:

$$h = \frac{1}{2}\mathbf{a}t^2 = \frac{e\mathbf{E}\ell^2}{2m\mathbf{v}^2}$$

(d) Using the known values, we obtain

$$h = \frac{e\mathbf{E}\ell^2}{2mv^2} = \frac{(1.6 \times 10^{-19}\ \text{C})(1000\ \text{N/C})(1.2\ \text{m})^2}{(2)(9.1 \times 10^{-31}\ \text{kg})(2.05 \times 10^7\ \text{m/s})^2} = 0.30\ \text{m}$$

6. (a) The frequency of the radiation photons is given by

$$f = \frac{c}{\lambda} = \frac{3 \times 10^8\ \text{m/s}}{5 \times 10^{-8}\ \text{m}} = 6.0 \times 10^{15}\ \text{Hz}$$

(b) The number of photons is

$$N = \frac{E_{\text{total}}}{E_{photon}}$$

Thus:

$$N = \frac{9.945 \times 10^{-16}\ J}{(6.0 \times 10^{15}\ \text{s}^{-1})(6.63 \times 10^{-34}\ \text{J} \cdot \text{s})} = 250$$

(c) The work function is equal to the product of the threshold frequency and Planck's constant:

$$W_o = hf_o = (6.63 \times 10^{-34}\ \text{J} \cdot \text{s})\ (2.5 \times 10^{15}\ \text{s}^{-1}) = 1.6575 \times 10^{-18}\ \text{J}$$

(d) The maximum kinetic energy is equal to the difference between the energy of one photon and the work function. Therefore:

$$KE_{\text{max}} = E_P - W_o = (3.978 \times 10^{-18}\ \text{J}) - (1.7575 \times 10^{-18}\ \text{J}) = 2.32 \times 10^{-18}\ \text{J} = 14.5\ \text{eV}$$

(e) Since 1 eV is the energy given to one electron accelerated through 1 V, the stopping potential is equal to 14.5 V in this case.

CHAPTER 3

Learning Strategies for Identifying Key Concepts

3.1 Introduction

Have you ever tried to do a physics problem only to quit in frustration because you didn't know how to get started? Many students often complain about this difficulty. Also, often students will say, after doing poorly on a test, that they "really studied hard" or "really knew the stuff." When asked how they studied, most will say that they reviewed their notes and looked at old homework assignments. A few industrious students may even have tried to do some extra problems.

Another factor revealed when students are interviewed about their study habits is that often they do not understand how the various parts of the material are connected. They memorize formulas and gain experience in solving certain types of problems. When faced with a challenging problem of a different kind, however, many students who study in this way may not even know how to start to solve it!

In physics, success requires more than the ability to memorize and use formulas. To solve a problem correctly, you must first understand what you are asked to do. Then you must access from your memory all of the information that may be related to the ideas involved in the problem. Next, you must decide which specific facts are relevant to the solution. Finally, you must decide on a path that will hopefully lead you to the correct solution. All of this mental process must be completed, on the AP examination, within an average of 15 minutes on a free-response problem (in a considerably shorter time on a multiple-choice question).

To succeed on this examination (or any other one), you must make sure that you understand and can apply many items of information that may seem, at first glance, to be unrelated. The ability to do this requires an organizational hierarchy of ideas called "concepts."

3.2 What Are Concepts?

If I were to say the word *big* or the word *digging* to you, what picture would you think of? What image comes to mind when you hear (or read) the word *atom*? Even though we all hear or use many of the same words, we develop different meanings or interpretations for them based on our own past experiences and ideas.

The mental images or ideas we attach to words are called **concepts**. Words are merely the labels we assign to concepts. A great deal of confusion and misunderstanding arises when we mix word labels with concepts. In physics, this fact is especially important for helping you understand the meanings of terms and ideas about the world. In the branch of physics known as mechanics, for example, many words are used that also occur very often in ordinary speech. These are words you grew up with and have come to associate with daily living experiences. Some of these words are *speed*, *force*, *momentum*, *strength*, *weight*, and *work.* Often, a student has conceptual difficulty in physics because he or she finds it hard to understand the different meanings that everyday words have when used in physics!

3.3 How Are Concepts Linked?

In this section, you will begin to see how concepts can be listed in a hierarchical, organizational way. The goal is to help you to study and learn more meaningfully. For example, if "energy" was our key concept of discussion, some terms associated with energy might be *kinetic, potential*, *work*, *motion*, *heat*, or even *photosynthesis.* This list could be made more meaningful by the inclusion of so-called linking words, such as *is*, *as, are*, *can*, *be*, and *with*. Verbs and verb phrases (*contains*, *is composed of*, *are made from*, etc.) can also be used. For example, we might start with "energy" and then say "Energy is the capacity to do work" or "Energy can depend on velocity or position." When concepts are linked together in a hierarchical way, a clearer view of what you do and do not understand can be obtained.

We began this chapter by considering the nature of concepts and their importance for understanding and studying physics. When you study, it is essential to pay attention to the organization of concepts. Since the goal of any examination is to assess how well you understand relevant concepts and their application, it is only natural to think next about the nature of problem solving and ways to improve your ability to solve novel and difficult physics problems.

CHAPTER 4

Problem Solving in Physics

4.1 What Is a Problem?

Consider the following situation. You are driving your car at 25 miles per hour. One hundred feet in front of you is a truck with a constant velocity of 20 miles per hour. When you are about 10 feet behind the truck, you decide to pass it by accelerating to 45 miles per hour. The highway has only two lanes, so you have to cross into the oncoming traffic lane. By the time you have reached the back of the truck, after starting this maneuver, you notice a car, about 1/4 mile away, coming at you with a velocity of 45 miles per hour. Do you have enough time to safely complete the maneuver?

Think for a moment about what is going on here. You have been presented with a realistic situation. A question introduced by the phrase "Do you have . . . " has been asked. What kind of answer is expected from you? Clearly, the answer prompted by the word *do* is either yes or no. But what information do you need before you can decide which answer is correct? In this case you have been given a "problem" to solve that is implicit from the question stated above.

A problem can be defined as a situation in which you want to achieve a goal but are unsure of how to go about achieving it. There are many elements to the problem presented above. Some information is explicit (for example, how fast you and the truck are going), and some information is implicit (it is never stated explicitly that you and the truck are going in the same direction; no acceleration by the truck is mentioned; it is assumed that your rate of acceleration is constant). In addition, the goal of the problem is implicit since, in order to answer yes or no to the question, you must first ascertain whether the distances covered simultaneously by you and the oncoming car will produce a number that can be interpreted as meaning either a successful or an unsuccessful completion of the maneuver.

In this chapter and the next one, you will explore the nature of problem solving and the various problem types to better understand where you usually succeed and where you have difficulty when solving a physics problem. Since the Advanced Placement Examination is timed, you must budget your time effectively. You will not have the luxury of examining the nature of a problem and sorting out its parts in detail. Nevertheless, by effective studying and reviewing you can develop a familiarity with certain common problem types and techniques and be prepared for more novel ones. This chapter and Chapter 5 will help you to develop an "intuition" about concepts and problems to handle any type you may encounter on an examination.

4.2 What Are the Structural Elements of a Problem?

The first elements of a typical problem are the **givens**, that is, the items of information that are explicitly provided. As you read a problem, the words that are associated with concepts begin to access information from your memory. What kind of information is retrieved, and in what form, depend on what you already know about the subject, the type of problem, your experience, and your expertise.

Some problems are difficult because the amount of given information is not well defined or is implicit. If you are used to solving certain types of problems, you come to expect what a problem should look like. Even so, identifying the givens is the first step. Then, after you initially read the problem, you begin to form a **representation** of it in your mind. This representation may begin with a redescription of the problem (perhaps as a mental image or mental model of the situation), followed by a translation of the problem into symbols that link concepts already known with the specific details of the present problem. The representation may be similar to a concept map in which "operators" tell your brain how to deal with particular concepts by using formulas or learned "rules of thumb" for problem solving. These representations can vary from solver to solver across a wide domain of problem types.

Forming a suitable representation for the problem is the key to getting started. The second concern is relevancy (choosing which information to consider and to incorporate into your solution path). As you learn, you actively interact with the given information and your own prior knowledge. You construct meanings based on your interpretations of circumstances.

As a simple example, consider the problem of a mass sliding down an inclined plane that is frictionless (see the accompanying figure). The length of the incline is l, and a mass M is starting from the top, which is height h above the ground. The problem is to determine the velocity of the mass when it reaches the bottom of the incline.

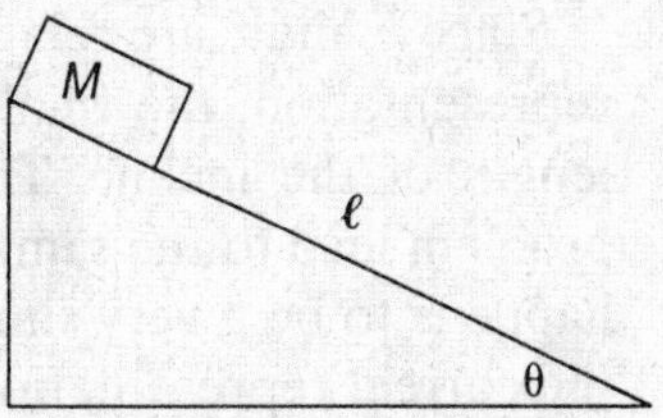

If the mass starts from rest, there are two ways to approach this problem. Suppose your first idea is to determine the acceleration of the mass down the incline. Since gravity acts on the mass, the acceleration down the incline is equal to

$$\mathbf{a} = \mathbf{g} \sin \theta$$

where **g** is the acceleration of gravity, equal to 9.8 meters per second squared. Now, since the time to go down the incline is not known, and we assume that the acceleration is constant (always ask yourself question such as "What assumptions am I making about this problem?" or "What representation have I chosen?"), we could try to determine to final velocity, **v**, by using a known expression from linear motion (kinematics) that does not explicitly involve time (does that mean that the concept "time" is irrelevant for this problem?):

$$\mathbf{v}^2 = 2\,\mathbf{a}\ell$$

This means that the final velocity at the bottom of the incline is given (after substituting for the acceleration) by

$$\mathbf{v} = \sqrt{2\mathbf{g}\ell \sin\theta}$$

Notice that both the mass and the height of the incline are absent from the final expression. Are these quantities, like the time, "irrelevant" to the problem? Clearly, what we use is dictated by how we choose to interpret and represent the problem. If we designate this problem as one of a class of kinematics problems, then certain expressions are independent of given quantities. However, did you observe that the height is implicit, since $h = \ell \sin\theta$?

There is another way to do this problem. If we consider the law of conservation of energy (since no friction is present), we can represent the problem in terms of the loss of potential energy balanced by the gain in kinetic energy. Mathematically this is stated as

$$M\mathbf{g}h = \frac{1}{2}M\mathbf{v}^2$$

Now, we simply cancel out the mass from both sides and solve for the velocity to get

$$\mathbf{v}^2 = 2\mathbf{g}h$$

Since h and ℓ are related, the answers are equivalent. Notice that, in this representation, the final expression is independent of the mass and the length of the incline. Thus, two equivalent representations of the same problem lead to the same final answer (as we would expect). This example happens to be a very simple one. With a really difficult problem, choosing the correct representation is the key to the correct solution.

The second elements in a problem are the **obstacles**. These are the factors that prevent you from immediately achieving your goal. In the example of Section 4.1, the obstacle to answering yes or no was the needing to know how long the passing maneuver would take and how much additional distance would be covered by each of the three vehicles (your car, the truck, and the oncoming car). In the example of the inclined plane, the obstacles depended on what representation you chose for the problem. In the motion representation, not knowing how long the mass takes to slide down the incline might be an obstacle for some students but not for others. You see that different solvers may encounter different obstacles.

Deciding on the proper method (or path) to solve a problem most efficiently is the main focus of **problem solving** as a process. In the following sections we will discuss several methods that have been identified by researchers as typical ways in which students solve physics problems. By studying these methods, you may recognize the way you solve problems; and, if you are not satisfied with your results, you can begin now to modify your procedures.

4.3 Problem-Solving Techniques

Problem solving consists of the mental and behavioral operations necessary to reach the goal of a problem. When you begin the solution process, you rely on stored knowledge about the particular problem and the subject area and on your past problem-solving experience.

A set procedure that, when followed, has been shown to solve a problem successfully is known as an **algorithm**. An algorithm may or may not make use of a formula. For example, the procedure for locating the image formed by a convex lens, using a ray diagram, is an example of an algorithm. On the other hand, given the mass and acceleration of an object, the use of the formula $\mathbf{F} = m\mathbf{a}$ to calculate the net force acting on the object is also an algorithm. Reliance on algorithms can sometimes hinder the ability to answer qualitative questions that require explanations.

4.4 Problem-Solving Heuristics

When an algorithm is not used, several other rules of thumb, or **heuristics**, have been identified as being helpful. These heuristics do not guarantee a successful conclusion, but they are often useful in moving toward the goal of a problem.

One simple heuristic that aids in the development of a successful representation of a problem is to redescribe the problem mentally. When you read a problem for the first time, you use your knowledge of reading comprehension to understand (parse) the sentences and interpret them mentally in terms of the conceptual knowledge required. Often, if a problem is poorly worded or if you have difficulty understand the meanings of some words ("lexical" difficulty), a redescription is useful.

One way to redescribe a problem is to rephrase it. Obviously, on an exam, your teacher will not be able to help you do this. When reviewing, however, you should practice rephrasing problems to help you handle this situation on a test. Another thing you can do is make a sketch of the problem situation. The old saying "A picture is worth a thousand words" is certainly true in problem solving. Also, if the problem is especially theoretical, putting in simple numbers sometimes will help you to understand the relationships involved.

A heuristic often used in mathematical proofs is *reductio ad absurdum* ("reducing to an absurdity"). In this heuristic, you try to establish the truth of something by first assuming that it is false. Following the rules of deductive logic, you proceed to analyze the situation until you reach an absurdity. You can then conclude that your original assumption about the falsity of the proposition was wrong, and it is indeed true. Although *reductio ad absurdum* is not often employed in the solution of physics problems, it is a method of logic that may occasionally be needed. In free-response questions, if something needs to be proved correct, you may on occasion find this heuristic useful.

Beginning physics students often use a heuristic called "working backward." They start with the goals and try to associate them with the givens. Usually, this means searching for a formula that contains the desired quantity and then determining whether the givens will fit into it. For example, in the inclined plane problem, where the goal was to determine the final velocity of the mass at the bottom, in the motion representation we established a formula for final velocity that was independent of time, and then proceeded to manipulate algebraically for an answer. This method of operation is all right for simple problems. For solving more difficult problems, however, greater conceptual knowledge is required since there may not exist a prior, explicit relationship among the quantities that enables us to immediately write an equation.

A heuristic commonly used by more experienced solvers is the "working forward" method. In this heuristic, you start with the givens and choose a representation that will link them together under the conditions of the laws of physics. From that broad viewpoint, mathematical relationships are established that can then be manipulated to find the solution. The energy representation of the inclined plane problem is an example of this methodology. Considering the law of conservation of energy to be basically responsible for the actions involved, we expressed that situation mathematically and then solved for velocity as a consequence of that law of physics!

Another heuristic to consider is "hill climbing." When you use hill climbing, you plan steps that will take you closer to your goal. In chess, for example, hill climbing is used when a move is made to put the opponent's king in check. Hill climbing may be helpful in solving a difficult physics problem. Suppose, for example, you are given a problem involving a suspension bridge. The goal is to determine whether a given load on the supported roadway will hold. If you are starting with a sketch, look at the incremental force elements on a given portion of the cable, and then state that the sum of all forces must remain zero, you have used the hill climbing heuristic. (The name "hill climbing" derives from the technique used by hikers to find their way out of a mountainous forest. If they know that the top of the mountain is above the tree line, thus enabling them to see their camp or a town, they will walk only in an uphill, or hill-climbing, direction.)

Related to hill climbing is another heuristic known as "means-ends analysis." In this heuristic, you break the problem into smaller, easier subgoals and proceed to solve them. The hope is that, considering the solutions to the subgoals, you will be able to solve the problem more efficiently. Problems that have steps labeled a, b, c, etc., call explicitly for means-ends analysis. A problem in which three subgoals are suppressed involves an implicit use of means-ends analysis since these prior steps, although not identified, must be solved in order to reach the final goal.

The final heuristic we will discuss is called the "method of analogies." Often, a difficult problem will have some similarity to a previously solved problem. It is also possible to use an analogy when understanding the behavior of a system. For example, certain types of electric circuits using alternating currents behave analogously to a mechanical oscillating system. In fact, the equations governing these systems are remarkably similar. The equations for rotational kinematics are similar to those of linear kinematics. Although the use of an analogy can often lead to a better understanding of a system, caution is needed since an analogy cannot replace an actual system.

CHAPTER 5

Problem-Solving Strategies for the AP Physics B Examination

5.1 Introduction

Your physics teacher has developed a very personal style for creating the tests given to you in class. Probably you have been prepared well to take the AP examination. If you live in New York State, you are familiar with the structure and format of a standardized physics examination, the Regents examination. If you live in any state, you have observed the structure and format of the College Board Achievement Test in Physics. Whereas the achievement test is entirely multiple choice, the Regents examination, like the AP test, contains a free-response part.

Achievement tests and state-mandated examinations are professionally designed to provide valid assessments of all students taking them. These examinations have undergone rigorous reliability and validity checks to make sure that they measure what they are supposed to. The Advanced Placement Physics Examination is no different in this respect. Published by the Educational Testing Service, the examination includes questions contributed by many teachers along strict guidelines. The graders, or readers, also follow strict guidelines for the awarding of points (especially partial credit). You will not have the luxury of having your own teacher grade your examination paper. The reader does not know who you are, what your strengths and weaknesses are, or how you approach problems or express yourself on an exam. Therefore, it is very important that you learn what is expected of you on the AP Physics Examination and that you express your thoughts clearly, concisely, and completely (the three C's). Although there may be some design flaws and/or careless writing on the examination that can be used to your advantage (if you know what to look for), it is foolish to rely on such flaws as aids to achieving a better grade.

5.2 The Structure of Multiple-Choice Questions

Whether you are comfortable or uncomfortable with multiple-choice questions, the fact remains that they are among the most popular formats for test items. Carefully constructed, they can be extraordinarily powerful in combining ease of scoring with a decent measure of cognitive behavior. The 70 multiple-choice questions on the AP Physics B Examination are worth 50 percent of your score.

We can divide a typical multiple-choice question into two parts. The first part, containing the problem statement, is called the "stem." The second part is referred to as the "options." In a typical question, five options are provided and you are requested to select the "best possible answer." This is not always the same as the "correct" answer, so be careful. The remaining options are referred to as "distractors."

Sometimes, an item writer will choose a distractor based on experience with the kinds of mistakes students often make when answering a similar question. While the use of such distractors has been termed "entrapment" by some students, the fact remains that you will have to cope with options of this type. Widely separated numbers, for example, 2, 50, 2000, and 10,000, provide a difficult set of options. Likewise, numbers that include one that clearly doesn't belong, are an obvious setup for guessing; a set such as 2, 5, 7, and 50 may lead an unwary student to chose 50 as the answer. On the other hand, the number set 2, 5, 7, and 8 makes it very difficult to guess the answer.

Another distinction in distractors involves the way they are written. Sometimes, one option is in a form different from the others, perhaps markedly longer or shorter or grammatically different.

Three basic types of multiple-choice questions are common to most examinations: recall, analysis, and synthesis questions.

Recall involves the direct retrieval of information from memory. Here is an example of a recall question:

> In a vector construction, two vectors are always drawn.
> (A) head to tail
> (B) head to head
> (C) tail to tail
> (D) any way desired
> (E) tail to head
> (The answer is option A.)

No advanced mental activity is required to answer a recall question, just memorization. Carefully written, however, recall questions can be notoriously tricky, and on the AP Physics B Examination, according to the ETS, 20 percent of the multiple-choice questions are recall questions.

Analysis requires the application of a set of procedures or algorithms that have been shown to be successful. For example, if you are presented with a series of wires or strings with weights hanging from them, and you are asked to determine whether the system will remain in equilibrium, you will have to *analyze* the situation, using Newton's laws for forces to find out the answer. This analysis will involve following a set procedure such as constructing vector diagrams or setting the algebraic formulas for the force components equal to zero. Here is an example of an analysis question:

A mass m is suspended vertically on a string attached to a fixture. A second mass M is attached by a string to the bottom of the first mass. The tension in the upper string is

(A) $(M + m)\mathbf{g}$ N
(B) $(Mm)\mathbf{g}$ N
(C) $(Mm / M + m)\mathbf{g}$ N
(D) $(M - m)\mathbf{g}$ N
(E) none of the above
(The answer is option A.)

Synthesis is a complex application of analysis and recall, coupled with judgment and decision making. When you *synthesize* something, you "build up" a conclusion by using deduction, induction, intuition, given information, analysis, and experience. The truck-passing problem discussed in Section 4.1 involves synthesis since, in actual experience, the decision of whether or not to begin the maneuver of passing is based on experience, knowledge, and quick problem-solving assessment skills.

5.3 Approaching the Multiple-Choice Questions

On the Advanced Placement Physics B Examination, you have 1.5 hours to answer 70 multiple-choice questions. That time limit means that on average you have a little over 1 minute to assess the nature of the question, recall information, do a calculation, and scan the options for distractors. Since the raw score for Section I is based on the number of correct questions answered, with a penalty for guessing, it is better to omit a question than to guess randomly. If, however, you can eliminate one or more of the options as clearly incorrect, it may be worth your while to make a considered guess. You should omit a question only as a last resort, with the intention of going back to it later. Since the ETS does not expect you to get every question correct, the highest score, 5, is awarded within a range of calculated scores based on the performance of all the test-takers. This "curve" can be used to your benefit if you approach the test wisely.

The fact that the examination was professionally designed and written means that great lengths were taken to make sure the questions are consistent with the intended level of the examination and that the distractors are, as far as possible, logical. Looking for inconsistencies in wording or numbers is a useful step in handling a difficult question, but there is no substitute for recalling the information needed and working out the analysis and synthesis questions. As you read a question, be sure you understand what the words mean and what concepts they refer to. Sometimes, the wording of a question is so standard that you can almost classify the question before you finish reading it. With enough practice, this kind of "categorization" can be very useful.

Another aspect of problem solving to be on the lookout for is the old "disguise" trick. Often a question will test your knowledge of a concept by using a semantic variation of it in a different context. For example, the concept "normal force" in statics might be replaced by "reaction force" when considering a ladder leaning against a wall. A useful philosophy to remember when approaching test questions is "It's not what you call it; it's what it is"!

5.4 Approaching the Free-Response Questions

The second part of the AP Physics B Examination consists of six free-response questions. Usually, you must calculate, make a vector or ray diagram, interpret a graph, or provide an explanation of some physical situation drawn from the main survey topics in physics. If we consider the following as subsections of physics: mechanics, heat, light, electricity and magnetism, and atomic and nuclear physics, we can see that there is room for multiple questions within a topic. Since mechanics includes kinematics (motion), dynamics (forces), and energy (as well as wave motion), a large percentage of problems can be taken from this area. However, no guarantee on the number of questions from a particular subtopic is ever implied by the ETS or this review book.

In this book, you will find a wide variety of problem types in each topical review chapter, as well as three practice examinations. Follow the solution guidelines carefully if you have difficulty with any of the problems. Even if you successfully solved the problems, reading the solutions may provide you with alternatives that offer a different perspective and greater insight into a particular problem.

The free-response questions are worth 50 percent of your exam grade, and great care must be used to make sure you include all necessary information, including units, throughout all calculations! It is also important to state, when beginning a problem, the laws or concepts of physics that you are assuming or using. The more you include, the easier it will be for the reader to grade your paper and to award you as many points as you deserve. On average, you will have about 15 minutes to solve each free-response question (a total of 1.5 hours is available for Section II). In summary, here are some useful hints to follow:

1. Always begin the problem by stating in mathematical terms or in words which underlying physics principle you are using. If the problem involves conservation of energy, for example, write down the general forms of the conservation laws used.
2. Always use and mention the proper SI units throughout the calculation. Make sure all units match on both sides of an equation and that the answer makes sense. This aspect is crucial. Too often, students rely on calculators to provide answers that they accept as correct without making the extra effort to see whether the answer is relevant or logical.
3. Communicate with the reader. Write as much as possible, but avoid wordiness or redundancy. Include explanations, charts, graphs, numbers—anything that can help your case. Remember that the reader has no knowledge of who you are or what you know.

4. Don't be afraid to use heuristics to solve the problems. Add numbers if they will help establish a relationship. Make a sketch, try analogies, use all the "tricks in the book" to help you manage a difficult situation. Above all, do not leave anything blank!
5. Read the directions and the problem statement carefully. Give the examiners what they want! Make sure you understand the meaning of every word and the context in which it appears.
6. Relax. Problem solving requires behavioral as well as mental activities. If you are nervous and stressed out, you will not do your best. Don't cram for the examination the night before. Staying up until four o'clock in the morning for last-minute studying will not help. If you have been reviewing consistently, using this book, and asking your teacher questions, a good night's sleep is the best last-minute preparation for the exam.

5.5 Summary

This chapter is the last of a series that attempts to show you how you can better organize your studying and learning to make test taking more effective. We explored the nature of problem solving together and discovered several rules of thumb, called "heuristics," that can help you to better understand how you approach a problem. We also examined the nature of multiple-choice questions and the strategies that exist for handling them. Finally, we looked at the free-response questions and the aspects of skills and knowledge that they require.

We are on a great adventure together. I have written this review book as a guide to help you through the complexities of physics. The book talks to you, not at you. We will be together for a long time as we review and study physics. If you are starting this book early in the year, the road ahead until May will be a long one. If you are using this book as preparation for the exam a few weeks before you will take it, I will try to lead you through the review as painlessly as possible. I want you to feel good about your physics experience.

We will now begin the task of reviewing topical material. If you need to brush up on some math skills, I suggest you begin with the Appendix and go over whatever material you need to review. Let's get started!

CHAPTER 6

Vectors

6.1 Coordinate Systems and Frames of Reference

We begin our review of physics with the idea that all observations and measurements are made relative to a suitably chosen frame of reference. In other words, when observations are made that will be the basis of future predictions, we must be careful to note from what point of view those observations are being made. For example, if you are standing on the street and see a car driving by, you observe the car and all of its occupants moving relative to you. However, to the driver and other occupants of the car, the situation is different: they may not appear to be in motion relative to themselves; rather, you appear to be moving backward relative to them.

If you were to get into your car, drive out to meet the other car, and travel at the same speed in the same direction, right next to the first car, there would be no relative motion between the two cars. These different points of view are known as **frames of reference**, and they are very important aspects of physics.

A coordinate system within a frame of reference is defined to be a set of reference lines that intersect at an arbitrarily chosen fixed point called the **origin**. In the Cartesian coordinate system, the reference lines are three mutually perpendicular lines designated x, y, and z (see Figure 6.1). The coordinate system must provide a set of rules for locating objects within that frame of reference. In the three-dimensional Cartesian system, if we define a plane containing the x- and y- coordinates (let's say a horizontal plane), then the z-axis specifies direction up or down.

It is often useful to compare observations made in two different frames of reference. In the example above, the motion of the occupants of the car was reduced to zero if we transformed our coordinate system to the car moving at constant velocity. In this case we say that the car is an **inertial frame of reference**. In such a frame, it is impossible to observe whether or not the reference frame is in motion if the observers are moving with it.

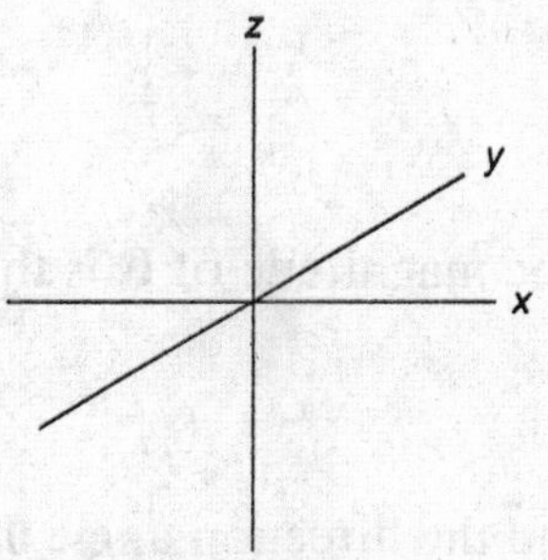

FIGURE 6.1

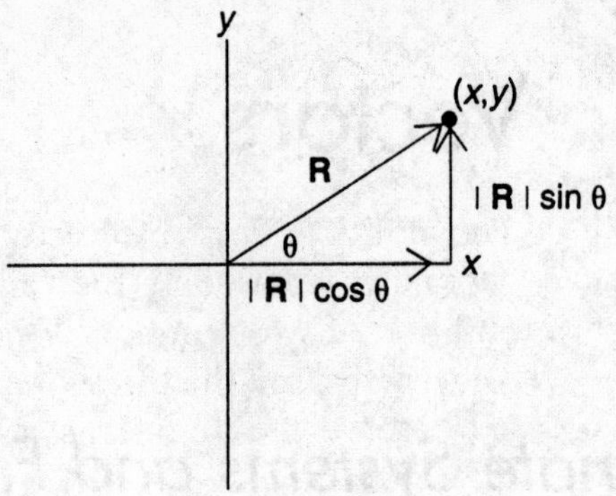

FIGURE 6.2

6.2 Vectors

Another way of locating the position of an object in the Cartesian system is with a directed line segment, or **vector**. If you draw an arrow, starting from the origin, to a point in space (see Figure 6.2), you have defined a position vector **R** whose magnitude is given by | **R** | and is equal to the linear distance between the origin and the point (x,y). The direction of the vector is given by the acute angle, indentified by the Greek letter θ, that the arrow makes with the positive x-axis. Any quantity that has both magnitude and direction is called a **vector quantity**. Any quantity that has only magnitude is a **scalar quantity**. Examples of vector quantities are force, velocity, weight, and displacement. Examples of scalar quantities are mass, distance, speed, and energy.

If we designate the magnitude of the vector **R** as r, and the direction angle is given by θ, then we have an alternative coordinate system called the **polar coordinate** system. In two dimensions, to locate the point in the Cartesian system (x,y) involves going x units horizontally and y units vertically. Additionally, we can show that (see Figure 6.2)

$$x = r\cos\theta \quad \text{and} \quad y = r\sin\theta$$

Having established this polar form for vectors, we can easily show that r and θ can be expressed in terms of x and y as follows:

$$r^2 = x^2 + y^2$$

$$\tan\theta = \frac{y}{x}$$

The magnitude of **R** is then given by

$$|\mathbf{R}| = r = \sqrt{x^2 + y^2}$$

and the direction angle θ is given by

$$\theta = \tan^{-1}\frac{y}{x}$$

6.3 Addition of Vectors

A. Geometric Considerations

The ability to combine vectors is a very important tool of physics. From a geometric standpoint, the "addition" of two vectors is not the same as the addition of two numbers. When we state that, given two vectors **A** and **B**, we wish to form the third vector **C** such that **A** + **B** = **C**, we must be careful to preserve the directions of the vectors relative to our chosen frame of reference.

One way to do this "addition" is by the construction of what is called a **vector diagram**. Vectors are identified geometrically by a directed arrow that has a "head" and a "tail." We will consider a series of examples. First, suppose a girl is walking from her house a distance of five blocks east and then an additional two blocks east. How can we represent these displacements vectorially? First, we must choose a suitable scale to represent the magnitude lengths of the vectors. In this case, let us just call the scale "one vector unit" or just "one unit," to be equal to one block of distance. Let us also agree that "east" is to the right (and hence "north" is directed up). A vector diagram for this set of displacements is given in Figure 6.3.

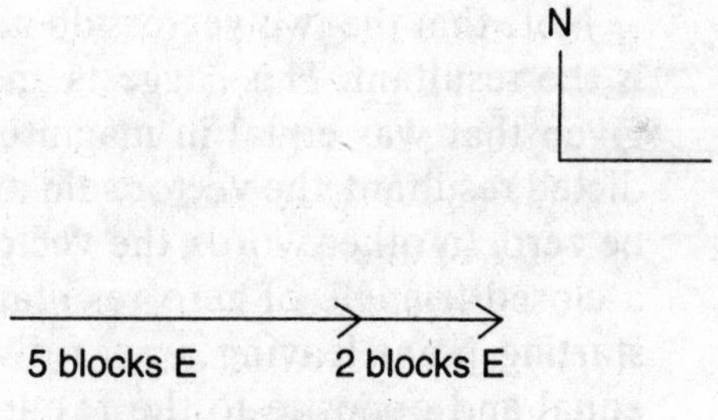

FIGURE 6.3

Now, for our second example, suppose the girl walks five blocks east and then two blocks northeast (that is, 45 degrees north of east). Since our intuition tells us that the final displacement will be in the general direction of north and east, we draw our vector diagram, using the same scale as before, so that the two vectors are connected head to tail. The vector diagram will look like Figure 6.4. The resultant is drawn from the tail of the first vector to the head of the second, forming a triangle (some texts use the "parallelogram" method of construction, which is equivalent). The direction of the resultant is measured from the tail of the vector inside the triangle.

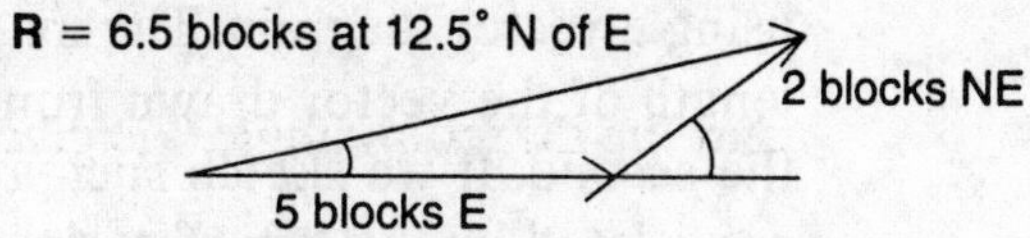

FIGURE 6.4

For our third example, suppose the girl walks five blocks east and then two blocks north. Figure 6.5 shows the vector diagram for this set of displacements.

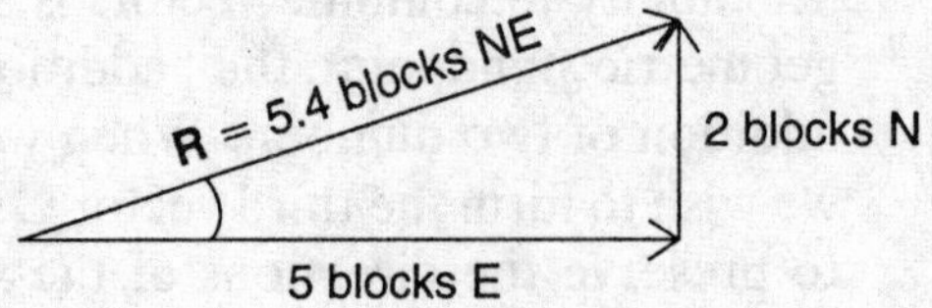

FIGURE 6.5

Finally, for our fourth example, suppose the girl walks five blocks east and then two blocks west. Her final displacement will be three blocks east of the starting point.

From these examples, we conclude that, as the angle between two vectors increases, the magnitude of their resultant decreases. Also, the magnitude of the resultant between two vectors is a maximum when the vectors are in the same direction (at a relative angle of 0 degree), and a minimum when they are in the opposite direction (at a relative angle of 180 degrees). It is important to remember that the vectors must be constructed head to tail and a suitable scale chosen for the system.

Note that the two vectors do not form a closed figure. The "missing link" is the resultant. This suggests an important concept. If a third vector was given that was equal in magnitude but opposite in direction to the predicted resultant, the vector sum of that resultant and the third vector would be zero. In other words, the vector sum of those three vectors would form a closed triangle of zero resultant, meaning that the girl returned to her starting point leaving a zero displacement. In physics, that third vector, equal and opposite to the resultant, is called the **equilibrant**. Figure 6.6 illustrates this concept.

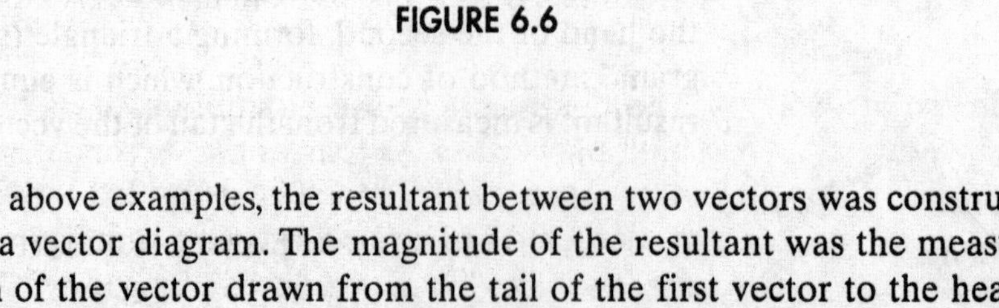

FIGURE 6.6

B. Algebraic Considerations

In the above examples, the resultant between two vectors was constructed using a vector diagram. The magnitude of the resultant was the measured length of the vector drawn from the tail of the first vector to the head of the second. If we sketch such a situation, we form a triangle whose sides are related by the **law of cosines** and whose angles are related by the **law of sines**.

Consider the vector triangle in Figure 6.7 with arbitrary sides a, b, and c and corresponding angles A, B, and C.

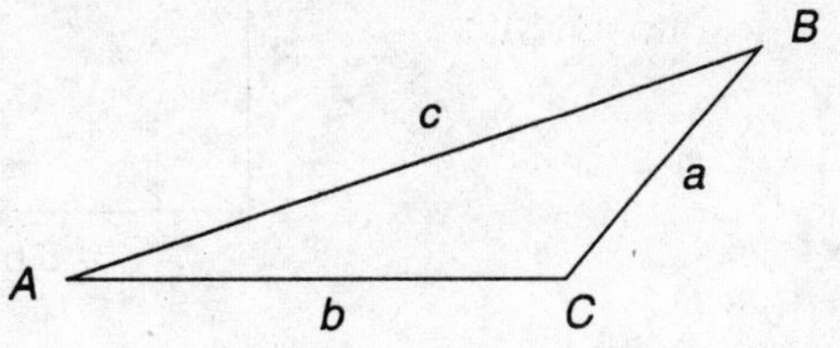

FIGURE 6.7

The law of cosines states that

$$c^2 = a^2 + b^2 - 2\,ab\cos C$$

The law of sines states that

$$\frac{a}{\sin A} = \frac{b}{\sin B} = \frac{c}{\sin C}$$

If we use the information given in our second example above, we see that in Figure 6.8 the vectors have the following magnitudes and directions:

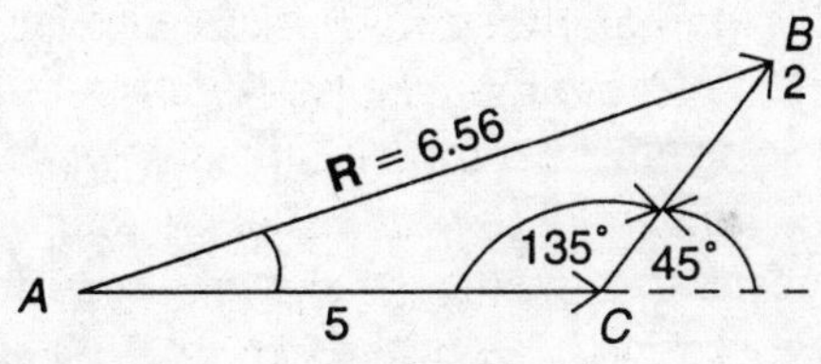

FIGURE 6.8

Using the law of cosines, we obtain the magnitude of the resultant in "blocks":

$$c = \sqrt{(2)^2 + (5)^2 - 2(2)(5)\cos 135} = 6.56$$

Using the law of sines, we find that the direction of the resultant is angle A:

$$\frac{6.56}{\sin 135} = \frac{2}{\sin A}$$

Angle A turns out to be equal to 12.45 degrees north of east.

C. Addition of Multiple Vectors

The discussion of the equilibrant leads to the idea of the addition of multiple vectors. As long as the vectors are constructed head to tail, multiple vectors can be added in any order. If the resultant is zero, the diagram constructed will be a closed geometric figure. This was shown in the case of three vectors forming a closed triangle, as in the example above. Thus, if the girl walks five blocks east, two blocks north, and five blocks west, the vector diagram will look like Figure 6.9, with the resultant displacement being equal to two blocks north.

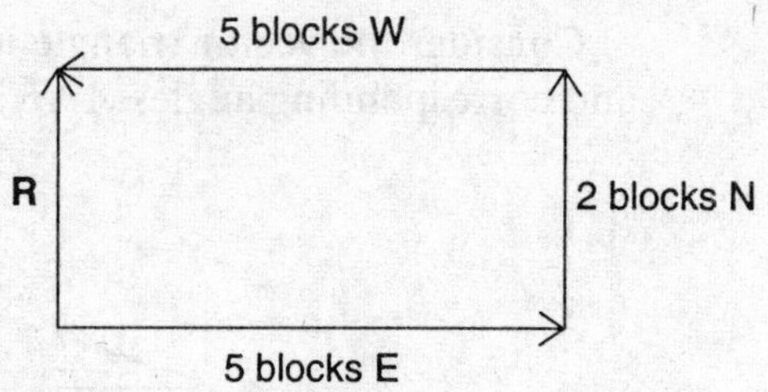

FIGURE 6.9

6.4 Subtraction of Vectors

The difference between two vectors can be understood by considering the process of displacement. Suppose that, in Figure 6.10, we identify two sets of points (x,y) and (u,v) in a coordinate system as shown. Each point can be located within the coordinate system by a position vector drawn from the origin to that point. The displacement of an object from point A to point B would be represented by the vector drawn from A to B. This vector is defined to be the difference between the two position vectors and is sometimes called $\Delta\mathbf{R}$, so that $\Delta\mathbf{R} = \mathbf{R}_2 - \mathbf{R}_1$.

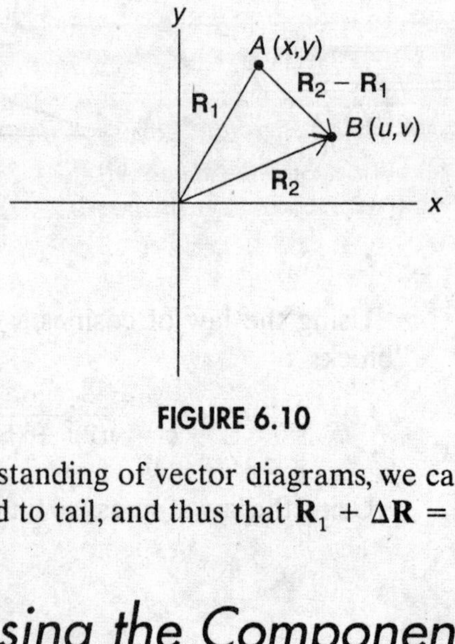

FIGURE 6.10

From our understanding of vector diagrams, we can see that $\mathbf{R}_1$ and $\Delta\mathbf{R}$ are connected head to tail, and thus that $\mathbf{R}_1 + \Delta\mathbf{R} = \mathbf{R}_2$!

6.5 Addition Methods Using the Components of Vectors

Any single vector in space can be **resolved** into two perpendicular components in a suitably chosen coordinate system. The methods of vector resolution were discussed in Section 6.2, but we can review them here. Given a vector (sketched in Figure 6.11) representing a displacement of 100 meters northeast (that is, making a 45-degree angle with the positive x-axis), we can observe that it is composed of an x and a y (a horizontal and a vertical) component that can be geometrically or algebraically determined.

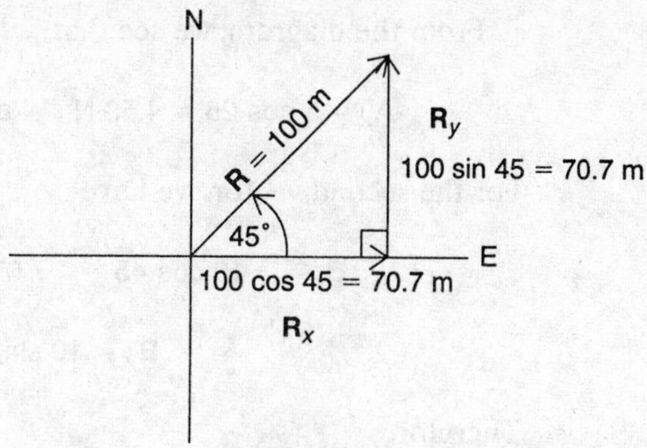

FIGURE 6.11

Geometrically, if we were to draw the 100-meter vector to scale at the correct angle, then projecting a perpendicular line down from the head of the given vector to the x-axis would construct the two perpendicular components. Algebraically, we see that if we have a given vector **R**, then, in the x direction, we have

$$\mathbf{R}_x = \mathbf{R} \cos \theta \qquad \text{and} \qquad \mathbf{R}_y = \mathbf{R} \sin \theta$$

where the magnitude of **R** is R.

This method of vector resolution can be useful when adding two or more vectors. Since all vectors in the same direction add up numerically, and all vectors in opposite directions subtract numerically, therefore, if we are given two vectors, the resultant between them will be found from the addition and subtraction of the respective components. In other words, if vector **A** has components $\mathbf{A}_x$ and $\mathbf{A}_y$, and if vector **B** has components $\mathbf{B}_x$ and $\mathbf{B}_y$, the resultant vector **C** will have components $\mathbf{C}_x$ and $\mathbf{C}_y$ such that

$$\mathbf{C}_x = \mathbf{A}_x + \mathbf{B}_x \qquad \text{and} \qquad \mathbf{C}_y = \mathbf{A}_y + \mathbf{B}_y$$

An example of this method is shown in Figure 6.12. Suppose we have two vectors, **A** and **B**, that represent tensions in two ropes applied at the origin of the coordinate system (let's say it's a box). The resultant force between these tensions (which are vector quantities) can be found by determining the respective x and y components of the given vectors.

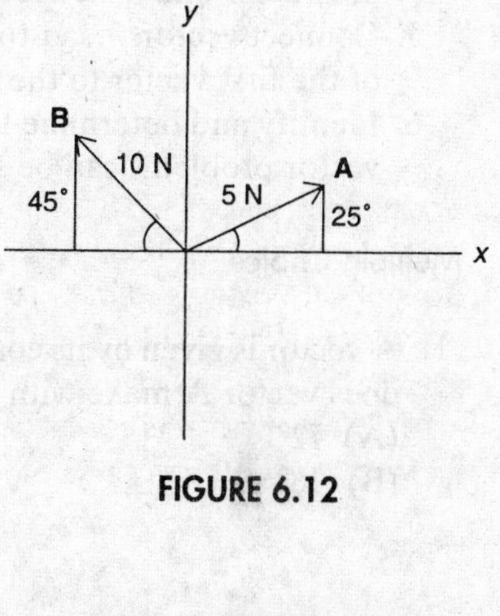

FIGURE 6.12

From the diagram, we see that

$$\mathbf{A}_x = 5 \cos 25 = 4.53 \text{ N} \quad \text{and} \quad \mathbf{A}_y = 5 \sin 25 = 2.11 \text{ N}$$

For the second vector, we have

$$\mathbf{B}_x = -10 \cos 45 = -7.07 \text{ N (since it is pointing left)}$$

$$\mathbf{B}_y = 10 \sin 45 = 7.07 \text{ N}$$

Therefore,

$$\mathbf{C}_x = 4.53 \text{ N} - 7.07 \text{ N} = -2.54 \text{ N} \quad \text{and} \quad \mathbf{C}_y = 2.11 \text{ N} + 7.07 \text{ N} = 9.18 \text{ N}$$

The magnitude of the resultant vector, **C**, is given by

$$|\mathbf{C}| = \sqrt{(-2.54)^2 + (9.18)^2} = 9.52 \text{ N}$$

The angle that vector **C** makes with the positive x-axis is about 105°.

Problem-Solving Strategies for Vectors

Vectors are a fundamental tool of physics. They provide a representation for physical quantities that are changing in both magnitude and direction. It is therefore essential that you understand the way in which vectors combine algebraically and geometrically. When solving a vector problem, be sure to:

1. Understand the frame of reference for the situation.
2. Select an appropriate coordinate system for the situation. Cartesian systems do not necessarily have to be vertical and horizontal (a mass sliding down an inclined plane is an example of a rotated system with the "x-axis" parallel to the incline).
3. Pick an appropriate scale for starting your vector diagram. For example, in a problem with displacement, a scale of 1 cm = 1 m might be appropriate.
4. Recognize the given orientation of the vectors as they correspond to geographical directions (N, E, S, W). Be sure to maintain the same directions as you draw your vector triangle or parallelogram. Use a protractor and a metric ruler.
5. Connect vectors head to tail, and connect the resultant from the tail of the first vector to the head of the last vector.
6. Identify and determine the components of the vectors. In most cases, vector problems can be simplified using components.

Practice Problems for Chapter 6

Multiple Choice

1. A vector is given by its components, $\mathbf{A}_x = 2.5$ and $\mathbf{A}_y = 7.5$. What angle does vector **A** make with the positive x-axis?
(A) 72°
(B) 18°

(C) 25°
(D) 50°
(E) 75°

2. Which pair of vectors could produce a resultant of 35?
(A) 15 and 15
(B) 20 and 20
(C) 30 and 70
(D) 20 and 60
(E) 20 and 70

3. A vector has a magnitude of 17 units and makes an angle of 20° with the positive x-axis. The magnitude of the horizontal component of this vector is
(A) 16 units
(B) 4.1 units
(C) 5.8 units
(D) 50 units
(E) 12 units

4. As the angle between a given vector and the horizontal axis increases from 0° to 90°, the magnitude of the vertical component of this vector
(A) decreases
(B) increases and then decreases
(C) decreases and then increases
(D) increases
(E) remains the same

5. Vector **A** has a magnitude of 10 units and makes an angle of 30° with the horizontal x-axis. Vector **B** has a magnitude of 25 units and makes an angle of 50° with the negative x-axis. What is the magnitude of the resultant between these two vectors?
(A) 20
(B) 35
(C) 15
(D) 45
(E) 25

6. Two concurrent vectors have magnitudes of 3 units and 8 units. The difference between these vectors is 8 units. The angle between these two vectors is
(A) 34°
(B) 56°
(C) 79°
(D) 113°
(E) 127°

7. Which of the following sets of displacements have equal resultants when performed in the order given?

I: 6 m east, 9 m north, 12 m west
II: 6 m north, 9 m west, 12 m east
III: 6 m east, 12 m west, 9 m north
IV: 9 m north, 6 m west, 12 m west

(A) I and IV
(B) I and II
(C) I, III, and IV
(D) I, II, IV
(E) II and IV

8. Which vector represents the direction of the two concurrent vectors shown below?

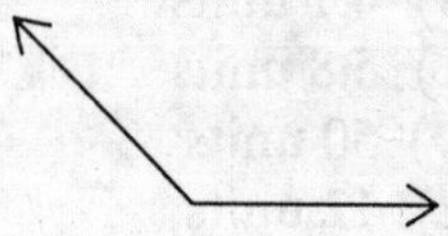

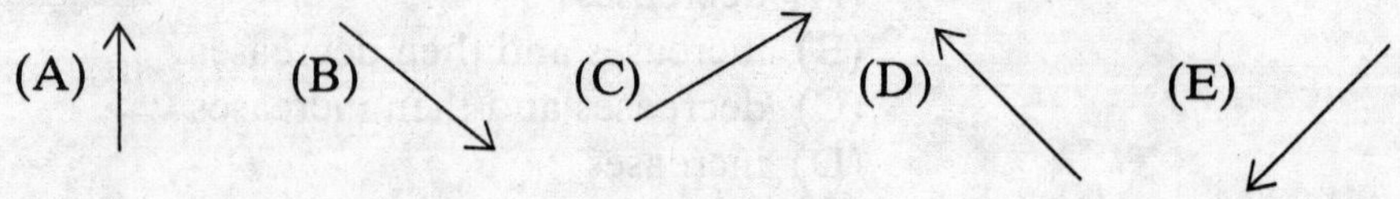

(A) (B) (C) (D) (E)

9. Three forces act concurrently on a point P as shown below. Which vector represents the direction of the resultant force on point P?

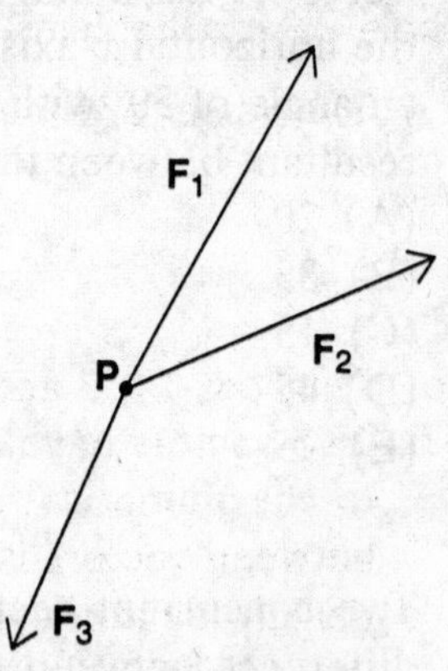

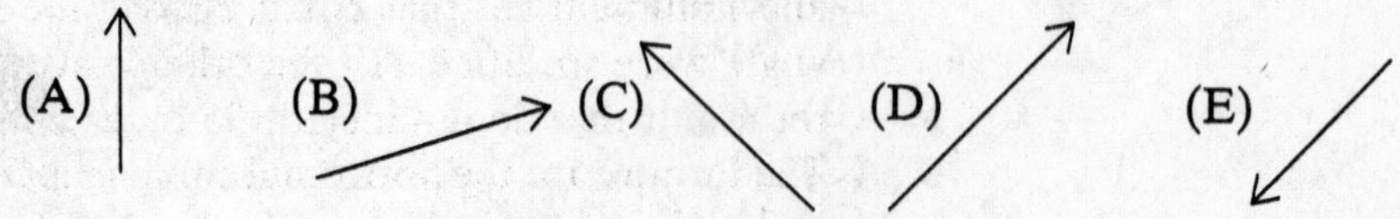

(A) (B) (C) (D) (E)

10. On a baseball field, first base is about 30 m away from home plate. A batter gets a "hit" and runs toward first base. She runs 3 m past the base and then runs back to stand on it. The magnitude of her final displacement from home plate is
(A) 27 m
(B) 30 m
(C) 33 m
(D) 36 m
(E) 40 m

Free Response

1. Using vector methods, prove that the line segment joining the midpoints of a triangle is parallel to the third side and equal to one-half of its magnitude.

2. Two vectors, **A** and **B**, are concurrent and attached at the tails with an angle θ between them. Given that each vector has components $\mathbf{A}_x$, $\mathbf{A}_y$ and $\mathbf{B}_x$, $\mathbf{B}_y$ respectively, use the law of cosines to show that

$$\cos\theta = \frac{A_xB_x + A_yB_y}{|A||B|}$$

3. A rectangular Cartesian coordinate system is rotated counterclockwise about the origin through an angle θ. Show that a point P that has coordinates (x,y) in the original coordinate system has coordinates (x', y') in the rotated system such that:

$$x' = x\cos + y\sin$$
$$y' = -x\sin\theta + y\cos$$

Solutions

Multiple-Choice Problems

1. **A** The angle for the vector to the positive x-axis is given by

$$\tan\theta = \frac{A_y}{A_x} = \frac{7.5}{2.5}$$

Thus $\tan\theta = 3$ and $\theta = 71.5°$ or, rounded off, 72°.

2. **B** Two vectors have a maximum resultant, whose magnitude is equal to the numerical sum of the vector magnitudes, when the angle between vectors is 0°. The resultant is a minimum at 180°, and the magnitude is equal to the numerical difference between the magnitudes. When this logic is used, only pair (20,20) produce a maximum and minimum set that could include the given value of 35 if the angle were specified. All the others have maximum and minimum resultants that do not include 35 in their range.

3. **A** The formula for the horizontal component of a vector **A** is $\mathbf{A}_x = |\mathbf{A}| \cos\theta$, where $|\mathbf{A}|$ is the magnitude of **A**. When the known values are used, values $\mathbf{A}_x = 17\cos 20 = 15.9$ units.

4. **D** The vertical component of a vector is proportional to the sine of the angle, which increases to a maximum at 90°.
5. **E** Form the components of each vector and then add these components, remembering the sign conventions; right and up are positive values. Thus, we have $\mathbf{A}_x = 10 \cos 30 = 8.66$ and $\mathbf{A}_y = 10 \sin 30 = 5$, $\mathbf{B}_x = -25 \cos 50 = -16.06$ and $\mathbf{B}_y = 25 \sin 50 = 19.15$.
   The components of the resultant are $\mathbf{C}_x = \mathbf{A}_x + \mathbf{B}_x = 8.66 - 16.06$, so $\mathbf{C}_x = -7.4$ unit and $\mathbf{C}_y = \mathbf{A}_y + \mathbf{B}_y = 5 + 19.15 = 24.15$. The magnitude of this resultant vector is given by

$$|\mathbf{C}| = \sqrt{\mathbf{C}_x^2 + \mathbf{C}_y^2} = \sqrt{(7.4)^2 + (24.15)^2}$$

   implying that $\mathbf{C} = 25$ units.
6. **C** Use the law of cosines where $a = 3$, $b = 8$, and $c = 8$, and solve for $\cos \theta$:

$$(8)^2 = (3)^2 + (8)^2 - 2(3)(8) \cos \theta$$

   Solving gives $\cos \theta = 0.1875$ and $\theta = 79°$.
7. **C** Vectors can be added in any order. The only requirement is that the vectors have the same magnitude and direction as they are shuffled. A look at the four sets of displacements indicates that I, III, and IV consist of the same vectors listed in different orders. These three sets will produce the same resultant.
8. **C** Sketch the vectors head to tail as if forming a vector triangle in construction. The resultant is drawn from the tail of the first vector to the head of the second. Choose the horizontal vector as the first one; then choice C is the general direction of the resultant.
9. **B** Sketch the vectors in any order, as shown below. Draw the resultant from the tail of the first vector to the head of the last.

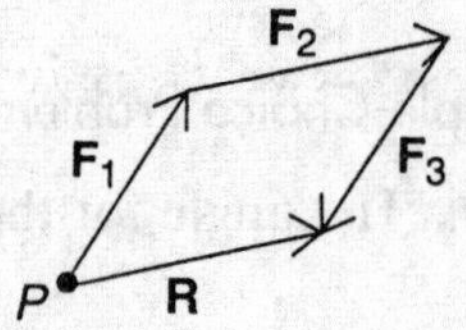

10. **B** The displacement is in the direction of first base and is equal in magnitude to the straight-line distance between home plate and first base (30 m).

Free-Response Problems

1. A typical triangle is shown on the following page. Let the sides be represented by vectors such that

$$\mathbf{DB} + \mathbf{BE} = \mathbf{DE} \text{ and } \mathbf{AB} + \mathbf{BC} = \mathbf{AC}$$

   Since our line is joining the midpoints, we can see that

$$\frac{1}{2}(\mathbf{AB}) + \frac{1}{2}(\mathbf{BC}) = \mathbf{DE}$$

and therefore

$$2(\mathbf{DE}) = \mathbf{AB} + \mathbf{BC} = \mathbf{AC}$$

The proof is complete.

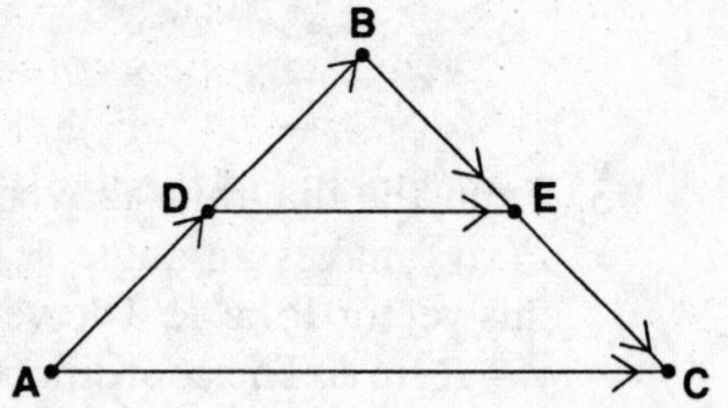

2. The situation is shown below. The "third" side of the vector triangle is **A − B**.

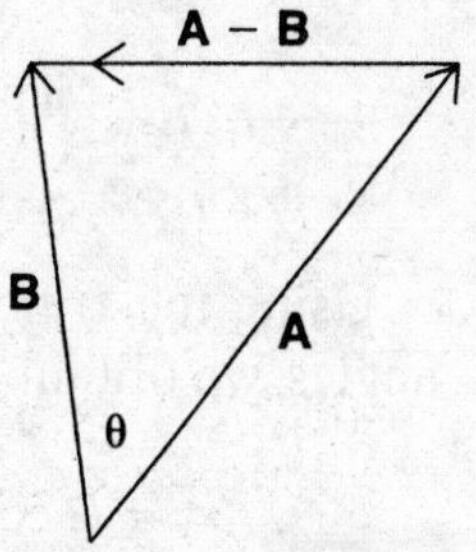

From the rules for vector subtraction, the components of **A − B** are $(\mathbf{A}_x - \mathbf{B}_y)$ and $(\mathbf{A}_y - \mathbf{B}_y)$. The law of cosines states that, for the given triangle,

$$|\mathbf{A} - \mathbf{B}|^2 = |\mathbf{A}|^2 + |\mathbf{B}|^2 - 2\,|\mathbf{A}|\,|\mathbf{B}|\cos\theta$$

Using our definitions of magnitudes and components, we have

$$(\mathbf{A}_x - \mathbf{B}_x)^2 + (\mathbf{A}_y - \mathbf{B}_y)^2 = \mathbf{A}_x^2 + \mathbf{A}_y^2 + \mathbf{B}_x^2 + \mathbf{B}_y^2 - 2\,|\mathbf{A}|\,|\mathbf{B}|\cos\theta$$

Expanding the left side and canceling like terms on both sides, we are left with

$$-2\mathbf{A}_x\mathbf{B}_x - 2\mathbf{A}_y\mathbf{B}_y = -2\,|\mathbf{A}|\,|\mathbf{B}|\cos\theta$$

Again, canceling like terms on both sides leaves us with the final expression as we solve for cos θ:

$$\cos\theta = \frac{\mathbf{A}_x\mathbf{B}_x + \mathbf{A}_y\mathbf{B}_y}{|\mathbf{A}|\,|\mathbf{B}|}$$

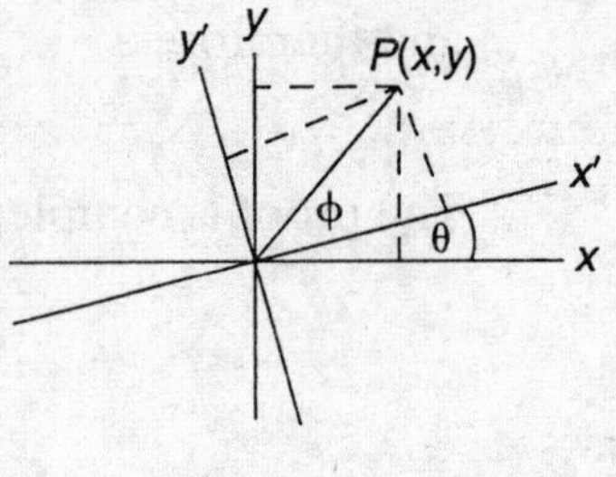

3. From the diagram above, we can see that the vector drawn to point $P(x,y)$ makes an angle ϕ to the original x-axis. Let the magnitude of this vector **P** be R. The vector will have components $x = R \cos \phi$ and $y = R \sin \phi$. The coordinate system is rotated counterclockwise through an angle θ as shown. Let vector **P** make an angle α to the new x-axis, the $x' =$ axis, such that $\alpha = \phi - \theta$. Thus, in the new rotated system, vector **P** has components given by $x' = R \cos \alpha$ and $y' = R \sin \alpha$. Therefore

$$x' = R \cos (\phi - \theta) \qquad \text{and} \qquad y' = R \sin (\phi - \theta)$$

Using the trigonometric identities for the difference between two angles, we obtain

$$x' = R \cos (\phi - \theta) = R \cos \phi \cos \theta + R \sin \phi \sin \theta$$

$$y' = R \sin (\phi - \theta) = R \sin \phi \cos \theta - R \cos \phi \sin \theta$$

But $x = R \cos \phi$ and $y = R \sin \phi$. Making that substitution and rearranging, we arrive at our transformation equations:

$$x' = x \cos \theta + y \sin \theta \qquad \text{and} \qquad y' = -x \sin \theta + y \cos \theta$$

CHAPTER 7

One-Dimensional Motion

7.1 Introduction

Motion involves the change in position of an object over time. When we observe an object moving, it is always with respect to a frame of reference. Since motion occurs in a particular direction, it is dependent on the choice of a coordinate system for that frame of reference. This fact leads us to the conclusion that there is a vector nature to motion that must be taken into account when we want to analyze how something moves.

In this chapter, we shall confine our discussions to motion in one dimension only. In physics, the study of motion is called **kinematics**. No hypotheses are made in kinematics concerning why something moves. Kinematics is a completely descriptive study of *how* something moves.

7.2 Average and Instantaneous Motion

Motion can take place either uniformly or nonuniformly. This means that, if an object is moving, relative to a frame of reference, the displacement changes, over a period of time, may be equal or unequal.

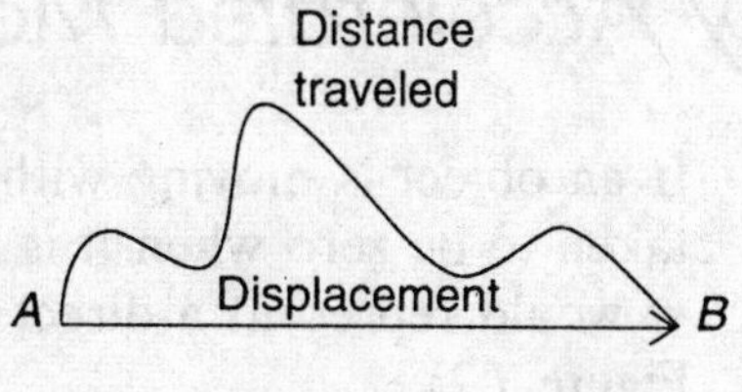

FIGURE 7.1 Displacement Versus Distance

If, in Figure 7.1, we consider the actual distance traveled by the object along some arbitrary path, we are dealing with a scalar quantity. The displacement vector **AB**, however, is directed along the line connecting points *A* and *B* (whether or not this is the actual route taken). Thus, when a baseball player hits a home run and runs around the bases, he or she may have traveled a distance of 360 feet (the bases are 90 feet apart), but the player's final displacement is zero (having started and ended up at the same place)!

If we are given the displacement vector of an object for a period of time Δt, we define the **average velocity**, $\bar{\mathbf{v}}$ to be equal to

$$\bar{\mathbf{v}} = \frac{\Delta \mathbf{x}}{\Delta t}.$$

This is a vector quantity since directions are specified. Numerically, we think of the average speed as being the ratio of the total distance traveled to the total elapsed time. The units of velocity are meters per second (m/s).

If we are interested in the velocity at any instant in time, we can define the **instantaneous velocity** to be the velocity, **v**, as determined at any precise time period. In a car, the speedometer registers instantaneous speed, which can become velocity if we take into account the direction of motion. If the velocity is constant, the average and instantaneous velocities are equal, and we can write simply

$$\Delta \mathbf{x} = \mathbf{v}\,\Delta t$$

It is possible that the observer making the measurements of motion is likewise in motion relative to the Earth. In this case, we consider the relative velocity between the two systems. If two objects, *a* and *b*, are moving in the same direction, the relative velocity between the objects is given by

$$\mathbf{v}_{\text{rel}} = \mathbf{v}_a - \mathbf{v}_b$$

In a similar way, if two objects, *a* and *b*, are approaching each other in opposite directions, the relative velocity between them is given by

$$\mathbf{v}_{\text{rel}} = \mathbf{v}_a + \mathbf{v}_b$$

7.3 Uniformly Accelerated Motion

If an object is moving with a constant velocity such that its position is taken to be zero when it is first observed, a graph of the expression $\mathbf{x} = \mathbf{v}t$ would represent a direct relationship between position and time (see Figure 7.2).

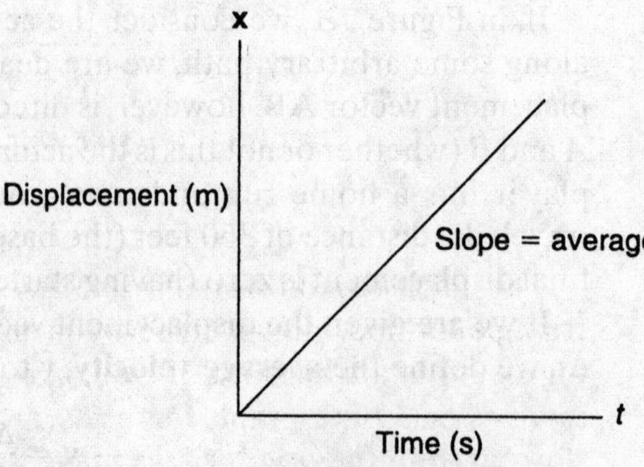

FIGURE 7.2

Since the line is straight, the constant slope (in which $\mathbf{v} = \Delta\mathbf{x}/\Delta t$) indicates that the velocity is constant throughout the time interval. If we were to plot velocity versus time for this motion, the graph might look like as shown in Figure 7.3.

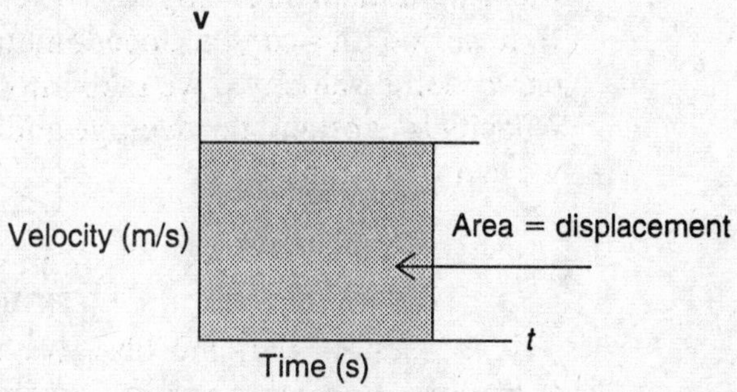

FIGURE 7.3

Notice that, for any time t, the area under the graph equals the displacement.

It is possible that the object is changing direction while maintaining a constant speed (uniform circular motion is an example of this situation), or that it is changing both speed and direction. In any case, if the velocity is changing, we say that the object is **accelerating**. If the velocity is changing uniformly, the object has uniform acceleration. In this case, a graph of velocity versus time would look like Figure 7.4.

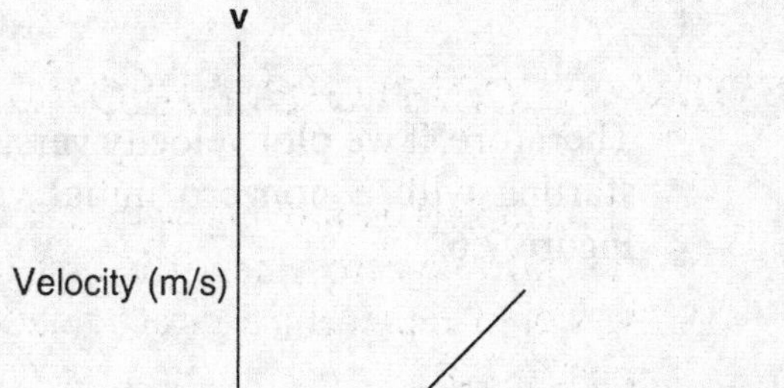

FIGURE 7.4

The displacement from $t = 0$ to any other time is equal to the area of the triangle formed. However, between any two intermediary times, the resulting figure is a trapezoid. If we make several measurements, the displacement versus time graph for uniformly accelerated motion is a parabola starting from the origin (if we make the initial conditions that, when $t = 0$, $x = 0$ and $\mathbf{v} = 0$; see Figure 7.5).

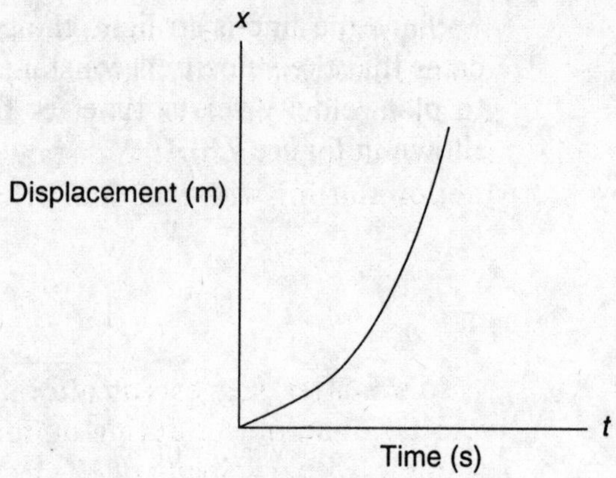

FIGURE 7.5

The slope of the velocity versus time graph is defined to be the average acceleration in units of meters per second squared (m/s^2). We can now write, for the average acceleration,

$$\bar{a} = \frac{\Delta \mathbf{v}}{\Delta t}$$

If the acceleration is taken to be constant in time, our expression for average acceleration can be written in a form that allows us to calculate the instantaneous final velocity after a period of acceleration has taken place. In other words, $\Delta \mathbf{v} = \mathbf{a}t$ (if we start our time interval from zero). If we define $\Delta \mathbf{v}$ to be equal to the difference between an initial and a final velocity, we can arrive at the fact that

$$\mathbf{v}_f = \mathbf{v}_i + \mathbf{a}t$$

Therefore, if we plot velocity versus time for uniformly accelerated motion starting with a nonzero initial velocity, we get a graph that looks like Figure 7.6.

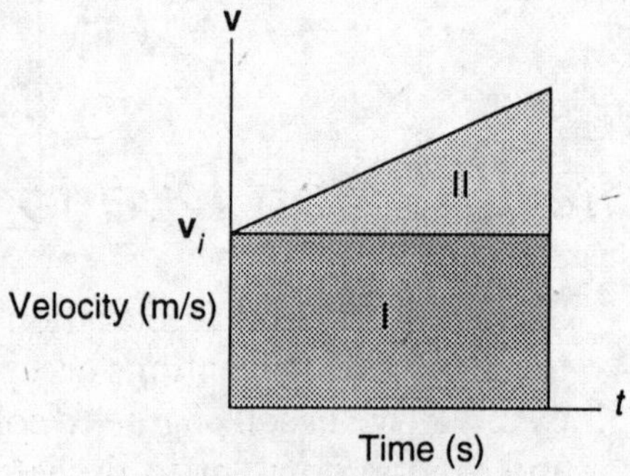

FIGURE 7.6

The displacement during any period of time will be equal to the total area under the graph. In this case, the total area will be the sum of two areas, one a triangle and the other a rectangle. The area of the rectangle, for some time t, is just $\mathbf{v}_i t$. The area of the triangle is one-half the base times the height. The "base" in this case is the time period, t, the "height" is the change in velocity, $\Delta\mathbf{v}$. Therefore, the area of the triangle is $(1/2)\Delta\mathbf{v}t$. If we recall the definition of $\Delta\mathbf{v}$ and the fact that $\mathbf{v}_f = \mathbf{v}_i + at$, we obtain the following formula for the distance traveled during uniformly accelerated motion starting with an initial velocity (assuming we start from the origin):

$$x = \mathbf{v}_i t + \frac{1}{2}\mathbf{a}t^2$$

This analysis suggests an alternative method of determining the average velocity of an object during uniformly accelerated motion. If we start, for example, with a velocity of 10 m/s and accelerate uniformly for 5 s at a rate of 2 m/s^2, the average velocity during that interval is the average of 10 m/s, 12 m/s, 14 m/s, 16 m/s, 18 m/s, and 20 m/s, which is just 15 m/s. Therefore, we can simply write

$$\bar{\mathbf{v}} = \frac{\mathbf{v}_i + \mathbf{v}_f}{2}$$

Occasionally, a problem in kinematics does not explicitly mention the time involved. For this reason it would be nice to have a formula for velocity that does not involve the time factor. We can derive one from all the other formulas. Since the above equation relates the average velocity to the initial and final velocities (for uniformly accelerated motion), we can write our displacement formula as

$$\mathbf{x} = \frac{\mathbf{v}_i + \mathbf{v}_f}{2}t$$

Now, since $\mathbf{v}_f = \mathbf{v}_i + at$, we can express the time as $t = (\mathbf{v}_f - \mathbf{v}_i)/a$. Therefore

$$x = \left(\frac{\mathbf{v}_i + \mathbf{v}_f}{2}\right)\left(\frac{\mathbf{v}_f - \mathbf{v}_i}{\mathbf{a}}\right)$$

$$= \left(\frac{\mathbf{v}_f^2 - \mathbf{v}_i^2}{2\mathbf{a}}\right)$$

7.4 Accelerated Motion Due to Gravity

Since velocity and acceleration are vector quantities, we need to consider the algebraic conventions accepted for dealing with various directions. For example, we usually agree to consider motion up or to the right as positive, and motion down or to the left as negative. In this way, negative velocity implies backward motion (since negative speed doesn't make sense). Negative acceleration, on the other hand, implies that the object is slowing down.

In Section 7.3, we considered the case of uniformly accelerated motion. A naturally occurring situation in which acceleration is constant involves motion due to gravity. Since gravity acts in the downward direction, its acceleration, common to all masses, is likewise taken to be in the downward direction. Notice that this convention may or may not imply deceleration. An object dropped from rest is accelerating as time passes, but in the downward or negative direction.

In physics, the acceleration due to gravity is generally taken to be −9.8 meter per second squared and is represented by the symbol **g**. As a vector quantity, **g** is negative and the direction of motion is reflected in either the position or the velocity equation. For example, if an object was dropped, the displacement in the −**y** direction would be given by

$$\mathbf{y} = -\frac{1}{2}\mathbf{g}t^2$$

If, however, the object was thrown down, with an initial velocity, we could write

$$\mathbf{y} = -\mathbf{v}_i t - \frac{1}{2}\mathbf{g}t^2$$

Finally, if the object was thrown upward, with some initial velocity, we would have

$$\mathbf{y} = \mathbf{v}_i t - \frac{1}{2}\mathbf{g}t^2$$

7.5 Graphical Analysis of Motion

We have seen that much information can be obtained if we consider the graphical analysis of motion. If complex changes in motion are taking place, visualization may provide a better understanding of the physics involved than algebra. The techniques of graphical analysis are as simple as slopes and areas. For example, we already know that, for uniformly accelerated motion, the graph of distance versus time is a parabola. Since the slope is changing, the instantaneous velocity can be approximated at a point by finding the slope of a tangent line drawn to a given point on the curve (see Figure 7.7).

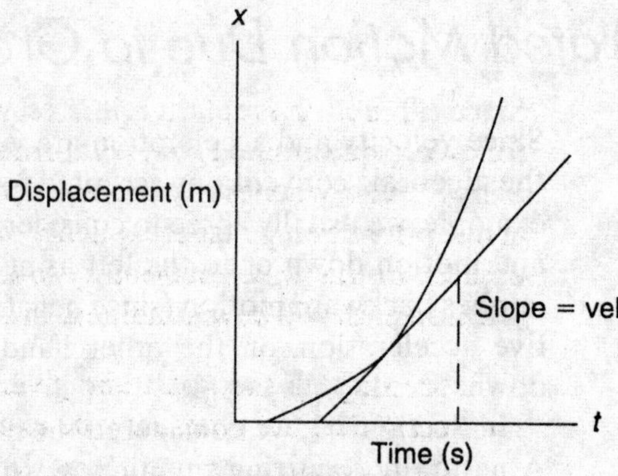

FIGURE 7.7

What would happen if an object accelerated from rest maintained a constant velocity for a while, and then slowed down to a stop? Using what we know about graphs of velocity and acceleration in displacement versus time, we might represent the motion as shown in Figure 7.8.

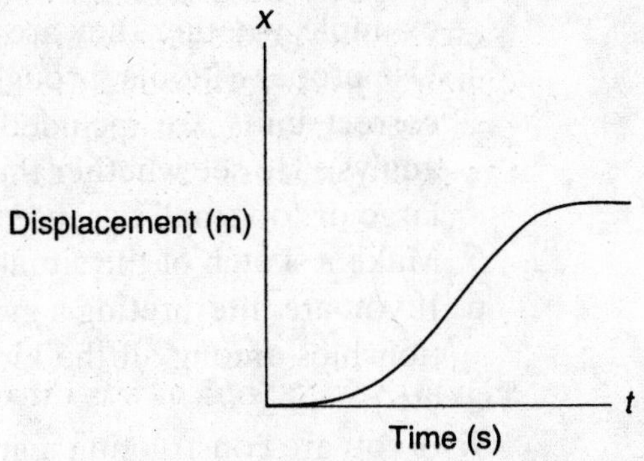

FIGURE 7.8

We can apply many instances of motion to graphs. In the case of changing velocity, consider the graph of velocity versus time for an object thrown upward into the air, reaching its highest point, changing direction, and then accelerating downward. This motion has a constant downward acceleration that, at first, acts to slow the object down, but later acts to speed it up. A graph of this motion is seen in Figure 7.9.

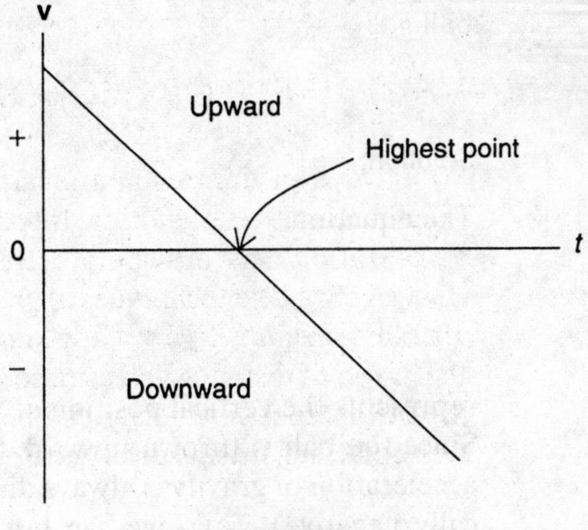

FIGURE 7.9

Problem-Solving Strategies for One-Dimensional Motion

Since all motion is relative, it is very important to always ask yourself the following question: "From what frame of reference am I viewing the situation?" Also, whenever you solve a physics problem, be sure to consider the assumptions being made, explicitly or implicitly, about the moving object or objects. In this way, your ability to keep track of what is relevant for your solution path will be maintained. In addition, it is suggested that you:

1. Identify all the goals and givens in the problem. Recall from Chapter 4 that the goals may be explicit or implicit. If a question is based on a decision or prediction, be sure to understand the algebraic requirements necessary to reach an answer.

2. Consider the "meaningfulness" of your solution or process. Does your answer or methodology make sense?
3. Choose a proper coordinate system and remember the sign conventions for algebraically treating vector quantities. In addition, make sure you understand the nature of the concepts being discussed (for example, whether they are vectors or scalars).
4. Use proper SI units throughout your calculations, and make sure that correct units are included in your final answer. Try "dimensional analysis" to see whether the answer makes sense. Perhaps it looks too large or too small because it is expressed in the wrong units.
5. Make a sketch of the situation if one is not provided.
6. If you are interpreting a graph, be sure you understand the interrelationships among all the kinematic variables discussed (slopes, areas, etc.).
7. If you are constructing a graph, label both axes completely, choose a proper scale for each axis, and draw neatly and clearly.
8. Try different problem-solving heuristics if you get stuck on a difficult problem.

Sample Problem:

A ball is thrown straight up into the air and, after being in the air for 9 s, is caught by a person 5 m above the ground. To what maximum height did the ball go?

Solution:

The equation

$$\mathbf{y} = \mathbf{v}_i t - \frac{1}{2}\mathbf{g}t^2$$

represents the vertical position of the ball above the ground for any time t. Since the ball is thrown upward, the initial velocity is positive, while the acceleration of gravity is always directed downward (and hence is algebraically negative). Thus, we can use the above equation to find the initial velocity when $\mathbf{y} = 5$ m and $t = 9$ s. Substituting these values, as well as the magnitude of $\mathbf{g}$ (9.8 m/s²) in the equation, we get $\mathbf{v}_i = 44.65$ m/s.

Now, to find the maximum height, we note that, when the ball rises to its maximum, its speed becomes zero since its velocity is changing direction. Since we do not know how long the ball takes to rise to its maximum height (we could determine this value if desired), we can use the formula

$$\mathbf{v}_f^2 - \mathbf{v}_i^2 = -2\mathbf{g}\mathbf{y}$$

When the final velocity equals zero, the value of $\mathbf{y}$ is equal to the maximum height. Using our answer for the initial velocity and the known value of $\mathbf{g}$, we find that $\mathbf{y}_{max} = 101.7$ m.

Practice Problems for Chapter 7

Multiple Choice

1. A ball is thrown upward with an initial velocity of 20 m/s. How long will the ball take to reach its maximum height?
(A) 19.6 s
(B) 9.8 s
(C) 6.3 s
(D) 3.4 s
(E) 2.04 s

2. An airplane lands on a runway with a velocity of 150 m/s. How far will it travel until it stops if its rate of deceleration is constant at $-3\ m/s^2$?
(A) 525 m
(B) 3214 m
(C) 6235 m
(D) 9813 m
(E) 10,435 m

3. A ball is thrown downward from the top of a roof with a speed of 25 m/s. After 2 s, its velocity will be
(A) 19.6 m/s
(B) −5.4 m/s
(C) −44.6 m/s
(D) 44.6 m/s
(E) −25 m/s

4. A rocket is propelled upward with an acceleration of $25\ m/s^2$ for 5 s. After that time, the engine is shut off, and the rocket continues to move upward. The maximum height, in meters, that the rocket will reach is
(A) 900
(B) 1000
(C) 1100
(D) 1200
(E) 1400

Questions 5–7 refer to the velocity versus time graph shown below.

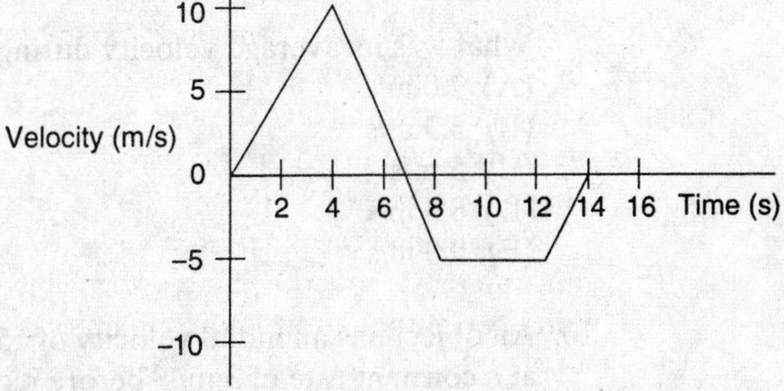

5. The total distance traveled by the object during the indicated 14 s is
(A) 7.5 m
(B) 25 m
(C) 62.5 m
(D) 77.5 m
(E) 82.1 m

6. The total displacement of the object during the 14 s indicated is
(A) 7.5 m
(B) 25 m
(C) 62.5 m
(D) 77.5 m
(E) 82.1 m

7. The average velocity, in meters per second, of the object is
(A) 0
(B) 0.5
(C) 2.5
(D) 4.5
(E) 5.6

8. What is the total change in velocity for the object whose acceleration versus time graph is given below?

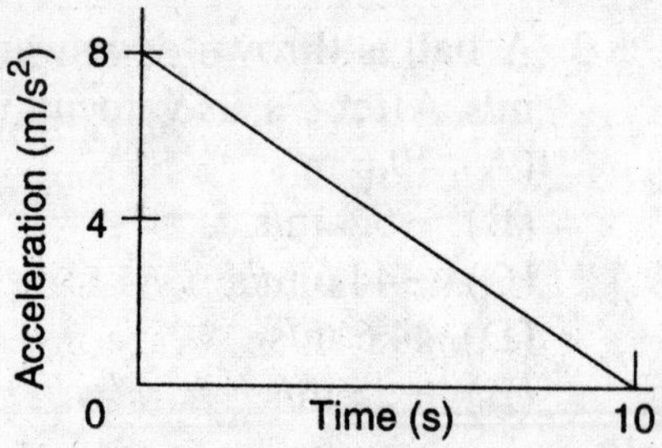

(A) 40 m/s
(B) −40 m/s
(C) 80 m/s
(D) −80 m/s
(E) 0 m/s

9. A particle moves along the x-axis subject to the following position function:

$$x(t) = 2t^2 + 3t - 1$$

What was its average velocity during the interval $t = 0$ to $t = 3$?
(A) 2.0 m/s
(B) 3.3 m/s
(C) 5 m/s
(D) 8.3 m/s
(E) 9.0 m/s

10. An object has an initial velocity of 15 m/s. How long must it accelerate at a constant rate of 3 m/s² before its average velocity is equal to twice its initial velocity?
(A) 5 s
(B) 10 s
(C) 15 s
(D) 20 s
(E) 25 s

Free Response

1. A particle has the acceleration versus time graph shown below:

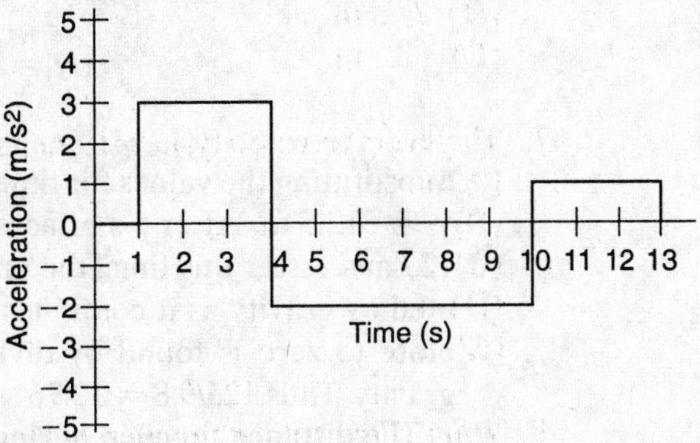

If the particle begins its motion at $t = 0$, with $v = 0$ and $x = 0$, make (a) a graph of velocity versus time and (b) a graph of position versus time for the particle's motion from $t = 0$ to $t = 13$ s.

2. A stone is dropped from a 75-m-high building. When this stone has dropped 15 m, a second stone is thrown downward with an initial velocity such that the two stones hit the ground at the same time. What was the initial velocity of the second stone?

3. A car is stopped at a traffic light. The instant the light turns green, it is passed by another car traveling at 17 m/s. The first car accelerates at a constant rate of 2.5 m/s² for a certain amount of time and then maintains a constant speed until it catches up to the second car. The total time involved is 60 s. (a) How far from the traffic light is the first car when it catches up to the second car? (b) How fast is the first car going when it passes the second car?

Solutions

Multiple-Choice Problems

1. **E** Given the initial velocity of 20 m/s, we know that the ball is decelerated by gravity at a rate of 9.8 m/s². Therefore, we need to know how long gravity will take to decelerate the ball to zero velocity. Clearly, from the definition of acceleration, dividing 20 m/s by 9.8 m/sec² gives the answer: 2.04 s.
2. **B** We do not know the time needed to stop, but we do know that the final velocity is zero. If we use the formula

$$v_f^2 - v_i^2 = 2ax$$

and substitute 150 m/s for the initial velocity and −3 m/s² for the deceleration, we get the answer: 3214 m.

3. **C** The initial velocity is −25 m/s downward, so $\mathbf{v} = -(25) - (9.8)(2) = -44.6$ m/s.
4. **C** The rocket accelerates from rest, so the first distance traveled in 5 s is given by

$$\mathbf{y}_1 = \frac{1}{2}\mathbf{a}t^2$$

Substituting the values for time (5 s) and acceleration (25 m/s²) gives $\mathbf{y}_1 = 312.5$ m. After 5 s of accelerating, the rocket has a velocity of 125 m/s. After this time, the engine stops and the rocket is decelerated by gravity as it continues to move upward. The time to decelerate to zero is found by dividing 125 m/s by the acceleration of gravity. Thus 125/9.8 = 12.76 s.

The distance traveled during that time is added to the first accelerated distance. The second distance is given by

$$y_2 = 125(12.76) - 4.9(12.76)^2 = 796.6 \text{ m}$$

The total distance traveled is therefore equal to 1108 m or, rounded off, 1100 m.
5. **C** The total distance traveled by the object in 14 s is equal to the total area under the graph. Breaking the figure up into triangles and rectangles, we find that their areas add up to 62.5 m (recall that distance is a scalar).
6. **A** The total displacement for the object is the sum of the positive (forward) and negative (backward) areas representing the fact that the object moves away from the origin and then back (as indicated by the velocity vs. time graph) going below the *x*-axis. Adding and subtracting the proper areas: 35 − 2.5 − 20 − 5 = 7.5 m for the final displacement.
7. **B** Average velocity is the change in displacement for the object over the change in time (not distance). Since from question 6 we know the displacement change to be 7.5 m in 14 s, the average velocity is therefore 0.53 m/s.
8. **A** The change in velocity for the object is equal to the area under the graph, which is equal to 1/2 (+8)(10) = +40 m/s.
9. **E** According to the formula, at $t = 0, x = -1$. When $t = 3$, $x = 26$. Thus $\Delta\mathbf{x} = 27$ m, and since average velocity is $\Delta\mathbf{x} / \Delta t$, the average velocity for 3 s is 9 m/s.
10. **B** For uniformly accelerated motion, the average velocity is

$$\bar{\mathbf{v}} = \frac{\mathbf{v}_f + \mathbf{v}_i}{2}$$

The question requires that the average velocity be equal to twice the initial velocity; thus, if the average velocity is 30 m/s, the final velocity attained must be 45 m/s. Now the question is, how long must the object accelerate from 15 m/s to achieve a speed of 45 m/s? A change in velocity of 30 m/s at a rate of 3 m/s² for 10 s is implied.

Free-Response Problems

1. (a) The acceleration graph given in the problem indicates constant acceleration from t = 1 to t = 3. Therefore, the area represents a constant change in velocity from 0 to 9 m/s. The second region corresponds to negative acceleration, which slows the object down and turns it around. We know this since the area is −12 m/s. This brings the graph from 9 m/s to −3 m/s (a change in direction). The last area is a change of 3 m/s which brings the velocity to 0 m/s. A graph of this motion is shown below, as desired:

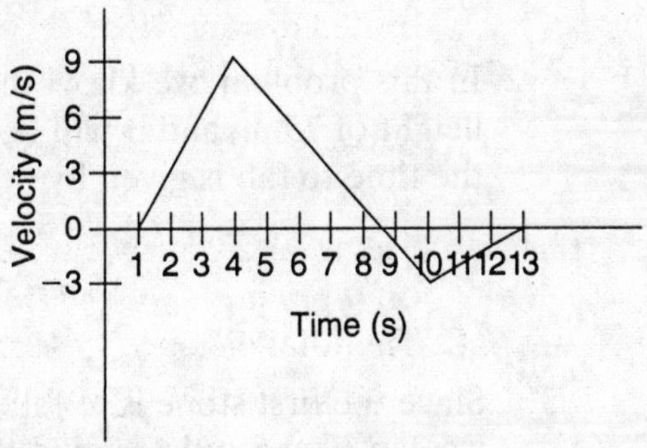

(b) To determine the corresponding position versus time graph, we note that, from t = 0 to t = 1 s, no motion has occurred. From t = 1 to t = 4 s, we have uniformly accelerated motion. The total distance traveled is equal to the area under the graph (which is a triangle of altitude 9 m/s and a base of 3 s.). This area is equal to 13. 5 m, and so we should sketch in a parabola starting at t = 1 and ending at t = 4. From t = 4 to about t = 7.5 s, the object is decelerating in the forward direction. Thus it continues to move forward, but at a slower rate. The total distance traveled in this segment is again equal to the area, which comes out to be 15.75 m. Since we have uniformly decelerated motion, we need an inverted parabola ending at about 30 m from the origin.

At this time, the object reverses direction and begins to accelerate backward from t = 7.5 until t = 10 s. The area of this segment is −3.75 m, which is subtracted from the ending point. Since the object is accelerating backward, there is a reversal of the parabola to reflect an increasingly negative slope until t = 10 s. From t = 10 to t = 13 s, the object slows down in the backward direction (the velocity graph is still below the x-axis). This last area is equal to 4.5 m, which is again subtracted. However, for this last segment, we need to show the slopes approaching zero as the velocity is zero at t = 13 s. A completed sketch of the displacement versus time graph is shown below:

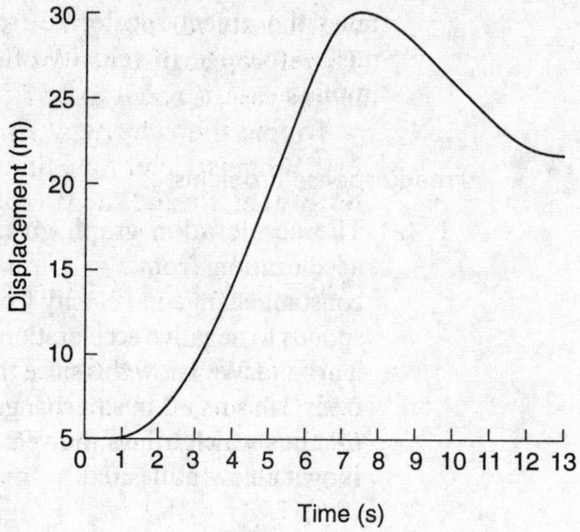

2. In this problem, we know that the first stone will be dropped from a height of 75 m, and it will be in free fall because of gravity. Therefore the time to fall is given by

$$t = \sqrt{\frac{2y}{g}} = 3.9 \text{ s}$$

Since the first stone is to fall 15 m before the second stone is dropped, we can likewise determine that $t = 1.75$ s to fall that distance. Thus, since the two stones must reach the ground at the same time, we know that the second stone must reach the ground after the first one has traveled for 3.9 s. Since the second stone is thrown when the distance fallen by the first stone is 15 m, we subtract 1.75 s from the total time of 3.9 s to get the second stone's duration of fall. That time is equal to 2.15 s. Since the second stone is thrown downward, it has a negative displacement, and so we can write

$$-75 = -\mathbf{v}_i(2.15) - \frac{1}{2}(9.8)(2.15)^2$$

This gives us a downward initial velocity of 24.34 m/s for the second stone.

3. (a) In this problem, when $t = 0$, the second car passes the first at a constant speed of 17 m/s. Since the entire episode lasts for 60 s, the second car travels a distance of 1020 m. This is the distance the first car is from the traffic light when it catches up to the second car.

(b) Now the first part of the first car's motion is an acceleration of 2.5 m/sec^2 for T seconds. After T seconds, the car travels at a constant speed for $60 - T$ s until it catches up to the second car. Thus, there are two sets of distances, one for the accelerated phase and one for the constant-velocity phase.

The distance traveled from rest during the acceleration phase is given by $1/2\ (2.5)T^2$. The velocity attained after T seconds is, of course, $2.5T$ m/s. This is the constant velocity for the second phase, which lasts for 60 − T s, since the total elapsed time is 60 s. Therefore, the distance for the second phase is given by $x = vt$, or, in this case, is equal to $2.5T\,(60 - T)$.

To find the velocity attained when the first car passes the second, we must determine time T. Since the total displacement must be 1020 m, we add the two phases to obtain

$$1020 = \frac{1}{2}(2.5)T^2 + (2.5T)(60 - T) = 1.25T^2 + 150T - 2.5T^2$$

We can solve for time T using the quadratic formula after we collect terms and bring 1020 over to the right side of the equation. Of the two solutions, only 7. 24 s is realistic (since the other term is greater than 60 s); therefore, the velocity in question is $(2.5)(7.24) = 18.1$ m/s.

CHAPTER 8

Two-Dimensional Motion

8.1 Relative Motion

In Chapter 7, we reviewed the basic elements of one-dimensional rectilinear motion. In this chapter, we will consider only two-dimensional motion. In one sense, one-dimensional motion can be viewed as two-dimensional motion by a suitable transformation of coordinate systems.

For example, consider the definition of displacement from Chapter 7. If we define a coordinate system for a reference frame, the location of a point in that frame is determined by a position vector drawn from the origin of that coordinate system to the point. If the point is displaced, the one-dimensional vector drawn from point *A* to point *B* is called the **displacement vector** and is designated as $\mathbf{B}-\mathbf{A}$ (see Figure 8.1).

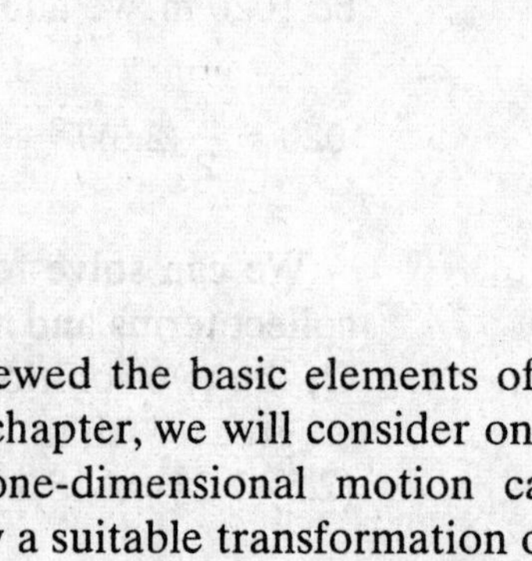

FIGURE 8.1

Even though the vector $\mathbf{B}-\mathbf{A}$ is one dimensional, we can resolve it into two components that represent mutually perpendicular and independent simultaneous motions. An example of this type of motion can be seen when a boat trying to cross a river or an airplane meeting a crosswind is considered. In the case of the boat, its velocity, relative to the river, is based on the properties of the engine and is measured by the speedometer on board. However, to a person on the shore, its **relative velocity** (or effective velocity) is different from what the speedometer in the boat may report. In Figure 8.2, we see such a situation with the river moving to the right at 4 meters per second and the boat moving upward across the page at 10 meters per second. If you like, we can call to the right "eastward" and up the page "northward."

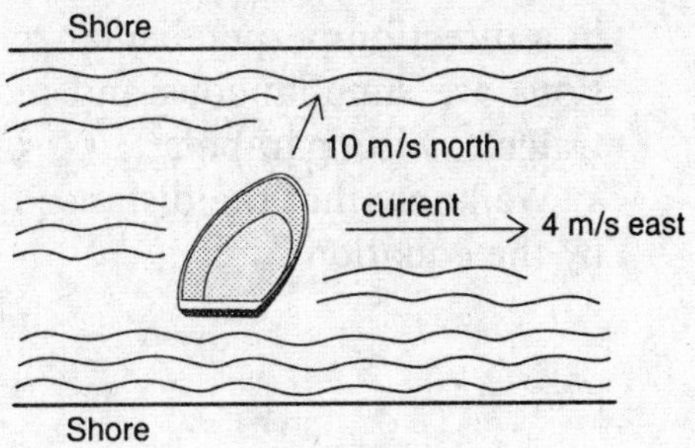

FIGURE 8.2

By vector methods, the resultant velocity relative to the shore is given by the Pythagorean theorem. The direction is found by means of a simple sketch (Figure 8.3) connecting the vectors head to tail to preserve the proper orientation. Numerically, we can use the tangent function or the law of sines.

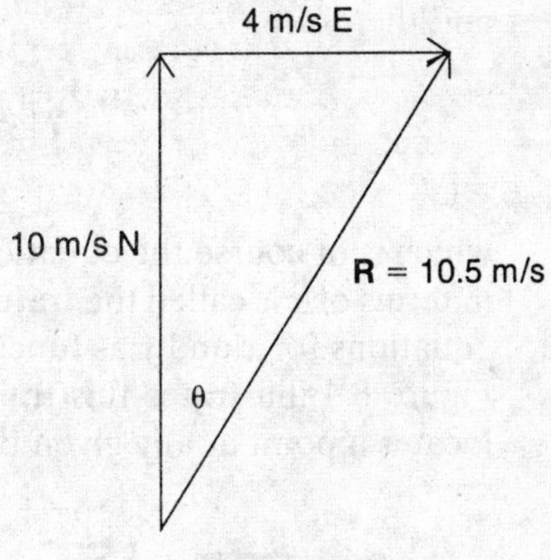

FIGURE 8.3

The resultant velocity is 10.5 meters per second at an angle of 22 degrees east of north.

In this chapter, we shall consider two-dimensional motion as viewed from the Earth frame of reference. Typical of this kind of two-dimensional motion is that of a projectile. Galileo Galilei was one of the pioneers in studying the mechanics in flying projectiles and the first to discover that the path of a projectile is a parabola.

8.2 Horizontally Launched Projectiles

If you roll a ball off a smooth table, you will observe that it does not fall straight down. With trial and error, you might observe that how far it falls will depend on how fast it is moving forward. Initially, however, the ball has no vertical velocity. The ability to "fall" is given by gravity, and the acceleration due to gravity is –9.8 meters per second squared. Since gravity acts in a direction perpendicular to the initial horizontal motion, the two motions are simultaneous and independent. Galileo demonstrated that the trajectory is a parabola.

We know that the distance fallen by a mass dropped from rest is given by the equation

$$|\mathbf{y}| = -\frac{1}{2}\mathbf{g}t^2$$

Since the ball that rolled off the table is moving horizontally, with some initial constant velocity, it covers a distance (called the **range**) of $x = |\mathbf{v}_{ix}|t$. Since the time is the same for both motions, we can first solve for the time, using the x equation, and then substitute it into the y equation. In other words,

$$t = \frac{x}{|\mathbf{v}_{ix}|}$$

and therefore

$$|\mathbf{y}| = -\frac{1}{2}\mathbf{g}\left(\frac{x}{\mathbf{v}_{ix}}\right)^2 = -\frac{\mathbf{g}x^2}{2\mathbf{v}_{ix}^2}$$

which is of course the equation of an inverted parabola. This equation of y in terms of x is called the **trajectory** of the projectile, while the two separate equations for x and y as functions of time are called **parametric equations.** Figure 8.4 illustrates this trajectory as well as a position vector **R**, which locates a point at any given time in space.

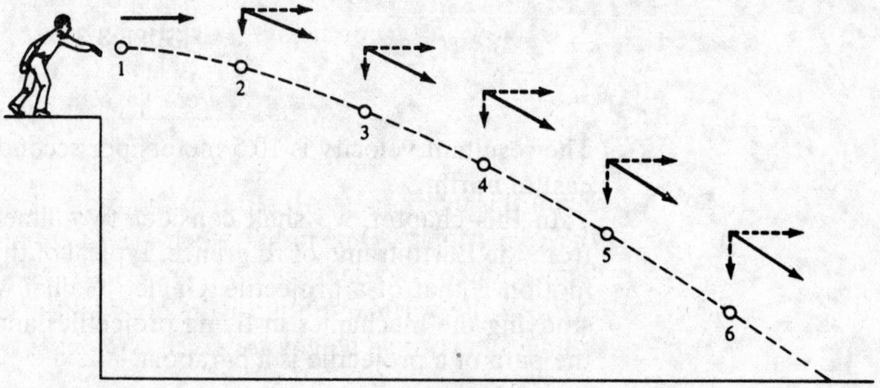

FIGURE 8.4

If the height from which a projectile is launched is known, the time to fall can be calculated from the equation for free fall. For example, if the height is 49 m, the time to fall is 3.16 s. If the horizontal velocity is 10 m/s, the maximum range will be 31.6 m. We can also follow the trajectory by determining how far the object has fallen when it is 10 m away from the base. Using the trajectory formula and the velocity given, we find that the answer is −4.9 m.

8.3 Projectiles Launched at an Angle

Suppose that a rocket on the ground is launched with some initial velocity at some angle θ. The vector nature of velocity allows us to immediately write the equations for the horizontal and vertical components of initial velocity:

$$\mathbf{v}_{ix} = \mathbf{v}\cos\theta \quad \text{and} \quad \mathbf{v}_{iy} = \mathbf{v}\sin\theta$$

Since each motion is independent, we can consider the fact that, in the absence of friction, the horizontal velocity will be constant while the y velocity will decrease as the rocket rises. When the rocket reaches its maximum height, its vertical velocity will be zero; then gravity will accelerate the rocket back down. It will continue to move forward at a constant rate. How long will the rocket take to reach its maximum height? From the definition of acceleration and the equations in Chapter 7, we know that this will be the time needed for gravity to decelerate the vertical velocity to zero, that is,

$$t_{up} = \frac{|\mathbf{v}_{iy}|}{|\mathbf{g}|} = \frac{|\mathbf{v}_i|\sin\theta}{|\mathbf{g}|}$$

The total time of flight will be just twice this time. Therefore, the range is the product of the initial horizontal velocity (which is constant) and the total time. In other words,

$$\text{Range} = 2\mathbf{v}_{ix}\,t_{up} = 2\mathbf{v}\cos\theta\, t_{up}$$

If we now substitute into this expression the time to go up, we get

$$\text{Range} = \frac{2\mathbf{v}_i\cos\theta\,\mathbf{v}_t\sin\theta}{\mathbf{g}} = \frac{\mathbf{v}_i^2\sin 2\theta}{\mathbf{g}}$$

From this expression, we see that the range is independent of the mass of the rocket and is maximum when sin 2θ equals 1. This occurs when the launch angle is 45 degrees.

Since the vertical motion is independent of the horizontal motion, the changes in vertical height are given one dimensionally as

$$\mathbf{y} = \mathbf{v}_{iy}\,t - \frac{1}{2}\mathbf{g}t^2$$

If we want to know the maximum height achieved, we simply use the value for the time to reach the highest point. To find the trajectory of the rocket, we first substitute for the value of the initial vertical velocity and then substitute for time. The time, t, is found from the fact that at all times $x = v_i\cos\theta t$. Solving for and then substituting, we obtain the following trajectory:

$$\mathbf{y} = \mathbf{v}_i\sin\theta\left(\frac{x}{\mathbf{v}_i\cos\theta}\right) - \frac{1}{2}\mathbf{g}\left(\frac{x}{\mathbf{v}_i^2\cos^2\theta}\right)$$

This simplifies to the final equation for the trajectory of the projectile:

$$y = (\tan\theta)\,x - \left(\frac{g}{2v_i^2 \cos^2\theta}\right)x^2$$

Of course, this equation also represents an inverted parabola. This trajectory is seen in Figure 8.5.

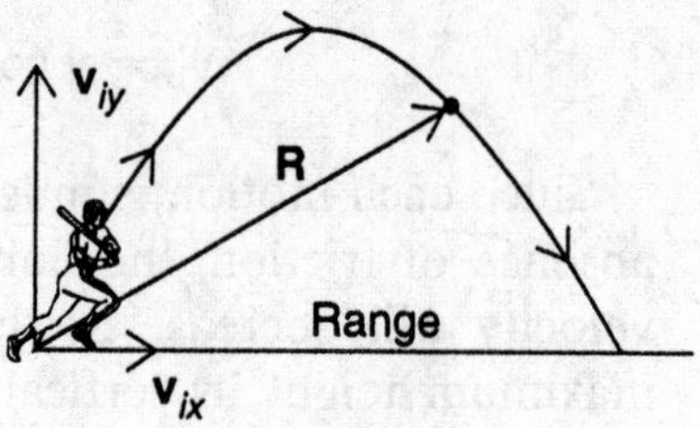

FIGURE 8.5

As an example, if a projectile is launched with an initial velocity of 100 m/s at an angle of 30°, the maximum range will be equal to 883.7 m. To find the maximum height, we could first find the time required to reach that height, but a little algebra will give us a formula for the maximum height independent of time. The maximum height can also be expressed as

$$y_{max} = \frac{v_i^2 \sin^2\theta}{2g}$$

Using the known numbers, we find that the maximum height reached is 127.55 m.

8.4 Uniform Circular Motion

Velocity is a vector. When velocity changes, the magnitude or direction, or both, can change. When the direction is the only quantity changing, as the result of a centrally directed deflecting force, the result is uniform circular motion. We will take up the discussion of deflecting forces in Chapter 9, but consider here an object already undergoing periodic, uniform circular motion. By this description we mean that the object maintains a constant speed as it revolves around a circle of radius R, in a period of time T. The number of revolutions per second is called the **frequency**, f.

Clearly, if the total distance traveled around the circle is its circumference, then the constant average velocity is given by $2\pi R/T$. Also, if the circle maintains a constant radius, the quantity $2\pi/T$ is called the **angular frequency** or **angular velocity**, $\boldsymbol{\omega}$. The units of $\boldsymbol{\omega}$ involve units related to arc length. Before going any further with this topic, we should digress a moment to discuss these units.

Imagine a circle of radius R as shown in Figure 8.6.

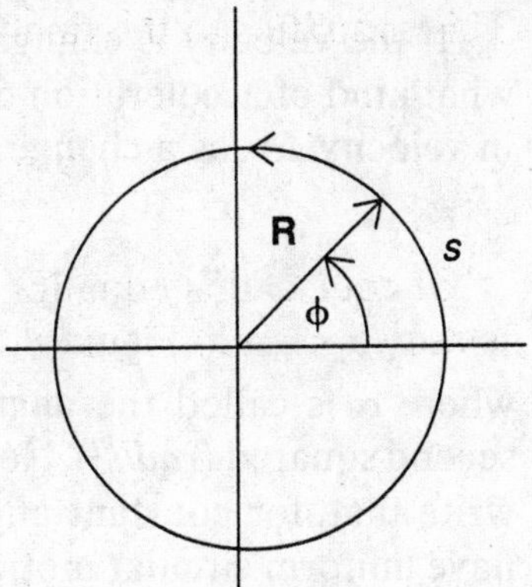

FIGURE 8.6

A point particle is moving counterclockwise around this circle, making an angle ϕ with the positive x-axis. A corresponding arc length s is associated with angle ϕ. From geometry, we know that the length of an arc s is equal to the circumference of the circle multiplied by the ratio of angle ϕ to the whole angle of the circle (360 degrees):

$$\mathbf{s} = 2\pi\mathbf{R}\left(\frac{\phi}{\text{whole-circle angle}}\right)$$

If we define the whole-circle angle to be equal to 2π and call the new unit "radians," we have

$$\mathbf{s} = \mathbf{R}\phi$$

which is a common formula from rotational dynamics in physics. The units of the angle are now such that 360 degrees corresponds to 2π radians. Thus, we have, for a uniformly changing angle in radians, the average angular velocity defined to be $\Delta\phi \,/\, \Delta t$. This is related to the linear velocity along the arc length by the formula

$$\frac{\Delta \mathbf{s}}{\Delta t} = R\frac{\Delta\phi}{\Delta t} = R\omega = \mathbf{v}$$

The units of angular velocity (or frequency) are now radians per second (rad/s). If we define the angular velocity as $\Delta\phi \,/\, \Delta t$, we can also write that $\Delta\phi = \omega\, \Delta t$, which looks remarkably similar to the linear formula $\Delta \mathbf{x} = \mathbf{v}\, \Delta t$.

Now, let us return to the idea of uniform circular motion. If the object is moving around a circle at a constant rate, its linear (tangential) and angular velocities are related by the angle swept out per second and the radius of the circle. We can see that, if we have an object on a rotating platform, or have a rotating solid, then the formula above informs us that all points have the same angular velocity but the linear velocity is directly proportional to the radius.

If the velocity is changing (as it is by virtue of its changing direction), what kind of acceleration does the object have? If we consider the change in velocity, Δv, as a change in the quantity $R\omega$, then clearly

$$\frac{\Delta \mathbf{v}}{\Delta t} = R\frac{\Delta \omega}{\Delta t} = R\alpha$$

where α is called the **angular acceleration** and has units of radians per second squared (*rad/s*^{2}). Notice that, analogously to linear motion, we could write that, for constant angular acceleration, $\Delta\boldsymbol{\omega} = \boldsymbol{\alpha}\,\Delta t$. However, if we have uniform circular motion, the angular frequency is not changing, so the angular acceleration is zero! Thus, we are still left with the question concerning the nature of the acceleration involved.

This confusion is cleared up easily if we recognize that, as angle ϕ changes, so do the position vector and the arc length. Consider the diagram in Figure 8.7.

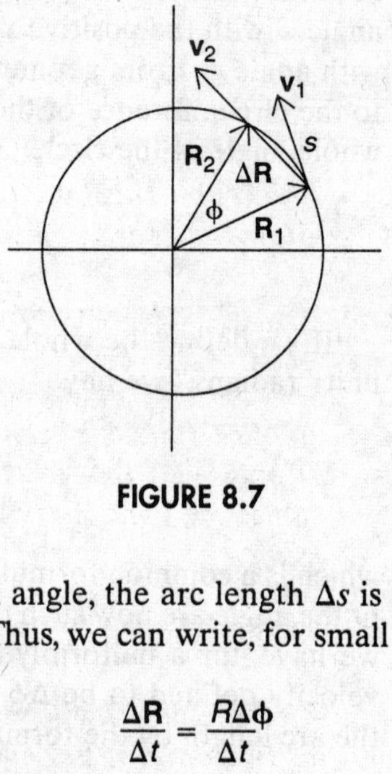

FIGURE 8.7

For small changes in angle, the arc length Δs is approximately equal to the displacement $\Delta\mathbf{R}$. Thus, we can write, for small approximations, that

$$\frac{\Delta \mathbf{R}}{\Delta t} = \frac{R\Delta\phi}{\Delta t}$$

This means that $\Delta\mathbf{R} / \mathbf{R} = \Delta\phi$. Since velocity is a vector, $\Delta\mathbf{v}$ is swept out in the same time as Δt and at the same angle, $\Delta\phi$. Thus

$$\frac{\Delta R}{R} = \frac{\Delta \mathbf{v}}{\mathbf{v}}$$

and so we can write

$$\frac{\Delta \mathbf{v}}{\Delta t} = \left(\frac{\mathbf{v}}{R}\right)\left(\frac{\Delta \mathbf{R}}{\Delta t}\right) = \frac{\mathbf{v}^2}{R} = \alpha_c$$

This quantity is known as the **centripetal acceleration**, and from the construction it is directed radially inward toward the center of the circle. The units are standard acceleration units. This quantity is different from the angular acceleration α, but is related to the angular velocity in the following way: since $\omega = \mathbf{v} / R$, we have that

$$\alpha_c = \frac{\mathbf{v}^2}{R} = \left(\frac{\mathbf{v}}{R}\right)\mathbf{v} = (\omega)(\omega R) = \omega^2 R$$

Finally, we can express the centripetal acceleration in terms of the period, T. Since we defined $\mathbf{v} = 2\pi R / T$, it immediately follows that

$$\alpha_c = \frac{4\pi^2 R}{T^2}$$

Problem-Solving Strategies for Two-Dimensional Motion

The key to solving projectile motion problems, or any other two-dimensional problem, is to remember that the horizontal and vertical motions are independent of each other. Therefore, using the formulas from Chapter 7 for one-dimensional motion can greatly reduce the complexity of a given problem. The following guidelines should also help:

1. Draw a sketch of the situation if none is provided.
2. Determine whether the components of motion are given in the problem. If not, try to determine the components of velocity and acceleration.
3. Keep in mind that accelerations given in one dimension do not affect the other. This fact results in the curved path.
4. Remember that velocity and acceleration are vectors and that both magnitudes and directions should be specified unless otherwise noted.
5. Choose a suitable frame of reference and coordinate system for the problem.
6. Ask yourself questions about the implications of each change in motion on the whole motion of the object.
7. Remember that trajectories are expressed in terms of position variables only, and that parametric equations usually relate positions with time.

Practice Problems for Chapter 8

Multiple Choice

1. A projectile is launched at an angle 45° with a velocity of 250 m/s. If air resistance is neglected, the magnitude of the horizontal velocity of the projectile at the time it reaches its maximum altitude is equal to
(A) 0 m/s
(B) 175 m/s
(C) 200 m/s
(D) 250 m/s
(E) 300 m/s

2. A projectile is launched horizontally with a velocity of 25 m/s from the top of a 75-m height. How many seconds will the projectile take to reach the bottom?
(A) 15.5
(B) 9.75
(C) 6.31
(D) 4.27
(E) 3.91

3. An object is launched from the ground with an initial velocity and angle such that the maximum height achieved is equal to the total range of the projectile. The tangent of the launch angle is equal to
(A) 1
(B) 2
(C) 3
(D) 4
(E) 5

4. At a launch angle of 45°, the range of a launched projectile is given by
(A) $\frac{\mathbf{v}_i^2}{\mathbf{g}}$
(B) $\frac{2\mathbf{v}_i^2}{\mathbf{g}}$
(C) $\frac{\mathbf{v}_i^2}{2\mathbf{g}}$
(D) $\sqrt{\frac{\mathbf{v}_i^2}{2\mathbf{g}}}$
(E) $\frac{2\mathbf{v}_i}{\mathbf{g}}$

5. A projectile is launched at a certain angle. After 4 s, it hits the top of a building 500 m away. The height of the building is 50 m. The projectile was launched at an angle of
(A) 14°
(B) 21°
(C) 37°
(D) 76°
(E) 85°

6. A projectile is launched at a velocity of 125 m/s at an angle of 20°. A building is 200 m away. At what height above the ground will the projectile strike the building?
(A) 50.6 m
(B) 90.2 m
(C) 104.3 m
(D) 114.6 m
(E) 125.6 m

7. The operator of a boat wishes to cross a 5-km-wide river that is flowing to the east at 10 m/s. He wishes to reach the exact point on the opposite shore 15 min after starting. With what velocity and in what direction should the boat travel?
(A) 11.2 m/s at 26.6° E of N
(B) 8.66 m/s at 63.4° W of N
(C) 11.2 m/s at 63.4° W of N
(D) 8.66 m/s at 26.6° E of N
(E) 5 m/s due N

8. An object is moving around a circle of radius 1.5 m at a constant velocity of 7 m/s. The frequency of the motion, in revolutions per second, is
(A) 0.24
(B) 0.53
(C) 0.67
(D) 0.74
(E) 0.98

9. A stereo turntable has a frequency of 33 rpm (revolutions per minute). A record of radius 15.25 cm is placed on the turntable and begins to rotate. The velocity of a point on the edge of the record is
(A) 2.16 m/s
(B) 22.23 m/s
(C) 0.53 m/s
(D) 7.62 m/s
(E) 13.5 m/s

10. In 3 s, an object moving around a circle sweeps out an angle of 9 rad. If the radius of the circle is 0.5 m, the centripetal acceleration of the object is
(A) 4.5 m/s^2
(B) 3 m/s^2
(C) 13.5 m/s^2
(D) 15 m/s^2
(E) 18 m/s^2

Free Response

1. A bomber is diving toward its target at an angle of 45° below the horizontal and at a speed of 320 m/s. When the bomber is 600 m above the ground, it releases its load, which then hits the target.
(a) How long will the bomb take to reach the target?
(b) What horizontal distance will the bomb travel?
(c) With what speed will it strike the target?

2. A projectile is launched at an angle of 40° with an initial velocity of 100 m/s. One hundred meters away is the beginning of a hill that slopes upward at an angle of 20°. The projectile strikes the hill a distance L up the slope. What is the value of this distance up the slope?

3. Two girls decide to have a swimming race in a river that flows with a velocity **u**. Each girl can swim with the same velocity **v**, relative to the water. One girl swims to a point across the river directly opposite her starting point and then swims back. The other girl swims downstream the same distance as the first girl swam and then swims back upstream.
(a) What is the ratio of the winning time to the losing time?
(b) Which girl wins the race?

Solutions

Multiple-Choice Problems

1. **B** The horizontal component of velocity remains constant in the absence of resistive forces and is equal to $\mathbf{v}_i \cos \theta$. Substituting the known numbers, we get $\mathbf{v}_x = (250)(0.7) = 175$ m/s.
2. **E** The time to fall is given by the free-fall formula from Chapter 7:

$$t = \sqrt{\frac{2\mathbf{y}}{\mathbf{g}}}$$

If we substitute the known numbers, we get 3.91 s for the time.
3. **D** Since the maximum height is equal to the range, we set these two equations equal to each other:

$$\frac{\mathbf{v}_i^2 \sin^2 \theta}{2\mathbf{g}} = \frac{\mathbf{v}_i^2 \sin 2\theta}{\mathbf{g}}$$

Recalling that $\sin 2\theta = 2 \sin \theta \cos \theta$, we solve for $\tan \theta$ and find that it equals 4.
4. **A** From the formula for range, we see that, at 45°, $\sin 2\theta = 1$, and so

$$R = \frac{\mathbf{v}_i^2}{\mathbf{g}}$$

5. **B** We know that, after 4 s, the projectile has traveled horizontally 500 m. Therefore, the horizontal velocity was a constant 125 m/s and is equal to $\mathbf{V}_i \cos \theta$. We also know that, after 4 s, the *y*-position of the projectile is 50 m. Thus we can write:

$$50 = 4\mathbf{v}_i \sin \theta - 4.9(4)^2 = 4\mathbf{v}_i \sin \theta - 78.4$$

Therefore, $\mathbf{v}_i \cos \theta = 125$, $\mathbf{v}_i \sin \theta = 32.1$, and $\tan \theta = 0.2568$, so $\theta = 14.4°$.
6. **A** The *x*-component of velocity is 93.97 m/s, and the *y*-component is 34.2 m/s. Since the projectile travels 200 m horizontally at 93.97 m/s, the time of flight $t = 2.128$ s. Substituting this time into our equation for the *y* position gives $y = 50.6$ m.
7. **C** The river is flowing at 10 m/s to the right (east) and the resultant desired velocity is 5 m/s up (north). Therefore, the actual velocity, relative to the river, is heading W of N. By the Pythagorean theorem, the velocity of the boat must be 11.2 m/s. The angle is given by the tangent function. In the diagram below, not drawn to scale but correct for orientation, $\tan \theta = 10/5 = 2$. Therefore, $\theta = 63.4°$ W of N.

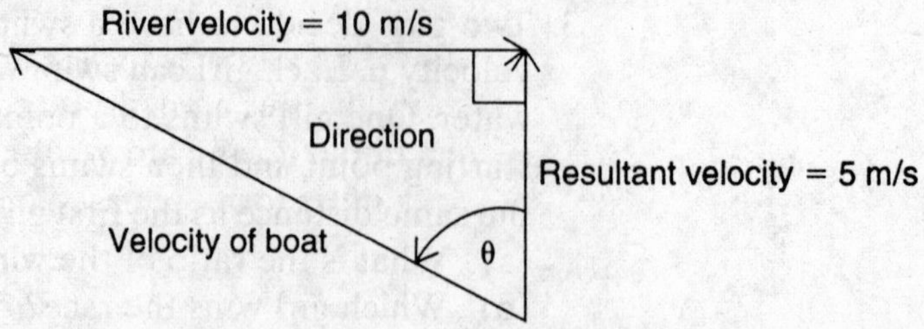

8. **D** The velocity is given by $\mathbf{v} = 2\pi R / T$, where T is the period, but the frequency f is just the reciprocal of the period. Thus, $\mathbf{v} = 2\pi R f$. We substitute the known numbers to obtain $f = 0.74$ rev/s.

9. **C** First we convert 33 rpm into radians per second. We note that there are 2π rad/rev and 60 s in 1 min. The conversion gives an angular frequency of 3.454 rad/s. Now we convert the radius to meters so that we are in SI units (MKS). Thus, $R = 0.1525$ m. Now we know that, for uniform circular motion, $\mathbf{v} = R\boldsymbol{\omega}$, so

$$\mathbf{v} = (0.1525 \text{ m})\ (3.454 \text{ rad/s}) = 0.53 \text{ m/s}$$

10. **A** If the object sweeps out 9 rad in 3 s, its angualr velocity is 3 rad/s. Since the radius is 0.5 m, the centripetal acceleration is given by

$$\alpha_c = \omega^2 R = (9)(0.5) = 4.5 \text{ m/s}^2$$

Free-Response Problems

1. (a) In this problem, we know that the bomber is on a descending flight path, so the angle below the horizontal implies a negative, vertical velocity. Since the plane is moving forward, we can treat its forward velocity as positive. Thus, following the problem-solving strategies, we should first make a sketch, as shown below, and then find the components of velocity.

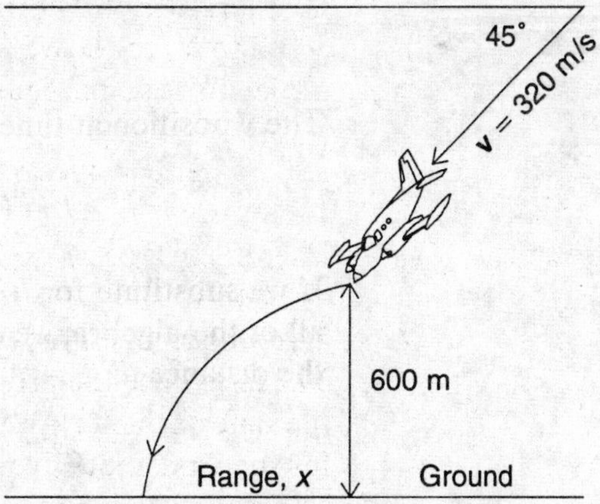

We determine the two component velocities, as $\mathbf{v}_x = 320 \cos 45 = 226.27$ m/s and $\mathbf{v}_y = 320 \sin 45 = 226.27$ m/s. The vertical distance traveled downward is algebraically given by -600 m, and so we can write for the time equation

$$-600 = -226.27t - 4.9t^2$$

Dividing all parts by 4.9, and rearranging into standard quadratic form, we get a quadratic equation for the time to fall 600 m with an initial downward velocity of 226.27 m/s; that is, we must use the quadratic formula based on

$$t^2 - 46.18t - 122.45 = 0$$

We keep only the positive solution, $t = 2.51$ s.

(b) Knowing the time to reach the target, we observe that the horizontal velocity of 226.27 m/s is constant, so the horizontal distance will be (226.27)(2.51) = 569 m.

(c) For the velocity of impact, we need only determine the changes in the vertical velocity. Gravity will accelerate the bomb downward at a rate of 9.8 m/s² for 2.51 s. Using our velocity-acceleration formula from Chapter 7, we find the final vertical velocity will be (−226.27) − (9.8)(2.51) = −250.87 m/s. The magnitude of the velocity of impact is determined by the Pythagorean theorem and is equal to 337.84 m/s.

2. Here is a sketch of this problem:

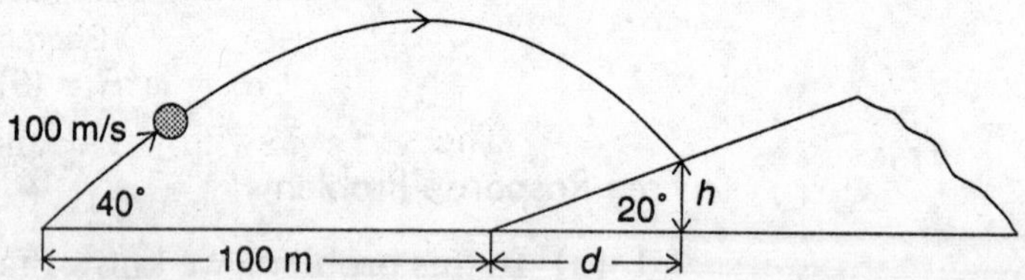

From the sketch, we know that tan 20 = h/d. We can also show that $\mathbf{v}_x = 100 \cos 40$ and $\mathbf{v}_y = 100 \sin 40$. Therefore

$$x = 100 + d = (100 \cos 40)t$$

or

$$t = \frac{100 + d}{100 \cos 40}$$

The y position at time t is given by

$$h = (100 \sin 40)t - 4.9t^2$$

If we substitute for h in terms of d, and t in terms of d, and apply all of the algebra, we are left with a single quadratic equation for the distance d:

$$d^2 - 370d - 90598.8 = 0$$

Using the quadratic formula, and keeping the positive root, we get $d = 538.3$ m and therefore $h = 195.9$ m. Applying the Pythagorean theorem, we find that the hypotenuse, ℓ, of the right triangle, which represents the distance up the slope, is 572.8 m.

3. (a) A sketch of the situation is given below. The river flows with velocity **u**, and each girl swims with velocity **v**. The girls travel equal distances, ℓ, and then back. If the first girl swims to a point directly opposite the starting point, she must swim in a direction slightly upstream so that her resultant direction ends up straight across.

Let's call the two directions perpendicular and parallel. The first swimmer crosses perpendicularly and swims slightly upstream with relative velocity **v**. The river flows downstream at velocity **u**. The desired resultant velocity is given by $\sqrt{\mathbf{v}^2 - \mathbf{u}^2}$. The total round-trip time is just twice the distance divided by this resultant velocity, or

$$t_1 = \frac{2\ell}{\sqrt{v^2 - u^2}}$$

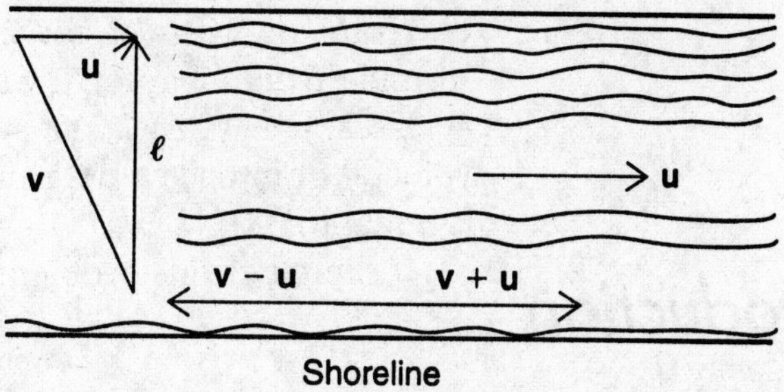

The second swimmer begins swimming downstream with relative velocity $\mathbf{v} + \mathbf{u}$ and then swims upstream at relative velocity $\mathbf{v} - \mathbf{u}$ (keeping the magnitude of the velocity positive). Each distance covered is ℓ, so the total time is given by

$$t_2 = \frac{\ell}{v + u} + \frac{\ell}{v + u} = \frac{2\ell V}{\sqrt{v^2 - u^2}}$$

If we take the ratio of these quantities we get

$$\frac{t_2}{t_1} = \sqrt{1 - \frac{u^2}{v^2}}$$

(b) This means that

$$t_2 = t_1\sqrt{1 - \frac{u^2}{v^2}}$$

Since $\mathbf{v}$ is greater than $\mathbf{u}$, the implication is that the second time (parallel) is less than the first time (perpendicular) and hence the second girl wins the race. The ratio factor is a key analogy to understanding the Michelson-Morley experiment that we will discuss in Chapter 27 on special relativity.

CHAPTER 9

Forces and Newton's Laws of Motion

9.1 Introduction

From our discussion in Chapter 6 of frames of reference, you should be able to convince yourself that, if two objects have the same velocity, the relative velocity between them is zero, and therefore one object looks as though it is at rest with respect to the other. In fact, it would be impossible to decide whether or not such an **"inertial"** observer was moving! Therefore, accepting this fact, we state that an object that appears to be at rest in the Earth frame of reference will simply be stated to be "at rest" relative to us (the observers).

9.2 Forces

Observations inform us that an inanimate object will not move freely of its own accord unless an interaction takes place between it and at least one other object. This interaction usually involves contact between the objects, although the gravity exerted by the Earth or any other body on the object does not involve any direct contact. This type of interaction is sometimes called an **action at a distance**. Electrostatic attraction and repulsion, as well as magnetic attraction and repulsion, are other examples of this effect.

When interaction occurs, we say that a **force** has been created between the objects. If an object was moving (relative to us), then the force may change the direction of the motion or it may change its speed. In other words, there will be a change in the velocity, which is a vector quantity; the magnitude and/or direction of the velocity will change. If no change occurs, we must conclude the presence of another force that resists the changes induced by the applied one. Friction is an example of an opposing force of this type.

In contrast to deflecting forces, other forces may be restorative. An example is a spring or other elastic material that has been stretched. Once the material has been elongated, it will snap back in an attempt to return to its original status.

If all the forces acting on an object produce no net change, the object is in a state of **equilibrium**. If the object is moving relative to us, we say that it is in a state of **dynamic equilibrium**. If the object is at rest relative to us, we say that it is in a state of **static equilibrium**.

9.3 Newton's Laws of Motion

In 1687, at the urging of his friend Edmund Halley, Isaac Newton published his greatest work. It was titled the *Mathematical Principles of Natural Philosophy*, but is more widely known by a shortened version, *The Principia*. In this book, Isaac Newton revolutionized the rational study of mechanics by the introduction of mathematical principles that all of nature was considered to obey. Using his newly developed ideas, Newton set out to explain the observations and analyses of Galileo Galilei and Johannes Kepler.

The ability of an object to resist a change in its state of motion is called **inertia**. This concept is the key to Newton's first law of motion:

> Every body continues in its state of rest, or of uniform motion in a straight line, unless it is compelled to change that state by forces acting on it.

In other words, an object at rest will tend to stay at rest, and an object in motion will tend to stay in motion, unless acted upon by an external force. By "rest," we of course mean the observed state of rest in a particular frame of reference. As stated above, the concept of "inertia" is taken to mean the ability of an object to resist a force attempting to change its state of motion. As we will subsequently see, this concept is covered under the new concept of **mass** (a scalar, as opposed to **weight**, a vector force).

If a mass has an unbalanced force incident upon it, the velocity of the mass is observed to change. The magnitude of this velocity change depends inversely on the amount of mass. In other words, a force directed along the direction of motion will cause a smaller mass to accelerate more than a larger mass. Newton's second law of motion expresses these observations as follows:

> The change of motion is proportional to the applied force, and is in the direction which that force acts.

The acceleration produced by the force is in the same direction as the force. This does not mean that the object's direction must remain the same. Mathematically, the second law is sometimes expressed as:

$$\mathbf{F} = m\mathbf{a}$$

However, to preserve the vector nature of the forces, and the fact that by "force" we mean "net force," we can write the second law as:

$$\mathbf{F}_{\text{net}} = \Sigma\mathbf{F} = m\mathbf{a}$$

The units of force are **newtons**; 1 newton (N) is defined as the force needed to give a 1-kilogram mass an acceleration of 1 meter per second squared. Thus 1 newton equals 1 kilogram-meter per second squared. This being the case, the weight of an object is given by

$$\mathbf{W} = m\mathbf{g}$$

where **g** is the acceleration due to gravity and the units of weight are newtons. In the SI system of units, the kilogram is taken as the standard unit of mass and corresponds to 9.8 newtons of weight, or about 2.2 English pounds.

Newton's third law of motion is crucial for understanding the conservation laws we will discuss later. It stresses the fact that forces are the result of mutual interactions and are thus produced in pairs. The third law is usually stated as follows:

For every action, there is an equal but opposite reaction.

When Newton wrote his second law of motion, his concept of "quantity of motion" was defined as the product of an object's mass and velocity. In modern times, this concept is known as **momentum**; it will be discussed in Chapters 11 and 12.

9.4 Static Applications of Newton's Laws

If we look more closely at Newton's second law of motion, we see an interesting implication. If the net force acting on an object is zero, the acceleration of the object will likewise be zero. Notice, however, that kinematically, zero acceleration does not imply zero motion! It simply indicates that the velocity of the object is not changing. If the object is in a state of rest and remains at rest (because of zero net forces), the object is in static equilibrium. Some interesting problems in engineering deal with the static stability of structures. Let's look at a simple example.

Place this book on a table. You will observe that it is not moving relative to you. Its state of rest is provided by the zero net force between the downward force of gravity and the upward reactive force of the table (pushing on the floor, which in turn pushes up on the table, etc.). Figure 9.1 shows this setup. The upward reactive force of the table, sometimes called the **normal force**, always acts perpendicular to the surface.

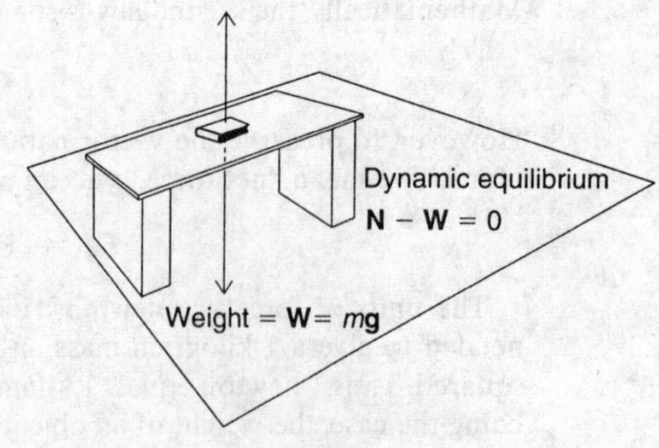

FIGURE 9.1

In this example, we have used both the second and third laws of motion. Remember: the second law is a vector equation, and so we must treat the sum of all vector forces in each direction separately! In this case, we have:

$$\Sigma F_y = \mathbf{N} - \mathbf{W} = 0$$

There are no forces in the *x*-directions to be "analyzed."

A slightly more complex problem would concern a mass suspended by two strings. The tensions in the strings support the mass and are thus vector forces acting at angles. In the problem illustrated in Figure 9.2, a 10-kilogram mass is suspended by two strings, making angles of 30 and 60 degrees, respectively, to the horizontal. The question is, "What are the tensions in the two strings?"

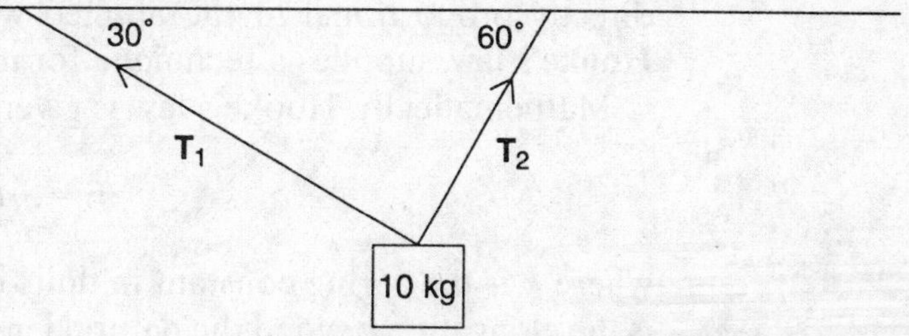

FIGURE 9.2

A useful heuristic for solving these types of problems is to construct what is called a "free-body diagram." In such a diagram, you "free" the body of its realistic constraints and redraw it, indicating the directions of all applied forces. You then use that diagram to set up your static equations for Newton's second law in both the *x*- and *y*-directions. The result is a system of two equations and two unknowns. In our example, a free-body diagram for both *x*- and *y*-directions would look like Figure 9.3.

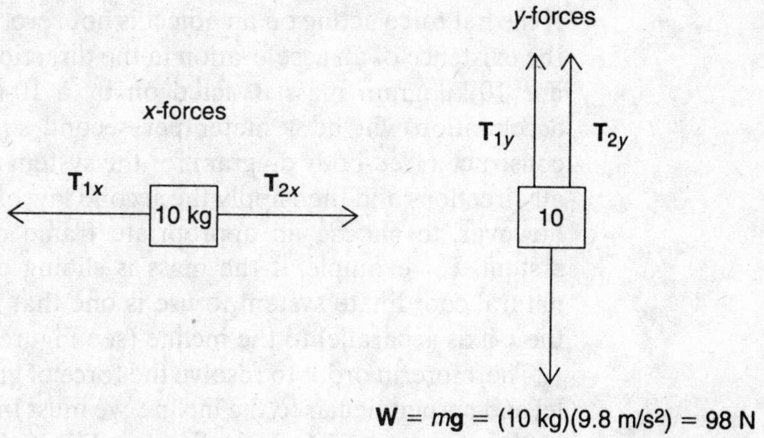

FIGURE 9.3

We can now set up our equations for Newton's second law, using the techniques of vector analysis reviewed in Chapter 6. We thus determine the *x*- and *y*-components of the tensions, which are given by $-\mathbf{T}_{1x} = -\mathbf{T}_1 \cos 30$ and $\mathbf{T}_{2x} = \mathbf{T}_2 \cos 60$. The negative sign is used since $\mathbf{T}_{1x}$ is to the left. Thus, in the *x*-direction we write

$$\Sigma \mathbf{F}_x = 0 = \mathbf{T}_2 \cos 60 - \mathbf{T}_1 \cos 30 = 0.5\,\mathbf{T}_2 - 0.866\,\mathbf{T}_1$$

Likewise, for the y-direction, we see that the 10-kg mass weighs 98 N. The downward pull of gravity is compensated for by the upward pull of the two vertical components of the tensions. In other words, we can write for the y-direction:

$$\Sigma \mathbf{F}_y = \mathbf{T}_1 \sin 30 + \mathbf{T}_2 \sin 60 - \mathbf{W} = 0.5\,\mathbf{T}_1 + 0.866\,\mathbf{T}_2 - 98$$

The two simultaneous equations can then be solved for $\mathbf{T}_1$ and $\mathbf{T}_2$. Performing the algebra, we find that $\mathbf{T}_1 = 48.97$ N and $\mathbf{T}_2 = 84.87$ N.

Another static situation occurs when a mass is hung from an elastic spring. It is observed that, when the mass is attached vertically to a spring that has a certain natural length, the amount of stretching, or elongation, is directly proportional to the applied weight. This relationship, known as **Hooke's law**, supplies a technique for measuring static forces.

Mathematically, Hooke's law is given as

$$\mathbf{F} = -k\mathbf{x}$$

where k is the spring constant in units of newtons per meter (N/m), and $\mathbf{x}$ is the elongation beyond the natural length. The negative is used to indicate that the applied force is restorative so that, if allowed, the spring will accelerate back in the opposite direction. As a static situation, a given spring can be calibrated for known weights or masses, and thus used as a "scale" for indicating weight or other applied forces.

9.5 Dynamic Applications of Newton's Laws

If the net force acting on an object is not zero, Newton's second law implies the existence of an acceleration in the direction of the net force. Therefore, if a 10-kilogram mass is acted on by a 10-newton force from rest, the acceleration will be 1 meter per second squared. Heuristically, we can construct a free-body diagram for the system to analyze all forces acting in all directions and then apply the second law of motion. We must be careful, however, to choose an appropriate frame of reference and coordinate system. For example, if the mass is sliding down a frictionless incline, a natural coordinate system to use is one that is rotated in such a way that the x-axis is parallel to the incline (see Figure 9.4).

Therefore, in order to resolve the force of gravity into components parallel and perpendicular to the incline, we must first identify the relevant angle in the geometry. This is outlined in Figure 9.4, and we can see that the magnitude of the downward component of weight along the incline is given by $-m\mathbf{g}\sin\theta$, where θ is the angle of the incline. The magnitude of the normal force, perpendicular to the incline, is therefore given by $|\mathbf{N}| = |m\mathbf{g}\cos\theta|$.

The direction of $m\mathbf{g}\cos\theta$ can be taken as inward into the incline's surface and provides the force necessary to keep the mass in contact with the surface. If friction were present (see Section 9.6), this force would be the main contributor to the frictional force, which would be directed opposite the direction of motion.

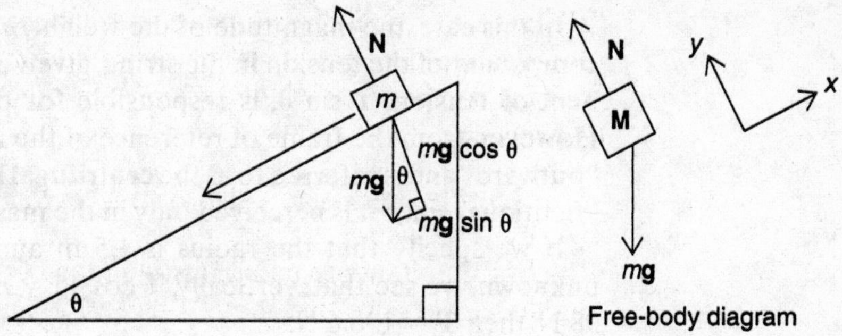

FIGURE 9.4

If, for example, the mass was 10 kg, the weight would be 98 N. If $\theta = 30°$, we would write for the x-forces:

$$\Sigma F_x = m\mathbf{a} = -mg \sin\theta = -98 \sin 30 = 49 \text{ N}$$

and since there is no acceleration in the y-direction, we would have:

$$\Sigma \mathbf{F}_y = 0 = \mathbf{N} - mg\cos\theta = \mathbf{N} - 98\cos 30 = \mathbf{N} - 8.49$$

Thus the normal force is equal to 8.49 N.

9.6 Central Forces

Consider a point mass moving around a circle, supported by a string making a 45-degree angle to a vertical post (the so-called **conical pendulum**). Let's analyze this situation, which is shown in Figure 9.5.

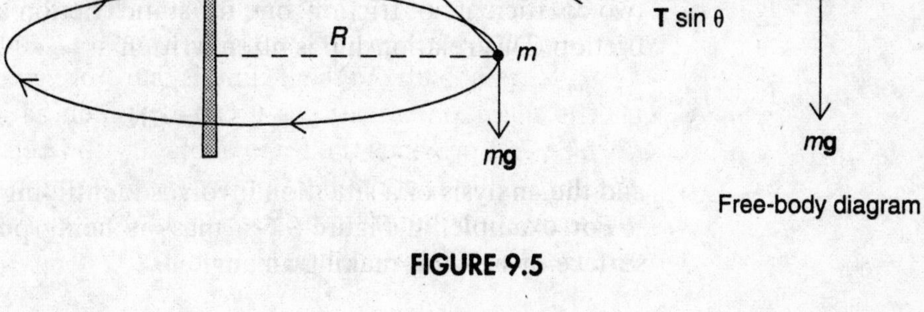

FIGURE 9.5

In this case, the magnitude of the weight, mg, is balanced by the upward component of the tension in the string, given by **T** cos θ. The inward component of tension, **T** sin θ, is responsible for providing a **centripetal force**. However, from the frame of reference of the mass, the force experienced is "outward" and is referred to as the **centrifugal force**. This force is often called "fictitious" since it is perceived only in the mass's frame of reference.

If we specify that the radius is 1.5 m and the velocity of the mass is unknown, we see that, vertically, **T** cos 45 = m**g**. This implies that, if m**g** = 98 N, then **T** = 138.6 N.

Horizontally, we see that

$$\mathbf{T}\sin 45 = \frac{Mv^2}{R}$$

where the expression for centripetal force is given by

$$\mathbf{F}_c = \frac{mv^2}{R}$$

using the logic of **F** = m**a**. Using our known information, we solve for velocity and find that **v** = 3.83 m/s. It is important to remember that the components of forces must be resolved along the principal axes of the chosen coordinate system.

9.7 Friction

Friction is a contact force between two surfaces that is responsible for opposing sliding motion. Even the smoothest surfaces are microscopically rough, with peaks and valleys like a mountain range. When an object is first moved, this friction plus inertia must be overcome. If a spring balance is attached to a mass and then pulled, the reading of the force scale when the mass first begins to move provides a measure of the static friction. Once the mass is moving, if we maintain a steady enough force, the velocity of movement will be constant. Thus, the acceleration will be zero, indicating that the net force is zero. The reading of the scale will then measure the kinetic friction. This reading will generally be less than the starting reading.

Observations show that the frictional force is directly related to the applied load pushing the mass into the surface. From our knowledge of forces, this fact implies that the normal force is responsible for this action. The proportionality constant linking the normal force with the frictional force is called the coefficient of friction and is symbolized by μ. There are two coefficients of friction, one for static friction and the other for kinetic friction. This relationship is often written as

$$\mathbf{f} = \mu\mathbf{N}$$

and the analysis of a situation involves identifying the normal force.

For example, in Figure 9.6 a mass is being pulled along a horizontal surface by a string, making an angle θ.

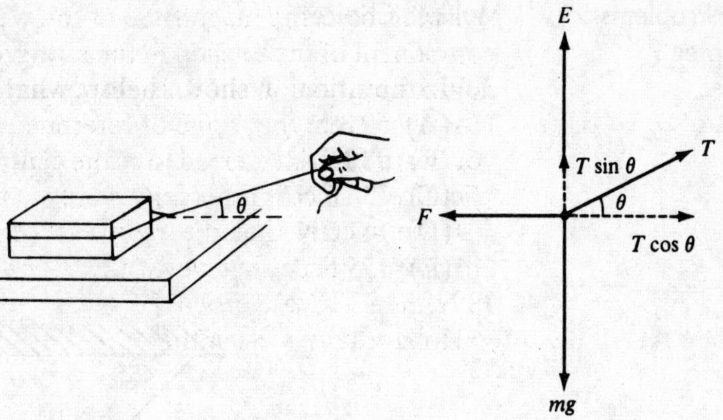

FIGURE 9.6

If we set up our equations of motion, we see that:

$$\Sigma \mathbf{F}_y = 0 = \mathbf{N} + \mathbf{F} \sin \theta - m\mathbf{g}$$

Thus the normal force is going to be less than the weight, *mg*, because of the upward component of the applied force. Therefore,

$$\mathbf{N} = m\mathbf{g} - \mathbf{F} \sin \theta$$

and the force of kinetic friction, given a coefficient of kinetic friction, μ_k, is written as:

$$\mathbf{f} = \mu_k \mathbf{N} = \mu_k(m\mathbf{g} - \mathbf{F} \sin \theta)$$

Problem-Solving Strategies for Forces and Newton's Laws of Motion

The key to solving force problems, whether static or dynamic, is to construct the proper free-body diagram. Remember that Newton's laws operate on vectors, and so you must be sure to resolve all forces into components once a frame of reference and a coordinate system have been chosen. Therefore, you should:

1. Choose a coordinate system.
2. Make a sketch of the situation if one is not provided.
3. Construct a free-body diagram for the situation.
4. Resolve all forces into perpendicular components based on the chosen coordinate system.
5. Write Newton's second law as the sum of all forces in a given direction. If the problem involves a static situation, set the summation equal to zero. If the situation is dynamic, set the summation equal to *m***a**. Be sure to include only applied forces in the diagram.
6. Find the normal force. It is always perpendicular to the surface.
7. Remember that the centripetal force is always directed inward toward the circular path and parallel to the plane of the circle. Gravity is always directed vertically downward.
8. Carefully solve your algebraic equations, using the techniques for simultaneous equations.

Practice Problems for Chapter 9

Multiple Choice

1. In the situation shown below, what is the tension in string 1?
   (A) 69.3 N
   (B) 98 N
   (C) 138.6 N
   (D) 147.6 N
   (E) 155 N

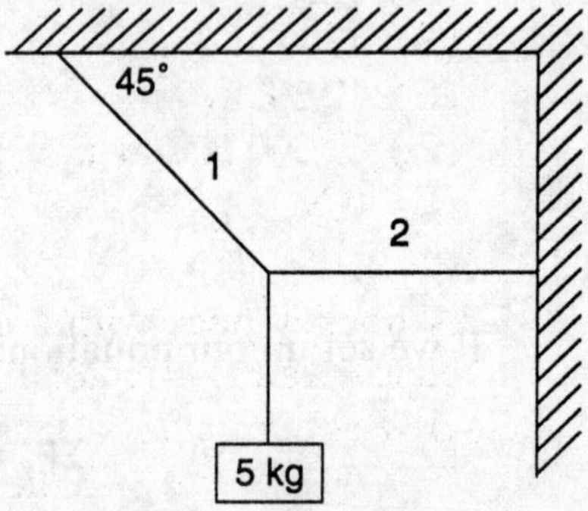

2. Two masses, M and m, are hung over a massless, frictionless pulley as shown below. If $M > m$, what is the downward acceleration of mass M?
   (A) g
   (B) $\frac{(M - m)\mathbf{g}}{(M + m)}$
   (C) $\left(\frac{M}{m}\right)\mathbf{g}$
   (D) $\frac{Mm\mathbf{g}}{M + m}$
   (E) $Mm\mathbf{g}$

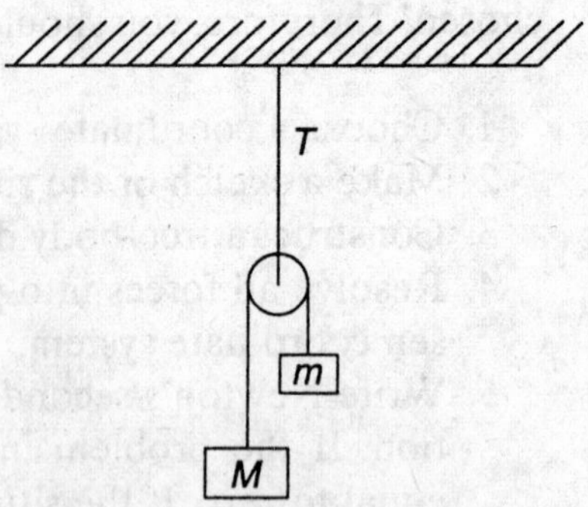

3. A 0.25-kg mass is attached to a string and swung in a vertical circle whose radius is 0.75 m. At the bottom of the circle, the mass is observed to have a speed of 10 m/s. What is the magnitude of the tension in the string at that point?
   (A) 2.45 N
   (B) 5.78 N

(C) 22.6 N
(D) 35.7 N
(E) 44.7 N

4. A car and driver have a combined mass of 1000 kg. The car passes over the top of a hill that has a radius of curvature equal to 10 m. The speed of the car at that instant is 5 m/s. What is the force of the hill on the car as it passes over the top?
(A) 7300 N up
(B) 7300 N down
(C) 12,300 N up
(D) 12,300 N down
(E) 0 N

5. A hockey puck with a mass of 0.3 kg is sliding along ice that can be considered frictionless. The puck's velocity is 20 m/s. The puck now crosses over onto a floor that has a coefficient of kinetic friction equal to 0.35. How far will the puck travel across the floor before it stops?
(A) 3 m
(B) 87 m
(C) 48 m
(D) 92 m
(E) 58 m

6. A spring with a stiffness constant $k = 50$ N/m has a natural length of 0.45 m. It is attached to the top of an incline that makes a 30° angle with the horizontal. The incline is 2.4 m long. A mass of 2 kg is attached to the spring, causing it to be stretched down the incline. How far down the incline does the end of the spring rest?
(A) 0.196 m
(B) 0.45 m
(C) 0.646 m
(D) 0.835 m
(E) 1.2 m

7. A 20-N force is pushing two blocks horizontally along a frictionless floor as shown below.

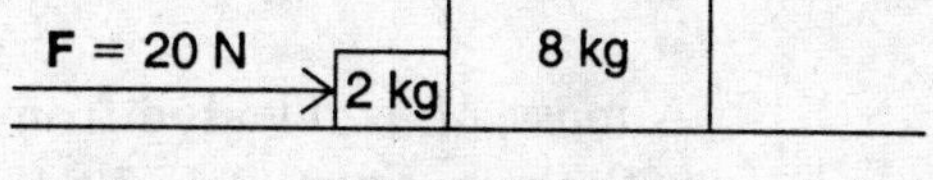

What is the force that the 8-kg mass exerts on the 2-kg mass?
(A) 4 N
(B) 8 N
(C) 16 N
(D) 20 N
(E) 24 N

8. A force of 20 N acts horizontally on a mass of 10 kg being pushed up a frictionless incline that makes a 30° angle with the horizontal, as shown below.

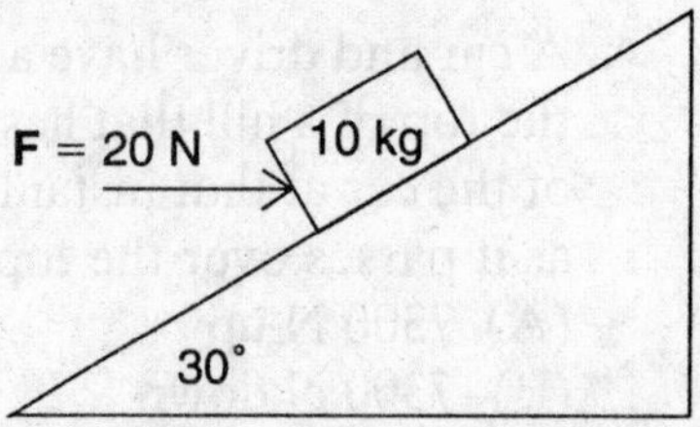

The magnitude of the acceleration of the mass up the incline is equal to
(A) 1.9 m/s²
(B) 2.2 m/s²
(C) 3.17 m/s²
(D) 3.87 m/s²
(E) 4.3 m/s²

9. According to the diagram below, what is the tension in the connecting string if the table is frictionless?
(A) 6.4 N

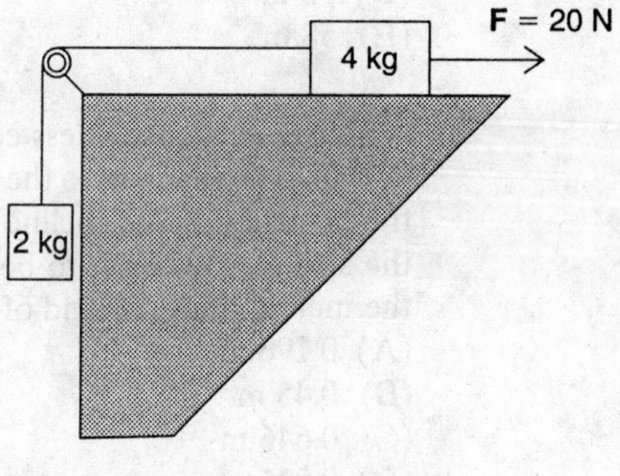

(B) 13 N
(C) 19.7 N
(D) 25 N
(E) 32 N

10. A mass, M, is released from rest on an incline that makes a 42° angle with the horizontal. In 3 s, the mass is observed to have gone a distance of 3 m. What is the coefficient of kinetic friction between the mass and the surface of the incline?
(A) 0.8
(B) 0.7
(C) 0.6
(D) 0.5
(E) 0.3

Free Response

1. A 3-kg block is placed on top of a 7-kg block as shown below.

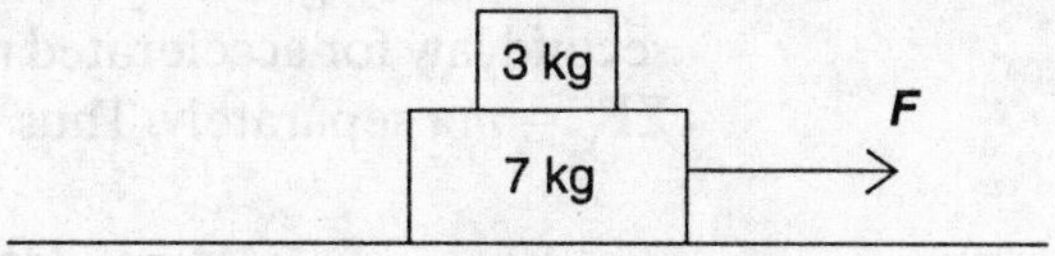

The coefficient of kinetic friction between the 7-kg block and the surface is 0.35. A horizontal force F acts on the 7-kg block.
   (a) Draw a free-body diagram for each block.
   (b) Calculate the magnitude of the applied force **F** necessary to maintain an acceleration of 5 m/s².
   (c) Find the minimum coefficient of static friction necessary to prevent the 3-kg block from slipping.

2. A curved road is banked at an angle θ, such that friction is not necessary for a car to stay on the road. A 2500-kg car is traveling at a speed of 25 m/s, and the road has a radius of curvature equal to 40 m.
   (a) Draw a free-body diagram for the situation described above.
   (b) Find angle θ.
   (c) Calculate the magnitude of the force that the road exerts on the car.

3. The "rotor" is an amusement park ride that can be modeled as a rotating cylinder, with radius R. A person inside the rotor is held motionless against the sides of the ride as it rotates with a certain velocity. The coefficient of static friction between a person and the sides is μ.
   (a) Derive a formula for the period of rotation T, in terms of R, g, and μ.
   (b) If $R = 5$ m and $\mu = 0.5$, calculate the value of the period T in seconds.
   (c) Using the answer to part (b), calculate the angular velocity ω in radians per second.

Solutions

Multiple-Choice Problems

1. **A** We need to apply the second law for static equilibrium. This means that we must resolve the tensions into their x- and y-components. For $\mathbf{T}_1$, we have $\mathbf{T}_1 \cos 45$ and $\mathbf{T}_1 \sin 45$. In equilibrium, the sum of all the x forces must equal zero. This means that $\mathbf{T}_1 \cos 45 = \mathbf{T}_2$ (since $\mathbf{T}_2$ is entirely horizontal). The y-component of $\mathbf{T}_1$ must balance the weight = mg = 49 N. Thus, $\mathbf{T}_1 \sin 45 = 49$ N and $\mathbf{T}_1 = 69.3$. N.
2. **B** The free-body diagrams for both masses, M and m, look like this:

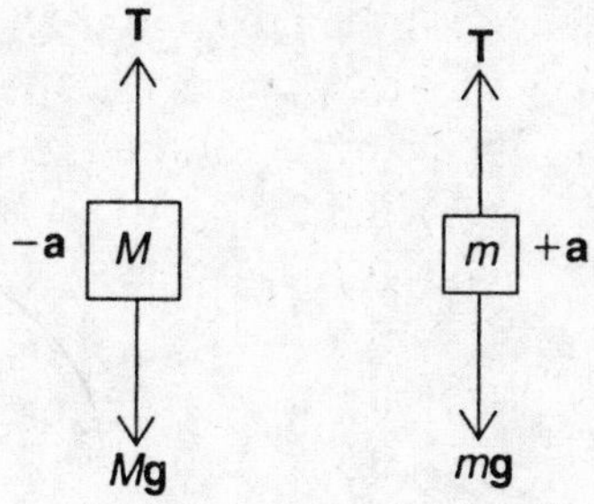

The large mass is accelerating downward, while the small mass is accelerating upward. The tension in the string is directed upward, while gravity, given by the weight, is directed downward. Using the second law for accelerated motion, we must show that $\Sigma \mathbf{F}_x = m\mathbf{a}$ and $\Sigma \mathbf{F}_y = m\mathbf{a}$ separately. Thus we have

$$\mathbf{T} - Mg = -Ma \quad \text{and} \quad \mathbf{T} - mg = ma$$

Eliminating the tension **T** and solving for **a** gives us $(M - m)\,\mathbf{g} / (M + m)$.

3. **D** A sketch of the situation is shown below:

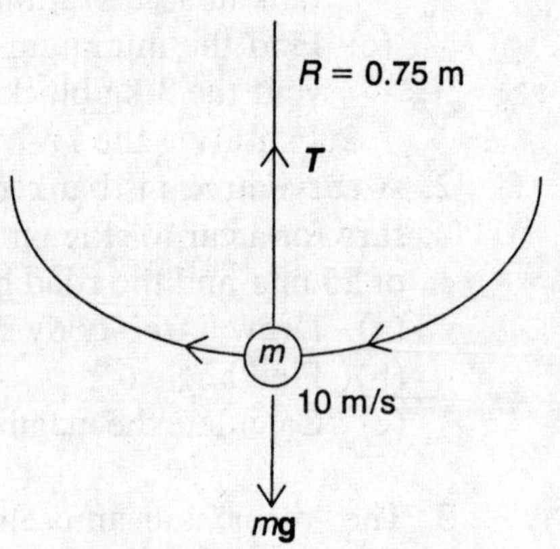

At the lowest point, the downward force of gravity is matched by the upward tension in the string. Thus we can write

$$\mathbf{T} - mg = \frac{mv^2}{R}$$

Substituting in the given values and solving for **T** gives us 35.7 N.

4. **A** As the car goes over the hill, the force that the hill exerts on the car is the normal force, **N**. This is modified, however, by the downward force of gravity. The combination produces (as in question 3) the centripetal force $\mathbf{F}_c$. Thus, we can write

$$\mathbf{N} - mg = \frac{-mv^2}{R}$$

The centripetal force, in this case, is directed downward, and hence is written as negative. A sketch is shown below. Substituting in the given values and solving for **N** gives 7300 N upward.

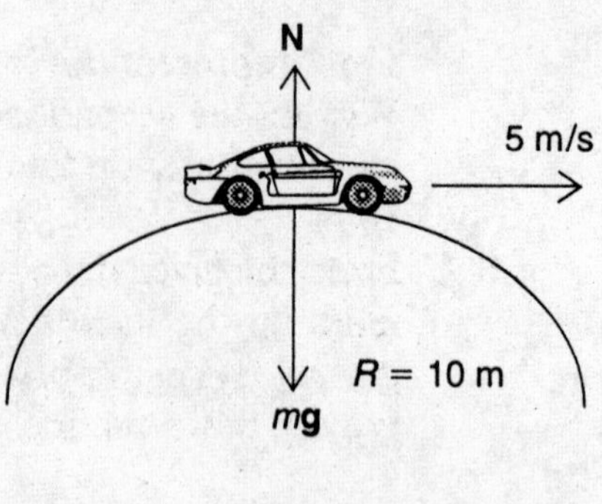

5. **E** With horizontal motion, the normal force is equal to the force of gravity. When the puck is moving with constant velocity, no net forces are acting on it. Thus, when friction acts to slow the puck down, the friction is the only net force. Therefore, we write

$$\mathbf{f} = \mu\mathbf{N} = \mu mg = -ma$$

(since the puck is decelerating). Substituting the known numbers gives a deceleration of -3.43 m/s². Now, the final velocity will be zero; and since the time to stop is unknown, we use the following kinematic expression to solve for the stopping distance:

$$-\mathbf{v}_i^2 = 2\mathbf{ax}$$

Substituting the known numbers, we obtain approximately 58 m as the distance the puck will travel before stopping.

6. **C** A sketch of the situation is given below. The spring constant is k = 50 N/m.

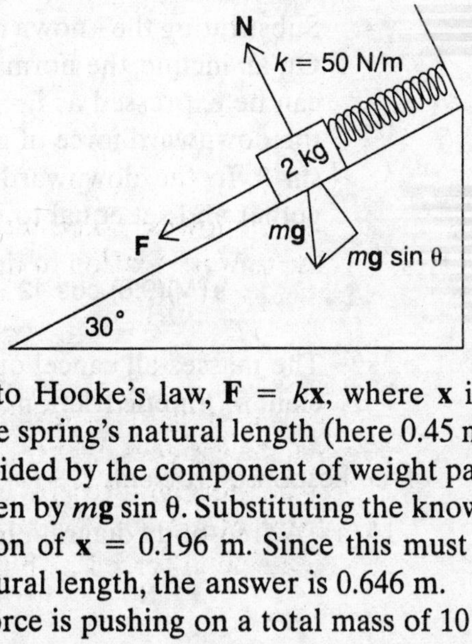

According to Hooke's law, $\mathbf{F} = k\mathbf{x}$, where $\mathbf{x}$ is the elongation in excess of the spring's natural length (here 0.45 m). The force, in this case, is provided by the component of weight parallel to the incline, which is given by $m\mathbf{g} \sin \theta$. Substituting the known numbers gives us an elongation of $\mathbf{x} = 0.196$ m. Since this must be in excess of the spring's natural length, the answer is 0.646 m.

7. **C** The 20-N force is pushing on a total mass of 10 kg. Thus, using $\mathbf{F} = m\mathbf{a}$, we have the acceleration of both blocks equal to 2 m/s². We draw a free-body diagram for the 2-kg mass as shown below.

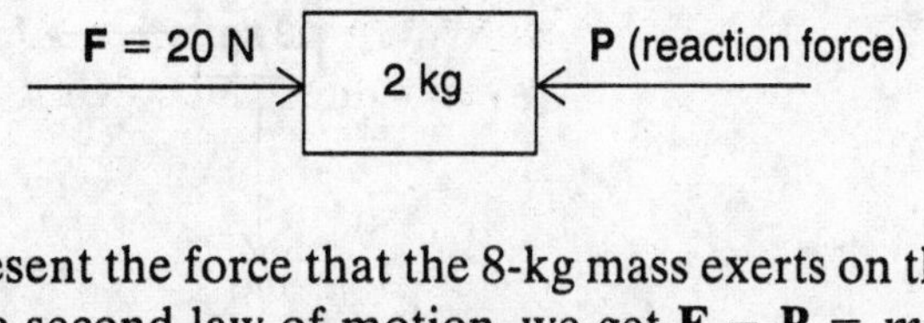

Let **P** represent the force that the 8-kg mass exerts on the 2-kg mass. Writing the second law of motion, we get $\mathbf{F} - \mathbf{P} = m\mathbf{a}$. To find **P**, we substitute the known numbers; $20 - \mathbf{P} = (2)(2) = 4$. Thus, $\mathbf{P} = 16$ N.

8. **C** From the given diagram, we see that the force necessary to move the mass up the incline must be in excess of the component force of gravity trying to push the mass down the incline. The component of gravity down the incline is always given by $m\mathbf{g} \sin \theta$. Resolving the

given force into a component parallel to the incline and a component perpendicular to the incline, we find that the force up the incline is, at the same angle, F cos θ. Thus, in general we would write:

$$\mathbf{F}\cos\theta - m\mathbf{g}\sin\theta = m\mathbf{a}$$

Substituting the known numbers gives **a** = 3.17 m/s².

9. **C** From the given diagram, we see that the 4-kg mass is accelerating to the right and the 2-kg mass is accelerating up. Thus we write that the sum of all forces, in each direction, equals *m***a**. In the *x*-direction we have (since the tension in the string will try to pull left), −**T** + 20 = 4**a**. In the *y*-direction, the tension pulls up against gravity. We therefore write **T** − 19.6 = 2**a**. Solving for **T** by eliminating **a**, we get **T** = 19.7 N.

10. **A** We know that the mass accelerates from rest uniformly in 3 s and goes a distance of 3 m. Thus, we can say that

$$d = \frac{1}{2}\mathbf{a}t^2$$

Substituting the known number gives us an acceleration of 0.67 m/s². On an incline, the normal force is given by *m***g** cos θ, and so friction can be expressed as **f** = μ*m***g** cos θ. Once again, this force opposes the downward force of gravity parallel to the incline, given by −*m***g** sin θ. In the downward direction, these two forces are added together and set equal to −*m***a**. Thus we write for this case

$$\mu(M)(9.8)\cos 42 - (M)(9.8)\sin 42 = -(M)(0.67)$$

The masses all cancel out, and solving for μ gives 0.8 as the coefficient of kinetic friction.

Free-Response Problems

1. (a) A free-body diagram for each of the two blocks is given below:

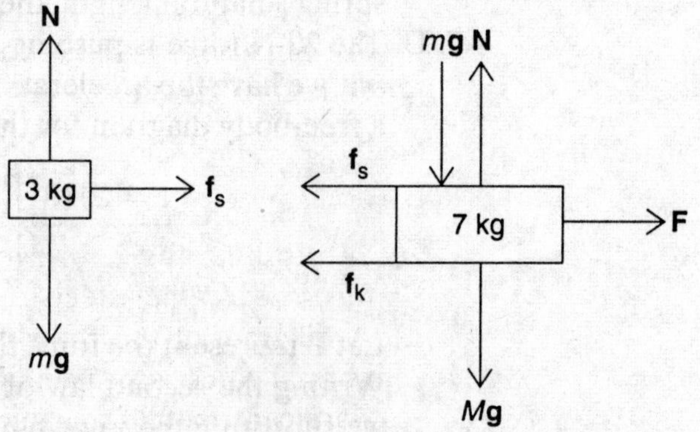

(b) The force of static friction between the two blocks is the force responsible for accelerating the 3-kg block to the right (hence the direction of friction in the free-body diagram). On the other hand, kinetic friction opposes the applied force, **F**, acting on the 7-kg block. Even so, the force **F** must accelerate both blocks combined. Thus, in the horizontal direction we can write that, for the second law of motion,

$$\mathbf{F} - \mathbf{f} = M\mathbf{a}$$

Also, since $\mathbf{f} = \mu\mathbf{N}$, we can write (since we have horizontal motion, the normal force is equal to the combined weights) $\mathbf{F} - (0.35)(10)(9.8) = (10)(5)$. Solving for **F**, we get $\mathbf{F} = 70.15$ N.

(c) Now, for the two blocks together, we know that static friction provides the force needed for the 3-kg block to accelerate at 5 m/s². The normal force on the "surface" is just the weight of the 3-kg block, as seen in the free-body diagram drawn in part (a). Thus $\mu(3)(9.8) = (3)(5)$. From this we get $\mu = 0.51$.

2. (a) A sketch of the situation and the free-body diagram are given below:

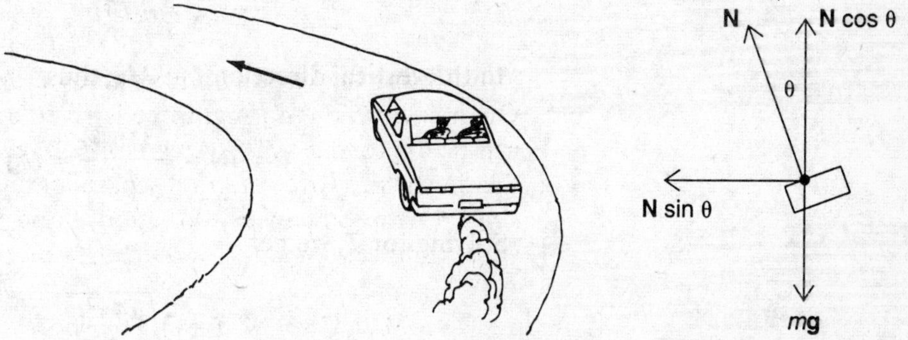

(b) In the coordinates chosen, the component of the normal force parallel to the plane of the curved road provides the centripetal acceleration. Thus we can write, in the absence of friction,

$$\mathbf{N} \sin \theta = \frac{\mathbf{v}^2}{r}$$

We can also see that $\mathbf{N} \cos \theta = m\mathbf{g}$. Thus, eliminating **N** from both equations gives us

$$\tan \theta = \frac{\mathbf{v}^2}{r\mathbf{g}}$$

Substituting the known numbers, we find that $\tan \theta = 1.59$ and $\theta = 57.8°$ (rather steep).

3. (a) A diagram of the rotor is seen on the following page. Here, the normal force is perpendicular to the person and opposes the inward centripetal force due to rotation. Friction acts along the walls against gravity, $m\mathbf{g}$, tending to slide the person down. Thus, the key to stability is to be fast enough to maintain equilibrium.

In the frame of reference of the person, there is an outward centrifugal force opposing the reaction force of the walls. Since $\mathbf{F} = m\mathbf{a}$,

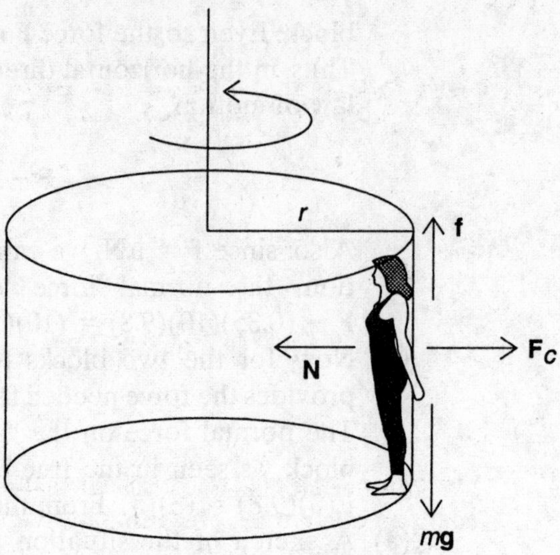

$$\mathbf{N} = \frac{4M\pi^2 r}{T^2}$$

In the vertical direction $\mathbf{f} = M\mathbf{g}$; thus

$$\mathbf{f} = \mu\mathbf{N} = \frac{\mu M 4\pi^2 r}{T^2} = M\mathbf{g}$$

Solving for T, we get

$$T = \sqrt{\frac{\mu 4\pi^2 r}{\mathbf{g}}}$$

This makes sense, since if the coefficient of friction is high, the rotation rate can be small, and thus a larger period!

(b) Substituting the known numbers gives $T = 10$ s.

(c) $W = 2\frac{\pi}{T} = \frac{6.28}{10} = 0.628$ rad/sec.

CHAPTER 10

Work and Energy

10.1 Work

Imagine we have two masses, m_1 and m_2. Now suppose that a separate force acts on each mass, providing individual acceleration according to Newton's second law of motion. How can we compare the "effects" of these two forces, $\mathbf{F}_1$ and $\mathbf{F}_2$? One thing we can do is observe their ratios:

$$\frac{\mathbf{F}_1}{\mathbf{F}_2} = \frac{m_1\mathbf{a}_1}{m_2\mathbf{a}_2} \tag{1}$$

One of the arguments of the Newtonian approach would be to compare the two forces relative to the time, t_1 or t_2, each force acts. Let us assume that they act simultaneously. Then we can write

$$\frac{\mathbf{F}_1 t}{\mathbf{F}_2 t} = \frac{m_1\mathbf{a}_1 t}{m_2\mathbf{a}_2 t} = \frac{m_1\mathbf{v}_1}{m_2\mathbf{v}_2} \tag{2}$$

where we have used the expression $\mathbf{v} = \mathbf{a}t$, assuming the objects start from rest.

Another way to relate the two forces is to consider the relative displacement through which each force acts. Let us assume they act through the same displacement, **d**. We can therefore write our ratio as

$$\frac{\mathbf{F}_1\mathbf{d}}{\mathbf{F}_2\mathbf{d}} = \frac{m_1\mathbf{a}_1\mathbf{d}}{m_2\mathbf{a}_2\mathbf{d}} = \frac{(1/2)m_1\mathbf{v}_1^2}{1/2m_2\mathbf{v}_2^2} \tag{3}$$

where, if we assume that the objects start from rest, we have used the expression $\mathbf{v}^2 = \mathbf{ad}$.

Comparing these two "representations" involves a comparison between vectors and scalars. The first comparison (equation 2) relates a *vector* quantity, **F***t*, expressed as the product of the force and the time (called the **impulse**). This quantity is proportional to the product of the mass and the velocity. However, in equation 3 the product of the magnitude force and distance, **Fd**, is a *scalar* quantity and is proportional to the product of the mass and the square of the velocity! This scalar quantity, **Fd**, is called the **work** done by the force.

Another way to think about this situation is to consider a graph of force versus displacement. Since an object's displacement is in the same direction as the net force applied, only the component of force acting in the direction of motion contributes to the work. Imagine that we have a constant force applied to an object. Figure 10.1 shows the graph of this relationship.

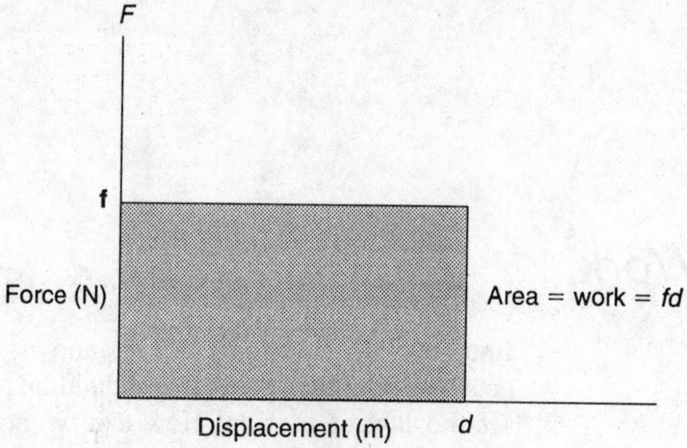

FIGURE 10.1

The area under the graph is equal to the work done. For variable forces, this method becomes most useful, and we can speak of the average force applied over the interval of distance displaced.

Based on equation 3, the units of work are defined to newton · meters (N · m), such that 1 newton · meter is equal to the work done by a 1-newton force displacing an object a distance of 1 meter. These units are also called **joules** (J). Using dimensional analysis, we see that, based on the definition of the newton in Chapter 9, 1 joule equals 1 kilogram · square meter per second squared.

The notion of work as a physical concept can be observed in the following way. It can be demonstrated that, if a mass m is dropped from a height h onto a nail, it will drive in the nail a distance x. If a mass of $4m$ is dropped from a height of $h/4$ onto a similar nail, the nail will be driven in the same amount. In other words, since the force of gravity provides the acceleration for the mass (i.e., its weight), this demonstration suggests that work (the effect of driving in nails) is equal to the product of force times displacement. In this case we could write, for work W,

$$W = mgh$$

Thus, for a given mass, the amount of work done depends on the height from which the mass is dropped; the greater the height, the more work.

10.2 Applications of the Work Concept

Suppose a mass of 10 kg is being pulled by a string making a 30° angle to the horizontal, as shown in Figure 10.2. The force in the string is 500 N, and the coefficient of friction between the mass and the ground, μ, is 0.2. How much work is done in displacing the mass a distance of 10 m?

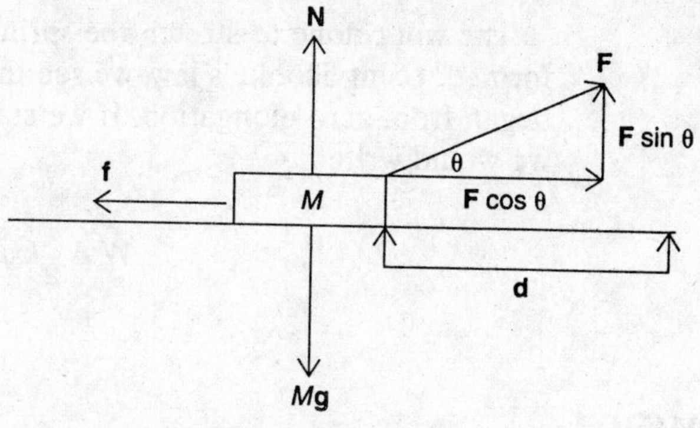

FIGURE 10.2

The horizontal component of the applied force is equal to **F** cos θ, and the vertical component is equal to **F** sin θ. The directions are based on the fact that the string pulls up and to the right. However, **F** cos θ is not the only horizontal force present; friction opposes the motion and is proportional to the normal force **N**. This normal force is not just the reaction force to the weight since the upward component of the string force contributes to a tendency to try and pull up the mass. Thus

$$\mathbf{N} = \mathbf{F} \sin \theta - Mg$$

and so the frictional force is

$$\mathbf{f} = \mu \mathbf{N} = \mu(\mathbf{F} \sin \theta - Mg)$$

The magnitude of the net horizontal force, which does the work, is therefore given by:

$$\mathbf{F}_{net} = \mathbf{F} \cos - \mu(\mathbf{F} \sin \theta - Mg)$$

It is the product of this net force and the displacement, **d**, that evaluates the amount of work, in joules. Substituting the known numbers gives us $W = 4026$ J.

As another example, consider the work done to stretch a spring. We know from Hooke's law that the elongation is directly proportional to the applied force, $\mathbf{F} = k\mathbf{x}$, where the stiffness constant, k, is in units of newtons per meter. This is not a constant force, and so the graph of force versus elongation would look as shown in Figure 10.3.

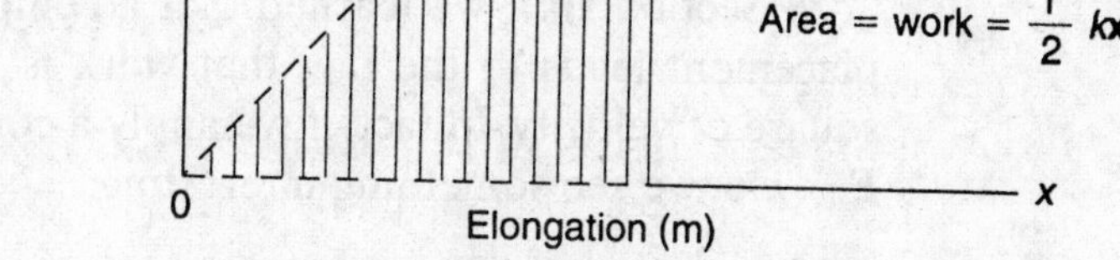

FIGURE 10.3

The work done to stretch the spring is equal to the area of the triangle formed. Using Hooke's law, we see that this turns out to be $(1/2)kx^2$ if we began from zero elongation. If we started at some other elongation, then we would write

$$W = \frac{1}{2}kx_f^2 - \frac{1}{2}kx_i^2$$

10.3 Power

It is often useful to consider the rate at which work is done. This rate, which would be expressed as the number of joules of work done per second, is called **power**. Algebraically we could write

$$\text{Power} = P = \frac{W}{t}$$

The units of power are joules per second, or **watts** (W). This relationship also implies that the work done is equal to the product of the power and the time (in seconds). If a constant force is applied, we can relate power to the average velocity attained. Since $P = W / t$ and $W = \mathbf{Fd}$, we can write:

$$P = \mathbf{F}\left(\frac{\mathbf{d}}{t}\right)$$

Recalling that the ratio of distance to time is the average velocity, we can say also:

$$P = \mathbf{Fv}$$

10.4 Energy

While performing experiments on the dynamics of pendulum motion, Galileo discovered that, if he introduced a nail or a peg at the vertical position of a swinging pendulum, thereby interrupting the original length of the pendulum, the pendulum bob would still swing up to its original height. On the way back, the pendulum would swing away from the nail or peg, resume its normal length, and still achieve the same height. Galileo could not interpret this fact in terms of forces, but we can now attribute the observations to the law of conservation of mechanical energy. To understand this concept better, let's return to our introduction to work.

In Section 10.1, we learned that a comparison between forces and displacement leads to the fact that work is proportional to mass times the square of velocity. In fact, if we apply a constant force to a mass and write $\mathbf{F} = m\mathbf{a}$, we see something interesting:

$$\mathbf{F}d = mad = \frac{1}{2}m(\mathbf{v}_f^2 - \mathbf{v}_i^2) = \frac{1}{2}m\mathbf{v}_f^2 - \frac{1}{2}m\mathbf{v}_i^2$$

The quantity (1/2) mv^2 is called the **kinetic energy** (*KE*) of the object and is defined to be the energy the object has by virtue of its being in motion relative to a frame of reference. This is crucial, since we can put ourselves into an inertial frame of reference in which the relative velocity observed is zero and the kinetic energy will be zero!

Work is therefore a measure of the change in kinetic energy; and since work implies the action of a force, we have established that forces are the agents of energy transfers. Thus we can define energy as the capacity to do work and define work as a measure of energy transferred. This relationship is known as the work-energy theorem. The units for kinetic energy are of course joules.

Another concept of energy is related to the position of an object. A mass sitting on a table has the ability to fall to the floor if allowed (the table exerts an upward force that prevents that from occurring). From our definition of energy, we can state that some type of positional energy exists within the mass. Experimentally, we know that, if we lift the mass slightly, it will land with a small velocity. However, if we lift the object very high, it will land with a large velocity. The displacement of the mass upward implies that work has been done to the object. The ability to fall is due to some kind of positional energy, which then converts itself into the kinetic energy of motion. In mechanics, this positional energy is known as **potential energy** (*PE*, or *U* in some textbooks). The units for potential energy are also joules.

If we recall the work-energy theorem, the gain in potential energy, by lifting, must be equal to the amount of work done (which we have previously shown to be equal to mgh). Therefore, there is a connection between potential energy and kinetic energy when we have vertical displacements in a gravitational field. However, just as in the case of kinetic energy, the frame of reference for potential energy is arbitrary, and we can define the zero base level to be anywhere. What is important is only how much energy is changing (remember that work and energy are scalars!). In summary, then, we can say that

$$W = \Delta KE \quad \text{or} \quad W = \Delta PE$$

10.5 Conservation of Energy

Suppose (see Figure 10.4) we lift a mass m a distance h above the ground. The minimum amount of force needed to overcome gravity is equal to the weight of the mass, mg. The work done is therefore equal to mgh. This quantity is also accompanied by a gain in potential energy since, if we release the mass, it will fall and gain velocity (i.e., it will gain kinetic energy). If the mass is allowed to fall from height h, what will its velocity be at the bottom?

Kinematically, we know that, if a mass is dropped from a height h, the time to fall is given by

$$t = \sqrt{\frac{2h}{g}}$$

Given the fact that the initial velocity is zero, the velocity at the bottom, just before impact, will be

$$\mathbf{v} = -\mathbf{g}t \quad \text{or} \quad \mathbf{v} = -\mathbf{g}\sqrt{\frac{2h}{\mathbf{g}}} = -\sqrt{2\mathbf{g}h}$$

(where the negative sign indicates the downward direction).

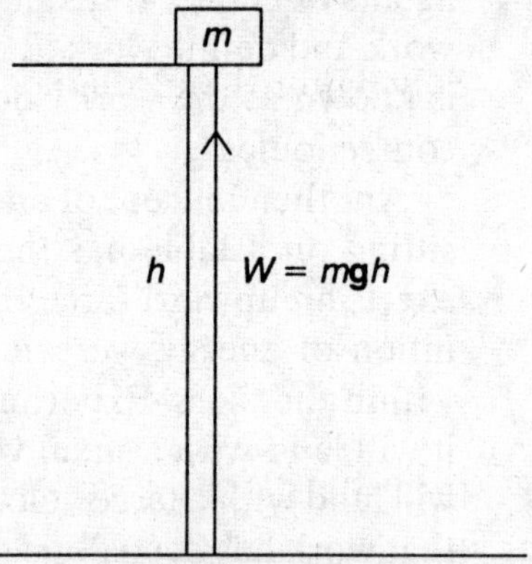

FIGURE 10.4

Now, since the work done to raise the mass is equal to the change (gain) in potential energy, the work done by gravity to accelerate the mass downward when released must derive from that potential energy. Since the work done through motion is equal to the change in kinetic energy, we can observe the fact that, as the mass falls, it loses potential energy and gains a proportional amount of kinetic energy. In the absence of any frictional forces, we can state that:

$$\Delta PE = \Delta KE$$

If we equate the fact that at the bottom the mass has lost all of its potential energy and gained all of its kinetic energy, then:

$$m\mathbf{g}h = \frac{1}{2}m\mathbf{v}^2$$

This implies, taking into account the direction of motion, that $\mathbf{v} = -\sqrt{2\mathbf{g}h}$ (as before). This discussion leads to the concept of the law of conservation of energy, which, briefly, states that energy is never created or destroyed. In the the absence of friction (which generates heat loss), the gain or loss of potential energy is balanced by a loss or gain of kinetic energy.

This conservation of energy concept applies to all mechanical systems, especially those involving springs and masses. Recall that the work done to compress (or stretch) a spring is given by $W = (1/2)kx^2$. This is also a measure of the potential energy stored in the spring. If a mass were moving on a frictionless table, at a velocity $\mathbf{v}$, toward an uncompressed spring and were to collide with it until the spring was fully compressed (and promptly absorbed all of the kinetic energy, causing the mass to stop), we could calculate the amount of compression as follows. If we assume that no energy is lost to heat (work by friction), the total energy before the interaction is contained in the kinetic energy of the mass. After the interaction, however, the energy is stored in the compressed spring as potential energy. We can therefore write that

$$\frac{1}{2}mv^2 = \frac{1}{2}kx^2$$

Solving for the amount, x of compression, gives

$$x = v\sqrt{\frac{m}{k}}$$

10.6 Conservative and Nonconservative Forces

If the work done by a force is independent of the path taken, the force is called a **conservative force**. This term implies that the mechanical energy of the system is conserved; that is, the sum of the potential and kinetic energies of the system remains constant in time. Gravity is an example of a conservative force, and so work done to or by a gravitational force (such as lifting or falling) is independent of the path taken.

As an example, consider a mass sliding down a frictionless incline of length ℓ. The magnitude of the component of gravity responsible for the acceleration down the incline is $-m\mathbf{g}\sin\theta$. Therefore, the work done by gravity is given by

$$W = -(m\mathbf{g}\sin\theta)\,\ell$$

As we saw in Chapter 9, in a right triangle the length ℓ is related to the height of the incline h so

$$h = \ell\sin\theta$$

Therefore, the work done down the incline can be written as $W = -m\mathbf{g}h$, which is just the loss of potential energy. The work done down the incline is exactly the same as the work done if the mass fell directly down from height h. An interesting aspect of this fact is that the accelerating force down the incline is less than the gravitational force (its weight), but the displacement is larger in magnitude. The extent to which we can ideally trade off effort versus displacement is called the **ideal mechanical advantage.**

Friction is an example of a **nonconservative force**. Since friction is derived from the contact between two surfaces, any change in path affects the length of time the contact takes place and therefore increases the effect of friction. The work done by friction can be expressed as the product of the frictional force and the displacement:

$$W_f = \mathbf{f}d$$

However, an implication of frictional work is the generation of heat, which reveals itself as an apparent nonconservation of mechanical energy. In other words, the work done by any nonconservative force, in which the change in total energy, ΔE, is not equal to zero, is given by:

$$W_{nc} = E_f - E_i$$

Problem-Solving Strategies for Work and Energy

1. Identify the types of energies involved in the situation.
2. Try to determine the initial energy of the system, which is usually the total energy.
3. If no friction is present, write the equations for the conservation of energy. Remember that, if a spring is involved, it has a different potential energy from gravity.
4. Remember that the work done is equal to the change in energy of the system.
5. For work problems, resolve forces into components in the direction of motion. This process involves vector analysis techniques. Identify the frame of reference involved.
6. Remember that work and energy are scalar quantities expressed in units of joules.
7. Keep in mind that, for any dynamics problem, especially one in which energy or work is not expressly stated as a concept, energy considerations may be useful in the solution.

Practice Problems for Chapter 10

Multiple Choice

1. Which of the following are the units for the spring constant, k?
   (A) $kg \cdot m^2/s^2$
   (B) $kg \cdot s^2$
   (C) $kg \cdot m/s$
   (D) kg/s^2
   (E) $kg \cdot m^2/s$

2. Which of the following is an expression for mechanical power?
   (A) $\mathbf{F}t/m$
   (B) $\mathbf{F}^2m/\mathbf{a}$
   (C) $\mathbf{F}m^2/t$
   (D) $\mathbf{F}m/t$
   (E) $\mathbf{F}^2t/m$

3. A pendulum consisting of a mass m attached to a light string of length ℓ is displaced from its rest position, making an angle θ with the vertical. It is then released and allowed to swing freely. Which of the following expressions represents the velocity of the mass when it reaches its lowest position?
(A) $\sqrt{2g\ell(1 - \cos\theta)}$
(B) $\sqrt{2g\ell \tan\theta)}$
(C) $\sqrt{2g\ell \cos\theta)}$
(D) $\sqrt{2g\ell(1 - \sin\theta)}$
(E) $\sqrt{2g\ell (\cos\theta - 1)}$

4. An engine maintains constant power on a conveyor belt machine. If the belt's velocity is doubled, the magnitude of its average acceleration
(A) is doubled
(B) is quartered
(C) is halved
(D) is quadrupled
(E) remains the same

5. A mass m is moving horizontally along a nearly frictionless floor with velocity **v**. The mass now encounters a part of the floor that has a coefficient of kinetic friction given by μ. The total distance traveled by the mass before it is slowed by friction to a stop is given by
(A) $2\mathbf{v}^2/\mu\mathbf{g}$
(B) $\mathbf{v}^2/2\mu\mathbf{g}$
(C) $2\mu\mathbf{g}v^2$
(D) $\mu\mathbf{v}^2/2\mathbf{g}$
(E) $\mu\mathbf{v}\mathbf{g}$

6. Two unequal masses are dropped simultaneously from the same height. The two masses will experience the same change in
(A) acceleration
(B) kinetic energy
(C) potential energy
(D) velocity
(E) momentum

7. A pendulum that consists of a 2-kg mass swings to a maximum vertical displacement of 17 cm above its rest position. At its lowest point, the kinetic energy of the mass is equal to
(A) 0.33 J
(B) 3.33 J
(C) 33.3 J
(D) 333 J
(E) 3333 J

8. A 0.3-kg mass rests on top of a spring that has been compressed by 0.04 m. Neglect any frictional effects, and consider the spring to be massless. Then, if the spring has a constant k equal to 2000 N/m, to what height will the mass rise when the system is released?
(A) 1.24 m
(B) 0.75 m
(C) 0.54 m
(D) 1.04 m
(E) 1.34 m

9. A box is pulled along a smooth floor by a force F, making an angle θ with the horizontal. As θ increases, the amount of work done to pull the box the same distance, d,
(A) increases
(B) increases and then decreases
(C) remains the same
(D) decreases and then increases
(E) decreases

10. As the time needed to run up a flight of stairs decreases, the amount of work done against gravity
(A) increases
(B) decreases
(C) remains the same
(D) increases and then decreases
(E) decreases and then increases

Free Response

1. A 1.3-kg sphere is dropped through a tall column of liquid. When the sphere has fallen a distance of 0.50 m, it is observed to have a velocity of 2.5 m/s.
   (a) How much work was done by the frictional "viscosity" of the liquid?
   (b) What is the average force of friction during the displacement of 0.5 m?

2. A 15-kg mass is attached to a massless spring by a light string that passes over a frictionless pulley as shown below. The spring has a force constant of 500 N/m and is unstretched when the mass is released. What is the velocity of the mass when it has fallen a distance of 0.3 m?

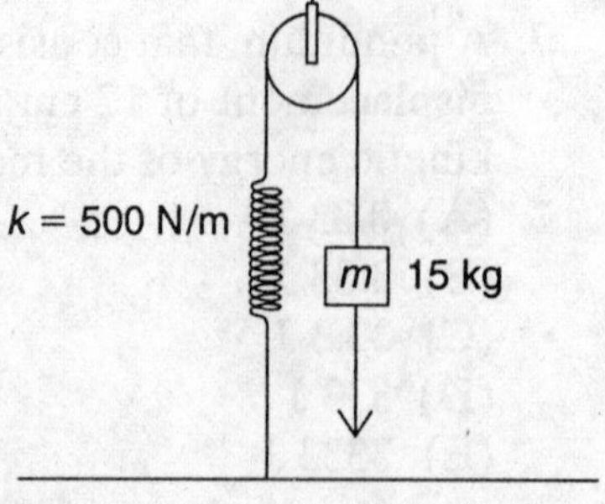

3. A 1.5-kg block is placed on a rough incline. The mass is connected to a massless spring by means of a light string passed over a frictionless pulley, as shown below. The spring has a force constant k equal to 100 N/m. The block is released from rest, and the spring is initially unstretched. The block moves down a distance of 16 cm before coming to rest. What is the coefficient of friction between the block and the surface of the incline?

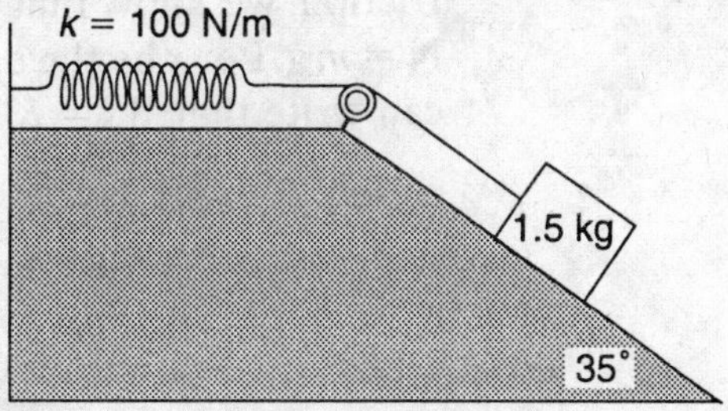

Solutions

Multiple-Choice Problems

1. **D** The units for the spring or force constant are provided by Hooke's law, $\mathbf{F} = k\mathbf{x}$, and are newtons per meter. Recall that 1 N = 1 kg · m/s², so dividing by m gives kg/s².

2. **E** Power is equal to work done divided by time. Therefore,

$$P = \frac{W}{t} = \frac{\mathbf{Fd}}{t}$$

Using some algebra and kinematics, we see that

$$P = \frac{\mathbf{Fd}}{t} = \mathbf{Fv} = \mathbf{F\,at} = \mathbf{F}\left(\frac{\mathbf{F}}{m}\right)t = \frac{\mathbf{F}^2 t}{m}$$

You could also get the answer by verifying which expression has units of joules per second.

3. **A** Consider the sketch below of the situation:

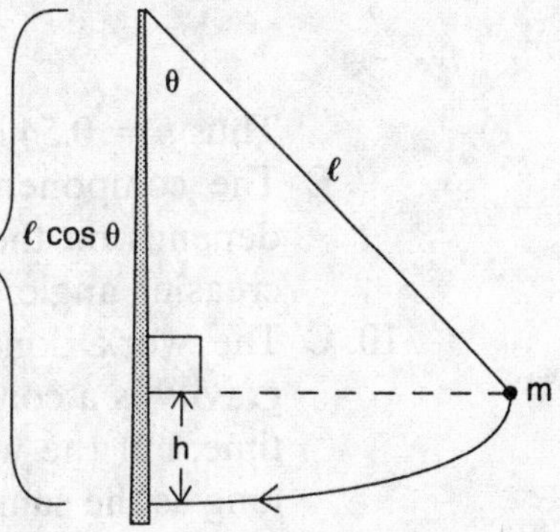

From the geometry of the sketch, note that

$$h = \ell - \ell\cos\theta = \ell(1 - \cos\theta)$$

If it is assumed that there is no friction, gravity is the only conservative force acting to do work. Therefore, $\Delta KE = \Delta PE$, and so, at the bottom,

$$\mathbf{v} = \sqrt{2\mathbf{g}h} = \sqrt{2\mathbf{g}\ell(1 - \cos\theta)}$$

4. **C** Power is equal to the product of the average force applied times the velocity. If the velocity is doubled, and the power is constant, the average force must be halved. Since $\mathbf{F} = m\mathbf{a}$, the average acceleration of the belt must be halved as well.
5. **B** The only applied force is friction, which is doing work to stop the mass. This work is being taken from the initial kinetic energy. For friction, we know that $\mathbf{f} = \mu\mathbf{N}$, and since the motion is horizontal, $\mathbf{N} = m\mathbf{g}$. Let x be the distance traveled while stopping; therefore, we can write that $W_f = KE$ and:

$$\frac{1}{2}mv^2 = \mu mgx$$

Solving for x, we get:

$$x = \frac{v^2}{2\mu g}$$

6. **D** Objects dropped simultaneously from the same height have the same constant acceleration, which is the change in velocity. The unequal masses will provide for different energies, but the velocity changes will be the same.
7. **B** Since we have a conservative system,

$$\Delta KE = \Delta PE = (2)(9.8)(0.17) = 3.33 \text{ J}$$

Remember to change 17 cm to 0.17 m!
8. **C** We are dealing with a conservative system, so the initial starting energy is just the potential energy of the compressed spring. This energy supplies the work needed to raise the mass a height h, which is a gain in gravitational potential energy. Thus we equate these two expressions and solve for the height:

$$\frac{1}{2}(2000)(0.4)^2 = (0.3)(9.8)h$$

Thus $h = 0.54$ m.
9. **E** The component of the applied force in the horizontal direction depends on the cosine of the angle. This value decreases with increasing angle. Thus the work decreases as well.
10. **C** The work done is independent of the time or path taken since gravity is a conservative force. The power generated is affected by time, but the work done to run up the stairs remains the same as long as the same mass is raised to the same height.

Free-Response Problems

1. (a) The change in potential energy is a measure of the initial energy and equals (0.75)(9.8)(2) = 14.7 J. After the sphere has fallen 2 m, its velocity is 5 m/s, so the kinetic energy is given by

$$KE = \left(\frac{1}{2}\right)(0.75)(5)^2 = 9.375 \text{ J}$$

The work done by friction is due to a nonconservative force that is equal to the difference between the final and initial energies:

$$E_f - E_i = 9.375 \text{ J} - 14.7 \text{ J} = -5.325 \text{ J}$$

Therefore, $W_f = -5.325$ J.

(b) The average frictional force is equal to the work done divided by the displacement of 2 m. Thus

$$\mathbf{f} = -2.67 \text{ N}$$

which of course is negative since it opposes the motion.

2. The loss of potential energy is balanced by a gain in elastic potential energy for the spring and in kinetic energy for the falling mass if we assume that the starting energy for the system is zero relative to the starting point for the mass. In the absence of friction, the displacement of the mass is equal to the elongation of the spring. Thus we can equate our energies and write:

$$0 = -mgh + \frac{1}{2}kx^2 + \frac{1}{2}mv^2$$

If we substitute the known numbers, we get

$$0 = -(15)(9.8)(0.3) + \left(\frac{1}{2}\right)(500)(0.3)^2 + \left(\frac{1}{2}\right)(15)(\mathbf{v}^2)$$

Solving for velocity $\mathbf{v}$ gives $\mathbf{v} = 1.7$ m/s.

3. In this problem, the work done by gravity down the incline is affected by the work done by friction. Together, the net work is applied to stretching the spring by an amount equal to the displacement of the mass. Thus we can say

$$W_g - W_f = W_s$$

where W_g is the work done by gravity, W_f is the work done by friction, and W_s is the work done to the spring. Hence:

$$mg \sin \theta d - \mu mg \cos \theta d = \frac{1}{2}kx^2$$

Substituting the known numbers, we get:

$$(1.5)(9.8)(0.16) \sin 35 - \mu(1.5)(9.8)(0.16) \cos 35 = \frac{1}{2}(100)(0.16)^2$$

Solving for the coefficient of friction gives $\mu = 0.036$.

CHAPTER 11

Impacts and Linear Momentum

11.1 Introduction

In Chapter 9, we discussed Isaac Newton's laws of motion. In the third law of motion, sometimes called the law of action and reaction, we considered the fact that an interaction between two objects in space creates a pair of impact forces that are equal and opposite. Thus, we conclude that forces do not act in isolation.

11.2 Internal and External Forces

Consider a system of two blocks with masses m and M $(M > m)$. If the blocks were to collide, the forces of impact would be equal and opposite. However, because of the different masses, the response to these forces (i.e., the changes in velocity) would not be equal. In the absence of any outside or external forces acting on the objects (such as friction or gravity), we say that the impact forces are internal.

To Newton, the "quantity of motion" discussed in his book, *The Principia* was the product of an object's mass and velocity. This quantity, called **linear momentum** or just **momentum**, is a vector quantity having units of kilogram · meters per second (kg · m/s). Algebraically, momentum is designated by the letter **p**, such that $\mathbf{p} = m\mathbf{v}$.

To understand Newton's rationale, consider the action of trying to change the motion of a moving object. Do not confuse this with the inertia of the object; here, both the mass and the velocity are important. Consider, for example, that a truck moving at a slow 1 meter per second can still inflict a large amount of damage because of its mass. Also, a small bullet, having a mass of perhaps 1 gram or less, does incredible damage because of its high velocity. In each case (see Figure 11.1) the damage is the result of a force of impact when the object is intercepted by something else. Let's now consider the nature of impact forces.

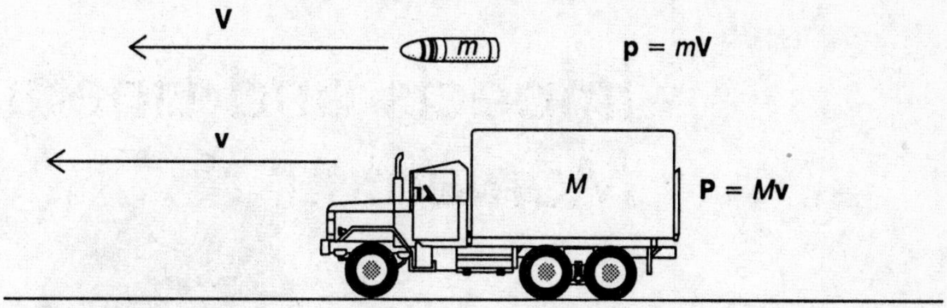

FIGURE 11.1 Comparison of the momentum of a truck with that of a bullet

11.3 Impact Forces and Momentum Changes

Consider a mass m moving with a velocity $\mathbf{v}$ in some frame of reference. If the mass is subjected to some external forces, then, by Newton's second law of motion, we can write that $\Sigma \mathbf{F} = m\mathbf{a}$. The vector sum of all the forces, referred to as the **net force**, is responsible for changing the velocity of the motion (in magnitude and/or direction).

If we recall the definition of acceleration as the rate of change or velocity, we can rewrite the second law of motion as

$$\mathbf{F}_{\text{net}} = m\left(\frac{\Delta \mathbf{v}}{\Delta t}\right)$$

This expression is also a vector equation and is equivalent to the second law of motion. If we make the assumption that the mass of the object is not changing, we can again rewrite the second law in the form

$$\mathbf{F}_{\text{net}} = \frac{\Delta m\mathbf{v}}{\Delta t} = \frac{\Delta \mathbf{p}}{\Delta t}$$

This expression means that the net external force acting on an object is equal to the rate of change of momentum of the object and is another alternative form of Newton's second law of motion. The **change in momentum** is a vector quantity in the same direction as the net force applied. Since the time interval is just a scalar quantity, we can multiply both sides by Δt to get

$$\mathbf{F}_{net}\Delta t = \Delta \mathbf{p} = m\Delta \mathbf{v} = m\mathbf{v}_f - m\mathbf{v}_i$$

The quantity, $\mathbf{F}_{\text{net}}\ \Delta t$, called the **impulse**, represents the effect of a force acting on a mass during a time interval Δt, and is likewise a vector quantity. From this expression, it can be stated that the impulse applied to an object is equal to the change in momentum of the object.

Another way to consider impulse is to look at a graph of force versus time for a continuously varying force (see Figure 11.2).

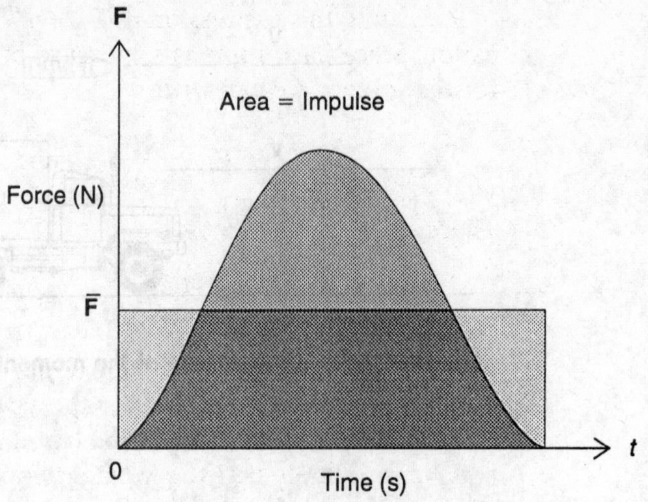

FIGURE 11.2

The area under this curve is a measure of the impulse in units of newton · seconds (N · s). Another way to view this concept is to identify the average force, $\overline{\mathbf{F}}$, such that the area of the rectangle formed by the average force is equal in area to the entire curve. This is more manageable algebraically, and we can write

$$\overline{\mathbf{F}}\,\Delta t = \Delta \mathbf{p}$$

As an example, consider the following problem: How long will an average braking force of 1500 N take to stop a 2500-kg car traveling with an initial velocity of 10 m/s? We substitute the given numbers into the formula for impulse and momentum change to get

$$(1500)\,\Delta t = (2500)(10)$$

The change in velocity is equal to 10 m/s because the object is stopping. Solving for the time, we find out that the braking force will take about 16.7 s.

11.4 The Law of Conservation of Linear Momentum

Newton's third law of motion states that for every action there is an equal but opposite reaction. This reaction force is present whenever we have an interaction between two objects in the universe. Suppose we have two masses, m_1 and m_2, that are approaching each other along a horizontal frictionless surface. Let $\mathbf{F}_{12}$ be the force that m_1 exerts on m_2, and let $\mathbf{F}_{21}$ be the force that m_2 exerts on m_1. According to Newton's law, these forces must be equal and opposite; that is, $\mathbf{F}_{12} = -\mathbf{F}_{21}$.

Rewriting this expression as $\mathbf{F}_{12} + \mathbf{F}_{21} = 0$ leads to an interesting implication. Since each force is a measure of the rate of change of momentum for that object, we can write

$$\mathbf{F}_{12} = \frac{\Delta \mathbf{p}_1}{\Delta t} \quad \text{and} \quad \mathbf{F}_{21} = \frac{\Delta \mathbf{p}_2}{\Delta t}$$

Therefore:

$$\frac{\Delta \mathbf{p}_1}{\Delta t} + \frac{\Delta \mathbf{p}_2}{\Delta t} = 0 \quad \text{and} \quad \frac{\Delta(\mathbf{p}_1 + \mathbf{p}_2)}{\Delta t} = 0$$

The change in the sum of the momenta is therefore zero, implying that the sum of the total momentum for the system ($\mathbf{p}_1 + \mathbf{p}_2$) is a constant all the time. This conclusion is called the **law of conservation of linear momentum**, and we say simply that the momentum is conserved.

Here is another way of writing this conservation statement in a general form for any two masses (after separating all initial and final terms):

$$m_1\mathbf{v}_{1i} + m_2\mathbf{v}_{2i} = m_1\mathbf{v}_{1f} + m_2\mathbf{v}_{2f}$$

Extension of the law of conservation of momentum to two or three dimensions involves the recognition that momentum is a vector quantity. Given two masses moving in a plane relative to a coordinate system, conservation of momentum must hold simultaneously in both the horizontal and vertical directions.These vector components of momentum can be calculated using the standard techniques of vector analysis used to resolve forces in components.

11.5 Elastic and Inelastic Collisions

During any collision between two pieces of matter, momentum is always conserved. This statement is not, however, necessarily true about kinetic energy. If two masses stick together after a collision, it is observed that the kinetic energy before the collision is not equal to the kinetic energy after it. If the kinetic energy is conserved as well as the momentum, the collision is described as **elastic**. If the kinetic energy is not conserved after the collision (e.g., energy being lost to heat or friction), the collision is described as **inelastic**.

As an example, suppose that a mass m has a velocity $\mathbf{v}$ while mass M is at rest along a horizontal frictionless surface. The two masses collide and stick together. What is the final velocity, $\mathbf{u}$, of the system? According to the law of conservation of momentum, the total momentum before the collision ($m\mathbf{v}$), must be equal to the total momentum after. Since the two masses are combining, the new mass of the system is $M + m$, and the new momentum is given by $(m + M)\mathbf{u}$. Thus, we find that:

$$\mathbf{u} = \frac{m\mathbf{v}}{m+M}$$

The initial kinetic energy is $(1/2)mv^2$. The final kinetic energy is given by

$$KE_f = \frac{1}{2}(m + M)\mathbf{u}^2 = \frac{1}{2}\left(\frac{m^2\mathbf{v}^2}{m + M}\right)$$

which is of course not equal to the initial kinetic energy.

If we have an elastic collision, we write both conservation laws to get two equations involving the velocities of the masses before and after the collision:

$$m_1\mathbf{v}_{1i} + m_2\mathbf{v}_{2i} = m_1\mathbf{v}_{1f} + m_2\mathbf{v}_{2f}$$

$$\frac{1}{2}m_1\mathbf{v}_{1i}^2 + \frac{1}{2}m_2\mathbf{v}_{2i}^2 = \frac{1}{2}m_1\mathbf{v}_{1f}^2 + \frac{1}{2}m_2\mathbf{v}_{2f}^2$$

If we cancel out the factor (1/2) in the second equation, and collect the expressions for each mass on each side, we can rewrite the two equations as

$$m_1(\mathbf{v}_{1i} - \mathbf{v}_{2i}) = m_2(\mathbf{v}_{2f} - \mathbf{v}_{2i})$$

$$m_1(\mathbf{v}_{1i}^2 - \mathbf{v}_{1f}^2) = m_2(\mathbf{v}_{2f}^2 - \mathbf{v}_{2i}^2)$$

The second equation is factorable and so can be simplified. Again rewriting the expressions, we get

$$m_1(\mathbf{v}_{1i} - \mathbf{v}_{1f}) = m_2(\mathbf{v}_{2f} - \mathbf{v}_{2i})$$

$$m_1(\mathbf{v}_{1i} + \mathbf{v}_{1f})(\mathbf{v}_{1i} - \mathbf{v}_{1f}) = m_2(\mathbf{v}_{2f} + \mathbf{v}_{2i})(\mathbf{v}_{2f} - \mathbf{v}_{2i})$$

If we take the ratio of the two expressions, we arrive at an interesting result after collecting terms:

$$\mathbf{v}_{1i} - \mathbf{v}_{2i} = -(\mathbf{v}_{1f} - \mathbf{v}_{2f})$$

This expression states that the relative velocity between the masses before the elastic collision is equal and opposite to the relative velocity between the masses after the elastic collision! Thus, there exists the characteristic "rebounding" observed during elastic collisions.

11.6 Motion in the Center of Mass Frame of Reference

When we first introduced the study of motion, we discussed the fact that all motion is relative to some chosen frame of reference. This frame can be "attached" to the moving mass; if the velocity is constant, the frame is called **inertial**. Another useful frame of reference is one connected with the **center of mass** of a system of masses.

Consider a collection of mass particles as shown in Figure 11.3. Let us identify an arbitrary mass particle m_i and its position vector r_i within the chosen coordinate system. If M represents the total mass of the system, such that $M = \Sigma m_i$, then the weighted distribution of mass relative to origin is given by the position vector $\mathbf{R}_{CM}$ as follows:

$$\mathbf{R}_{CM} = \frac{\Sigma m_i \mathbf{r}_i}{\Sigma m_i}$$

where CM stands for "center of mass." In other words, the center of mass for the system is the point where all of the mass can be considered concentrated and is a "weighted" mean position for the mass distribution.

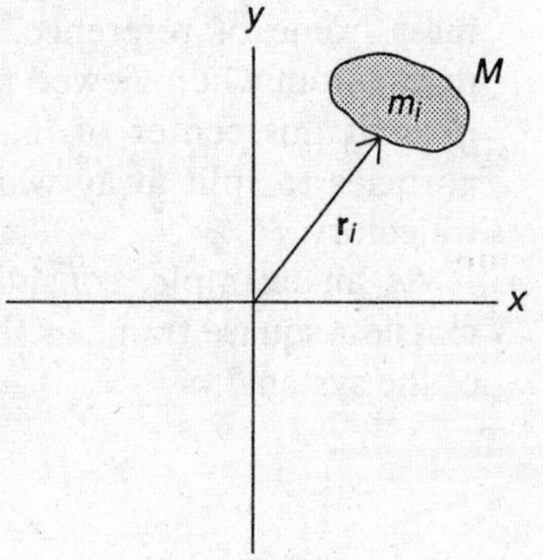

FIGURE 11.3

Another way of writing the expression for center of mass is

$$MR_{CM} = \Sigma m_i r_i = m_1 r_1 + m_2 r_2 + \ldots + m_n r_n$$

Since this is a vector equation, the center-of-mass-position vector can be resolved into *x*- and *y*-components for the center of mass as follows:

$$x_{CM} = \frac{m_1 x_1 + m_2 x_2 + \ldots + m_n x_n}{M}$$

$$y_{CM} = \frac{m_1 y_1 + m_2 y_2 + \ldots + m_n y_n}{M}$$

Dynamically, some interesting effects happen in the center-of-mass frame of reference. First, any coordinate system attached to this frame of reference can provide for zero initial kinetic energy and momentum. Second, if we allow the system to move in a time Δt, we can write

$$M\left(\frac{\Delta \mathbf{R}_{CM}}{\Delta t}\right) = \Sigma m_i \left(\frac{\Delta \mathbf{r}_i}{\Delta t}\right)$$

This means that $M\mathbf{v}_{CM} = \Sigma m_i \mathbf{v}_i$ and we can state that the total momentum for the system can be viewed as the momentum of the center of mass (where the total mass is considered to be concentrated). Additionally, if the system is accelerating, we can state that

$$M\left(\frac{\Delta \mathbf{v}_{CM}}{\Delta t}\right) = \Sigma m_i\left(\frac{\Delta \mathbf{v}_i}{\Delta t}\right)$$

$$M\mathbf{a}_{CM} = \Sigma m_i \mathbf{a}_i$$

The implication of this statement is that, if an external force is applied to each mass in the system, the responses to the force can be viewed as a single force acting on the center of mass to produce a translational acceleration (as opposed to a rotation; see Chapter 12), since $\mathbf{F} = m\mathbf{a}$.

These redescriptions of the dynamics of a collection of masses suggest that the motion or interaction effects may appear simpler in the center-of-mass frame of reference. For example, a projectile in motion has zero momentum when viewed from the center-of-mass frame of reference. The path of this center of mass is a parabola. An explosion will cause the particles to split away while the center of mass continues in its original trajectory.

As an example, consider four masses arranged on the corners of a massless square frame as shown in Figure 11.4. Where is the center of mass of the system?

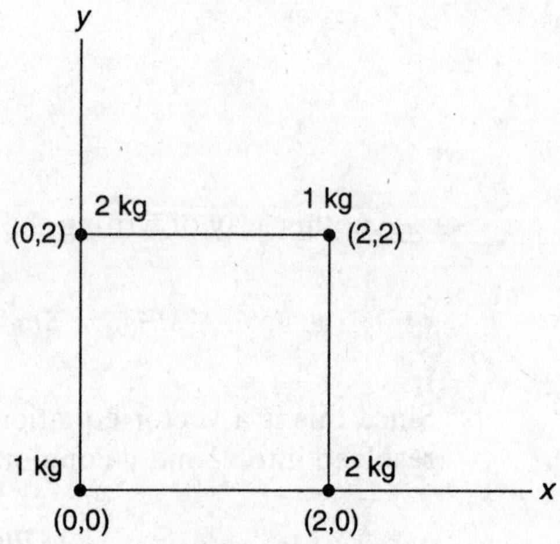

FIGURE 11.4

Using our formulas for the x- and y-components of the center of mass, we get $M = 6$ kg, and $X_{CM} = 1$ unit and $Y_{CM} = 1$ unit.

Thus $\mathbf{R}_{CM} = (1,1)$, which is in the middle of the square.

Problem-Solving Strategies for Impacts and Linear Momentum

In any matter interaction, momentum is always conserved. Therefore, when you read a problem that does not state explicitly that momentum is involved, you can safely assume, in the case of collision or an impact, that momentum is conserved, and you should write the equations for the conservation of momentum. The kinetic energy, however, is not necessarily conserved unless the collision is elastic. In summary, you should:

1. Decide whether an impact or a collision is involved. If there is a collision, observe whether it is elastic or inelastic.

2. Remember that, if the collision is inelastic, masses will usually stick together, so be sure to determine the new combined mass.
3. If the collision is elastic, write the equations for the conservation of both momentum and kinetic energy.
4. Remember that the impulse given to a mass is equal to its change in momentum. The change in momentum is a vector quantity in the same direction as the impulse or net force.
5. Be sure to take into account algebraically any reversal of directions, and remember the sign conventions for left, right, up, and down motions.
6. Keep in mind that motions may be simpler if studied in the center-of-mass frame of reference. In such a frame, one considers the motion of the center of mass, as well as the motions of mass particles relative to the center of mass.
7. Remember that in two dimensions the center of mass will follow a smooth path after an internal explosion since the forces involved were internal and the initial momentum in that frame was zero. For example, for a projectile launched at an angle and then exploded the center of mass still follow the regular parabolic trajectory.

Practice Problems for Chapter 11

Multiple Choice

1. Which of the following expressions, where **p** represents the linear momentum of the particle, is equivalent to the kinetic energy of a moving particle?
(A) $m\mathbf{p}^2$
(B) $m^2/2\mathbf{p}$
(C) $2\mathbf{p}/m$
(D) $\mathbf{p}/2m$
(E) $\mathbf{p}^2/2m$

2. Two carts having masses 1.5 kg and 0.7 kg, respectively, are initially at rest and are held together by a compressed massless spring. When released, the 1.5-kg cart moves to the left with a velocity of 7 m/s . What is the velocity and direction of the 0.7-kg cart?
(A) 15 m/s right
(B) 15 m/s left
(C) 7 m/s left
(D) 7 m/s right
(E) 0 m/s

3. The product of an object's instantaneous momentum and its acceleration is equal to its
(A) applied force
(B) kinetic energy
(C) power output
(D) net force
(E) displacement

4. A ball with a mass of 0.15 kg has a velocity of 5 m/s. It strikes a wall perpendicularly and bounces off straight back with a velocity of 3 m/s. The ball underwent a change in momentum equal to
(A) 0.30 kg · m/s
(B) 1.20 kg · m/s
(C) 0.15 kg · m/s
(D) 5 kg · m/s
(E) 7.5 kg · m/s

5. What braking force is supplied to a 3000-kg car traveling with a velocity of 35 m/s that is stopped in 12 s?
(A) 29,400 N
(B) 3000 N
(C) 8750 N
(D) 105,000 N
(E) 150 N

6. A 0.1-kg baseball is thrown with a velocity of 35 m/s. The batter hits it straight back with a velocity of 60 m/s. What is the magnitude of the average impulse exerted on the ball by the bat?
(A) 3.5 N · s
(B) 2.5 N · s
(C) 7.5 N · s
(D) 9.5 N · s
(E) 12.2 N · s

7. A 1-kg object is moving with a velocity of 6 m/s to the right. It collides and sticks to a 2-kg object moving with a velocity of 3 m/s in the same direction. How much kinetic energy was lost in the collision?
(A) 1.5 J
(B) 2 J
(C) 2.5 J
(D) 3 J
(E) 0 J

8. A 2-kg mass moving with a velocity of 7 m/s collides elastically with a 4-kg mass moving in the opposite direction at 4 m/s. The 2-kg mass reverses direction after the collision and has a new velocity of 3 m/s. What is the new velocity of the 4-kg mass?
(A) −1 m/s
(B) 1 m/s
(C) 6 m/s
(D) 4 m/s
(E) 5 m/s

9. A mass m is attached to a massless spring with a force constant k. The mass rests on a horizontal frictionless surface. The system is compressed a distance x from the spring's initial position and then released.

The momentum of the mass when the spring passes its equilibrium position is given by
(A) $x\sqrt{mk}$
(B) $x\sqrt{k/m}$
(C) $x\sqrt{m/k}$
(D) $x\sqrt{k^2m}$
(E) xmk

10. Three equal masses are arranged at the vertices of a massless triangular frame such that the coordinates of each mass, m, are given as follows in the x,y-plane: (0,0), (1,2), and (2,0). The coordinates of the center of mass of this system are
(A) (1,1)
(B) $(1, \frac{2}{3})$
(C) $(\frac{1}{2}, \frac{1}{2})$
(D) $(\frac{1}{2}, \frac{3}{4})$
(E) (0, 0)

Free Response

1. Two blocks with masses 1 kg and 4 kg, respectively, are moving on a horizontal frictionless surface. The 1-kg block has a velocity of 12 m/s, and the 4-kg block is ahead of it, moving at 4 m/s, as shown in the diagram below. The 4-kg block has a massless spring attached to the end facing the 1-kg block. The spring has a force constant k equal to 1000 N/m.

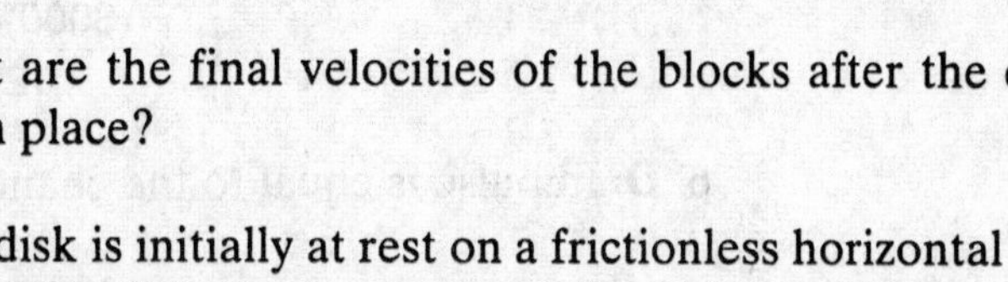

(a) What is the maximum compression of the spring after the collision?
(b) What are the final velocities of the blocks after the collision has taken place?

2. A 0.4-kg disk is initially at rest on a frictionless horizontal surface. It is hit by a 0.1-kg disk moving horizontally with a velocity of 4 m/s. After the collision, the 0.1-kg disk has a velocity of 2 m/s at an angle of 43° to the positive x-axis.
(a) Determine the velocity and direction of the 0.4-kg disk after the collision.
(b) Determine the amount of kinetic energy lost in the collision.

3. A 50-kg girl stands on a platform with wheels on a frictionless horizontal surface as shown below. The platform has a total mass of 1000 kg and is attached to a massless spring with a force constant k equal to 1000 N/m. The girl throws a 1-kg ball with an initial velocity of 35 m/s at an angle of 30° to the horizontal.
(a) What is the recoil velocity of the platform-girl system?
(b) What is the elongation of the spring?

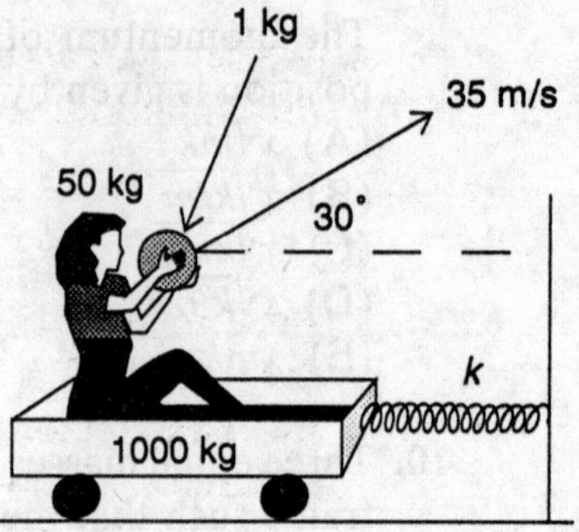

Solutions

Multiple-Choice Problems

1. **E** If we multiply the formula for kinetic energy by the ratio *m/m*, we see that the formula for kinetic energy becomes

$$KE = \left(\frac{1}{2m}\right)(m^2)(v^2) = \frac{p^2}{2m}$$

2. **A** Momentum is conserved, so (1.5)(7) = 0.7**v**. Thus **v** = 15 m/s. The direction is to the right since in a recoil the masses go in opposite directions.
3. **C** An object's instantaneous momentum times its acceleration will equal its power output in units of joules per second or watts.
4. **B** The change in momentum is a vector quantity. The rebound velocity is in the opposite direction, so $\Delta \mathbf{v} = 5 - (-3) = 8$ m/s. The change in momentum is

$$\Delta \mathbf{p} = (0.15)(8) = 1.20 \text{ kg} \cdot \text{m/s}$$

5. **C** The formula is $\mathbf{F}\,\Delta t = m\,\Delta \mathbf{v}$. Solving for the force, we get

$$\mathbf{F} = \frac{(3000)(35)}{12} = 8750 \text{ N}$$

6. **D** Impulse is equal to the change in momentum, which is

$$\Delta \mathbf{p} = (0.1)[35 - (-60)] = 9.5 \text{ N} \cdot \text{s}$$

because of the change in direction of the ball.
7. **D** First, we find the final velocity of this inelastic collision. Momentum is conserved, so we can write (1)(6) + (2)(3) = (3)**v**′ since both objects are moving in the same direction. Thus **v**′ = 4 m/s. The initial kinetic energy of the 1-kg object is 18 J, while the initial kinetic energy of the 2-kg mass is 9 J. Thus the total initial kinetic energy is 27 J. After the collision, the combined 3-kg object has a velocity of 4 m/s and a final kinetic energy of 24 J. Thus, 3 J of kinetic energy has been lost.
8. **B** Momentum is conserved in this elastic collsion but the directions are opposite, so we must be careful with negative signs. We therefore write (2)(7) − (4)(4) = −(2)(3) + 4**v**′and get **v**′ = 1 m/s.

9. **A** We set the two energy equations equal to solve for the velocity at the equilibrium position. Thus

$$\frac{1}{2}kx^2 = \frac{1}{2}mv^2$$

since no gravitational potential energy is involved, and we write that the velocity is $\mathbf{v} = x\sqrt{k/m}$. Now momentum $\mathbf{p} = m\mathbf{v}$, so we multiply by m and factor the "mass" back under the radical sign, where it is squared so that we get $\mathbf{p} = x\sqrt{mk}$.

10. **B** Using our formulas for the x- and y-positions of the center of mass, we get the following results from our data:

in the x-direction: $X_{CM} = \dfrac{m(0) + m(1) + m(2)}{3m} = 1$ unit

in the y-direction $Y_{CM} = \dfrac{m(0) + m(0) + m(2)}{3m} = \dfrac{2}{3}$ unit

Free-Response Problems

1. (a) Upon impact, the spring becomes compressed, but both blocks are still in motion. Therefore, for an instant, we have an inelastic collision, and momentum is of course conserved. Thus we can write for the moment of impact

$$m_1\mathbf{v}_{1i} + m_2\mathbf{v}_{2i} = (m_1 + m_2)\mathbf{v}_f$$

Solving for the final velocity, we get $\mathbf{v}_f = 5.6$ m/s. Using the initial values for the velocities, we find that the initial kinetic energies are 72 J and 32 J for the 1-kg and 4-kg blocks, respectively. Thus the total initial kinetic energy is 104 J. Using the final velocity of 5.6 m/s and the combined mass of 5 kg, we get a final kinetic energy of 78.4 J. The difference in kinetic energy of 25.6 J is used to compress the spring in this inelastic collision. Using the formula for the work done against a spring, $(1/2)kx^2$, we get $x = 0.05$ m for the maximum compression of the spring after the collision.

(b) After the collision has taken place, the two blocks again separate. If we treat the situation as elastic, since we assume that the work done to compress the spring will be used by the spring in rebounding, we can use the initial velocities as a "before" condition for momentum and kinetic energy, and seek to solve for the two final velocities of the blocks after the rebound has taken place. To find both velocities, we need two equations, and we use the conservation of kinetic energy in this case to assist us. Thus we write

$$m_1\mathbf{v}_{1i} + m_2\mathbf{v}_{2i} = m_1\mathbf{v}_{1f} + m_2\mathbf{v}_{2f}$$

and for the kinetic energy

$$\frac{1}{2}m_1\mathbf{v}_{1i}^2 + \frac{1}{2}m_2\mathbf{v}_{2i}^2 = \frac{1}{2}m_1\mathbf{v}_{1f}^2 + \frac{1}{2}m_2\mathbf{v}_{2f}^2$$

Substituting the known numbers, we obtain for the momentum $28 = \mathbf{v}_{1f} + 4\mathbf{v}_{2f}$, and for the kinetic energy we get $208 = \mathbf{v}_{1f}^2 + 4\mathbf{v}_{2f}^2$.

If we solve for $\mathbf{v}_{1f}$ from the momentum equation, square the result, and substitute into the kinetic energy equation, we obtain a factorable quadratic equation for $\mathbf{v}_{2f}$:

$$\mathbf{v}_{2f}^2 - 11.2\mathbf{v}_{2f} + 28.2 = (\mathbf{v}_{2f} - 7.2)(\mathbf{v}_{2f} - 4) = 0$$

Of the two choices for the second final velocity, only one provides a physically meaningful set of solutions. This is so because the first mass must rebound, and hence its final velocity must be negative. Our final answers are therefore $\mathbf{v}_{2f} = 7.2$ m/s and $\mathbf{v}_{1f} = -0.8$ m/s.

2. (a) This is a two-dimensional collision, and we consider the conservation of momentum in each direction, before and after. In the x-direction, we have only the initial momentum of the 0.1-kg disk with a velocity of 4 m/s. After the collision, the 0.1 kg disk has an x-component of momentum given by (0.1)(2) cos 43.

The 0.4-kg disk had initially zero momentum and now has some unknown velocity at some unknown angle, θ, to the x-axis. Let us assume that the angle is below the x-axis, so that the x-component will be positive and the y-component negative. If our assumption is correct, we will get a positive answer for θ. A negative answer will let us know that the assumption is incorrect. The x-component of final momentum for the 0.4-kg disk is given by $(0.4)\mathbf{v}_{2f}\cos\theta$, and the y-component by $-(0.4)\mathbf{v}_{2f}\sin\theta$. We can therefore write for the x-direction:

$$(0.1)(4) + 0 = (0.1)(2)\cos 43 + (.4)\mathbf{v}_{2f}\cos\theta$$

and for the y-direction:

$$0 = (0.1)(2)\sin 43 - (0.4)\mathbf{v}_{2f}\sin\theta$$

Solving for the angles and velocities in each we get the following two equations:

$$\mathbf{v}_{2f}\sin\theta = 0.34 \quad \text{and} \quad \mathbf{v}_{2f}\cos\theta = 0.635$$

Taking the ratio gives $\tan\theta = 0.535$ and $\theta = 28°$. Substituting this angle gives us the final velocity for the 0.4-kg disk: 0.72 m/s.

(b) To find the loss of kinetic energy, we calculate the total initial and final kinetic energies. Using the given data, we find that the initial kinetic energy is 0.8 J. Using our final data, we get a total final kinetic energy of 0.3 J. Thus 0.5 J of kinetic energy has been lost.

3. (a) In this problem, the x-component of the velocity provides the impulse to elongate the spring using recoil. Thus we have that the velocity of the ball is 35 cos 30 = 25.98 m/s. Using conservation of momentum, we state that (1)(25.98) = (1050)$\mathbf{v}'$. Thus $\mathbf{v}'$ = 0.0247 m/s in the negative x-direction, so the recoil velocity of the platform-girl system can be expressed as $\mathbf{v}' = -0.0247$ m/s.

(b) This recoil velocity provides kinetic energy that does work to elongate the spring. Thus we have

$$\left(\frac{1}{2}\right)(1050)(0.0247^2) = 0.32 = \left(\frac{1}{2}\right)(1000)x^2$$

Solving for x gives $x = 0.025$ m for the elongation of the spring.

CHAPTER 12

Torque and Angular Momentum

12.1 Introduction

In Chapter 11, we discussed the fact that, if a single force is directed toward the center of mass of an extended object, the result is a linear or translational acceleration in the same direction as the force. If, however, the force is directed away from the center of mass, then the result is a rotation about the center of mass. In addition, if the object is constrained by a fixed pivot point, the rotation will take place about that pivot (e.g., a hinge). These observations are summarized in Figure 12.1.

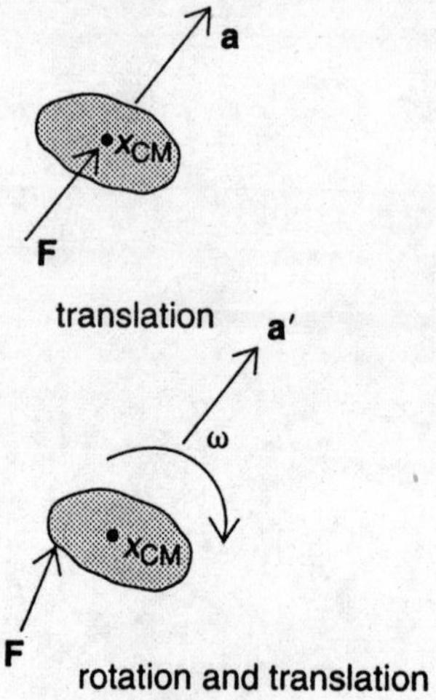

FIGURE 12.1

12.2 Parallel Forces and Moments

If two forces are used, it is possible to prevent the rotation if these forces are parallel and are of suitable magnitudes. If the object is free to move in space, translational motion may result (see Figure 12.2).

As an example of parallel forces, consider two people on a seesaw, as shown in Figure 12.3. The two people have weights $\mathbf{W}_1$ and $\mathbf{W}_2$, respectively, and are sitting distances d_1 and d_2 from the fixed pivot point (called the **fulcrum**). From our discussion about forces, we see that the tendency of each force (provided by gravity), is to cause the seesaw to rotate about the

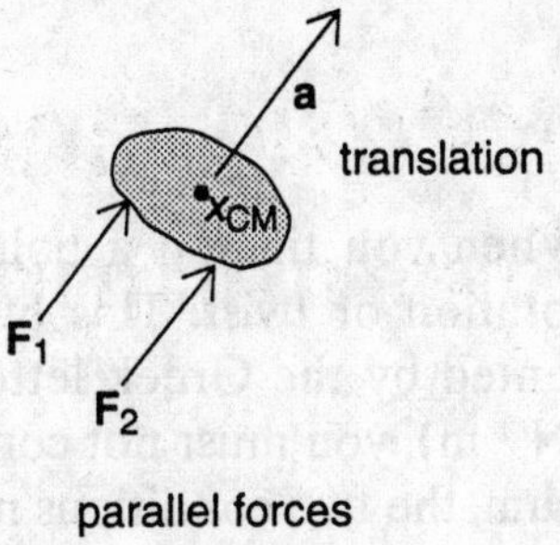

FIGURE 12.2

fulcrum. Force W_1 will tend to cause a counterclockwise rotation; force W_2, a clockwise rotation. Arbitrarily, we state that a clockwise rotation is taken as being a negative, while counterclockwise is taken as positive. What factors will influence the ability of the two people to remain in "balance"; that is, what conditions must be met so that the system remains in rotational equilibrium (it is already in a state of translational equilibrium and constrained to remain that way)?

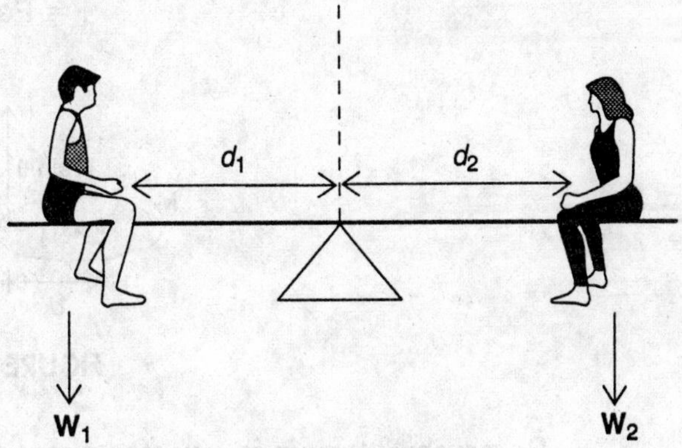

FIGURE 12.3

Through experiments, you can show that distances d_1 and d_2 (called **moment arm distances**) play a crucial role since we take the weights as being constant. If the two weights were equal, it should not be a surprise to learn that $d_1 = d_2$. In these examples, the weight of the seesaw is taken to be negligible (this is not a realistic scenario).

It turns out that, if W_2 is greater, that person must sit closer to the fulcrum. If equilibrium is to be maintained, the following condition must hold:

$$(W_1)(d_1) = (W_2)(d_2)$$

These are force and distance products, but they do not represent work in the translational sense because the two vectors are not parallel or resolvable into parallel components. In rotational motion, the product of a force and a perpendicular moment arm distance (relative to a fulcrum) is called **torque**. Let us now consider some more examples of torques and equilibrium.

12.3 Torque

When you tighten a bolt with a wrench, you apply a force to create a rotation or twist. This twisting action, called torque in physics, is represented by the Greek letter τ. Even though its units are newton · meters (N · m), you must not confuse it with translational work. In static equilibrium, the two conditions met are that the vector sum of all forces acting on the object equals zero and that the vector sum of all torques equals zero:

$$\Sigma \mathbf{F} = 0 \quad \text{and} \quad \Sigma \tau = 0$$

When we say that $\boldsymbol{\tau} = \mathbf{F}d$, d is the moment arm distance from the center of mass, or the pivot point, and **F** is the force perpendicular to the vector displacement. If the force is applied at some angle θ to the object, as seen in Figure 12.4, the component of the force, perpendicular to the vector displacement out from the pivot, is taken as the force used. Algebraically this is stated as

$$\tau = Fd \sin \theta$$

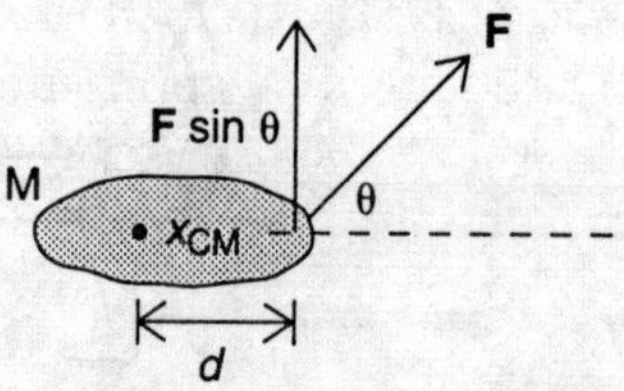

FIGURE 12.4

Remember: torque is a vector quantity, but work is not! The direction of the torque is taken as either positive or negative, depending on whether the rotation is counterclockwise or clockwise.

As an example, consider a light string wound around a frictionless and massless wheel, as shown in Figure 12.5. The free end of the string is attached to a 1.2-kg mass that is allowed to fall freely. The wheel has a radius of 0.25 m. What torque is produced?

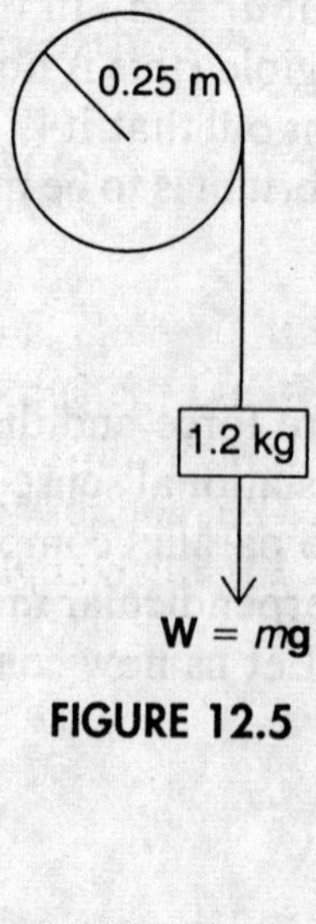

FIGURE 12.5

The force acting at right angles to the center of the wheel is the weight of the mass, given by

$$\mathbf{W} = m\mathbf{g} = (1.2)(9.8) = 11.76 \text{ N}$$

The radius serves as the moment arm distance, $d = 0.25$ m, so we can write

$$\tau = -Fd = (11.76)(0.25) = -2.94 \text{ N} \cdot \text{m}$$

The torque is negative since the falling weight induces a clockwise rotation in this example.

12.4 More Static Equilibrium Problems Using Forces and Torques

In the following example (see Figure 12.6), a hinged rod (considered massless) is attached to a wall with a string (and, of course, by the hinge). The string is considered massless, and makes an angle θ with the horizontal. A mass M is attached to the end of the rod, whose length is ℓ. What is the tension **T** in the string?

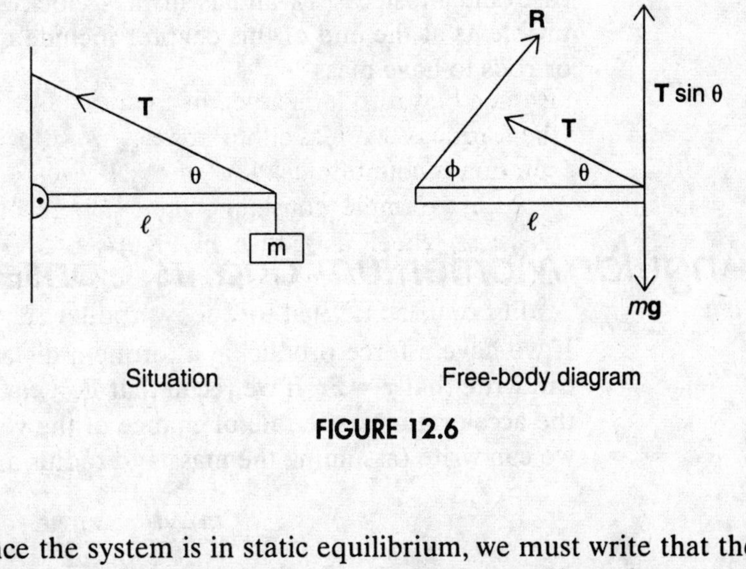

FIGURE 12.6

Since the system is in static equilibrium, we must write that the sum of all forces and the sum of all torques equal zero. If we choose to focus on the pivot, then all forces acting through that point do not contribute any torques. The reaction force **R** is the response of the wall to the rod and acts at some unknown angle ϕ. Thus we state that

$$\Sigma\tau = 0 \quad \text{and} \quad \Sigma\mathbf{F} = 0$$

For the forces, we see from the free-body diagram in Figure 12.6 that in the x-direction

$$\Sigma \mathbf{F}_x = 0 = \mathbf{R} \cos \phi - \mathbf{T} \cos \theta$$

and in the y-direction

$$\Sigma \mathbf{F}_y = 0 = \mathbf{R} \sin \phi + \mathbf{T} \sin \theta - mg$$

Since $\mathbf{T} \sin \theta = m\mathbf{g}$, it follows that $\mathbf{R} \sin \phi = 0$ by direct substitution. Hence, angle ϕ is also equal to zero, and the reaction force is directed horizontally along the rod.

For the torques, we see that the component of tension perpendicular to the rod contributes a counterclockwise torque, while the hanging weight contributes a clockwise torque:

$$\Sigma \tau = 0 = (\mathbf{T} \sin \theta)\, \ell - mg\ell$$

We could specifiy the length of the rod, but it is clear from the torque equation that the length can be eliminated. We can also immediately write

$$\mathbf{T} = \frac{m\mathbf{g}}{\sin \theta}$$

Suppose $m = 10$ kg and $\theta = 30°$. Then $\mathbf{T} = 196$ N. With this information, we see that $\mathbf{R} \sin \phi$ equals zero and that $\mathbf{R} \cos \phi = \mathbf{R}_x = 169.7$ N.

It should be noted that, if the rod is considered to have mass, the torque produced by the rod is its weight taken from the center of mass ($\ell/2$ in this case and most cases), and is always clockwise (negative). The practice problems at the end of this chapter include questions allowing for beams or rods to have mass.

12.5 Angular Momentum and Its Conservation

If we have a force producing a torque a distance $\mathbf{r}$ from a pivot point we can write that $\boldsymbol{\tau} = \mathbf{Fr}$. If we recall that $\mathbf{F} = m\mathbf{a}$, we can write $\boldsymbol{\tau} = m\mathbf{ar}$. Now, the acceleration is the rate of change of the velocity; that is, $\mathbf{a} = \Delta\mathbf{v} / \Delta t$, so we can write (assuming the mass and radius are constant)

$$\tau = \frac{m\,\Delta\mathbf{vr}}{\Delta t} = \frac{\Delta\, m\mathbf{vr}}{\Delta t} = \frac{\Delta\mathbf{L}}{\Delta t}$$

The quantity $m\mathbf{vr}$, called the **angular momentum** (designated by the letter **L**), is analogous to the linear momentum discussed in Chapter 11. Also, just as a force is equal to a change in linear momentum over time, a torque is equal to the rate of change of angular momentum. Thus torque is analogous to force in its characteristics to produce rotations. Angular momentum is a vector quantity, and its units are kilogram · square meters per second (kg · m²/s).

If the net torque acting on a system is zero, then the rate of change of angular momentum is zero, and we say that the angular momentum has been conserved. An example of this concept occurs when an ice skater starts to spin and draws her arms inward. Since angular momentum is conserved, the response to a decrease in radius is an increase in angular velocity, **ω**, so she spins faster. As a ratio we can state that, for two given times t_1 and t_2,

$$\frac{\mathbf{v}_1}{\mathbf{v}_2} = \frac{r_2}{r_1}$$

From Chapter 8 we know that angular velocity can be expressed as $\omega = \mathbf{v}/r$, so we can also write

$$\frac{\omega_1}{\omega_2} = \frac{r_2^2}{r_1^2}$$

Another example of a system in which no net torque is acting is the solar system. Since (as we shall see in Chapter 14) the force of gravity is radial, it acts parallel to the radius vector swept out from the Sun, thus producing zero torque. Kepler's laws of planetary motion will be seen as a consequence of the law of conservation of angular momentum.

Problem-Solving Strategies for Torque and Angular Momentum

Solving torque problems is similar to solving static equilibrium problems with Newton's laws. In fact, Newton's laws provide the first condition for static equilibrium (the vector sum of all forces equals zero). This fact means that you should once again draw a free-body diagram of the situation.

In rotational static equilibrium, the vector sum of all torques must equal zero. Remember that torque is a vector even though its units are newton · meters. We take clockwise torques as negative and counterclockwise torques as positive. Any force going through the chosen pivot point (or fulcrum) does not contribute any torques. Therefore, it is wise to choose a point that eliminates the greatest number of forces. Also, remember that only the components of forces that are perpendicular to the direction of a radius displacement from the pivot (called the moment arm) are responsible, a situation that usually involves the sine of the force's orientation angle.

In rotational motion, angular momentum is conserved if no external torques act on an isolated system. This is analogous to the statement that linear momentum is conserved if no external forces act on the system (translationally).

Practice Problems for Chapter 12

Multiple Choice

1. A point mass m is undergoing uniform circular motion with an angular frequency ω in a horizontal circle of radius r. Which of the following is a representation of the angular momentum of the mass?
   (A) $mr^2\omega$
   (B) mr^2/ω
   (C) $r\omega^2/m$

(D) $mr\omega$
(E) $m\omega$

2. A skater extends her arms, holding a 2-kg mass in each hand. She is rotating about a vertical axis at a given rate. She brings her arms inward toward her body in such a way that the distance of each mass from the axis changes from 1 m to 0.50 m. Her rate of rotation (neglecting the mass of the skater) will
(A) be doubled
(B) be halved
(C) be quadrupled
(D) be quartered
(E) remain the same

3. A 45-kg girl is sitting on a seesaw 0.6 m from the balance point, as shown below. How far, on the other side, should a 60-kg boy sit so that the seesaw will remain in balance?

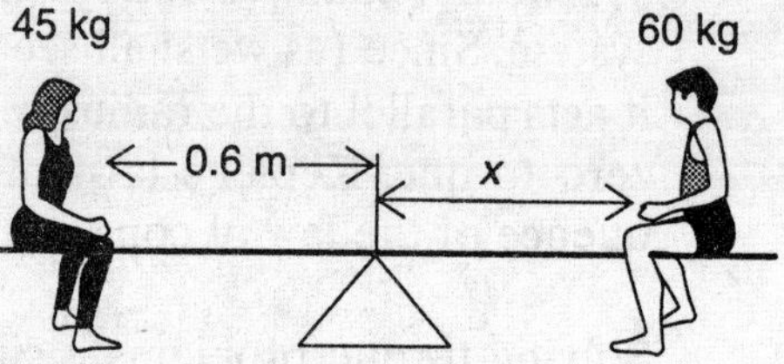

(A) 0.30 m
(B) 0.35 m
(C) 0.40 m
(D) 0.45 m
(E) 0.50 m

4. A balanced meter stick is shown below. The distance from the fulcrum is shown for each mass except the 10-g mass. What is the approximate position of the 10-g mass, based on the diagram?

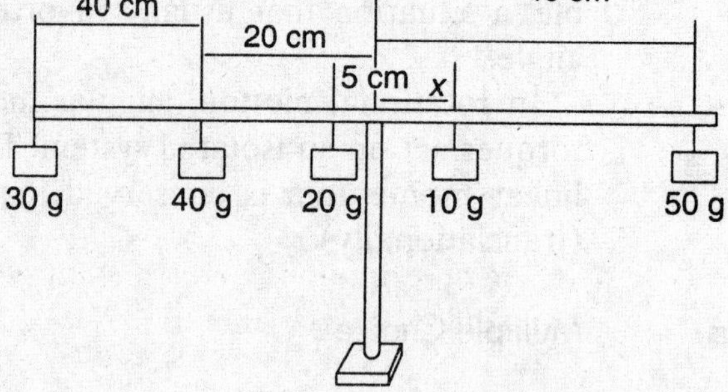

(A) 7 cm
(B) 9 cm
(C) 10 cm
(D) 15 cm
(E) 21 cm

5. A 1-kg mass swings in a verical circle after having been released from a horizontal position with zero initial velocity. The mass is attached to a massless rigid rod of length 1.5 m. The angular momentum of the mass, in kilogram · square meters per second, when it is in its lowest position is approximately
(A) 4
(B) 5
(C) 8
(D) 10
(E) 12

6. A rock with a mass of 0.05 kg is swung overhead in a horizontal circle of radius 0.3 m at a constant rate of 5 revolutions per second. The angular momentum of the rock is
(A) 0.14 kg · m²/s
(B) 0.0056 kg · m²/s
(C) 0.32 kg · m²/s
(D) 1.32 kg · m²/s
(E) 2.45 kg · m²/s

7. A solid cylinder consisting of an outer radius R_1 and an inner radius R_2 is pivoted on a frictionless axle as shown below. A string is wound around the outer radius and is pulled to the right with a force $\mathbf{F}_1$ = 3 N. A second string is wound around the inner radius and is pulled down with a force $\mathbf{F}_2$ = 5 N. If R_1 = 0.75 m and R_2 = 0.35 m, what is the net torque acting on the cylinder?

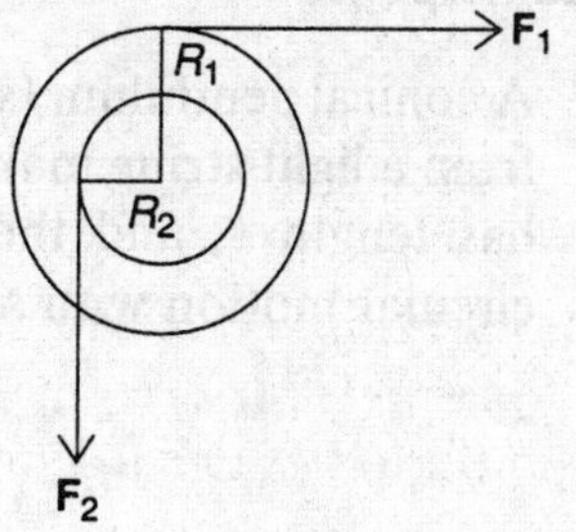

(A) 2.25 N · m
(B) −2.25 N · m
(C) 0.5 N · m
(D) −0.5 N · m
(E) 0 N · m

Answer questions 8 and 9 based on the following diagram. The rod is considered massless.

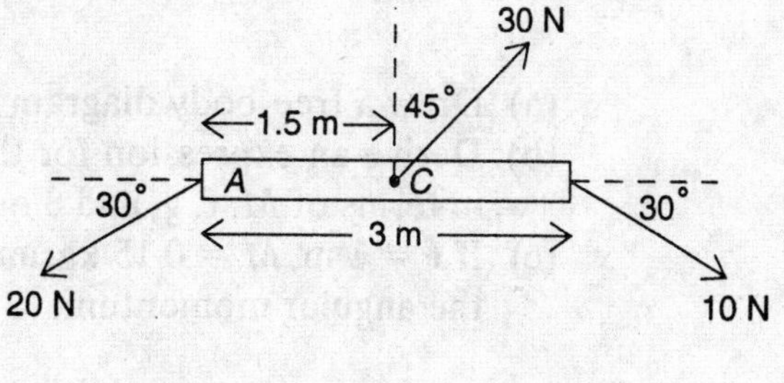

8. What is the net torque about an axis through point A?
   (A) 16.5 N · m
   (B) 15.2 N · m
   (C) −5.5 N · m
   (D) −7.8 N · m
   (E) 6 N · m

9. What is the net torque about an axis through point C?
   (A) 3.5 N · m
   (B) 7.5 N · m
   (C) −15.2 N · m
   (D) 5.9 N · m
   (E) 7 N · m

10. A small disk of mass 2 kg slides on a frictionless horizontal surface, and is constrained to move in a circular path by a light, rigid rod of length 0.5 m. The disk is undergoing uniform circular motion at a velocity of 4 m/s at any instant. A piece of putty, with a mass of 0.4 kg, is dropped onto the disk. If the radius of the circular path remains constant, what is the new velocity of the disk-putty system?
    (A) 1.5 m/s
    (B) 2.25 m/s
    (C) 3.3 m/s
    (D) 4.0 m/s
    (E) 5 m/s

Free Response

1. A conical pendulum (see Chapter 9) consists of a point mass suspended from a light string making a vertical angle θ, as shown below. The string has length ℓ, and the mass is M. The mass is undergoing uniform circular motion with an instantaneous velocity **v**.

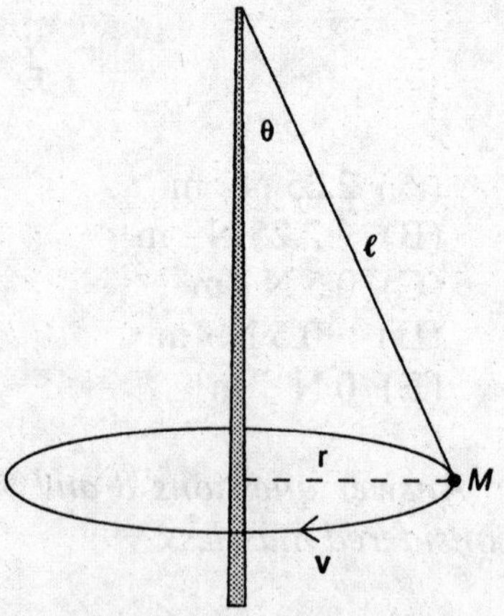

   (a) Draw a free-body diagram for this situation.
   (b) Derive an expression for the square of the angular momentum L in terms of M, ℓ, g, and θ only.
   (c) If $\ell = 1$ m, $M = 0.15$ kg, and $\theta = 10°$, determine the magnitude of the angular momentum.

2. A 500-N person stands 2.5 m from a wall against which a horizontal beam is attached. The beam is 6 m long and weighs 200 N (see diagram below). A cable attached to the free end of the beam makes an angle of 45° to the horizontal and is attached to the wall.

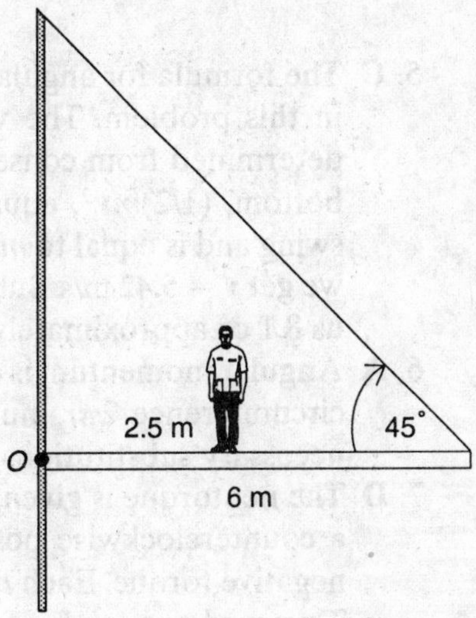

(a) Draw a free-body diagram of this situation.
(b) Determine the magnitude of the tension in the cable.
(c) Determine the reaction force that the wall exerts on the beam.

3. A uniform ladder of length ℓ and weight 100 N rests against a smooth vertical wall. The coefficient of static friction between the bottom of the ladder and the floor is 0.5.
(a) Draw a free-body diagram of this situation.
(b) Find the minimum angle, θ, that the ladder can make with the floor so that the ladder will not slip.

Solutions

Multiple-Choice Problems

1. **A** Angular momentum is the quantity $m\mathbf{v}\mathbf{r}$. Since $\mathbf{v} = r\boldsymbol{\omega}$, upon substitution we get $\mathbf{L} = mr^2\boldsymbol{\omega}$.
2. **C** The ratio of spin rates (angular velocity) is proportional to the inverse ratio of distance from the axis of rotation. Since the distance is decreasing by two times, the spin rate must increase by four times.
3. **D** To remain in balance, the two torques must be equal. The force on each side is given by the weight, $m\mathbf{g}$. The moment arm distances are 0.6 m and x. Since the factor $\mathbf{g}$ will appear on both sides of the torque balance equation, we can eliminate it and write

$$(45)(0.6) = (60)x \quad \text{implies} \quad x = 0.45 \text{ m}$$

4. **E** In this problem, again, the sum of the torques on the left must equal the sum of the torques on the right. We could convert all masses to

kilograms and all distances to meters, but in the balance equation the same factors appear on both sides. Therefore, for simplicity and time efficiency, we can simply write

$$(30)(40) + (40)(20) + (20)(5) = (10)x + (50)(40) \quad \text{implies} \quad x = 21 \text{ cm}$$

5. **C** The formula for angular momentum is $m\mathbf{v}r$; $m = 1$ kg and $r = 1.5$ m in this problem. The velocity at the bottom of the swing can be determined from conservation of energy. The kinetic energy at the bottom, $(1/2)m\mathbf{v}^2$, equals the loss of potential energy during the swing and is equal to $m\mathbf{g}h$, where $h = r = 1.5$ m. Solving for velocity, we get $\mathbf{v} = 5.42$ m/s. Substituting in for the angular momentum gives us 8.1 or approximately 8 kg · m²/s.
6. **A** Angular momentum is expressed as $m\mathbf{v}r$. The velocity is given by the circumference, $2\pi r$, multiplied by the frequency, 5 rev/s. Making the necessary substitutions gives us an answer of 0.14 kg · m²/s.
7. **D** The net torque is given by the vector sum of all torques. $\mathbf{F}_2$ provides a counterclockwise positive torque, while $\mathbf{F}_1$ provides a clockwise negative torque. Each radius is the necessary moment arm distance. Thus we have

$$\tau_{net} = (5)(0.35) - (3)(0.75) = -0.5 \text{ N} \cdot \text{m}$$

8. **A** In this problem, the net torque about point A implies that the force passing through point A does not contribute to the net torque. Also, we need the components of the remaining forces perpendicular to the beam. From the diagram, we see that the 30-N force acts counterclockwise (positive), while the 10-N force acts clockwise (negative). Thus:

$$\tau_{net} = (30)(\cos 45)(1.5) - (10)(\sin 30)(3) = 16.5 \text{ N} \cdot \text{m}$$

9. **B** In this problem, since the pivot is now set at point C, we can eliminate the 30-N force passing through point C as a contributor to the torque. Again, we see that the 20-N force will act in a counterclockwise direction, while the 10-N force will act clockwise. Each force is 1.5 m from the pivot. We also need the component of each force perpendicular to the beam. Thus:

$$\tau_{net} = (20)(\sin 30)(1.5) - (10)(\sin 30)(1.5) = 7.5 \text{ N} \cdot \text{m}$$

10. **C** Angular momentum is conserved since the dropping of the putty does not add a net torque to the system. Thus we can state that $m_1\mathbf{v}_1r_1 = m_2\mathbf{v}_2r_2$. The radius is remaining the same, and the mass is increasing by 0.4 kg. Therefore

$$(2)(4)(0.5) = (2.4)(\mathbf{v}_2)(0.5) \quad \text{implies} \quad \mathbf{v}_2 = 3.3 \text{ m/s}$$

Free-Response Problems

1. (a) A free-body diagram for the conical pendulum appeared in Chapter 9 and is reproduced below:

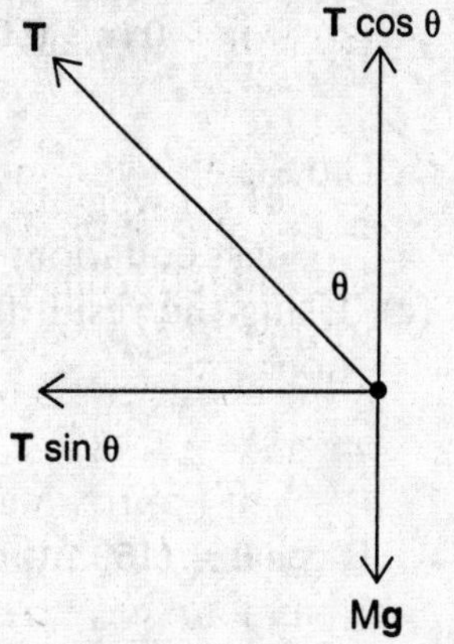

(b) We know that $\mathbf{L} = m\mathbf{v}r$, with a point mass in this case. Thus $\mathbf{L}^2 = m^2\mathbf{v}^2r^2$. From the geometry we can see that $r = \ell \sin\theta$, and from Chapter 9 we know that

$$\mathbf{v}^2 = rg\tan\theta = \frac{\ell\sin\theta\, g\sin\theta}{\cos\theta} = \frac{\ell g\sin^2\theta}{\cos\theta}$$

Making the necessary substitutions, we get

$$\mathbf{L}^2 = \frac{M^2 g\ell^3\sin^4\theta}{\cos\theta}$$

(c) Using the given numbers, we find that $\mathbf{L}^2 = 2.077 \times 10^{-05}$. This implies that

$$\mathbf{L} = 4.56 \times 10^{-03}\ \text{kg}\cdot\text{m}^2/\text{s}$$

2. (a) The free-body diagram for this situation appears below:

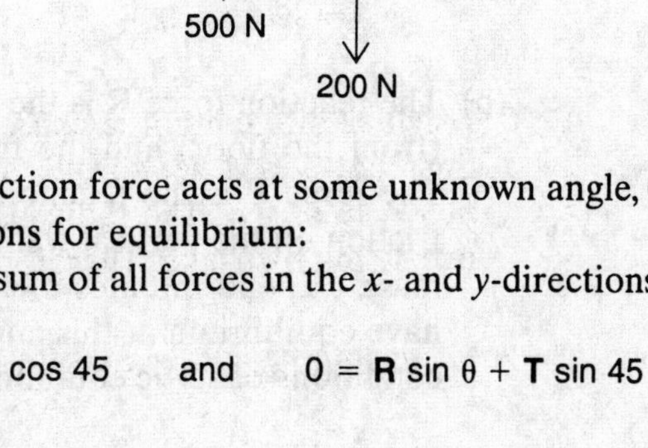

(b) The reaction force acts at some unknown angle, θ. We use our two conditions for equilibrium:
1. The sum of all forces in the x- and y-directions must equal zero:

$$0 = \mathbf{R}\cos\theta - \mathbf{T}\cos 45 \quad \text{and} \quad 0 = \mathbf{R}\sin\theta + \mathbf{T}\sin 45 - 500\ \text{N} - 200\ \text{N}$$

2. The sum of all torques through contact point O must be zero, thus eliminating the reaction force **R**:

$$0 = -(500)(2.5) - (200)(3) + \mathbf{T} \sin 45(6)$$

Both weights produce clockwise torques! Solving for **T** in the last equation, we get **T** = 153.21 N.

(c) Using the result from part (b), we can rewrite the first two equations as:

$$\mathbf{R} \cos \theta = (153.21) \cos 45 = 107.25 \text{ N} \quad \text{and} \quad \mathbf{R} \sin \theta = 592.75 \text{ N}$$

Taking the ratio of these two equations gives us tan θ = 5.5268; therefore θ = 79.7°. Since we know the angle at which the reaction force acts, we can simply write

$$\mathbf{R} \cos 79.7 = 107.25 \quad \text{implies} \quad \mathbf{R} = 602.37 \text{ N}$$

3. (a) A sketch of the situation and its free-body diagram are given below:

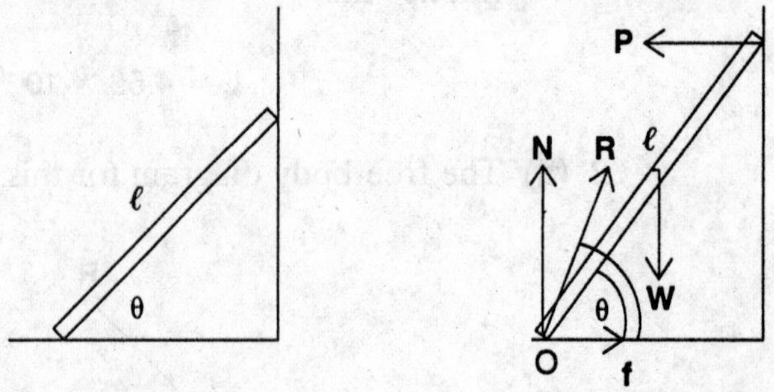

Situation Free-body diagram

(b) The reaction force **R** is the vector resultant of the normal force **N** (from the floor) and the frictional force **f** that opposes slippage. The force **P** is the reaction force of the vertical wall; there is no friction on the vertical wall. The weight **W** acts from the center of mass, ℓ/2, and initiates a clockwise torque (if allowed). Since we have equilibrium at this angle, we can write our equations for the conditions of static equilibrium.

1. The sum of all x- and y-forces must be equal to zero. Horizontally, friction is an opposing force, as well as the reaction force, **P**: $0 = \mathbf{f} - \mathbf{P}$. Vertically, we can write $0 = \mathbf{N} - \mathbf{W}$. Since $\mathbf{W} =$ 100N, then $\mathbf{N} =$ 100N. Now, for no slippage, $\mathbf{f} \leqq \mu\mathbf{N}$, thus $\mathbf{f} = (0.5)(100) = 50\text{N} = \mathbf{P}$.
2. The sum of the torques must be zero. We need the component of **P** perpendicular to the ladder. From the geometry, we see that this is **P** sin θ. Also, the component of weight perpendicular to the ladder is **W** cos θ. Thus, for the sum of all torques equals zero, we write:

$$0 = \mathbf{P}\ell \sin\theta - \mathbf{W}(\ell/2)\cos\theta$$

The length of the ladder is therefore irrelevant and can be canceled out. Since we know that $\mathbf{P} = 50$ N and $\mathbf{W} = 100$ N, we find that $\tan\theta = \mathbf{W}/2\mathbf{P} = 1.0$. Therefore $\theta = 45°$.

CHAPTER 13

Oscillatory Motion

13.1 Simple Harmonic Motion: A Mass on a Spring

From Hooke's law in Chapter 9, we know that a spring will become elongated by an amount directly proportional to the force applied. The force constant, k, relates to the specific amount of force (in newtons) needed to stretch or compress the spring by 1 meter:

$$\mathbf{F} = -k\mathbf{x}$$

The negative sign indicates that the force is restorative. One could easily use Hooke's law without the negative sign in the proper context.

Suppose we have a spring with a mass attached to it horizontally in such a way that the mass rests on a flat frictionless surface as shown in Figure 13.1.

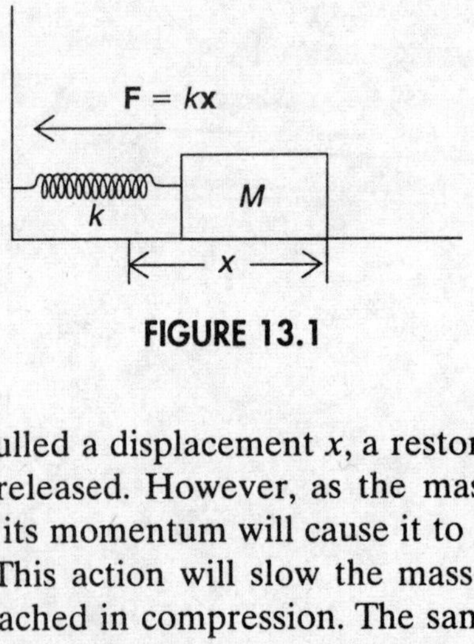

FIGURE 13.1

If the mass M is pulled a displacement x, a restoring force of $\mathbf{F} = -k\mathbf{x}$ will act on it when released. However, as the mass accelerates past its equilibrium position, its momentum will cause it to keep going, thus compressing the spring. This action will slow the mass down until the same displacement, $\mathbf{x}$, is reached in compression. The same restoring force will then accelerate the mass back and forth, creating oscillatory motion with a certain period T (in seconds) and frequency f (in hertz or cycles per second). The SI unit for frequency is reciprocal seconds (s^{-1}).

Now, according to Newton's second law of motion, $\mathbf{F} = m\mathbf{a}$, so when the mass was originally extended, the restoring force $\mathbf{F} = -k\mathbf{x}$ would also produce an instantaneous accleration, given by $\mathbf{F} = m\mathbf{a}$. In other words, $\mathbf{a} = -(k/m)\ \mathbf{x}$. The fact that the acceleration is directly proportional to the displacement (but in the opposite direction) is characteristic of a special kind of oscillatory motion called **simple harmonic motion**. From this expression, it can be shown that the acceleration is zero at the equilibrium point (where $x = 0$).

We can build up a qualitative picture of this type of motion by considering a displacement versus time graph for this mass-spring system. Suppose we have the system at rest so that the spring is unstretched. We now pull the mass to the right a distance A (called the **amplitude**) and release the mass. This action creates a restoring force that will pull the mass to the left toward the equilibrium point. The velocity will become greater and greater, reaching a maximum as the mass passes through the equilibrium point (at which $\mathbf{a} = 0$). The mass will then move toward the left, slowing down as it compresses the spring (since the accleration is in the opposite direction). The mass stops momentarily when $x = -A$ (because of conservation of energy) and then accelerates again to maintain simple harmonic motion (in the absence of friction).

A graph of displacement versus time (see Chapter 7) would look like a graph of the **cosine** function since the mass is beginning at some distance from the origin. We could consider the motion in progress from the point of view of the origin, in which case the graph would be of the **sine** function (some textbooks use this format). Figure 2 shows the characteristics of acceleration and deceleration as the mass oscillates in a period T with a frequency f (for arbitrary units of displacement and time).

From Chapter 10, we know that the maximum energy of a compressed (or stretched) spring is given by $E = (1/2)kA^2$, for $x = A$ as in our example. Thus the constraining points $X = \pm A$ define the limits of oscillation for the mass.

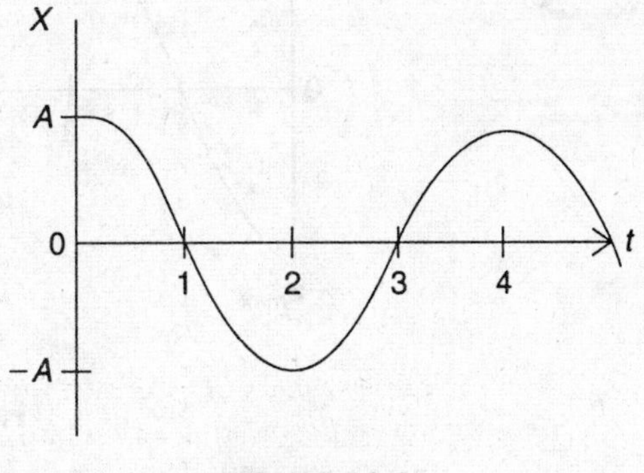

FIGURE 13.2

A graph of velocity versus time can be built up qualitatively in much the same way. Recall that the slope of the displacement versus time graph represents the instantaneous velocity. From Figure 13.2, you can see that, at $t = 0$, the graph is horizontal, indicating that $\mathbf{v} = 0$. The increasingly negative slope shows that the mass is accelerating "backward" until, at $t = 1$, the line is momentarily straight, indicating maximum velocity when $x = 0$. The slope now gradually approaches zero at $t = 2$, indicating that the mass is slowing down as it approaches $x = -A$. The cycle then repreats itself, producing a graph similar to Figure 13.3.

Finally, analyzing the velocity graph with slopes, we produce an acceleration versus time graph. When $t = 0$, the line is momentarily straight with a negative slope indicating a maximum negative acceleration. When the mass crosses the equilibrium point, velocity is maximum but acceleration is

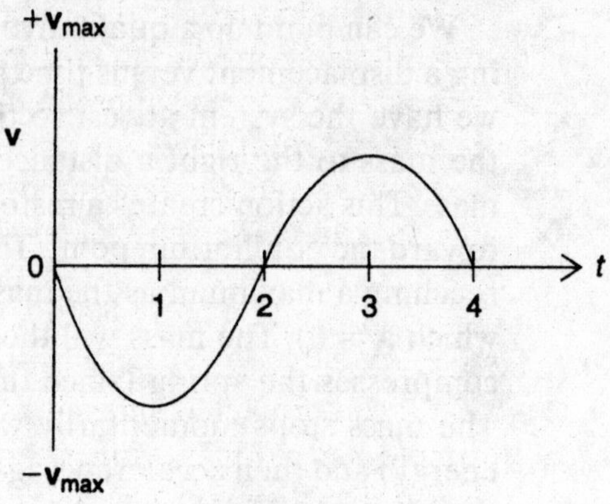

FIGURE 13.3

momentarily zero. The acceleration (proportional to displacement), reaches a maximum once again when $x = -A$. The cycle repeats itself, producing Figure 13.4. Notice that the acceleration graph is approximately the negative of the displacement graph, as expected!

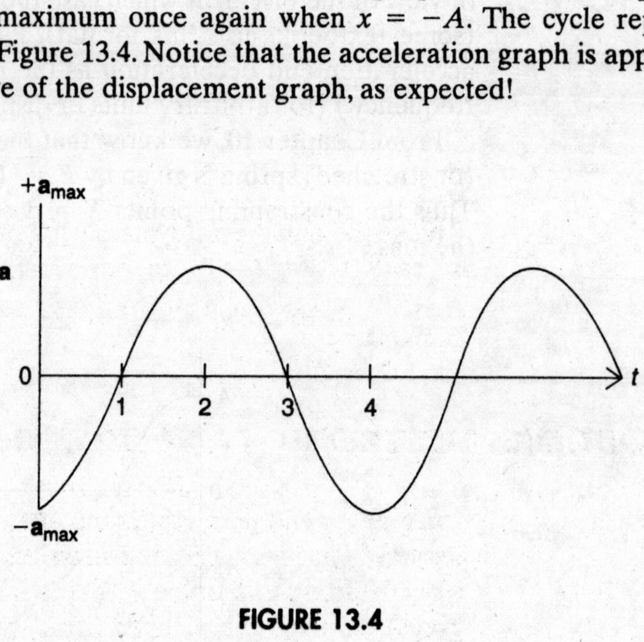

FIGURE 13.4

To derive the period of oscillation for the mass-spring system, we can consider another form of periodic motion already discussed: uniform circular motion. If a mass is attached to a rotating turntable and then turned onto its side, a projected shadow of the rotating mass simulates simple harmonic motion (Figure 13.5).

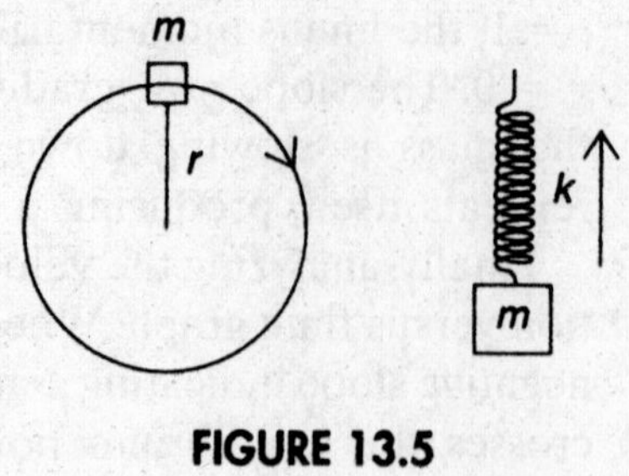

FIGURE 13.5

In this simulation, the radius r acts like the amplitude A, and the frequency and period of the rotation can be adjusted so that, when the shadow appears next to a real oscillating system, it is difficult to decide which one is actually rotating.

From our understanding of uniform circular motion, we know that the magnitude of the centripetal acceleration is given by

$$\mathbf{a}_c = \frac{4\pi^2 r}{T^2}$$

Since the projected sideways view of this motion appears to approximate simple harmonic motion, we can let the radius r be approximated by the linear displacement x and write

$$\mathbf{a}_x = \frac{4\pi^2 x}{T^2}$$

Since $\mathbf{a} = (k/m)\mathbf{x}$ in simple harmonic motion, we can now write

$$\left(\frac{k}{m}\right)x = \frac{4\pi^2 x}{T^2}$$

$$T = 2\pi\sqrt{\frac{m}{k}}$$

This is the equation for the period of an oscillating mass-spring system in seconds. To find the frequency of oscillation, recall that $f = 1/T$. Also, recall that the angular frequency (velocity) is expressed as $\boldsymbol{\omega} = 2\pi/T$, which implies that $\boldsymbol{\omega} = \sqrt{k/m}$.

13.2 Simple Harmonic Motion: The Simple Pendulum

Imagine a pendulum consisting of a mass M (called a bob) and a string of length ℓ that is considered massless (Figure 13.6). The pendulum is displaced through an angle θ that is much less than 1 radian (about 57 degrees). Under these conditions, the pendulum approximates simple harmonic motion and the period of oscillation is independent of amplitude.

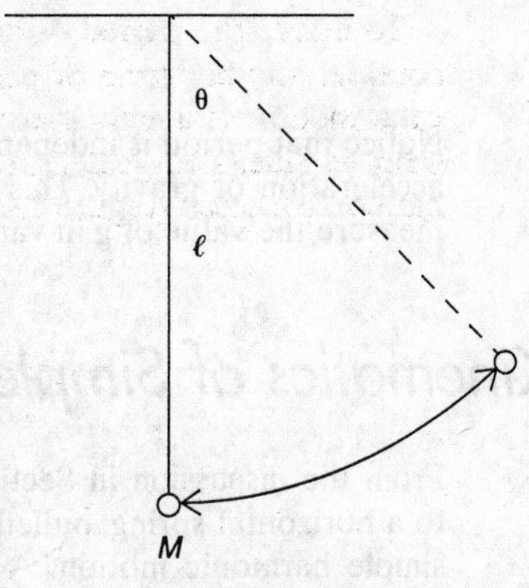

FIGURE 13.6

When the pendulum swings through an arc of length s, it appears to be following a straight path for a suitably chosen small period of time or small section of the arc. In this approximation, we can imagine the pendulum as being accelerated down an incline. The oscillations occur because gravity accelerates the pendulum back to its lowest position. Its momentum maintains the motion through that point, and then the constraining action of the string (providing a centripetal force) causes the pendulum to swing in an upward arc. Conservation of energy will bring the pendulum to the same vertical displacement (or cause it to swing through the same arc length) and then momentarily stop until gravity begins to pull it down again.

If we imagine that an incline of set angle θ is causing the acceleration, then, from our discussions of kinematics, we know that $\mathbf{a} = -\mathbf{g} \sin \theta$ (where the angle is measured in radians). Now, if θ is sufficiently less than 1 radian, we can write that $\sin \theta \approx \theta$ and therefore that

$$\mathbf{a} = -\mathbf{g} \sin \theta \approx -\mathbf{g}\, \theta \approx \frac{\mathbf{g}s}{\ell}$$

In the above equation we used the known relationship from trigonometry that, in radian measure, if s is the arc length and ℓ corresponds to the effective "radius" of swing, then $s = \ell\theta$.

It should be remembered that these are only approximations, but for angles of about 10 or 20 degrees the approximations are fairly accurate. Since the pendulum now approximates simple harmonic motion, we know that we can find a suitable rotational motion that, when viewed in projection (as well as the pendulum swing being viewed in projection), simulates our simple harmonic motion. Therefore, in a similar fashion to that in Section 13.1, we can write

$$\mathbf{a} = \frac{4\pi^2 s}{T^2} = \frac{\mathbf{g}s}{\ell}$$

where the arc length s is the amplitude of swing in this case.

If we solve for the period T, we finally get

$$T = 2\pi \sqrt{\frac{\ell}{\mathbf{g}}}$$

Notice that period is independent of mass but is very sensitive to the local acceleration of gravity. This becomes an excellent way to independently measure the value of **g** in various locations.

13.3 The Kinematics of Simple Harmonic Motion

From the discussion in Section 13.1, we know that, if a mass is attached to a horizontal spring, pulled to one side, and then released, it undergoes simple harmonic motion. A graph of displacement versus time for this motion can be expressed in terms of a cosine function, as was shown.

Algebraically, at $t = 0$, $x = A$ (the amplitude), and $\mathbf{v} = 0$. Thus we can write

$$\mathbf{x} = A \cos(\omega t + \phi)$$

We recall from Chapter 8 that the angular frequency ω is in units of radians per second (rad/s), and so the product ωt is an angle in units of radians. The angle ϕ, called the **phase angle**, can be used to adjust the initial condition for the starting point at $t = 0$. If this angle is suitably chosen, we can convert the formula for displacement to $\mathbf{x} = A \sin \boldsymbol{\omega} t$ (which some textbooks present as the displacement).

Let us use our first formula for displacement and choose $\phi = 0$ so that $x = A \cos \omega t$. Since $\boldsymbol{\omega} = 2\pi / T$, we can write $\mathbf{x} = A \cos (2\pi/T)t$. Thus, when $t = 0, x = A$; and when $t = T/2$, $x = -A$ (as expected, since $T/2$ is one-half period of oscillation). The velocity of the mass is maximum when the mass passes through the point $x = 0$, and this occurs at one-quarter of a period, $T/4$. From Chapter 8 we recall that in uniform circular motion $\mathbf{v} = r\boldsymbol{\omega}$. In this case, we associate the amplitude A with the equivalent circular radius r so that $\mathbf{v}_{max} = A\boldsymbol{\omega}$. In a similar fashion, we can show that the acceleration is $\mathbf{a} = -\boldsymbol{\omega}^2 A$.

From Chapter 10 we know that the work done to compress a spring is also equal to the potential energy stored in the spring. This value is expressed as $(1/2)kx^2$. If the system is set into oscillation by stretching the spring by an amount $x = A$, the maximum energy possessed by the oscillating system is given by $U = (1/2)kA^2$. As the mass oscillates, it reaches maximum velocity when it passes through $x = 0$. At that point, the potential energy of the spring is zero; and since we are treating the cases without friction, the loss of potential energy is balanced by this gain in kinetic energy:

$$KE_{max} = \frac{1}{2} mv_{max}^2 = \frac{1}{2} mA^2\omega^2$$

Thus we can now write that, for conservation of energy,

$$\frac{1}{2} mA^2\omega^2 = \frac{1}{2} kA^2$$

which implies that $\boldsymbol{\omega} = \sqrt{k/m}$, as expected.

If we want to treat cases in which the mass is between the two extremes of $x = 0$ and $x = \pm A$, we note that the spring will still possess some elastic potential energy (no gravitational potential energy is involved since the mass is oscillating horizontally). This implies that

$$\frac{1}{2} kA^2 = \frac{1}{2} mv^2 + \frac{1}{2} kx^2$$

If we solve for velocity, we get

$$\mathbf{v} = \pm \sqrt{\frac{k}{m}(A^2 - x^2)}$$

Sample Problem:

A body executes simple harmonic motion with a displacement that varies in time according to the relationship $\mathbf{x} = 0.02 \cos \pi t$.

(a) Find the amplitude, angular frequency, frequency, and period for the body.
(b) Find the maximum velocity attained by the body.
(c) If the body is a mass of 0.3 kg attached to a spring, find the force constant k.
(d) Find the velocity when $t = 0.2$ s.

Solution:

(a) From this chapter we know that $\mathbf{x} = A \cos \omega t$, and so $A = 0.02$ m and $\omega = \pi$ rad/s. Now, $\omega = 2\pi f$, so, solving for frequency, we get $f = 0.5$ Hz. Period $T = 1/f$, so $T = 2$ s.
(b) For the maximum velocity, $\mathbf{v}_{max} = A\omega = (0.02)(3.14) = 0.0628$ m/s.
(c) Recall that in simple harmonic motion $\omega = \sqrt{k/m}$. Using $\omega = 3.14$ rad/s and $m = 0.3$ kg, we find that $k = 2.96$ N/m.
(d) When $t = 0.2$ s, $x = 0.02 \cos [(\pi)0.2]$. The argument of the cosine function is in radians, so we find that $x = 0.016$ m. Now the velocity at that position (i.e., time) is given by

$$\mathbf{v} = \pm \sqrt{\frac{k}{m}(A^2 - x^2)}$$

Substituting the known numbers gives $v = \pm 0.037$ m/s.

Problem-Solving Strategies for Oscillatory Motion

Keep in mind the following facts:

1. Simple harmonic motion is related to circular motion and is characterized by the fact that the acceleration varies directly with the displacement (but in the opposite direction).
2. A simple pendulum approximates simple harmonic motion only if its displacement angle is much less than 1 radian (about 57 degrees). The period will be independent of amplitude and mass under these circumstances.
3. It is sometimes easier to use energy considerations since the equations involve scalars and no free-body diagrams have to be drawn.
4. For pendulum or pendulum-like problems, if $\theta \ll 1$ radian, then $\sin \theta \approx \tan \theta \approx \theta$.

Practice Problems for Chapter 13

Multiple Choice

1. What is the length of a pendulum whose period, at the Equator, is 1 s?
(A) 0.15 m
(B) 0.25 m
(C) 0.30 m

(D) 0.45 m
(E) 1.0 m

2. On a planet, an astronaut determines the acceleration of gravity by means of a pendulum. She observes that the 1-m-long pendulum has a period of 1.5 s. The acceleration of gravity, in meters per second squared, on the planet is
(A) 7.5
(B) 15.2
(C) 10.2
(D) 26.3
(E) 17.5

3. When a 0.05-kg mass is attached to a vertical spring, it is observed that the spring stretches 0.03 m. The system is then placed horizontally on a frictionless surface and set into simple harmonic motion. What is the period of the oscillations?
(A) 0.75 s
(B) 0.12 s
(C) 0.35 s
(D) 1.3 s
(E) 2.3 s

4. A mass-spring system is observed to have a period of oscillation equal to 1.45 s. If the amplitude of the oscillations is 0.12 m, the maximum velocity attained by the mass is
(A) 0.17 m/s
(B) 0.32 m/s
(C) 12.08 m/s
(D) 0.03 m/s
(E) 0.52 m/s

5. Which of the following is an expression for the maximum velocity of an oscillating mass-spring system?
(A) $\sqrt{Ak/m}$
(B) $\sqrt{A^2mk}$
(C) $\sqrt{A^2m/k}$
(D) $\sqrt{A^2k/m}$
(E) Akm

6. A mass of 0.5 kg is connected to a massless spring with a force constant k of 50 N/m. The system is oscillating on a frictionless horizontal surface. If the amplitude of the oscillations is 2 cm, the total energy of the system is
(A) 0.01 J
(B) 0.1 J
(C) 0.5 J

(D) 0.3 J
(E) 0.2 J

7. A mass of 0.3 kg is connected to a massless spring with a force constant k of 20 N/m. The system oscillates horizontally on a frictionless surface with an amplitude of 4 cm. What is the velocity of the mass when it is 2 cm from its equilibrium position?
(A) 0.28 m/s
(B) 0.08 m/s
(C) 0.52 m/s
(D) 0.15 m/s
(E) 0.34 m/s

8. If the length of a simple pendulum is doubled, its period will
(A) decrease by 2
(B) increase by 2
(C) decrease by $\sqrt{2}$
(D) increase by $\sqrt{2}$
(E) remain the same

9. The pendulums of two grandfather clocks have the same length. One clock (A) runs faster than the other clock (B). Which of the following statements is true?
(A) Pendulum A is more massive.
(B) Pendulum B is more massive.
(C) Pendulum A swings through a smaller arc.
(D) Pendulum B swings through a smaller arc.
(E) None of the above statements is correct.

10. A 2-kg mass is oscillating horizontally on a frictionless surface when attached to a spring. The total energy of the system is observed to be 10 J. If the mass is replaced by a 4-kg mass, but the amplitude of oscillations and the spring remain the same, the total energy of the system will be
(A) 10 J
(C) 5 J
(C) 20 J
(D) 3.3 J
(E) 15.5 J

Free Response

1. A mass M is attached to two springs with force constants k_1 and k_2 respectively. The mass can slide horizontally over a frictionless surface. Two arrangements, (a) and (b), for the mass and springs are shown below. In each case, determine the period of oscillation.

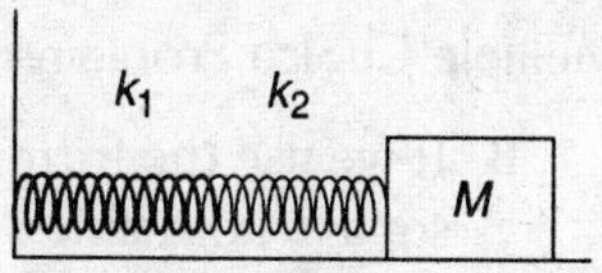

(a)

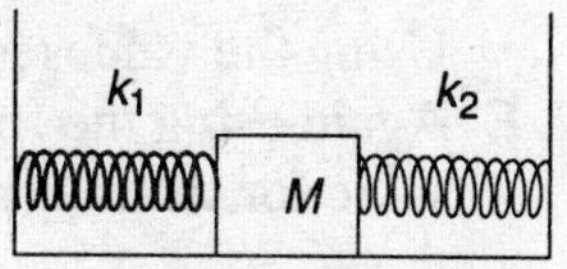

(b)

2. A mass M is attached to two light elastic strings both having length ℓ and both made of the same material. The mass is displaced vertically upward by a small displacement $\Delta \mathbf{y}$ such that equal tensions $\mathbf{T}$ exist in the two strings, as shown below. The mass is released and begins to oscillate up and down. Assume that the displacement is small enough so that the tensions do not change appreciably.

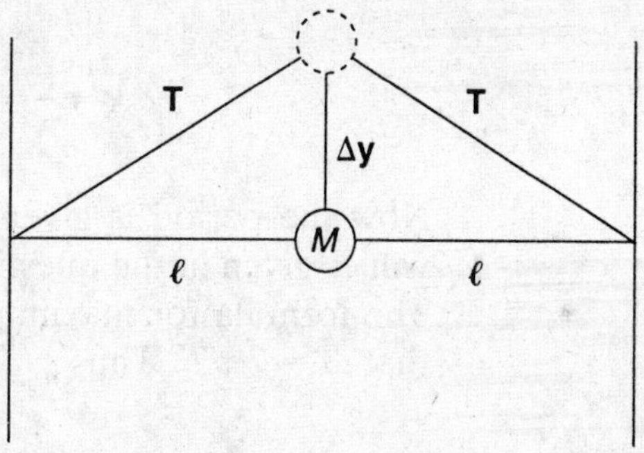

(a) What is the net restoring force that acted on the mass when it was initially displaced and held at rest?
(b) What is the frequency of oscillation?

3. A block of mass of 0.5 kg rests on top of a flat rectangular plate. The system is undergoing simple harmonic motion, as shown below, with a period of 2.7 Hz. The plate rests on a horizontal frictionless surface. The coefficient of static friction between the block and the plate is 0.4.
(a) Draw a free-body diagram for the block.
(b) What is the maximum amplitude of oscillation such that the block will not slip?
(c) If the spring has a force constant k of 1000 N/m, what is the total energy possessed by the system?

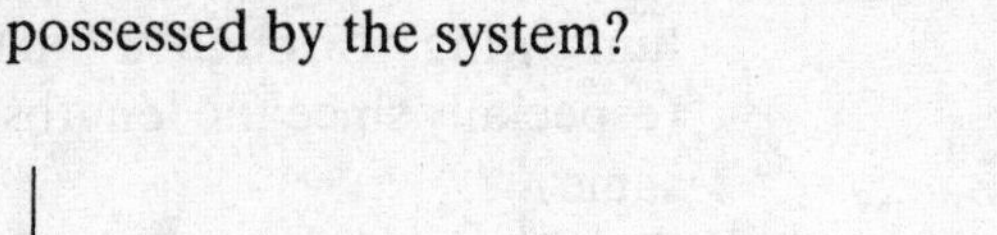

Solutions

Multiple-Choice Problems

1. **B** If we use the formula for the period of a pendulum, $T = 2\pi\sqrt{l/\mathbf{g}}$, and square both sides, we can solve for the length:

$$\ell = T^2 \frac{\mathbf{g}}{4\pi^2}$$

Using the values given in the question, we find that $\ell = 0.25$ m.

2. **E** Again using the formula for the period of a pendulum, this time we solve for the magnitude of the acceleration of gravity:

$$\mathbf{g} = \frac{4\pi\ell}{T^2}$$

Using the values given in the question, we find that $\mathbf{g} = 17.5$ m/s^2.

3. **C** We first find the spring constant. From $\mathbf{F} = k\mathbf{x}$, we see that

$$\mathbf{F} = m\mathbf{g} = (0.05)(9.8) = 0.49 \text{ N}$$

Thus

$$k = \frac{\mathbf{F}}{x} = \frac{0.49}{0.03} = 16.3 \text{ N/m}$$

Now the period is given by the formula $T = 2\pi\sqrt{m/k}$. Using the values given in the question, we find that $T = 0.35$ s.

4. **E** The formula for maximum velocity is $\mathbf{V}_{max} = A\boldsymbol{\omega}$. Also, we recall that $\boldsymbol{\omega} = 2\pi/T$. Thus

$$\mathbf{v}_{max} = 2\pi\frac{A}{T} = 0.52 \text{ m/s}$$

using the given values.

5. **D** Since $\mathbf{v}_{max} = A\boldsymbol{\omega}$ and $\boldsymbol{\omega} = \sqrt{k/m}$, bringing A back under the radical sign makes the equation equal to $\sqrt{A^2k/m}$.

6. **A** The formula for total energy is $E = (1/2)kA^2$. Using the values given in the question, we get $E = 0.01$ J.

7. **A** The formula for any intermediary velocity is $\mathbf{v} = \sqrt{(k/m)(A^2 - x^2)}$. Before substituting the known values, we must change centimeters to meters: 4 cm = 0.04 m and 2 cm = 0.02 m. Then, using these values for amplitude and position, we find that $\mathbf{v} = 0.28$ m/s.

8. **D** Since the period of a pendulum varies directly as the square root of the length, if the length is doubled, the period increases by $\sqrt{2}$.

9. **C** If clock A runs faster, its period is quicker and therefore its pendulum swings through a smaller arc to maintain the faster period (especially since the lengths of pendulum A and pendulum B are the same).

10. **A** The maximum energy in the mass-spring system can be expressed independently of the mass; it depends on the force constant and the square of the amplitude. Thus, if the spring and the amplitude of oscillations remain the same, so will the total energy of the system (10 J).

Free-Response Problems

1. (a) When mass M is stretched a distance x, spring k_1 is stretched distance x_1 and spring k_2 is stretched distance x_2. At the point of connection, Newton's third law states that the forces must be equal and opposite. Thus we can write

$$k_1x_1 = k_2x_2$$

Since $x = x_1 + x_2$, we have $x_2 = x - x_1$, and so

$$\begin{aligned} k_1x_1 &= k_2(x - x_1) \\ &= k_2x - k_2x_1 \\ k_1x_1 + k_2x_1 &= k_2x \\ k_2x &= (k_1 + k_2)x_1 \\ x_1 &= \left(\frac{k_2}{k_1 + k_2}\right)x \end{aligned}$$

is the expression for the displacement of k_1.

Now, for any spring, let's say spring 1:

$$\mathbf{F}_1 = k_1\mathbf{x}_1 = \left(\frac{k_1k_2}{k_1 + k_2}\right)\mathbf{x}_1$$

Let's call $(k_1k_2/\ k_1 + k_2) = k'$, so

$$\mathbf{F}_1 = k'\mathbf{x}_1$$

This is in the form of the equation for simple harmonic motion and therefore is equal to $m\mathbf{a}$ by Newton's second law:

$$m\mathbf{a} = k'\mathbf{x}_1$$

Thus

$$T = 2\pi\sqrt{\frac{m}{k'}} = 2\pi\sqrt{\frac{m(k_1 + k_2)}{k_1\ k_2}}$$

This is the period of oscillation for arrangement (a).

(b) In this case, each spring is displaced the same distance as the mass, since the springs are on either side of the mass. Thus we can write

$$\mathbf{F} = -(k_1 + k_2)\mathbf{x}_1$$

and set $\mathbf{k}' = k_1 + k_2$. We therefore have the equation for the period of oscillation

$$T = 2\pi\sqrt{\frac{m}{k_1 + k_2}}$$

for arrangement (b).

2. (a) In the diagram, we can see that, since Δy is small, $\theta = \Delta y/\ell$. Now, since θ (in radians) is small, $\theta \approx \sin\theta \approx \Delta y/\ell$. From the geometry, we see that the net restoring force is given by

$$\Sigma \mathbf{F} = -2\mathbf{T}\sin\theta = \frac{-2\mathbf{T}\,\Delta \mathbf{y}}{\ell}$$

(b) Since this situation is approximating simple harmonic motion, we can write

$$\mathbf{F} = -k\mathbf{y}$$

$$\frac{-2\mathbf{T}\,\Delta \mathbf{y}}{\ell} = -k\,\Delta \mathbf{y}$$

$$k = \frac{2\mathbf{T}}{\ell}$$

and

$$\omega = 2\pi f = \sqrt{\frac{k}{m}} = \sqrt{\frac{2\mathbf{T}}{\ell m}}$$

$$f = \frac{1}{2\pi}\sqrt{\frac{2\mathbf{T}}{\ell m}}$$

3. (a) A free-body diagram for the block is shown below:

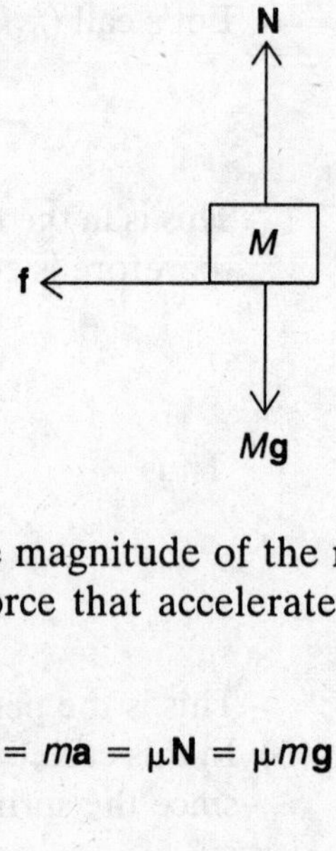

(b) The formula for the magnitude of the maximum acceleration is $\mathbf{a} = A\omega^2$. Now the force that accelerates the block is the force of static friction. Thus

$$\mathbf{f} = m\mathbf{a} = \mu\mathbf{N} = \mu m\mathbf{g}$$

and

$$\mu m\mathbf{g} = A\omega^2$$

These equations are for the maximum amplitude (acceleration; force); although, technically, they should be expressed in the form of "less than or equal to," we are interested here in the maximum values. Thus, since $\omega = 2\pi f$ (where f is the frequency, given as 2.7 Hz), we can solve for the maximum amplitude of oscillation, A, which is 0.0136 m.

(c) The total energy of the system at maximum amplitude is given by $E = (1/2)kA^2$. Substituting the known values gives $A = 0.0929$ J.

CHAPTER 14

Gravitation

14.1 Kepler's Laws of Planetary Motion

In the early seventeenth century, in an effort to support the belief by Copernicus that the Sun was the center of the universe, Johannes Kepler developed three laws of planetary motion. Briefly, these laws state that:

1. All the planets orbit the Sun in elliptical paths.
2. A planet sweeps out an equal area of space in an equal amount of time in its orbit.
3. The ratio of the cube of a planet's mean distance from the Sun and the square of its period is a constant.

We can understand Kepler's first law by looking at Figure 14.1. An ellipse consists of two fixed points, called **foci** (one point is a **focus**). An **ellipse** is defined to be the set of all points such that the sum of the distances to the two fixed points, from anywhere, equals a constant. Thus, if a point P is a distance P_{f1} from the first focal point and a distance P_{f2} from the second, then $P_{f1} + P_{f2}$ is always a constant. In the solar system, the Sun is located at one of the foci. The extent to which an ellipse differs from a circle is referred to as its **eccentricity**.

The second law can be understood from the law of conservation of angular momentum. In Figure 14.1, if it takes 1 month to go from point A to point B on the ellipse and 1 month to go from point C to point D, then Kepler's second law asserts that the areas swept out (as outlined) are equal. From our knowledge of forces, we suspect that the force acting on the planet increases as distance decreases since, as the planet gets closer, it begins to accelerate in its orbit and the centripetal acceleration directed toward the center also increases.

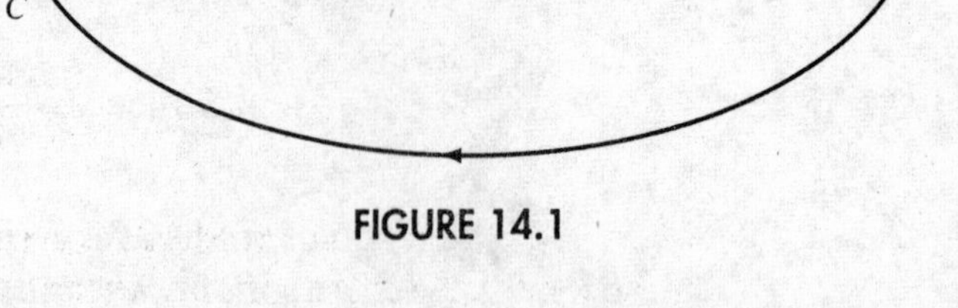

FIGURE 14.1

The eccentricity of the planetary orbits is so small that they can almost be considered circles. Therefore, since the force acting on the planets is radial, we know from Chapter 12 that, if the force is parallel to the radius vector from the pivot or action point (in this case, the Sun), no net torque acts on the system. In that case, there is no change in the angular momentum of the system (it is conserved). Therefore, as the planet gets closer to the Sun, it must orbit faster in order to maintain the same amount of angular momentum. In Section 14.2 we will look at Newton's law of universal gravitation and explain in more detail the meaning behind Kepler's second law.

Kepler's third law of motion can be written mathematically in the form

$$\frac{R^3}{T^2} = K_s = 3.35 \times 10^{18}\ \mathrm{m^3/s^2}$$

This constant is the same for all planets in the solar system whose R is the mean radius and T is the period. The universality of Kepler's third law lies in the fact that for any system (such as the Earth-Moon system) a suitable "Kepler's constant" can be found. The Moon obeys Kepler's laws, as do also the satellites of Jupiter and stars in distant galaxies!

14.2 Newton's Law of Universal Gravitation

We already know that all objects falling near the surface of the Earth have the same acceleration, given by $\mathbf{g} = 9.8\ \mathrm{m/s^2}$. The value of this constant can be determined from the independence of the period of a pendulum on the mass of the bob. This "empirical" verification is independent of any "theory" of gravity.

The weight of an object on the Earth is given by $\mathbf{W} = m\mathbf{g}$, which represents the magnitude of the force of gravity due to the Earth that is acting on the object. From our discussion in Chapter 8, we know that gravity causes a projectile to assume a parabolic path. Isaac Newton, in his book *The Principia*, extended the idea of projectile motion to an imaginary situation in which the velocity of the projectile was so great that the object would fall and fall, but the curvature of the Earth would bend away and leave the projectile in "orbit." Newton conjectured that this might be the reason why the Moon orbits the Earth. At one time was the Moon falling toward the Earth like the proverbial apple?

To answer this question, Newton first had to determine the centripetal acceleration of the Moon based on observations from astronomy. He knew the relationship between centripetal acceleration and period. We have written that relationship as

$$\mathbf{a}_c = \frac{4\pi^2 R}{T^2}$$

where R is the distance to the Moon (in meters) and T is the orbital period (in seconds). From astronomy we know that $R = 3.8 \times 10^8$ m, and since the

Moon orbits the Earth in 27.3 days, we have $T = 2.3 \times 10^6$ s. Using these values, we find that $\mathbf{a}_c = 2.8 \times 10^{-3}$ m/s^2.

Using the formula for centripetal acceleration, Newton was able to observe that, since $\mathbf{F} = m\mathbf{a}$ by his second law, the formula for centripetal force is given by (recall Chapter 9)

$$\mathbf{F}_c = \frac{M4\pi^2R}{T^2}$$

Using Kepler's third law of planetary motion, and setting M equal to the mass of the Moon, Newton could express the force of gravity in the form

$$\mathbf{F}_g = \frac{M_{\text{Moon}}4\pi^2\,K_{\text{Earth}}}{R^2}$$

Then Kepler's constant could be evaluated for the Earth-Moon system by using Kepler's third law.

Using his third law of motion, Newton realized that the force that the Earth exerts on the Moon should be exactly equal, but opposite, to the force that the Moon exerts on the Earth (observed as tides). This relationship implied that the constant K should be dependent on the mass of the Earth, and this mutual interaction implied that the force of gravity should be proportional to the product of both masses. In other words, Newton's law of gravity could be expressed as

$$\mathbf{F}_g = \frac{GM_1M_2}{R^2}$$

This is a vector equation in which the force of gravity is directed inward toward the center of mass for the system (in this case, near the center of the Earth). Since the Earth is many times more massive than the Moon, the Moon orbits the Earth, and not vice versa.

The value of G, called the universal gravitational constant, was experimentally determined by Henry Cavendish in 1795. In modern units $G = 6.67 \times 10^{-11}\, N \cdot \text{m}^2/\text{kg}^2$. If we recognize that $\mathbf{F} = m\mathbf{a}$, and then if we consider M_1 to equal the mass of an object of mass m, and M_2 equal to the mass of the Earth, M_E, the acceleration of a mass m near the surface of the Earth is given by

$$\mathbf{a} = \frac{GM_E}{R_E^2}$$

where R_E is the radius of the Earth in meters. Using known values for these quantities, we discover that $\mathbf{a} = 9.8$ m/s^2 $= \mathbf{g}$!

Thus we have a theory that accounts for the value of the known acceleration due to gravity. In fact, if we replace the mass of the Earth by the mass of any other planet, and the radius of the Earth by the corresponding radius of the other planet, the above formula allows us to determine the vaue of $\mathbf{g}$ on any planet or astronomical object in the universe! For example, the value of $\mathbf{g}$ on the Moon is approximately 1.6 meters per second squared, or about one-sixth the value on the Earth. Thus, objects on the Moon weigh one-sixth as much as they do on the Earth.

Now, Newton's prediction for the acceleration of the Moon toward the Earth is that the value of **g** decreases as the square of the distance from the Earth. The ancient Greek astronomers discovered that the mean distance to the Moon is approximately equal to 60 times the radius of the Earth. Thus, the acceleration of the Moon should be 1/3600 of the acceleration of an object near the Earth's surface: **a** = 9.8 / 3600 = 0.0028 m/s^2! Newton's theory of gravity was confirmed in one simple, triumphant demonstration. Further proof came when his friend Edmund Halley used Newton's law to predict that a certain comet (now known as Halley's comet) would return every 76 years, appearing next in 1758.

14.3 Newton's Interpretation of Kepler's Laws

We are now in a position to discuss Kepler's third law of planetary motion in light of Newton's law of gravitation. First, we should observe that Newton's "theory" merely describes the relationship between two masses and their displacement from each other. It is a vector law, so the familiar rules for vector mechanics will apply. However, as Newton himself wrote, nowhere is the "cause" of gravity discussed. In *The Principia*, his seminal work, Newton himself boldly states that he "frames no hypotheses" regarding the origin of the force of gravity.

Nevertheless, the theory allows us to understand the meaning behind Kepler's laws. For example, we have noted that Kepler's second law can be thought of as a consequence of the law of conservation of angular momentum. The reason why the shapes of the orbits of the the planets are elliptical was determined by Newton and has something to do with the amount of total energy available to a particular planet when it formed. We will not go into more detail on this topic.

Kepler's third law relates the distance of a planet from the Sun and the velocity of its orbit about the Sun:

$$\frac{R^3}{T^2} = K_S$$

To begin, let us write the equation for the force of gravity between a planet and the Sun:

$$\mathbf{F} = \frac{GM_P M_S}{R^2}$$

Recall now that, if the eccentricities of ellipses are small, the ellipses can be treated approximately as though they were circles. In this case, the mean radius of the orbit can be thought of as the radius of a circular path in which a centripetal force (provided by gravity) acts on the planet:

$$\frac{M_P 4\pi^2 R}{T^2} = \frac{GM_P M_S}{R^2}$$

The mass of the planet can be eliminated from both sides, and we are left with an equation that depends simply on the mass of the Sun and the distance to the Sun (which is Kepler's law!):

$$\frac{R^3}{T^2} = \frac{GM_S}{4\pi^2} = k_S$$

If we want to know the value of the constant for an Earth-centered system, simply use the mass of the Earth instead of the Sun's mass in the equation above. The mass of the Sun is approximately 2×10^{30} kilograms, and the mass of the Earth is approximately 6×10^{24} kilograms.

Kepler's third law implies that, for any system, the ratio of distance cubed to time squared is a constant for any two intervals of time:

$$\frac{R_1^{\ 3}}{T_1^2} = \frac{R_2^{\ 3}}{T_2^{\ 2}}$$

We can use this relationship to find any corresponding period for any given distance from the center of the Earth (or Sun) if we know any "standard." For example, if we take the Earth system and use the Moon's motion as our standard, we can compute the orbital period of an artificial satellite or spacecraft (recognizing that R is actually the sum of the height above the surface of the Earth and the Earth's radius).

This leads directly to the concept of geostationary or geosynchronous orbits. At an altitude of about 22,000 miles, the orbital period of an orbiting spacecraft is exactly equal to the rotational period of the Earth (about 24 hours). The spacecraft (or satellite) appears to remain stationary above a specified point on the Earth. These satellites are used for communication relays and weather forcasting since a series of them, strategically placed, can always monitor a given region of the Earth's surface.

14.4 Gravitational Energy

In Chapter 10 we saw that the amount of work done (by or against gravity) when vertically displacing a mass is given by the change in the gravitational potential energy:

$$\Delta PE = \Delta\ m\mathbf{g}h$$

We now know that the value of **g** is not constant but varies inversely with the square of the distance from the center of the Earth. Also, since we want the potential energy to become weaker the closer we get to the Earth, we can use the results of Section 14.2 to rewrite the potential energy formula as

$$PE = \frac{-GM_oM_E}{R_E}$$

This equation is valid if an object is located near the surface of the Earth. Actually, we should have used a distance variable $R = R_E + h$ (where h is the height above the surface). If h is very small compared with the radius of the Earth, it can effectively be eliminated from the equation.

The "escape velocity" from the gravitational force of the Earth can be determined by considering the situation where an object has just reached infinity, with zero final velocity, given some initial velocity at any direction away from the surface of the Earth. We designate that escape velocity as $\mathbf{v}_{esc}$, and state that, when the final velocity is zero (at infinity), the total energy must be zero, which implies

$$\frac{1}{2}M_o\mathbf{v}_{esc}^{\;2} = \frac{GM_oM_E}{R_E}$$

The mass of the object can be eliminated from the relationship, leaving

$$\mathbf{v}_{esc} = \sqrt{\frac{2GM_E}{R_E}}$$

An object can leave the surface of the Earth with any velocity. There is, however, one minimum velocity at which if the spacecraft coasted, it would not fall back to the Earth because of gravity.

The orbital velocity can be determined by assuming that we have an approximately circular orbit (see Chapter 8). In this case, we can set the centripetal force equal to the gravitational force:

$$\frac{GM_oM_E}{R_E^{\;2}} = \frac{M_o\mathbf{v}_o^{\;2}}{R_E}$$

Eliminating the mass of the object from the equation leaves

$$\mathbf{v}_{orbit} = \sqrt{\frac{GM_E}{R_E}}$$

Sample Problem:

(a) What is the magnitude of the acceleration due to gravity at an altitude of 400 km above the surface of the Earth?

(b) What percentage loss in the weight of an object results?

Solution:

(a) The formula for the acceleration due to gravity above the Earth's surface is

$$\mathbf{g} = \frac{GM_E}{(R_E + h)^2}$$

We have $M_E = 5.98 \times 10^{24}$ kg, $R_E = 6.38 \times 10^6$ m, $h = 400$ km $= 0.4 \times 10^6$ m. Substituting these values, as well as the known value for G, given in Section 14.2, we get $g = 8.67$ m/s^2.

(b) The fractional change in weight is found by comparing the value of g at 400 km to its value at the Earth's surface: $8.67/9.8 = 0.885$. Thus, there is an 11.5% loss of weight at that height.

Sample Problem:

Three uniform spheres of masses 1 kg, 2 kg, and 4 kg are placed at the corners of a right triangle as shown below. The positions relative to the coordinate system indicated are also shown. What is the magnitude of the resultant gravitational force on the 4-kg mass if we consider that mass to be fixed?

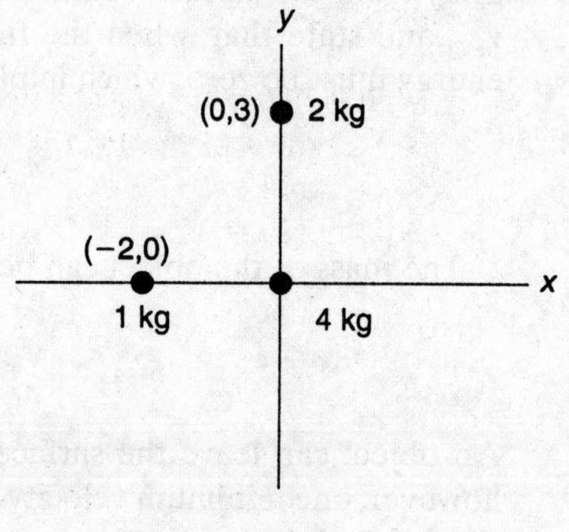

Solution:

In this problem, we have to determine separately the force of gravitational attraction between each of the smaller masses and the 4-kg mass. The 1-kg mass will be attracted to the right along the x-axis, and the 2-kg mass will be attracted downward along the y-axis.

We begin by calculating the force between the 1-kg mass and the 4-kg mass:

$$\mathbf{F}_{1-4} = \frac{(6.67 \times 10^{-11})(1)(4)}{(-2)^2} = 6.67 \times 10^{-11}\ \text{N}$$

The direction is to the right and is therefore considered positive.

For the 2-kg mass and the 4-kg mass, the downward direction is taken as negative:

$$\mathbf{F}_{2-4} = \frac{(6.67 \times 10^{-11})(2)(4)}{(-3)^2} = 5.93 \times 10^{-11}\ \text{N}$$

The magnitude of the resultant force is given by the Pythagorean theorem:

$$\mathbf{F} = \sqrt{(6.67 \times 10^{-11})^2 + (5.93 \times 10^{-11})^2} = 8.92 \times 10^{-11}\ \text{N}$$

Problem-Solving Strategies for Gravitation

There are not many special considerations for solving problems involving Kepler's laws or Newton's law of gravitation. You should remember the connection between Kepler's second law and the law of conservation of angular momentum, and the connection between Kepler's third law and Newton's law of gravity. Also, remember that each "system" has its own "Kepler's constant" that an orbiting object obeys.

Keep in mind that gravity is a force and therefore a vector quantity. Distances are measured in meters from the center of masses of each object; therefore if an object is above the surface of the Earth, you must add the height to the radius of the Earth. If you remember that the force of gravity is an inverse-square-law relationship, you may be able to deduce an answer from logic rather than algebraic calculations, which take time.

Practice Problems for Chapter 14

Multiple Choice

1. What is the value of **g** at a height above the Earth's surface that is equal to the radius of the Earth?
(A) 9.8 N/kg
(B) 4.9 N/kg
(C) 6.93 N/kg
(D) 2.45 N/kg
(E) 1.6 N/kg

2. A planet has half the mass of the Earth and half the radius. Compared to the acceleration due to gravity near the surface of the Earth, the acceleration of gravity near the surface of this other planet is
(A) twice as much
(B) one-fourth as much
(C) half as much
(D) the same
(E) zero

3. Which of the following is an expression for the acceleration of gravity with uniform density ρ and radius R?
(A) $G\,(4\pi\rho/3R^2)$
(B) $G\,(4\pi\rho R^2/3)$
(C) $G\,(4\pi\rho/3R)$
(D) $G\,(4\pi R\rho/3)$
(E) None of these is correct.

4. Given that the mean radius of the Moon's orbit is 3.84×10^8 m and its period is 2.36×10^6 s, at what altitude above the surface of the Earth does a geostationary satellite orbit? (The radius of the Earth is 6.38×10^6 m.)
(A) 4.23×10^7 m
(B) 3.59×10^7 m
(C) 6.2×10^8 m
(D) 2.2×10^7 m
(E) 5.8×10^7 m

5. What is the orbital velocity of a satellite at a height of 300 km above the surface of the Earth? (The mass of the Earth is approximately 6×10^{24} kg, and its radius is 6.4×10^6 m.)
(A) 5.42×10^1 m/s
(B) 1.15×10^6 m/s

(C) 7.7×10^3 m/s
(D) 6×10^6 m/s
(E) 3×10^8 m/s

6. What is the escape velocity from the Moon, given that the mass of the Moon is 7.2×10^{22} kg and its radius is 1.778×10^6 m?
(A) 1.64×10^3 m/s
(B) 2.32×10^3 m/s
(C) 2.69×10^6 m/s
(D) 5.38×10^6 m/s
(E) 3×10^8 m/s

7. A "black hole" theoretically has an escape velocity that is greater than or equal to the velocity of light (3×10^8 m/s). If the effective mass of the black hole is equal to the mass of the Sun (2×10^{30} kg), what is the effective "radius" (called the "Schwarzchild radius") of the black hole?
(A) 3×10^3 m
(B) 1.5×10^3 m
(C) 8.9×10^6 m
(D) 4.45×10^6 m
(E) 0 m

8. Kepler's second law of planetary motion is a consequence of the law of conservation of
(A) linear momentum
(B) charge
(C) energy
(D) mass
(E) angular momentum

9. What is the gravitational force of attraction between two trucks, each of mass 20,000 kg, separated by a distance of 2 m?
(A) 0.057 N
(B) 0.013 N
(C) 0.0067 N
(D) 1.20 N
(E) 0 N

10. The gravitational force between two masses is 36 N. If the distance between masses is tripled, the force of gravity will be
(A) the same
(B) 18 N
(C) 9 N
(D) 4 N
(E) 27 N

Free Response

1. Four masses are arranged at the corners of a rectangle as shown below. Consider the 2-kg mass to be fixed.

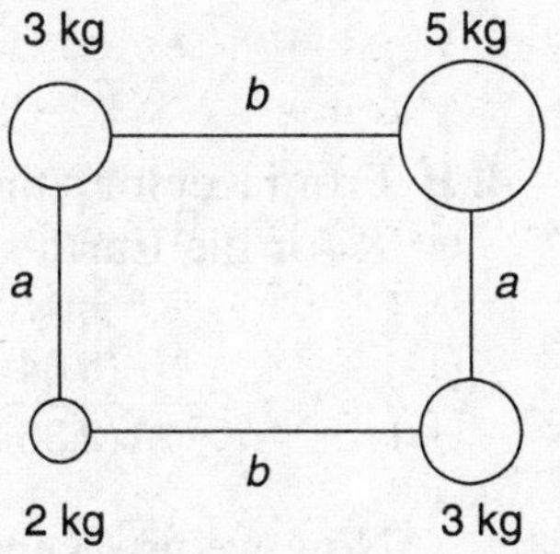

   (a) Derive an expression for the x- and y-components of the resultant force acting on the 2-kg mass.
   (b) If $a = 0.1$ m and $b = 0.2$ m, what are the magnitude and the direction of the resultant gravitational force?

2. A satellite orbits a planet of uniform density ρ, mass M, and radius R at a height h above the surface of the planet. The orbital period of the satellite is T.
   (a) Derive an expression for the density of the planet in terms of h, R, G, and T only.
   (b) What is the approximate density if $h \ll R$?

3. Find the magnitude of the gravitational field strength **g** at a point P along the perpendicular bisector between two equal masses, M and M, that are separated by a distance $2b$ as shown below:

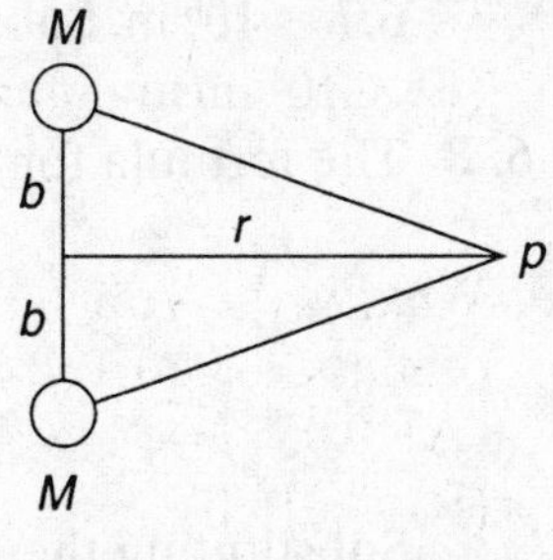

Solutions

Multiple-Choice Problems

1. **D** The value of **g** varies inversely with the square of the distance from the center of the Earth; therefore, if we double the distance from the center (as in this case), the value of **g** decreases by one-fourth: $1/4(9.8) = 2.45$. Since $\mathbf{g} = \mathbf{F} / m$, alternative units are newtons per kilogram.
2. **A** If, using the formula for **g**, we take half the mass, the value decreases by one-half. If we decrease the radius by half, the value will increase by four times. Combining both effects results in an overall increase of two times.

3. **D** The formula for **g** is $\mathbf{g} = GM/R^2$. The planet is essentially a sphere of mass M, radius R, and density ρ (with $M = V\rho$; where V is the volume). The volume of the planet is given by $V = 4/3\pi R^3$. Making the substitutions yields:

$$\mathbf{g} = G\frac{4\pi R\rho}{3}$$

4. **B** From Kepler's third law, we can determine the value of the constant K for the Earth system by using the data for the Moon:

$$\frac{(3.84 \times 10^8)^3}{(2.36 \times 10^6)^2} = 1.01664 \times 10^{13} \ \text{m}^3/\text{s}^2$$

Now, we use Kepler's third law again, but this time with a period of 86,400 s (which equals the 24-h period of a geostationary orbit) and the above constant for K:

$$\frac{R^3}{T^2} = K = 1.01664 \times 10^{13} = \frac{R^3}{(86{,}400)^2}$$

Solving for R (don't forget to take the cube root!) yields R = 42,338,119 m as the distance of the satellite from the center of the Earth. To get the answer, we must subtract the radius of the Earth, which is given in the question, leaving $h = 3.59 \times 10^7$ m.

5. **C** The formula for orbital velocity is

$$\mathbf{v}_{\text{orbit}} = \sqrt{\frac{GM}{R}}$$

where R is the distance from the center of the Earth. In this case we must add 300 km = 300,000 m to the radius of the Earth. Thus, $R = 6.7 \times 10^6$ m. Substituting the given values yields $\mathbf{v}_{\text{orbit}} = 7728$ or 7.7×10^3 m/s.

6. **B** The formula for escape velocity is

$$\mathbf{v}_{\text{esc}} = \sqrt{\frac{2GM_{\text{moon}}}{R_{\text{moon}}}}$$

Substituting the given values yields $\mathbf{v}_{\text{esc}} = 2324$ or 2.32×10^3 m/s.

7. **A** From question 6, we know that the escape velocity is given by $\mathbf{v}_{\text{esc}} = \sqrt{2GM/R}$. To find R, we need to square both sides, and then solve for the radius. This yields $R = 2GM/v^2$. Substituting the given values yields $R = 3000$ or 3×10^3 m. (This is only a "theoretical" size for the black hole. As an interesting exercise, try calculating the value of **g** on such an object!)

8. **E** Kepler's second law can be explained in terms of the conservation of angular momentum. Since the force of gravity is radial, the net torque acting on a planet in the solar system is zero. Therefore, the change in angular momentum is zero and so this quantity is conserved.

9. **C** We use the formula for gravitational force:

$$\mathbf{F} = \frac{GM_1M_2}{R^2}$$

Substituting the given values (don't forget to square the distance!) yields $\mathbf{F} = 0.0067$ N.

10. **D** The force of gravity is an inverse-square-law relationship. This means that, as the distance is tripled, the force is decreased by one-ninth. One-ninth of 36 N is 4 N.

Free-Response Problems

1. (a) We can see from the diagram that the force along b is only horizontal and that the force along a is only vertical. The force connecting the 2-kg and 5-kg masses is directed along the diagonal of the rectangle. The length of the diagonal can be found by using the Pythagorean theorem.

If θ is the acute angle from the positive x-axis, then $\tan\theta = a / b$. Thus we see that the x-component of the diagonal force involves the vector component involving $\cos\theta$, while the y-component involves $\sin\theta$. We can combine these ideas to write, for the magnitudes of the components of the resultant force on the 2-kg mass,

$$\mathbf{F}_x = \frac{G(2)(3)}{b^2} + \frac{G(2)(5)}{a^2 + b^2}\cos\theta$$

$$\mathbf{F}_y = \frac{G(2)(3)}{a^2} + \frac{G(2)(5)}{a^2 + b^2}\sin\theta$$

(b) To find the magnitude and the direction of the net resultant force, we first need the value of θ. We know that $\tan\theta = a / b$. Given that $a = 0.1$ m and $b = 0.2$ m, we find that $\theta = 26.57°$. Therefore, $\cos\theta = 0.8944$ and $\sin\theta = 0.4473$. Using the values above, we find that $\mathbf{F}_x = 2.19 \times 10^{-8}$ N and $\mathbf{F}_y = 4.6 \times 10^{-8}$ N. The magnitude of the resultant gravitational force is given by the Pythagorean theorem: $\mathbf{F} = 5.09 \times 10^{-8}$ N.

To find the direction of the resultant, we note that, since we consider the 2-kg mass to be fixed, and gravity is attractive, the resultant force is directed toward the lower left part of the page. Specifically, we recall from our work on vectors that, if ϕ is the direction of the resultant, then $\tan\phi = \mathbf{F}_y / \mathbf{F}_x$. Now, both $\mathbf{F}_x$ and $\mathbf{F}_y$ are directed in what we have, by convention, termed "negative" directions. However, from trigonometry, we recall that the tangent function is positive (since we have a ratio of two negative numbers) in the third quadrant. Thus, taking the ratio, we find that $\tan\phi = 2.1$ and thus $\phi = 64.5°$ below the negative x-axis (244.5°).

2. (a) The formula for density is $\rho = M / V$. Since the planet is a sphere, we can write

$$\rho = \frac{3M}{4\pi R^3}$$

From Kepler's third law, we know also that

$$T^2 = \frac{4\pi^2}{GM} r^3 = \frac{4\pi^2}{GM}(R + h)^3$$

where we have used $r = R + h$. Now, factoring out an R leaves us with

$$T^2 = \frac{4\pi^2}{GM} R^3 \left(\frac{1 + h}{R} \right)^3$$

Solving for the cube of the radius, which appears in the density formula, we get

$$R^3 = \frac{GMT^2}{4\pi^2(1 + h/R)^3}$$

We must now substitute this expression for the cube of the radius into the first density formula. Canceling out all like terms leaves us with our desired expression (independent of mass!):

$$\rho = \frac{3\pi}{GT^2}\left(1 + \frac{h}{R}\right)^3$$

If $h \ll R$, then $h / R \ll 1$, and so the term can be eliminated as an approximation. Thus, for small heights above the surface of the planet (relative to the radius of the planet) we can write

$$\rho = \frac{3\pi}{GT^2}$$

3. Let's designate as $\mathbf{g}_1$ the field strength at P caused by the top mass and designate as $\mathbf{g}_2$ the field strength at point P due to the bottom mass. Both of these field strengths are accelerations and therefore vectors. The distance from point P to the line connecting the masses is r, and the midpoint distance connecting the masses is b. Therefore, the distance from point P to each mass is given by the Pythagorean theorem and is equal to $\sqrt{r^2 + b^2}$.

The direction of each acceleration $\mathbf{g}$ is directed toward each mass from point P. Since each mass is identical and the distance to each mass is the same, the angles formed by the vectors to the x-axis are the same. Let's call each angle θ such that $\tan \theta = b / r$ in magnitude.

From the above analysis we can conclude that

$$\mathbf{g}_1 = \mathbf{g}_2 = \frac{GM}{r^2 + b^2}$$

The vector components of each field strength result in a symmetrical cancellation of the y-components. This is true since the direction of $\mathbf{g}_1$ is toward the upper left, and thus its x-component is directed to the left and its y-component is directed upward. Field strength $\mathbf{g}_2$ has an x-component that is also directed to the left and equal in magnitude to the x-component of $\mathbf{g}_1$. The y-component of $\mathbf{g}_2$ is directed downward and is also equal in magnitude to the y-component of $\mathbf{g}_1$. Since these two vectors are equal and opposite, they will sum to zero and will not contribute to the net resultant field (which is just directed horizontally to the left).

What remains to be done is to determine the expression for the x-component of $\mathbf{g}_1$ or $\mathbf{g}_2$ and then multiply by 2. Since $\mathbf{g}_{1x} = \mathbf{g}_1 \cos\theta$, we can see from the geometry that

$$\cos\theta = \frac{r}{\sqrt{r^2 + b^2}}$$

Combining results gives

$$\mathbf{g}_{\text{net}} = \frac{2GMr}{(r^2 + b^2)^{3/2}}$$

CHAPTER 15

Temperature and Heat

15.1 Introduction

We have already learned that friction is a nonconservative force. When work is done against friction, the kinetic energy of the system is not conserved. Where does the energy go? Observations made by touch indicate that even though the mass and shape of the system may stay the same, the mass "feels" different. This sensation is attributable to a form of energy we call **heat**.

15.2 Temperature and Its Measurement

Temperature can be defined as the relative measure of heat flow. In other words, temperature is a measure of the extent to which two bodies differ in heat content. We can state even more simply that temperature is a measure of how "hot" or "cold" a body is (relative to your own body or another standard or arbitrary reference). Human touch is unreliable in measuring temperature since what feels hot to one person may feel cool to another.

During the seventeenth century, Galileo invented a method for measuring temperature using water and its ability to react to changes in heat content by expanding or contracting. Figure 15.1 shows a simple "thermometer" that consists of a beaker of water in which is inverted a tube with a circular bulb at the top. When heat is added to the beaker, the level of water will rise.

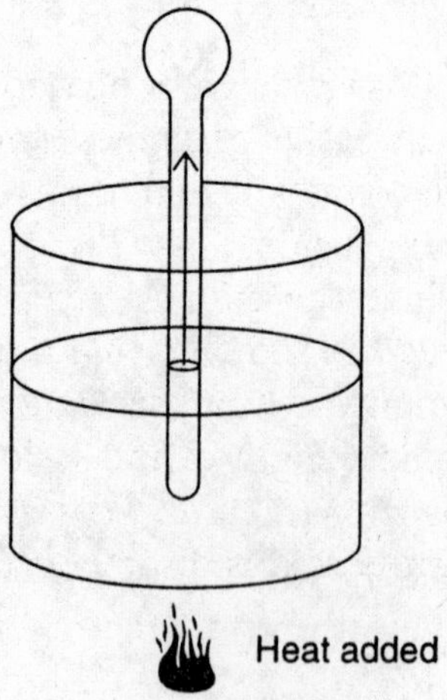

FIGURE 15.1

For two reasons, however, water is not the best substance to use to measure temperature. First, water has a relatively high freezing and low boiling point; second, it has a peculiar variation in density as a function of temperature because of its chemical structure. Even so, the phenomenon of "thermal expansion" is an important topic not only in this context but also for engineering buildings, roads, and bridges. We will discuss this aspect in more detail later in the chapter.

Most modern thermometers use mercury or alcohol in a small capillary tube. In the metric system, the standard sea-level points of reference are the freezing point (0 degree) and boiling point (100 degrees) of water. This temperature scale, formerly known as the centrigrade scale, is now called the Celsius scale after Anders Celsius. (The English Farenheit system is not used in physics.)

One difficulty with the Celsius scale is that the zero mark is not a true zero since some substances freeze at temperatures below zero. Some gases, such as oxygen and hydrogen, do not even condense until their temperatures reach far below 0 degree Celsius. The discovery of a theoretical "absolute zero" temperature resulted in the so-called absolute or Kelvin temperature scale. A temperature of −273 degrees Celsius is redefined as "absolute zero" on the Kelvin scale. An easy way to convert from Celsius to Kelvin is to add the number 273 to the Celsius temperature. This just adds a scale factor that preserves the metric scale of the Celsius reading. In other words, there is still a 100-degree difference in temperature between melting ice and boiling water—273 K and 373 K, respectively. (Note that neither the word "degrees" nor the degree sign is used in expressing Kelvin temperatures.)

15.3 Thermal Expansion of Solids, Liquids, and Gases

You know from your previous studies in science that matter exists in three states: solid, liquid, and gas. These states react differently when heat is applied because of their different structures.

A. Solids

A metal rod, when heated, will expand linearly. When a sidewalk is constructed, the spacing between slabs allows for expansion. Similarly, on a bridge you will sometimes see metal spacers in the roadway, again to allow for expansion.

Since the expansion of most solids is linear, experiments can be performed to indicate that a direct relationship exists between the fractional amount of expansion and the change in temperature. If we let ℓ_o be the original length of the solid, and let ℓ be the new length of the solid after expansion, then $\Delta\ell / \ell_o$ represents the fractional change in length. It is this quantity that is directly proportional to the change in temperature:

$$\frac{\Delta\ell}{\ell_o} = \alpha\Delta T$$

where α, called the **coefficient of linear expansion**, is in units of 1 / degrees Celsius. Notice that this relationship is dimensionless since the ratio of length to length cancels the units out. Some selected coefficients of linear expansion are given in Table 15.1.

TABLE 15.1 Selected Coefficients of Linear Expansion ($\times 10^{-6}$)

Aluminum	23
Brass	19
Concrete	12
Copper	17
Glass: Pyrex	3.2
Lead	30
Silver	51
Steel	12

The expression for the fractional change in length can also be written in the form

$$\ell = \ell_o(1 + \alpha\,\Delta T)$$

For some solids, there is a change in area as well. Since area can be considered as length squared, we can write the area change as

$$A = \ell^2 = \ell_o^2\,(1 + \alpha\,\Delta T)^2 = A_o(1 + 2\alpha\,\Delta T + \alpha^2\,\Delta T^2)$$

If α is $\ll 1$, then, to a first approximation,

$$A = A_o(1 + 2\alpha\,\Delta T)$$

We can infer from this expression that the coefficient of area expansion for a solid is approximately twice the value of the coefficient of linear expansion.

In a similar way, we can observe that, if any volume changes occur in the solid, then, following the logic that volume is length cubed, we can write (again assuming that $\alpha \ll 1$):

$$V = V_o(1 + 3\alpha\,\Delta T)$$

The coefficient of volume expansion for solids is approximately three times the value of the linear expansion coefficient.

B. Liquids and Gases

Liquids and gases expand in volume only. We define the volume relationship to be similar to the linear relationship for solids:

$$\frac{\Delta V}{V_o} = \beta\,\Delta T$$

A list of some values for volume expansions is given in Table 15.2.

TABLE 15.2 Selected Coefficients of Volume Expansion ($\times 10^{-6}$)

Acetone	150
Air	3670
Ethanol	1100
Mercury	180
Water	210

As an example, consider the following problem. A copper rod is 0.5 m in length at 20°C. What is its length at 100°C?

To answer this question, we note in Table 15.1 that the coefficient of linear expansion for copper is 17; therefore, $\alpha = 17 \times 10^{-6}\ C^{-1}$. Using the formula for linear expansion, we find that for an 80° change in temperature $\Delta\ell = 6.8 \times 10^{-4}$ m. Thus, $\ell = 0.50068$ m, the length of the copper rod at 100°C.

15.4 Heat Capacity

You may have noticed that during the hottest days of summer the water in a pool, lake, or ocean is usually much cooler than the air. Similarly, if equal masses of water and sand are placed under sunlamps, it can be observed that the temperature of the sand rises faster than the temperature of the water. Additional experiments reveal that equal masses (same shapes and sizes) of different metals, when heated to the same temperature and then placed on a plate of wax, melt the wax to different depths.

The observations imply that different substances maintain different heat capacities when equal masses and equal changes in temperature are compared. In physics, a quantity of heat is designated by the letter Q; and any change in heat, ΔQ, is usually accompanied by a change in temperature, ΔT; these two quantities are directly proportional to each other.

Historically, the unit of heat content has been the calorie. One calorie is defined to be the amount of heat needed to raise the temperature of 1 gram of water by 1 degree Celsius. Using this definition, scientists define the specific heat capacity of any substance to be equal to the amount of heat needed to raise the temperature of 1 gram of the substance by 1 degree Celsius, with water having a specific heat equal to 1 calorie per gram per degree Celsius.

The heat content of a substance also depends on how much of the substance is involved. Thus, algebraically, we can write

$$\Delta Q = mc\,\Delta T$$

where c is the specific heat capacity of the substance in units of calories per gram · degree Celsius (cal 1 g · °C).

Experiments in the nineteenth century by physicist James Joule revealed that, if 4.19 joules of mechanical work is done, 1 calorie of heat is added. In the standard SI units of physics (to be followed in this book), the unit for heat is the same as the unit for all energy, the joule. The fact that 4.19 joules is equivalent to 1 calorie is referred to as the "mechanical equivalent of heat." Thus, to convert from calories to joules, we simply multiply by 4.19. We must be careful, however, since in SI units we should be using kilograms instead of grams. Through factor analysis, we can convert to kilojoules when kilograms are used. Thus the units of specific heat can be expressed as kilojoules per kilogram · degree Celsius (kJ / kg · °C) (provided that we use Celsius temperatures and kilograms for mass). Some specific heats are presented in Table 15.3.

As an example, consider the following problem. How much heat was added to 250 g of copper that was heated from 20° C to 100°C? To answer this question, we look at Table 15.3 and find that the specific heat of copper is 0.39 kJ / kg · °C. Since 250 g = 0.25 kg , and $\Delta T = 80°$, we find that

$$\Delta Q = (0.25)(0.39)(80) = 7.8 \text{ kJ}$$

TABLE 15.3 Specific Heats of Selected Substances (kJ / kg · °C)

Substance	Specific Heat (kJ / kg · °C)
Alcohol (ethyl)	2.43 (liq.)
Aluminum	0.90 (sol.)
Copper	0.39 (sol.)
Iron	0.45 (sol.)
Lead	0.13 (sol.)
Mercury	0.14 (sol.)
Silver	0.24 (sol.)
Tungsten	0.13 (sol.)
Water:	
Ice	2.05 (sol.)
Liquid water	4.19 (liq.)
Steam	2.10 (gas)
Zinc	0.39 (sol.)

15.5 Conservation of Heat

When heat is transferred from one substance to another, all of the energy transferred is conserved. It is quite possible that some of the heat is "leaked" to the environment, but even so, all of the heat is accounted for. In an ideal situation, an isolated system will allow for the direct transfer of heat without the gain or loss of heat to the environment being considered. In such a situation we can write that the heat gained by one substance is equal to the heat lost by the other; that is, $\Delta Q_{gain} = \Delta Q_{loss}$.

Consider the following problem. A 0.05-kg block of lead, at a temperature of 100°C, is placed in 2 kg of water at a temperature of 20°C. What is the final temperature of the mixture when equilibrium has been achieved?

Using Table 15.3, we locate the specific heats of lead (0.13) and water (4.19). Since we are making a comparison, we must make sure all units are consistent. The masses are given in kilograms, so everything is correct. We can now state that the final temperature reached by the mixture will involve equal changes in heat content:

$$M_W c_W \, \Delta T_w = M_L c_L \, \Delta T_L$$

$$(2)(4.19)(T_f - 20) = (0.05)(0.13)(100 - T_f)$$

The different forms of the expressions for ΔT are used to keep the change in temperature a positive value. Solving for the final temperature of the mixture, we obtain $T_f = 20.06°C$ (not much change in temperature!).

15.6 Latent Heat and Changes of State

In Section 15.5 we observed that a change in temperature implies a change in heat content (and vice versa). However, you may have observed that, when water boils, its temperature does not change even though more heat is being added! This apparent contradiction can be explained by recognizing that, when water boils, it changes into steam. Therefore, instead of changing the temperature, the heat being added is doing work to change the state of the water from a liquid to a gas (vaporization). Similar observations demonstrate that, when water freezes, its temperature does not go below zero degree Celsius (assuming the water is relatively pure).

The amount of heat needed to change the state of a substance is referred to a **latent** (or hidden) heat. Specifically, in going from a liquid to a gas (or vice versa), this heat is called the **latent heat of vaporization**. In changing from a liquid to a solid (or vice versa), this heat is the **latent heat of fusion**. Both of these quantities are measured in units of joules per gram (J / g) or kilojoules per kilogram (kJ / kg). A list of some latent heats is given in Table 15.4.

TABLE 15.4 Latent Heats of Fusion and Heats of Vaporization for Selected Substances

Substance	Heat of Fusion (kJ / kg)	Heat of Vaporization (kJ / kg)
Aluminum	396	10,500
Copper	205	4790
Iron	267	6290
Lead	25	866
Mercury	11	295
Silver	105	2370
Water	334	2260
Zinc	113	1770

For any change of state, if L represents the appropriate latent heat, we can write that $\Delta Q = m\,L$ (with the mass expressed in kilograms). Notice also that the latent heat of vaporization is larger than the latent heat of fusion for all substances.

As an example, consider a 20-g block of ice at −15°C. Heat is added until the block becomes 20 g of steam at 120°C. How much heat was added (assume no losses)?

We first note that this is a five-step problem. First, the ice heats up to its melting point. Second, the ice melts. Third, the water heats up to its boiling point (assume the block is at sea level). Fourth, the water vaporizes into steam. Fifth, the steam heats up to 120°C.

Each of these five steps can be expressed algebraically using the results of this and the preceding section:

1. $\Delta Q = mc\,\Delta T = (0.02)(2.05)(15) = 0.615$ kJ
2. $\Delta Q = mL = (0.02)(335) = 6.7$ kJ
3. $\Delta Q = mc\,\Delta T = (0.02)(4.19)(100) = 8.38$ kJ
4. $\Delta Q = mL = (0.02)(2260) = 45.2$ kJ
5. $\Delta Q = mc\,\Delta T = (0.02)(2.01)(20) = 0.804$ kJ

Total $\Delta Q = 61.699$ kJ

If we were to make a graph of the change in heat versus the change in temperature, we could see these five steps as five distinct regions. In the regions corresponding to the three states of matter (solid, liquid, and gas), we would see three diagonal lines corresponding to the direct relationship between change in temperature and change in heat content. Two horizontal lines indicating no change in temperature would denote regions where the state was changing. The length of each line would be proportional (not equal) to the two latent heats. A typical graph of this type is shown in Figure 15.2.

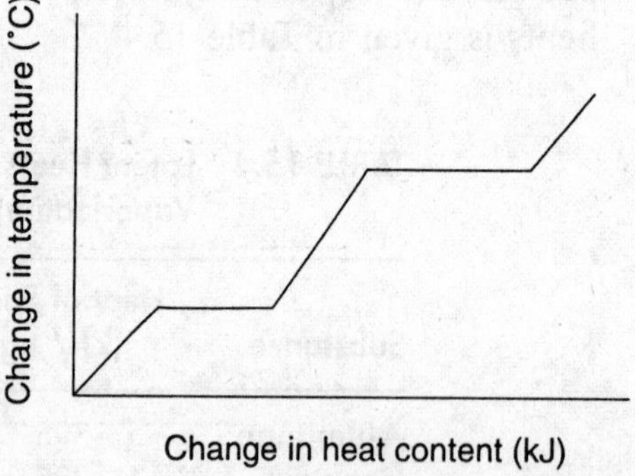

FIGURE 15.2

To find the value of the latent heat quantity desired, we simply measure the length of each horizontal line and divide by the mass (since the units are kilojoules per kilogram). The slopes of the diagonal lines are related to the specific heats (but reciprocally). From the formula for heat transfer within a substance, we can show that $c = \Delta Q / m\,\Delta T$. This is actually the reciprocal of the slope, divided by the mass. Thus, a substance has a high specific heat if it has a line of small slope (indicating that a large amount of heat is required to change the temperature of the substance by a small amount).

15.7 Heat Flow and Thermal Conductivity

Heat can flow through a substance by the process of conduction. Metals are good conductors of heat because they contain a large number of free electrons (this characteristic also makes metals good conductors of electricity). If we consider a small rectangular slab of material, the rate at which heat flows from one side to the other, through a thickness Δx, can be shown to be related to the variation in temperature, ΔT, from one side to the other:

$$\frac{\Delta Q}{\Delta t} = kA\frac{\Delta T}{\Delta x}$$

where k, called the **coefficient of thermal conductivity**, is in units of watts per meter · degree Celsius (W / m · °C). The quantity A is the cross-sectional area of the slab of thickness Δx (see Figure 15.3). Also, the quantity $\Delta T / \Delta x$ is sometimes referred to as the **temperature gradient**. A list of some coefficients of thermal conductivity (rated at 25 degrees Celsius) is given in Table 15.5.

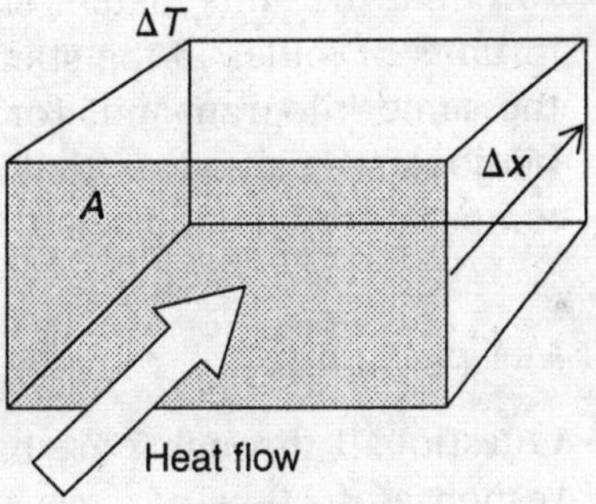

FIGURE 15.3

TABLE 15.5 Coefficients of Thermal Conductivity for Selected Substances

Substance	Coefficient of Thermal Conductivity (W / m · °C)
Air	0.0234
Aluminum	238
Concrete	0.8
Copper	397
Glass (Pyrex)	0.8
Gold	314
Ice	2.0
Iron	79.5
Lead	34.7
Silver	427
Wood	0.08

Another useful way to look at the expression for heat flow is to divide by the cross-sectional area A. If we define the left-hand side of the equation to be H, which is the rate of heat flow per unit area, in units of watts per square meter (W / m^2), then H can be referred to as a **heat flux** since it indicates the power generated per unit area. This aspect of heat flow is very important in engineering construction. Thus, we can write

$$H = \frac{k\,\Delta T}{\Delta x}$$

as the expression for heat flux.

Problem-Solving Strategies for Temperature and Heat

There are no special considerations to be concerned with when solving problems involving heat transfer or heat flow. Make sure, however, that you are aware of the proper units as shown in the tables.

For example, suppose you are given a problem involving a bullet that is shot into a block of wood and are asked to find the change in temperature for the wood. The kinetic energy of the bullet will be transferred to heat as it enters the wood (let us assume that the wood will not move when struck by the bullet). To compare the two energies, kinetic and heat, we must make sure that the units match. The kinetic energy (using kilograms for mass) is in units of joules in the standard formula from mechanics. However, with the same kilogram unit for mass, the thermal energy will be in units of kilojoules—a situation that can lead to inconsistent values for changes in temperature, specific heats, or thermal conductivity.

Practice Problems for Chapter 15

Multiple Choice

Questions 1 through 7 are based on the graph below, which represents the response of 2.0 kg of a gas at 140° C. The gas is releasing heat at a rate of 6 kJ / min.

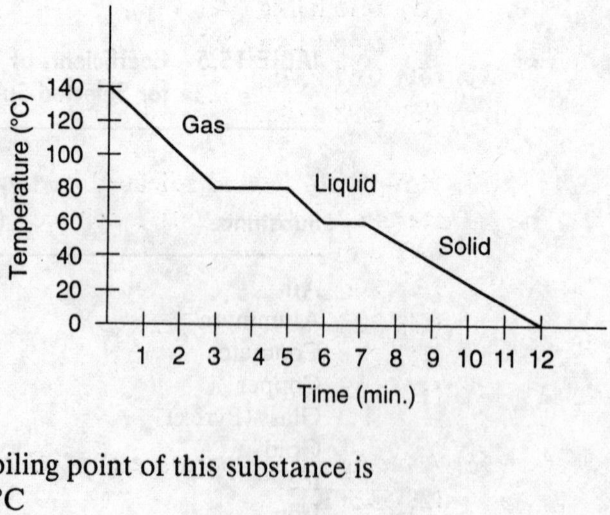

1. The boiling point of this substance is
   (A) 0°C
   (B) 60°C
   (C) 80°C
   (D) 140°C
   (E) There is not enough information to determine.

2. The melting point of this substance is
   (A) 0°C
   (B) 60°C
   (C) 80°C
   (D) 140°C
   (E) There is not enough information to determine.

3. The heat of vaporization of this substance is
   (A) 80 kJ/kg
   (B) 12 kJ/kg
   (C) 6 kJ/kg
   (D) 2 kJ/kg
   (E) 24 kJ/kg

4. The heat of fusion of this substance is
   (A) 3 kJ/kg
   (B) 6 kJ/kg
   (C) 12 kJ/kg
   (D) 20 kJ/kg
   (E) 24 kJ/kg

5. Compared to the specific heat in the gas state, the specific heat of this substance as a solid is
   (A) greater
   (B) less
   (C) the same
   (D) sometimes greater, sometimes less
   (E) There is not enough information to determine.

6. The specific heat of the substance in the liquid state is
   (A) 0.02 kJ/kg · °C
   (B) 0.15 kJ/kg · °C
   (C) 0.45 kJ/kg · °C
   (D) 0.62 kJ/kg · °C
   (E) 0.98 kJ/kg · °C

7. How much heat is released by the substance from the time the gas starts to condense until it completely solidifies?
   (A) 4 kJ
   (B) 8 kJ
   (C) 12 kJ
   (D) 24 kJ
   (E) 34 kJ

8. A change in temperature of 50°C is equal to a change of
   (A) 323 K
   (B) 273 K
   (C) −223 K
   (D) 100 K
   (E) 50 K

9. In an experiment, 0.02 kg of a substance is heated in a bath of boiling water until its temperature is approximately 100°C. The substance is then placed in an insulated container that is holding 0.10 kg of water at 25° C. The final equilibrium temperature of the mixture is 32°C. The specific heat of substance, in kilojoules per kilogram · degree Celsius, is
   (A) 2.16
   (B) 2.095
   (C) 2.57
   (D) 4.19
   (E) 1.0

10. A steel rod is heated from 20°C to 200°C. If the rod is originally 0.45 m long (and considered to be thin so that it expands linearly), by what percentage did the rod expand?
   (A) 0.09%
   (B) 0.216%
   (C) 0.24%
   (D) 0.15%
   (E) 0.45%

Free Response

1. Two square slabs of thicknesses d_1 and d_2 , with cross-sectional areas A_1 and A_2, have outward-facing temperatures of T_1 and T_2 ($T_2 > T_1$), respectively. Also, the two slabs are in face-to-face contact with each other and have thermal conductivities of k_1 and k_2, respectively:
   (a) Derive an expression for the temperature at the boundary where the two slabs touch.
   (b) If each slab has sides of length 0.25 m, $d_1 = 0.01$ m and $d_2 = 0.03$ m, $T_1 = 50$°C and $T_2 = 100$°C, $k_1 = 9 \times 10^{-6}$ W / m · °C and $k_2 = 15 \times 10^{-6}$ W /m · °C, calculate the value of the temperature at the boundary between the two slabs.

2. Concrete sections are poured into a sidewalk at a temperature of 15°C. Each slab has a length of 5 m. If the concrete is to reach a temperature of 60°C, what minimum spacing must the engineer allow for so that no buckling will occur in the sidewalk?

3. A Pyrex flask calibrated at 25°C is filled to the 150-mL mark with liquid acetone at 40°C. (Assume the flask is initally in equilibrium with acetone.)
   (a) What is the volume of the acetone when it is cooled to 25°C?
   (b) What is the percentage change in the volume of the flask itself compared to the change in the acetone?

Solutions

Multiple-Choice Problems

1. **C** Since the substance starts as a gas (when $t = 0$ min), the temperature at which it changes from a gas to a liquid is the boiling point. According to the graph, this occurs at 80°C.

2. **B** Since the substance became a liquid at 80°C, the next transition occurs at a temperature of 60°C, where the substance changes from a liquid to a solid.
3. **C** During the transition from gas to liquid (t = 3 min to t = 5 min), 12 kJ of heat is released. This corresponds to the heat of vaporization if we divide by the mass. Thus, 12 kJ / 2 kg = 6 kJ / kg.
4. **A** During the transition from liquid to solid (t = 6 min to t = 7 min), 6 kJ of heat has been released. Thus, the heat of fusion is 6 kJ / 2 kg = 3 kJ / kg.
5. **A** The change in temperature for both complete states is 60°C. The gas begins at t = 0 min and starts changing phase at t = 3 min. The solid begins at t = 7 min and ends at t = 12 min. Since the slope of the gas phase is larger, the corresponding specific heat is smaller since a shorter time is required to change the temperature of the gas than the temperature of the solid.
6. **B** The liquid slope begins at t = 5 min and ends at t = 6 min. Thus 6 kJ of heat has been released. The corresponding change in temperature is 20°C. The mass is 2 kg. Using our formula for specific heat, we have

$$c = \frac{6 \text{ kJ}}{(20°\text{C})(2 \text{ kg})} = 0.15 \text{ kJ / kg} \cdot °\text{C}$$

7. **D** The gas starts to condense at t = 3 min and completely solidifies at t = 7 min. Thus 4 min has elapsed. The rate of 6 kJ / min implies that 24 kJ was released during that time period.
8. **E** A *change* of 50°C is equal to a *change* of 50 K. We do not have to convert 50°C to Kelvin units since what we are interested in is the *change*!
9. **A** Since heat is conserved, the heat gained equals the heat lost. The hot substance will lose heat, and the water will gain an equal amount. Therefore we can write

$$(0.02)c(68) = (0.1)(4.19)(7)$$

Solving for the specific heat yields c = 2.16 kJ / kg · °C.
10. **B** Table 15.1 gives us 12 for the coefficient of linear expansion of steel, so $\alpha = 12 \times 10^{-6}$. Now, the percentage change in expansion is related to the fractional change in expansion multiplied by 100. Thus, using our formula:

$$\alpha \, \Delta T = (12 \times 10^{-6})(180) = 0.00216$$

and multiplying the answer by 100 gives us the percentage change: 0.216%.

Free-Response Problems

1. (a) At equilibrium, the rate of heat transfer between the two slabs must be the same. Thus we can write

$$\frac{k_1A(T - T_1)}{d_1} = \frac{k_2A(T_2 - T)}{d_2}$$

where T is the equilibrium temperature at the boundary interface. Solving for T yields the final result for part (a):

$$T = \frac{k_1d_2T_1 + k_2d_1T_2}{k_1d_2 + k_2d_1}$$

which is independent of area!

(b) Substitute all of the given numbers in the expression above to get the numerical value of T: 67.86°C.

2. This is actually a simple problem once we recognize that the minimum expansion distance for the concrete slabs is just the change in length, $\Delta\ell$.

$$\Delta\ell = \ell\alpha\,\Delta T = (5)(12 \times 10^{-6})(45) = 0.0027 \text{ m}$$

3. (a) The volume of the acetone when cooled to 25°C can be determined from a modified version of the volume-expansion formula:

$$V = V_o(1 + \beta\,\Delta T = (150)(1 + (150 \times 10^{-6})(-15)) = 149.66 \text{ mL}$$

(b) We know that

$$\Delta V_{\text{acetone}} = (\beta\,\Delta T)_{\text{acetone}} \quad \text{and} \quad \Delta V_{\text{flask}} = (\beta\,\Delta T)_{\text{flask}}$$

Now, for the same initial volume and change in temperature, we can state that

$$\frac{\Delta V_{acetone}}{\Delta V_{flask}} = \frac{\beta_{acetone}}{\beta_{Pyrex}} = \frac{150 \times 10^{-6}}{3(3.2 \times 10^{-6})} = \frac{1}{6.4 \times 10^{-2}}$$

which implies a 6.4% comparison.

CHAPTER 16

Thermodynamics and the Kinetic Theory of Gases

16.1 Pressure

Pressure is defined to be the measure of the force per unit area applied to matter. Mathematically, we can write this as

$$P = \frac{\mathbf{F}}{A}$$

and the units are newtons per square meter, or **Pascals**. The choice of pascals (Pa) as the unit of pressure reflects the use of standard SI units in this review book and most textbooks.

Pressure is measured using a barometer. One of the first barometers was developed by Evangelista Torricelli (a student of Galileo's); it consists of a dish of mercury and an inverted tube. As Figure 16.1 shows, the tube is inverted into the dish of mercury. The outside air pressure pushes down on the liquid in the dish, forcing some of it up into the tube. When equilibrium has been reached (a pressure difference creates a force and does work on a liquid by displacing it), the level of mercury can be calibrated to read the air pressure. At sea level, this height corresponds to 76 cm and is referred to as 1 atmosphere (atm) of pressure.

We can calculate the amount of air pressure in such a tube at zero degree Celsius and sea level (a condition referred to by chemists as STP, an acronym for Standard Temperature and Pressure) by recognizing that the air pressure forcing the level up is balanced by the weight of the fluid pushing the liquid down. Thus, in equilibrium, if $P = \mathbf{F} / A$, the force is equal to the weight of the column of liquid (given by the product $m\mathbf{g}$). In the tube, we have a liquid with density ρ and volume V at a height h. In the tube, $V = Ah$, and so $A = V / h$. The mass of liquid in the tube is related to the density and volume ($\rho = m / V$) so that $m = \rho V$.

Combining all these ideas, we can rewrite the pressure formula (for a column of liquid exposed to the air) as

$$P = \rho \mathbf{g} h$$

If we substitute the density of mercury, which is 13.6×10^3 kilograms per cubic meter, we find that 1 atmosphere equals 1.01×10^5 newtons per square meter, or 101 kilopascals (kPa) of pressure.

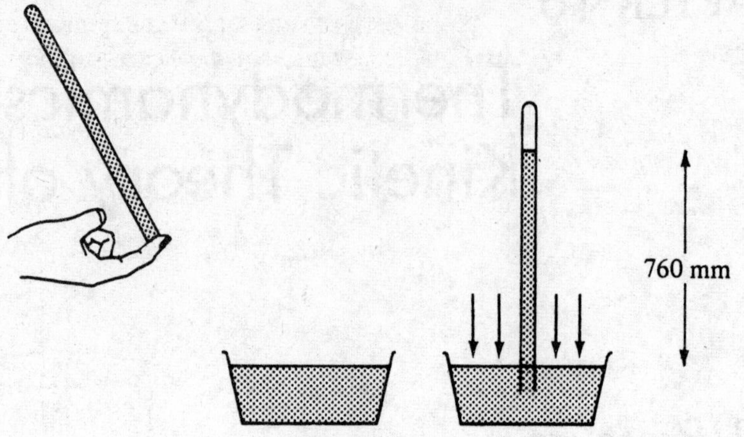

FIGURE 16.1

16.2 Molar Quantities

Under the conditions of STP, most gases behave according to a simple relationship among their pressures, volumes, and absolute temperatures. This **equation of state** applies to what is referred to as an **ideal gas**. A real gas, however, is very complex, and a large number of variables are required to understand all of the intricate movements taking place within it.

To help us understand ideal gases, we introduce a quantity called the **molar mass**. In thermodynamics (and chemistry), the molar mass or **gram-molecular mass** is defined to be the mass of a substance that contains 6.02 $\times 10^{23}$ molecules. This number is called **Avogadro's number** (N_A), and 1 mole of an ideal gas occupies a volume of 22.4 liters at zero degree Celsius. For example, the gram-molecular mass of carbon is 12 grams, while the gram-molecular mass of oxygen is 32 grams. If m represents the actual mass, the number of moles of gas is given by the relationship $n = m / M$, where M equals the gram-molecular weight. For example, 64 grams of oxygen equals 2 moles, and 36 grams of carbon equals 3 moles.

16.3 The Ideal Gas Law Equation of State

Imagine that we have an ideal gas in a sealed, insulated chamber such that no heat can escape or enter. Figure 16.2 shows an external force placed on the piston at the top of the chamber so that the pressure change causes the piston to move down. The chamber is a cylinder with cross-sectional area A and height h. If a constant force **F** is applied, work is done to move the piston (frictionless) a distance h. Thus , $W = \mathbf{F}h$, and since $h = V / A$, the work done is

$$W = \frac{\mathbf{F}V}{A} = PV$$

In other words, the work done (in this case) is equal to the product of the pressure and the volume.

If the temperature of the gas remains constant, this relationship is known as **Boyle's law** and can be expressed as

$$PV = \text{constant}$$

or

$$P_1V_1 = P_2V_2$$

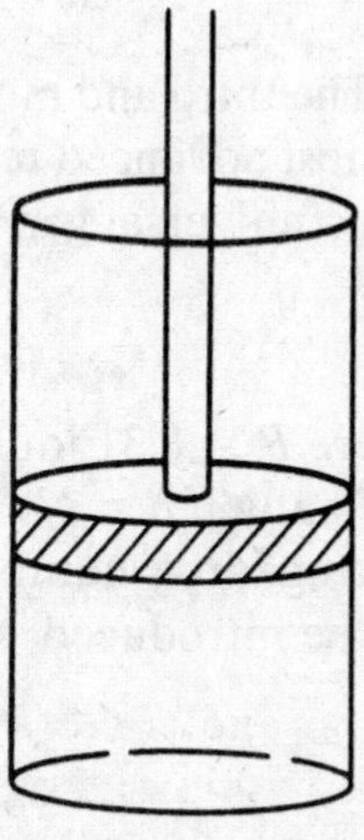

FIGURE 16.2

A graph of Boyle's law is a hyperbola, and this fact will be important when considering the subject of heat engines in Section 16.5.

Experiments demonstrate that, if a gas is enclosed in a chamber of constant volume, there is a direct relationship between the pressure in the chamber and the absolute Kelvin temperature of the gas: the ratio of pressure to absolute temperature in an ideal gas always remains constant (indicated by a diagonal, straight-line graph at constant volume). We can write this relationship algebraically as:

$$\frac{P}{T} = \text{constant}$$

or

$$\frac{P_1}{T_1} = \frac{P_2}{T_2}$$

where the temperatures must be in Kelvin units.

French scientist Jacques Charles (and, independently, Joseph Gay-Lussac) developed a relationship, commonly known as **Charles's law**, between the volume and the absolute temperature of an ideal gas at constant pressure. This law states that the ratio of volume and absolute temperature in an ideal gas remains constant; that is,

$$\frac{V_1}{T_1} = \frac{V_2}{T_2}$$

The three gas laws—pressure-temperature law, Boyle's, and Charles's—can be summarized by the one **ideal gas law**, which has four forms:

The first form is a direct consequence of all three gas laws:

$$\frac{P_1V_1}{T_1} = \frac{P_2V_2}{T_2}$$

where the temperatures must be in Kelvin units.

The second form states that the product of pressure and volume, divided by the absolute temperature, remains a constant:

$$\frac{PV}{T} = \text{constant}$$

The third and more general form of the ideal gas law (and the one found in most advanced textbooks) includes the number of moles of gas involved and a universal gas constant R:

$$PV = nRT$$

where $R = 8.31$ joules per mole · Kelvin (J / mol · K).

Finally, if $n = N / N_A$, where N is the actual number of molecules and N_A is Avogadro's number, a constant $k = R / N_A$, called **Boltzmann's constant,** can be introduced, and the ideal gas law takes the form

$$PV = NkT$$

Again, the temperatures must always be in Kelvin units. Additionally, if we express the volume in liters, the pressure in atmospheres, and the temperature in Kelvins, the number of moles, n, is given by

$$n = (12.2)\frac{PV}{T}$$

16.4 The First Law of Thermodynamics

If work is being done to an ideal gas at constant temperature, Boyle's law states that the work done is equal to the product of the pressure and the volume (this product remaining constant). A graph of Boyle's law, seen in Figure 16.3, is a hyperbola. Pressure and volume changes that include temperature changes and are adiabatic obey a different kind of inverse relationship, in which the volume is raised to a higher exponential power (making the hyperbola steeper). We will encounter these kinds of curves in Section 16.5.

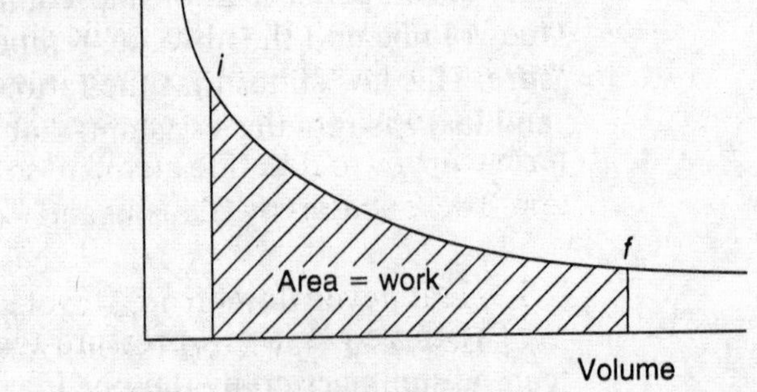

FIGURE 16.3

The pressure versus volume diagram for Boyle's law shows that the area enclosed by the curve from some initial state to a final state is equal to the work done.

The **first law of thermodynamics** is basically the law of conservation of energy. Let ΔQ represent the change in heat energy supplied to a system, ΔU represent the change in internal molecular energy, and ΔW represent the amount of net work done by the system. Then the first law of thermodynamics states that

$$\Delta Q = \Delta U + \Delta W$$

In thermodynamics, certain terms are often used and are worth defining:

Isothermal means "constant temperature."
Isobaric means "constant pressure."
Isochoric means "constant volume."

An example of the application of each term is shown in Figure 16.4 in a pressure versus volume diagram.

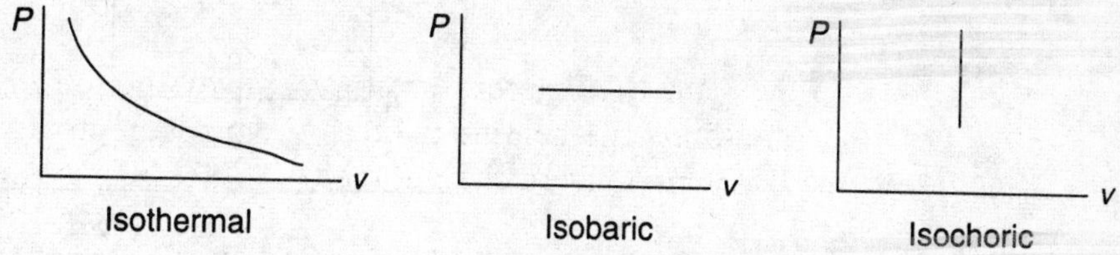

FIGURE 16.4

16.5 The Second Law of Thermodynamics and Heat Engines

No system is ideal. When a machine is manufactured and operated, heat is always lost because of friction. This friction creates heat that can be accounted for by the law of conservation of energy. Recall that heat flows from a hotter body to a cooler body. Thus, if there is a reservoir of heat at high temperature, the system will draw energy from that reservoir (hence its name). Only a certain amount of energy is needed to do work, so the remainder, if any, is released as exhaust at a lower temperature. This phenomenon was investigated by a French physicist named Sadi Carnot. Carnot was interested in the cyclic changes that take place in a heat engine, which converts thermal energy into mechanical energy.

In the nineteenth century, German physicist Rudolf Clausius coined the term *entropy* to describe an increase in the randomness or disorder of a system. These studies by Clausius and Carnot can be summarized as follows:

1. Heat never flows from a cooler to a hotter body of its own accord.
2. Heat can never be taken from a reservoir without something else happening in the system.
3. The entropy of the universe is always increasing.

These three statements embody the **second law of thermodynamics**: it is impossible to construct a cyclical machine that produces no other effect than to transfer heat continuously from one body to another at higher temperature.

Connected with the second law of thermodynamics is the concept of a reversible process. Heat flows spontaneously from hot to cold, and this action is irreversible unless acted upon by an outside agent. A system may be reversible if it passes from the initial to the final state by way of some intermediary equilibrium states. This reversible process, which can be represented on a pressure versus volume diagram, was studied extensively by Carnot.

Consider the simple Carnot cycle shown in Figure 16.5.

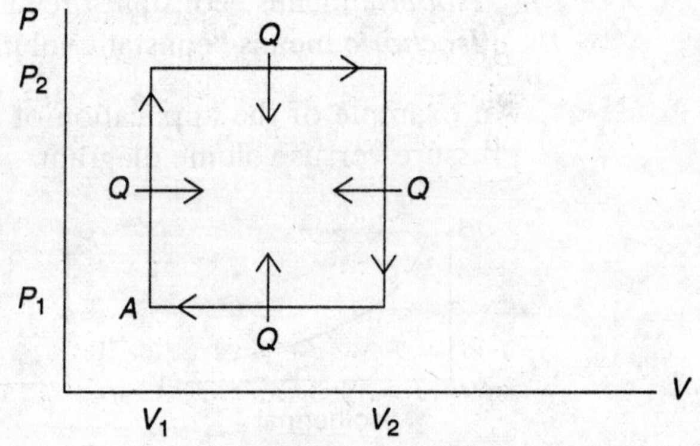

FIGURE 16.5

To change the system from P_1 to P_2 isochorically, heat must be supplied and the temperature will rise. Now, because of the pressure change, we allow the gas to expand isobarically from (P_2,V_1) to (P_2,V_2). The gas is doing work to expand so we supply energy to replace whatever is lost. Now, suppose we allow the system to cool by placing it in contact with a reservoir at lower temperature. If cooling is to occur isochorically from P_2 back to P_1 at the same volume, additional energy must again be added to the system from the outside. Finally, we allow the gas to contract from V_2 to V_1 isobarically. The temperature will decrease according to Charles's law, so additional energy must be supplied.

In each isochoric change, $\Delta W = 0$ since there were no changes in volume. During isobaric changes,

$$\Delta W_2 = P_2(V_2 - V_1) \quad \text{and} \quad \Delta W_1 = P_1(V_1 - V_2)$$

The net work is equal to $(P_2 - P_1)(V_2 - V_1)$ and would be equal to the area of the rectangle in Figure 16.5.

A Carnot cycle in which adiabatic temperature changes occur is shown in Figure 16.6.

The isothermal changes occur from A to B and from C to D. The adiabatic changes are represented by segments BC and AD, in which no heat is gained or lost. Therefore, heat must be added in segment AB and

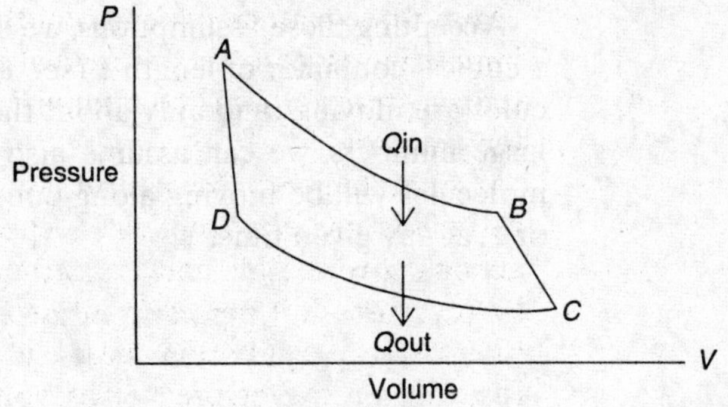

FIGURE 16.6

released in CD. In other words, there is an isothermal expansion in AB at a temperature T_1. Heat is absorbed from the reservoir, and work is done. BC represents an adiabatic expansion in which an insulator has been placed in the container of the gas. The temperature falls, and work is done. In CD, we have an isothermal compression when the container is connected to a reservoir of temperature T_2 that is lower than T_1. Heat is released in this process, and work is done. Finally, in DA, the gas is compressed adiabatically and work is done. The total work done would be equal to the area of the figure enclosed by the graph.

The efficiency of this "heat engine" is given by the fractional ratio between the total work done and the original amount of heat added:

$$\text{Efficiency} = \frac{W}{Q_1} = 1 - \frac{Q_2}{Q_1}$$

The reason is that the net work done in one cycle is equal to the net heat transferred ($Q_1 - Q_2$), since the change in internal energy is zero. If we use Kelvin temperatures, we can write

$$\text{Efficiency} = 1 - \frac{T_2}{T_1}$$

where $T_1 > T_2$ and both temperatures are in Kelvin units.

16.6 The Kinetic Theory of Gases

Six assumptions are made for the kinetic theory of gases:

1. All gases consist of very large numbers of molecules, and the separations between molecules are large compared with the molecular sizes.
2. Collectively the molecules obey Newton's laws of motion, but individually the molecules move randomly.
3. The molecules undergo elastic collisions with each other.
4. The forces between molecules are neglible except during a collision.
5. The gas involved at any time is a pure gas.
6. The gas is in thermal equilibrium with the walls of the container.

Accepting these assumptions, we imagine that such a gas is contained in a cubical container of length ℓ (see Figure 16.7). We suppose that N molecules are moving randomly about the container. Under the assumption of large numbers, we can assume also that approximately one-third of the molecules will be moving along one of the principal coordinate axes, x, y, or z, at any given time.

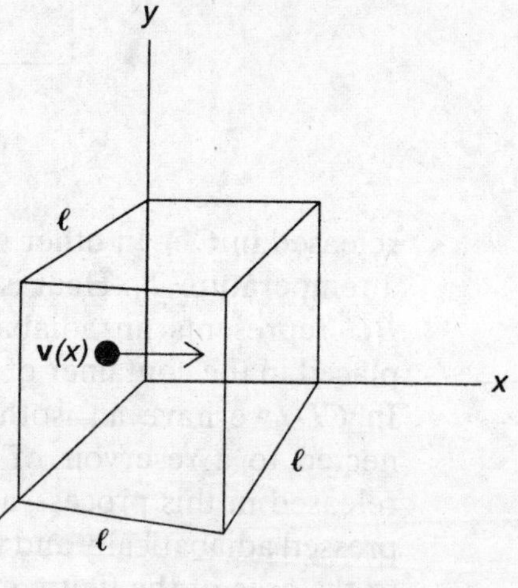

FIGURE 16.7

We imagine one molecule of mass M moving from one side of the container horizontally to the other with a constant horizontal velocity $\mathbf{v}$. The molecule has a momentum $M\mathbf{v}$ in the x-direction. If an elastic collision takes place with one of the walls, the magnitude of the change in momentum will be $2M\mathbf{v}$.

In a time t, the distance traveled by the molecule will equal to $\mathbf{v}t$. Since the round-trip distance is 2ℓ, the total number of round trips is given by $\mathbf{v}t / 2\ell$. Thus, in time t, the total change in momentum for this molecule is given by $M\mathbf{v}^2t/\ell$. The change in momentum is equal to the impulse applied to the molecule. Hence, if we divide the change in momentum by the time, the result is equal to the average force applied and we can state that

$$F = M\frac{\mathbf{v}^2}{\ell}$$

The total force on the wall is the sum of all such terms, and the total pressure will be the total force divided by the area of the wall. Since we have $N/3$ molecules in the x-direction moving with some average velocity $\overline{\mathbf{v}}_x$, what we need is the average of the squares of the velocities. If we divide the force by the area, we end up with the cube of the length of a side of the container, ℓ^3, which equals the volume V.

The final expression will be the pressure exerted on the wall in the x-direction. Now, we know that, for all three directions, we have equally probable average velocities. Thus the average of the squares of the velocities in the three directions is just one-third of the average of the square of the actual velocity. Therefore, the final expression for the pressure will be

$$P = \left(\frac{N}{3}\right)\left(\frac{M}{V}\right)\overline{\mathbf{v}^2}$$

where v is the actual velocity. Rearranging this expression, we see that the pressure is proportional to twice the average kinetic energy of the molecules (at constant volume):

$$PV = \frac{2}{3}N(KE_{avg})$$

where $KE_{avg} = (1/2)M\overline{v^2}$. This is the kinetic theory equivalent of the ideal gas law derived in Section 16.3.

If we recall that $PV = NkT$, where the temperature T is in Kelvin, we can write that the absolute temperature is proportional to the average kinetic energy of the molecules:

$$T = \frac{2}{3k}\left(\frac{1}{2}M\overline{v^2}\right)$$

The average kinetic energy can also be expressed as $KE_{avg} = (3/2)kT$, and the square root of $\overline{v^2}$, called the **root mean square velocity**, can be written as

$$\mathbf{v}_{\mathbf{rms}} = \sqrt{\frac{3kT}{M}}$$

If we let m represent the molecular mass, usually expressed in units of grams per mole, the magnitude of the root mean square velocity can be written as:

$$\mathbf{v}_{\mathbf{rms}} = \sqrt{\frac{3RT}{m}}$$

Finally, the change in internal energy, ΔU, is given by the expression

$$\Delta U = \frac{3}{2}nRT$$

where $R = 8.31$ joules per mole.

16.7 Heat Capacities of Gases

The molar heat capacity of a monatomic gas is based on the fact that the only contribution to the total internal energy of the gas is the translational kinetic energy of the molecules. If a quantity of heat ΔQ is supplied to the gas, either the internal energy will change or work will be done by the system. If we specify that no work is to be done, then

$$\Delta Q = \Delta U = \frac{3}{2}R\,\Delta T \text{ per mole.}$$

Thus we define the molar heat capacity of the gas at constant volume as

$$c_V = \frac{\Delta Q}{\Delta T} = \frac{3}{2} R$$

in units of calories per mole · Kelvin (cal/mol · K). For all monatomic gases, the molar heat capacities are the same, but the specific heat capacities (the heat capacities per gram) differ.

If we allow work to be done on the monatomic gas, we can define the molar specific heat at constant pressure. First, if work is done, then

$$\Delta Q = \Delta U + P\,\Delta V$$

From the ideal gas law, if P is constant, then $P\,\Delta V = R\,\Delta T$. Thus,

$$\Delta Q = \frac{3}{2} R\,\Delta T + R\,\Delta T = \frac{5}{2} R\,\Delta T$$

and

$$c_p = \frac{5}{2} R$$

Also,

$$\Delta Q = nc_p\,\Delta T$$

For diatomic gases, the molar specific heat at constant volume is equal to $(5/2)R$, and the molar heat capacity at constant pressure is equal to $(7/2)R$. The ratio of heat capacities, γ, can be written as

$$\gamma = \frac{c_P}{c_V}$$

For monatomic gases $\gamma = 1.67$, and for diatomic gases $\gamma = 1.4$.

Finally, we can note that

$$c_P - c_V = R$$

Sample Problem:

Twenty cubic meters of an ideal gas is at 50°C and at a pressure of 50 kPa. If the temperature is raised to 200°C, and the volume is compressed by half, what is the new pressure of the gas?

Solution:

We must first change all temperatures to Kelvin units:

$$50°\text{C} = 323\text{ K} \quad \text{and} \quad 200°\text{C} = 473\text{ K}$$

We now use the ideal gas law for two sets of conditions:

$$\frac{P_1 V_1}{T_1} = \frac{P_2 V_2}{T_2}$$

Substituting the appropriate values, we get

$$\frac{(50)(20)}{323} = \frac{(P_2)(10)}{473}$$

Solving for the pressure gives $P_2 = 146.4$ kPa.

Problem-Solving Strategies for Thermodynamics and the Kinetic Theory of Gases

It is important to remember that all temperatures must be converted to Kelvin units before doing any calculations. Also, since the units for the gas constant R and Boltzmann's constant k are in SI units, all masses or molecular masses must be in kilograms. For example, the molecular mass of nitrogen is usually given as 28 grams per mole. However, in an actual calculation, this must be converted to 0.028 kilogram per mole.

You also should remember that, unless a comparison relationship is used (such as Boyle's law or the preceding sample problem), all pressures must be in units of pascals (not kilopascals, atmospheres, or centimeters of mercury) and all volumes must be in cubic meters. However, in a comparison relationship, the chosen units are irrelevant (except for temperature, which is always in Kelvins), and you can use atmospheres for pressure, or liters (1 liter = 1000 cubic centimeters) for volume. The molar specific heat capacities depend on the number of moles, not the number of grams (the specific heat capacity).

Practice Problems for Chapter 16

Multiple Choice

1. At constant temperature, an ideal gas is at a pressure of 30 cm of mercury and a volume of 5 L. If the pressure is increased to 65 cm of mercury, the new volume will be
(A) 10.8 L
(B) 2.3 L
(C) 0.43 L
(D) 1.7 L
(E) 5.6 L

2. At constant volume, an ideal gas is heated from 75°C to 150°C. The original pressure was 1.5 atm. After heating, the pressure will be
(A) doubled
(B) halved
(C) the same
(D) less than doubled
(E) quadrupled

3. At constant pressure, 6 m^3 of an ideal gas at 75°C is cooled until its volume is halved. The new temperature of the gas will be
(A) 174°C
(B) 447°C
(C) −99°C
(D) 37.5°C
(E) 100°C

4. Water is used in an open-tube barometer. If the density of water is 1000 kg/m^3, what will be the level of the column of water at sea level?
(A) 10.3 m
(B) 12.5 m
(C) 13.6 m
(D) 11.2 m
(E) 9.7 m

5. As the temperature of an ideal gas increases, the average kinetic energy of its molecules
(A) increases, then decreases
(B) decreases
(C) remains the same
(D) decreases, then increases
(E) increases

6. The product of pressure and volume is expressed in units of
(A) pascals
(B) kilograms per newton
(C) watts
(D) joules
(E) newtons

7. Which of the following is equivalent to 1 Pa of gas pressure?
(A) $1\ kg/s^2$
(B) $1\ kg \cdot m / s$
(C) $1\ kg \cdot m^2/s^2$
(D) $1\ kg/m \cdot s^2$
(E) 1 kg/m

8. What is the efficiency of a heat engine that performs 700 J of useful work from a reservoir of 2700 J?
(A) 74%
(B) 26%
(C) 35%
(D) 65%
(E) 50%

9. Hydrogen has a molecular mass of 2 g / mole, while oxygen has a molecular mass of 32 g / mole. At the same temperature, the molecular velocity of hydrogen, as compared to the molecular velocity of oxygen, is
(A) one-fourth
(B) one-sixteenth
(C) four times greater
(D) 16 times greater
(E) the same

10. Given that the molecular mass of hydrogen is 2 g / mole, what is its molecular velocity at a temperature of 27°C?
(A) 1933 m/s
(B) 61.2 m/s

(C) 3745 m/s
(D) 580 m/s
(E) 360 m/s

Free Response

1. (a) How many molecules of helium are required to fill a balloon with a diameter of 50 cm at a temperature of 27°C?
   (b) What is the average kinetic energy of each molecule of helium?
   (c) What is the average velocity of each molecule of helium?
2. An engine absorbs 2000 J of heat from a hot reservoir and expels 750 J to a cold reservoir during each operating cycle.
   (a) What is the efficiency of the engine?
   (b) How much work is done during each cycle?
   (c) What is the power output of the engine if each cycle lasts for 0.5 s?
3. A monatomic ideal gas undergoes a reversible process as shown in the pressure versus volume diagram below:

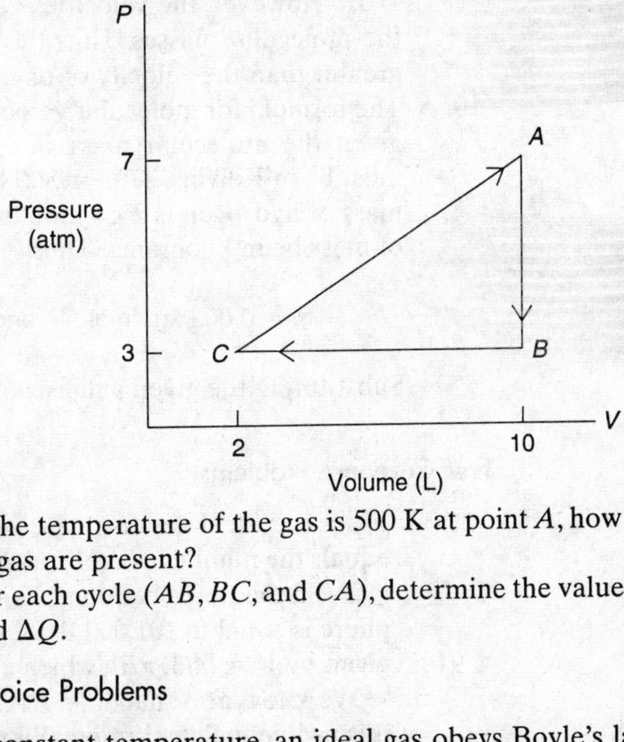

   (a) If the temperature of the gas is 500 K at point A, how many moles of gas are present?
   (b) For each cycle (AB, BC, and CA), determine the values of ΔW, ΔU, and ΔQ.

Solutions

Multiple-Choice Problems

1. **B** At constant temperature, an ideal gas obeys Boyle's law. Since we are making a two-position comparison, we can use the given units for pressure and volume. Substituting the given values into Boyle's law, we obtain (30)(5) = (65)(V_2), which implies that V_2 = 2.3 L.
2. **D** At constant volume, the changes in pressure are directly proportional to the changes in absolute Kelvin temperature. Therefore, even though the Celsius temperature is being doubled, the Kelvin temperature is not! Thus, the new pressure must be less than doubled.

   Alternatively, you can calcluate the new pressure since 75°C = 348 K and 150°C = 423 K. Thus 1.5 / 348 = P_2 / 423, and P_2 = 1.8 atm (less than double). Again, since a comparison relationship is involved, we can keep the pressure in atmospheres for convenience.

3. **C** This is a Charles's law problem, and the temperatures must be in Kelvin units. Since 75°C = 348 K, we can write that 6 / 348 = 3 / T_2. However, the volume change is directly proportional to the Kelvin temperature change. Thus T_2 = 174 K = −99°C.
4. **A** The formula for pressure is $P = \rho gh$. The density of water is 1000 kg/m³, and g = 9.8 m/s². We also know that at sea level P = 101 kPa, which must be converted to pascals or newtons per square meter. Thus $h = P / \rho g$, and making the necessary substitutions gives h = 10.3 m (a very large barometer over 35 ft tall!).
5. **E** The absolute temperature of an ideal gas is directly proportional to the average kinetic energy of its molecules. Hence, the average kinetic energy increases with temperature.
6. **D** The units of the product PV are joules, the units of energy.
7. **D** One pascal is equivalent to 1 N/m², but 1 N is equal to 1 kg · m/s². Thus the final equivalency is 1 kg · m²/s².
8. **B** Efficiency = (700 J/2700 J) × 100% = 26%.
9. **C** The ratio of the molecular masses of oxygen and hydrogen is 32 / 2 = 16. However, the velocities vary inversely as the square roots of the molecular masses. Thus the velocity of hydrogen is four times greater than the velocity of oxygen at the same temperature.
10. **A** The formula for molecular velocity (the root mean square velocity), given the molecular mass, is $v_{rms} = \sqrt{3RT/m}$. The temperature T must be in Kelvins; 27°C = 300 K. Also, even though the molecular mass of hydrogen is 2 g / mol, the equation demands that the units of mass be in kilograms! Thus

$$m = 0.002 \text{ kg / mol} \quad \text{and} \quad R = 8.31 \text{ J / mol}$$

Substituting the given values we get v_{rms} = 1933 m/s .

Free-Response Problems

1. (a) From the ideal gas formula, we know that $PV = NkT$, where N equals the number of molecules and k is Boltzmann's constant. For a 50-cm-diameter balloon, the radius will be 0.25 m. One atmosphere is equal to 101,000 Pa of pressure. The volume of a sphere is given by $V = (4/3)\pi R^3$, which equals 0.065 m³ upon substitution.

We know also that $N = PV / kT$, where T is equal to 300 K in this problem. Substituting all known values gives

$$N = \frac{(101{,}000)(0.065)}{(1.38 \times 10^{-23})(300)} = 1.59 \times 10^{24} \text{ molecules}$$

(b) The average kinetic energy of each molecule is equal to

$$\overline{KE} = \frac{3}{2}kT = (1.5)(1.38 \times 10^{-23})(300) = 6.21 \times 10^{-21} \text{ J}$$

(c) The average velocity of each molecule is given by

$$v_{rms} = \sqrt{\frac{3RT}{m}} = \sqrt{\frac{(3)(8.31)(300)}{0.004}} = 1367 \text{m/s}$$

2. (a) The efficiency of the heat engine is given by the formula

$$e = \frac{\Delta Q}{Q_{hot}} = \frac{2000 - 750}{2000} = 0.625 \text{ or } 62.5\%$$

(b) The work done during each cycle is equal to

$$\Delta Q = 2000 - 750 = 1250 \text{ J}$$

(c) The power output each cycle equals the work done divided by the time:

$$P = \frac{1250}{0.5} = 2500 \text{ W}$$

3. (a) Since we know the pressure, volume, and absolute temperature of the ideal (monatomic) gas at point A, we can use the ideal gas law, $PV = nRT$, to find the number of moles, n.

First, however, we must be in standard units: 7 atm = 707,000 Pa, and since 1 L = 0.001 m^3, then 10 L = 0.01 m^3. Thus:

$$n = \frac{(707{,}000)(0.01)}{(8.31)(500)} = 1.7 \text{ moles of gas}$$

(b) i. The cycle AB is isochoric, and so

$$\Delta W = 0$$

Thus, $\Delta U = \Delta Q$. Now, as the pressure decreases from 7 atm to 3 atm, the absolute temperature decreases proportionally. Thus we can write

$$\frac{7}{500} = \frac{3}{T_B}$$

which implies that the absolute temperature at point B is equal to 214.29 K. To find the change in the internal energy, we recall that

$$\Delta U = \frac{3}{2} nR\,\Delta T = (1.5)(1.7)(8.31)(-285.7) =$$
$$-6054 \text{ J} = \Delta Q \text{ also!}$$

ii. The cycle BC is isobaric, and the decrease in volume from 10 L to 2 L is accompanied by a corresponding decrease in absolute temperature. We know from step (i) that the temperature at B is 214.29 K, so we can use Charles's law to find the temperature at point C. Also, the work done is negative since we are expelling energy to reduce pressure and volume. We can therefore write

$$\frac{10}{214.29} = \frac{2}{T_C}$$

which implies that the absolute temperature at point C is equal to 42.86 K. Therefore $\Delta T = -171.43$ K.

Now, in this process, work is done to compress the gas, and $W = P\,(V_C - V_B)$. The pressure is constant at $P = 3$ atm $=$ 303,000 Pa, and $\Delta V = -8$ L $= -0.008$ m³.
Thus

$$\Delta W = (303{,}000)(-0.008) = -2424 \text{ J}$$

To find ΔU, we note that the temperature change of the 1.7 moles was -171.43 K, and so

$$\Delta U = (1.5)(1.7)(8.31)(-171.43) = -3632.69 \text{ J}$$

To find ΔQ, we use the first law of thermodynamics:

$$\Delta Q = \Delta U + \Delta W = -3632.69 - 2424 = -6057 \text{ J}$$

iii. The last part of the reversible cycle puts back all the work and energy, a total of 12,111 J of heat (the sum of ΔQ in steps i and ii), that was removed in the first two steps. Thus, for CA,

$$\Delta Q = +12{,}111 \text{ J}$$

In a similar way, the total change in internal energy equaled -9686.69 J. Thus, in cycle CA,

$$\Delta U = +\,9686.69 \text{ J}$$

Finally,

$$\Delta W = \Delta Q - \Delta U = 12{,}111 - 9686.69 = 2424.31 \text{ J}$$

Notice that, since no work was done in step i, this is approximately equal to the work done in step ii!

CHAPTER 17

Electrostatics

17.1 The Nature of Electric Charges

The ancient Greeks used to rub pieces of amber on wool or fur. The amber was then able to pick up small objects that were not made of metal. The Greek word for amber was *elektron* (ελεκτρον)—hence the term ***electric***. The pieces of amber would retain their attractive property for some time, so the effect appears to have been **static**. The amber acted differently from magnetic ores (lodestones), naturally occurring rocks that attract only metallic objects.

In modern times, hard rubber, such as ebonite, is used with cloth or fur to dramatically demonstrate the properties of electrostatic force. If you rub an ebonite rod with cloth and then bring it near a small cork sphere painted silver (called a "pith ball") and suspended on a thin thread, the pith ball will be attracted to the rod. When the ball and rod touch each other, the pith ball will be repelled. If a glass rod that has been rubbed with silk is then brought near the pith ball, the ball will be attracted to the rod. If you touch the pith ball with your hand, the pith ball will return to its normal state.

In the nineteenth century, chemical experiments to explain these effects showed the presence of molecules called **ions** in solution. These ions possessed similar affinities for certain objects, such as carbon or metals, placed in the solution. These objects are called **electrodes**. The experiments confirmed the existence of two types of ions, **positive** and **negative**. The effects they produce are similar to the two types of effects produced when ebonite and glass are rubbed. Even though both substances attract small objects, these objects become **charged** oppositely when rubbed, as indicated by the behavior of the pith ball. Further, chemical experiments coupled with an atomic theory demonstrated that in solids it is the negative charges that are transferred. Additional experiments by Michael Faraday in England during the first half of the nineteenth century suggested the existence of a single, fundamental carrier of **electric charge**, which was later named the **electron**. The corresponding carrier of positive charge was termed the **proton**.

The essentially neutral condition of all matter is due to the balance of charges in atoms that contain equal numbers of protons and electrons. Ions consist of atoms or molecules that contain more or fewer electrons compared to protons. When an acid is placed in a solution, it dissociates itself into positive and negative ions. When ebonite is rubbed with cloth, electrons are transferred to the ebonite, giving it a net negative charge (leaving the cloth positive).

17.2 The Detection and Measurement of Electric Charges

When ebonite is rubbed with cloth, only the part of the rod in contact with the cloth becomes charged. The charge remains localized for some time (hence the name *static*). For this reason, among others, rubber, along with plastic and glass, is called an **insulator**. A metal rod held in your hand cannot be charged statically for two reasons. First, metals are **conductors**; that is, they allow electric charges to flow through them. Second, your body is a conductor, and any charges placed in the metal rod are conducted out through you (and into the Earth). This effect is called **grounding**. The silver-coated pith balls mentioned in Section 17.1 can become statically charged because they are suspended by thread, which is an insulator. They can be used to detect the presence and sign of an electric charge, but they are not very helpful in obtaining a qualitative measurement of the magnitude of charge they possess.

An instrument that is often used for qualitative measurement is the **electroscope**. One form of electroscope consists of two "leaves" made of gold foil (Figure 17.1a). The leaves are vertical when the electroscope is uncharged. As a negatively charged rod is brought near, the leaves diverge. If we recall the hypothesis that only negative charges move in solids, we can understand that the electrons in the knob of the electroscope are repelled down to the leaves through the conducting stem. The knob becomes positively charged, as can be verified with a charged pith ball, as long as the rod is near but not touching (Figure 17.1b). Upon contact, electrons are directly transferred to the knob, stem, and leaves. The whole electroscope then becomes negatively charged (Figure 17.1c). The extent to which the leaves are spread apart is an indication of how much charge is present (but only qualitatively). If you touch the electroscope, you will ground it and the leaves will collapse together.

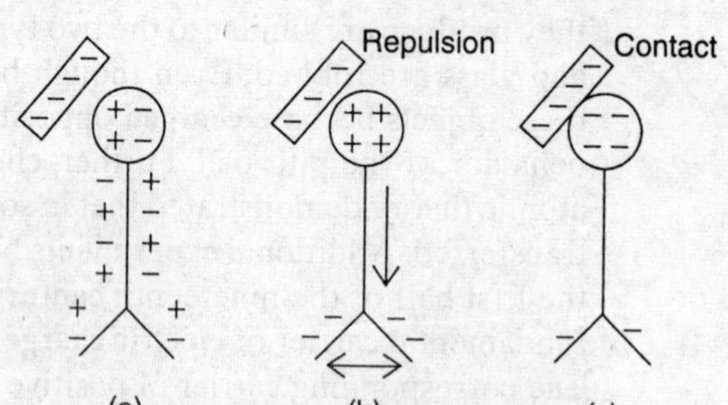

FIGURE 17.1

The electroscope can also be charged by **induction**. If you touch the electroscope shown in Figure 17.1b with your finger when the electroscope is brought near (see Figure 17.2a), the repelled electrons will be forced out into your body. If you remove your finger, keeping the rod near, the electroscope will be left with an overall positive charge by induction (Figure 17.2b).

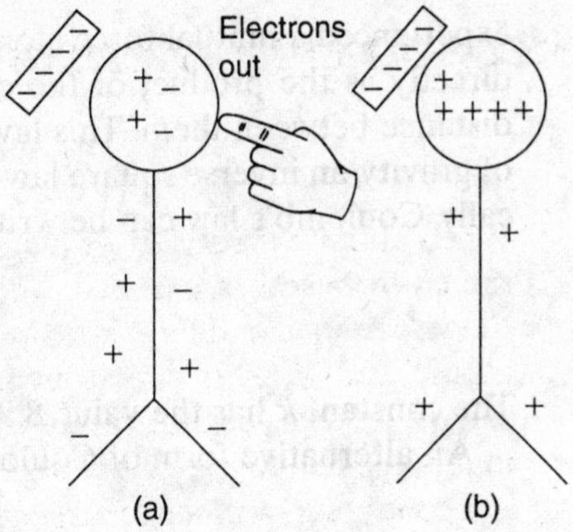

FIGURE 17.2

Finally, we can state that electric charges, in any distribution, obey a conservation law. When we transfer charge, we always maintain a balanced accounting. Suppose we have two charged metal spheres. Sphere A has $+5$ elementary charges, and sphere B has a $+1$ elementary charge (thus both are positively charged). The two spheres are brought into contact. Which way will charges flow? Negative charges always flow from a higher concentration to a lower one, and sphere B has an overall greater negative tendency (since it is less positive). Upon contact, it will give up negative charges until equilibrium is achieved. Notice that it is only the excess charges that flow out of the countless numbers of total charges in the sphere! A little arithmetic shows that sphere B will give up two negative charges, leaving it with an overall charge of $+3$. Sphere A will gain the two negative charges, reducing its charge to $+3$. If the two spheres are separated, each will have $+3$ elementary charges.

17.3 Coulomb's Law

From Sections 17.1 and 17.2, we can conclude that like charges repel each other while unlike charges attract. The electrostatic force between two charged objects can act through space and even a vacuum. This property makes electrostatic force similar to the force of gravity. However, there are two key differences (other than the fact that charge and mass are two different physical quantities). First, gravity always attracts, whereas electrostatic force can either repel or attract, depending on the sign of the charges. Second, charge is relativistically invariant. Therefore, unlike mass, which can actually vary as an object's velocity approaches the speed of light (see Chapter 25), electric charge remains observationally the same in any frame of reference, regardless of whether the frame is accelerating or moving at a constant velocity.

In the SI system of units, charge is measured in **coulombs** (C). In the late eighteenth century, the nature of the electrostatic force was studied by French scientist Charles Coulomb. He discovered that the force between two point charges (designated as q_1 and q_2), separated by a distance r, experienced a mutual force along a line connecting the charges that varied directly as the product of the charges and inversely as the square of the distance between them. This law, known as **Coulomb's law**, is, like the law of gravity, an inverse square law acting on matter at a distance. Mathematically, Coulomb's law can be written as

$$\mathbf{F} = \frac{kq_1q_2}{r^2}$$

The constant k has the value $8.9875 \times 10^9 \approx 9 \times 10^9$ N · m²/C².

An alternative form of Coulomb's law is

$$\mathbf{F} = \left(\frac{1}{4\pi\epsilon_0}\right)\frac{q_1q_2}{r^2}$$

The new constant, ϵ_0, is called the **permittivity of free space** or **permittivity of the vacuum** and has a value of 8.8542×10^{-12} C²/N · m². In the SI system, one elementary charge is designated as e and has a magnitude of 1.6×10^{-19} C.

Coulomb's law, like Newton's law of universal gravitation, is a vector equation. The direction of the force is along a radial vector connecting the two point sources. It should be noted that Coulomb's law applies only to point sources (or to sources that can be treated as point sources, such as charged spheres). If we have a distribution of point charges, the net force on one charge is the vector sum of all the other electrostatic forces. This aspect of force addition is sometimes termed **superposition.**

17.4 The Electric Field

Another way to consider the force between two point charges is to recall that the force can act through free space. If a charged sphere has charge $+Q$, and a small test charge $+q$ is brought near it, the test charge will be repelled according to Coulomb's law. Everywhere, the test charge will be repelled along a radial vector out from charge $+Q$. We can state that, even if charge $+Q$ is too small to be visible, the influence of the electrostatic force can be observed and measured (since charges have mass and $\mathbf{F} = m\mathbf{a}$ as usual).

In this way, charge $+Q$ is said to set up an electric field, which pervades the space surrounding the charge and produces a force on any other charge that enters the field (just as a gravitational field does). The strength of the electric field, **E**, is defined to be the measure of the force per unit charge experienced at a particular location. In other words,

$$\mathbf{E} = \frac{\mathbf{F}}{q},$$

and the units are newtons per coulomb (N/C). The electric field strength **E** is a vector quantity since it is derived from the force (a vector) and the charge (a scalar).

An illustration of this situation is given in Figure 17.3. Charge $+Q$ is represented by a charged sphere drawn as a circle. A small positive test charge, $+q$, is brought near and repelled along a radial vector r drawn outward from charge $+Q$. In fact, anywhere in the vicinity of charge $+Q$, the test charge will be repelled along an outward radial vector. We therefore draw these **force field lines** as radial vectors coming out from charge $+Q$.

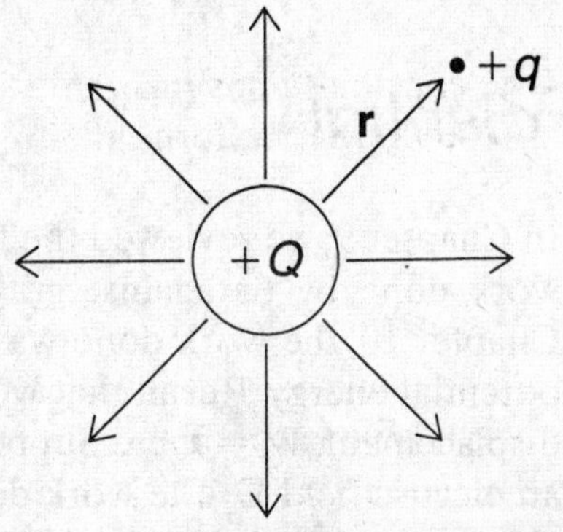

FIGURE 17.3

By convention, we always consider the test charge to be positive. Since the force varies according to Coulomb's law, the electric field strength **E** will also vary, depending on the location of the test charge (we assume that it and the main charge remain constant in magnitude). Thus, we can write

$$\mathbf{E} = \frac{F}{q} = \frac{kQ}{r^2} = \left(\frac{1}{4\pi\epsilon_0}\right)\frac{Q}{r^2}$$

We can also interpret field strength by observing the density of field lines per square meter. With point charges, the radial nature of their construction causes the field lines to converge near the surface of the charge, Q indicating a relative increase in field strength. In Section 17.5, we will encounter a configuration in which the field strength remains constant throughout.

There are several other configurations of electric field lines that we can consider. In Figure 17.4, the field between two point charges, with different arrangements of signs, is illustrated. Notice that the field lines are always

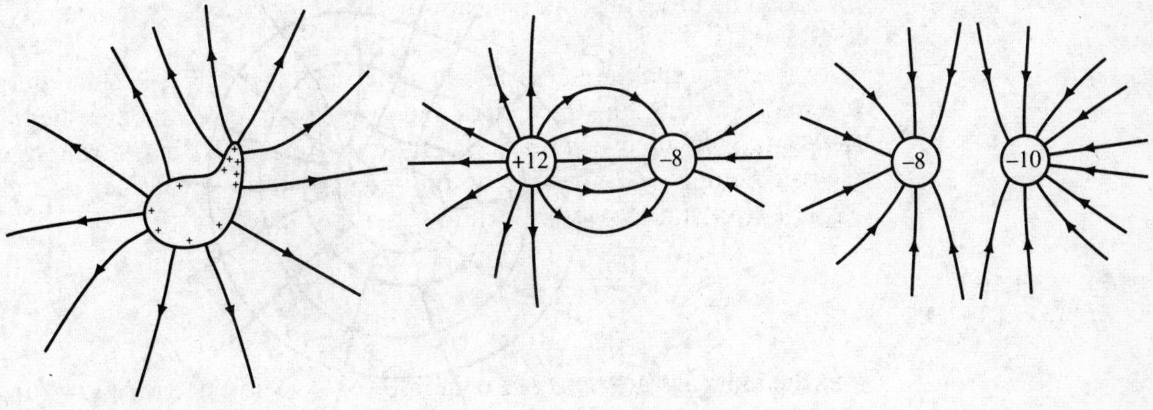

FIGURE 17.4

perpendicular to the "surface" of the source and that they never cross each other. Additionally, between two like charges the electric field is zero. This fact can be extended to the idea that the electric field inside a hollow conducting sphere is zero, and all of the charges reside on the surface of the sphere.

The arrows on the field lines always indicate the direction in which a positive test charge would move.

17.5 Electric Potential

In Chapter 9, we reviewed the fact that gravity is a conservative force. Any work done by or against gravity is independent of the path taken. In Chapter 10, the work done was measured as a change in the gravitational potential energy. Recall that work is equal to the magnitude of force times displacement, $W = \mathbf{F}\,\Delta x$. Suppose that the force is acting on a charge q in an electric field $\mathbf{E}$. The work done by or against the electric field, which is also a conservative field, is given by

$$W = \mathbf{E}q\,\Delta r \text{ (in one dimension, radially).}$$

Since the electrostatic force is conservative, the work done should be equal to the change in the electrical potential energy between two points, A and B.

These two points cannot be just anywhere in the field. Consider the original electric field diagram in Figure 17.3. If test charge $+q$ is a distance r from source charge $+Q$, it will experience a certain radial force whose magnitude is given by Coulomb's law. At any position around the source, at a distance r, we can observe that the test charge will experience the same force. The localized potential energy will be the same as well. The set of all such positions defines a circle of radius r (actually a sphere in three dimensions), called an **equipotential surface**.

Figure 17.5 shows a series of equipotential "curves" or varying radii. Since the electric field is conservative, work is done by or against the field only when a charge is moved from one equipotential surface to another. To

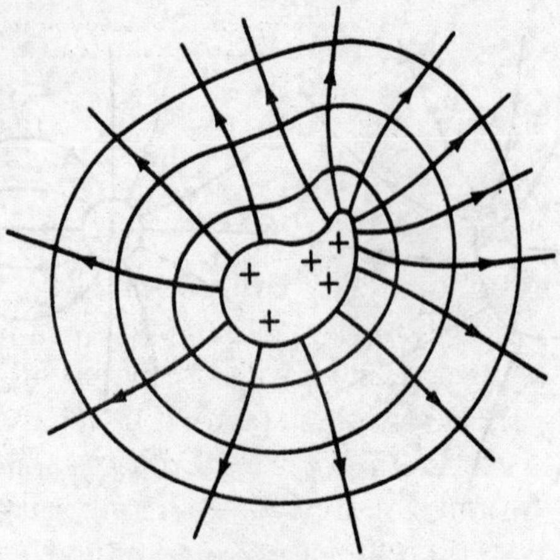

FIGURE 17.5

better understand this effect, we define a quantity called the **electric potential**, which is a measure of the magnitude of electrical potential energy per unit charge at a particular location in the field. Thus, the work done per unit charge, in moving from equipotential surface A to equipotential surface B, is a measure of what is called the **potential difference** or **voltage**.

Thus we define V to be the potential difference ($V_A - V_B$) and to be equal to W / q, and so the units of potential difference are joules per coulomb (J/C) or **volts**. Since $W = \mathbf{E}_q \, \Delta r$, calculating the work can be difficult if the electric field can vary (as in the case of a point source). However, if we can find a configuration in which the electric field is uniform, **E** becomes a constant. Since potential difference is the work done per charge, we see that $V = \mathbf{E} \, \Delta r$. The units of electric field strength can now be defined in terms of the potential difference between two points. Usually, one of those points is infinity, and the potential is defined to be zero there. The localized electric potential is then given by $V = kQ / r$, using Coulomb's law. In a uniform electric field, we can now define the electric field strength, $\mathbf{E} = V / d$, and the units are volts / meter (V / m).

The desired configuration is one in which two charged parallel plates are separated by a distance d. If each side is oppositely charged, then (see Figure 17.6) the electric field (and hence the electric force on a test charge within the field) is uniform. If a charge q and mass m enters the electric field with a velocity v, the charge will be subject to an electrical force **F** such that $\mathbf{F} = m\mathbf{a}$. In this case, $\mathbf{F} = \mathbf{E}q$, and the kinematics of charged particles in uniform electric fields can be developed in an analogous manner to the kinematics of particles in a uniform gravitational field. The applications of this kinematics extends into the fields of electronics and atomic theory.

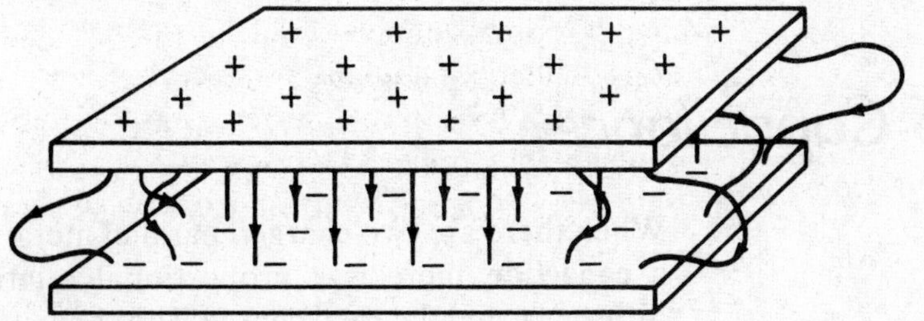

FIGURE 17.6

Some sign conventions have been developed for dealing with electric potential. By agreement, we state that a positive test charge, in a uniform electric field, will lose potential energy as it moves in the direction of the field. In other words, if the change in electrical potential energy is given by ΔU, then $\Delta U = -q\mathbf{E}d$. Consequently, the charge, because of the conservation of energy, will gain kinetic energy as it moves in the direction of the field.

Another convenient unit of electrical energy is the **electron-volt** (eV). By definition, if one elementary charge experiences a potential difference of

1 volt, its energy (or the work done to transfer the charge) is equal to 1 electron-volt. Consequently, we can state that 1 electron-volt = 1.6×10^{-19} joule.

Charges flow when a difference in potential exists, just as water flows when there is a difference in pressure. To maintain a constant flow of charge (current), a continuous potential difference must be maintained. Chemically, this is achieved through the use of a **battery** and attached conducting wires, which can create a potential difference between two points. In the case of two parallel plates (see Figure 17.7), the potential difference sets up an electric field between the plates. If a conductor is placed between the plates, charge can flow. If there is no conductor, charge is simply stored on the plates. If an insulating material such as wax or paper (called a **dielectric**) is placed between the plates, static charges can be stored to a much higher concentration. This situation defines a simple **parallel-plate capacitor**.

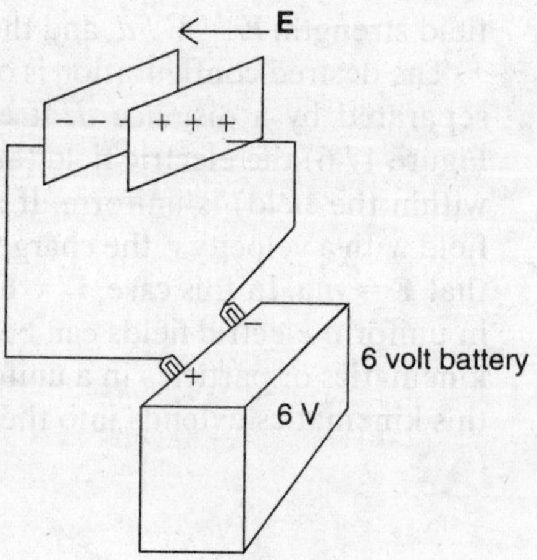

FIGURE 17.7

17.6 Capacitance

When there are two charged parallel metal plates in a configuration called a **capacitor**, there is a proportional relationship between the potential difference and the total charge. The capacitance, C, of a capacitor is defined to be the ratio of the charge on either conductor and the potential difference between the conductors:

$$C = \frac{Q}{V}$$

This is a positive scalar quantity that is essentially a measure of the capacitor's ability to store charge. The reason is that, for a given capacitor, the ratio Q / V is a constant since potential difference increases as the charge on either capacitor increases.

The SI unit of capacitance is the **farad** (F). The types of capacitors used in electronic devices have capacitances that range from microfarads to picofarads.

In this section we deal only with simple parallel-plate capacitors. However, in general, if there is a spherical distribution of charge, the electric field, at some point r, is given by:

$$\mathbf{E} = \left(\frac{1}{4\pi\epsilon_0}\right)\left(\frac{Q}{r^2}\right) = \left(\frac{Q}{\epsilon_0}\right)\left(\frac{1}{4\pi r^2}\right) = \frac{Q}{\epsilon_0 A}$$

Now, with two parallel plates, the electric field is uniform and is given by $\mathbf{E} = Vd$, and A is the area of the rectangular plates. The potential difference is then given by:

$$V = \mathbf{E}d = \frac{Qd}{\epsilon_0 A}$$

Finally, given the definition of capacitance, we can write

$$C = \frac{Q}{V} = \frac{Q}{Qd/\epsilon_0 A} = \frac{\epsilon_0 A}{d}$$

The implication of the last formula is that the capacitance of the parallel-plate capacitor is directly proportional to the area of the plates and inversely proportional to their separation.

The energy stored in a capacitor can be studied by recognizing that the definition of capacitance can be written as $Q = CV$. This direct relationship between plate charge and voltage will produce a diagonal straight line if we plot a graph of charge versus voltage (see Figure 17.8).

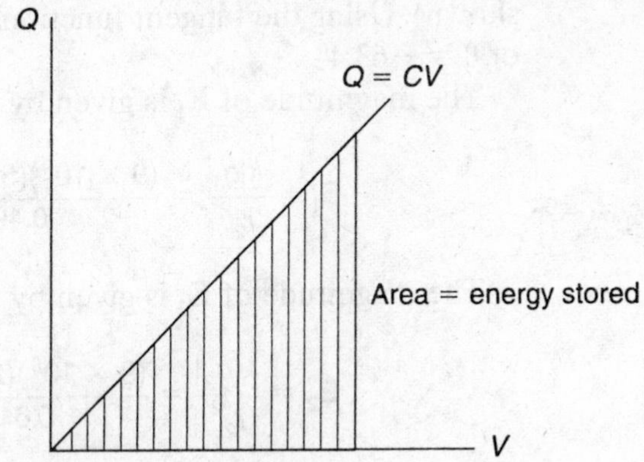

FIGURE 17.8

Notice that the units of QV are joules (the units of work). The area under the diagonal line is equal to the amount of energy stored in the capacitor. This energy is given by $E = (\tfrac{1}{2})CV^2$. The behavior of capacitors in electrical circuits will be reviewed in Chapter 18.

Sample Problem:

A charge of 5 μC is located at the origin of a Cartesian coordinate system. A second charge of −2 μC is placed horizontally 0.35 m to the right of the first charge. What is the magnitude of the strength of the electric field at location (0,0.7m)?

Solution:

First draw a sketch of the situation, as shown below:

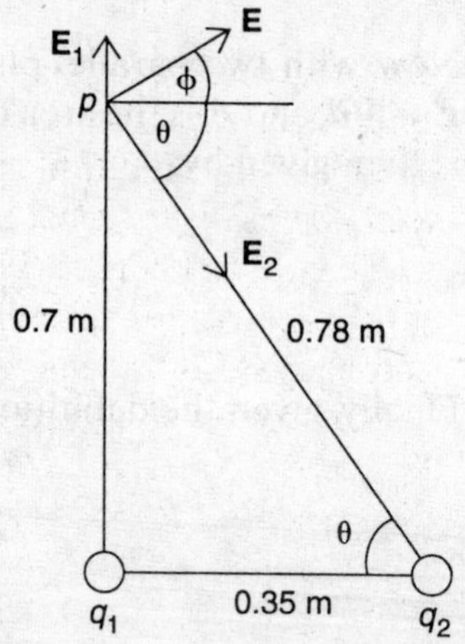

The electric field is a vector at a particular point p. The direction of the vector is the direction a positive test charge would take. Since q_1 is positive, the direction is up away from q_1. However, charge q_2 is negative, and so the electric field vector is directed along a line from point p to charge q_2. Using the given information and the Pythagorean theorem, we find that this distance is 0.78 m. The law of superposition states that the net electric field at point p will be equal to the vector sum of the two fields $\mathbf{E}_1$ and $\mathbf{E}_2$ (as shown). Using the tangent function, we find that vector $\mathbf{E}_2$ makes an angle of $\theta = -63.4°$.

The magnitude of $\mathbf{E}_1$ is given by

$$\mathbf{E}_1 = \frac{k|q_1|}{r_2^{\,2}} = \frac{(9 \times 10^9)(5 \times 10^{-6})}{0.49} = 9.18 \times 10^4 \text{ N/C}$$

The magnitude of $\mathbf{E}_2$ is given by

$$\mathbf{E}_2 = \frac{k|q_2|}{r_2^{\,2}} = \frac{(9 \times 10^9)(2 \times 10^{-6})}{0.6125} = 2.9 \times 10^4 \text{ N/C}$$

Now, the resultant field $\mathbf{E}$ is the vector sum of these two. Recall that, if we resolve vectors into components, we can simply add the components and then recombine, using the Pythagorean theorem. $\mathbf{E}_1$ is already in the positive y-direction and so has no other components. The direction of $\mathbf{E}_2$ is $-63.4°$ and has components given by $\mathbf{E}_2 \cos\theta$ and $\mathbf{E}_2 \sin\theta$. Since the cosine function is positive in the fourth quadrant,

$$\mathbf{E}_{2(x)} = \mathbf{E}_2 \cos\theta = 2.9 \times 10^4 \cos(-63.4) = 12985 \text{ N/C}$$

and

$$\mathbf{E}_{2(y)} = \mathbf{E}_2 \sin\theta = 2.9 \times 10^4 \sin(-63.4) = -25930.47 \text{ N/C}$$

The magnitudes of the components of the net electric field are found by simply adding like components:

$$\mathbf{E}_y = 65869.53 \text{ N/C} \quad \text{and} \quad \mathbf{E}_x = 12985 \text{ N/C}$$

Using the Pythagorean theorem will give us the magnitude of the net electric field strength at point P. We find that $\mathbf{E} = 67{,}137$ N/C.

Problem-Solving Strategies for Electrostatics

The preceding sample problem reminds us that we are dealing with vector quantities when the electrostatic force and field are involved. Drawing a sketch of the situation and using our techniques from vector constructions and algebra were most effective in solving the problem.

Be sure to keep track of units. If a problem involves potential or capacitance, remember to maintain the standard SI system of units, which are summarized in the appendices.

Remember that electric field lines are drawn as though they followed a "positive" test charge and that Coulomb's law applies only to point charges. The law of superposition allows you to combine the effects of many forces (or fields) using vector addition. Additionally, symmetry may allow you to work with a reduced situation that can be simply doubled or quadrupled. In this aspect, a careful look at the geometry of the situation is called for.

If the electric field is uniform, the charges in motion will experience a uniform acceleration that will allow you to use Newtonian kinematics to analyze the motion. Electrons in oscilloscopes are an example of this kind of application.

Potential and potential difference (voltage) are scalar quantities usually measured relative to the point at infinity in which the localized potential is taken to be zero. In a practical sense, it is the change in potential that is electrically significant, not the potential itself.

Practice Problems for Chapter 17

Multiple Choice

1. An insulated metal sphere, A, is charged to a value of $+Q$ elementary charges. It is then touched and separated from an identical but neutral insulated metal sphere, B. This second sphere is then touched to a third identical and neutral insulated metal sphere C. Finally, spheres A and C are touched and then separated. Which of the following represents the distribution of charge on each sphere, respectively, after the above process has been completed?
   (A) $Q/3, Q/3, Q/3$
   (B) $Q/4, Q/2, Q/4$
   (C) $3Q/8, Q/4, 3Q/8$
   (D) $3Q/8, Q/2, Q/4$
   (E) None of these is correct.

2. Electrical appliances are usually grounded in order to
   (A) maintain a balanced charge distribution
   (B) prevent the buildup of heat on them
   (C) run properly using household electricity
   (D) prevent the buildup of an overloaded circuit
   (E) prevent the buildup of static charges on their surfaces

3. Two point charges experience a force of repulsion equal to 3×10^{-4} N when separated by 0.4 m. If one of the charges is 5×10^{-4} C, what is the magnitude of the other charge?
(A) 1.07×10^{-11} C
(B) 2.7×10^{-11} C
(C) 3.2×10^{-9} C
(D) 5×10^{-4} C
(E) 0 C

4. A parallel-plate capacitor has a capacitance of C. If the area of the plates is doubled, while the separation between the plates is halved, the new capacitance will be
(A) $2C$ F
(B) $4C$ F
(C) $C/2$ F
(D) C F
(E) $C/4$ F

5. What is the capacitance of a parallel-plate capacitor made of two aluminum plates, 4 cm in length on a side and separated by 5 mm ?
(A) 2.832×10^{-11} F
(B) 2.832×10^{-10} F
(C) 2.832×10^{-12} F
(D) 2.832×10^{-9} F
(E) 1 F

6. If 10 J of work is required to move 2 C of charge in a uniform electric field, the potential difference present is equal to
(A) 20 V
(B) 12 V
(C) 8 V
(D) 5 V
(E) 10 V

7. Which of the following diagrams represents the equipotential curves in the region between a positive point charge and a negatively charged parallel plate?

(A) 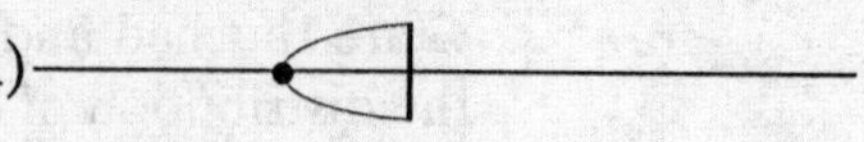

(B) 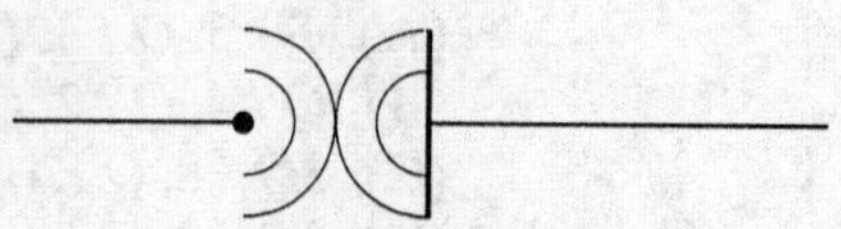

(C) 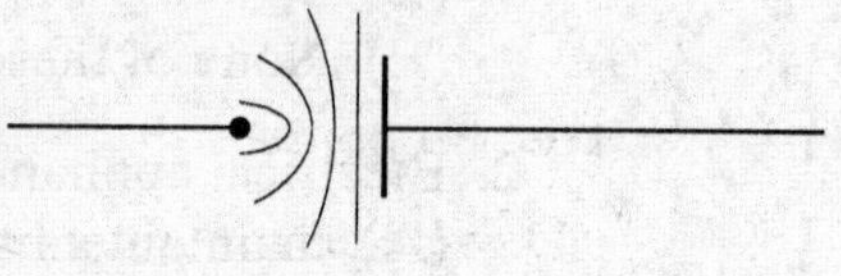

(D) 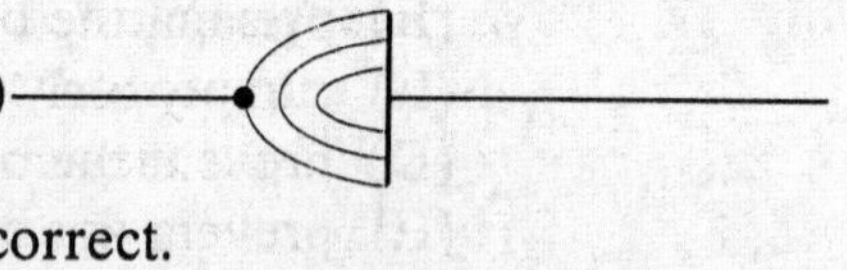

(E) None of these is correct.

8. An electron is placed between two charged parallel plates as shown below. Which of the following statements is true?

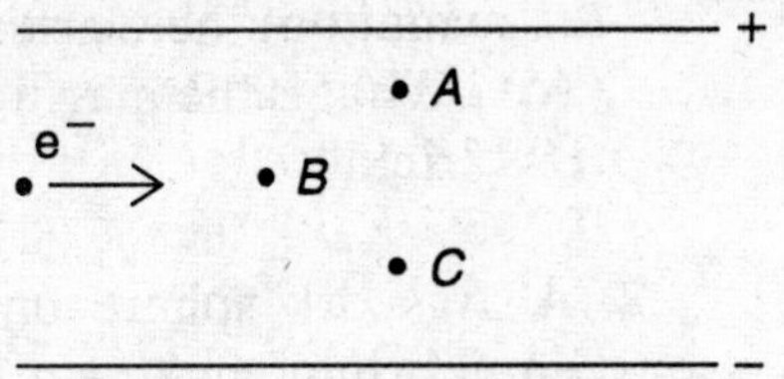

I. The electrostatic force is greater at *A* than at *B*.
II. The work done from *A* to *B* to *C* is the same as the work done from *A* to *C*.
III. The electrostatic force is the same at points *A* and *C*.
IV. The electric field strength decreases as the electron is repelled upward.

(A) I and II
(B) I and III
(C) II and III
(D) II and IV
(E) I and IV

9. How much kinetic energy is given to a doubly ionized helium atom due to a potential difference of 1000 V?
(A) 3.2×10^{-16} eV
(B) 1000 eV
(C) 2000 eV
(D) 3.2×10^{-19} eV
(E) Not enough information is given.

10. Which of the following is equivalent to 1 F of capacitance?

(A) $\frac{C^2 \cdot s^2}{kg \cdot m^2}$

(B) $\frac{kg \cdot m^2}{C^2 \cdot s^2}$

(C) $\frac{C}{kg \cdot s}$

(D) $\frac{Cm}{kg^2 \cdot s}$

(E) $C \cdot m / s$

Free Response

1. An electron enters a uniform electric field between two parallel plates vertically separated with **E** = 400 N / C. The electron enters with an initial velocity of 4×10^7 m/s. The length of each plate is 0.15 m.
(a) What is the acceleration of the electron?
(b) How long does the electron travel through the electric field?

(c) If it is assumed that the electron enters the field level with the top plate, which is negatively charged, what is the vertical displacement of the electron during that time?
(d) What is the magnitude of the velocity of the electron as it exits the field?

2. A 1-g cork sphere on a string is coated with silver paint. It is in equilibrium, making a 10° angle in a uniform electric field of 100 N/C as shown below. What is the charge on the sphere?

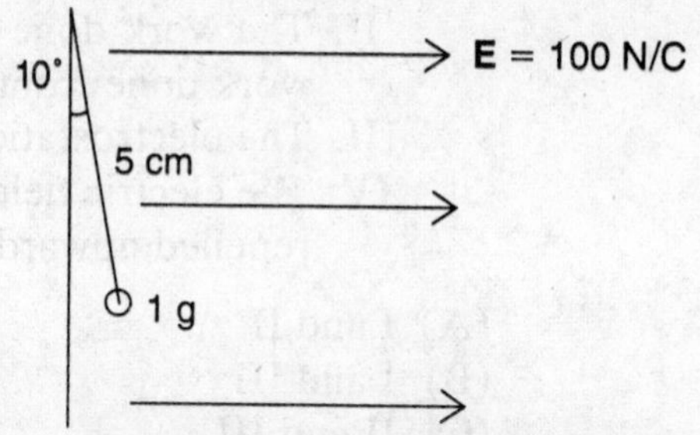

3. Four identical point charges ($Q = +3\ \mu C$) are arranged in the form of a rectangle as shown below. What are the magnitude and the direction of the net electric force on the charge in the lower left corner due to the other three charges?

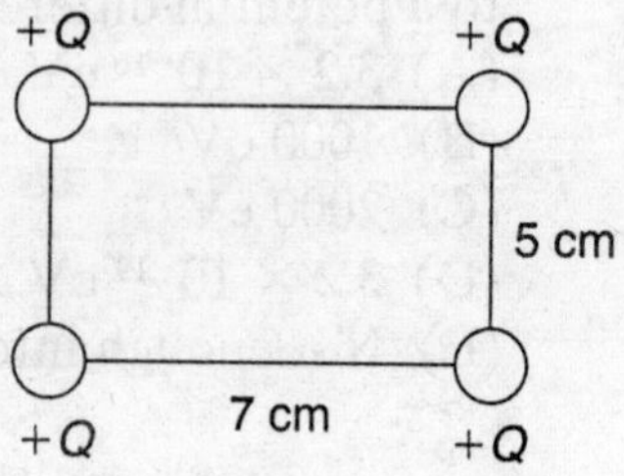

Solutions

Multiple-Choice Problems

1. **C** We use the conservation of charge to determine the answer. Sphere A has $+Q$ charge, and B has zero. When these spheres are touched and separated, each will have one-half of the total charge, which was $+Q$. Thus, each now has $+Q/2$.

   When B is touched with C, which also has zero charge, we again distribute the charge evenly by averaging. Thus, B and C will now each have $+Q/4$, while A still has $+Q/2$.

   Finally, when A and C are touched, we take the average of $+Q/4$ and $+Q/2$, which is $+3Q/8$.

   The final distribution is therefore $3Q/8, Q/4, 3Q/8$.
2. **E** Electrical appliances are grounded to prevent the buildup of static charges on their surfaces.
3. **A** We use Coulomb's law to calculate the answer. Everything is given except one charge. The working equation therefore looks like this:

$$3 \times 10^{-4} = \frac{(9 \times 10^{9})(5 \times 10^{-4})\, q}{(0.4)^2}$$

$$q = 1.07 \times 10^{-11}\ \text{C}$$

4. **B** The formula for the capacitance of a parallel-plate capacitor is $C = \epsilon_0 A/d$. Therefore, if the area is doubled and the separation distance halved, the capacitance increases by four times and is equal to 4 *C* F.
5. **C** We use the formula from question 4, but first all measurements must be in meters or square meters. Converting the given lengths yields 4 cm = 0.04 m and 5 mm = 0.005 m. Then $A = (0.04)(0.04) = 0.0016$ m^2 and $d = 0.005$ m. Using the formula and the value for the permittivity of free space given in the chapter, we get $C = 2.832 \times 10^{-12}$ F.
6. **D** Potential difference is the work done per unit charge. Thus

$$V = \frac{W}{q} = \frac{10}{2} = 5V$$

7. **C** The equipotential curves around a point charge are concentric circles. The equipotential curves between two parallel plates are parallel lines (since the electric field is uniform). The combination of these two produces the diagram shown in choice C.
8. **C** The electric field is the same at all points between two parallel plates since it is uniform. Thus the force on an electron is the same everywhere. Also, we stated in the chapter that the electric field, like gravity, is a conservative field. This means that work done to or by the field is independent of the path taken. Thus both statements II and III are true.
9. **C** One electron-volt is defined to be the energy given to one elementary charge through 1 V of potential difference. A doubly ionized helium atom has +2 elementary charges. Since the potential difference is 1000 V, the kinetic energy is 2000 eV. When using electron-volt units, we eliminate the need for the small numbers associated with actual charges of particles.
10. **A** One farad is defined to be 1 C / V. One volt is 1 J / C. One joule is 1 kg · m² / s². The combination results in

$$\frac{C^2 \cdot s^2}{kg \cdot m^2}$$

Free-Response Problems

1. (a) Since the electron is in a uniform electric field, the kinematics of the electron follows the standard kinematics of mechanics. Since $\mathbf{F} = m\mathbf{a}$ and $\mathbf{F} = -e\mathbf{E}$, $\mathbf{a} = -e\mathbf{E} / m$ (the negative sign is needed since an electron is negatively charged). Using the information given in the problem and the values for the charge and mass of the electron from the Appendix, we get

$$\mathbf{a} = \frac{-(1.6 \times 10^{-19})(400)}{9.1 \times 10^{-31}} = -7.03 \times 10^{13} \text{ m/ s}^2$$

   (b) The electron is subject to a uniform acceleration in the downward direction. The path will therefore be a parabola, and the electron will be a projectile in the field. The initial horizontal velocity remains constant, and therefore the time is given by the expression

$$t = \frac{\ell}{\mathbf{v}_0} = \frac{0.15}{4 \times 10^7} = 3.75 \times 10^{-9}\ \text{s}$$

(c) If we take the initial entry level as zero in the vertical direction, the electron has initially zero velocity in that direction. Thus, the vertical displacement is given by $\mathbf{y} = (1/2)\mathbf{a}t^2$. Using the information from parts (a) and (b), we get

$$\mathbf{y} = -(1/2)(7.03 \times 10^{13})(3.75 \times 10^{-9})^2 = -4.94 \times 10^{-4}\ \text{m}$$

(d) The magnitude of the velocity as the electron exits the field, after time t has elapsed, is given by the vector nature of two-dimensional motion. The horizontal velocity is the same throughout the encounter and is equal to 4×10^7 m/s. The vertical velocity is given by $\mathbf{v}_y = -\mathbf{a}t$ since there is no initial vertical velocity. Using the information from the previous parts, we find that

$$\mathbf{v}_y = -(7.03 \times 10^{13})(3.75 \times 10^{-9}) = -2.6 \times 10^5\ \text{m/s}$$

Now the magnitude of the velocity is given by the Pythagorean theorem since the velocity is the vector sum of these two component velocities:

$$\mathbf{v} = \sqrt{4 \times 10^7)^2 + (2.6 \times 10^5)^2} = 40{,}000{,}845\ \text{m/s} \approx 4 \times 10^7\ \text{m/s}$$

The result is not a significant change in the magnitude of the initial velocity. There is of course a significant change in direction. The angle of this change can be determined by the tangent function if desired.

2. If the sphere is in equilibrium, the vector sum of all forces acting on it must equal zero. There are several forces involved. Mechanically, gravity acts to create a tension in the string. This tension has an upward component that directly balances the force of gravity ($m\mathbf{g}$) acting on the sphere. A second horizontal component acts to the left and counters the horizontal electrical force established by the field and the charge on the sphere. A free-body diagram looks like this:

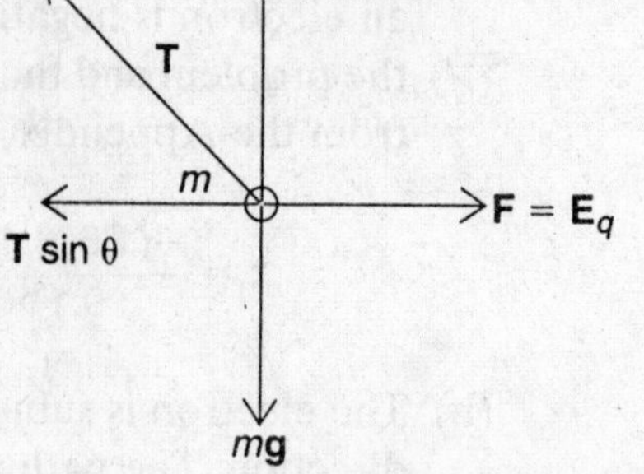

From the diagram, we see that **T** cos θ = *m***g**, where θ = 10° and *m* = 1 g = 0.001 kg. Thus, **T** = 0.00995 N, using our known value for the acceleration due to gravity, *g*. Now, in the horizontal direction, **T** sin θ = $\mathbf{E}_q$ and **E** = 100 N / C. Using all known values given and derived, we arrive at

$$q = 1.75 \times 10^{-5}\ \text{C}$$

3. Since all the charges are positive, the lower-left-corner charge will experience mutual repulsions from the other three. A diagram showing these forces appears below:

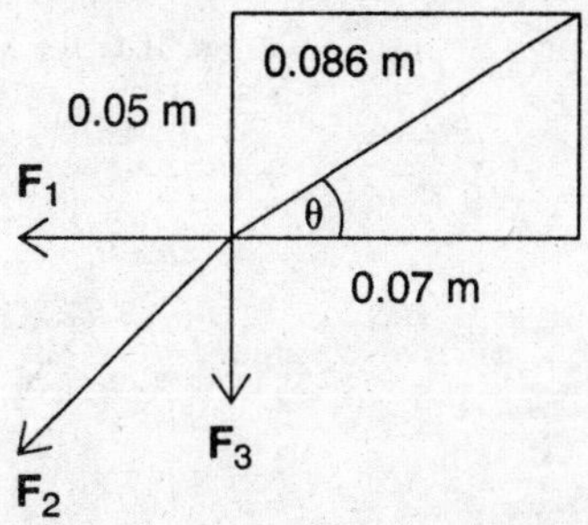

The magnitude of each force is given by Coulomb's law. The diagonal distance was determined using the Pythagorean theorem. The three force magnitudes are therefore calculated to be:

$$\mathbf{F}_1 = \frac{(9 \times 10^9)(3 \times 10^{-6})(3 \times 10^{-6})}{(0.07)^2} = 16.53\ \text{N}$$

$$\mathbf{F}_2 = \frac{(9 \times 10^9)(3 \times 10^{-6})(3 \times 10^{-6})}{(0.086)^2} = 10.95\ \text{N}$$

$$\mathbf{F}_3 = \frac{(9 \times 10^9)(3 \times 10^{-6})(3 \times 10^{-6})}{(0.05)^2} = 32.4\ \text{N}$$

Now, $\mathbf{F}_1$ acts to the left and $\mathbf{F}_3$ acts downward, so no further vector reductions are necessary. However, $\mathbf{F}_2$ acts at some angle toward the lower left, given by θ. To find the angle, we recall that tan θ = 5 / 7, which implies that θ = 35.53°. Both components of $\mathbf{F}_2$ will be negative by our sign convention of Chapter 6.

We can now write

$$\mathbf{F}_2(x) = -10.95 \cos 35.53 = -8.91\ \text{N}$$

and

$$\mathbf{F}_2(y) = -10.95 \sin 35.53 = -6.36\ \text{N}$$

The resultant or net force acting on the lower-left-corner charge is the vector sum of these charges. We can find the components of this force by simply adding up the forces in the same directions:

$$\mathbf{F}_x = -16.53 - 8.91 = -25.44\ \text{N}$$

$$\mathbf{F}_y = -32.40 - 6.36 = -38.76\ \text{N}$$

The magnitude of the net force **F** is given by the Pythagorean theorem and is equal to 46.36 N. The direction of this force is given by

$$\tan \phi = \frac{F_y}{F_x} = \frac{38.76}{25.44} = 1.523$$

This implies that $\phi = 56.72°$ relative to the negative x axis.

CHAPTER 18

Electric Circuits

18.1 Current and Electricity

In Chapter 17 we observed that, if two points have a potential difference between them, and they are connected with a conductor, negative charges will flow from a higher concentration to a lower one. This aspect of charge flow is very similar to the flow of water in a pipe due to a pressure difference.

Moving electric charges are referred to as electric **current**, which measures the amount of charge passing a given point every second. The units of measurement are coulombs per second (C / s). Algebraically, we designate current by the capital letter *I* and state that

$$I = \frac{\Delta Q}{\Delta t}$$

In electricity, it is the battery that supplies the potential difference needed to maintain a continuous flow of charge. In the nineteenth century, physicists thought that this potential difference was an electric force, called the **electromotive force** (emf), that pushed an electric fluid through a conductor. Today, we know that an emf is not a force, but rather a potential difference measured in volts. Do not be confused by the designation emf in the course of reviewing or of solving problems!

From chemistry, recall that a battery uses the action of acids and bases on different metals to free electrons and maintain a potential difference. In the process, two terminals, designated positive and negative, are created. When a conducting wire is attached and looped around to the other end, a complete circle of wire (a **circuit**) is produced, allowing for the continuous flow of charge. The battery acts like a pump, forcing electrons off the positive side onto the negative side using chemical reactions (see Figure 18.1). The mov-

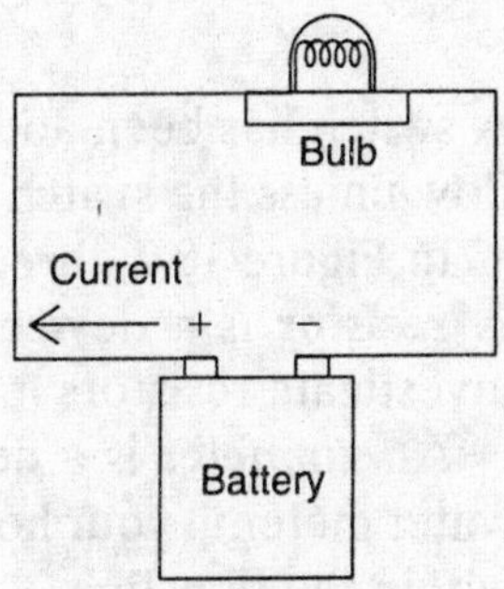

FIGURE 18.1

ing electrons can then do work since they carry energy. This work is the electricity with which we have become so familiar in our modern world.

The diagram in Figure 18.1 shows a simple electric circuit. The direction of the conventional current, in most college textbooks, is from the positive terminal. To maintain a universal acceptance of concepts and ideas (recall our earlier discussions of concepts and labels), schematic representations for electrical devices were developed and accepted by physicists and electricians worldwide. These schematics are used when drawing or diagramming an electric circuit, and it is important that you be able to interpret and draw them to fully understand this topic. In Figure 18.2, schematics for some of the most frequently encountered electrical devices are presented.

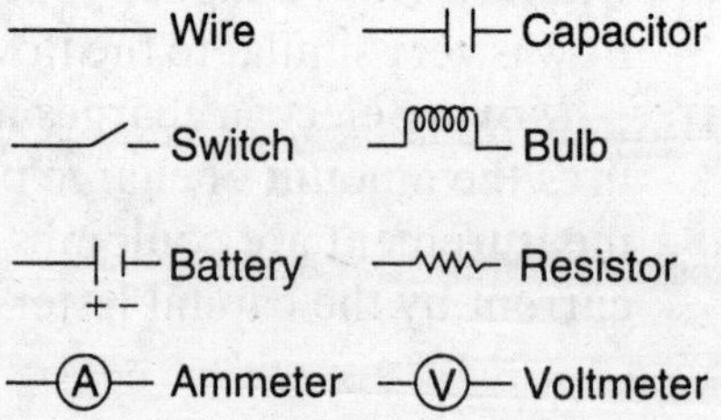

FIGURE 18.2 Electrical Schematic Diagrams

The simple circuit shown in Figure 18.1 can now be diagrammed schematically as in Figure 18.3.

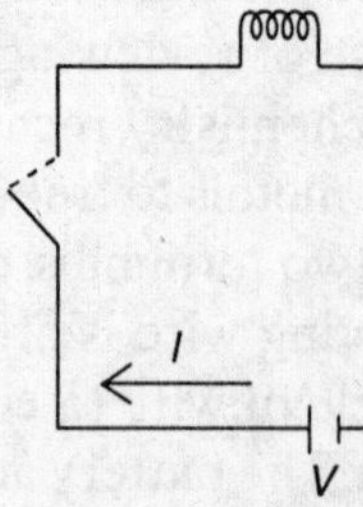

FIGURE 18.3

A switch has been added to the schematic; of course the charge would not flow unless the switch was closed.

In Figure 18.2, three schematics appear that we have not yet discussed. A **resistor** is a device whose function is to oppose the current. We will investigate resistors in more detail in the next section.

An **ammeter** is a device that measures the current. You can locate the water meter in your house or apartment building and notice that it is placed within the flow line. The reason is that the meter must measure the flow of water per second through a given point. An ammeter is placed within an electric circuit in much the same way. This is referred to as a "series connection," and it maintains the singular nature of the circuit. In practical terms, you can imagine cutting a wire in Figure 18.3 and hooking up the bare leads to the two terminals of the ammeter.

A **voltmeter** is a device that measures the potential difference, or voltage, between two points. Unlike an ammeter, the voltmeter cannot be placed within the circuit since it will effectively be connected to only one point. A voltmeter is therefore attached in a "parallel connection," creating a second circuit through which only a small amount of current flows to operate the voltmeter. In Figure 18.4, the simple circuit is redrawn with the ammeter and voltmeter placed.

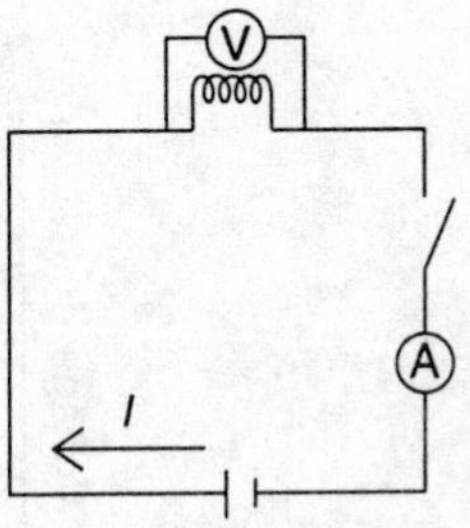

FIGURE 18.4

For simple circuits, there will be no observable difference in readings if the ammeter and voltmeter are moved to different locations. However, there is a slight difference in the emf across the terminals of the battery and the emf across the bulb. The first emf reflects the work done by the battery not only to move charge through the circuit but also to move charge across the terminals of the battery. This is sometimes referred to as the **terminal emf** or **internal emf**.

18.2 Electrical Resistance

In Figure 18.4, a simple electric circuit is illustrated with measuring devices for voltage and current. If a light bulb is left on for a long time, two observations can be made. First, the bulb gets hot because of the action of the electricity and the filament. The light produced by the bulb is caused by the heat of the filament. Second, the current in the ammeter will begin to decrease.

These two observations are linked to the idea of electrical resistance. Friction generates heat. The interaction of flowing electrons and the molecules of a wire (or bulb filament) creates an electrical friction called **resistance**. This resistance is temperature dependent since, from the kinetic theory, an increase in temperature will increase the molecular activity and therefore interfere to a greater extent with the flow of current.

In the case of a light bulb, it is this resistance that is desired in order for the bulb to do its job. Resistance along a wire or in a battery, however, is unwanted and must be minimized. In more complicated circuits, a change in current flow is required to protect devices, and so special resistors are manufactured that are small enough to easily fit into a circuit. While resistance is the opposite of conductance, we do not want to use insulators as resistors since insulators will stop the flow altogether. Therefore, a range of materials, indexed by "resistivity," is catalogued in electrical handbooks to assist scientists and electricians in choosing the proper resistor for a given situation.

If the temperature can be maintained at a constant level, a simple relationship between the voltage and the current in a circuit is revealed: as the voltage is increased, a greater flow of current is observed. This direct relationship was investigated theoretically by a German physicist named Georg Ohm and is called **Ohm's law** (see Figure 18.5).

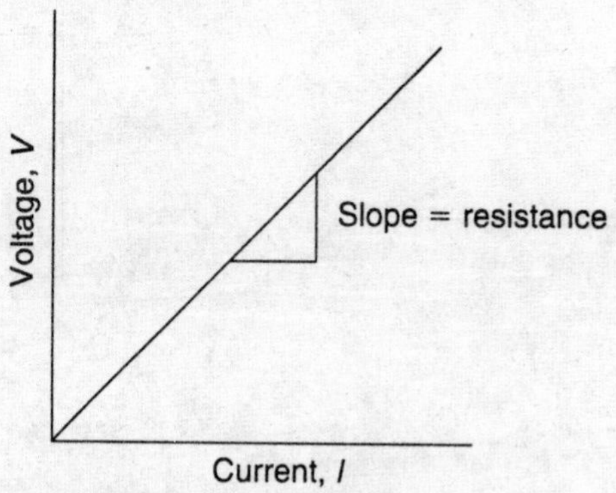

FIGURE 18.5 Ohm's Law

Ohm's law states that in a circuit at constant temperature the ratio of the voltage to the current remains constant. The slope of the line in Figure 18.5 represents the resistance of the circuit, which is measured in units of Ohms (Ω). Algebraically, we can write Ohm's law as

$$R = \frac{V}{I} \quad \text{or} \quad V = IR$$

Not all conductors obey Ohm's law. Semiconductors and liquid conductors, for example, do not.

Other factors also affect the resistance of a conductor. We have already discussed the effects of temperature and material type (resistivity). Resistivity is designated by the Greek letter ρ (rho). In a wire, electrons try to move through, interacting with the molecules that make up the wire. If the wire has a small cross-sectional area, the chances of interacting with a bound molecule increase and thus the resistance of the wire increases. If the length of the wire is increased, the greater duration of interaction time will also increase the resistance of the wire. In summary, these resistance factors all contribute to the overall resistance of the circuit.

Algebraically, we may write these relationships (at constant temperature) in the following form:

$$R = \frac{\rho L}{A}$$

Where L is the length in meters and A is the cross-sectional area in units of m^2. The resistivity (ρ) is measured in units of ohm · meters ($\Omega \cdot m$) and is usually rated at 20 degrees Celsius.

In the accompanying table, the resistivities of various materials are presented. Since the ohm is a standard (SI) unit, be sure that all lengths are in meters and areas are in square meters.

TABLE 18.1 Resistivities of Selected Materials at 20°C

Substance	Resistivity, ρ ($\Omega \cdot m$)
Aluminum	2.83×10^{-8}
Carbon	3.5×10^{-5}
Copper	1.69×10^{-8}
Gold	2.44×10^{-8}
Nichrome	100×10^{-8}
Platinum	10.4×10^{-8}
Silver	1.59×10^{-8}
Tungsten	5.33×10^{-8}

18.3 Electrical Power and Energy

Electricity produces energy that, in turn, can be used to produce light and heat. Electricity can do work to turn a motor. Having measured the voltage and current in a circuit, we can determine the amount of power and energy being produced in the following way. The units of voltage (potential difference) are joules per coulomb (J / C) and are a measure of the energy supplied to each coulomb of charge flowing in the circuit. The current, I, measures the total number of coulombs per second flowing at any given time. The product of the voltage and the current (VI) is therefore a measure of the total power produced since the units will be joules per second (watts):

$$P = VI$$

The electrical energy expended in a given time t (in seconds) is simply the product of the power and the time:

$$\text{Energy} = Pt = VIt = I^2Rt$$

In the second equation we used Ohm's law ($V = IR$) to express the energy in another form. This energy could be related to heat if we considered, for example, a direct transfer of energy into some water. The rise in temperature could then be computed. Note that the electrical energy is expressed in joules, while specific heats involve kilojoules and kilograms. To be consistent, you should convert either to joules or to kilojoules, but maintain the use of kilograms for mass!

18.4 Resistors in Series and Parallel Circuits

A. Series Circuits

A series circuit consists of two or more resistors sequentially placed within one circuit. An example is seen in Figure 18.6.

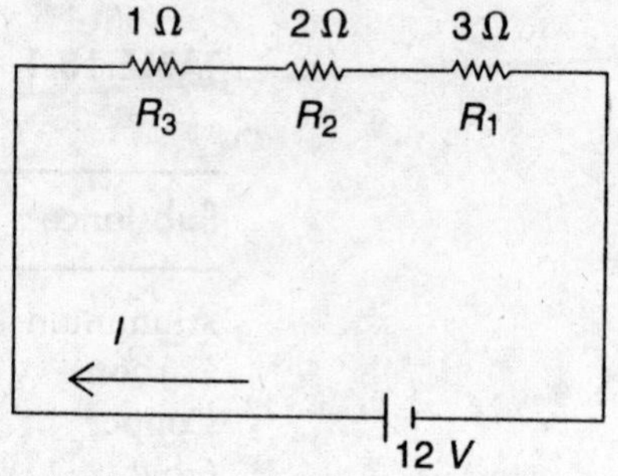

FIGURE 18.6 Series Circuit

We need to ask two questions. First, what is the effect of adding more resistors in series to the overall resistance in the circuit? Second, what effect does adding the resistors in series have on the current flowing in the circuit?

A look at the series circuit shows that it is still one continuous loop. Therefore, if there is a break in one place (let's say one light bulb goes out), the entire circuit will shut down. Experiments reveal that the current is the same through the entire circuit, because actually there is only one circuit. However, these experiments show also that the terminal emf across the battery is essentially equal to the sum of the emf's across all of the resistors. There exists a "potential drop" across each resistor.

One way to think about this circuit is to imagine a series of doors, one after the other. As people exit through one door, they must wait to open another. The result is to drain energy out of the system and decrease the number of people per second leaving the room. In an electric circuit, adding more resistors in series decreases the current (with the same voltage) by increasing the resistance of the circuit.

Algebraically, all of these observations can be summarized as follows. In resistors R_1, R_2, and R_3, we have currents I_1, I_2, and I_3. Each of these three currents is equal to each other current and to the circuit current I:

$$I = I_1 = I_2 = I_3$$

However, the voltage across each of these resistors is less than the source voltage V. If all three resistors were equal, each voltage would be equal to one-third of the total source voltage. In any case, we have

$$V = V_1 + V_2 + V_3$$

Using Ohm's law ($V = IR$), we can rewrite this expression as

$$IR = I_1R_1 + I_2R_2 + I_3R_3$$

However, the three currents are equal, so they can be canceled out of the expression. This leaves us with

$$R = R_1 + R_2 + R_3$$

In other words, when resistors are added in series, the total resistance of the circuit increases as the sum of all the resistances. This fact explains why the current decreases as more resistors are added. In our example, the total resistance of the circuit is

$$1\ \Omega + 2\ \Omega + 3\ \Omega = 6\ \Omega$$

Since the source voltage is 12 V, Ohm's law provides for a circuit current of 12 / 6 = 2 A. The voltage across each resistor can now be determined from Ohm's law since each gets the same current of 2 A. Thus,

$$V_1 = (1)(2) = 2\text{ V};\quad V_2 = (2)(2) = 4\text{ V};\quad V_3 = (3)(2) = 6\text{ V}$$

The voltages in a series circuit add up to the total, and not unexpectedly we have

$$2\text{ V} + 4\text{ V} + 6\text{ V} = 12\text{ V}$$

It should be noted that, when batteries are connected in series (positive to negative), the effective voltage increases additively as well.

B. Parallel Circuits

A parallel circuit consists of two or more resistors connected across each other to a common point of potential difference. An example of a parallel circuit is seen in Figure 18.7.

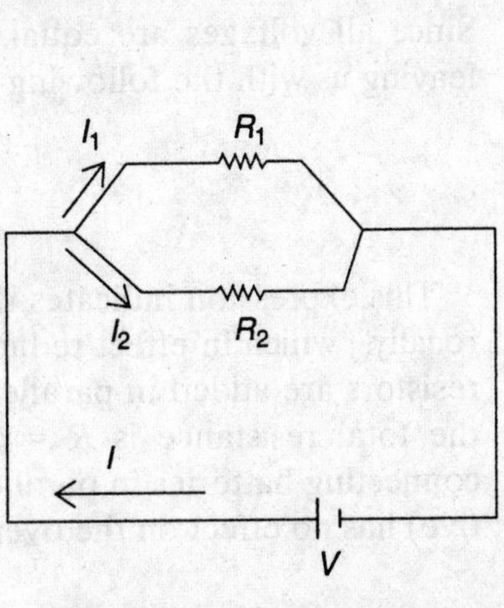

FIGURE 18.7 Parallel Circuit

In this circuit, a branch point is reached in which the current I is split into I_1 and I_2. Since each resistor is connected to a common potential point, experiments verify that the voltage across each resistor equals the source voltage V. Thus, in this circuit it is the current that is shared; the voltage is the same. Another feature of the parallel circuit is the availability of alternative paths. If one part of the circuit is broken, current can flow through the other path. While each branch current is less than the total circuit current I, the effect of adding resistors in parallel is to increase the effective circuit current by decreasing the circuit resistance R.

To understand this effect further, imagine a set of doors placed next to each other along a wall in a room. Unlike the series connection (in which the doors are placed one after the other), the parallel-circuit analogy involves placing the doors next to each other. Even though each door will have fewer people per second going through it at any given time, the overall effect is to allow, in total, more people to exit from the room. This is analogous to reducing the circuit resistance and increasing the circuit current (at the same voltage).

Algebraically, we can express these observations as follows. We have two resistors, R_1 and R_2, with currents I_1 and I_2. Voltmeters placed across the two resistors would indicate voltages V_1 and V_2, which would be essentially equal to the source voltage V; that is, in this example,

$$V = V_1 = V_2$$

Ammeters placed in the circuit would reveal that the circuit current I is equal to the sum of the branch currents I_1 and I_2; that is,

$$I = I_1 + I_2$$

Using Ohm's law, we see that

$$\frac{V}{R} = \frac{V_1}{R_1} + \frac{V_2}{R_2}$$

Since all voltages are equal, they can be canceled from the expression, leaving us with the following expression for resistors in parallel:

$$\frac{1}{R} = \frac{1}{R_1} + \frac{1}{R_2}$$

This expression indicates that the total resistance is determined "reciprocally," which in effect reduces the total resistance of the circuit as more resistors are added in parallel. If, for example, $R_1 = 10\ \Omega$ and $R_2 = 10\ \Omega$, the total resistance is $R = 5\ \Omega$ (in parallel)! It should be noted that connecting batteries in parallel (positive to positive and negative to negative) has no effect on the overall voltage of the combination.

18.5 Combination Circuits and Networks

In Figure 18.8, a circuit that consists of resistors in series and parallel is presented. The key to reducing such a circuit is to decide whether it is, overall, a series or parallel circuit. In Figure 18.8, an 8-Ω resistor is placed

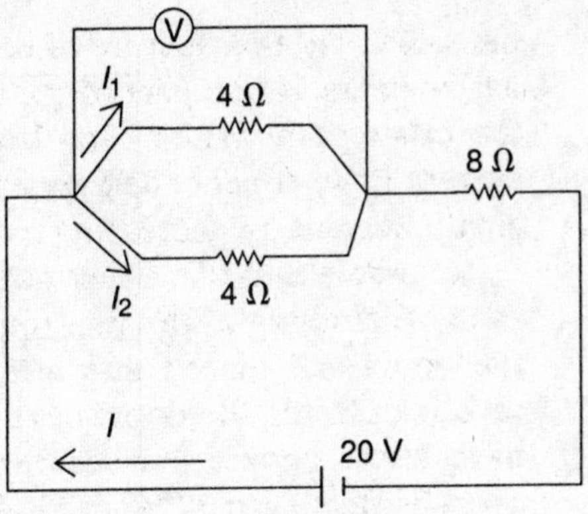

FIGURE 18.8

in series with a parallel branch containing two 4-Ω resistors. The problem is to reduce the circuit to only one resistor and then to determine the circuit current, the voltage across the branch, and the current in each branch.

To reduce the circuit and find the circuit resistance R, we must first reduce the parallel branch. Thus, if R_e is the equivalent resistance in the branch, then

$$\frac{1}{R_e} = \frac{1}{4} + \frac{1}{4}$$

This implies that $R_e = 2\ \Omega$ of resistance. The circuit can now be thought of as a series circuit between a 2-Ω resistor and an 8-Ω resistor. Thus,

$$R = 2\ \Omega + 8\ \Omega = 10\ \Omega$$

Since the circuit voltage is 20 V, Ohm's law states that the circuit current is

$$I = \frac{V}{R} = \frac{20}{10} = 2\text{ A}$$

In a series circuit, the voltage drop across each resistor is shared proportionally since the same current flows through each resistor. Thus, for the branch,

$$V = IR_e = (2)(2) = 4\text{ V}$$

To find the current in each part of the parallel branch, we recall that in a parallel circuit the voltage is the same across each resistor. Thus, since the two resistors are equal, each will get half of the circuit current; thus each current is 1 A.

The above procedure for reducing can be used in a large number of combination circuits. However, in Figure 18.9, we show a circuit in which this procedure will not work because of the presence of a second emf in a branch. Analysis of this type of circuit, sometimes called a **network**, requires the use of two laws stated in the nineteenth century by physicist Gustav Kirchhoff (Kirchhoff's laws).

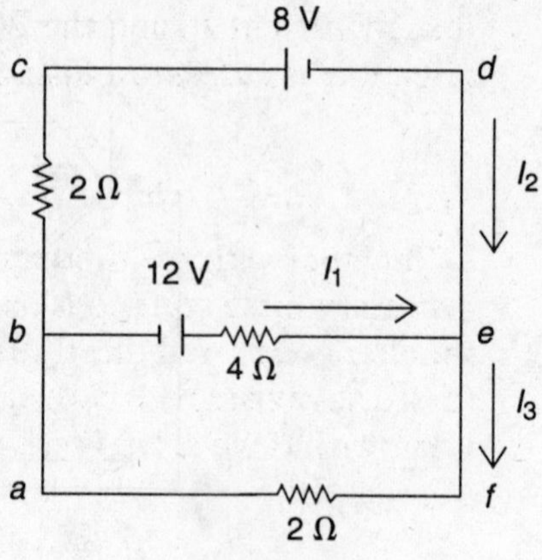

FIGURE 18.9

The directions of the currents, I_1, I_2, I_3, are given arbitrarily, and the directions of the battery terminals are reversed. This has an important effect on the determination of the values of the three currents, which is the problem. Kirchhoff's first law states that the sum of all currents entering a junction point must be equal to the sum of all currents leaving that junction point. Kirchhoff's second law states that the sum of the emf's across all of the elements around any closed loop must be equal to zero.

Kirchhoff's laws are just restatements of the laws of conservation of charge and energy, respectively. In an analogous situation, water flows through a closed system with many branches, but no leaks. In our example, we can see that $I_1 + I_2 = I_3$ at junction point *e*.

There are also some useful heuristics to consider as problem-solving strategies. Imagine that we traverse a loop in the clockwise direction. First, if a resistor is crossed in the direction of the current, the potential across that resistor is written as $-$IR. Second, if the resistor is crossed in the direction opposite the current, the potential is written as $+IR$. Third, if a source of emf is crossed from negative to positive, we state that the potential is $+V$. Fourth, if the source of emf is crossed from positive to negative, we state that the potential is $-V$. Fifth, it is useful to consider the first four rules while imagining that we traverse each loop in a clockwise direction. It should be noted that the junction rule applies only $n - 1$ times if there are n junctions. Since we will be ending up with a system of equations, we must make sure that we have enough equations to equal all of the unknowns.

We have applied the junction rule at point *e*; let's continue the example for loops. Let's go clockwise around loop *abefa*. The emf is crossed from negative to positive; and the resistor on the top is crossed in the direction of current I_1, while the resistor on the bottom is crossed in the direction of current I_3. Using Kirchhoff's second law, we have

$$12 - 4(I_1) - 2(I_3) = 0$$

Let's now look clockwise at loop *bcdeb*. The emf on the top is crossed from positive to negative, the second emf on the bottom is also crossed from positive to negative, the 4-Ω resistor is crossed in the opposite direction to current I_1, and the 2-Ω resistor on the side is crossed in the same direction as current I_2. Using Kirchhoff's second law, we have

$$-8 - 12 + 4(I_1) - 2(I_2) = 0$$

Together with the first equation relating the three currents, we have our necessary three equations and three unknowns. These three must be solved simultaneously for the three currents, using known algebraic techniques (more advanced matrix techniques, such as Cramer's rule, can also be used if known). If we solve these equations, we find that

$$I_1 = 3.2 \text{ A}, \qquad I_2 = -3.6 \text{ A}, \qquad \text{and } I_3 = -0.4 \text{ A}$$

The negative sign means that the original directions for these currents should have been reversed.

18.6 Capacitors in Circuits

A. Capacitors in Series

We know from Chapter 17 that the capacitance of a parallel-plate capacitor is given by $C = Q / V$. Suppose we have a series of capacitors connected to a potential difference V as shown in Figure 18.10.

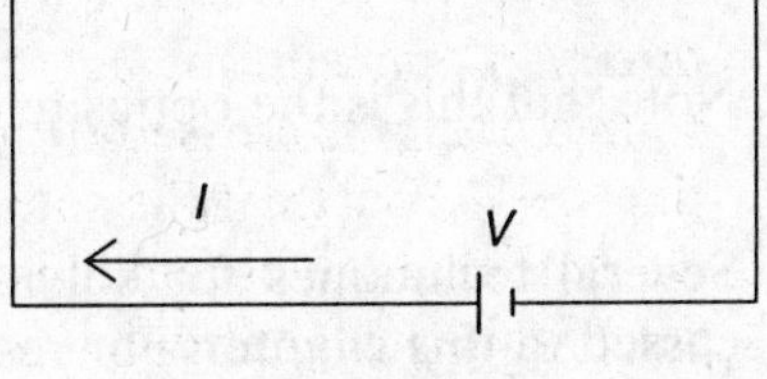

FIGURE 18.10

In this circuit, the magnitude of the charge must be the same on all plates because the left plate of C_1 becomes $+Q$ and the right plate of C_2 becomes $-Q$. By induction, the right plate of C_1 becomes $-Q$ and the left plate of C_2 becomes $+Q$. Additionally, the voltage across each capacitor is shared proportionally so that $V_1 + V_2 = V$ (just like the situation with resistors in series). Thus,

$$\frac{Q}{C_1} + \frac{Q}{C_2} = \frac{Q}{C}$$

and

$$\frac{1}{C_1} + \frac{1}{C_2} = \frac{1}{C} \quad \text{(for a series combination)}$$

Note that this is the opposite of the relationship for resistors in series. Be sure not to confuse them!

A parallel combination of capacitors is shown in Figure 18.11.

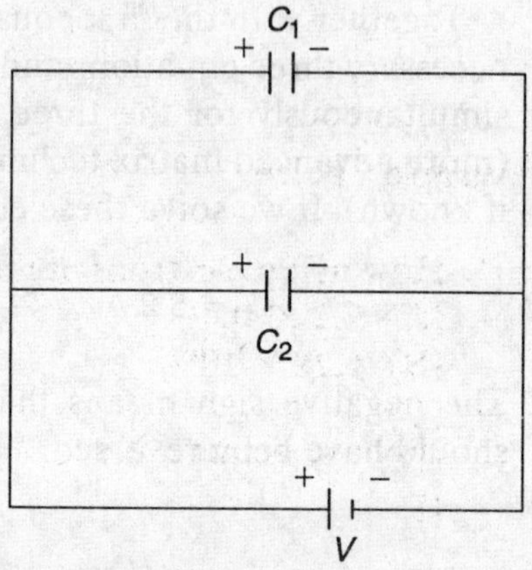

FIGURE 18.11

In this circuit, the current branches off, and so each capacitor is charged to a different total charge, Q_1 and Q_2. The equivalent total charge is $Q = Q_1 + Q_2$, and the voltage across each capacitor is the same as the source emf voltage. Thus,

$$CV = C_1V + C_2V$$

and

$$C = C_1 + C_2 \quad \text{(for a parallel combination)}$$

Note that this is the opposite of the relationship for resistors in parallel.

Problem-Solving Strategies for Electric Circuits

Several techniques for solving electric circuit problems have been discussed in this chapter. For resistances with one source of emf, we use the techniques of series and parallel circuits. Ohm's law plays a big role in measuring the potential drops across resistors and the determination of currents within the circuit.

When working with a combination circuit, try to reduce all subbranches first, as well as any series combinations. The goal is to be left with only one equivalent resistor and then use Ohm's law to identify the various missing quantities. Drawing a sketch of the circuit (if one is not already provided) is essential. Also, remember that in most college textbooks, the direction of current is taken from the positive terminal of a battery. This is opposite to the way current is presented in most high school physics textbooks.

In a network with two or more emf's, you must use Kirchhoff's rules. While the directions of the currents are arbitrary, it is important to remember that Kirchhoff's rules are based on the laws of conservation of charge and energy. Take care that enough equations are presented to solve for all the missing information.

In solving a network problem, you can choose to traverse the loop either clockwise or counterclockwise. You must, however, be consistent throughout and remember the accepted sign conventions when crossing emf's and meeting currents. Working slowly and carefully will minimize careless errors.

Practice Problems for Chapter 18

Multiple Choice

1. How many electrons are moving through a current of 2 A for 2 s?
   (A) 3.2×10^{-19}
   (B) 6.28×10^{18}
   (C) 4
   (D) 2.5×10^{19}
   (E) 1

2. How much electrical energy is generated by a 100-W light bulb turned on for 5 min?
   (A) 20 J
   (B) 500 J
   (C) 3000 J
   (D) 15,000 J
   (E) 30, 000 J

3. What is the current in a 5-Ω resistor due to a potential difference of 20 V?
   (A) 25 A
   (B) 4 A
   (C) 0.20 A
   (D) 5 A
   (E) 20 A

4. A 20-Ω resistor has 10 A of current in it. The power generated is
   (A) 2000 W
   (B) 2 W
   (C) 200 W
   (D) 4000 W
   (E) 20 W

5. What is the value of resistor R in the circuit shown below?
   (A) 20 Ω
   (B) 2 Ω
   (C) 4 Ω
   (D) 12 Ω
   (E) 10 Ω

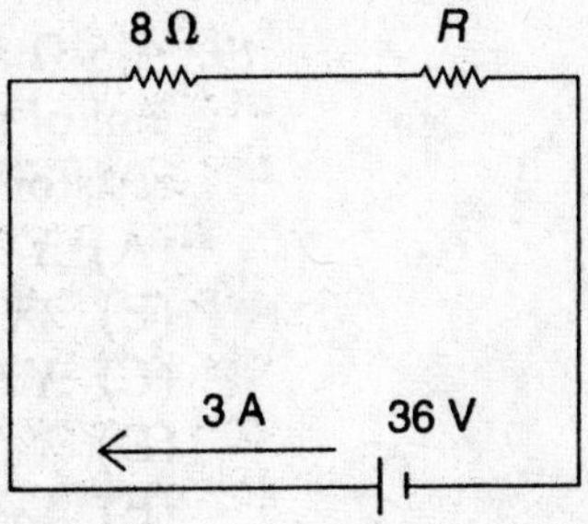

6. What is the equivalent capacitance of the circuit shown below?
(A) 2 F
(B) 8 F
(C) 5 F
(D) 10 F
(E) 15 F

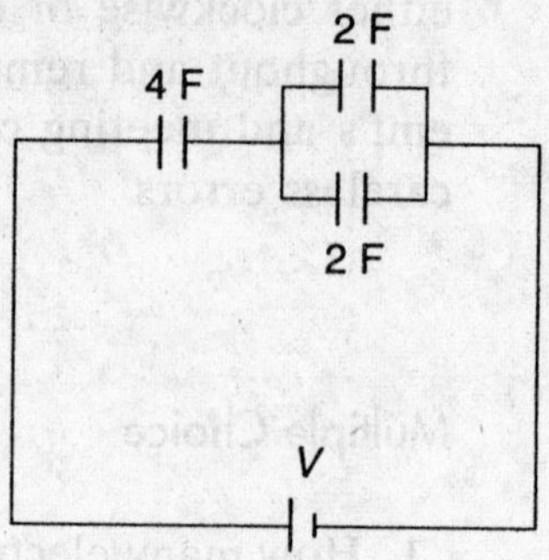

Answer questions 7 and 8 based on the circuit below:

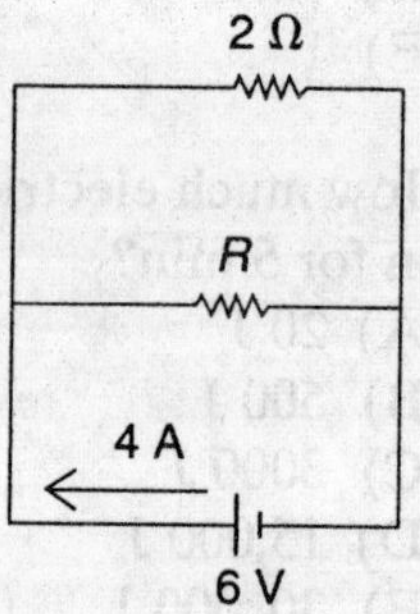

7. If the current in the circuit above is 4 A, then the power generated by resistor R is
(A) 6 W
(B) 18 W
(C) 24 W
(D) 7 W
(E) 16 W

8. What is the value of resistor R in the circuit above?
(A) 4 Ω
(B) 3 Ω
(C) 5 Ω
(D) 6 Ω
(E) 8 Ω

9. A 5-Ω and a 10-Ω resistor are connected in series with one source of emf of negligible internal resistance. If the energy produced in the 5-Ω resistor is X, then the energy produced in the 10-Ω resistor is
(A) X
(B) $2X$
(C) $X/2$
(D) $X/4$
(E) $4X$

10. Four equivalent light bulbs are arranged in a circuit as shown below. Which bulb(s) will be the brightest?
(A) *A*
(B) *B*
(C) *C*
(D) *D*
(E) both *C* and *D*

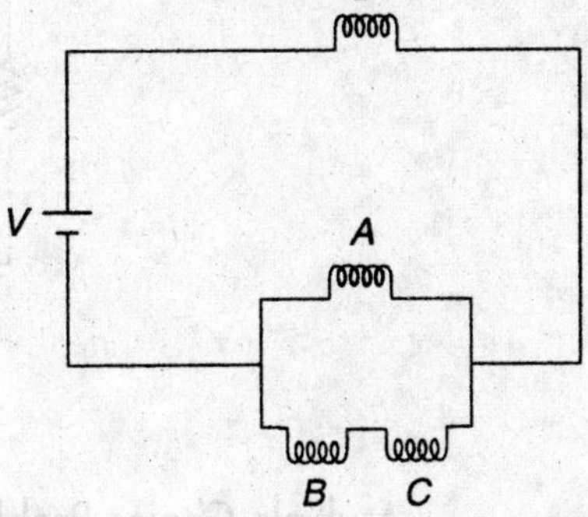

Free Response

1. A 30-Ω heating coil is placed into 250 g of water at a temperature of 25° C. If the coil is connected to a 120-V supply and turned on for 2 min, what will be the new temperature of the water? Assume that all of the energy is directed into the water and there are no losses to the environment.

2. Based on the circuit shown below:

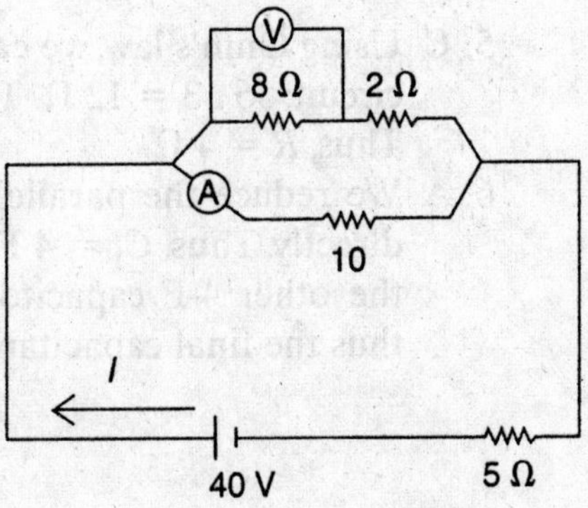

(a) Determine the equivalent resistance of the circuit.
(b) Determine the value of the circuit current *I*.
(c) Determine the value of the reading of ammeter A.
(d) Determine the value of the reading of voltmeter V.

3. Determine the values of the three currents shown in the network circuit below.

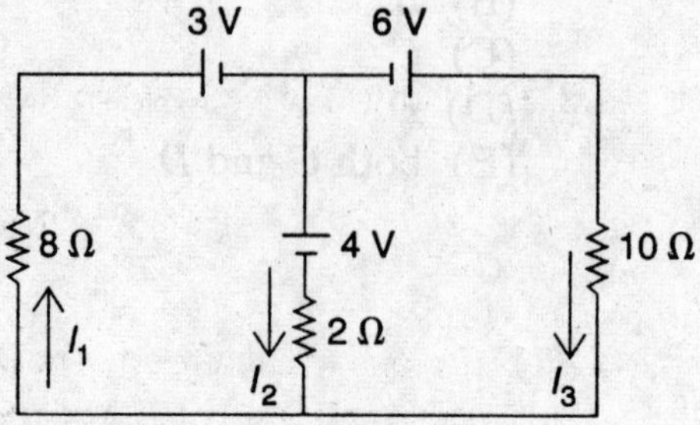

Solutions

Multiple-Choice Problems

1. **D** By definition, 1 A of current measures 1 C of charge passing through a circuit each second. One coulomb is the charge equivalent of 6.28 $\times$ 10^{18} electrons. In this question, we have 2 A for 2 s. This is equivalent to 4 C of charge or 2.5 $\times$ 10^{19} electrons.
2. **E** Energy is equal to the product of power and time. The time must be in seconds; 5 min = 300 s. Thus

$$\text{Energy} = (100)(300) = 30{,}000 \text{ J}$$

3. **B** Using Ohm's law, we have

$$I = \frac{V}{R} = \frac{20}{5} = 4 \text{ A}$$

4. **A** We know that $P = VI$, and using Ohm's law ($V = IR$), we get

$$P = I^2R = (100)(20) = 2000 \text{ W}$$

5. **C** Using Ohm's law, we can determine the equivalent resistance of the circuit: 36 / 3 = 12 Ω. The two resistors are in series, so 12 = 8 + R. Thus, R = 4 Ω.
6. **A** We reduce the parallel branch first. In parallel, capacitors add up directly. Thus, C_1 = 4 F. Now, this capacitor would be in series with the other 4-F capacitor. In series, capacitors add up reciprocally; thus the final capacitance is

$$\frac{1}{C} = \frac{1}{4} + \frac{1}{4}$$

This implies that C = 2 F.
7. **A** In a parallel circuit, all resistors have the same potential difference across them. The branch currents must add up to the source current (4 A, in this case). Thus, using Ohm's law, we can see that the current in the 2-Ω resistor is I = 6 / 2 = 3 A. Thus, the current in

resistor R must be equal to 1 A. Since $P = VI$, the power in resistor R is

$$P = (6)(1) = 6 \text{ W}$$

8. **D** Using Ohm's law, we have,

$$R = \frac{V}{I} = \frac{6}{1} = 6\ \Omega$$

9. **B** In a series circuit, the two resistors have the same current but proportionally shared potential differences. Thus, since the 10-Ω resistor has twice the resistance of the 5-Ω resistor in series, it has twice the potential difference. Therefore, with the currents equal, the 10-Ω resistor will generate twice as much energy, that is, 2 X, when the circuit is on.
10. **D** The fact that all the resistors (bulbs) are equal means that the parallel branch will reduce to an equivalent resistance less than that of resistor D. The remaining series circuit will produce a greater potential difference across D than across that equivalent resistor. With the currents equal at that point, resistor D will generate more power than the equivalent resistance. Thus, with the current split for the actual parallel part, even less energy will be available for resistors A, B, and C. Bulb D will be the brightest.

Free-Responses Problems

1. We need to assume that all of the electrical energy produced is converted into heat. The electrical energy is given by the expression $E = VIt$. Using Ohm's law, we find that

$$I = \frac{V}{R} = \frac{120}{30} = 4 \text{ A}$$

In this case, the time, t, is 120 s.

Thus, $E = (120)(4)(120) = 57{,}600$ J. Now, in water, $Q = mc\,\Delta T$. Since the specific heat of water is 4.19 kJ / kg · °C, we need to convert to joules by multiplying by 1000. Also, m = 250 g = 0.25 kg. Thus,

$$57{,}600 = (0.25)(4190)(\Delta T)$$

This implies that ΔT = 54.98°C. Since this is added to the water, the new temperature will be approximately 80°C.

2. (a) The first thing we need to do is to reduce the series portion of the parallel branch. The equivalent resistance there is 8 Ω + 2 Ω = 10 Ω. Now, this resistance is in parallel with the other 10-Ω resistor. The equivalent resistance is found to be 5 Ω for the entire parallel branch. This equivalent resistance is in series with

the other 5-Ω resistor, making a total equivalent resistance of 10 Ω.

(b) We can determine the circuit current using Ohm's law:

$$I = \frac{V}{R} = \frac{40}{10} = 4 \text{ A}$$

(c) To determine the reading of ammeter A, we must first understand that the potential drop across the 5-Ω resistor on the bottom is equal to 20 V since

$$V = IR = (4)(5) = 20$$

Now, the equivalent resistance of the parallel branch is also 5 Ω, and therefore across the entire branch there is also a potential difference of 20 V (in a series circuit, the voltages must add up—in this case, to 40 V). In a parallel circuit, the potential difference is the same across each portion. Thus, the 10-Ω resistor has 20 V across it. Using Ohm's law, we find that this implies a current reading of 2 A for ammeter A.

(d) If, from part (c), ammeter A reads 2 A, the top branch must be getting 2 A of current as well (since the source current is 4 A). Thus, using Ohm's law, we can find the voltage across the 8-Ω resistor:

$$V = IR = (2)(8) = 16 \text{ V}$$

3. We begin by applying the junction rule. From the diagram, we see that

$$I_1 = I_2 + I_3$$

Now, we apply the loop rule for both loops by going clockwise around each one. For the left loop, we cross the emf's from the positive side to the negative side. These are treated as "negatives" in our equations. Both resistors are crossed in the direction of each current, and so the potential drop across each of these is taken as a positive value. Thus, we write:

$$-3 - 4 + 2(I_2) + 8(I_1) = 0$$

For the right loop, we cross the emf's from the negative side and write them as positive values. The 10-Ω reisistor is crossed in the direction of I and the 2-Ω resistor is crossed in the opposite direction of I_2. For this loop we can write:

$$4 + 6 - 2(I_2) + 10(I_3) = 0$$

The three equations must be solved for I_1, I_2, and I_3. We first substitute for I_1 in the second equation. This leaves us with:

$$-7 + 2(I_2) + 8(I_2) + 8(I_3) = 0$$

$$10 - 2(I_2) + 10(I_3) = 0$$

Eliminating I_2 in both equations leads to $I_3 = -0.74$ A. Substitution back leads to $I_2 = 1.292$ A. Finally, using the first equation, we get $I_1 = 0.552$ A. The negative sign for I_3 means that our original direction for I_3 was incorrect.

CHAPTER 19

Magnetism

19.1 Magnetic Fields and Forces

When two statically charged point objects approach each other, each exerts a force on the other that varies inversely with the square of their separation distance. We can also state that one of the charges creates an electrostatic field around itself, and this field transmits the force through space.

When we have a wire carrying current, we no longer consider the effects of static fields. A simple demonstration reveals that, when we arrange two current-carrying wires parallel to each other so that the currents are in the same direction, the wires will be attracted to each other with a force that varies inversely with their separation distance and directly with the product of the currents in the two wires. If the currents are in opposite directions, the wires are repelled. Since this is not an electrostatic event, we must conclude that a different force is responsible.

The nature of this force can be further understood when we consider the fact that a statically charged object, such as an amber stone, cannot pick up small bits of metal. However, certain naturally occurring rocks called **lodestones** can attract metal objects. The lodestones are called **magnets** and can be used to **magnetize** metal objects (especially those made from iron or steel).

If a steel pin is stroked in one direction with a magnetic lodestone, the pin will become magnetized as well. If an iron rail is placed in the earth for many years, it will also become magnetized. If cooling steel is hammered while lying in a north-south line, it too will become magnetized (heating will eliminate the magnetic effect). If the magnetized pin is placed on a floating cork, the pin will align itself along a general north-south line. If the cork's orientation is shifted, the pin will oscillate around its original equilibrium direction and eventually settle down along this direction. Finally, if another magnet is brought near, the "compass" will realign itself toward the new magnet.

Each of these experiences suggests the presence of a magnetic force, and we can therefore consider the actions of this force through the description of a magnetic field. If a magnet is made in the shape of a rectangular bar (see Figure 19.1), the orientation of a compass, moved around the magnet, demonstrates that the compass aligns itself tangentially to some imaginary field lines that were first discussed by English physicist Michael Faraday. In general, we label the north-seeking pole of the magnet as N and the south-seeking pole as S. We also observe that these two opposite poles behave in a similar way to opposite electric charges: like poles repel, while unlike poles attract.

A fundamental difference between these two effects is that magnet poles never appear in isolation. If a magnet is broken in two pieces, each new magnet has a pair of poles. This phenomenon continues even to the atomic level. There appear, at present, to be no magnetic monopoles naturally occurring in nature. (New atomic theories have postulated the existence of magnetic monopoles, but none has as yet been discovered.)

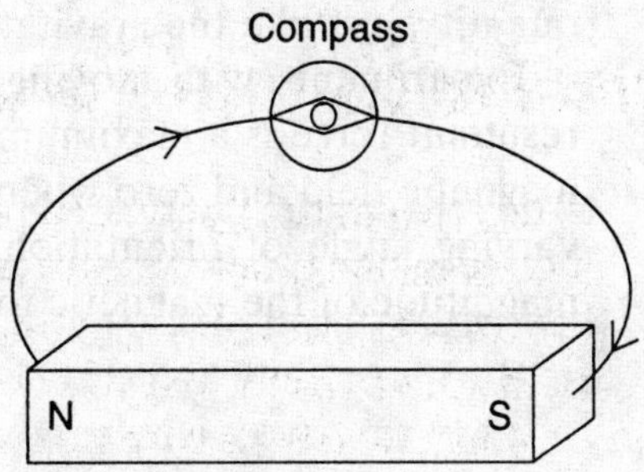

FIGURE 19.1

Small pieces of iron (called "filings") can be used as miniature compasses to illustrate the characteristics of the magnetic field around magnets made of iron or similar alloys. The ability of a metal to be magnetized is called its **permeability**; substances such as iron, cobalt, and nickel have among the highest permeabilities. These substances are sometimes called **ferromagnets**.

In Figure 19.2, several different magnetic field configurations are shown. By convention, the direction of the magnetic field is taken to be from the north pole of the magnet to the south pole.

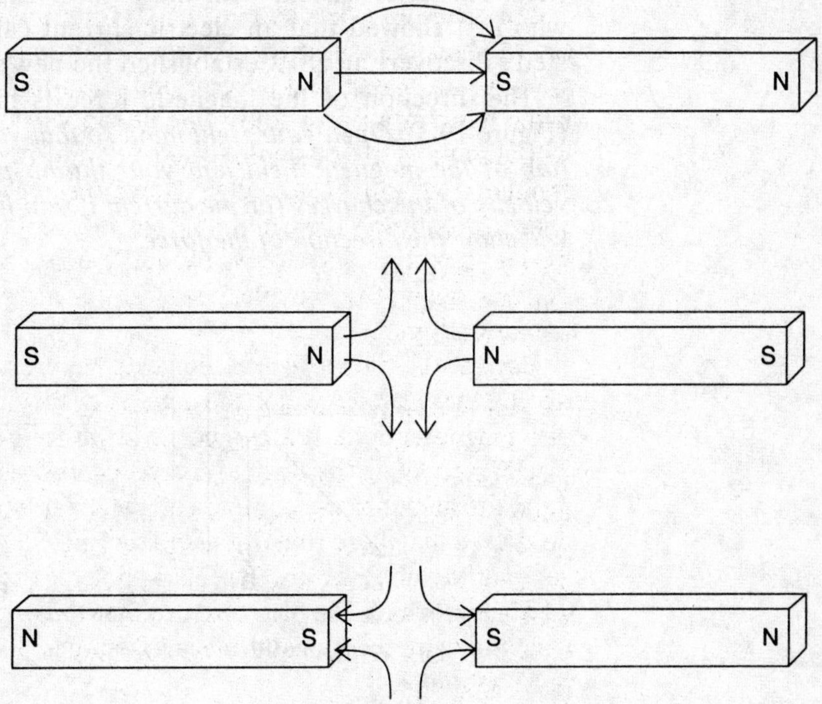

FIGURE 19.2

19.2 Magnetic Force on a Moving Charge

If a moving electric charge enters a magnetic field, it will experience a force that depends on its velocity, charge, and orientation with respect to the field. The force will also depend on the magnitude of the magnetic field strength (designated as **B** algebraically). This field strength is a vector quantity, just like the gravitational and electrical field strengths.

Experiments with moving charges in a magnetic field reveal that the resultant force is a maximum when the velocity, **v**, is perpendicular to the magnetic field and zero when the velocity is parallel to the field. With this varying angle of orientation θ and a given charge *Q*, we find that the magnitude of the magnetic force is given by:

$$\mathbf{F} = \mathbf{B}Q\mathbf{v} \sin \theta$$

Since the units of force must be newtons, the units for the magnetic field strength **B** must be newton · seconds per coulomb · meter (N · s / C · m). Recall that the newton · second is the unit for an impulse. We can think of the magnetic field as a measure of the impulse given to 1 coulomb of charge moving a distance of 1 meter in a given direction. Additionally, if we have a beam of charges, we effectively have an electric current. The units (seconds per coulomb) can be interpreted as the reciprocal of amperes, and so the strength of the magnetic field, in a current-carrying wire is given in units of newtons per ampere · meter (N / A · m).

In the SI system, this combination is called a **tesla**; 1 tesla is equal to 1 newton per ampere · meter. Thus, an electric current carries a magnetic field. This is consistent with the earliest experiments by Hans Oersted, who first showed that an electric current can influence a compass. Oersted's discovery, in 1819, established the new science of **electromagnetism**.

The direction of the magnetic force is given by a "**right-hand rule**" (Figure 19.3): *Open your right hand so that your fingers point in the direction of the magnetic field and your thumb points in the direction of the velocity of the charges (or the current if you have a wire). Your open palm will show the direction of the force.*

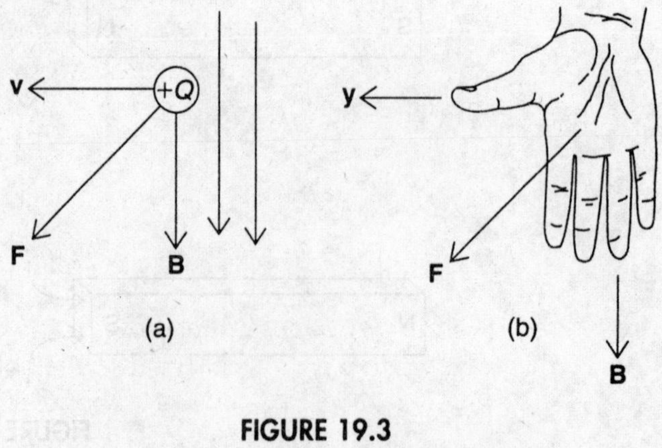

FIGURE 19.3

Figure 19.4 illustrates that, if the velocity and magnetic field are perpendicular to each other, the path of the charge in the field is a circle of radius *R*. The direction, provided by the right-hand rule, is the direction that a positive test charge would take. Thus, the direction for a negative charge would be opposite to what the right-hand rule predicted.

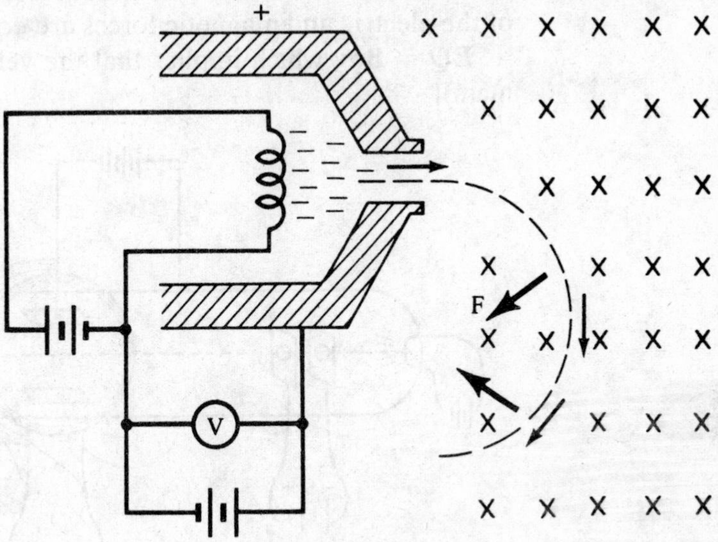

FIGURE 19.4

The circular path arises because the induced force is always at right angles to the deflected path when the velocity is initially perpendicular to the magnetic field. This path is similar to the circular path of a stone being swung in an overhead horizontal circle while attached to a string.

In the frame of reference of the moving charge, the inward magnetic force is apparently balanced by an outward centrifugal force. This relationship is given by:

$$m\frac{\mathbf{v}^2}{R} = \mathbf{B}Qv$$

where *m* is the mass of the charge.

This relationship can be used to determine the radius of the path:

$$R = m\frac{\mathbf{v}}{Q\mathbf{B}}$$

This expression assumes that the velocity and mass of the charge are known independently. Even if we wish to use this expression to find the mass of the charge (as used in a mass spectrograph):

$$m = \frac{RQ\mathbf{B}}{\mathbf{v}}$$

we still must know what the velocity is independent of the mass of the charge.

One way to determine the velocity of the charge, independently from the mass, is to pass the charge through both an electric and a magnetic field, as in a cathode ray tube. As shown in Figure 19.5, if the electric field is horizontal, the charges will be attracted or repelled along a horizontal line. If the magnetic field is vertical, the right-hand rule will force the charges along the same horizontal line. Careful adjustment of both fields (keeping the velocity perpendicular to the magnetic field) can lead to a situation where the effect of one field balances out the effect from the other and the charges remain undeflected. In that case, we can write that the magnitudes of the electric and magnetic forces are equal:

$\mathbf{E}Q = \mathbf{B}q\mathbf{v}$ which implies that the velocity $\mathbf{v} = \mathbf{E} / \mathbf{B}$ (independent of mass)!

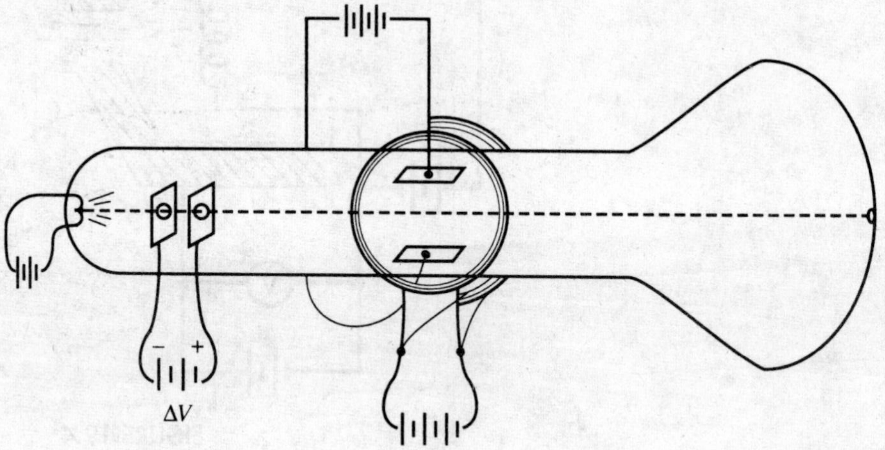

FIGURE 19.5

If the velocity is not perpendicular to the magnetic field when it first enters, the path will be a spiral because the velocity vector will have two components. One component will be perpendicular to the field (and create a magnetic force that will try to deflect the path into a circle), while the other component will be parallel to the field (producing no magnetic force and maintaining the original direction of motion). This situation is illustrated in Figure 19.6.

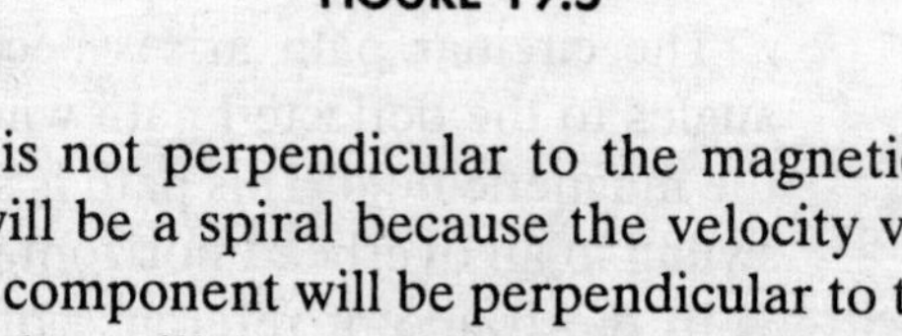

FIGURE 19.6

19.3 Magnetic Fields Due to Currents in Wires

A. A Long, Straight Wire

If a compass is placed near a long, straight wire carrying current, the magnetic field produced by the current will cause the compass to align tangent to the field. Placing the compass at varying distances reveals that the strength of the field varies inversely with the distance from the wire and varies directly with the amount of current.

The shape of the magnetic field is a series of concentric circles (Figure 19.7) whose rotational direction is determined by a right-hand rule: *Grasp the wire with your right hand. If your thumb points in the direction of the current, your fingers will curl around the wire in the same direction as the magnetic field.*

A schematic for the three-dimensional nature of the field is sometimes used. For an emerging field, we use a series of dots; for an inward field, we use a series of X's.

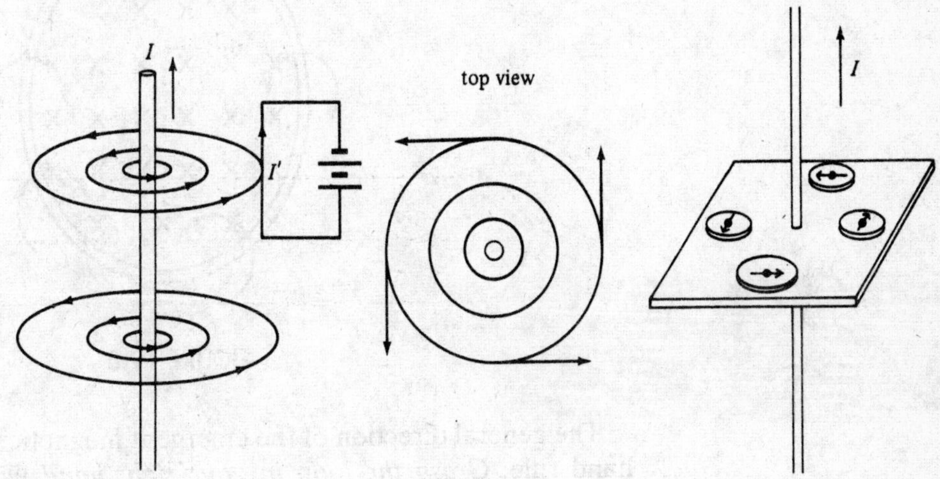

FIGURE 19.7

The magnitude of the magnetic field strength at some distance r from the wire is given by

$$\mathbf{B} = \frac{\mu I}{2\pi r}$$

where μ is the permeability of the material around the wire in units of newtons per square ampere (N / A^2). In air, the value of μ is approximately equal to the permeability of a vacuum:

$$\mu_0 = 4\pi \times 10^{-7}\ N/A^2$$

This equation is therefore usually written in the form

$$\mathbf{B} = \frac{\mu_0 I}{2\pi r}$$

B. A Loop of Wire

Imagine a straight wire with current that has been bent into the shape of a loop with radius r. Each of the circular magnetic fields now interacts in the center of the loop. In Figure 19.8, we see that the effect of all of these subfields is to produce one concentrated field, pointing inward or outward, at the center.

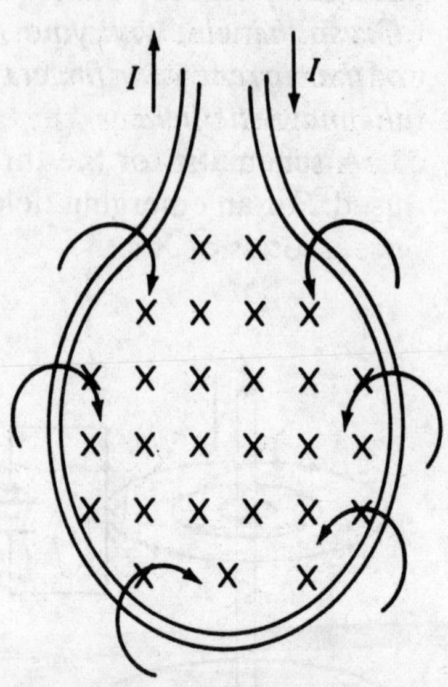

FIGURE 19.8

The general direction of the emergent magnetic field is given by a right-hand rule: *Grasp the loop in your right hand with your fingers curling around the loop in the same direction as the current. Your thumb will now show the direction of the magnetic field.* Figure 19.9 illustrates this rule.

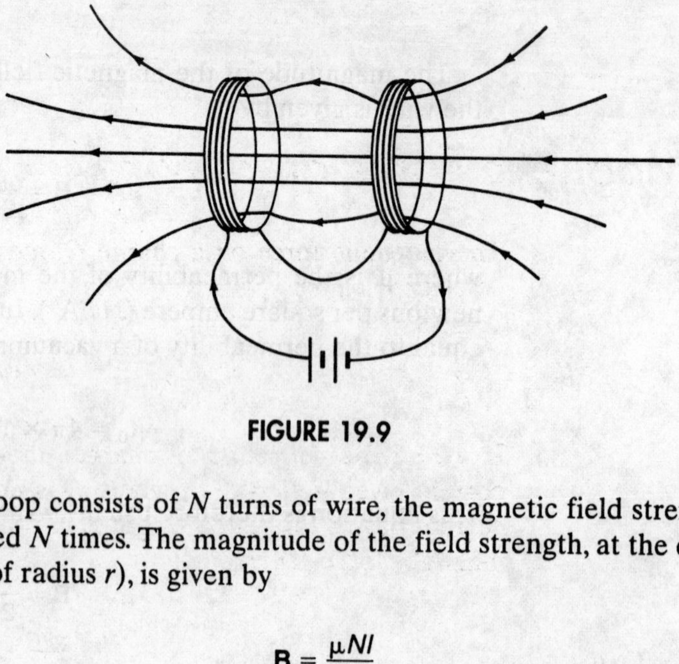

FIGURE 19.9

If the loop consists of N turns of wire, the magnetic field strength will be increased N times. The magnitude of the field strength, at the center of the loop (of radius r), is given by

$$\mathbf{B} = \frac{\mu N I}{2r}$$

The strength of the field can also be increased by changing the permeability of the core. If the wire is looped around iron, the field is stronger than if the wire were looped around cardboard. Also, if the loop's radius is smaller, the field is more concentrated at the center and thus stronger.

C. A Solenoid

If the loop described in Section B is stretched out to a length L, in the form of a spiral, we have what is called a **solenoid** (Figure 19.10). This is the basic form for an electromagnet, in which wire is wrapped around an iron nail and then connected to a battery. The strength of the field will increase with the number of turns, the permeability of the core, and the amount of current in the wire:

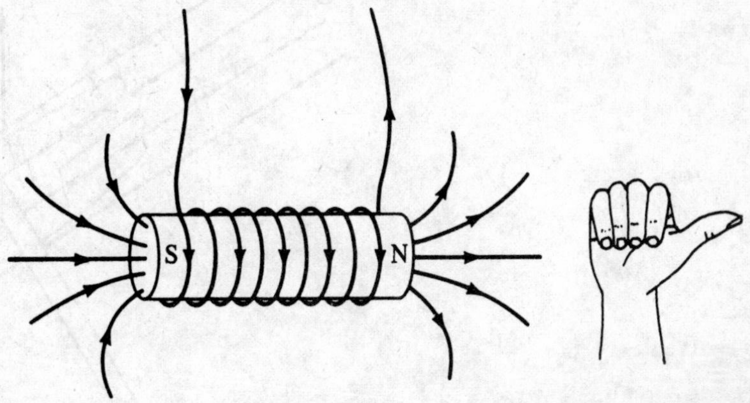

FIGURE 19.10

The direction of the magnetic field is given by another right-hand rule: *Grasp the solenoid with your right hand so that your fingers curl in the same direction as the current. Your thumb will point in the direction of the emergent magnetic field.*

19.4 Magnetic Force on a Wire

The magnetic force on a charge Q, moving in a magnetic field **B** with a velocity v, is given by

$$\mathbf{F} = \mathbf{B}qv \sin \theta.$$

If we have a collection of charges, then effectively we have an electric current given by $I = Q / t$, where Q is now the total charge present. If the current passes through a length L in time t, we can state that the induced magnetic force is given by:

$$\mathbf{F} = \mathbf{B}IL \sin \theta$$

If the charges are contained within a wire and the wire is perpendicular to the magnetic field, the force is given simply by

$$\mathbf{F} = \mathbf{B}IL.$$

Again, the direction of the force is given by a right-hand rule (Figure 19.11): *Point the fingers of your right hand in the direction of the magnetic field so that your thumb points in the direction of the current. The palm of your hand will show the direction of the force.*

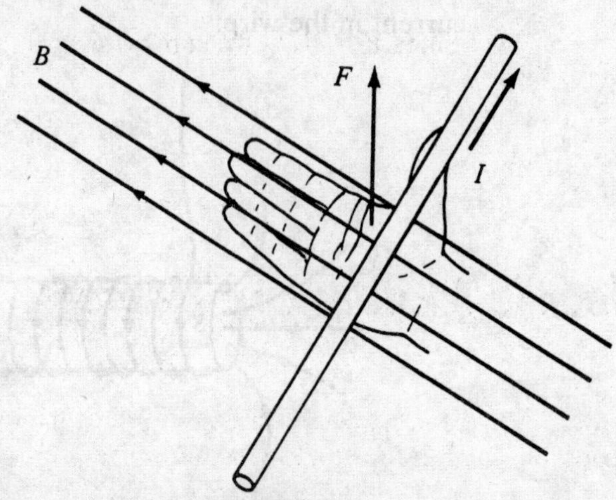

FIGURE 19.11

19.5 Magnetic Force Between Two Wires

Imagine that you have two straight wires with currents going in the same direction (Figure 19.12). Each wire creates a circular magnetic field around itself so that, in the region between the wires, the net effect of each field is to weaken the other field relative to the other side. This difference produces a net inward attractive force.

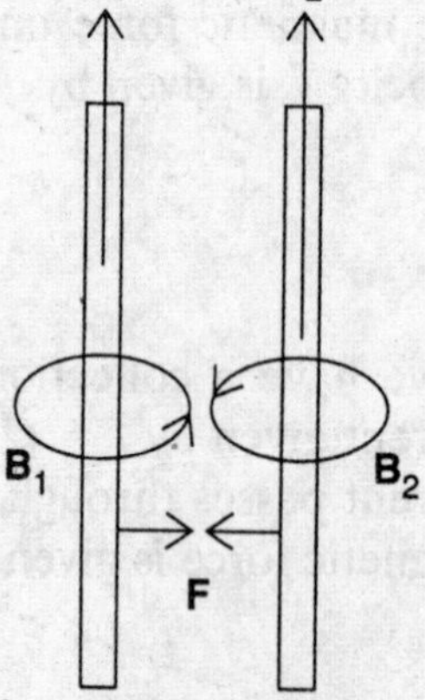

FIGURE 19.12

If the current in one wire is reversed, the force will become repulsive.

The magnitude of the force between the wires, at a distance r, can be determined if we consider the fact that one wire sets up the external field that acts on the other. If we want the magnetic force on wire 2 due to wire 1, we can write

$$\mathbf{B}_1 \frac{\mu_0 I_1}{2\pi r}$$

Since $\mathbf{F} = \mathbf{B}IL$, we can write

$$\mathbf{F}_{12} = \frac{\mu_0 I_1 I_2 L}{2\pi r}$$

19.6 Electric Motors and Meters

A. Torque on the Current in a Loop of Wire

Imagine a rectangular loop of wire with current. If the plane of the loop is parallel to an external magnetic field (see Figure 19.13), a net torque will be produced that will cause the loop to rotate about an axis perpendicular to the field.

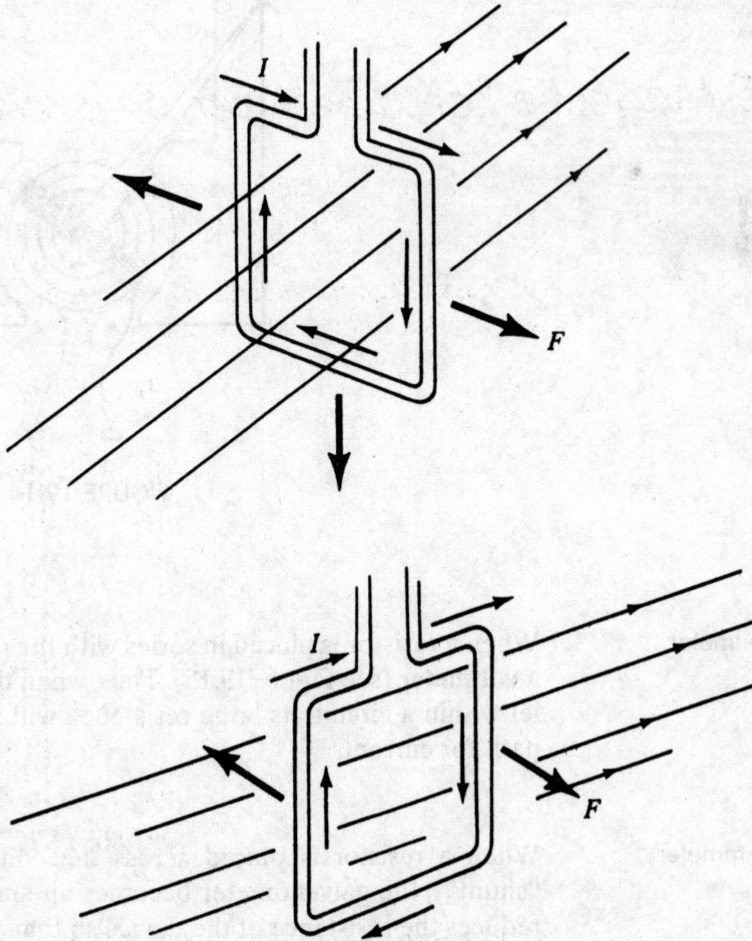

FIGURE 19.13

The torque can be observed using the right-hand rule. On the right side a downward force is produced, while on the left side there is an upward force. This combination causes the rotation of the loop. The torque effect will continue until the plane of the loop is perpendicular to the field. At that point, the net force (and torque) will be zero. With the loop vertical, angular momentum may allow the loop to continue to rotate until it is once again in the original horizontal position.

B. A Galvanometer

A **galvanometer** is a device that detects small amounts of electric current. A simple galvanometer consists of a coil of wire with a pointer attached. The coil is placed in an external magnetic field (see Figure 19.14) so that, when current flows through the coil, the torque produced will cause the pointer to deflect along a calibrated scale.

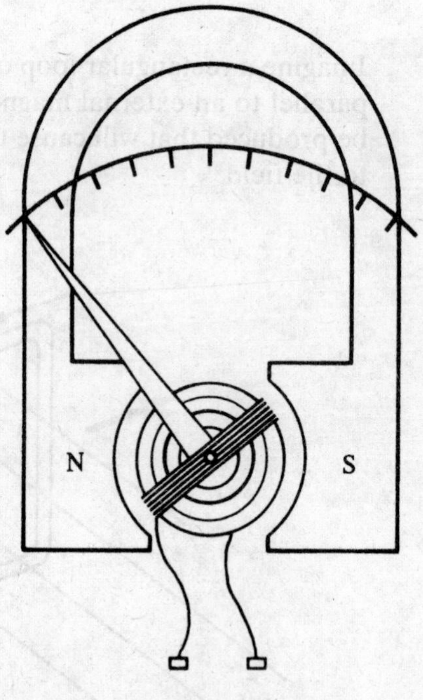

FIGURE 19.14

C. A Voltmeter

When a resistor is placed in series with the coil, the galvanometer becomes a **voltmeter** (see Figure 19.15). Thus, when the voltmeter is placed in parallel within a circuit, its large resistance will imply a low parallel resistance path for current.

D. An Ammeter

When a resistor is placed across the coil of a galvanometer (called a "shunt"), the galvanometer becomes an **ammeter** (see Figure 19.16). This reduces the resistance of the device so that, when the ammeter is placed in series within a circuit to measure current, only a small amount of current will be used to operate the ammeter.

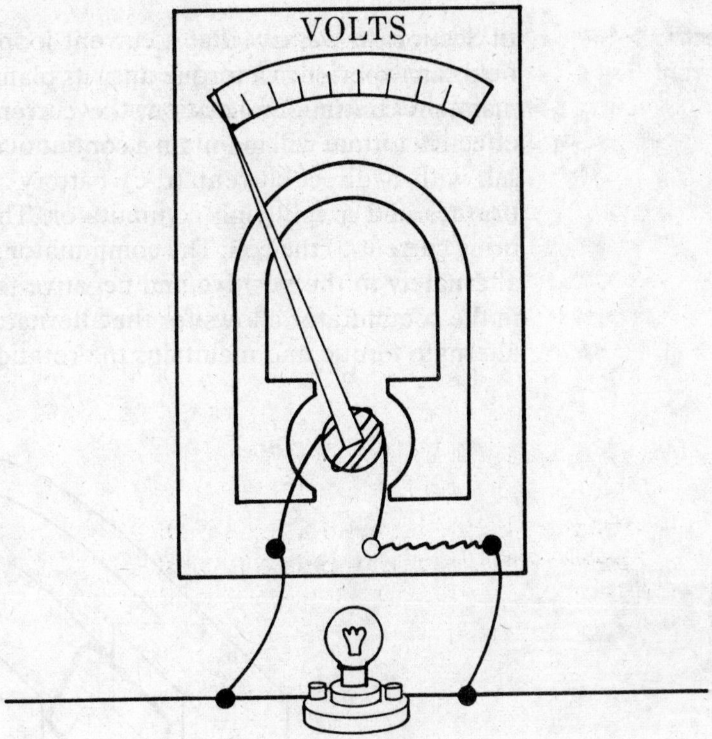

FIGURE 19.15

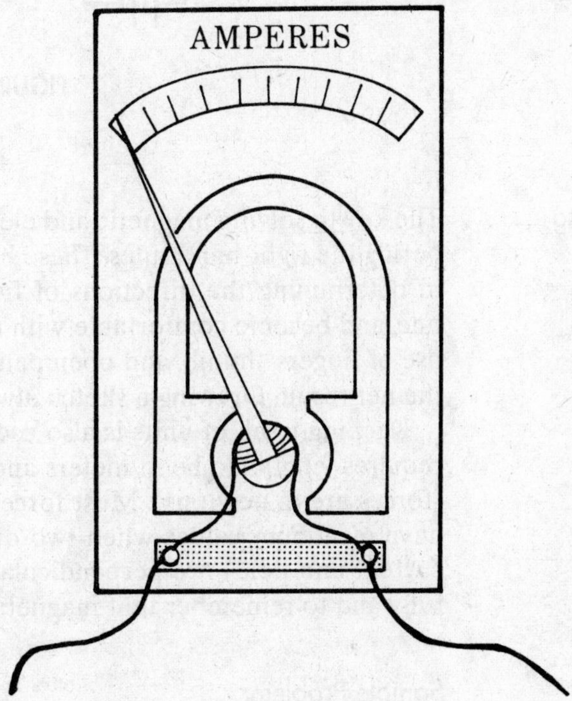

FIGURE 19.16

E. The Electric Direct-Current Motor

In Section A, we saw that a current loop placed in an external magnetic field can experience a torque until its plane is perpendicular to the field. To maintain continuous rotation, the current must be reversed so that the effective torque will maintain a continuous rotational direction. This reversal, with a direct-current (d-c) battery, is achieved through the use of brushes and a split-ring commutator. The brushes are metal strips that bring current to the coil. The commutator is a metal band that is connected alternately to the positive and negative terminals of the battery. The split in the commutator allows for the alternation of the current that creates an alternate torque and maintains the rotation (see Figure 19.17).

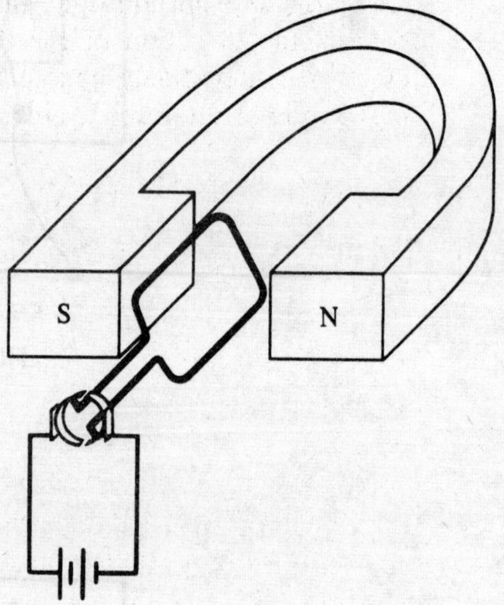

FIGURE 19.17

Problem-Solving Strategies for Magnetism

The key to solving magnetic and electromagnetic field problems is remembering the right-hand rules. These heuristics have been shown to be useful in determining the directions of field interaction forces. Memorize each one, and become comfortable with its use. Some rules are familiar in their use of fingers, thumb, and open palm. Make sure, however, that you know the net result. Drawing a sketch always helps.

Keeping track of units is also useful. The tesla is an SI unit and as such requires lengths to be in meters and velocities to be in meters per second (forces are in newtons). Most force interactions are angle dependent and have maximum values when two quantities (usually velocity and field or current and field) are perpendicular. Be sure to read each problem carefully and to remember that magnetic field **B** is a vector quantity!

Sample Problem:

An electron enters a magnetic field perpendicularly as shown below. The strength of the magnetic field is 100 T. If the velocity of the electron is

17,000 m/s, what is the magnitude and direction of the induced magnetic force on the electron?

B

XXXXXXXXXXXXXXXX

$e- \rightarrow \mathbf{V}$

XXXXXXXXXXXXXXXX

XXXXXXXXXXXXXXXX

Solution:

Using the appropriate right-hand rule, we know that, if the electron were a proton, the direction of the induced force would be upward. Since the electron is negatively charged, the direction is reversed downward. The magnitude of the force is given by

$$\mathbf{F} = \mathbf{B}Q\mathbf{v}$$

where $\mathbf{v} = 17,000$ m/s, $\mathbf{B} = 100$ T, and $Q = 1.6 \times 10^{-19}$ C. Thus,

$$\mathbf{F} = 2.72 \times 10^{-13} \text{ N}.$$

Practice Problems for Chapter 19

Multiple Choice

1. A charge moves in a circular orbit of radius R due to a uniform magnetic field. If the velocity of the charge is doubled, the orbital radius will become
   (A) $2R$
   (B) R
   (C) $R/2$
   (D) $4R$
   (E) $R/4$

2. Inside a solenoid, the magnetic field
   (A) is zero
   (B) decreases along the axis
   (C) increases along the axis
   (D) is uniform
   (E) increases, then decreases along the axis

3. A proton enters a magnetic field of 10 T and an electric field of 2000 N / C in such a way that it passes through both fields undeflected. The velocity of the proton will become
   (A) 2000 m/s
   (B) 200 m/s
   (C) 200,000 m/s
   (D) 20,000 m/s
   (E) 2,000,000 m/s

4. Which of the following measures will decrease the strength of the magnetic field of a solenoid ?
   (A) Increase the permeability of the core.
   (B) Increase the temperature of the solenoid.
   (C) Increase the current.
   (D) Increase the number of turns of wire.
   (E) All of these measures will decrease the strength.

5. An electron crosses a perpendicular magnetic field as shown below. The direction of the induced magnetic force is
   (A) to the right
   (B) to the left
   (C) up the page
   (D) out of the page
   (E) into the page

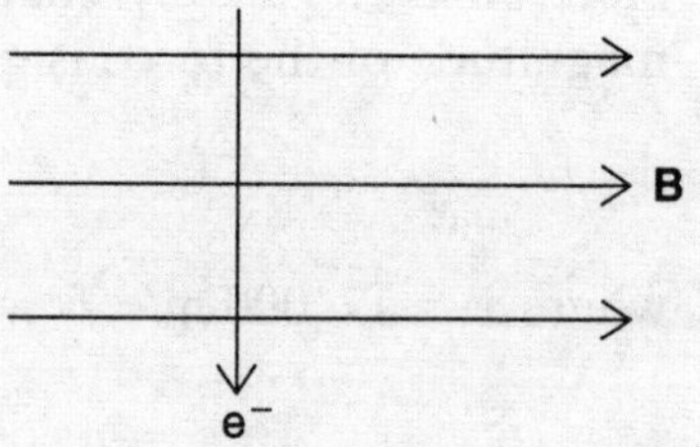

6. Three centimeters from a long, straight wire, the magnetic field produced by the current is determined to be equal to 3×10^{-5} T. The current in the wire must be
   (A) 2.0 A
   (B) 4.5 A
   (C) 1.5 A
   (D) 3 A
   (E) 5.0 A

7. In which direction does the compass needle point when it is placed near the straight wire carrying current in the direction shown below?
   (A) *A*
   (B) *B*
   (C) *C*
   (D) *D*
   (E) The direction will vary.

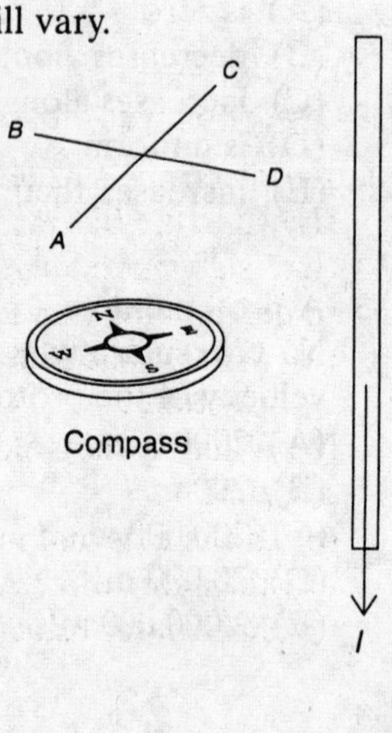

8. Magnetic field lines determine
   (A) only the direction of the field
   (B) the relative strength of the field
   (C) both the relative strength and the direction of the field
   (D) only the shape of the field
   (E) All of the preceding are correct.

9. What is the direction of the magnetic field at point A above the wire carrying current?
   (A) Out of the page
   (B) Into the page
   (C) Up the page
   (D) Down the page
   (E) To the right

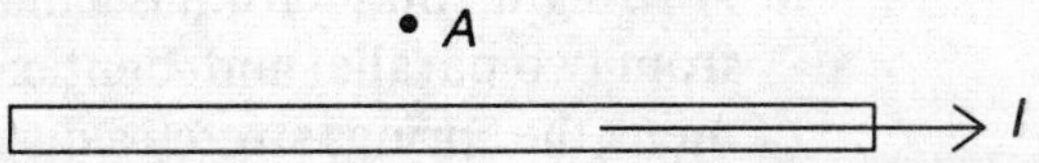

10. In which situation below did an electron enter the magnetic field at a nonright angle?
   (A) A
   (B) B
   (C) C
   (D) D
   (E) None of the preceding is correct.

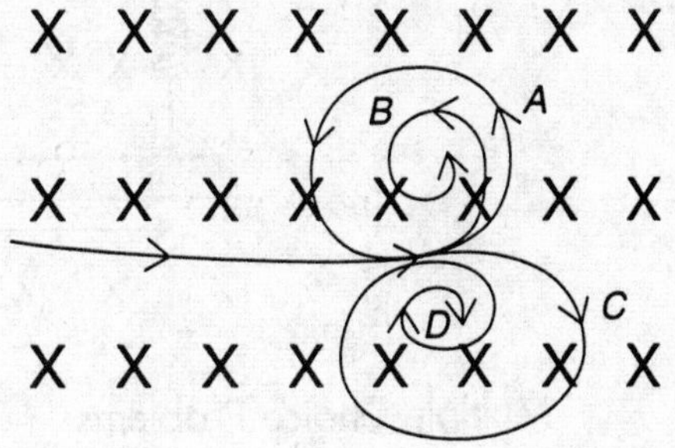

Free Response

1. An electron is accelerated by a potential difference of 12,000 V as shown in the following diagram. The electron enters a cathode ray tube that is 20 cm in length and the external magnetic field causes the path to deflect along a vertical screen for a distance y.
   (a) What is the kinetic energy of the electron as it enters the cathode ray tube?
   (b) What is the velocity of the electron as it enters the cathode ray tube?
   (c) If the external magnetic field has a strength of 4×10^{-5} T, what is the value of y? Assume that the field has a negligible effect on the horizontal velocity.

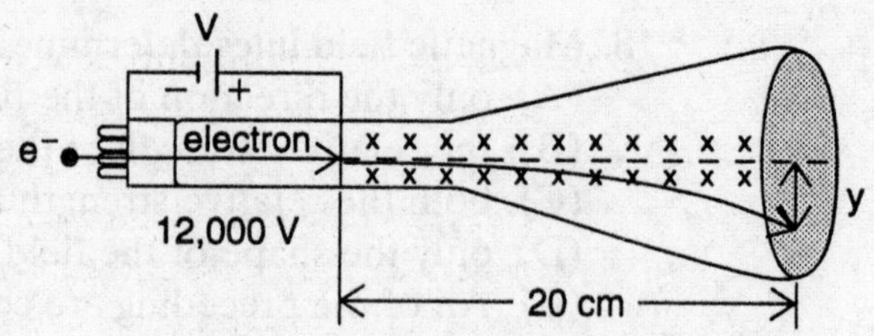

2. A proton enters a magnetic field perpendicularly with a velocity **v**.
   (a) Derive an expression for the angular frequency ω in terms of charge, mass, and field strength.
   (b) If the field strength is 2 T, what is the value of the angular frequency?
   (c) If the radius of the path is 2.2 mm, what is the linear velocity of the proton?

3. A straight conductor has a mass of 15 g and is 4 cm long. It is suspended from two parallel and identical springs as shown below. In this arrangement, the springs stretch a distance of 0.3 cm. The system is attached to a rigid source of potential difference equal to 15 V, and the overall resistance of the circuit is 5 Ω. When current flows through the conductor, an external magnetic field is turned on and it is observed that the springs stretch an additional 0.1 cm. What is the strength of the magnetic field?

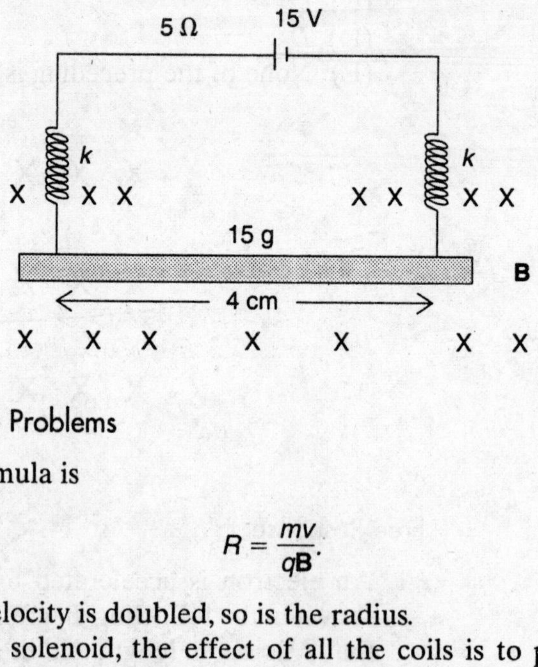

Solutions

Multiple-Choice Problems

1. **A** The formula is

$$R = \frac{mv}{q\mathbf{B}}.$$

If the velocity is doubled, so is the radius.

2. **D** Inside a solenoid, the effect of all the coils is to produce a long, uniform magnetic field.

3. **B** Using the formula and substituting the appropriate numbers gives

$$v = \frac{E}{\mathbf{B}} = \frac{2000}{10} = 200 \text{ m / s}.$$

4. **B** Increasing the temperature of the solenoid will increase the resistance of the coils. This, in turn, will decrease the current and hence decrease the strength of the magnetic field.

5. **E** Using the right-hand rule, we place the fingers of the right hand along the line of the magnetic field and point the thumb in the direction of the velocity. The palm points outward. However, since the particle is an electron, and the right-hand rule is designed for a positive charge, we must reverse the direction and say that the force is directed inward (into the page).

6. **B** The formula is

$$\mathbf{B} = \frac{\mu_0 I}{2\pi r} = \frac{(2 \times 10^{-7})I}{r}$$

Recalling that $r = 3$ cm $= 0.03$ m, we substitute all the given values to obtain $I = 4.5$ A.

7. **C** Imagine a circle surrounding the wire and use the right-hand rule. The direction of the circle would be clockwise if you were to look down on it. In this orientation, the field goes from right to left. On the left side, the needle will enter the page, and in perspective that is the *C* direction.

8. **C** Magnetic field lines were introduced by Michael Faraday to determine both the direction of the field and its relative strength (a stronger field is indicated by a greater line density).

9. **A** Using the right-hand rule, we find that the circle surrounding the wire will have its field coming out of the page at point *A*.

10. **D** When a charged particle (here, an electron) enters a magnetic field at an angle other than 90°, it takes a spiral path. Using the right-hand rule and reversing for the negative charge gives us *D* for the desired situation (the path is seen in perspective since the field is inward).

Free-Response Problems

1. (a) The kinetic energy of the electron is the product of its charge and potential difference. Thus,

$$KE = (1.6 \times 10^{-19})(12{,}000) = 1.92 \times 10^{-15}\text{ J}$$

(b) The formula for the velocity, when the mass and kinetic energy are known, is

$$\mathbf{v} = \sqrt{\frac{2KE}{m}} = \sqrt{\frac{(2)\,(1.92 \times 10^{-15})}{9.1 \times 10^{-31}}} = 6.5 \times 10^{7}\text{ m / s}$$

(c) The magnetic force will cause a downward uniform acceleration, which can be found from Newton's second law, $\mathbf{F} = m\mathbf{a}$. The force will be due to the magnetic force, $\mathbf{F} = qv\mathbf{B}$. Thus, $\mathbf{a} = \frac{qv\mathbf{B}}{m}$. Using our known values, we get

$$\mathbf{a} = 4.57 \times 10^{14}\text{ m/s}^2$$

Now, for linear motion downward (recall projectile motion), $\mathbf{y} = (1/2)\mathbf{a}t^2$. The time to drop y meters is the same time required to go 20 cm (0.20 m), assuming no change in horizontal velocity. Thus,

$$t = \frac{x}{\mathbf{v}} = \frac{0.20}{6.5 \times 10^7} = 3 \times 10^{-9}\ \text{s}.$$

This implies that, upon substitution, $y = 0.00205$ m $= 2.05$ mm.

2. (a) We know that $\mathbf{v} = q\mathbf{B}r / m$ and $\boldsymbol{\omega} = \mathbf{v} / r$. Thus,

$$\boldsymbol{\omega} = \frac{q\mathbf{B}}{m}$$

(b) Substituting the known values gives

$$\boldsymbol{\omega} = 1.9 \times 10^8\ \text{rad/s}.$$

(c) Now we have

$$\mathbf{v} = \boldsymbol{\omega}\, r = (0.0022)(1.9 \times 10^8) = 4.2 \times 10^8\ \text{m/s}$$

3. The effect of the conductor is to stretch both springs. Since we have two parallel springs of equal force constant k, we know from our work on oscillatory motion (Chapter 13) that the effective spring constant is equal to $2k$. Thus:

$$\mathbf{F} = 2k\,\Delta\mathbf{x}$$

where $\Delta x = 0.003$ m. Thus, the weight of the conductor is

$$\mathbf{W} = m\mathbf{g} = (0.015)(9.8) = 0.147\ \text{N}$$

and $k = 24.5$ N / m. Now, the magnetic force, $\mathbf{F} = \mathbf{B}IL$, is responsible for another elongation, x. Since $\mathbf{F} = k\mathbf{x}$, we have (with both springs attached)

$$\mathbf{B}IL = (24.5)(0.002) = 0.0490\ \text{N}.$$

The length of the conductor is 4 cm = 0.04 m; and using Ohm's law, we know that the current is $I = 15 / 5 = 3$ A. Thus, we find that

$$\mathbf{B}(3)(0.04) = 0.0490 \quad \text{implies} \quad \mathbf{B} = 0.4\ \text{T}.$$

CHAPTER 20

Electromagnetic Induction

20.1 Induced Motional EMF in a Wire

We know from Oersted's experiments, mentioned in Chapter 19, that a current in a wire generates a magnetic field. We also know that the field of a solenoid approximates that of an ordinary bar magnet. A third fact is that the magnetic property of a material (called its **permeability**) influences the strength of its magnetic field. Additionally, the interactions between fields lead to magnetic forces that can be used to operate an electric meter or motor.

A question can now be raised: Can a magnetic field be used to induce a current in a wire? The answer, investigated in the early nineteenth century by French scientist Andre Ampere, is yes. However, the procedure is not as simple as placing a wire in a magnetic field and having a current "magically" arise!

A simple experimental setup is shown in Figure 20.1. A horseshoe magnet is arranged with a conducting wire attached to a galvanometer. When the wire rests in the magnetic field, the galvanometer registers zero current. If the wire is then moved through the field in such a way that its motion "cuts across" the imaginary field lines, the galvanomter will register the presence of a small current. If, however, the wire is moved through the field in such a way that its motion remains parallel to the field, again no current is present. This experiment also reveals that a maximum current, for a given

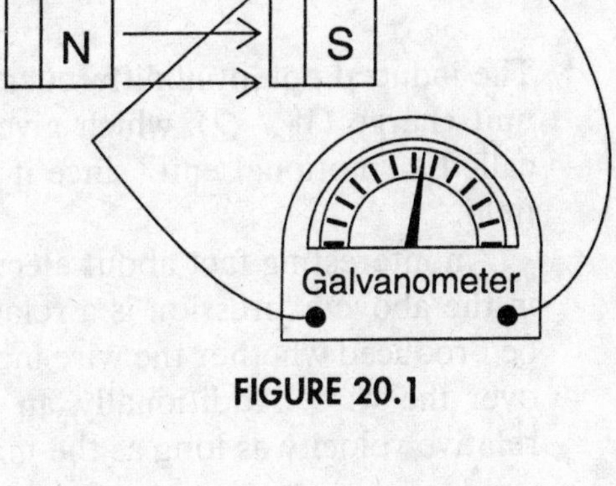

FIGURE 20.1

velocity, occurs when the wire moves perpendicularly through the field (which suggests a dependency on the sine of the orientation angle).

The phenomenon described above is known as **electromagnetic induction**. The source of the induced current is the establishment of a **motional emf** due to the change in something called the **magnetic flux**, which we will define shortly.

If the wire is moved up and down through the field in Figure 20.1, the galvanometer shows that the induced current alternates back and forth according to a right-hand rule. The fingers of the right hand point in the direction of the magnetic field; the thumb points in the direction of the velocity of the wire. Finally, the open palm indicates the direction of the induced current.

Now, since a parallel motion through the field implies no induced current, if the wire is moved at any other angle, only the perpendicular component contributes to the induction process. Additionally, it can be demonstrated that the magnitude of the induced current varies directly with the velocity of the wire, the length of wire in the field, and the strength of the external field. Since current is related to potential difference (emf) through Ohm's law ($V = IR$), we can write

$$\text{emf} = \mathbf{B}\ell\mathbf{v} \tag{1}$$

where **v** is the perpendicular velocity component.

The derivation of this expression involves a reconsideration of the induced magnetic force on a charge in an external magnetic field. Recall that, if **v** is a perpendicular velocity component, $\mathbf{F} = \mathbf{B}q\mathbf{v}$ is the expression for the magnitude of the induced magnetic force on a charge q. Now, the wire in our situation contains charges that will experience a force **F** if we can get them to move through an external field. Physically moving the entire wire accomplishes this task. The direction of the induced force, determined by the right-hand rule, is along the length of the wire. If we let Q represent the total charge per second, we can write

$$\mathbf{F} = \mathbf{B}Q\mathbf{v} \tag{2}$$

The charges experience a force as long as they are in the magnetic field. This situation occurs for a length ℓ, and the work done by the force is given by $W = \mathbf{F}\ell$. Thus

$$W = \mathbf{B}Q\mathbf{v}\ell \tag{3}$$

The induced potential difference (emf) is a measure of the work done per unit charge (W / Q), which gives us emf $= \mathbf{B}q\mathbf{v}$. This emf is sometimes called a "motional emf" since it is due to the motion of a wire through a field.

An interesting fact about electromagnetic induction is that the velocity in the above expression is a relative velocity, that is, the induced emf can be produced whether the wire moves through the field or the field changes over the wire! Additionally, an emf can be induced even if there is no relative velocity as long as the magnetic field is changing.

Figure 20.2 is a simple illustration of this effect.

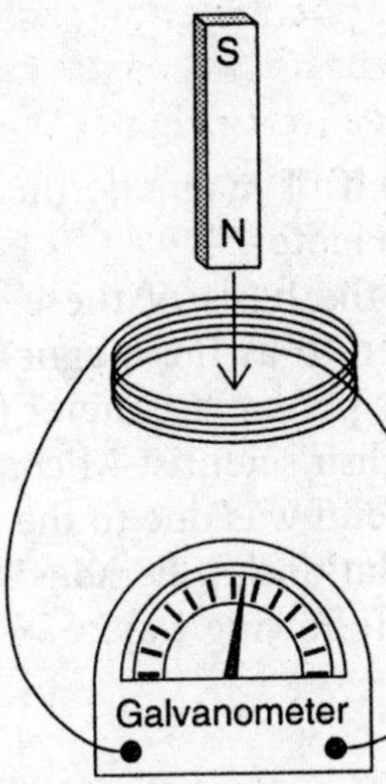

FIGURE 20.2

In Figure 20.2, a bar magnet is thrust into and out of a coil in which there are N turns of wire. The number of coils is related to the overall length ℓ in equation 1. The galvanometer registers the alternating current in the coil as the magnet is inserted and withdrawn. Varying the velocity affects the amount of current as predicted. Moving the magnet around the outside of the coils generates only a weak current. The concept of relative velocity is illustrated if the magnet is held constant and the coil is moved up and down over the magnet.

20.2 Magnetic Flux and Faraday's Law of Induction

In Figure 20.3, there is a circular region of cross-sectional area A. An external magnetic field **B** passes through the region at an angle θ to the region. The perpendicular component of the field is given by

$$\mathbf{B}_\perp = \mathbf{B} \cos \theta$$

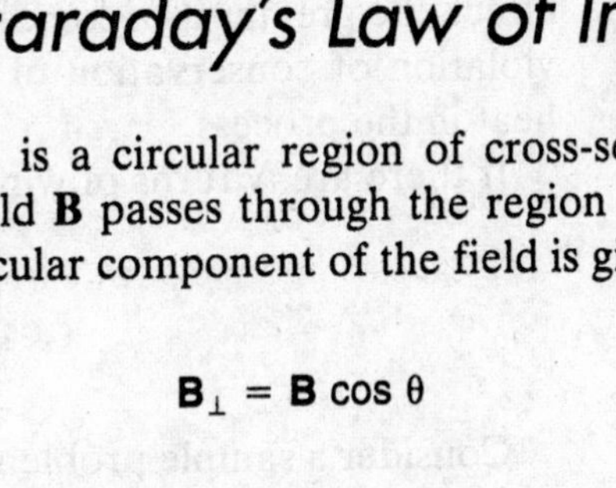

FIGURE 20.3 Magnetic Flux

The magnetic flux, Φ, is defined as the product of the perpendicular component of the magnetic field and the cross-sectional area A:

$$\Phi = \mathbf{B}A \cos \theta$$

The unit of magnetic flux is the **weber** (Wb); 1 weber equals 1 tesla per square meter.

On the basis of these ideas, the magnetic field strength is sometimes referred to as the **magnetic flux density** and can be expressed in units of webers per square meter (Wb / m²).

English scientist Michael Faraday demonstrated that the induced motional emf was due to the rate of change of the magnetic flux. We now call this relationship **Faraday's law of electromagnetic induction** and express it in the following way:

$$\text{emf} = -\left(\frac{\Delta\Phi}{\Delta t}\right)$$

The negative sign is used because another relationship, known as **Lenz's law**, states that an induced current will always flow in a direction such that its magnetic field opposes the magnetic field that induced it. Lenz's law is just another way of expressing the law of conservation of energy. Consider the experiment in Figure 20.2. When the magnet is inserted through the coil, an induced current flows. This current, in turn, produces a magnetic field that is directed either into or out of the coil, along the same axis as the bar magnet.

If the current had a direction such that the "pole" of the coil attracted the pole of the bar magnet, more energy would be derived from the effect than is possible in nature. Thus, according to Lenz's law, the current in the coil will have a direction so that the new magnetic field will oppose the magnetic field of the bar magnet. The more one tries to overcome this effect, the greater it becomes. The opposition of fields in this way prevents violation of conservation of energy and can generate a large amount of heat in the process.

If there are N turns of wire in the coil, Faraday's law becomes:

$$\text{emf} = -N\left(\frac{\Delta\Phi}{\Delta t}\right)$$

Consider a sample problem. A coil is made of 10 turns of wire and has a diameter of 5 cm. The coil is passing through the field in such a way that the axis of the coil is parallel to the field. The strength of the field is 0.5 T. What is the change in the magnetic flux? Also, if an average emf of 2 V is observed, for how long was the flux changing?

The change in the magnetic flux is given by

$$\Delta\Phi = -\mathbf{B}A = -\mathbf{B}\pi r^2 = -(0.5)(3.14)(0.025)^2 = -9.8 \times 10^{-4}\ \text{Wb}$$

The time is therefore given by

$$\Delta t = N\left(\frac{\Delta\Phi}{\text{emf}}\right) = 10\left(\frac{9.8 \times 10^{-4}}{2}\right) = 4.9 \times 10^{-3}\text{ s}$$

20.3 Generators

Using Faraday's law, we can demonstrate an electromagnetic generator. In Figure 20.4, wire is shaped into a coil loop and wound around an armature. This armature is connected to a shaft that is easily rotated. Wires from the coil are connected to two slip rings that have no gaps in them, and each ring is then connected to a metallic brush. The remaining wires can be connected to a galvanometer, as shown, or to a mechanical device.

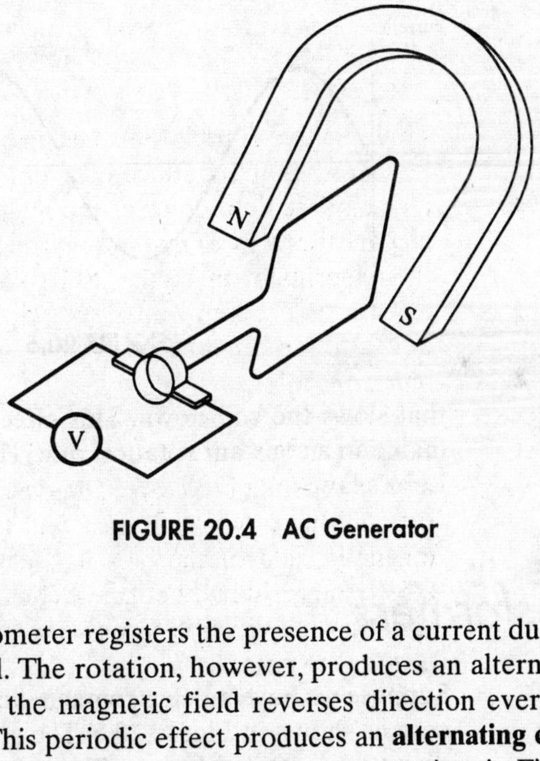

FIGURE 20.4 AC Generator

The galvanometer registers the presence of a current due to the induced emf in the coil. The rotation, however, produces an alternating current as the change in the magnetic field reverses direction every half-turn (see Figure 20.5). This periodic effect produces an **alternating current**, which is sinusoidal in shape. The graph of voltage versus time in Figure 20.5 would follow an equation of the form

$$V = V_{max} \cos 2\pi f t$$

where f is the frequency of alternation.

If commutator rings (with gaps) are used instead of slip rings, the alternating current can be converted into **direct current**. The commutator rings act like **full-wave rectifiers**, permitting only current in one direction to pass through the circuit. An electronic **diode** can also act as a rectifier in an alternating current (a-c) circuit, such as a radio.

The current induced in the coil will in turn produce a magnetic field. This changing magnetic field will **self-induce** the coil and produce a **back emf**

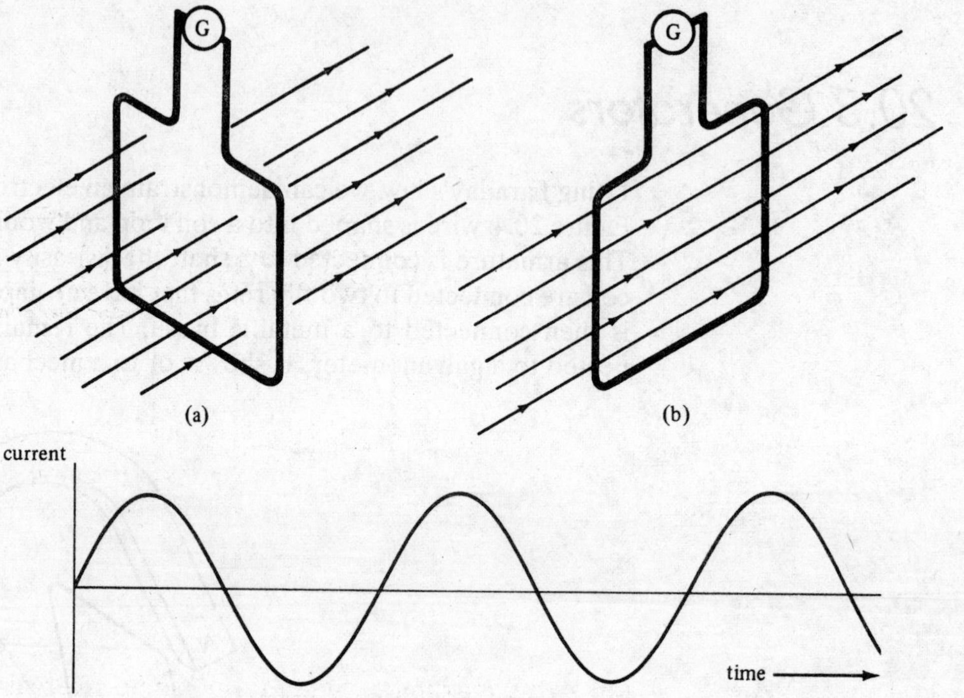

FIGURE 20.5

that slows the coil down. This effect often occurs in an electric motor to maintain a constant rotation rate. The back emf is a direct consequence of Lenz's law.

20.4 Transformers

Suppose we have an electromagnet consisting of a solenoid with a soft-iron core as shown in Figure 20.6. The solenoid is connected to a switch and a direct-current (d-c) battery. There are N turns of wire on the solenoid (now called the "primary"). Near the primary is a second solenoid (known as the "secondary") that is connected to a galvanometer. The secondary consists of n turns of wire around an iron core. The two solenoids are near each other, but not touching.

When the switch is initially closed on the primary, the galvanometer registers the presence of a current in the secondary that quickly goes to zero. With a steady current flowing through the primary, the galvanometer in the secondary registers zero. However, when the switch is initially opened, the galvanometer again registers a current in the opposite direction and then quickly approaches zero once again.

The ability of one solenoid to induce an emf in another is called **mutual induction** and is responsible for a phenomenon known as the **transformer effect**. When the switch was initially closed, the current in the primary built

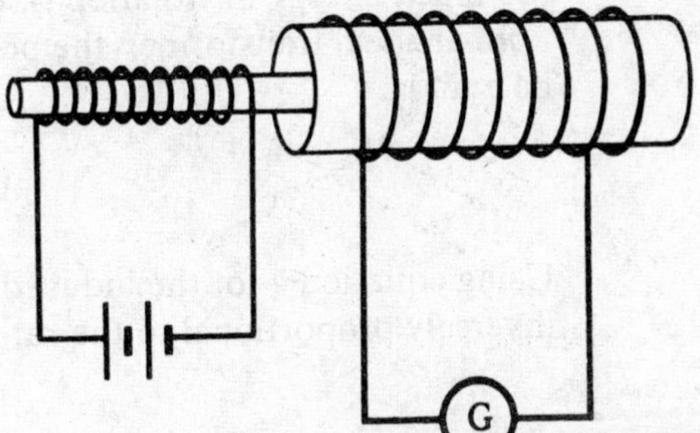

FIGURE 20.6

up to its maximum value during some interval of time. This changing current also generates a changing magnetic field. The changing field can move through space to the secondary and hence induce an emf there, based on the core material and the number of turns of wire. If a specially designed a-c voltmeter was attached, the induced emf could be measured.

Experimentally, it was determined that, with a smaller number of turns in the secondary, the voltage reading goes down. If the number of turns in the secondary is greater, then the induced emf will be greater as well.

The system described above is known as a **transformer**. A simple transformer is shown in Figure 20.7.

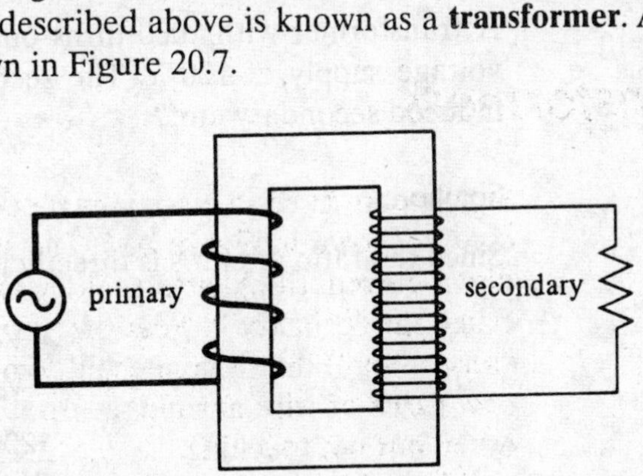

FIGURE 20.7 Step-up Transformer

If we induce a larger emf, we have a **step-up transformer**. With a lower emf, we have a **step-down transformer**. In either case, the induced emf is proportional to the ratio of the number of turns of wire in both solenoids. If we let N_1 be the number of turns in the primary and N_2 be the number of turns in the secondary, then

$$\frac{V_1}{V_2} = \frac{N_1}{N_2} \tag{4}$$

where V_1 and V_2 are the emf's in the primary and secondary, respectively.

It should be noted that Lenz's law plays a role here as well. The induced current in the secondary, given by Ohm's law if the resistance of the secondary is known, will in turn generate an opposing magnetic field in itself and the primary. This constant back emf will prevent the build-up of too much energy in violation of the law of conservation of energy.

In an ideal transformer, the power generated in the two solenoids would be equal:

$$V_1 I_1 = V_2 I_2 \tag{5}$$

Using equation 4 for the induced emf's, we find that the ratio of currents is inversely proportional to the ratio of turns:

$$\frac{I_1}{I_2} = \frac{N_2}{N_1} \tag{6}$$

Thus, as voltages are stepped up, the currents are stepped down. When electricity is brought to your home, the power company steps up the voltage in high-voltage lines to reduce the current. This has the effect of lowering the "joule heating " losses, which are proportional to the current. Outside your home, the transformers attached to telephone poles step down the voltage, and this is the supply brought to your main electrical box. Transformers are used in many electrical devices and are most obvious in electric train and racing car sets.

Sample Problem:

A transformer with 1000 turns on its primary coil is connected to an a-c voltage supply, of 120 V. The secondary coil has 200 turns. What is the induced secondary emf?

Solution:

Since the ratio of emf's is directly proportional to the ratio of turns:

$$\frac{V_1}{V_2} = \frac{N_1}{N_2}$$

$$\frac{120}{V_2} = \frac{1000}{200}$$

Thus, $V_2 = 24$ V(a-c).

Problem-Solving Strategies for Electromagnetic Induction

When solving electromagnetic problems, keep in mind that vector quantities are involved. The directions of these vectors are usually determined by the right-hand rules. Additionally, remember Lenz's law: **An induced current will always flow in a direction such that its magnetic field opposes the magnetic field that induced it**, which plays a role in many applications.

When solving problems in electromagnetic induction, it is important to remember the right-hand rules. Also, keep in mind that the induced emf is proportional to the change in the magnetic flux, not the magnetic field.

Practice Problems for Chapter 20

Multiple Choice

1. The back emf of a motor is at a maximum when
   (A) the speed of the motor is constant
   (B) the speed of the motor is at its maximum value
   (C) the motor is first turned on
   (D) the speed of the motor is increasing
   (E) the motor is turned off

2. A bar magnet is pushed through a flat coil of wire. The induced emf is greatest when
   (A) the north pole is pushed through first
   (B) the magnet is pushed through quickly
   (C) the magnet is pushed through slowly
   (D) the south pole is pushed through first
   (E) the magnet rests in the coil

3. The magnetic flux through a wire loop is independent of
   (A) the shape of the magnetic field
   (B) the area of the loop
   (C) the strength of the magnetic flux
   (D) the orientation of the magnetic field and the loop
   (E) none of the preceding

4. A flat, 300-turn coil has a resistance of 3 Ω. The coil covers an area of 15 cm^2 in such a way that its axis is parallel to an external magnetic field. At what rate must the magnetic field change in order to induce a current of 0. 75 A in the coil?
   (A) 0.0075 T/s
   (B) 2.5 T/s
   (C) 0.0005 T/s
   (D) 5 T/s
   (E) 15 T/s

5. When a loop of wire is turned in a magnetic field, the direction of the induced emf changes every
   (A) one-quarter revolution
   (B) two revolutions
   (C) one revolution
   (D) one-half revolution
   (E) The direction never changes.

6. A wire of length 0.15 m is passed through a magnetic field with a strength of 0.2 T. What must be the velocity of the wire if an emf of 0.25 V is to be induced?
   (A) 8.3 m/s
   (B) 6.7 m/s
   (C) 0.0075 m/s
   (D) 0.12 m/s
   (E) 7.6 m/s

Answer questions 7–9 based on the following information:

The primary coil of an ideal transformer has 200 turns, while the secondary coil has 50 turns. The power generated in the primary coil is 600 W when the coil is connected to a 120-V a-c supply.

7. What is the power generated in the secondary coil?
   (A) 1200 W
   (B) 60 W
   (C) 2400 W
   (D) 150 W
   (E) 600 W

8. What is the current in the secondary coil?
   (A) 5 A
   (B) 10 A
   (C) 0.2 A
   (D) 20 A
   (E) 2 A

9. The induced emf in the secondary coil is equal to
   (A) 60 V
   (B) 480 V
   (C) 300 V
   (D) 120 V
   (E) 30 V

10. A loop of wire is rotated through 360° across an external magnetic field. During one period of revolution, the induced emf in the coil will change in
    (A) magnitude only
    (B) direction only
    (C) both magnitude and direction
    (D) neither magnitude nor direction
    (E) first magnitude and then direction

Free Response

1. A horizontal conducting bar is free to slide along a pair of vertical bars, as shown on page 269. The conductor has length ℓ and mass M. As it slides vertically downward under the influence of gravity, it passes through an outward-directed, uniform magnetic field. The resistance of

the entire circuit is R. Find an expression for the terminal velocity of the conductor (neglect any frictional effects due to sliding).

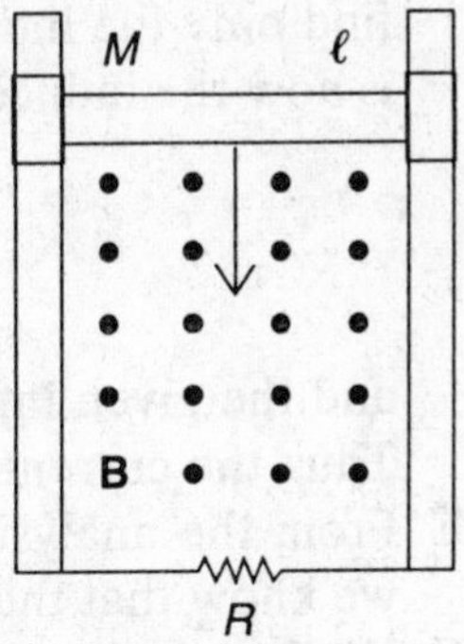

2. A motor with a series of coils that have a total resistance of 20 Ω is operated with a 120-V power supply. While the motor is running at maximum speed, the current in the coils is measured to be 2 A. What is the back emf at that time?

3. (a) A small cylindrical magnet is dropped into a long copper tube. The magnet takes longer to emerge than the predicted free-fall time. Give an explanation for this effect.
   (b) A generator consists of a coil of wire connected to a crank shaft, surrounded by four horseshoe magnets. The wires from the coils are connected to a light socket into which a bulb can be inserted. A boy who begins to turn the shaft with no bulb in the socket finds the shaft very easy to turn. However, as his teacher inserts the bulb, the shaft become more difficult to turn. Explain this effect.

Solutions

Multiple-Choice Problems

1. **B** The back emf is proportional to the rate of change of magnetic flux and opposes the ability of the motor to turn. It is at its greatest value when the speed of the motor is a maximum.
2. **B** The motional emf is equal to $\mathbf{B}\ell\mathbf{v}$, where $\mathbf{v}$ is the velocity of the bar magnet. Thus, the induced emf is greatest when the magnet is pushed through quickly.
3. **A** The magnetic flux is independent of the shape of the wire loop.
4. **D** The formula for the rate of change of magnetic flux is emf $= -N(\Delta\Phi / \Delta t)$. Using the given values and Ohm's law, we get for the magnitude of the flux change

$$\left(\frac{\Delta\Phi}{\Delta t}\right) = \frac{(0.75)(3)}{300} = 0.0075 \text{ Wb/s}$$

Our question concerns the rate of change of the magnetic field. In a situation in which the axis of the coil is parallel to the magnetic field, $\Phi = \mathbf{B}A$, where $A = 0.0015$ m^2. Thus $\Delta\mathbf{B}/\Delta t = 5$ T/s.

5. **D** In an a-c generator, the emf reverses direction every one-half revolution.
6. **A** The motional emf is given by emf $= \mathbf{B}\ell\mathbf{v}$. Thus, using the given values, we find that $\mathbf{v} = 8.3$ m/s.

7. **E** In an ideal transformer, the power in the secondary coil is equal to the power in the primary coil, which is 600 W.
8. **D** Since the power in the secondary coil is equal to 600 W, we need to find only the induced secondary emf ($P = VI$, where the voltage V is now the induced emf). Using the transformer equations

$$\frac{V_1}{V_2} = \frac{N_1}{N_2}$$

and the given information, we find that the secondary emf is 30 V. Thus, the current is 20 A.
9. **E** From the analysis for problem 8, using the transformer equations, we know that the secondary induced emf is equal to 30 V.
10. **C** While rotating through the magnetic field, the induced emf goes through a maximum and minimum magnitude, as well as a reversal in direction.

Free-Response Problems

1. Initially, the bar is accelerated downward by the force of gravity, given by $\mathbf{F} = M\mathbf{g}$. The resistance R, in conjunction with the induced current I, produces an emf equal to IR and also to the product $\mathbf{B}\ell\mathbf{v}$. The magnetic force due to the current I is given by $\mathbf{B}I\ell$. Combining all these ideas, we get that at terminal velocity

$$M\mathbf{g} = I\ell\mathbf{B} \quad \text{and} \quad I = \frac{\mathbf{B}\ell\mathbf{v}}{R}$$

Thus

$$\mathbf{v}_t = \frac{M\mathbf{g}R}{\ell^2\mathbf{B}^2}$$

2. When the motor is first turned on, the current in the motor is given by

$$I = \frac{\text{emf}}{R} = 6\text{ A}$$

At maximum speed the current is 2 A and is given by

$$I = \frac{\text{emf} - \text{emf}_{\text{back}}}{R}$$

Thus

$$\text{emf}_{\text{back}} = \text{emf} - IR = 120 - (2)(20) = 80\text{ V}$$

3. (a) Copper is not highly magnetic. However, because of Lenz's law, the currents set up in the tube produce an upward magnetic field opposing the original field. The result is to slow down the magnet's terminal velocity, as compared to the normal uniformly accelerated motion.

   (b) The back emf produced by the generator takes effect when the bulb makes electrical contact. The resistance will increase the more the boy tries to overcome it by turning the shaft faster.

CHAPTER 21

Waves and Sound

21.1 Pulses

A pulse is a single vibratory disturbance in a medium. An example of a pulse is seen in Figure 21.1. If a string fixed at both ends and made taut, under a tension T (in newtons), is given a quick up and down snap, an upwardly pointing pulse is directed from the left to the right. The pulse appears to travel with a velocity v down the string. In actuality, the energy transferred to the string causes segments to vibrate up and down successively. This effect produces the illusion of a continuous pulse. Only energy is transferred by the pulse, and because the vibration is perpendicular to the apparent direction of motion, the pulse is said to be **transverse**. The **amplitude** of the pulse is the displacement of the disturbance above the level of the string.

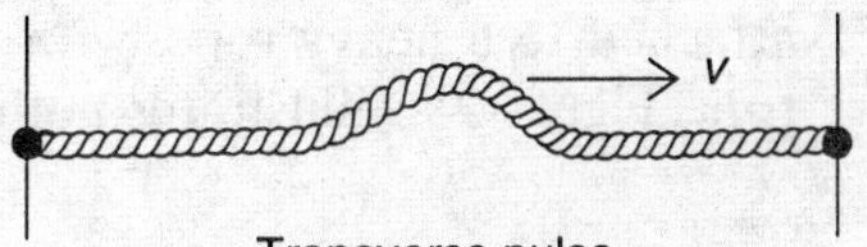

Transverse pulse

FIGURE 21.1

If the tension in the string is increased, the velocity appears to increase. If a heavier string is used (greater mass per unit length), the pulse appears to move slower. Careful measurements of these observations leads to the following equation for the velocity of the pulse:

$$v = \sqrt{\frac{T}{M/\ell}}$$

where T is the tension in newtons, M is the mass in kilograms, and ℓ is the length of the string in meters.

When the pulse reaches one boundary, the energy transferred is directed upward against the wall, creating an upward force. Since the wall is rigid, the reaction to this action is a downward force. The string responds by being displaced downward and is reflected back. The result of this boundary interaction, illustrated in Figure 21.2, is observed as an inversion of the pulse upon reflection. Some energy is lost in the interaction, but most is reflected back with the pulse.

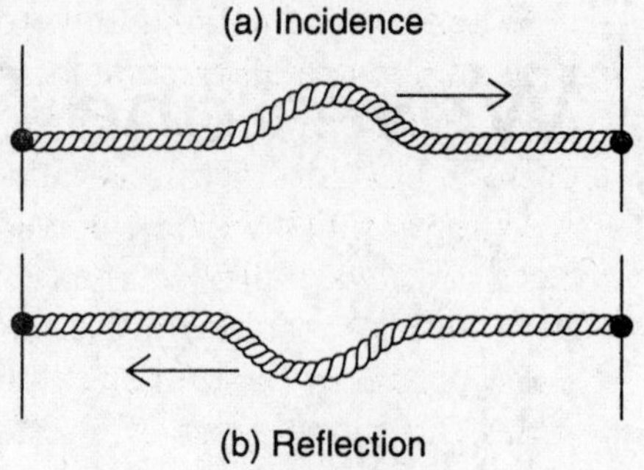

FIGURE 21.2

At a nonrigid boundary, say between two strings of different masses (but equal tensions), a different effect occurs. When the pulse reaches the nonrigid boundary, the upward displacement causes the second string to also be displaced upward. The magnitude of the second displacement depends on the mass density and tension in the second string. Thus, the transmitted pulse has an upward orientation and may travel with a larger or smaller velocity, depending, in this case, on the mass density.

The reflected pulse will be upward in orientation since no inversion takes place with a nonrigid boundary unless the difference between the two media (as measured by the second string's inertia) is large enough to behave as a semirigid boundary. As an example, consider a light string attached to a heavy rope, with the pulse traveling from the string to the rope. Figure 21.3 illustrates both cases.

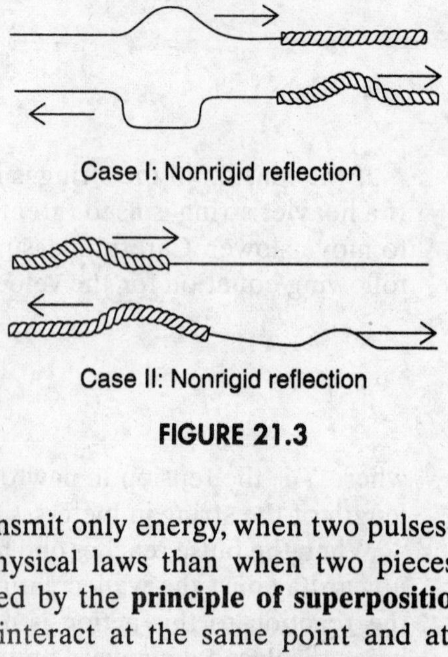

FIGURE 21.3

Since pulses transmit only energy, when two pulses interact, they obey a different set of physical laws than when two pieces of matter interact. Pulses are governed by the **principle of superposition**, which states that, when two pulses interact at the same point and at the same time, the interaction produces a single pulse whose amplitude displacement is equal to the sum of the displacements of the original two pulses. After the interaction, however, both pulses continue in their original directions of motion, unaffected by the interaction. Sometimes, this interaction is called **interference**.

When a pulse with an upward displacement interacts with another pulse with an upward displacement, the resulting pulse has a displacement larger than that of either original pulse (equal to the numerical sum of these pulses). This interaction is called **constructive interference.**

When a pulse with an upward displacement interacts with a pulse that has a downward displacement, the interaction is called **destructive interference**, and the resulting pulse has a smaller displacement than either original pulse (equal to the numerical difference of these pulses). Figure 21.4 illustrates these two types of interferences; *a* and *b* designate the two original amplitudes and *p* is a point on the string.

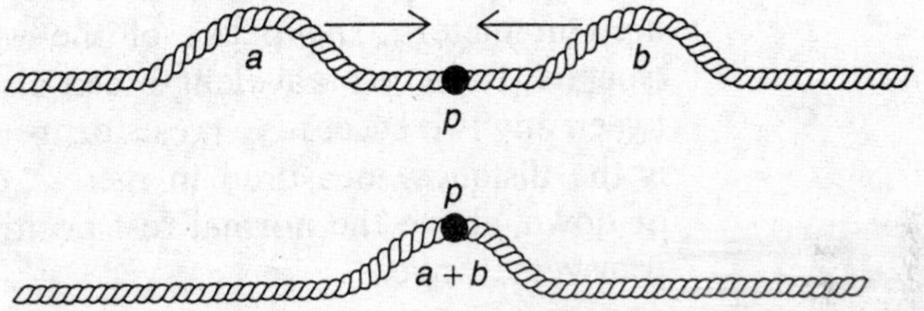

(a) Constructive interference

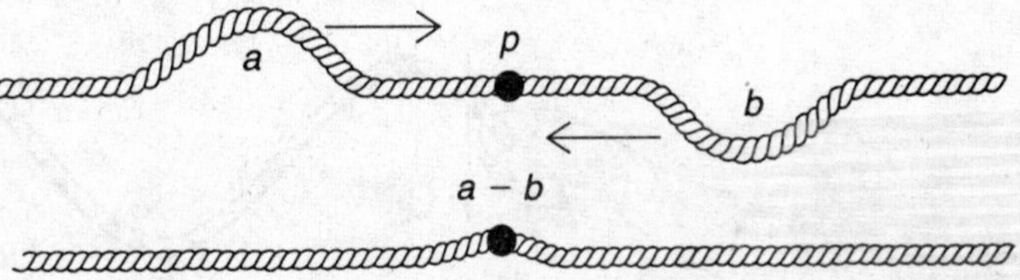

(b) Destructive interference

FIGURE 21.4

In the destructive interference case, it is possible, if the amplitudes are equal, that the interaction will momentarily cancel out both pulses. In any case, the orientation of the resulting pulse depends on the magnitude of each amplitude.

21.2 Wave Motion

If a continuous up and down vibration is given to the string in Figure 21.1, the resulting set of transverse pulses is called a **wave train** or just a **series of waves**. Whereas the pulse was just an upward- or downward-oriented, transverse disturbance, a wave consists of a complete up and down segment. Waves are thus periodic disturbances in a medium. The number of waves per second is called the **frequency**, designated by the letter *f* and expressed in units of reciprocal seconds (s^{-1})or **Hertz** (Hz). The time required to complete one wave cycle is called the **period**, designated by the capital letter T and expressed in seconds. The frequency and period of a wave are reciprocals of each other, so that $f = 1 / T$.

Like pulses, waves transmit only energy. The particles in the medium vibrate only up and down as the transverse waves approach and pass a given point. Since there is a contiuous series of waves, many points in the medium will be moving up or down in unison. The **phase** of a wave is defined to be the relative position of a point on a wave with respect to another point on the same wave.

The distance between any two successive points in phase is a measure of the **wavelength**, designated by the Greek letter λ (lambda) and measured in meters. The peaks of the wave are called **crests**; the valleys, **troughs**. Thus, one wavelength can also be measured as the distance between any two successive crests or troughs. The **amplitude**, A, of the wave is the distance, measured in meters, of the maximum displacement, up or down, above the normal rest position. Figure 21.5 illustrates a typical transverse wave.

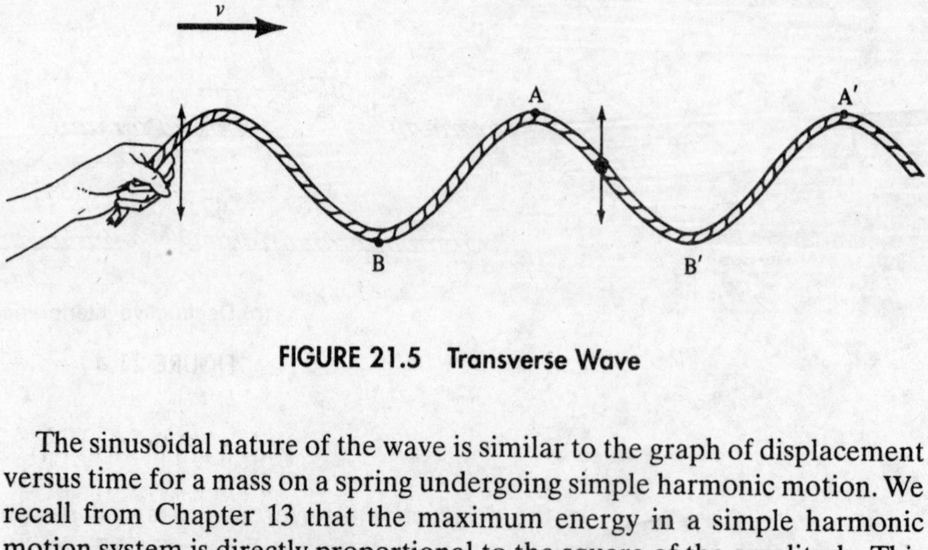

FIGURE 21.5 Transverse Wave

The sinusoidal nature of the wave is similar to the graph of displacement versus time for a mass on a spring undergoing simple harmonic motion. We recall from Chapter 13 that the maximum energy in a simple harmonic motion system is directly proportional to the square of the amplitude. This is indeed the case with a simple wave motion like the one described in Figure 21.5. In this illustration we can identify points a, b, and c as all in phase. Points d and e are also in phase, and the distance from d to e can also be used to measure the wavelength. Finally, the velocity of the transverse wave is given by the equation $\mathbf{v} = f\lambda$.

Since each wave carries energy, it should not be surprising that the frequency is also proportional to the energy of a wave. The amplitude is related to what we might consider the wave's **intensity**. In sound, this property might be called **volume**. The frequency, however, measures the **pitch** of the wave. Waves of higher frequency transmit, at the same amplitude, more energy per second than waves of lower frequency.

There are many different kinds of frequencies that interact with human senses. It is worthwhile, therefore, to recall that the prefix *kilo-* represents 10^3, the prefix *mega-* represents 10^6, and the prefix *giga-* represents 10^9.

21.3 Types of Waves

In physics we usually deal with two types of waves, mechanical and electromagnetic. Waves that result from the vibration of a physical medium (a drum, a string, water, etc.) are called **mechanical waves**. Waves that result from electromagnetic interactions (light, X rays, radio waves, etc.) are called **electromagnetic waves**. These electromagnetic waves are special since they do not require a physical medium to carry them.

Also, all electromagnetic waves are transverse in nature. Physicists know this because of an analogous behavior with mechanical waves. Imagine a long string as shown in Figure 21.5. We can set up transverse vibrations in the spring by shaking it up and down. The resulting transverse waves can be analyzed as before.

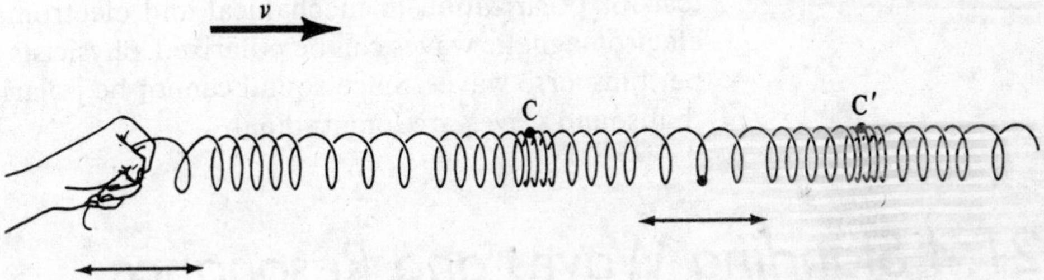

FIGURE 21.6 Longitudinal Wave

Another way to set up periodic disturbances in the spring is to pull the spring back and forth along its longitudinal axis. The resulting disturbances consist of regions of compressions and expansions that appear to travel parallel to the disturbances themselves. These waves are called **longitudinal** (Figure 21.6) or **compressional** waves. Sound is an example of a longitudinal wave. The vibrations of an object in the air create pressure differences that alternately expand and contract the air and that, when impacted on our ears, create the phenomenon known as **sound**.

In a transverse wave, the vibrations must be perpendicular to the direction of apparent motion. However, if we cut a plane containing the directions of vibration, we find that there are many possible three-dimensional orientations in which the vibrations can still be considered perpendicular to the direction of travel. Thus, we can select one or more planes containing our chosen vibrational orientation. For example, a sideways vibration is just as "transverse" as an up and down or diagonal vibration. This selection process, known as **polarization** (see Figure 21.7), applies only to transverse waves.

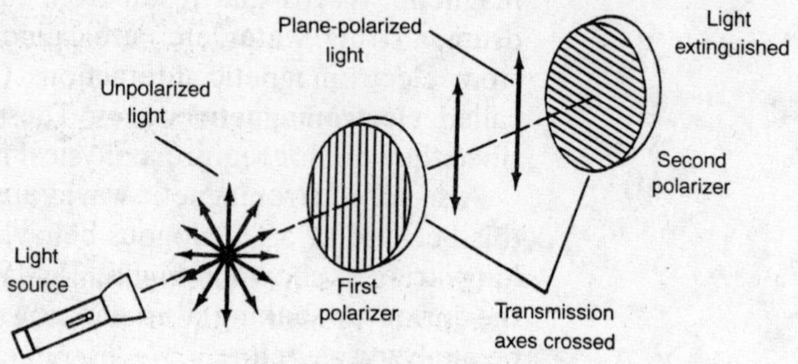

FIGURE 21.7 Used with permission of Prentice Hall, Needham, MA.

In a longitudinal wave, there is only one way to make the vibrations parallel to the direction of travel. Special devices have been developed to test for polarization in mechanical and electromagnetic waves. Since all electromagnetic waves can be polarized, physicists conclude that they must be transverse waves. Since sound cannot be polarized, physicists conclude that sound waves are longitudinal.

21.4 Standing Waves and Resonance

Consider Figure 21.1 again. There are several ways in which we can make the taut string vibrate transversely. One way is make the entire string move up and down as a single unit. This is the easiest frequency mode of vibration possible and is called the **fundamental mode**. If we increase the frequency, something interesting happens. The waves reaching a boundary reflect off it inverted and match perfectly, in amplitude and frequency, the remaining incoming waves. In this situation, the apparent horizontal motion of the wave stops and we have a **standing wave**, which appears to be segmented by **nodal points**. These nodal points correspond to points where no appreciable displacement takes place.

Figure 21.8 shows a standing wave in various vibrational modes. Figure 21.8a illustrates the fundamental mode. In Figure 21.8b we see the second mode, in which one nodal point appears. This nodal point occurs at the one-half wavelength mark, so that, for a string of length ℓ, $\lambda = \ell$ (at this frequency). In the fundamental mode of Figure 21.8a, $\lambda = 2\ell$. In Figure 21.8c, there are two nodal points and $\lambda = 2\ell / 3$.

This standing-wave pattern is a form of interference, and with sound the nodal points would be determined by a significant drop in intensity. With light, we would observe a darker region relative to the surrounding area. With a string, we would see the characteristic segmented pattern shown in Figure 21.8.

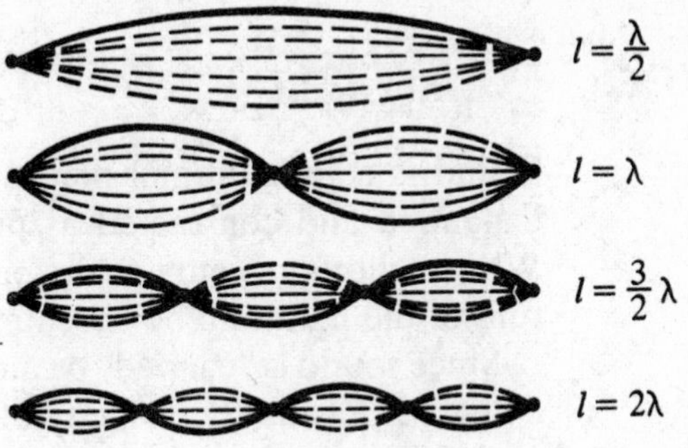

FIGURE 21.8

Standing waves can be manipulated so that the maximum points continuously reinforce themselves. This buildup of wave energy due to the constructive interference of standing waves is called **resonance**. Resonance can also be induced by an external agent.

All objects have a natural vibrating frequency. When a glass or bell is struck, only one fundamental characteristic frequency of vibration is heard (actually, the sound is a complex mixture of vibrations). If, however, two identical tuning forks, *A* and *B*, are held close together, then the phenomenon of resonance can be observed. If tuning fork *A* is struck, the waves emanating from it strike fork *B*. Since the frequency of these waves match the natural vibrating frequency of fork *B*, that fork will begin to vibrate (see Figure 21.9).

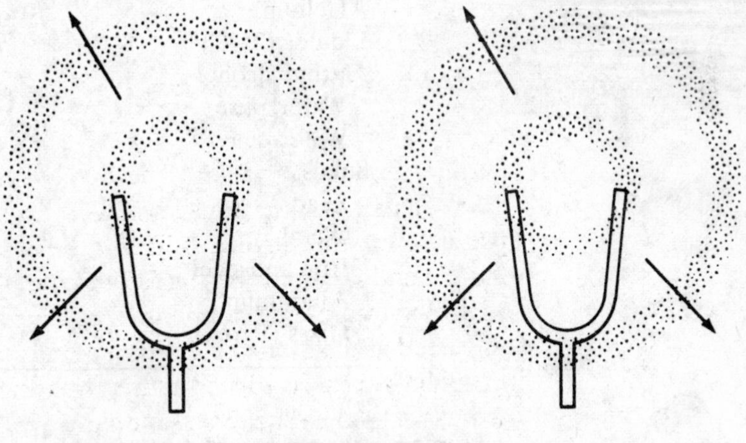

FIGURE 21.9 Resonance in Two Identical Tuning Forks

Resonance also explains how an opera singer can shatter a crystal wine glass. More important, it explains why soldiers are ordered to "break march" when crossing a bridge. The rhythmic marching can set up a resonance vibration and perhaps collapse the bridge. In November 1940, a resonance vibration caused by a light gale wind generated catastrophic torsional vibrations in the Tacoma Narrows Bridge in Washington State. The violent convulsions were photographed and are shown as a classic illustration of the principle of resonance. Nicknamed "Galloping Gertie," the bridge has become a testament to the need for engineers to be very careful when considering the possible effects of resonance.

21.5 Sound

Sound is a longitudinal mechanical wave. Air molecules are alternately expanded and contracted as pressure differences move through the air. When lightning occurs, the expansion of air due to the very high temperature of the lightning bolt creates the violent sound known as thunder.

Since sound is "carried" by air molecules, it is temperature dependent. At 0 degree Celsius, the velocity of sound in air is 331 meters per second. For each 1-degree rise in temperature, the velocity of sound increases by 0.6 meter per second. The study of sound is called **acoustics**, and longitudinal waves in matter are sometimes termed **acoustical waves.**

The ability of sound waves to pass through matter depends on the structure of the molecules involved. Thus, sound travels slower in a gas, in which the molecules have more random motion, than in a liquid or a solid, which has a more "rigid" structure. In Table 21.1 the velocities of sound in selected substances are listed.

TABLE 21.1 Velocities of Sound in Selected Substances

Substance	Velocity (m/s)
Gases (0°C)	
Carbon dioxide	259
Air	331
Helium	965
Liquids (25°C)	
Ethyl alcohol	1207
Water, pure	1498
Water, sea	1531
Solids	
Lead	1200
Wood	~4300
Iron and steel	~5000
Aluminum	5100
Glass (Pyrex)	5170

Human hearing can detect sound in a range from 20 to 20,000 hertz. Sound waves exceeding a frequency of 20,000 hertz are called **ultrasonic** waves. The amplitude of the sound wave is the intensity of **loudness** of the wave, while the frequency relates to the **pitch**. When two sound waves interfere, the regions of constructive and destructive interference produce the phenomena known as **beats**. The number of beats per second is equal to the frequency difference.

Interference, for any kind of wave, is dependent on what is called the **path-length difference**. Consider two point sources of sound, A and B, and a receiver some distance away. If the distance from source A to the receiver is ℓ_A and the distance from source B to the receiver is ℓ_B, the receiver will be at a point of constructive interference if the path-length difference, $\ell_A - \ell_B$, is equal to a whole multiple of the wavelength, $n\lambda$. Destructive interference will occur if the path-length difference is equal to an odd multiple of the half-wavelengths, $(n + 1/2)\lambda$.

Another phenomenon associated with interference is **diffraction.** When a wave encounters a boundary, the wave appears to bend around the corners of the boundary. This effect, known as **diffraction**, occurs because at the corners the wave behaves like a point source and creates circular waves. These waves, because of their shape, reach behind the corners, and this continuous effect gives the illusion of wave bending. In Figure 21.10a, we observe a series of straight waves, made in a water tank, and the resulting diffraction at a corner. Figure 21.10b shows the diffraction of waves as they pass through a narrow opening. Interference and diffraction will be discussed in more detail in Chapter 22 on light.

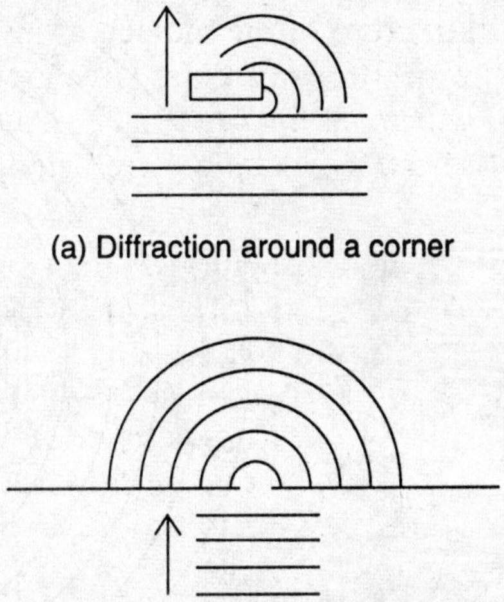

(a) Diffraction around a corner

(b) Diffraction through a narrow opening

FIGURE 21.10

The intensity of sound is measured in units called **decibels** (dB). Human hearing does not respond to changes in intensity in a linear fashion. Because of this fact, the decibel system is a logarithmic (base 10) system in which the intensity, β, is measured in decibels using the relationship

$$\beta = 10 \log \frac{I}{I_0}$$

where I is the intensity in units of watts per square meter, and I_0 is taken to be the barely audible intensity 10^{-12} watt per square meter. Some common decibel measurements are presented in Table 21.2.

TABLE 21.2 Sound Intensities

Sound	Intensity (dB)
Whisper	30
Conversation	60
Loud sound	70–90
Deafening sound	100
Painful sound	120
Damaging sound	140

21.6 The Doppler Effect

Almost everyone has had the experience of hearing a siren pass by. Even though the siren is emitting a sound at a single frequency, the changing position of the siren, relative to the hearer, produces an apparent change in the frequency. As the siren approaches, the pitch is increased; as the siren passes, the pitch is decreased. This phenomenon is called the **Doppler effect.**

Let us imagine a point source sending out waves in a circular fashion. In the static case shown in Figure 21.11a, the listeners at points *A* and *B* both experience the same frequency of waves as a listener located at the source *S*.

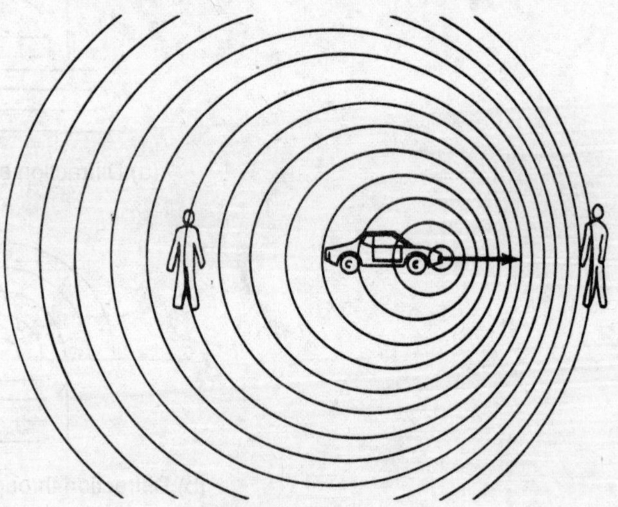

FIGURE 21.11

However, in Figure 21.11b the source is moving; let's say toward point *A*. Then, for each period of time *T* between waves, the circular waves will not be concentric. In other words, the spacing between each two successive waves will be reduced by an amount equal to the distance traveled by the source in time *T*. Thus, an apparent increase in frequency is experienced at point *A*, while at point *B* there is an apparent decrease in frequency.

The relationships governing this change in frequency are given by the formulas

$$f = f_0\left(\frac{\mathbf{v}}{\mathbf{v} - \mathbf{v}_S}\right)$$

and

$$f = f_0\left(\frac{\mathbf{v}}{\mathbf{v} + \mathbf{v}_S}\right)$$

where $\mathbf{v}$ is the wave velocity in the medium and $\mathbf{v}_S$ is the relative velocity of the source. The first equation is used when the source is approaching a receiver, and the second equation when the source is receding from a receiver.

If the source velocity equals the wave velocity, a very strong interference pattern builds up in front of the source. If, however, the source velocity exceeds the wave velocity, the source will be "outrunning" its own waves. This phenomenon occurs when ducks land on the water and when airplanes break the sound barrier. The regions of constructive interference are termed **shock waves.**

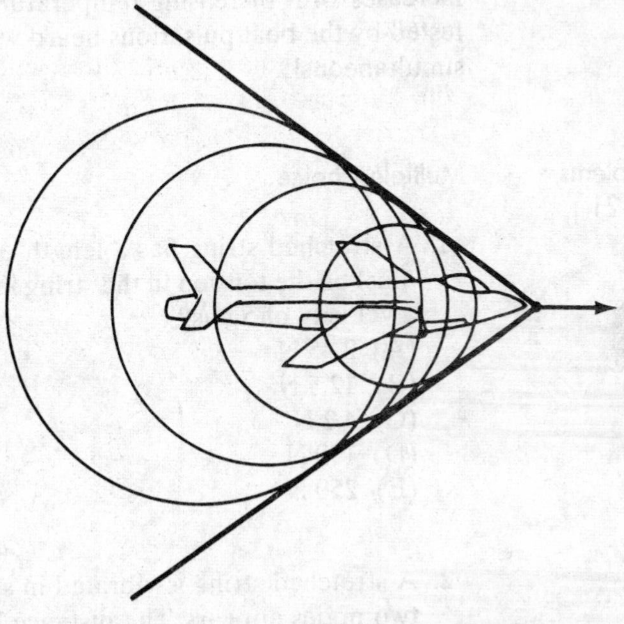

FIGURE 21.12 Shock Wave Pattern

The ratio of the source velocity to the wave velocity is called the **Mach number** in honor of Austrian physicist Ernst Mach. At Mach 1, the source is traveling at the wave velocity. The **sonic boom** made by supersonic aircraft is an example of shock waves in air as in Figure 21.12.

Sample Problem:

A sound wave emits a frequency of 350 Hz. If the air temperature is 15°C, what is the wavelength of the sound?

Solution:

The speed of sound increases from 331 m/s by 0.6 m/s for each degree above 0°C. At 15°C, therefore, the speed of sound is 340 m/s. Then, since $\mathbf{v} = f\lambda$, the wavelength $\lambda = 0.97$ m.

Problem-Solving Strategies for Waves and Sound

Solving wave motion problems involves remembering the basic physical concepts involved. For transverse waves, the only particle motion in the medium will be up and down. If a series of waves is presented, you must resist the temptation of viewing labeled points as beads on a wire. As a wave approaches a point, it will first go up and then go down. Points that are in phase are either going up at the same time or going down at the same time.

Transverse waves can be polarized, meaning that you can select a preferred axis to contain the vibrations and have them remain perpendicular to the direction of apparent wave motion. Longitudinal waves cannot be polarized, and the vibrations remain parallel to the apparent direction of wave motion.

Sound waves travel through a medium, and their speed is determined by the molecular structure of the matter involved. In air, the speed of sound increases with increasing temperature. Sound wave interference is manifested by the beat pulsations heard when two frequencies are experienced simultaneously.

Practice Problems for Chapter 21

Multiple Choice

1. A stretched string has a length of 1.5 m and a mass of 0.25 kg. What must be the tension in the string in order for pulses in the string to have a velocity of 5 m/s?
   (A) 2.45 N
   (B) 12.5 N
   (C) 4.2 N
   (D) 150 N
   (E) 250 N

2. A stretched string is vibrated in such a way that a standing wave with two nodes appears. The distance between the nodes is 0.2 m. What is the wavelength of the standing wave?
   (A) 0.4 m
   (B) 0.3 m
   (C) 0.2 m
   (D) 0.6 m
   (E) 0.8 m

3. What is the wavelength of sound produced at a frequency of 300 Hz when the air temperature is 20°C?
   (A) 1.10 m
   (B) 1.30 m
   (C) 0.80 m
   (D) 1.14 m
   (E) 1.2 m

4. Two tuning forks are vibrating simultaneously. One fork has a frequency of 256 Hz; the other, a frequency of 280 Hz. The number of pulsational beats per second heard will be
   (A) 256
   (B) 536
   (C) 1.1
   (D) 0.91
   (E) 24

5. In a stretched string with a constant tension T, as the frequency of the waves increases, the wavelength
   (A) increases
   (B) decreases
   (C) remains the same
   (D) increases, then decreases
   (E) decreases, then increases

6. What is the period of a wave that has a frequency of 12,000 Hz?
   (A) 36.25 s
   (B) 0.000083 s
   (C) 0.0275 s
   (D) 12,000 s
   (E) 0.012 s

7. Sound waves travel fastest in
   (A) a vacuum
   (B) air
   (C) water
   (D) wood
   (E) Not enough information is provided.

8. The amplitude of a sound wave is related to its
   (A) pitch
   (B) loudness
   (C) frequency
   (D) resonance
   (E) wavelength

9. At 25°C, a sound wave takes 3 s to reach a receiver. How far away is the receiver from the source?
   (A) 1038 m
   (B) 993 m
   (C) 1215 m
   (D) 1068 m
   (E) 887 m

10. How many times more intense is a 100-dB sound than a 60-dB sound?
   (A) 10^4
   (B) 400
   (C) 40
   (D) 4
   (E) 100

Free Response

1. A jet engine's noise is coming into a window 1.0 m wide by 1.2 m high. If the sound level is 140 dB, at what rate does energy enter the window?

2. What must be the tension in a 0.25-m string with a mass of 0.30 kg so that its fundamental frequency mode is 400 Hz?

3. A train whistle has a natural frequency of 1500 Hz. If the train is approaching a station at a velocity of 30 m/s, what is the frequency perceived by a person standing at the station? (Assume that the air temperature is 30°C).

Solutions

Multiple-Choice Problems

1. **C** The formula for wave velocity in a string is

$$\mathbf{v} = \sqrt{\frac{\mathbf{T}}{M/\ell}}$$

Using the given information and solving for tension leads to **T** = 4.2 N.

2. **A** Standing-wave nodes occur at half-wavelength intervals. Thus,

$$\lambda = 2(0.2) = 0.4 \text{ m}$$

3. **D** At 20°C, the speed of sound is 331 + (0.6)(20) = 343 m/s. Since **v** = $f\lambda$, we get a wavelength of λ = 1.14 m.

4. **E** The number of beats per second is equal to the frequency difference: 280 − 256 = 24.

5. **B** Since **v** = $f\lambda$ and since, for constant tension, the velocity is constant, as the frequency increases, the wavelength decreases.

6. **B** Frequency and period are reciprocals of each other. Thus

$$T = \frac{1}{12{,}000} = 0.000083 \text{ s}$$

7. **D** Because of molecular arrangement, sound travels faster in solids than in liquids, or gases.

8. **B** Amplitude is related to the intensity of a wave. In sound, wave intensity is perceived as loudness.

9. **A** At 25°C, the speed of sound is 331 + (0.6)(25) = 346 m/s. Since **x** = **v***t*,

$$\mathbf{x} = (346)(3) = 1038 \text{ m}$$

10. **A** The decibel scale is defined in such a way that a difference of 10 dB corresponds to a difference (ratio) of 10 times in intensity. Thus a 40 dB difference equals 10,000 times difference in intensity.

Free-Response Problems

1. The formula for sound level in decibels is

$$\beta = 10 \log \frac{I}{I_0}$$

where I_0, a barely audible intensity, equals 10^{-12} W/m². In our problem $\beta = 140$ dB, and we must solve for intensity I. If we divide by 10, substitute for I_0, and then exponentiate by raising each side as a power of 10, we get, after cross multiplying, $I = 100$ W/m².

The rate of energy per second is the power emitted, in watts. We must multiply 100 W/m² by the area of our window, which is 1.2 m². Thus, the rate at which energy is emitted is 120 W.

2. At fundamental frequency, we have

$$\lambda = 2\ell = (2)(0.25) = 0.5 \text{ m}$$

Now, $\mathbf{v} = f\lambda$, which means that

$$\mathbf{v} = (400)(0.5) = 200 \text{ m/s}$$

We can now use the formula for the velocity in a fixed string:

$$\mathbf{v} = \sqrt{\frac{\mathbf{T}}{M/\ell}}$$

Solving for the tension gives $\mathbf{T} = 48{,}000$ N.

3. At 30°C, the velocity of sound is 331 + (0.6)(30) = 348 m/s. The Doppler formula for a stationary observer and an approaching source is

$$f = f_0\left(\frac{\mathbf{v}}{\mathbf{v} - \mathbf{v}_S}\right)$$

where $f_0 = 1500$ Hz, $\mathbf{v}_S = 30$ m/s, and $\mathbf{v} = 348$ m/s. Solving for frequency, we get $f = 1641.5$ Hz.

CHAPTER 22

Light

22.1 Electromagnetic Waves

In Chapter 20, we reviewed aspects of electromagnetic induction. In one example, we observed how the changing magnetic flux in a solenoid can influence a second solenoid not physically attached to the primary. This **mutual induction** involves the transfer of energy through space by means of an oscillating magnetic field. Experiments in the late nineteenth century by German physicist Heinrich Hertz confirmed what Scottish physicist James Clerk Maxwell had asserted theoretically in 1864: that oscillating electromagnetic fields travel through space as transverse waves and that they travel with the same speed as does light.

Light is just one form of electromagnetic radiation that travels in the form of transverse waves. We know that these waves are transverse because they can be polarized, as discussed in Chapter 21. The speed of light is approximately equal to 3×10^8 meters per second and is designated by the letter c.

Light waves can be coherent if they are produced in a way that maintains a constant phase-amplitude relationship (see Chapter 21). **Lasers** produce coherent light of one wavelength. (The word *laser* is an acronym for *l*ight *a*mplification by the *s*timulated *e*mission of *r*adiation.)

Experiments by Sir Isaac Newton in the seventeenth century showed that "white light," when passed through a prism, contains the colors red, orange, yellow, green, blue, and violet (abbreviated as ROYGBV). Each color of light is characterized by a different wavelength and frequency. The wavelengths range from about 3.5×10^{-7} meter for violet light to about 7.0×10^{-7} meter. Small wavelengths are sometimes measured in **angstroms**, (Å); 1 angstrom is equal to 1×10^{-10} meter. In more modern textbooks, the units **nanometers** (nm) are used; 1 nanometer is equal to 1×10^{-9} meter.

Together with other electromagnetic waves, such as radio waves, X rays, and infrared waves, light occupies a special place in the so-called **electromagnetic spectrum** because we can "see" it. A sample electromagnetic spectrum is presented in Figure 22.1.

Since electromagnetic waves are "waves," they all obey the relationship $c = f\lambda$, where c is the speed of light, discussed above. With this in mind,

High frequency — Low frequency

Gamma rays	X rays	Ultraviolet	Light: Blue … Red	Infrared	Micro-waves	Radio waves

Short wavelength — Long wavelength

FIGURE 22.1 Electromagnetic Spectrum

gamma rays have frequencies in the range of 10^{25} hertz and wavelengths in the range of 10^{-13} meter. These properties make gamma rays very small but very energetic. They are sometimes referred to as "cosmic rays" since they often originate in the cores of exploding stars and galaxies.

22.2 Shadows

One property of light that is most useful is its ability to travel in a straight line. We do not always perceive the wave nature of light. If two sticks are placed on the ground, it is possible to mark a straight line by sighting along first one and then the other. This can be accomplished because light travels in a line. If, however, an opaque object is placed in the path of a beam of light, the object will be reflected and a **shadow** will appear in the region behind the object. If a point source of light is used, the rays of light will emerge radially in all directions. Figure 22.2 shows that, if an object is placed in the path of the point source, a clear shadow is formed and a simple geometric relationship exists between the object and the shadow image.

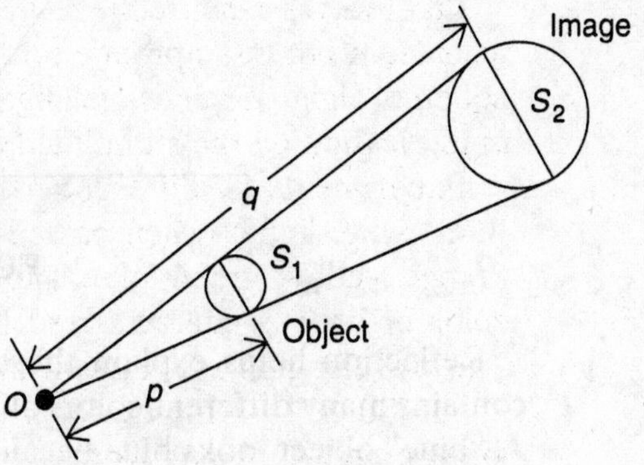

FIGURE 22.2

If p and q represent the object and image distances, respectively, from the source, and S_1 and S_2 represent the object and image sizes, respectively, we can write that for a point source of light

$$\frac{p}{q} = \frac{S_1}{S_2}$$

Closer examination reveals that the edges of the shadow are not sharp; a distinctive "fuzziness" is associated with all shadows. This irregularity was first examined in the seventeenth century by an Italian physicist named Grimaldi, and attributed to the diffraction of light around the edges of the object. This evidence for the wave nature of light was used by Grimaldi, along with a Dutch contemporary named Christian Huygens, as the basis of a "wave theory of light" advanced in the seventeenth century to counter Isaac Newton's "corpuscular theory of light." Wave interference patterns were first demonstrated for light in 1801 by English physicist Thomas Young, and the corpuscular theory of light was forgotten until the discovery of the **photoelectric effect** at the end of the nineteenth century.

22.3 Reflection

Reflection is the ability of light to seemingly bounce off a surface. This phenomenon does not reveal the wave nature of light, and the notion of wavelength or frequency rarely enters into a discussion of reflection. If light is incident on a flat mirror, the angle of incidence is measured with respect to a line perpendicular to the surface of the mirror and called the **normal**.

In Figure 22.3 the **law of reflection**, which states that the angle of incidence equals the angle of reflection, is illustrated. Note that the angles of incidence and reflection and the normal are all coplanar.

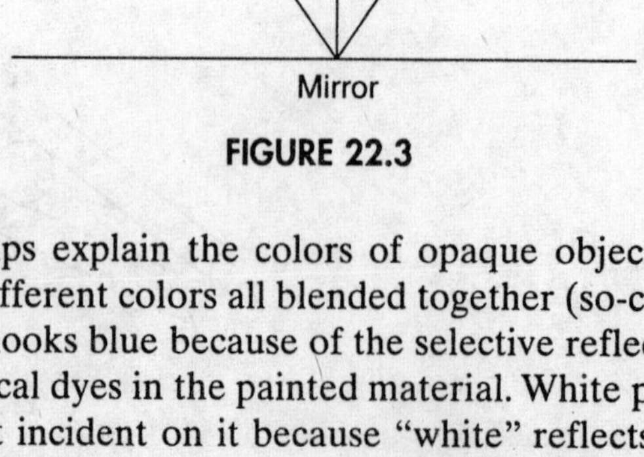

FIGURE 22.3

Reflection helps explain the colors of opaque objects. Ordinary light contains many different colors all blended together (so-called white light). A "blue" object looks blue because of the selective reflection of blue light due to the chemical dyes in the painted material. White paper assumes the color of the light incident on it because "white" reflects all colors. Black paper absorbs all colors (and of course nothing can be painted a "pure" color). If light of a single wavelength can be isolated (using a laser, for example), the light is said to be **monochromatic**. If all of the waves of light are moving in phase, the light is said to be **coherent**. The fact that laser light is both monochromatic and coherent contributes to its strength and energy.

If a concave or convex mirror is used, the law of reflection still holds, but the curved shapes affect the direction of the reflected rays. Figure 22.4a shows that a concave mirror converges parallel rays of light to a **focal point** that is described as **real** since the light rays really cross. In Figure 22.4b, we see that a convex mirror causes the parallel rays to diverge away from the mirror. If we extend the rays backward in imagination, they appear to originate from a point on the other side of the mirror. This point is called the **virtual focal point** since it is not real. The human eye will always trace a ray of light back to its source in a line. This deception of the eye is responsible for images in some mirrors appearing to be on the "other side" of the mirror (**virtual images**). Image formation in mirrors will be discussed in more detail in Chapter 23.

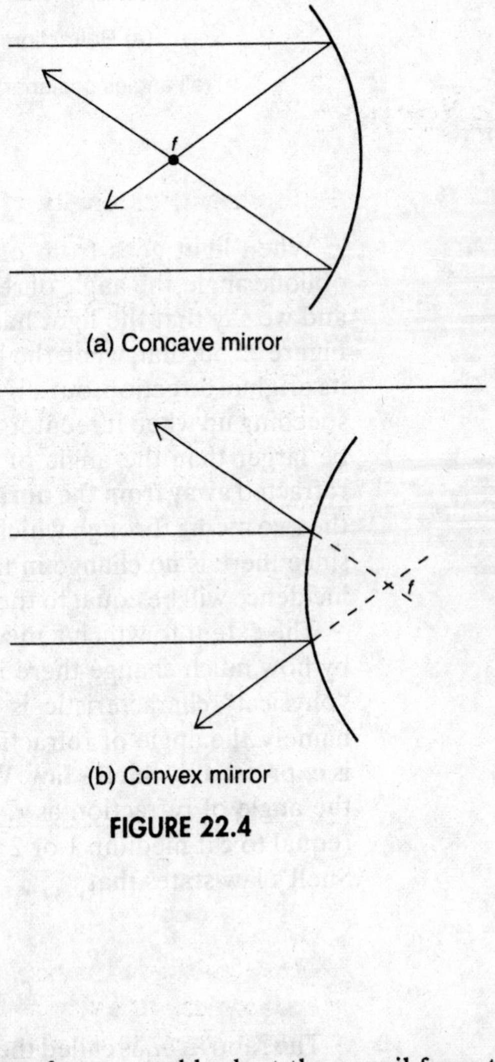

FIGURE 22.4

22.4 Refraction

Place a pencil in a glass of water and look at the pencil from the side. The apparent bending of the pencil is due to refraction (Figure 22.5a). When light passes obliquely from one transparent medium to another, there is a uniform change in the speed of light. When this occurs, the light appears to bend toward or away from the normal. If there is no change in speed, as when light passes from benzene to Lucite, for example, there will be no refraction at any angle (Figure 22.5b). If the light is incident at an angle of zero degrees to the normal, there will again be no refraction, whether or not there is a change in speed (Figure 22.5c).

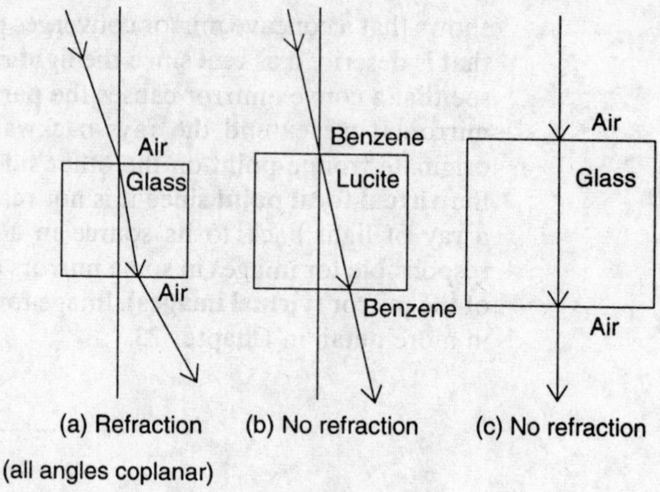

FIGURE 22.5

When light goes from one medium to another and slows down, at an oblique angle, the angle of refraction will be less than the angle of incidence, and we say that the light has been refracted **toward the normal**. Notice, in Figure 22.5a, that, when the light reemerges into the air, it will be parallel to its original direction, but slightly offset. This is due to the fact that the light is speeding up when it reenters the air. In that case, the angle of refraction will be larger than the angle of incidence, and we say that the light has been refracted **away from the normal**. Remember that, if the optical properties of the two media through which light passes are the same, no refraction occurs since there is no change in the speed of the light. In that case, the angle of incidence will be equal to the angle of refraction (no deviation).

The extent to which a medium is a good refracting medium is measured by how much change there is in the speed of light passing through it. This "physical" characteristic is manifested by a "geometric" characteristic, namely, the angle of refraction. The relationship between these quantities is expressed by **Snell's law**. With the angle of incidence designated as i and the angle of refraction as r, and with $\mathbf{v}_1$ the velocity of light in medium 1 (equal to **c** if medium 1 or 2 is air) and $\mathbf{v}_2$ the velocity of light in medium 2, Snell's law states that

$$\frac{\sin i}{\sin r} = \frac{\mathbf{v}_1}{\mathbf{v}_2} = \frac{n_2}{n_1}$$

The ratio n_2/n_1 is called the **relative index of refraction**. If medium 1 is air, then, by definition, the **absolute index of refraction**, n, of air (and a vacuum) is taken to be equal to 1.00, although it is actually slightly larger (1.00029; see the accompanying Table 22.1). Snell's law can now be written in the form

$$\frac{\sin i}{\sin r} = \frac{\mathbf{c}}{\mathbf{v}_2} = \mathbf{n}_2$$

Note that, when light is refracted, there is no change in the frequency of the light, only a change in wavelength.

TABLE 22.1 Absolute Indices of Refraction of Selected Media

Substance	Index of Refraction
Air (vacuum)	1.00
Water	1.33
Alcohol	1.36
Quartz	1.46
Lucite	1.50
Benzene	1.50
Glass	
Crown	1.52
Flint	1.61
Diamond	2.42

The particular colors of visible light all have specific frequencies. When these colors are used in a refraction experiment, they produce angles of refraction since they travel at different speeds in media other than air (or a vacuum). Substances that allow the frequencies of light to travel at different speeds are called **dispersive media**. This aspect of refraction explains why a prism allows one to see a colored, "continuous" spectrum and, additionally, why red light (at the low-frequency end) emerges on top (see Figure 22.6).

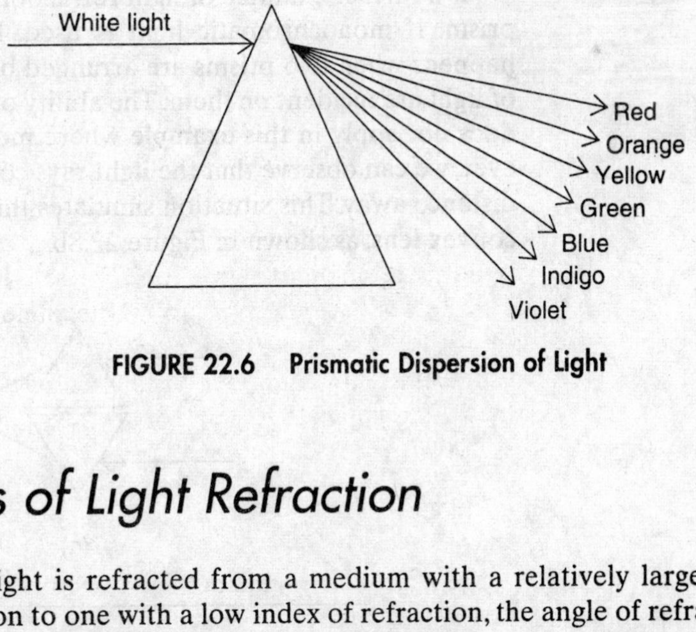

FIGURE 22.6 Prismatic Dispersion of Light

22.5 Applications of Light Refraction

When light is refracted from a medium with a relatively large index of refraction to one with a low index of refraction, the angle of refraction can be quite large. Note, however, that, although the relative index of refraction can be less than 1.00, the absolute index of refraction cannot.

Figure 22.7 illustrates a situation in which the angle of incidence is at some critical value θ_c such that the angle of refraction equals 90 degrees. This can occur only when the relative index of refraction is less than 1.00, as stated above.

If the angle of incidence exceeds this critical value, the angle of refraction will exceed 90 degrees and the light will appear to be internally reflected, a phenomenon aptly called **total internal reflection**. The ability of diamonds to sparkle in sunlight is due to total internal reflection and a relatively small critical angle of incidence (due to a diamond's high index of refraction). Fiber optics communication, in which information is processed along hair-thin glass fibers, works because of total internal reflection.

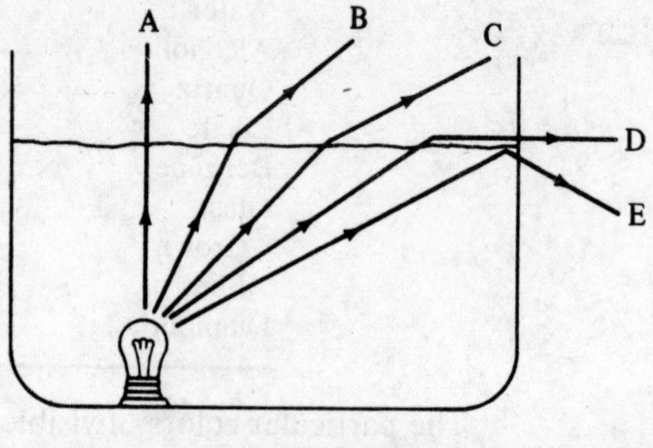

FIGURE 22.7

The critical angle can be determined from the relationship

$$\sin \theta_c = \frac{n_2}{n_1} \ (n_2 < n_1)$$

As a further example of light refraction, consider the refraction due to a prism. If monochromatic light is used, Figure 22.8a demonstrates what happens when two prisms are arranged base to base and two parallel rays of light are incident on them. The ability of the prism to disperse white light does not apply in this example where monochromatic light is used. However, we can observe that the light rays converge to a real focal point some distance away. This situation simulates the effect of refraction by a double convex lens, as shown in Figure 22.8b.

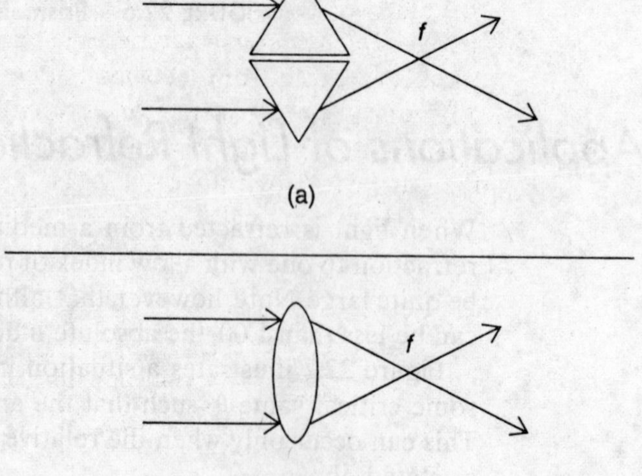

FIGURE 22.8

The focal length is dependent on the frequency of light used; red light will produce a greater focal length than violet light in a convex lens.

If the prisms are placed vertex to vertex, as in Figure 22.9a, the parallel rays of light will be diverged away from an apparent virtual focal point. This simulates, as shown in Figure 22.9b, the effect of a double concave lens.

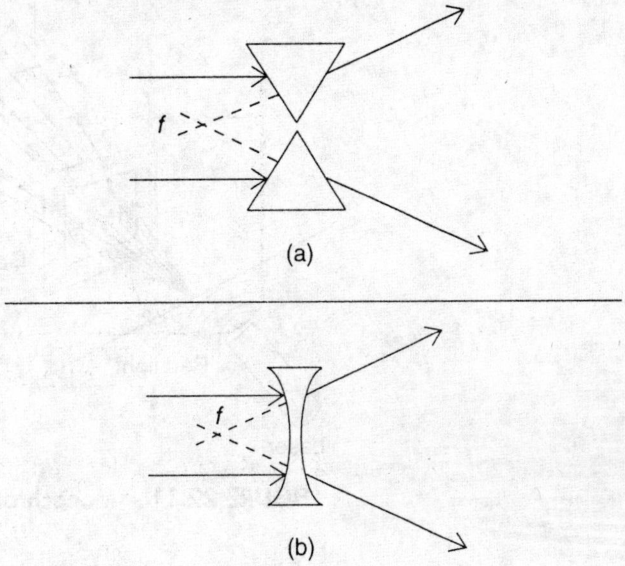

FIGURE 22.9

22.6 Interference and Diffraction of Light

The ability of light to diffract and exhibit an interference pattern is evidence of the wave nature of light. In Section 22.2, we saw that the diffraction of light occurs in connection with shadows. Light interference can be observed by using two or more narrow slits. Multiple-slit diffraction is achieved with a plastic "grating" onto which over 5000 lines per centimeter are scratched.

Figure 22.10 shows that, if white light is passed through the grating, a series of continuous spectra appears. Interestingly, this continuous spectrum is reversed from the way it appears in dispersion. The reason for this difference is that diffraction is wavelength dependent. When a narrow opening is used, the short-wavelength violet rays are diffracted least and the longer red rays most.

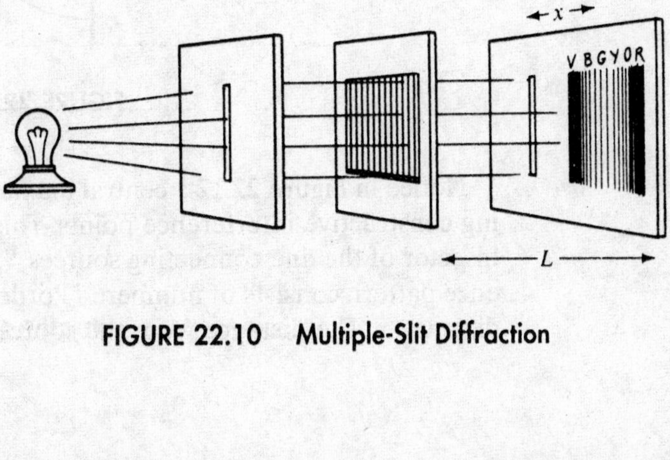

FIGURE 22.10 Multiple-Slit Diffraction

With monochromatic light, an alternating pattern of bright and dark regions appears. If a laser is used, the pattern appears as a series as dots representing regions of constructive and destructive interference (see Figure 22.11). The dots are evenly spaced throughout.

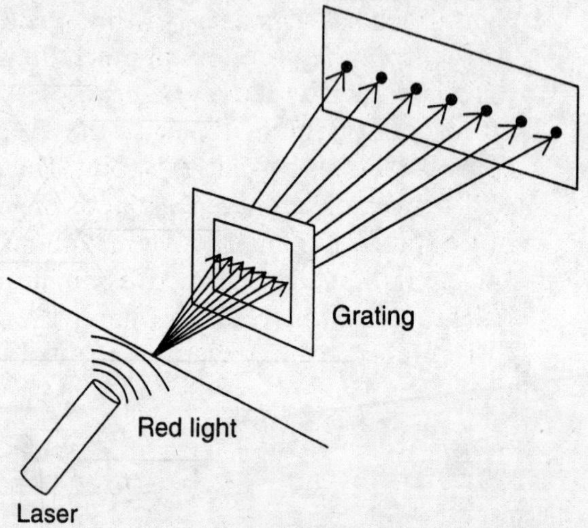

FIGURE 22.11 Monochromatic Diffraction Pattern

The origin of this pattern can be understood if we consider a water-tank analogy. Suppose two point sources are vibrating in phase in a water tank. Each source produces circular waves that overlap in the region in front of the sources. Where crests meet crests, there is constructive interference; where crests meet troughs, destructive interference. This situation is illustrated in Figure 22.12.

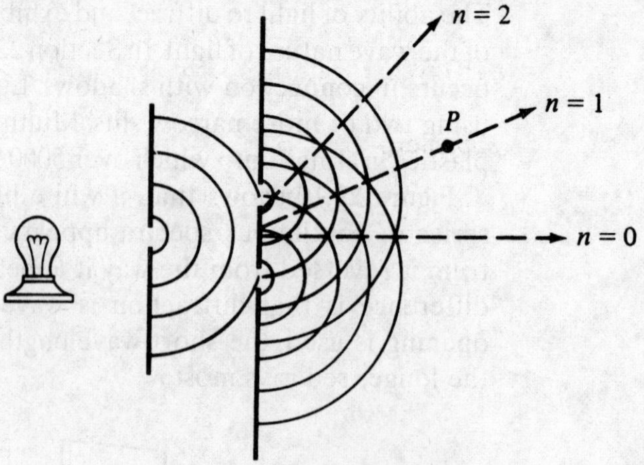

FIGURE 22.12

Notice in Figure 22.12 a central maximum built up by a line of intersecting constructive interference points. This line lies along the perpendicular bisector of the line connecting sources S_1 and S_2. The symmetrical interference pattern consists of numbered "orders" that are evenly separated by a distance x. The distance from the sources to the screen along the perpendicular bisector is labeled L. The wavelength of each wave, measured by the spacing between each two concentric circles, is of course represented by λ, and the separation between the sources is designated as d.

In Young's double-slit experiment, the two explicit sources in the water tank are replaced by two narrow slits in front of a monochromatic ray of light. Each slit acts as a new point source of light that interferes with the waves from the other slit in much the same way as Figure 22.12 illustrates (this is known as **Huygen's principle**). The central maximum is called the "0- order maximum" because the difference in path length from the two sources (slits) is zero at this point. The next order is first order because the path-length difference is equal to one wavelength, and so on as discussed in Chapter 21. Constructive maximum points occur at whole multiples of wavelength, while destructive minimum points occur at odd multiples of half-wavelengths (refer to Chapter 22 for review).

The relationship governing the variables discussed above is given by the equation

$$n\frac{\lambda}{d} = \frac{x}{L}$$

where n represents the desired order.

If θ is an angle measured from the midpoint between the slits and a particular order, the ratio x / L is approximately equal to $\sin \theta$, and the diffraction formula becomes:

$$n\lambda = d \sin \theta$$

Sample Problem:

A ray of monochromatic light, in air, is incident on a diamond ($n = 2.42$) at an angle of 30°.

(a) What is the angle of refraction in the diamond?
(b) What is the velocity of light in the diamond?

Solution:

(a) We use Snell's law to solve this part, recalling that the index of refraction of air is 1.00. We can therefore write

$$\frac{\sin 30}{\sin r} = 2.42$$

$$\sin r = 0.2066$$

Therefore

$$r = 12°$$

(b) The velocity of light in any substance (coming from air) is given by:

$$\mathbf{v} = \frac{\mathbf{c}}{n}$$

where n is equal to the absolute index of refraction. Thus

$$\mathbf{v} = \frac{3 \times 10^8}{2.42} = 1.24 \times 10^8 \text{ m/s}$$

Problem-Solving Strategies for Light

Remember that light is an electromagnetic wave. Therefore it can travel through a vacuum. Reflection and refraction do not, by themselves, verify the wave nature of light. Diffraction and interference are evidence of the wave nature of light, and the ability of light to be polarized, using special Polaroid filters, is evidence that light is a transverse wave.

Keep in mind that, when light refracts, the frequency of the light is not affected. Since the velocity changes, so does the wavelength in the new medium. If the velocity in the medium is frequency dependent, the medium is said to be "dispersive." Light waves can be coherent if they are produced in a fashion that maintains constant phase-amplitude relationships. Lasers produce coherent light of one wavelength.

When doing refraction problems, remember that the light refracts toward the normal if it enters a medium of higher index of refraction and refracts away from the normal if it enters a medium of lower index of refraction. The absolute index of refraction of a substance can never be less than 1.00.

Practice Problems for Chapter 22

Multiple Choice

1. What is the frequency of a radio wave with a wavelength of 2.2 m?
(A) 3×10^8 Hz
(B) 1.36×10^8 Hz
(C) 7.3×10^{-9} Hz
(D) 2.2×10^8 Hz
(E) 2.2 Hz

2. A ray of light is incident from a layer of crown glass ($n = 1.52$) upon a layer of water ($n = 1.33$). The critical angle of incidence for this situation is equal to
(A) 32°
(B) 41°
(C) 49°
(D) 61°
(E) 75°

3. The relative index of refraction between two media is 1.20. Compared to the velocity of light in medium 1, the velocity of light in medium 2 will be
(A) greater by 1.2 times
(B) reduced by 1.2 times
(C) the same
(D) The velocity will depend on the two media.
(E) The velocity will depend on the angle of incidence.

4. What is the approximate angle of refraction for a ray of light incident from air on a piece of quartz at a 37° angle?
(A) 24°
(B) 37°
(C) 42°
(D) 66°
(E) 75°

5. What is the velocity of light in alcohol ($n = 1.36$)?
(A) 2.2×10^8 m/s
(B) 3×10^8 m/s
(C) 4.08×10^8 m/s
(D) 1.36×10^8 m/s
(E) None of the preceding values is correct.

6. If the velocity of light in a medium depends on its frequency, the medium is said to be
(A) coherent
(B) refractive
(C) resonant
(D) diffractive
(E) dispersive

7. If the intensity of a monochromatic ray of light is increased while the ray is incident on a pair of narrow slits, the spacing between maxima in the diffraction pattern will be
(A) increased
(B) decreased
(C) the same
(D) increased or decreased, depending on the frequency
(E) increased or decreased, depending on the slit separation

8. In the diagram below, a source of light (*S*) sends a ray toward the boundary between two media in which the relative index of refraction is less than 1. The angle of incidence is indicated by *i*. Which ray best represents the path of the refracted light?

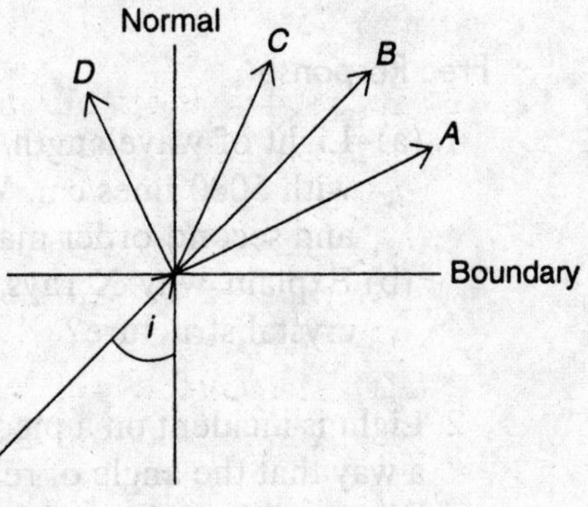

(A) *A*
(B) *B*
(C) *C*
(D) *D*
(E) Either *A* or *C*

9. A coin is placed at the bottom of a clear trough filled with water (n = 1.33) as shown below. Which point best represents the approximate location of the coin as seen by someone looking into the water?
(A) *A*
(B) *B*
(C) *C*
(D) *D*
(E) The perceived location depends on the depth of the water.

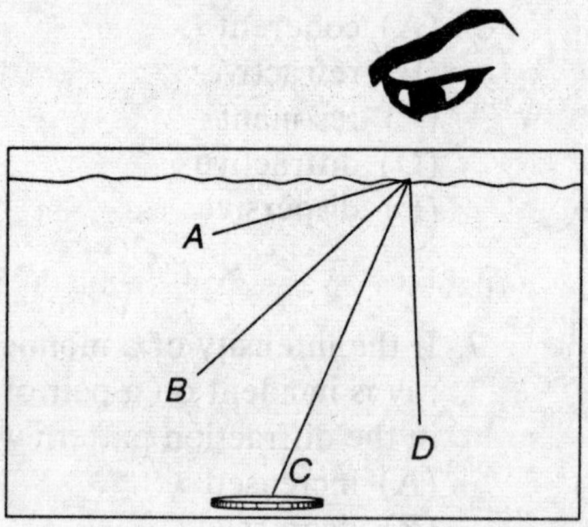

10. If, in question 9, the water is replaced by alcohol (n = 1.36), the coin will appear to be
(A) higher
(B) lower
(C) the same
(D) higher or lower, depending on the depth of the alcohol
(E) Not enough information is provided to answer the question.

Free Response

1. (a) Light of wavelength 700 nm is directed onto a diffraction grating with 5000 lines/cm. What are the angular deviations of the first- and second-order maxima from the central maxima?
(b) Explain why X rays, rather than visible light, are used to study crystal structure?

2. Light is incident on a piece of flint glass (n = 1.66) from the air in such a way that the angle of refraction is exactly half the angle of incidence. What are the values of the angles of incidence and the angle of refraction?

3. A ray of light passing through air is incident on a piece of quartz (n = 1.46) at a angle of 25°, as shown below. The quartz is 1.5 cm thick. Calculate the deviation d of the ray as it emerges back into the air.

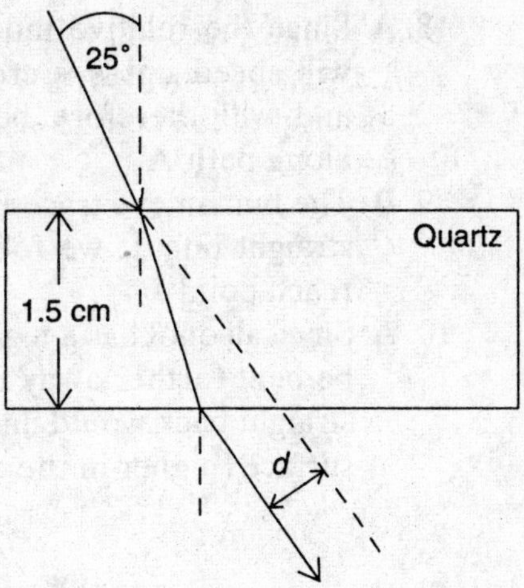

Solutions

Multiple-Choice Problems

1. **B** The velocity of light in air is given by the formula $\mathbf{c} = f\lambda$. The wavelength is 2.2 m, and the velocity of light in air is 3×10^8 m/s. Substituting known values gives us

$$f = 1.36 \times 10^8 \text{ Hz}$$

2. **D** The critical angle of incidence is given by the formula

$$\sin \theta_c = \frac{n_2}{n_1}$$

where $n_2 = 1.33$ and $n_1 = 1.52$. Substitution yields a value of 61° for the critical angle.

3. **B** The velocity relationship is given by the formula

$$\frac{\mathbf{v}_1}{\mathbf{v}_2} = n_2 / n_1$$

Since the relative index of refraction is defined to be equal to the ratio n_2 / n_1, we see that $\mathbf{v}_1 = 1.2\ (\mathbf{v}_2)$. Thus, compared to $\mathbf{v}_1$, $\mathbf{v}_2$ is reduced by 1.2 times.

4. **A** Snell's law in air is given by

$$\frac{\sin i}{\sin r} = n_2$$

The absolute index of refraction for quartz is 1.46. Substitution yields a value of 24° for the angle of refraction.

5. **A** Compared to the velocity of light in air, the velocity of light in any other transparent substance (here, alcohol) is given by the formula $\mathbf{v} = \mathbf{c} / n$. In this case, $n = 1.36$, and so the velocity of light is equal to 2.2 × 108 m/s.

6. **E** By definition, a medium is said to be "dispersive" if the velocity of light is dependent on its frequency.

7. **C** The position and separation of interference maxima are independent of the intensity of the light.

8. **A** Since the relative index of refraction is less than 1, the light ray will speed up as it crosses the boundary between the two media and will therefore bend away from the normal, approximately along path A.
9. **B** The human eye traces a ray of light back to its apparent source as a straight line. If we follow the line from the eye straight back, we reach point *B*.
10. **A** Since alcohol has a higher absolute index of refraction, the light will be bent further away from the normal. Tracing that imaginary line straight back would imply that the image would appear closer to the surface (higher in the alcohol).

Free-Response Problems

1. (a) The general formula for diffraction is

$$n\lambda = d \sin \theta$$

where θ is the angle of deviation from the center. For the first-order maximum, $n = 1$, and d is equal to the reciprocal of the number of lines per meter. Thus, we must convert 5000 lines / cm to 500,000 lines / m. Now,

$$\sin \theta = \frac{n\lambda}{d} = \frac{(1)(7 \times 10^{-7})}{500{,}000} = 0.35$$

and

$$\theta = 20.5^\circ$$

For the second-order maximum, we have $n = 2$. Thus

$$\sin \theta = \frac{(2)(7 \times 10^{-7})}{500{,}000} = 0.7$$

and

$$\theta = 44.4^\circ$$

(b) X rays are used to study crystal structure because of their very small wavelengths. These wavelengths are comparable to the spacings between lattices in a crystal and thus make it possible for the X rays to be diffracted from the different layers. Visible light has wavelengths that are much greater than these spacings and so are not affected by them. The use of X rays to probe crystals was one of the first diagnostic applications of these rays in atomic physics at the beginning of the twentieth century.

2. We want the angle of refraction to be equal to half the angle of incidence. This means that $i = 2r$. Now, since the light ray is initially in air ($n = 1.00$), Snell's law can be written:

$$\frac{\sin i}{\sin r} = n\,(\text{glass})$$

Substituting our requirement that $i = 2r$ gives

$$\frac{\sin 2r}{\sin r} = 1.66$$

Now, we recall the following trigonometric identity:

$$\sin 2\theta = 2 \sin \theta \cos \theta$$

Thus

$$\frac{2 \sin r \cos r}{\sin r} = 1.66$$

and

$$2 \cos r = 1.66$$

Therefore

$$\cos r = 0.83$$

and

$$r = 34°$$

which means that

$$i = 68°$$

3. The diagram from the problem has been redrawn as shown below. From our knowledge of refraction, we know that angle θ must be equal to 25°. Angle r is given by Snell's law:

$$\frac{\sin 25}{\sin r} = 1.46$$

$$\sin r = \frac{\sin 25}{1.46} = 0.2894$$

$$r = 16.8°$$

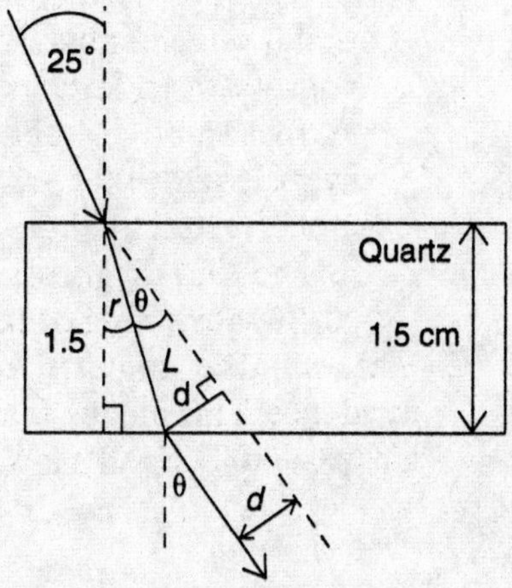

Now, angle ϕ is equal to the difference between the angle of incidence and the angle of refraction:

$$\phi = 25° - 16.8° = 8.2°$$

Since the quartz is 1.5 cm in thickness, the length of the light ray, in the quartz, at the angle of refraction, can be determined from $\cos r = 1.5 / \ell$. This implies that $\ell = 1.57$ cm. Now, since we know the length of the diagonal ℓ, and the angle ϕ, the deviation d is just part of the right triangle in our diagram. Thus

$$\sin \phi = \frac{d}{\ell}$$

and

$$d = \ell \sin \phi = (1.57) \sin 8.2 = 0.224 \text{ cm.}$$

CHAPTER 23

Geometrical Optics

23.1 Image Formation in Plane Mirrors

When you look at yourself in a plane mirror, your image appears to be directly in front of you and on the other side of the mirror. Everything about your image is the same as you, the person, except for a left-right reversal. Since no light can be originating from the other side of the mirror, your image is termed **virtual**.

The formation of a virtual image in a plane mirror is illustrated in Figure 23.1. Using an imaginary point object, we construct two rays of light that merge radially from the object because of ambient light from its environment. Each light ray is incident on the plane mirror at some arbitrary angle and is reflected off at the same angle (relative to the normal). Geometrically, we construct these lines using the law of reflection and a protractor. Since the rays diverge from the object, they continue to diverge after reflection. The human eye, however, perceives the rays as originating from a point on the other side of the mirror and in a direct line with the object.

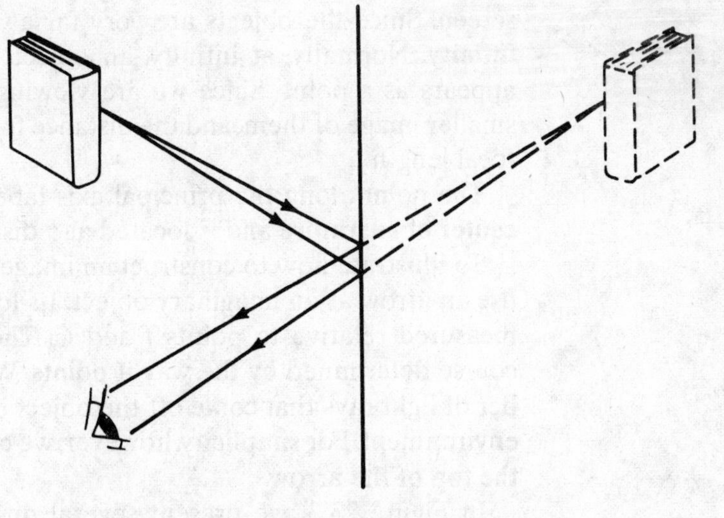

FIGURE 23.1 Plane Mirror

23.2 Image Formation in Curved Mirrors

A. Concave Mirrors

In Chapter 22, we saw that, if we use a concave or convex mirror, the shape will cause parallel rays of light to either converge or diverge. In Figure 23.2 a typical concave mirror is illustrated. The shape of the bisecting axis, called the **principal axis**, should be parabolic in cross section. If the curvature of the mirror is too large, a defect known as **spherical aberration** occurs and distorts the images seen. The real images formed by concave mirrors can be projected onto a screen. The focal length can be determined by using parallel rays of light and observing the point at which they converge.

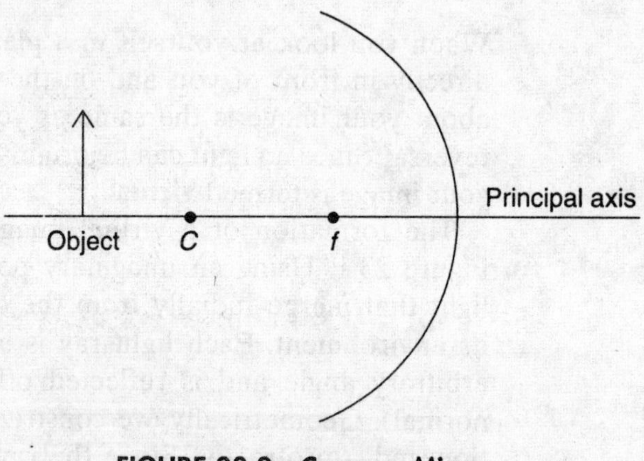

FIGURE 23.2 Concave Mirror

Another, more interesting method is to aim the mirror out the window at distant objects. Again, the images of those objects can be focused onto a screen. Since the objects are very far away, they are considered to be **at infinity**. Normally, at infinity, an object sends parallel rays of light and appears as a point. Since we are viewing extended objects, we project a smaller image of them, and the distance from the screen to the mirror is the focal length f.

The point along the principal axis labeled C on Figure 23.2 marks the **center of curvature** and is located at a distance $2f$.

To illustrate how to construct an image formed by a concave mirror, we use an arrow as an imaginary object. Its location along the principal axis is measured relative to points f and C. The orientation of the arrow is of course determined by the way it points. We could choose an infinite number of light rays that come off the object because of ambient light from its environment. For simplicity, however, we choose two rays that emerge from the top of the arrow.

In Figure 23.3, we present several different concave-mirror constructions. The first light ray is drawn parallel to the principal axis and then reflected through the focal point f. The second light ray is drawn through the focal point and then reflected parallel to the principal axis. The point of intersection (below the principal axis in cases I, II, and III) indicates that the image appears inverted at the location marked in the diagram.

From cases I, II, and III in Figure 23.3, we can see that the real images are always inverted. Additionally, as the object is moved closer to the mirror, the image gets larger and appears to move further away from the mirror. Notice that, when the object is at point C, as in case II, the image is also at point C and is the same size. When the object is at the focal point,

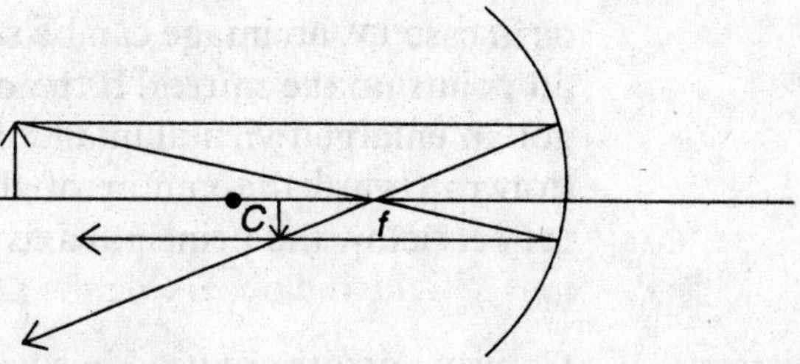

Case I—object beyond *C*; image is real, is between *f* and *C*, is smaller

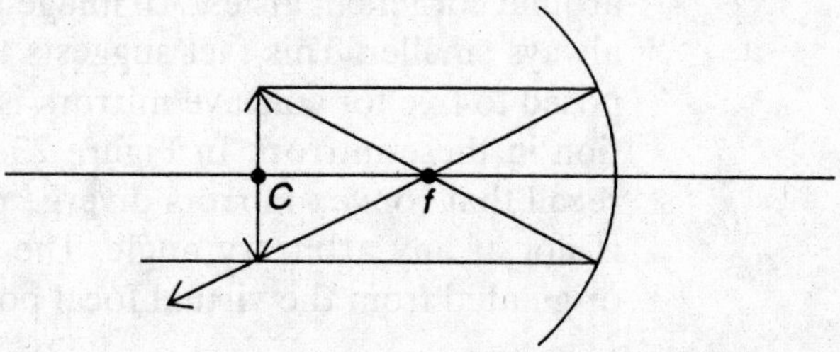

Case II—object at *C*; image is real, is at point *C*, is the same size

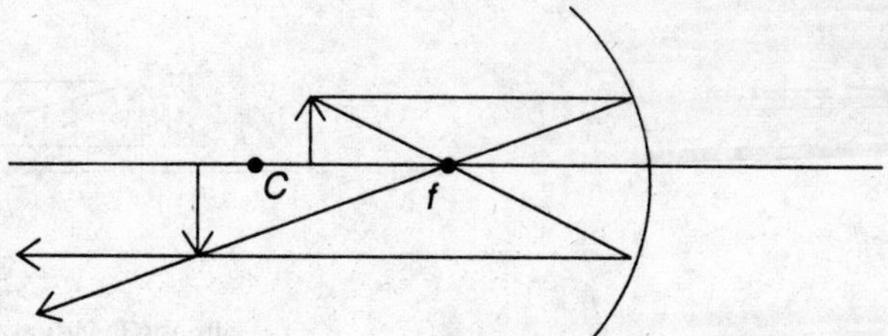

Case III—object between *f* and *C*; image is real, is beyond *C*, is larger

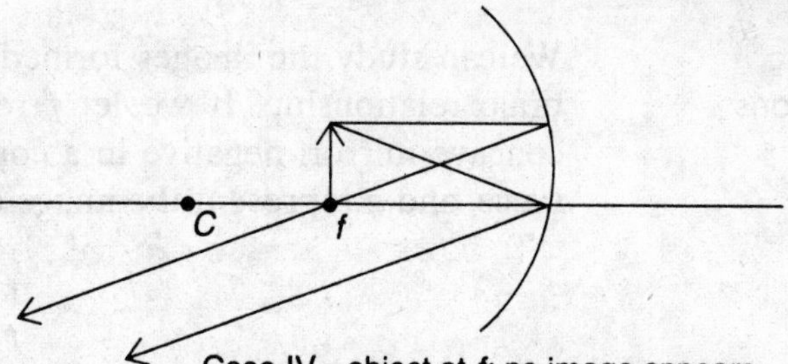

Case IV—object at *f*; no image appears

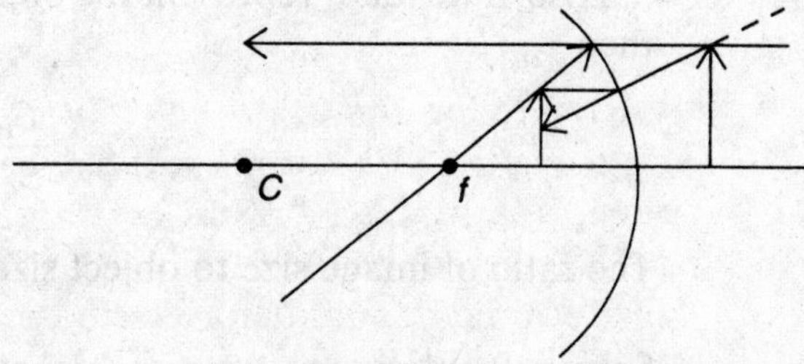

Case V—object between *f* and the mirror; image is virtual, is larger

FIGURE 23.3

as in case IV, no image can be seen since the light is reflected parallel from all points on the mirror. If the object is moved even closer, as in case V, we get an enlarged virtual image that is erect. In case IV, a light ray has been drawn toward the center of the mirror; by the law of reflection, it will reflect below the principal axis at the same angle of incidence.

B. Convex Mirrors

Convex mirrors are used in a variety of situations. In stores or elevators, for example, they have the ability to reveal images (although distorted) from around corners in aisles. An image in a convex mirror is always virtual and always smaller. This fact suggests that only one case construction, as opposed to five for concave mirrors, is necessary to understand image formation in these mirrors. In Figure 23.4, we show a sample construction and recall that convex mirrors diverge parallel rays. This divergence, however, is not at any arbitrary angle. The divergent ray is directed as though it originated from the virtual focal point.

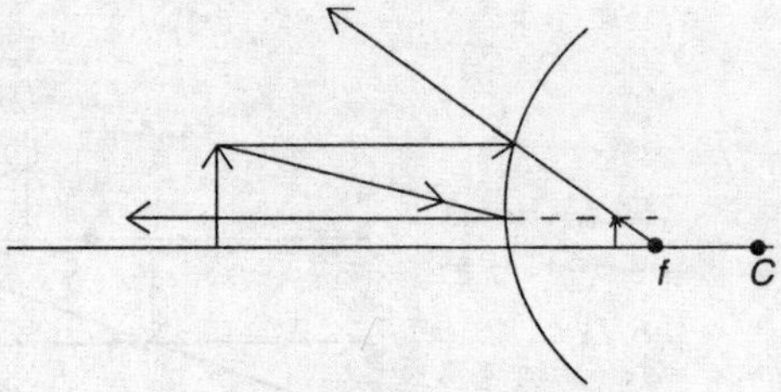

Image is virtual, erect, and smaller.

FIGURE 23.4 Convex Mirror

C. Algebraic Considerations

We can study the images formed in curved mirrors by means of an algebraic relationship. If we let f represent the focal length (positive in a concave mirror; negative in a convex mirror), p represent the object distance, and q represent the image distance, then, for a curved mirror,

$$\frac{1}{f} = \frac{1}{p} + \frac{1}{q}$$

Also, if we let S_o represent the object size and S_i represent the image size, then

$$\frac{S_i}{S_o} = \frac{q}{p}$$

The ratio of image size to object size is called the **magnification**.

Sample Problem:

A 10-cm-tall object is placed 20 cm in front of a concave mirror with a focal length of 8 cm. Where is the image located, and what is its size?

Solution:

Using the first formula presented above, we can write

$$\frac{1}{8} = \frac{1}{20} + \frac{1}{q}$$

Solving for the image distance, we obtain $q = 13.3$ cm. This is consistent with case I as illustrated in Figure 23.3.

The image size can be obtained from the expression

$$S_i = S_o\left(\frac{q}{p}\right) = 10\left(\frac{13.3}{20}\right) = 6.7 \text{ cm}$$

23.3 Image Formation in Lenses

A. Converging Lenses

When discussing the formation of images in lenses, we usually invoke what is called the **thin lens approximation**; that is, we consider that the light begins to refract from the center of the lens. As a result any curvature effects can be ignored. Since the top and the bottom of the lens are tapered like a prism, however, a defect known as **chromatic aberration** can sometimes occur. This defect causes the different colors of light to disperse in the lens and focus at different places because of their different frequencies and velocities in the lens material.

Figure 23.5 shows a series of cases in which a double convex lens is constructed as a straight line, using the thin lens approximation. The symmetry of the lens creates two real focal points, one on either side, and instead of considering the center of curvature (as in the curved mirror cases), we employ point $2f$ as an analogous location for reference. Our object is again an arrow drawn along the principal axis, which bisects the lens.

From Chapter 22, we know that a light ray parallel to the principal axis will refract through the focal point. Therefore, a light ray originating from the focal point will refract parallel to the principal axis. We will use these two light rays to construct most of our images.

Notice that in case IV no image is produced, and we had to draw a different light ray passing through the optical center of the lens. In case V an enlarged virtual image is produced on the same side as the object. This is an example of a simple magnifying glass.

B. Diverging Lenses

A concave lens will diverge parallel rays of light away from a virtual focal point. Figure 23.6 illustrates a typical ray construction for a diverging lens. Again, if we assume the thin lens approximation, we will draw the lens itself as a line for ease of construction. The context of the problem tells us that the drawing represents a concave, not a convex, lens.

To construct the image, we have drawn a parallel light ray that then diverges away from the focal point. The second light ray is drawn through the optical center of the lens. The resulting virtual image will be erect and smaller and will be in front of the object. This will be true for any location of the object, so only one sample construction is necessary.

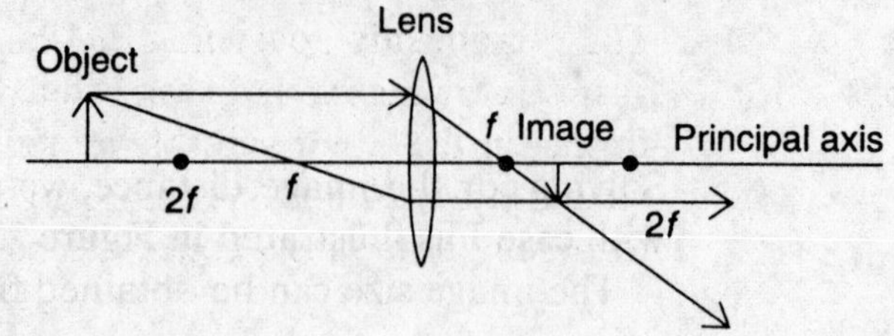

Case I—object beyond 2*f*; image is between *f* and 2*f*, is real, is smaller

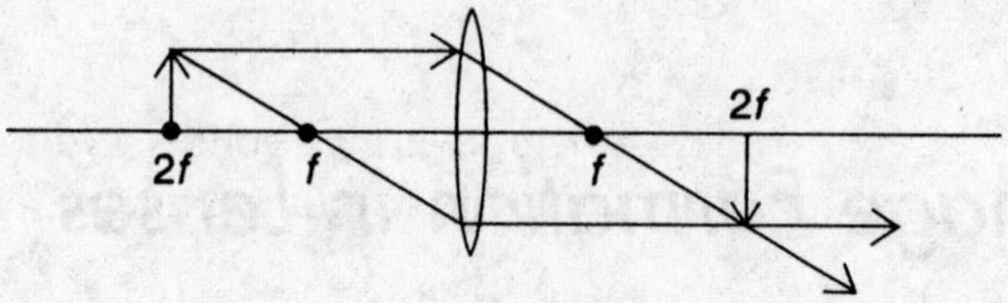

Case II—object at 2*f*; image is at 2*f*; is real, is same size

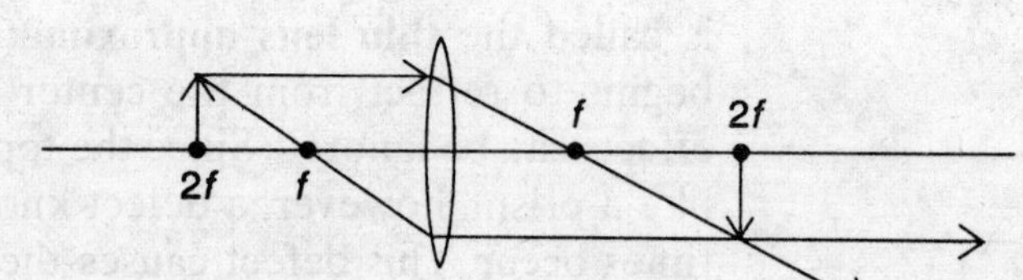

Case III—object between *f* and 2*f*; image is beyond 2*f*, is real, is larger

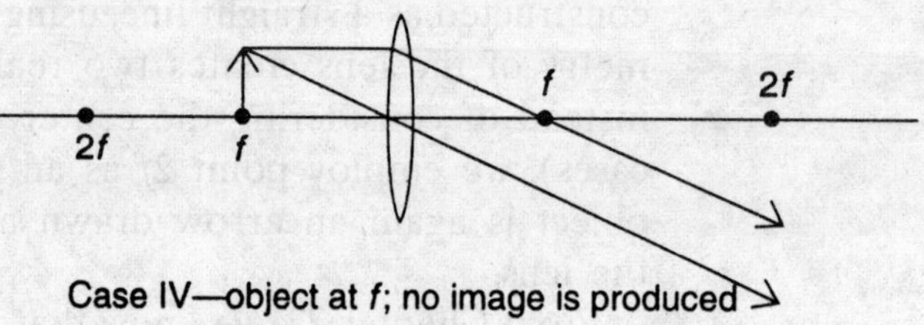

Case IV—object at *f*; no image is produced

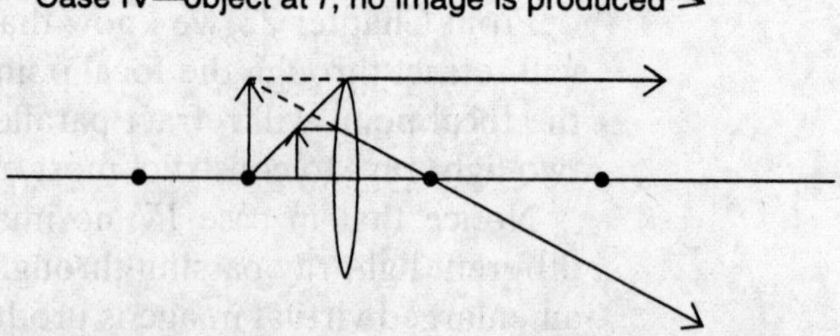

Case V—object between *f* and the lens; image is behind object, is virtual, is larger

FIGURE 23.5

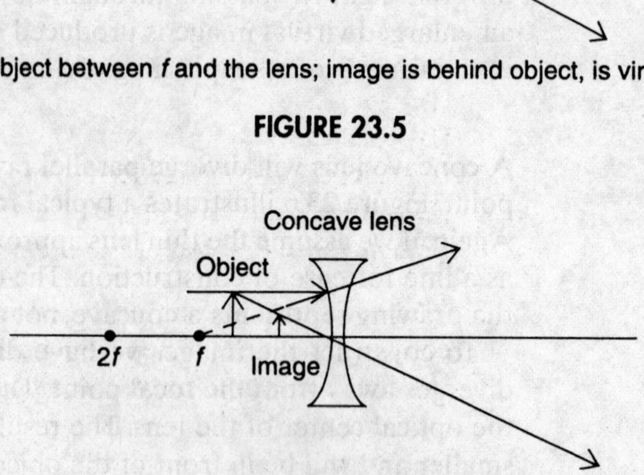

FIGURE 23.6

C. Algebraic Considerations

The relationship governing the image formation in a thin lens is the same as it was for a curved mirror. Positive image distances occur when the image forms on the other side of the lens. A negative image distance implies a virtual image. A positive focal length implies a convex lens, while a negative focal length implies a concave lens. Therefore, as before, we can write

$$\frac{1}{f} = \frac{1}{p} + \frac{1}{q}$$

and

$$\frac{S_i}{S_o} = \frac{q}{p}$$

If two converging lenses are used in combination, separated by some distance x, the combined magnification, m, of the system is given by

$$m = m_1 m_2$$

Problem-Solving Strategies for Geometrical Optics

To solve ray-diagram problems, you must remember the types of light rays and understand how they reflect and refract using mirrors and lenses. Numerically, keep in mind that positive focal lengths imply concave mirrors and convex lenses.

Memorize all of the cases illustrated in this chapter, and remember that real images are always inverted. Even if a given problem does not require a construction, draw a sketch. Additionally, remember that the focal length of a lens is dependent on the frequency of light used and the material of which the lens is made.

Practice Problems for Chapter 23

Multiple Choice

1. Which material will produce a converging lens with the longest focal length?
   (A) Lucite
   (B) Crown glass
   (C) Flint glass
   (D) Quartz
   (E) Diamond

2. An object is placed in front of a converging lens in such a way that the image produced is inverted and larger. If the lens were replaced by one with a larger index of refraction, the size of the image would
   (A) increase
   (B) decrease
   (C) increase or decrease, depending on the degree of change
   (D) remain the same
   (E) increase or decrease depending on the wavelength of the light

3. You wish to make an enlarged reproduction of a document using a copying machine. When you push the enlargement button, the lens inside the machine moves to a point
   (A) equal to f
   (B) equal to $2f$
   (C) between f and $2f$

(D) beyond $2f$
(E) less than f

4. A negative image distance means that the image formed by a concave mirror will be
(A) real
(B) erect
(C) inverted
(D) smaller
(E) both (B) and (D)

5. Real images are always produced by
(A) plane mirrors
(B) convex mirrors
(C) concave lenses
(D) convex lenses
(E) both (B) and (C)

6. The focal length of a convex mirror with a radius of curvature of 8 cm is
(A) 4 cm
(B) −4 cm
(C) 8 cm
(D) −8 cm
(E) 16 cm

7. An object appears in front of a plane mirror as shown below:

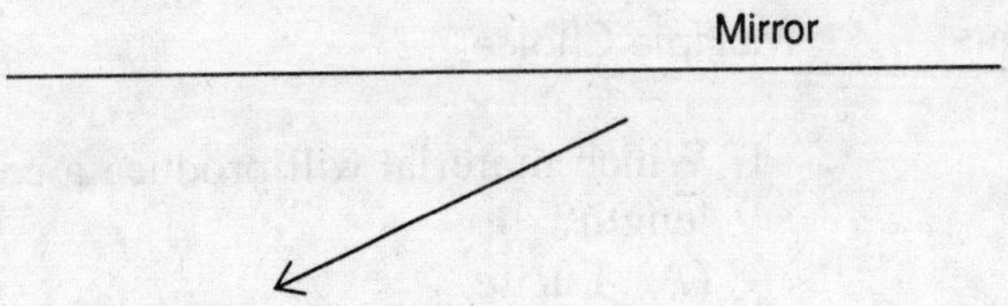

Which of the following diagrams represents the reflected image of this object?

(A) 

(B) 

(C) 

(D) 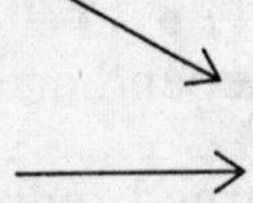

(E) 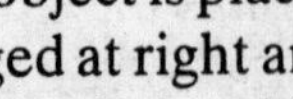

8. An object is placed in front of, and exactly between, two mirrors that are hinged at right angles to each other. How many images of the object will be seen if the object is viewed from a point directly behind the object?
(A) One
(B) Two

(C) Three
(D) Four
(E) Five

9. An object is located 15 cm in front of a converging lens. An image twice as large as the object appears on the other side of the lens. The image distance must be
(A) 15 cm
(B) 30 cm
(C) 45 cm
(D) 60 cm
(E) 75 cm

10. A 1.6-meter-tall person stands 1.5 m in front of a vertical plane mirror. The height of his image is
(A) 0.8 m
(B) 2.6 m
(C) 3.2 m
(D) 4.5 m
(E) 1.6 m

Free Response

1. Using a geometric-ray diagram construction, prove Newton's version of the lens equation:

$$f^2 = d\,d'$$

where f is the focal length of the lens, d is the distance from the object to the focal point, and d' is the distance of the image from the other focal point.

2. Prove that, if two thin convex lenses are touching, the effective focal length of the combination is given by the formula

$$\frac{1}{f} = \frac{1}{f_1} + \frac{1}{f_2}$$

3. An object is 25 cm in front of a converging lens with a 5-cm focal length. A second converging lens, with a focal length of 3 cm, is placed 10 cm behind the first one.
(a) Locate the image formed by the first lens.
(b) Locate the image formed by the second lens if the first image is used as an "object" for the second lens.
(c) What is the combined magnification of this combination of lenses?

Solutions

Multiple-Choice Problems

1. **D** The longest focal length will be produced by the material that refracts the least, that is, has the smallest index of refraction. Of the five choices, quartz has the lowest index of refraction.
2. **B** The lens formula can be rewritten as

$$q = \frac{pf}{p - f}$$

If the object remains in the same position relative to the lens, then using a larger index of refraction will imply a smaller focal length. The image will move closer to the lens and consequently will be smaller.

3. **C** To produce an enlarged real image, the object must be located between *f* and 2*f*.
4. **B** In a concave mirror, a negative image distance implies a virtual image, which is enlarged and erect.
5. **D** Only a convex lens or a concave mirror can produce a real image.
6. **B** The radius of curvature of a spherical mirror is twice the focal length. However, in a convex mirror, the focal length is taken to be negative.
7. **B** The reflected image must point "away" from the mirror but on the other side, flipped over.
8. **C** A sketch of the situation appears below. Each mirror will have one image, but an image will also be seen at the vertex point.

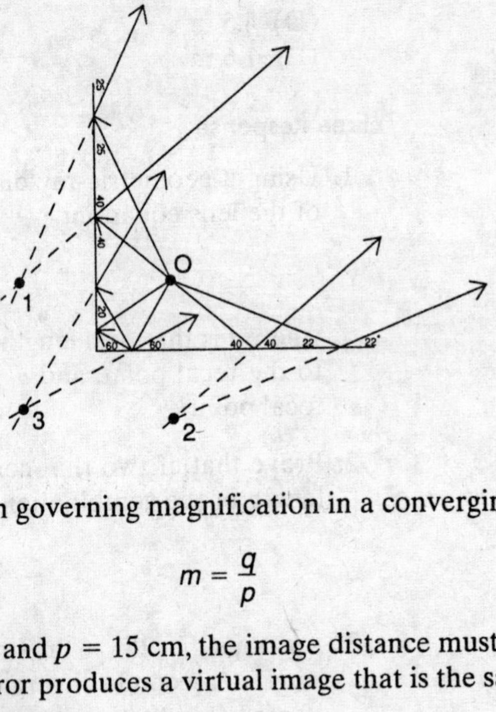

9. **B** The equation governing magnification in a converging lens is

$$m = \frac{q}{p}$$

Since $m = 2$ and $p = 15$ cm, the image distance must be $q = 30$ cm.

10. **E** A plane mirror produces a virtual image that is the same size as the object in all cases.

Free-Response Problems

1. A drawing of the situation is given below:

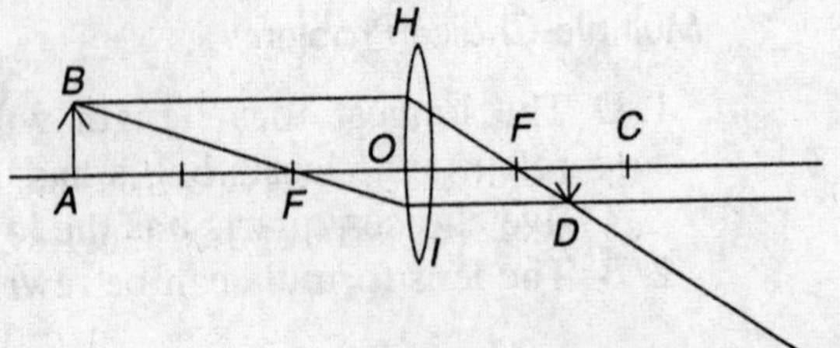

In this construction, we have used the thin lens approximation. On the left side of the lens,

$$AF = d \quad \text{and} \quad FO = f \text{ (focal length)}$$

On the right side,

$$FO = f \quad \text{and} \quad FC = d'$$

Since we have a thin lens,

$$AB = OH \quad \text{and} \quad OI = CD$$

Now, we have ΔFAB similar to ΔFOI and ΔFOH similar to ΔFCD. Thus, the following sides are in proportion:

$$AB / OI = AF / FO$$

$$OH / CD = FO / FC$$

Thus, $f / d = d' / f$, using the relationships defined above. Therefore,

$$f^2 = dd'$$

as desired.

2. If we have two lenses in contact, the image of the first lens becomes a "negative" object for the second lens. For the first lens, we have

$$\frac{1}{f_1} = \frac{1}{p} + \frac{1}{q_1}$$

where p is the object distance for the combination. For the second lens, we must now have

$$\frac{1}{f_2} = \frac{1}{q_1} + \frac{1}{q_2}$$

If we combine these equations, we obtain

$$\frac{1}{f_1} + \frac{1}{f_2} = \frac{1}{p} + \frac{1}{q_2}$$

Since the two thin lenses are in contact, $q_2$can be considered the image distance from the first lens also. Therefore, if we set

$$\frac{1}{p} + \frac{1}{q_2} = \frac{1}{f}$$

the combination of two thin lenses in contact behaves equivalently as a single lens with a focal length f, so that

$$\frac{1}{f} = \frac{1}{f_1} + \frac{1}{f_2}$$

3. (a) For the first lens, we have $f = 5$ cm and $p = 25$; thus

$$q = \frac{pf}{p-f} = \frac{(25)(5)}{25-5} = \frac{125}{20}$$

and the location of the image formed by the first lens is given by $q = 6.25$ cm.

(b) Since $d = 10$ cm for the second lens (its distance from the first lens) and $q = 6.25$ for the first lens, the image q now serves as the new "object" at a distance $p' = 10 - 6.25 = 3.75$. The focal length of the second lens is 3 cm; therefore, the distance q' of the image formed by the second lens is

$$q' = \frac{(3.75)(3)}{3.75-3} = 15 \text{ cm}$$

(c) The combined magnification of the system is equal to the product of the separate magnifications. Since $m = q / p$, in general, we have

$$m_1 = \frac{6.25}{25} = 0.25$$

$$m_2 = \frac{15}{3.75} = 4$$

Therefore, the combined magnification of this conbination of lenses is given by

$$m = m_1 m_2 = (0.25)(4) = 1$$

CHAPTER 24

Quantum Theory

24.1 Photoelectric Effect

Light has a very interesting effect on certain metals. Imagine a piece of zinc placed on top of an electroscope and charged negatively by contact (in a vacuum). If the zinc is exposed to various frequencies of light, it is determined that light in the ultraviolet region causes the electroscope to discharge (see Figure 24.1). This phenomenon does not occur, however, when the zinc and electroscope are charged positively.

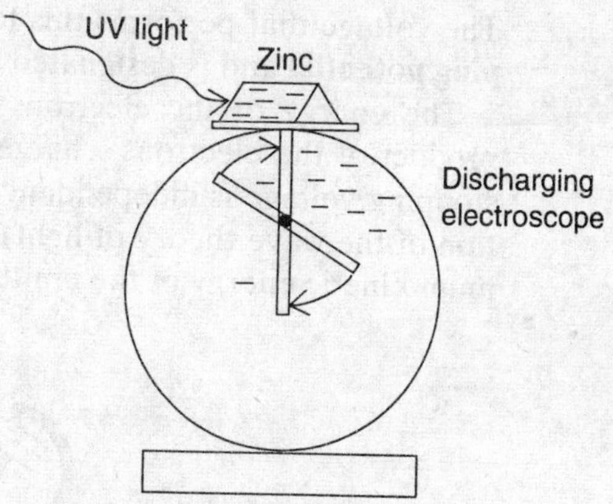

FIGURE 24.1

The conclusion is that the ultraviolet light causes the zinc to emit electrons, that, in turn, cause the electroscope to discharge. This phenomenon, called the **photoelectric effect**, defines a new view of light that has come to be known as the **quantum theory**. Developed by Albert Einstein, the quantum theory has been extended to particles as well as electromagnetic waves and forms the basis of modern physics.

The photoelectric effect can be studied in a more quantitative way. Figure 24.2 shows an evacuated tube that contains a photoemissive material. Many metals exhibit the photoelectric effect. On the other side of the tube is a collecting plate. The tube is connected to a microammeter, which can be used to measure the current generated by the emitted electrons. When exposed to light of suitable frequency, the ammeter will implicitly measure the number of electrons emitted per second. This number is sensitive only to the intensity of the electromagnetic wave applied. The minimum frequency that emits electrons is called the **threshold frequency** and is designated as f_0.

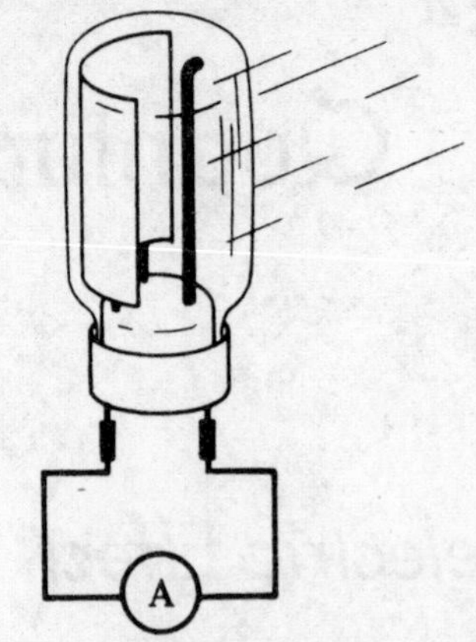

FIGURE 24.2

To measure the energy of the emitted electrons, we insert in the circuit a source of potential difference (Figure 24.3) such that the negative electrons approach a negatively charged side. This will create a braking force; and if we select the voltage properly, we can stop the current completely. The voltage that performs this feat is called the **stopping voltage** or **stopping potential** and is designated as V_0.

The energy of the electrons stopped by this voltage is equal to the product of the electrons' charge and the stopping voltage, eV_0. Since the stopping voltage is independent of the intensity of the light used (a violation of the wave theory of light), the stopping voltage measures the maximum kinetic energy of the emitted electrons.

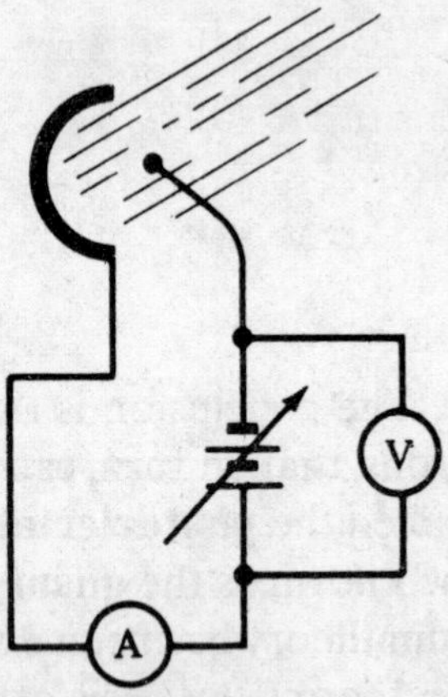

FIGURE 24.3

As the frequency of light is slowly increased, there is a change in the maximum kinetic energy of the electrons. The fact that this energy is independent of the intensity of the light was used by Einstein to demonstrate that light consists of discrete or **quantized** packets of energy called **photons**. The energy of a given photon is directly proportional to its frequency.

To clarify this relationship, Figure 24.4 illustrates a typical graph of maximum kinetic energy versus frequency.

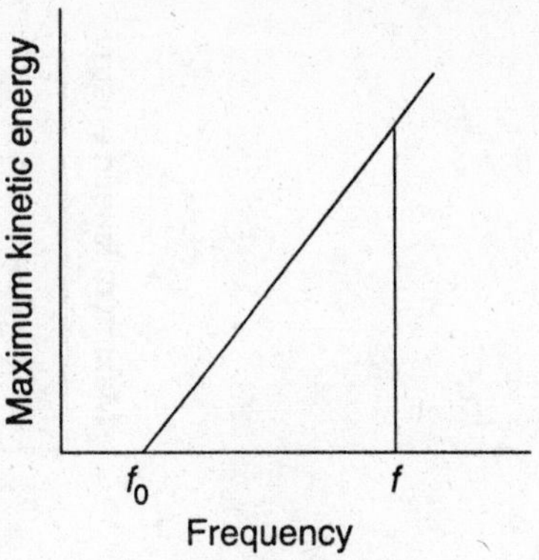

FIGURE 24.4

Starting with the threshold frequency, the graph is a straight line. For any frequency point, *f*, the slope of the line is given by

$$\text{Slope} = \frac{KE_{max}}{f - f_0} = h$$

This slope, referred to as **Planck's constant** and symbolized as *h,* has a value of

$$h = 6.63 \times 10^{-34}\ \text{J/Hz} = 6.63 \times 10^{-34}\ \text{J} \cdot \text{s}$$

Planck's constant originally appeared in the theoretical work of German physicist Max Planck. His mathematical discovery in 1900 of an **elementary quantum of action** helped explain the nature of radiation emitted from hot bodies. Planck's constant became a part of Einstein's quantum theory of light and Bohr's quantum theory of the hydrogen atom.

The above equation can be solved for the maximum kinetic energy:

$$KE_{max} = hf - hf_0$$

In this expression, known as the **photoelectric equation**, hf represents the energy of the original photon, while hf_0, called the **work function**, is a property of the metal. The quantity hf_0 is a measure of the minimum amount of energy needed to free an electron. It is designated in some textbooks by the Greek letter phi (ϕ) and in others by W_0. In this book, we use the latter designation for the work function.

Experiments with various metals yield some interesting results. Even though the different metals all have different threshold frequencies, they all obey the same photoelectric equation and have the same slope, *h*. A typical comparison graph of three metals, *A*, *B*, and *C*, is shown in Figure 24.5.

Einstein was awarded the Nobel Prize for Physics in 1921, the same year that he published his celebrated paper on special relativity. Because of the controversy over relativity, the Nobel committee awarded the prize on the basis of Einstein's theoretical work in 1905 on the quantum theory of light. His suggestion of the photoelectric effect, whereby light behaves as packets of quantized energy (photons), was in direct conflict with the prevailing

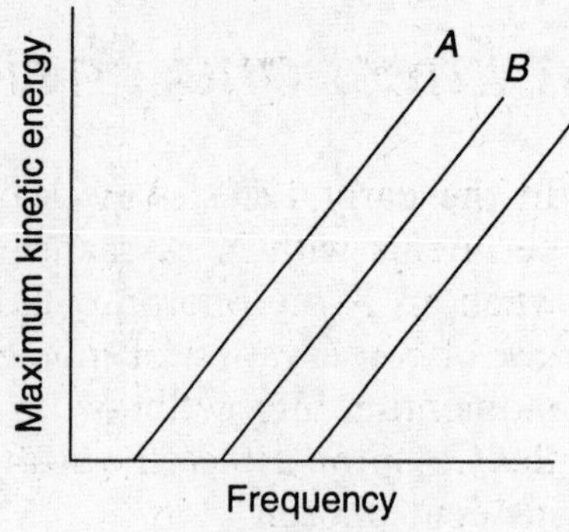

FIGURE 24.5

wave theory of light, as demonstrated by interference and diffraction. Thus, physicists in the early twentieth century were presented with a **dual nature of light**.

In the wave theory of light, the intensity of light is related to its amplitude and is measured with a **photometer**. The intensity of light energy varies inversely as the square of the distance from the source. In the quantum theory, however, light intensity is related to the number, N, of photons:

$$N = \frac{\text{Detected energy}}{\text{Energy of a photon}}$$

In the photoelectric effect, when the intensity is varied, only the number of photons, not their kinetic energy, is changed. Modern instruments used to measure light intensity now include **photoelectric photometers** that determine how many photons are entering the device. In telescopes and video cameras, image detectors use **charge coupled devices** (CCD's) to work with small numbers of photons.

Sample Problem:

Light with a frequency of 2×10^{15} Hz is incident on a piece of copper.
(a) What is the energy of the light in joules and in electron volts?
(b) If the work function for copper is 4.5 eV, what is the maximum kinetic energy, in electron volts, of the emitted electrons?

Solution:

(a) The energy in joules is given by $E = hf$. Thus,

$$E = hf = (6.63 \times 10^{-34})(2 \times 10^{15}) = 1.326 \times 10^{-18}\ \text{J}$$

Since 1 eV $= 1.6 \times 10^{-19}$ J, we have

$$E = 8.28\ \text{eV}$$

(b) To find the maximum kinetic energy, we simply subtract the work function from the photon energy:

$$KE_{max} = 8.28 - 4.5 = 3.79\ \text{eV}$$

24.2 Compton Effect and Photon Momentum

In the early 1920s, American physicist Arthur Compton conducted experiments with X rays and graphite. He was able to demonstrate that, when an X-ray photon collides with an electron, the collision obeys the law of conservation of momentum. The scattering of photons due to this momentum interaction is known as the **Compton effect** (Figure 24.6). In the Compton effect, the scattered photon has a lower frequency than the incident photon.

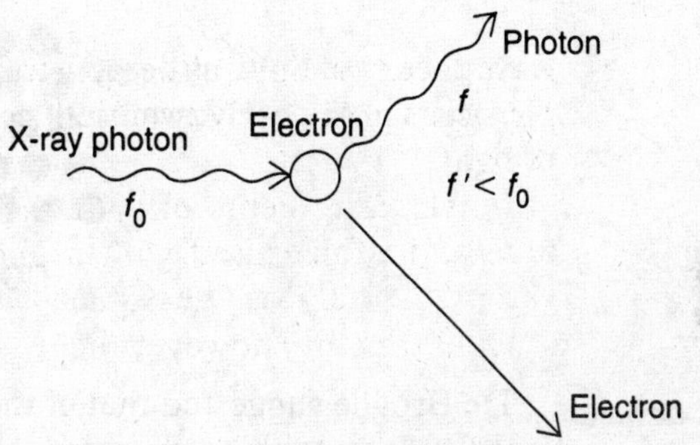

FIGURE 24.6

The momentum of the photon is given by the relationship $\mathbf{p} = h / \lambda$. Thus X rays, because of their very high frequency, possess a large photon momentum. Even though we state that photons can have momentum, they do not possess what is called **rest mass**. If light can have momentum as well as wavelength, the question now raised is, "Can particles have wavelength as well as momentum?"

24.3 Matter Waves

If a beam of X rays is incident on a crystal of salt, the pattern that emerges is characteristic of the scattering of particles, not waves. If, however, a beam of electrons is incident on a narrow slit (Figure 24.7), the pattern that emerges is a typical wave diffraction pattern. Electron diffraction is one example of the dual nature of matter, which, under certain conditions, exhibits a wave nature. The circumstances are determined by experiment. If you perform an interference experiment with light, you will demonstrate its wave properties. If you do a photoelectric effect experiment, light will reveal its "particlelike" properties.

In the 1920s, French physicist Louis de Broglie used the dual nature of light to suggest that matter can have a "wavelike" nature, as indicated by its de Broglie wavelength. Since a photon's momentum is given by $\mathbf{p} = h / \lambda$, the wavelength can be transposed to give $\lambda = h / \mathbf{p}$.

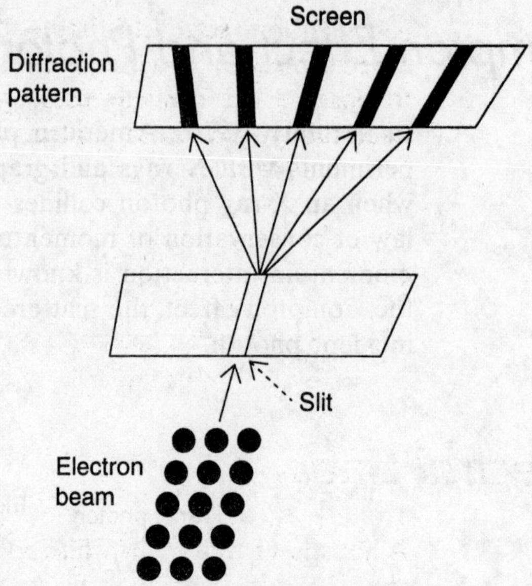

FIGURE 24.7

De Broglie suggested that, if the momentum of a particle, $\mathbf{p} = m\mathbf{v}$, has a magnitude suitable to overcome the small magnitude of Planck's constant, a significant wavelength can be observed. The criterion, since mass is in the denominator of the expression for wavelength, is that the mass be extremely small (on the atomic scale). Thus, while electrons, protons, and neutrons might have wave characteristics, a falling stone, because of its large mass, would not exhibit any wavelike effects. The equation for the de Broglie wavelength of a particle is given by

$$\lambda = \frac{h}{m\mathbf{v}}$$

Sample Problem:

Find the de Broglie wavelength for each of the following:
(a) A 10-g stone moving with a velocity of 20 m/s.
(b) An electron moving with a velocity of 1×10^7 m/s.

Solution:

(a) Since $m = 10$ g $= 0.01$ kg, and $\lambda = h / m\mathbf{v}$, we have

$$\lambda = \frac{6.63 \times 10^{-34}}{(0.01)(20)} = 3.315 \times 10^{-33} \text{ m}$$

(b) In this part we have

$$\lambda = \frac{h}{m\mathbf{v}} = \frac{6.63 \times 10^{-34}}{(9.1 \times 10^{-31})(1 \times 10^7)} = 7.3 \times 10^{-11} \text{ m}$$

This aspect of particle motion, on a small scale, leads to the so-called **Heisenberg uncertainty principle**. Developed by Werner Heisenberg, also in the 1920s, this states that because of the wave nature of small particles (on an atomic scale) it is impossible to determine precisely both the simultaneous position and momentum of the particle. Any experimental attempt to observe the particle, using photon detection, will cause an inherent uncertainty since those photons will interact with the particles. Mathematically, the Heisenberg uncertainty principle states that

$$\Delta x \, \Delta \mathbf{p} \geq \frac{h}{2\pi}$$

where h is Planck's constant.

24.4 Spectral Lines

A hot source that emits white light is said to be **incandescent**. Its light, when analyzed with a prism, is broken up into a continuous spectrum of colors. (A **spectroscope** is a device that uses either a prism or a grating to create a spectrum.) If a colored filter is used over the incandescent source, light of only that one color will be emitted, and the spectrum will appear as a continuous band of that color.

If hydrogen gas contained at low pressure in a tube is electrically sparked, the gas will emit a bluish light. If that light is analyzed with a spectroscope, a discrete series of colored lines ranging from red to violet, rather than a continuous band of color, is revealed. When sparked, other chemical elements also show characteristic **emission line spectra** that are useful for chemical analysis.

Figure 24.8 illustrates a typical hydrogen spectral series in the visible range of the electromagnetic spectrum. This series is often called the **Balmer series** in honor of Jakob Balmer, a Swiss mathematician who empirically studied the hydrogen spectrum in the late nineteenth century. In Figure 24.8, a hydrogen tube is excited and its light is passed through a narrow slit to provide a point source. This light is then passed through a prism or grating. Many emission lines are produced, but only the first four,

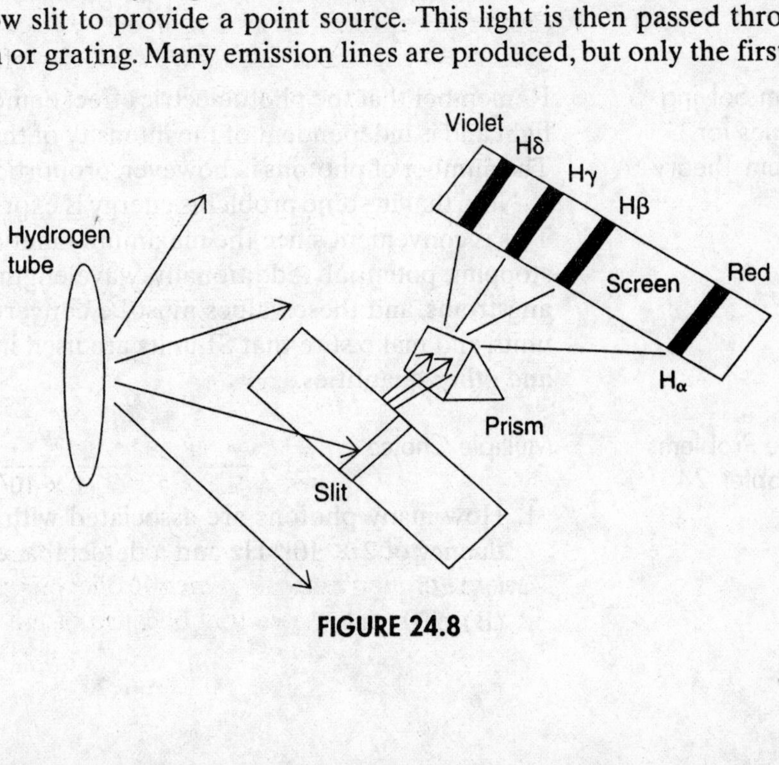

FIGURE 24.8

designated as Hα (red), Hβ, Hλ, and Hδ (violet), are illustrated here. The wavelengths range from about 656 to about 400 nanometers.

It was Balmer, who first demonstrated, in 1884, that the visible hydrogen spectrum obeys the following empirical (nontheoretical) relationship, where λ is measured in angstroms:

$$\lambda\ (\text{Å}) = 3645.6\left(\frac{n^2}{n^2 - 4}\right)$$

Here $n = 3, 4, 5, \ldots$.

Balmer did not understand the significance of the integral index *n,* but it was clear that the light emitted by atomic compounds is not continuous but discrete (quantized). An alternative form of the Balmer formula allows for additional insight. If we solve for the **wave number,** 1 / λ, we will have a relationship that is directly proportional to the emitted energy of the photons. For the Balmer series, this expression (in SI units) takes the form

$$\frac{1}{\lambda} = R\left(\frac{1}{2^2} - \frac{1}{n^2}\right)$$

The constant *R*, known as the **Rydberg constant**, has a value of

$$R = 1.097 \times 10^7\ \text{m}^{-1}$$

Several other emission line series for hydrogen have been discovered in the ultraviolet region (Lyman series) and in the infrared region (Paschen series). In each case, a similar version of the Balmer formula appears:

$$\text{Lyman UV: } \frac{1}{\lambda} = R\left(\frac{1}{1^2} - \frac{1}{n^2}\right), \text{ where } n = 2,3,4, \ldots$$

$$\text{Paschen IR: } \frac{1}{\lambda} = R\left(\frac{1}{3^2} - \frac{1}{n^2}\right), \text{ where } n = 4,5,6, \ldots$$

Problem-Solving Strategies for Quantum Theory

Remember that the photoelectric effect demonstrates the particle nature of light and is independent of the intensity of the electromagnetic waves used. The number of photons is, however, proportional to the intensity of energy.

Note that in some problems energy is expressed in units of electron volts. This is convenient since the maximum kinetic energy is proportional to the stopping potential. Additionally, wavelengths are sometimes expressed in angstroms, and these values must be converted to meters. Be careful with units, and make sure that SI units are used in equations involving energies and other quantities.

Practice Problems for Chapter 24

Multiple Choice

1. How many photons are associated with a beam of light having a frequency of 2×10^{16} Hz and a detectable energy of 6.63×10^{-15} J?
(A) 25
(B) 500

(C) 135
(D) 8
(E) 80

2. A photoelectric experiment reveals a maximum kinetic energy of 2.2 eV for a certain metal. The stopping potential for the emitted electrons is
(A) 1.2 V
(B) 1.75 V
(C) 3.5 V
(D) 4.2 V
(E) 2.2 V

3. The work function for a certain metal is 3.7 eV. What is the threshold frequency for this metal?
(A) 9×10^{14} Hz
(B) 2×10^{15} Hz
(C) 7×10^{14} Hz
(D) 5×10^{15} Hz
(E) 3.5×10^{15} Hz

4. In which kind of waves do the photons have the greatest momentum?
(A) Radio waves
(B) Microwaves
(C) Red light
(D) Ultraviolet
(E) X ray

5. What is the momentum of a photon associated with yellow light that has a wavelength of 5500 Å?
(A) 1.2×10^{-27} kg · m/s
(B) 1.2×10^{-37} kg · m/s
(C) 1.2×10^{-17} kg · m/s
(D) 1.2×10^{-30} kg · m/s
(E) 5000 kg · m/s

6. What is the de Broglie wavelength for a proton ($m = 1.67 \times 10^{-27}$ kg) with a velocity of 6×10^7 m/s?
(A) 1.5×10^{14} m
(B) 1.5×10^{-14} m
(C) 4.8×10^{-11} m
(D) 6.6×10^{-15} m
(E) 3×10^8 m

7. What is the velocity of an electron with a de Broglie wavelength of 3×10^{-10} m?
(A) 3×10^8 m/s
(B) 2.4×10^6 m/s
(C) 7.28×10^4 m/s
(D) 1.5×10^7 m/s
(E) 5.7×10^5 m/s

8. Which of the following is a formula for photon momentum?
   (A) $\mathbf{p} = Ec$
   (B) $\mathbf{p} = Ec^2$
   (C) $\mathbf{p} = E / c$
   (D) $\mathbf{p} = mc^2$
   (E) $\mathbf{p} = E + c$

9. Which of the following statements is correct about emission line spectra?
   (A) All of the lines are evenly spaced.
   (B) All elements in the same chemical family have the same spectra.
   (C) Only gases emit emission lines.
   (D) All lines result from discrete energy differences.
   (E) All of the preceding statements are correct.

10. Which of the following is equivalent to the units, joule · seconds, of Planck's constant?
   (A) kg · m/s
   (B) kg · m/s^2
   (C) kg · m^2/s
   (D) kg · m^2/s^2
   (E) kg / s

Free Response

1. (a) Starting with the Balmer formula for wavelength in angstroms:

$$\lambda\,(\text{Å}) = 3645.6\left(\frac{n^2}{n^2 - 4}\right)$$

derive the alternative version of the Balmer formula in units of reciprocal meters (m^{-1}):

$$\frac{1}{\lambda} = R\left(\frac{1}{4} - \frac{1}{n^2}\right)$$

where $R = 1.097 \times 10^7\ m^{-1}$.

(b) What is the wavelength of the photon associated with $n = 4$?

2. (a) Explain the implication of Planck's constant being larger than its present value.
   (b) Explain the basic theory behind electron diffraction.

3. The threshold frequency for calcium is 7.7×10^{14} Hz.
   (a) What is the work function, in joules, for calcium?
   (b) If light of wavelength $2.5 \times 10^{-7}\ m$ is incident on calcium, what will be the maximum kinetic energy of the emitted electrons?
   (c) What is the stopping potential for the electrons emitted under the conditions in part (b)?

Solutions

Multiple-Choice Problems

1. **B** If E equals the total detectable energy and E_p equals the energy of a photon, then

$$N = \frac{E}{E_p} = \frac{E}{hf} = \frac{6.63 \times 10^{-15}\ J}{1.326 \times 10^{-17}\ J} = 500$$

2. **E** By definition, 1 eV is the amount of energy given to one electron when placed in a potential difference of 1 V. Thus, if $KE_{max} = 2.2$ eV, the stopping potential must be equal to 2.2 V.
3. **A** The formula for the work function is $W_0 = hf_0$. The work function must be expressed in units of joules before dividing by Planck's constant:

$$f_0 = \frac{(3.7)(1.6 \times 10^{-19})}{6.63 \times 10^{-34}} = 8.9 \times 10^{14} \text{ Hz}$$

4. **E** Since $\mathbf{p} = h / \lambda$, the waves with the smallest wavelength will have the greatest photon momentum. Of the five choices, an X-ray photon has the smallest wavelength and thus the greatest momentum.
5. **A** The wavelength must first be converted to meters; then we can use $\mathbf{p} = h / \lambda$:

$$\mathbf{p} = \frac{6.63 \times 10^{-34}}{(5500)(1 \times 10^{-10})} = 1.2 \times 10^{-27} \text{ kg} \cdot \text{m/s}$$

6. **D** The formula for the de Broglie wavelength is $\lambda = h / m\mathbf{v}$. Substituting the known values gives

$$\lambda = \frac{6.63 \times 10^{-34}}{(1.67 \times 10^{-27})(6 \times 10^{7})} = 6.6 \times 10^{-15} \text{ m}$$

7. **B** Using the de Broglie formula for wavelength gives $\mathbf{v} = h / m\lambda$. Substituting the known values, we obtain

$$\mathbf{v} = \frac{6.63 \times 10^{-34}}{(9.1 \times 10^{-31})(3 \times 10^{-10})} = 2.4 \times 10^{6} \text{ m/s}$$

8. **C** We have that $\mathbf{p} = h / \lambda$ and that $E = hf = hc / \lambda$. Thus, $E = \mathbf{p}c$, and so $\mathbf{p} = E / c$.
9. **D** Spectral emission lines are different for every atom or molecule, and the lines are not evenly spaced. They do, however, arise from energy difference transitions as discussed in Chapter 25.
10. **C** The units of Planck's constant are joule · seconds; and since 1 J = 1 kg · m²/s², the units for h are kilogram · square meters per second (kg · m²/s). These units are also the units for angular momentum!

Free-Response Problems

1. (a) To derive the Rydberg formula, we need to rewrite the Balmer formula in terms of meters:

$$\lambda \text{ (m)} = 3.6456 \times 10^{-7}\left(\frac{n^2}{n^2 - 4}\right)$$

Now, we take the reciprocal of each side:

$$\frac{1}{\lambda} = \frac{n^2 - 4}{3.6456 \times 10^{-7}\, n^2}$$

We distribute the denominator into the two factors in the numerator:

$$\frac{1}{\lambda} = \frac{1}{3.6456 \times 10^{-7}}\left(\frac{1}{1} - \frac{4}{n^2}\right)$$

and, finally, factor out a 4:

$$\frac{1}{\lambda} = \frac{4}{3.6456 \times 10^{-7}}\left(\frac{1}{4} - \frac{1}{n^2}\right) = 1.097 \times 10^{7}\left(\frac{1}{4} - \frac{1}{n^2}\right) = R\left(\frac{1}{4} - \frac{1}{n^2}\right)$$

(b) To find the wavelength associated with $n = 4$, we substitute $n = 4$ to get

$$\frac{1}{\lambda} = 2056875 \text{ m}^{-1}$$

which means that

$$\lambda = 4.861 \times 10^{-7} \text{ m}$$

2. (a) If Planck's constant were larger than its present value, an implication would be that the uncertainty principle, $\Delta \mathbf{p}\, \Delta x \geq h/2\pi$, would apply to a domain of larger magnitude and we would see quantum effects occur at larger sizes as well.

(b) Electron diffraction is based on the wave theory of matter. Since an electron has a sufficiently small mass, its de Broglie wavelength is large enough to be diffracted by small openings and thus to exhibit seemingly common wave properties. Scanning electron microscopes, although much more complex in theory, use the same basic principle.

3. (a) The work function is given by

$$W_0 = hf_0 = (6.63 \times 10^{-34})(7.7 \times 10^{14}) = 5.1 \times 10^{-19} \text{ J}$$

(b) The frequency associated with a wavelength of 2.5×10^{-7} m is given by

$$f = \frac{c}{\lambda} = \frac{3 \times 10^{8}}{2.5 \times 10^{-7}} = 1.2 \times 10^{15} \text{ Hz}$$

The energy of the associated photon is equal to

$$E = hf = 7.956 \times 10^{-19} \text{ J}$$

The maximum kinetic energy of the emitted electrons is equal to the difference between this energy and the work function:

$$KE_{max} = 7.956 \times 10^{-19} - 5.1 \times 10^{-19} = 2.856 \times 10^{-19} \text{ J}$$

(c) This maximum kinetic energy is equal to the product of the electron charge and the stopping potential. Thus:

$$V_0 = \frac{KE_{max}}{e} = \frac{2.856 \times 10^{-19}}{1.6 \times 10^{-19}} = 1.785 \text{ V}$$

CHAPTER 25
The Atom

25.1 Atomic Structure and Rutherford's Model

In 1896, French physicist Henri Becquerel was studying the phosphorescent properties of uranium ores. Certain rocks glow after being exposed to sunlight, and many physicists at that time were examining the light emanations from these ores.

One day, while engaged in such a study, Becquerel placed a piece of uranium ore in a drawer on top of some sealed photographic paper. Several days later, he found to his surprise that the paper had been exposed even though no light was incident on it! His conclusion was that radiation emitted by the uranium had penetrated the sealed envelope and exposed the paper.

Subsequent work by Marie and Pierre Curie revealed that this natural radioactivity, as they called it, came from the uranium itself and was a consequence of its instability as an atom. Also, Ernest Rutherford discovered (see Figure 25.1) that the radiation emitted yielded particles that were useful for further atomic studies.

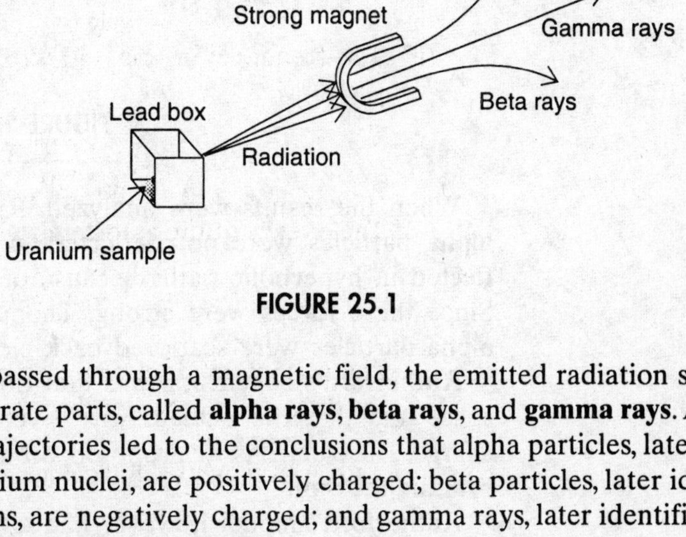

FIGURE 25.1

When passed through a magnetic field, the emitted radiation split into three separate parts, called **alpha rays**, **beta rays**, and **gamma rays**. Analysis of their trajectories led to the conclusions that alpha particles, later identified as helium nuclei, are positively charged; beta particles, later identified as electrons, are negatively charged; and gamma rays, later identified to be photons, are electrically neutral.

J. J. Thomson, using the data available at the end of the nineteenth century, devised an early model of the atom based on the fact that all atoms are electrically neutral. After concluding that the atom is positively charged and that electrons are also associated with it, Thomson's model proposed that the atom consisted of a relatively large, uniformly distributed, positive mass with negatively charged electrons embedded in it like raisins in a pudding (see Figure 25.2).

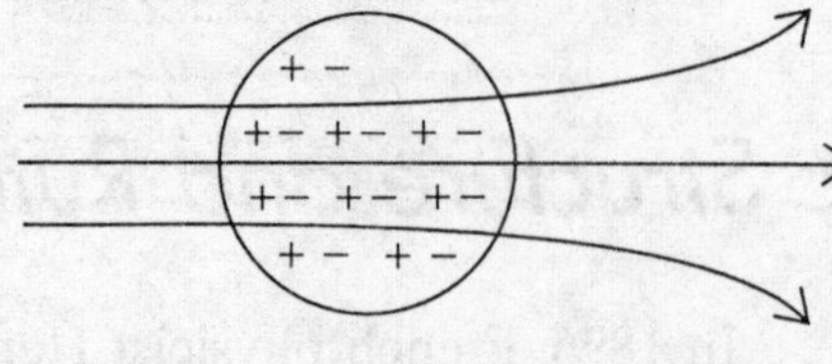

FIGURE 25.2 Thomson's Model of the Atom

In 1911, Rutherford and his coworkers decided to test Thomson's model using alpha-particle scattering. In the Thomson model, the positive charge was uniformly distributed. Since the negative electrons were embedded inside the nucleus, the Coulomb force of attraction would weaken the deflecting force on a passing positively charged alpha particle.

Rutherford's procedure was to aim alpha particles at a thin metal foil (he used gold) and observe the scattering pattern on a zinc sulfide screen (Figure 25.3).

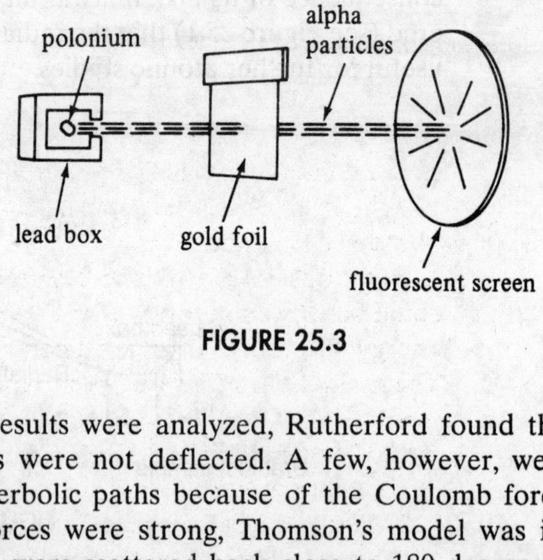

FIGURE 25.3

When the results were analyzed, Rutherford found that most of the alpha particles were not deflected. A few, however, were strongly deflected in hyperbolic paths because of the Coulomb force of repulsion. Since these forces were strong, Thomson's model was incorrect. Some alpha particles were scattered back close to 180 degrees (Figure 25.4).

Rutherford's conclusion was that the atom consisted mostly of empty space and that the nucleus was a very small, densely packed, positive charge. The electrons, he proposed, orbited around the nucleus like planets orbiting the Sun.

Rutherford's model, however, had several major problems, including the fact that it could not account for the appearance of discrete emission line spectra. In Rutherford's model the electrons continuously orbited around the nucleus. This circular, "accelerated" motion should produce a continuous band of electromagnetic radiation, but it did not. Additionally, the

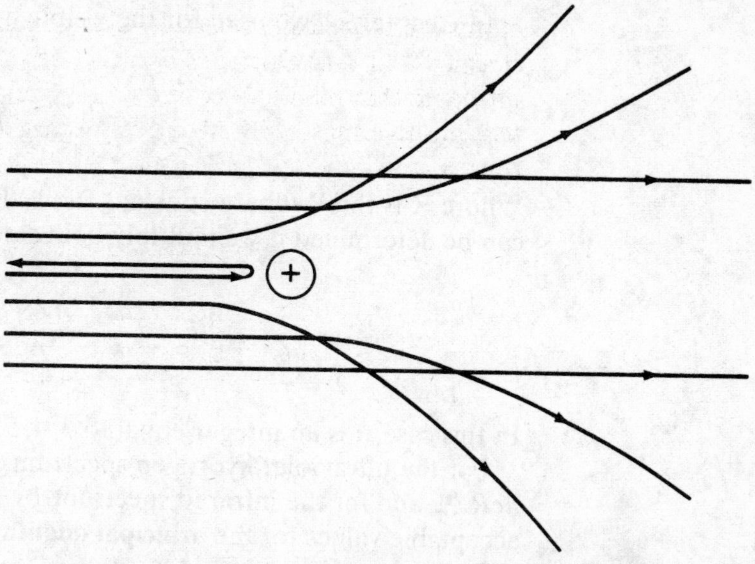

FIGURE 25.4 Alpha Particle Scattering Trajectories

predicted orbital loss of energy would cause an atom to disintegrate in a very short time and thus break apart all matter. This phenomenon, too, did not occur.

25.2 The Bohr Model

Niels Bohr, a Danish physicist, decided in 1913 to study the hydrogen spectral lines again. Years earlier, Einstein had proposed a quantum theory of light, developing the concept of a photon and completely explaining the photoelectric effect.

Bohr observed that the Balmer formula for the hydrogen spectrum could be viewed in terms of energy differences. He then realized that these energy differences involved a new set of postulates about atomic structure. The main ideas of his theory are these:

1. Electrons do not emit electromagnetic radiation while in a given orbit (energy state).
2. Electrons cannot remain in any arbitrary energy state. They can remain only in discrete or quantized energy states.
3. The angular momentum of an electron is quantized (by an integer index n) and is proportional to Planck's constant.
4. Electrons emit electromagnetic energy when they make transitions from higher energy states to lower energy states. The lowest energy state is the **ground state**.
5. Absorption spectra (dark lines appearing on an otherwise continuous-colored spectrum) occur because of transitions from lower to higher energy states as emitted light is absorbed by a cooler gas in front and reradiated.

In Chapter 24, we used for the visible hydrogen spectrum the formula:

$$\frac{1}{\lambda} = R\left(\frac{1}{4} - \frac{1}{n^2}\right)$$

Where R is the Rydberg constant. Now, the energy of the emitted photon can be determined if we multiply both sides by the quantity hc:

$$E_p = \frac{hc}{\lambda} = \frac{hcR}{4} - \frac{hcR}{n^2}$$

In this case, n is an integer equal to 3, 4, 5, ...

For the ultraviolet hydrogen spectrum, the factor $hcR / 4$ is replaced by $hcR / 1$, and for the infrared spectrum, by the factor $hcR / 9$. In those cases, acceptable values for the **principal quantum number**, n, would also change.

Since electrons appear to be "bound" to a nucleus (because of attractive Coulomb forces), forces designate the energy levels as increasingly negative as an electron gets closer to the nucleus, with $n = 1$ being the ground state. Thus, we can qualitatively write

$$E_n = -\frac{hcR}{n^2}$$

The energy states are then given as $E_1 = -13.6$ eV, $E_2 = -3.4$ eV, $E_3 = -1.5$ eV, E4 = -0.84 eV, etc.

These energy states have been derived qualitatively on the basis of the appearance of emission line spectra. The genius of Niels Bohr enabled him to begin with the electrical Coulomb forces and the quantized angular momentum and then to derive theoretically the same relationship for the hydrogen spectrum as we just described qualitatively.

Bohr knew that from Rutherford's experiments that the average radius of a hydrogen atom is 5.3×10^{-11} meter. The circumference of this orbit would therefore be equal to

$$C = 2\pi r = (6.28)(5.3 \times 10^{-11}) = 3.3 \times 10^{-10} \text{ m}$$

To better understand how angular momentum is quantized, let us use an argument that was advanced 10 years after Bohr's theory but is more illustrative. Recall that an electron has a wavelength inversely proportional to its momentum, $\lambda = h / m\mathbf{v}$. Physicists suspected, using Rutherford's model, that the orbital velocity of an electron is about 2.2×10^6 meters per second. The wavelength associated with this velocity is given by:

$$\lambda = \frac{h}{mv} = \frac{(6.63 \times 10^{-34})}{(9.1 \times 10^{-31})(2.2 \times 10^6)} = 3.3 \times 10^{-10} \text{m}$$

This wavelength is exactly the same as the circumference derived above!

If we state that the wavelength corresponds to a closed standing wave (see Figure 25.5) that is a multiple of the circumference (a two-dimensional standing wave), we can write

$$n\lambda = 2\pi r = \frac{nh}{mv}$$

If we transpose some of the variables, we can rewrite this expression in the form

$$\mathbf{L} = mvr = \frac{nh}{2\pi}$$

The quantity mvr, designated by the letter L, is, in a classical sense, the angular momentum of the electron. The expression above is Bohr's statement about the quantization of the angular momentum. The angular momentum is proportional to Planck's constant divided by 2π, and the units of Planck's constant are consistent with those for angular momentum! Some examples of orbital standing waves are shown in Figure 25.5.

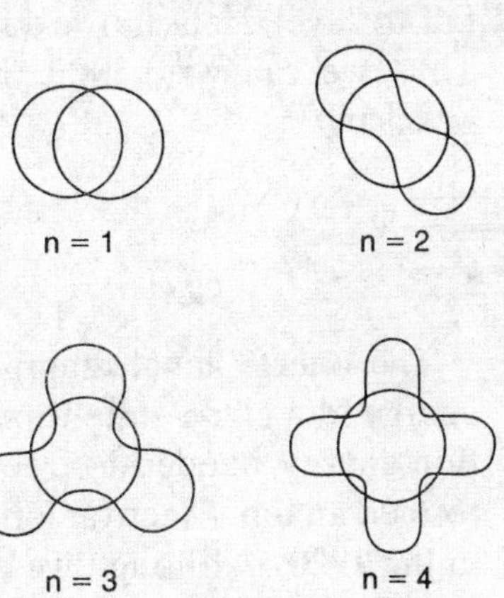

FIGURE 25.5 Electron Standing Waves

Bohr was able to derive the fact that the energy levels are determined by

$$E_n = -\frac{2\pi^2 k^2 m e^4}{n^2 h^2} = -\frac{13.6\text{eV}}{n^2}$$

where k is Coulomb's constant, m is the mass of an electron, e is the charge of an electron, h is Planck's constant, and n is the principal quantum number, equal to the energy level (ground state and excited states).

Bohr's expression completely matches the empirical and qualitative energy-level values suggested by the emission line spectra in the absence of any quantum theory (except that $E = hf$ for photons). According to the Bohr theory, the energy of a photon is equal to the energy difference between two energy states (Figure 25.6).

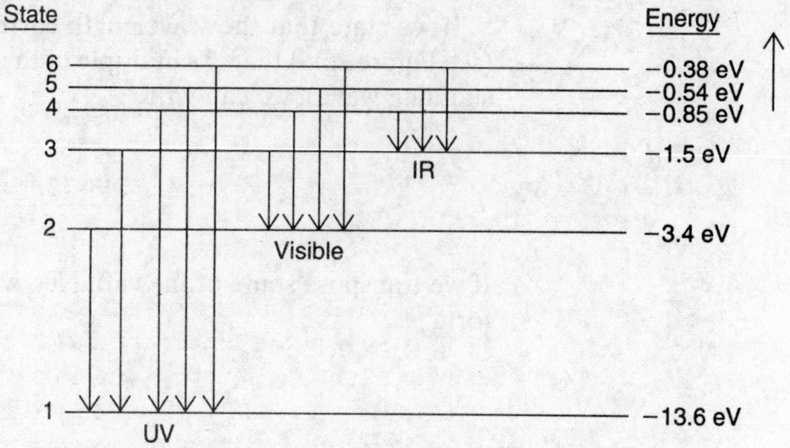

FIGURE 25.6 Energy Level Diagram for Hydrogen

The different spectral series arise from transitions from higher energy states to specified lower energy states. The ultraviolet Lyman series occurs when electrons fall to level 1; the visible Balmer series, when electrons fall to level 2; the infrared Paschen series, when electrons fall to level 3. Thus, we can write that the energy, in joules, for an emitted photon is given by

$$f = \frac{E_{initial} - E_{final}}{h}$$

The energy level diagram for hydrogen is shown in Figure 25.6. The energy in a given state represents the amount of energy, called the **ionization energy**, needed to free an electron from the atom. A charged atom is termed an **ion**. Electron ionization energies were confirmed by experiment in the 1920s. Although we designate the levels mathematically as negative so that the ionization level will have a value of zero, the energies are positive quantities. Even though hydrogen has only one electron, the many atoms of hydrogen in a sample of this gas, coupled with the different probabilities of electrons being in any one particular state, produce the multiple lines that appear in the visible spectrum when the gas is "excited."

Sample Problem:

What is the wavelength of a photon emitted when an electron makes a transition in a hydrogen atom from level 5 to level 3?

Solution:

From level 5 to level 3 involves an energy difference of

$$E = (-0.54 \text{ eV}) - (-1.50 \text{ eV}) = 0.96 \text{ eV} = 1.536 \times 10^{-19} \text{ J}$$

Now, the frequency of the photon will be equal to

$$f = \frac{1.536 \times 10^{-19}}{6.63 \times 10^{-34}} = 2.3 \times 10^{14}\ \text{Hz}$$

The wavelength of this photon is given by

$$\lambda = \frac{c}{f} = \frac{3 \times 10^{8}}{2.3 \times 10^{14}} = 1.29 \times 10^{-6}\text{m}$$

(which is in the infrared part of the electromagnetic spectrum).

It is important to remember that an electron will make a transition from a lower to a higher energy state only when it absorbs a photon equal to a given possible ("allowed") energy difference. This is the nature of the quantization of the atom; the electron can exist only in a specified energy state. To change states, the electron must either absorb or emit a photon whose energy is proportional to Planck's constant and equal to the energy difference between two energy states.

The Heisenberg uncertainty principle, discussed in Chapter 24, introduces the element of "probability" in describing the nature of electron orbits and energy states. This subject is studied in the science of **quantum mechanics**, developed by Erwin Schrödinger and Werner Heisenberg.

25.3 Quantum Mechanics and the Electron Cloud Model

The success of the Bohr model was limited to the hydrogen atom and certain hydrogen-like atoms (atoms with one electron in the outermost shell; single-ionized helium is an example). The wave nature of matter led to a problem in predicting the behavior of an electron in a strict Bohr energy state.

In 1926, physicist Erwin Schrödinger developed a new mechanics of the atom, then called **wave mechanics**, but later termed **quantum mechanics**. In the wave mechanics of Schrödinger, the position of an electron was determined by a mathematical function called the **wave function**. This wave function was related to the probability of finding an electron in any one energy state. A **wave equation**, called the **Schrödinger equation**, was derived using ideas about time-dependent motion in classical mechanics.

The energy states of Bohr were now replaced by a probability "cloud." In this **cloud model** the electrons are not necessarily limited to specified orbits. A cloud of uncertainty is produced, with the densest regions corresponding to the highest probability of an electron being in a given state.

The use of probability to explain the structure of the atom led to intense debates between the proponents of the new quantum mechanics and one of its fiercest opponents, Albert Einstein. Einstein, who had helped to develop the quantum theory of light 20 years earlier, was not convinced that the universe could be determined by probability. To paraphrase, Einstein said he could not believe that God would play dice with the Universe. "God is subtle," he said, "but not malicious."

At about the same time that Schrödinger introduced his wave mechanics, Werner Heisenberg developed his **matrix mechanics** for the atom. Instead of using a wave analogy, Heisenberg developed a purely abstract, mathematical theory using matrices. Working with Heisenberg, Wolfgang Pauli advanced the so-called **Pauli exclusion principle**, which states that two electrons having the same spin orientations cannot occupy the same quantum state at the same time.

The new **quantum mechanics** was born when the two rival theories were shown to be equivalent. Electron spin was experimentally verified, and the theory proved to be more successful than the older Bohr theory in explaining atomic and molecular structures and leading to new ideas about solid-state physics and the subsequent development of lasers.

Problem-Solving Strategies for the Atom

Understanding Bohr's postulates is a key element in solving atomic structure and spectra problems. Semiclassical ideas about Coulomb's law, energy, and uniform circle motion were used by Bohr.

You should either memorize the energy level diagram for hydrogen or else remember that the levels are inversely proportional to the square of the principal quantum number n and directly proportional to the factor -13.6 eV. However, in a frequency or wavelength calculation, you must convert these energies back to joules.

Practice Problems for Chapter 25

Multiple Choice

1. How much energy is needed to ionize a hydrogen atom in the $n = 4$ state?
(A) 0.85 eV
(B) 13.6 eV
(C) 12.75 eV
(D) 10.2 eV
(E) 3.4 eV

2. Which electron transition will emit a photon with the greatest frequency?
(A) $n = 1$ to $n = 4$
(B) $n = 5$ to $n = 2$
(C) $n = 3$ to $n = 1$
(D) $n = 7$ to $n = 3$
(E) $n = 1$ to $n = 3$

3. An electron in the ground state of a hydrogen atom can absorb a photon with any of the following energies except
(A) 10.2 eV
(B) 12.1 eV
(C) 12.5 eV
(D) 12.75 eV
(E) 13.06 eV

4. What is the frequency of a photon emitted in an electron transition from $n = 3$ to $n = 1$ in a hydrogen atom?
   (A) 1.83×10^{34} Hz
   (B) 2.92×10^{15} Hz
   (C) 1.7×10^{15} Hz
   (D) 4.7×10^{14} Hz
   (E) 3.3×10^{15} Hz

5. Which of the following statements about the atom is correct?
   (A) Orbiting electrons can sharply deflect passing alpha particles.
   (B) The nucleus of the atom is electrically neutral.
   (C) The nucleus of the atom deflects alpha particles into parabolic trajectories.
   (D) The nucleus of the atom contains most of the atomic mass.
   (E) None of the preceding statements is correct.

6. Which of the following statements about the Bohr theory reflect how it differs from classical predictions about the atom?

   I. An electron can orbit without a net force acting.
   II. An electron can orbit about a nucleus.
   III. An electron can be accelerated without radiating energy.
   IV. An orbiting electron has a quantized angular momentum that is proportional to Planck's constant.

   (A) I and II
   (B) I and III
   (C) III and IV
   (D) II and IV
   (E) I and IV

7. What is the maximum angle by which an alpha particle can be deflected by a nucleus?
   (A) 30°
   (B) 60°
   (C) 90°
   (D) 135°
   (E) 180°

8. An electron makes a transition from a higher energy state to the ground state in a Bohr atom. As a result of this transition
   (A) the total energy of the atom is increased
   (B) the force of attraction on the electron is increased
   (C) the energy of the ground state is increased
   (D) the charge on the electron is increased
   (E) the electron's energy remains the same

9. How many different photon frequencies can be emitted if an electron is in excited state $n = 4$ in a hydrogen atom?
   (A) 1
   (B) 3

(C) 5
(D) 6
(E) 8

10. A radioactive atom emits a gamma ray photon. As a result
    (A) the energy of the nucleus is decreased
    (B) the charge in the nucleus is decreased
    (C) the ground-state energy is decreased
    (D) the force on an orbiting electron is decreased
    (E) None of the preceding statements is correct.

Free Response

1. (a) Using Coulomb's law and an assumed circular orbit, derive an expression for the orbital velocity of an electron in the ground state of a hydrogen atom.
   (b) Using the Bohr quantized standing wave hypothesis, use the results of part (a) to show that in the ground state:

$$r = \frac{h^2}{mke^2 4\pi^2}$$

   (c) Using all known values of the quantities in part (b), calculate the classical radius of a ground-state hydrogen atom.

2. (a) Using the fact that the electrical potential energy for an orbiting ground-state electron in a hydrogen atom is given by

$$U = -\frac{ke^2}{r}$$

   use the result for problem 1(a) to show that the expression for the total energy of the atom is given by:

$$E = -\frac{ke^2}{2r}$$

   (b) The total energy for the ground-state hydrogen atom is −13.6 eV. Using this fact, derive the ground-state radius for the atom using the expression, in part (a) and compare it with the results obtained for problem 1.

3. (a) Using the information in problems 1 and 2, show that the energy levels in a hydrogen atom are given by the formula

$$E_n = -\frac{2\pi^2 k^2 m e^4}{h^2 n^2}$$

   (b) Using the known values in the above expression, show that the equation in part (a) reduces to

$$E_n = -\frac{13.6\text{ eV}}{n^2}$$

Solutions

Multiple-Choice Problems

1. **A** In the $n = 4$ state, the energy level is -0.85 eV. Thus, to ionize the electron in this state, $+ 0.85$ eV must be supplied.
2. **C** Transitions to level 1 produce ultraviolet photons that have frequencies greater than those produced by transitions to other levels.
3. **C** An electron in the ground state can absorb a photon that has an energy equal to the energy difference between the ground state and any other level. Only 12.5 eV is not such an energy difference.
4. **B** The energy difference from level 3 to level 1 is 12.1 eV. The emitted frequency is.

$$f = \frac{E}{h} = \frac{(12.1)(1.6 \times 10^{-19})}{6.63 \times 10^{-34}} = 2.92 \times 10^{15}\text{ Hz}$$

5. **D** "The nucleus of the atom contains most of the atomic mass" is a correct statement.
6. **C** The Bohr theory challenged classical theories by stating that an electron can be accelerated without radiating energy (statement III) and that its angular momentum is quantized and proportional to Planck's constant (statement IV).
7. **E** Rutherford's experiments revealed that some alpha particles are back-scattered through angles as large as 180°.
8. **B** As an electron gets closer to the nucleus, the force of attraction on the electron increases.
9. **D** There are six possible photon frequencies emitted from state $n = 4$: (1) $n = 4$ to $n = 1$, (2) $n = 4$ to $n = 3$, (3) $n = 4$ to $n = 2$, (4) $n = 3$ to $n = 2$, (5) $n = 3$ to $n = 2$, (6) $n = 2$ to $n = 1$.
10. **A** Since photons do not have any rest mass, their emission releases nuclear energy only.

Free-Response Problems

1. (a) Assuming a circular orbit for the electron, we set the Coulomb force equal to the centripetal force:

$$\frac{ke^2}{r^2} = \frac{mv^2}{r}$$

Solving for velocity **v**, we get

$$\mathbf{v} = e\sqrt{\frac{k}{mr}}$$

(b) Using the standing wave hypothesis for $n = 1$, we have:

$$\lambda = 2\pi r = \frac{h}{mv} = \frac{h}{me\sqrt{k / mr}}$$

We square both sides to obtain

$$4\pi^2 r^2 = \frac{h^2 mr}{m^2 e^2 k}$$

Finally, solving for r gives

$$r = \frac{h^2}{mke^2 4\pi^2}$$

(c) Using the known values for the physical quantities, we have

$$r = \frac{(6.63 \times 10^{-34})^2}{(9.1 \times 10^{-31})(9 \times 10^9)(1.6 \times 10^{-19})^2 4(3.14)^2} = 5.3 \times 10^{-11}\text{m}$$

2. (a) The total energy is equal to the sum of the kinetic and potential energies and is given by

$$E = \frac{1}{2} mv^2 - \frac{ke^2}{r}$$

Substituting for the velocity expression in problem 1(a) above, we get

$$E = \frac{1}{2} m\left(\frac{e^2 k}{mr}\right) - \frac{ke^2}{r} = \frac{ke^2}{2r} - \frac{2ke^2}{2r} = -\frac{ke^2}{2r}$$

(b) We are given that, for $n = 1$, $E = -13.6$ eV, and we need to convert this energy to joules:

$$E = -(13.6)(1.6 \times 10^{-19}) = -2.176 \times 10^{-18}\ \text{J}$$

Solving for the radius r gives

$$r = \frac{(9 \times 10^9)(1.6 \times 10^{-19})^2}{2(2.176 \times 10^{-18})} = 5.3 \times 10^{-11}\ \text{m}$$

which is the same answer obtained in problem 1.

3. (a) If we go back to the standing wave hypothesis, then, for any quantum number n,

$$\lambda = \frac{nh}{mv}$$

and

$$r = \frac{n^2h^2}{mke^2 4\pi^2}$$

Now, if we substitute this radius formula into the total energy formula, we get

$$E = -\frac{ke^2}{2r} = -\frac{ke^2}{2}\left(\frac{me^2k4\pi^2}{n^2h^2}\right) = -\frac{2\pi^2mk^2e^4}{n^2h^2}$$

(b) If we substitute all known values for the quantities (except n), we get

$$E = -\frac{2.167 \times 10^{-18}\,\text{J}}{n^2} = -\frac{13.54\text{eV}}{n^2}$$

CHAPTER 26

The Nucleus

26.1 Nuclear Structure and Stability

The experiments of Hans Geiger and Ernest Marsden (under Rutherford's supervision) in 1911 confirmed that the nucleus of an atom is compact and positively charged. Experiments on nuclear masses using a **mass spectrograph**, which deflects the positively charged nuclei into curved paths with different radii, confirmed that the estimate of nuclear mass was too low. The nucleus could not, therefore, be made entirely of positively charged protons.

Physicists theorized that another electrically neutral particle, called the **neutron**, must be present since (a) all of the charge on the nucleus could be accounted for by the presence of the protons, (b) more neutral mass was needed, and (c) a method for countering the repulsive Coulomb forces created by the protons was required.

Thus, the question of nuclear stability depended on the particular structure of the nucleus. The work on radioactive decay by Rutherford and Marie and Pierre Curie confirmed that the radioactive disintegration of an atom is a nuclear phenomenon and is tied to stability as well.

The basic structure of the atom, using a Bohr-Rutherford planetary model, consists of a nucleus with a certain number of protons and neutrons (together called **nucleons**). The number of protons characterizes an element since no two elements have the same number of protons. This **atomic number**, Z, also measures the relative charge on the nucleus. The **mass number**, A, is a measure of the total number of nucleons (protons plus neutrons) in the nucleus. Both of these numbers are whole numbers, but the actual nuclear mass is not a whole number.

Since an atom is electrically neutral, the initial numbers of protons and electrons are the same. Schematically, an atom is designated by a capital letter, possibly followed by one lower-case letter, indicating the element it represents, with the two nuclear numbers A and Z written as a superscript and a subscript, respectively, on the left-hand side. For an unknown element X we write $^{A}_{Z}X$. The designation $^{1}_{1}H$ represents the element hydrogen, with one nucleon (a proton) and an atomic number of 1. Some elements have **isotopes**, that is, nuclei with the same number of protons but different numbers of neutrons. For example, the element helium is designated as $^{4}_{2}He$, where the 4 indicates 2 protons and 2 neutrons. An isotope of this atom is helium-3, designated as $^{2}_{3}He$. Some nuclear structures are illustrated in Figure 26.1.

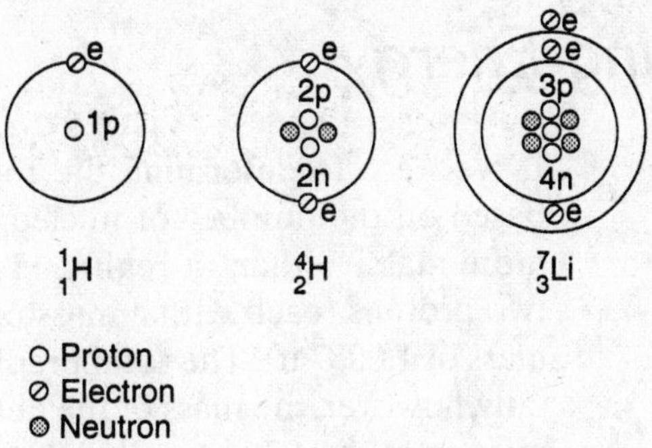

FIGURE 26.1 Nuclear Structures

A neutron is slightly more massive than a proton. A proton mass is approximately equal to

$$m_p = 1.673 \times 10^{-27} \text{kg}$$

and a neutron mass to

$$m_n = 1.675 \times 10^{-27} \text{kg}$$

Nuclear masses are usually expressed in **atomic mass units** (u). One atomic mass unit is defined to be equal to one-twelfth the mass of a carbon-12 isotope:

$$1 \text{u} = 1.66 \times 10^{-27} \text{ kg}$$

On this scale, the proton's mass is given as 1.0078 atomic mass units, and the neutron's mass is given as 1.0087 atomic mass units.

If one looks at all stable isotopes of known nuclei, something qualitatively interesting emerges. Experiments show that lighter nuclei have about the same number of protons as neutrons. However, heavier stable nuclei have more neutrons than protons. This suggests that the neutrons must somehow help overcome the repulsive forces in a tightly packed positive nucleus. Also, this **strong nuclear force** must operate within the short distances in an atomic nucleus. Unstable, radioactive nuclei lie off this stability curve (see Figure 26.2); and as they decay, the alpha, beta and other particle emissions **transmute** the original nucleus into a more stable one.

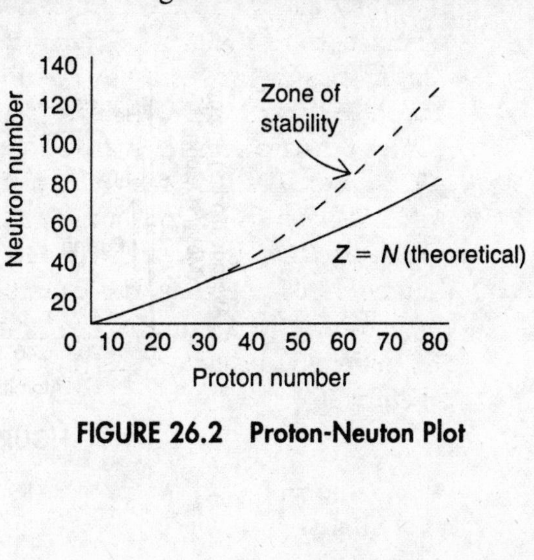

FIGURE 26.2 Proton-Neuton Plot

26.2 Binding Energy

If we were to determine the total mass of a particular isotope, say ${}^{4}_{2}He$, based on the number of nucleons, we would arrive at a nucleus that was more massive than in reality. For example, the helium-4 nucleus contains two protons (each with a mass of 1.0078 u) and two neutrons (each with a mass of 1.0087 u). The total predicted mass would be 4.0330 u. Experimentally, however, the mass of the helium-4 nucleus is found to be 4.0026 u. The difference of 0.0304 u, called the **mass defect**, is proportional to the **binding energy** of the nucleus.

Using Einstein's special theory of relativity (Chapter 27), we know that mass can be converted to energy. The energy equivalent of 1 atomic mass unit is equal to 931.5 million electron volts (MeV). The binding energy of any nucleus is therefore determined by using the relationship

$$BE\text{ (MeV)} = \text{Mass defect} \times 931.5\text{ MeV / u}$$

In our example, the binding energy of the helium-4 nucleus is

$$BE = 0.0304 \times 931.5 = 28.3\text{ MeV}$$

It is useful to think about the average binding energy per nucleon, which is equal to BE / A, where A = the mass number of the element. Thus, for helium-4, where A = 4,

$$\text{Avg } BE = \frac{28.3}{4} = 7.08\text{ MeV per nucleon}$$

In Figure 26.3, a graph of average binding energy per nucleon is plotted against atomic number Z. The graph shows that a maximum point is reached at about $Z = 26$ (iron). The greater the average binding energy, the greater the stability of the nucleus. Thus, since hydrogen isotopes have less stability than helium isotopes, the **fusion** of hydrogen into helium increases the stability of the nucleus through the release of energy. Likewise, the unstable uranium isotopes yield more stable nuclei if they are split (**fission**) into lighter nuclei (also releasing energy).

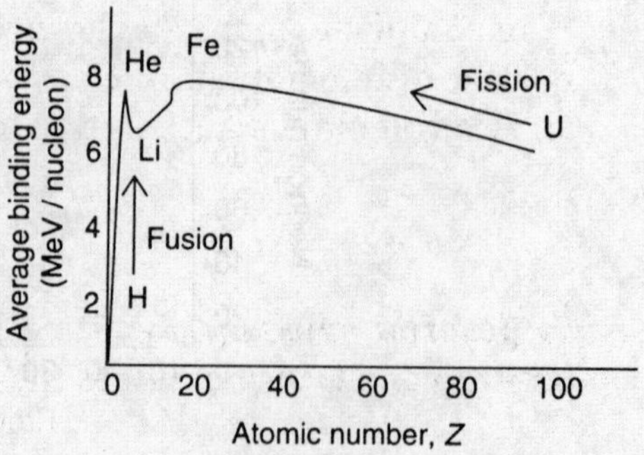

FIGURE 26.3

26.3 Radioactive Decay

Radioactivity was discovered in 1895 by Henri Becquerel, and the relationship between radioactivity and nuclear stability was studied by Pierre and Marie Curie. Ernest Rutherford pioneered the experiments of nuclear bombardment and introduced the word **transmutation** into the nuclear physics vocabulary. The discovery of alpha- and beta-particle emission from nuclei led to the use of these particles to probe the structure of the nucleus in the first decades of the twentieth century. Subsequent research showed the existence of positively charged electrons called **positrons**, and even negatively charged protons!

The question of how these particles could originate from a nucleus was answered using Einstein's theory of mass-energy equivalence ($E = mc^2$). Schematically, we have the following designations for some of these particles:

Proton (hydrogen nucleus): ${}^{1}_{1}\text{H}$	Neutron: ${}^{1}_{0}\text{n}$
Alpha particle (helium nucleus): ${}^{4}_{2}\text{He}$	Positron (positive electron): ${}^{0}_{1}\text{e}$
Beta particle (electron): ${}^{0}_{-1}\text{e}$	Photon: ${}^{0}_{0}\gamma$

When ${}^{238}_{92}\text{U}$, an isotope of uranium, decays, it emits an alpha particle according to the following equation:

$${}^{238}_{92}\text{U} \rightarrow {}^{234}_{90}\text{Th} + {}^{4}_{2}\text{He}$$

When, in turn, the radioactive thorium isotope decays, it emits a beta particle

$${}^{234}_{90}\text{Th} \rightarrow {}^{234}_{91}\text{Pa} + {}^{0}_{-1}\text{e}$$

In the first example, both the atomic number and the mass number changed as the uranium transmuted into thorium. In the decay of the thorium nucleus, however, only the atomic number changed. The reason is that in beta decay a neutron in the nucleus is converted into a proton, an electron, energy, and a particle called an **antineutrino**. At this time (1995), there is no evidence that neutrinos have any mass, although some theories require that they do.

In addition to alpha and beta decay, there are several other scenarios for nuclear disintegration. In **electron capture**, an isotope of copper captures an electron into its nucleus and transmutes into an isotope of nickel:

$${}^{64}_{29}\text{Cu} + {}^{0}_{-1}\text{e} \rightarrow {}^{64}_{28}\text{Ni}$$

In **positron emission**, the same isotope of copper decays by emitting a positron and transmutes into the same isotope of nickel:

$${}^{64}_{29}\text{Cu} \rightarrow {}^{0}_{1}\text{e} + {}^{64}_{28}\text{Ni}$$

The rate of nuclear decay is characterized by the element's **half-life**, that is, the time required for half of a given amount of radioactive substance to decay. For a sample with N nuclei, the number, ΔN, that decay in a time Δt is proportional to the number N:

$$\frac{-\Delta N}{\Delta t} = \lambda N$$

where λ is called the **decay constant**. The solution to this equation is given by

$$N = N_0 e^{-\lambda t}$$

where N_0 is the number of nuclei present when $t = 0$ and e is the base of the natural logarithm system, approximately equal to 2.7.

The meaning of the constant λ is as follows. In a time $\tau = 1 / \lambda$, called the **characteristic time**, the number of nuclei is equal to $1 / e$ or 37 percent of the original amount. The half-life is related to the characteristic time. Let T represent the half-life; then

$$T = 0.693\tau$$

The "activity" of a radioactive substance is the number of decays that occur per second:

$$\text{Activity} = R = -\frac{\Delta N}{\Delta t} = \lambda N = \left(\frac{0.693}{T}\right) N_o$$

The SI unit of decay rate (decays per second) is the **becquerel** (Bq). A graph of radioactive decay is shown in Figure 26.4.

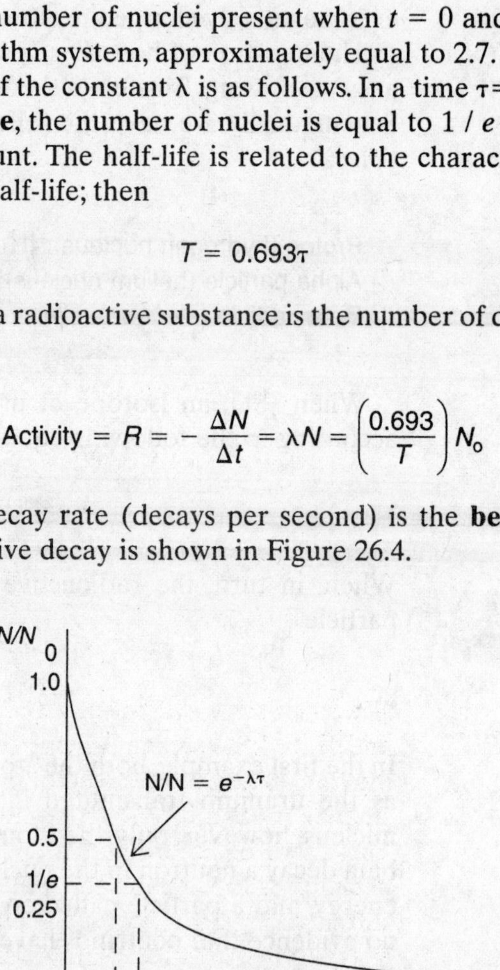

FIGURE 26.4

An alternative way of expressing the decay relationship is as follows. Let T represent the half-life, t be any time (in the same units), and m_0 be, the original mass at time $t = 0$. The mass remaining after time t can therefore be given by

$$m = \frac{m_0}{2^{t/T}} - N = \frac{N_0}{2^{t/T}}$$

This expression eliminates the need to use natural logarithms, but so-called common logarithms will still be required. Also eliminated is the necessity to know the decay constant and the characteristic time. Consider the following sample problem.

Sample Problem:

Radon ($^{222}_{86}Rn$) has a half-life of 3.8 days. Suppose we start with 0.03 kg. How many days will it take to have 0.001 kg remaining?

Solution:

Our starting formula is

$$\frac{m}{m_0} = \frac{1}{2^{t/T}}$$

We take the logarithm of both sides:

$$\log\left(\frac{m}{m_0}\right) = \log\left(\frac{1}{2^{t/T}}\right) = \log\left(\frac{1}{2}\right)^{t/T} = \left(\frac{t}{T}\right)\log\frac{1}{2}$$

We need to solve for time *t*:

$$t = T\frac{\log(m\,/\,m_0)}{\log 0.5} = (3.8)\frac{\log 0.33}{\log 0.5} = 18.7 \text{ days}$$

26.4 Fission

Nuclear fission was discovered in 1939 by German physicists Otto Hahn and Fritz Strassman. When $^{235}_{92}U$, an isotope of uranium, absorbs a slow-moving neutron, the resulting instability will split the nucleus into two smaller (but still radioactive) nuclei and release a large amount of energy. The curve in Figure 26.3 shows that the binding energy per nucleon for uranium is lower than the values for other, lighter nuclei. The increase in stability (a gain in potential energy) is accompanied by a loss of kinetic energy. One possible uranium fission reaction could occur as follows:

$$^{235}_{92}U + {}^{1}_{0}n \rightarrow {}^{140}_{54}Xe + {}^{94}_{38}Sr + 2\,{}^{1}_{0}n + 200 \text{ MeV}$$

In controlled fission reactions, water or graphite is used as a **moderator** to slow the neutrons since they cannot be slowed by electromagnetic processes. The production of two additional neutrons means that a chain reaction is possible. In a fission reactor, cadmium control rods adjust the reaction rates to desirable levels.

In the production of plutonium as a fissionable material, another isotope of uranium, $^{238}_{92}U$, is used. First, the uranium absorbs a neutron to form neptunium, a rare element. The neptunium then decays to form plutonium:

$$^{238}_{92}U + ^{1}_{0}n \rightarrow ^{239}_{92}U \rightarrow ^{239}_{93}Np + ^{0}_{-1}e$$

$$^{239}_{93}Np \rightarrow ^{239}_{94}Pu + ^{0}_{-1}e$$

26.5 Fusion

The binding energy curve (Figure 26.3) indicates that, if hydrogen can be fused into helium, the resulting nucleus will be more stable and energy can be released. In a fusion reaction, isotopes of hydrogen known as deuterium ($^{2}_{1}H$) and tritium ($^{3}_{1}H$) are used. The following equations represent one kind of hydrogen fusion reaction:

$$^{1}_{1}H + ^{1}_{1}H \rightarrow ^{2}_{1}H + ^{0}_{1}e + 0.4 \text{ Mev}$$

$$^{1}_{1}H + ^{2}_{1}H \rightarrow ^{3}_{2}He + 5.5 \text{ Mev}$$

$$^{3}_{2}He + ^{3}_{2}He \rightarrow ^{4}_{2}He + 2\,^{1}_{1}H + 12.9 \text{ Mev}$$

In this reaction, hydrogen is first fused into deuterium. The deuterium is then fused with hydrogen to form the isotope helium-3. Finally, the helium-3 isotope is fused into the stable element helium.

In a different reaction, the isotope tritium is fused with deuterium to form the stable element helium in one step:

$$^{2}_{1}H + ^{3}_{1}H \rightarrow ^{4}_{2}He + ^{1}_{0}n + 17.6 \text{ MeV}$$

Problem-Solving Strategies for the Nucleus

Solving nuclear equations requires that you remember two rules. First, make sure that you have conservation of charge. That means that all of the atomic numbers, which measure the number of protons (and hence the charge) should add up on both sides. However, to get the actual charge, you must multiply the atomic number by the proton charge in units of coulombs.

The second rule to consider is the conservation of mass. The mass numbers that appear as superscript should add up. Any missing mass should be accounted for by the appearance of energy (sometimes designated by the letter Q). The mass energy equivalence is that 1 u is equal to 931.5 MeV. This second rule applies to problems involving binding energy and mass defect. Remember that an actual nucleus has less mass than the sum of its nucleons!

Practice Problems for Chapter 26

Multiple Choice

1. How many neutrons are in a nucleus of $^{213}_{84}Po$?
   (A) 84
   (B) 129
   (C) 213
   (D) 297
   (E) 546

2. The nitrogen isotope $^{13}_{7}N$ emits a beta particle as it decays. The new isotope formed is
(A) $^{14}_{7}N$
(B) $^{13}_{6}C$
(C) $^{13}_{8}O$
(D) $^{14}_{8}O$
(E) Not enough information is provided.

3. The half-life of a radioactive material is 5 years. After 20 years, how much of a 75-g sample of the material remains?
(A) 4.68 g
(B) 3.75 g
(C) 18.75 g
(D) 15 g
(E) 22.4 g

4. Which radiation has the greatest ability to penetrate matter?
(A) X ray
(B) Alpha particle
(C) Gamma ray
(D) Beta particle
(E) Positron

5. As a sample of radioactive material decays, its half-life
(A) increases, then decreases
(B) decreases, then increases
(C) increases
(D) decreases
(E) remains the same

6. As a radioactive material undergoes nuclear disintegration,
(A) its atomic number always remains the same
(B) its mass number never increases
(C) its mass number never decreases
(D) it always emits an alpha particle
(E) None of the preceding statements is correct.

7. If all of the following particles had the same velocity, which one would have the shortest wavelength?
(A) Alpha particle
(B) Beta particle
(C) Neutron
(D) Proton
(E) Positron

8. Which of the following statements is correct about nuclear isotopes?
(A) They all have the same binding energy.
(B) They all have the same mass number.
(C) They all have the same number of nucleons.
(D) They all have the same number of protons.
(E) All of these statements are correct.

9. In the following nuclear reaction, an isotope of aluminum is bombarded by alpha particles:

$$^{27}_{13}Al + ^{4}_{2}He \rightarrow ^{30}_{15}P + Y$$

Quantity Y must be
(A) a neutron
(B) an electron
(C) a positron
(D) a photon
(E) a proton

10. When a gamma-ray photon is emitted from a radioactive nucleus, which of the following occurs?
(A) The nucleus goes to an excited state.
(B) The nucleus goes to a more stable state.
(C) An electron goes to an excited state.
(D) The atomic number of the nucleus decreases.
(E) The number of nucleons decreases.

Free Response

1. (a) If 75 g of a radioactive sample decays to 30 g in 3.5 years, what is the half-life of this substance?
(b) Make a chart of mass versus time, in units of half-lives, for a total of six half-lives.
(c) Make a graph (appropriately scaled) of time, in half-lives, versus mass on the set of axes below.

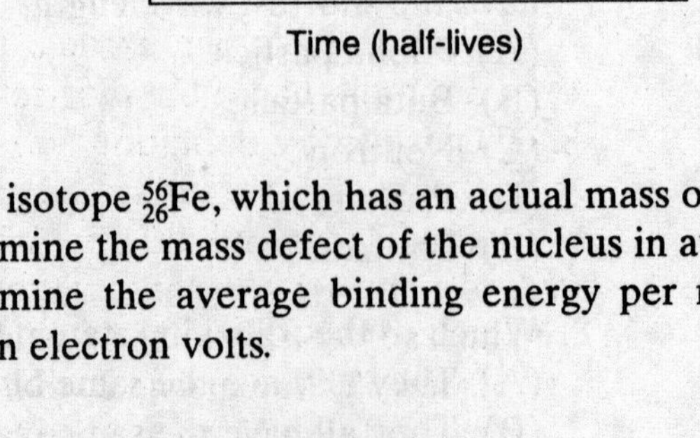

2. Given the isotope $^{56}_{26}Fe$, which has an actual mass of 55.934939 u:
(a) Determine the mass defect of the nucleus in atomic mass units.
(b) Determine the average binding energy per nucleon in units of million electron volts.

3. In the early decades of this century, F. W. Aston, the inventor of the mass spectrograph, developed the concept of the nuclear "packing fraction," given by the formula

$$f = \frac{M - A}{A}$$

where M is the mass of the isotope in atomic mass units, and A is the whole mass number. Aston recognized that the nuclear masses are very close to whole numbers.

(a) Determine the packing fraction, f, for each of the following nuclear isotopes (packing fractions are usually multiplied by a factor of 10^4 for convenience):

i. $^{1}_{1}$H: mass = 1.0078252 u	v. $^{16}_{8}$O: mass = 15.994915
ii. $^{4}_{2}$He: mass = 4.0026033 u	vi. $^{56}_{26}$Fe: mass = 55.934939 u
iii. $^{9}_{4}$Be: mass = 9.01211858 u	vii. $^{184}_{74}$W: mass = 183.9510
iv. $^{12}_{6}$C: mass = 12.000000 u	viii. $^{238}_{92}$U: mass = 238.05076 u

(b) Make a graph of packing fraction ($\times 10^4$), versus mass number, A, for each isotope, and compare this graph with the one in Figure 26.3 for binding energy.

Solutions

Multiple-Choice Problems

1. **B** The number of neutrons is given by

$$N = A - Z = 213 - 84 = 129$$

2. **C** The emission of a beta particle involves the transformation of a neutron into a proton and an electron. Thus, the total number of nucleons (Z) remains the same, but the number of protons increases by one. The new isotope is therefore oxygen-13.
3. **A** For this material, 20 years corresponds to 4 half-lives. If we take just half of the given amount, compounded over 20 years (counting every fifth year), we end up with 4.68 g.
4. **C** Gamma rays have the greatest energy with the greatest penetration power.
5. **E** The half-life is preset by Nature. It is not affected by the decay process itself.
6. **B** In nuclear *disintegration*, the nucleus always either loses mass or releases energy in the form of photons.
7. **A** From Chapter 24, we know that, at the same velocity, the particle with the largest mass will have the shortest wavelength. Of the four choices, the alpha particle, being a helium nucleus, has the largest mass and hence the shortest wavelength.
8. **D** Isotopes, by definition, are of the same chemical element. Hence they must have the same number of protons (but different numbers of neutrons and different binding energies).
9. **A** We must have conservation of charge and mass. The subscripts already add up to 15 on each side, so we are left with a subscript of 0 for Y; the particle is therefore neutral. The superscripts on the right must add up to 31 to balance. Since the missing particle needs a superscript of 1, particle Y is a neutron.
10. **B** When radioactive nuclei emit photons, they settle down to a more stable state since no mass has been lost.

Free-Response Problems

1. (a) We use the formula:

$$m = \frac{m_0}{2^{t/t_h}}$$

If we transpose some variables, we can rewrite this expression in the form

$$2^{t/t_h} = \frac{m_0}{m}$$

Now, taking the logarithm of each side and, using the rules of exponents, we get

$$\frac{t}{t_h}\log 2 = \log\left(\frac{m_0}{m}\right)$$

We now substitute all given values: $t = 3.5$ years, $m_0 = 75$ g, and $m = 30$ g. Solving for the half-life, we get 2.648 years.

(b) Knowing the half-life, we can get a sense of the decay rate. The half-life is the time required for half of a given amount of radioactive material to decay. We start with 75 g when $t = 0$ and list for six half-lives:

t (yr)	*m* (gm)
0	75
2.648	37.5
5.296	18.75
7.944	9.375
10.592	4.6875
13.240	2.343
15.888	1.170

(c) We plot a graph of mass versus time, in half-lives, below:

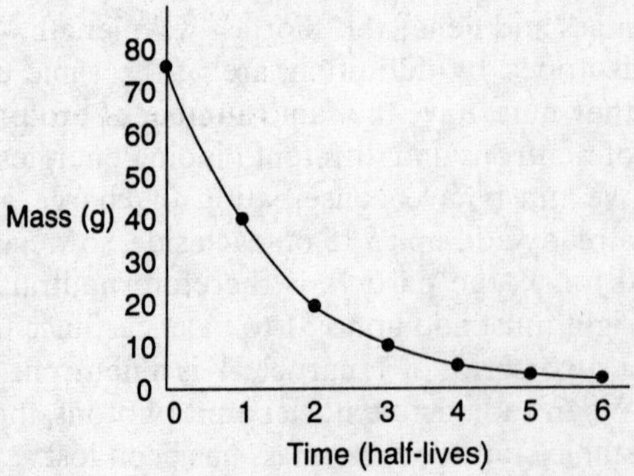

2. (a) The actual mass of iron-56 is 55.934939 u. The total additive mass is determined by noting that this isotope of iron has 26 protons and 30 neutrons. Each proton has a mass of 1.0078 u, and each neutron has a mass of 1.0087 u. Thus the total constituent mass is

$$26\ (1.0078) = 26.2028\ \text{u}$$
$$30\ (1.0087) = 30.\ 2610\ \text{u}$$
$$\text{Total mass} = 56.4638\ \text{u}$$

The mass defect of the nucleus is therefore the difference between this mass and the actual mass:

$$\text{Mass defect} = 56.463800 - 55.934939 = 0.528861\ \text{u}$$

(b) The binding energy is given by

$$BE = 0.528861 \times 931.5 = 492.63402\ \text{MeV}$$

The average binding energy per nucleon is

$$\text{Avg. } BE = \frac{492.63402}{56} = 8.797\ \text{MeV}$$

3. (a) We calculate the packing fraction for each isotope. The fractions have been multiplied by a factor of 10^4 as is customary:

i. $f = 78$
ii. $f = 6.5$
iii. $f = 13.465$
iv. $f = 0$
v. $f = -3.178$
vi. $f = -11.6$
vii. $f = -2.663$
viii. $f = 2.13$

(b) No agreed physical significance is attached to Aston's packing fraction. It is revealing, however, that the graph of packing fraction versus mass number resembles somewhat the binding energy curve flipped over.

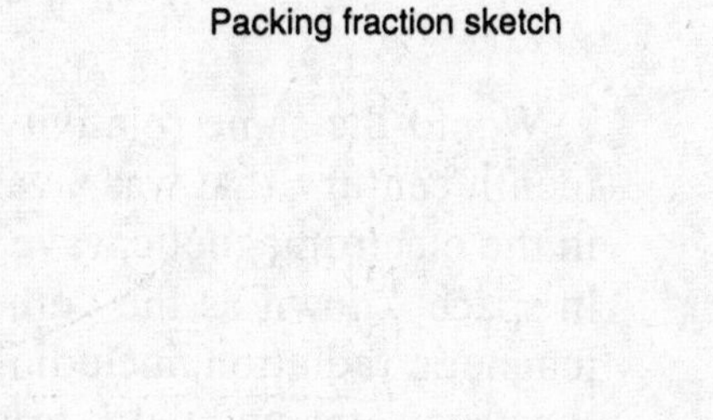

Packing fraction sketch

CHAPTER 27

Special Relativity

27.1 Frames of Reference and the Postulates of Relativity

We end our review of physics exactly where we began. All motion is relative. However, when we discussed relative motion in Chapter 6, we restricted ourselves to inertial frames of reference moving at velocities much less than the velocity of light (300,000 km / s). This aspect of restricted relativity, known as **Galilean relativity**, is illustrated in Figure 27.1

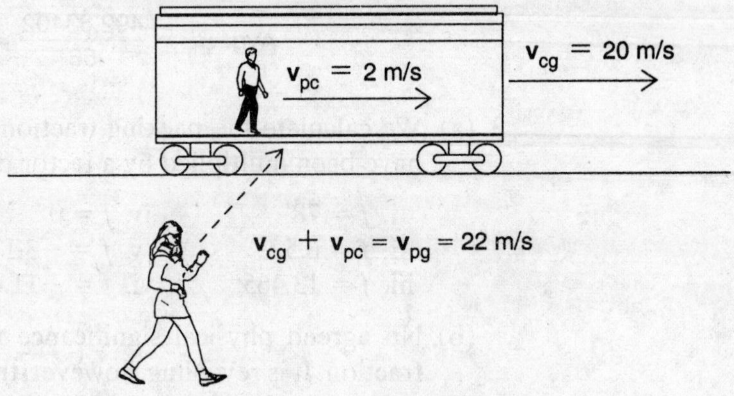

FIGURE 27.1 Galilean Relativity

where we see a person walking inside a moving frame of reference. The velocity of the center of gravity of the frame is $\mathbf{v}_{cg}$ = 20 meters per second relative to the Earth. Inside the frame, the person is walking in the direction of motion with a velocity of $\mathbf{v}_{pc}$ = 2 meters per second relative to the frame. To an observer on the Earth, outside the frame, the relative velocity of the person walking is given by

$$\mathbf{v}_{pg} = \mathbf{v}_{cg} + \mathbf{v}_{pc} = 22 \text{ m/s to the right.}$$

Would the same relativity transformations apply to light? In the nineteenth century, that was a valid research question. Physicists who believed in the electromagnetic wave theory of light had speculated that a material in space, known as the "ether," was responsible for transmitting electromagnetic radiation, including light, through space. In a fashion similar to the way water undulates to transmit water waves, the ether was supposed to move in a transverse manner to carry light. It was suggested that, as the Earth rotated on its axis, the velocity of light might be different in a direction away from the rotation of the Earth (say, perpendicularly).

As an analogy, consider the situation in Figure 27.2. Imagine two swimmers of equal ability. Each can swim with maximum velocity c. A course is set up in a river with a current velocity $\mathbf{v}$, and three rafts are placed at equal distances from each other. One swimmer will go across the river and swim back. The other will swim downstream to a raft and then upstream back to the start. Both swimmers will cover the same effective distance, $2L$.

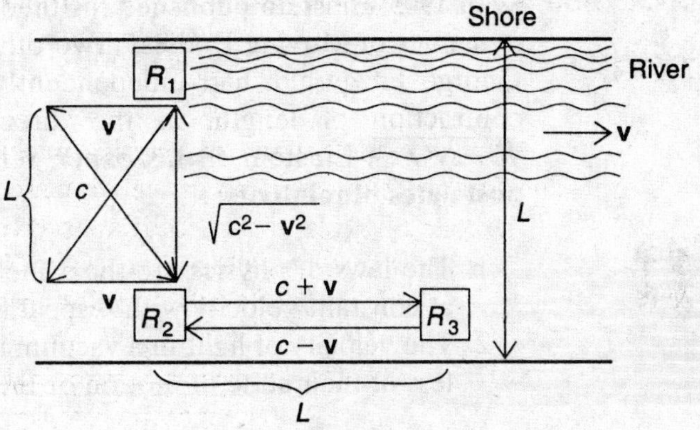

FIGURE 27.2

Let's consider the first person, who swims parallel to the current. When she travels with the current, her relative velocity is $c + \mathbf{v}$. When she travels against the current, her relative velocity is $c - \mathbf{v}$. Since her round-trip distance is $2L$, her total travel time, t_1, is given by

$$t_1 = \frac{L}{c + \mathbf{v}} + \frac{L}{c - \mathbf{v}} = \frac{2Lc}{c^2 - \mathbf{v}^2}$$

Now, let's consider the person who swims across the current. To head straight across, she must swim slightly upstream at her maximum velocity, $\mathbf{c}$. Her relative velocity across the river is therefore given by $\sqrt{\mathbf{c}^2 - \mathbf{v}^2}$. The total distance she travels is again equal to $2L$. Thus, her round-trip time, t_2, is given by

$$t_2 = \frac{2L}{\sqrt{\mathbf{c}^2 - \mathbf{v}^2}}$$

Now, the question is, who wins the race? The answer can determined by looking at the ratio of times:

$$\frac{t_1}{t_2} = \frac{2L\mathbf{c} / (\mathbf{c}^2 - \mathbf{v}^2)}{2L / \sqrt{\mathbf{c}^2 - \mathbf{v}^2}} = \frac{1}{\sqrt{1 - \mathbf{v}^2 / \mathbf{c}^2}}$$

Since this ratio is greater than 1, $t_1 > t_2$ and so the second swimmer wins the race.

In 1887, an experiment was performed by two physicists, Albert Michelson and Edward Morley. They were attempting to establish a difference between the velocity of light in the direction of the Earth's rotation and the velocity of light in a direction perpendicular to the Earth's rotation. To their surprise, the "race" turned out to be a tie! The velocity of light was found to be the same in all directions. In fact, the velocity of light is an **invariant**; in other words, for all observers, no matter where they are or how they are measuring, the velocity of light, in a vacuum, has the same value! This is the starting point of Albert Einstein's **special theory of relativity**.

In 1905, Einstein published his theory under the title "On the Electrodynamics of Moving Bodies." Two other physicists, Hendrik Lorentz and George Fitzgerald, had independently theorized that there might be a contraction of length, in the direction of motion, by a factor of $\sqrt{1 - \mathbf{v}^2/\mathbf{c}^2}$. Einstein, in his paper, refined this idea more clearly as the **postulates of relativity**:

1. The laws of physics are the same for all frames of reference moving at constant velocity with respect to one another.
2. The velocity of light in a vacuum is the same for all observers regardless of their state of motion or the motion of the source of light.

27.2 Length Contraction and Time Dilation

In the theory of special relativity, the proper or rest measurement of length, L_0, is contracted in the direction of motion according to the formula

$$L = L_0\sqrt{1 - \mathbf{v}^2/\mathbf{c}^2}$$

Another consequence of special relativity is the breakdown of **Absolute time**. In Isaac Newton's *The Principia*, all measurements of space and time were made relative to an absolute fixed frame of reference (the stars). Einstein proposed that even the concept of time is relative. In relativity, a moving clock keeps slower time than one at rest. By this we mean that the time interval between two events is longer in a moving frame of reference than when viewed by a stationary observer. This phenomenon is called **time dilation**; and if t_0 is the "proper time" measured in the moving frame of reference, then the time t observed in the fixed frame is

$$t = \frac{t_0}{\sqrt{1 - \mathbf{v}^2/\mathbf{c}^2}}$$

Confirmation of these predictions can be found in cosmic ray particles called "muons." These particles are created in the nuclear collisions of particle accelerators on Earth and in the ionosphere and magnetosphere surrounding the Earth. In a laboratory, muons have a lifetime of approximately 2.2 microseconds (2.2×10^{-6} s). At velocities of about $0.998c$, they can travel only 0.66 kilometer before decaying. How is it possible for them to be detected on Earth if they are created high in the atmosphere? The answer is time dilation. Using Einstein's formula and the velocity of the muons as measured on Earth, we find that, while the frame of reference moving with the muon would observe a lifetime of 2.2 microseconds, we on Earth would observe a lifetime of:

$$t = \frac{2.2 \times 10^{-6}}{\sqrt{1 - (0.998\mathbf{c})^2 / \mathbf{c}^2}} = 34.8 \times 10^{-6}\ \text{s} = 34.8\ \mu\text{s}$$

This is a lifetime increased almost 16 times. Therefore, the muons can travel about 16 times further (about 10.4 km). As far as the muons are concerned, the distance they travel in their 2.2 microsecond lifetime is contracted according to the relativity formula for length contraction.

Sample Problem:

Imagine a meter stick moving relative to the Earth with a velocity of 0.85**c**. By what factor will its length appear to be contracted?

Solution:

Using the length contraction formula, we have

$$\frac{L}{L_0} = \sqrt{1 - (0.85\,\mathbf{c})^2 / \mathbf{c}^2} = 0.53$$

which is approximately one-half the rest length of the meter stick.

27.3 Relativistic Velocity Transformations

In Galilean relativity, if a person is walking toward the front of a moving train at 2 meters per second relative to the train, and the train has a velocity of 20 meters per second relative to the Earth, then the velocity of the person relative to the Earth is 22 meters per second (see Figure 27.1). One might think that, if the train turns on its headlight, the velocity of the photons emitted will also be additive in the same way as the person's velocity.

This prediction, in fact, does not occur. The second postulate of relativity states that the velocity of light is invariant. It remains the same for all inertial observers. At velocities close to the velocity of light, the transformation equation that governs the relative velocity observed is

$$\mathbf{v}' = \frac{\mathbf{v} + \mathbf{u}}{1 + \mathbf{uv} / \mathbf{c}^2}$$

where **u** is the velocity of the frame of reference, **v** is the velocity relative to the frame of reference, and **v**′ is the velocity observed by a stationary observer. If the object is moving in the opposite direction, we would use $-\mathbf{v}$ instead of $\mathbf{v}$. This equation governs all bodies and reduces to the familiar sum of velocities $(\mathbf{u} + \mathbf{v})$ if $\mathbf{v} \ll \mathbf{c}$.

Sample Problem:

What is the observed velocity of a photon emitted by the light of a spacecraft that has a velocity of 0.95**c** relative to the Earth?

Solution:

We know that the answer should be equal to **c**, but let's prove it anyway. In this problem, $\mathbf{v} = \mathbf{c}$ and $\mathbf{u} = 0.95\mathbf{c}$. Therefore the observed velocity, $\mathbf{v}'$, is given by

$$\mathbf{v}' = \frac{\mathbf{c} + 0.95\mathbf{c}}{1 + (0.95\mathbf{c})(\mathbf{c}) / \mathbf{c}^2} = \frac{1.95\mathbf{c}}{1 + 0.95} = \mathbf{c}$$

27.4 Relativistic Mass and Energy

When we introduced Newton's laws of motion, we discussed the meaning of inertia. Inertia is the property of matter that resists a net force that would change its state of motion. In Newtonian mechanics, we tend to associate the inertia of an object with its "mass" (actually, its inertial mass). In all Newtonian interactions, the mass of an object remained the same unless something physical was happening to it (like an explosion or a rocket using fuel).

Einstein, in his paper on special relativity, demonstrated that inertial mass can vary if the velocity of the mass approaches the velocity of light. Experimental evidence for this phenomenon is observed in the mass of high-speed electrons accelerated by magnetic fields. According to special relativity, the **rest mass**, m_0, varies according to the formula

$$m = \frac{m_0}{\sqrt{1 - \mathbf{v}^2 / \mathbf{c}^2}}$$

We can see now why it is impossible for a mass to exceed the velocity of light in a vacuum. As velocity **v** approaches the velocity of light **c**, the mass of the object increases and is undefined if $\mathbf{v} = \mathbf{c}$. The relativistic momentum, $\mathbf{p} = m\mathbf{v}$, can now be expressed as:

$$p = m\mathbf{v} = \frac{m_0\mathbf{v}}{\sqrt{1 - \mathbf{v}^2 / \mathbf{c}^2}}$$

In his analysis of mechanics, Einstein also introduced the most famous equation of the twentieth century. Any object, with a rest mass of m_0, has an equivalent rest energy given by

$$E_0 = m_0\mathbf{c}^2$$

This equation is the origin of the binding energy factor of 931.5 MeV per atomic mass unit.

If the object is in motion, it has an equivalent energy given by

$$E = mc^2 = \frac{m_0 c^2}{\sqrt{1 - v^2 / c^2}}$$

This energy is the sum of the object's kinetic energy and its rest energy. Thus, the kinetic energy is given by

$$KE = mc^2 - m_0 c^2 = \frac{m_0 c^2}{\sqrt{1 - v^2 / c^2}} - m_0 c^2$$

For low velocities, this expression reduces to the familiar, classical expression

$$KE = \left(\frac{1}{2}\right) m_0 v^2$$

We can link the relativistic energy to the momentum in the following way. In classical mechanics,

$$KE = \left(\frac{1}{2}\right) m_0 v^2 = \frac{p^2}{2} m_0$$

Using the relativistic forms for the total energy E and the momentum $\mathbf{p}$, we get

$$E^2 = p^2 c^2 + (m_0 c^2)^2$$

Sample Problem:

What is the rest energy for a 60-kg student?

Solution:

We use the rest-energy formula to find the answer:

$$E_0 = m_0 c^2 = (60)(9 \times 10^{16}) = 5.4 \times 10^{18}\ \text{J}$$

Problem-Solving Strategies for Special Relativity

Relativity problems can be somewhat confusing. The key is to remember the various frames of reference involved. When dealing with relative velocities, you will need one of them to serve as the inertial frame for the observation. In other words, you can have observations from a stationary (the Earth) or from a moving (say, a spaceship) frame.

Be sure to follow the equations carefully and to memorize them for use on the examination. Try not to let your intuition about classical mechanics influence the concepts in relativity. Time and space are relative concepts, and even the notion of simultaneity is suspect since time measurements depend on the frame of reference. Thus, two events that may appear to be simultaneous in one frame may not be simultaneous in another.

Practice Problems for Chapter 27

Multiple Choice

1. Which of the following statements is a postulate of special relativity?
   (A) All motion is relative.
   (B) An object can never go faster than the velocity of light in any medium.
   (C) Accelerated frames of reference produce fictitious forces.
   (D) The laws of physics are equivalent in all inertial frames of reference.
   (E) All laws of physics reduce to Newton's laws at low velocity.

2. What is the perceived length of a meter stick if it is moving with a velocity of $0.5c$ relative to the Earth?
   (A) 0.87 m
   (B) 0.75 m
   (C) 0.50 m
   (D) 0.25 m
   (E) 0.35 m

3. What is the energy equivalent of an electron at rest?
   (A) 931.5 MeV
   (B) 0.017 MeV
   (C) 0.512 MeV
   (D) 535 MeV
   (E) 675 MeV

4. The observed mass of a moving object is three times its rest mass. What is the velocity of the object relative to the Earth?
   (A) $(2\sqrt{2})\mathbf{c} / 3$
   (B) $\mathbf{c}$
   (C) $3\,\mathbf{c}$
   (D) $(2\sqrt{2})\mathbf{c}$
   (E) $\mathbf{c} / 3$

5. An observer is moving with a velocity of $0.95c$ in a direction perpendicular to a rod of length L. The observer will measure the length of the rod to be
   (A) equal to L
   (B) less than L
   (C) greater than L
   (D) zero
   (E) more or less, depending on the velocity

6. A subatomic particle called a "pion" has an observed laboratory lifetime of 2.6×10^{-8} s. If the pion is observed to have a velocity of $0.93c$ relative to the laboratory, by what factor is the lifetime of the pion observed to increase?
(A) 1.35
(B) 3.6
(C) 1.75
(D) 2.72
(E) 0.56

7. An observer on the Earth sees a cosmic particle coming toward her at a velocity of $0.96c$ when it is at an altitude of 1850 m. What is the altitude of the particle as measured from a frame of reference moving with the particle?
(A) 130 m
(B) 518 m
(C) 768 m
(D) 6607 m
(E) 9833 m

8. A pendulum is set swinging inside a spaceship moving at a velocity of $0.91\mathbf{c}$ relative to the Earth. The period is measured to be equal to 2.5 s inside the spaceship. What is the period to a stationary observer outside the spaceship?
(A) 3 s
(B) 6.03 s
(C) 1.03 s
(D) 4.27 s
(E) 2.3 s

9. A boy is standing on a platform that is moving with a velocity of $0.75\mathbf{c}$ relative to a stationary observer. The boy throws a ball in the forward direction with a velocity of $0.60\mathbf{c}$ relative to himself. What is the velocity of the ball relative to the stationary observer?
(A) $0.15\mathbf{c}$
(B) $1.35\ \mathbf{c}$
(C) $0.93\ \mathbf{c}$
(D) $0.82\ \mathbf{c}$
(E) $0.75\ \mathbf{c}$

10. For the situation described in problem 9, if the mass of the ball, relative to the thrower, is 150 g, what is the mass relative to the stationary observer?
(A) 408 g
(B) 187.5 g
(C) 226.7 g
(D) 334.2 g
(E) 150 g

Free Response

1. (a) What is the relativistic kinetic energy of an electron moving with a velocity of 0.9**c** ?
   (b) Use the binomial expansion series to show that for low velocities the relativistic formula for kinetic energy reduces to the classical expression $(1/2)m_0\mathbf{v}^2$.

2. (a) Starting with the expressions for the relativistic total energy E and momentum **p**, show that

$$E^2 = \mathbf{p}^2\mathbf{c}^2 + (m_0\mathbf{c}^2)^2$$

   (b) If a photon has no rest mass, derive an expression for the momentum of the photon in terms of its energy E.
   (c) Explain why the expression $E^2 - \mathbf{p}^2\mathbf{c}^2$ is a relativistic invariant (that is, it has the same value in any frame of reference), whereas the quantities E and **p** are not invariants.

3. A proton has a kinetic energy of 3.5×10^{-11} J.
   (a) What is the velocity of the proton?
   (b) By what factor has the mass of the proton been increased?

Solutions

Multiple-Choice Problems

1. **D** "The laws of physics are equivalent in all inertial frames of reference" is one of Einstein's postulates of relativity.
2. **A** We use the length contraction formula with $L_0 = 1.0$ m:

$$L = L_0\sqrt{1 - \mathbf{v}^2 / \mathbf{c}^2} = 1.0\sqrt{1 - (0.5\mathbf{c})^2 / \mathbf{c}^2} = 0.87\text{ m}$$

3. **C** We use the mass-energy relationship for a stationary electron:

$$E_0 = m_0\mathbf{c}^2 = (9.1 \times 10^{-31})(9 \times 10^{16}) = 8.14 \times 10^{-14}\text{ J} = 0.512\text{ MeV}$$

4. **A** We use the relativistic mass relationship:

$$m = \frac{m_0}{\sqrt{1 - \mathbf{v}^2 / \mathbf{c}^2}}$$

$$3m_0 = \frac{m_0}{\sqrt{1 - \mathbf{v}^2 / \mathbf{c}^2}}$$

$$\sqrt{1 - \mathbf{v}^2 / \mathbf{c}^2} = \frac{1}{3}$$

Now, we square each side and solve for velocity **v**:

$$1 - \frac{\mathbf{v}^2}{\mathbf{c}^2} = \frac{1}{9}$$

$$\frac{\mathbf{v}^2}{\mathbf{c}^2} = \frac{8}{9}$$

$$\mathbf{v} = \frac{(2\sqrt{2})\mathbf{c}}{3}$$

5. **A** If the rod is laid along the *x*-axis and the motion is in the *y*-direction, no change will be observed in the length of the rod.
6. **D** We use the time dilation formula and solve for the ratio t/t_0:

$$\frac{t}{t_0} = \frac{1}{\sqrt{1 - (0.93\mathbf{c})^2 / \mathbf{c}^2}} = 2.72$$

7. **B** We use the length contraction formula since an observer moving with the particle will perceive a shorter distance:

$$L = 1850\sqrt{1 - (0.96\mathbf{c})^2 / \mathbf{c}^2} = 518\,\text{m}$$

8. **B** We use the time dilation formula to measure the observed period:

$$t = \frac{2.5}{\sqrt{1 - (0.91\mathbf{c})^2 / \mathbf{c}^2}} = 6.03\,\text{s}$$

9. **C** We use the relativistic velocity formula for both objects moving in the same direction relative to the stationary observer:

$$\mathbf{v} = \frac{0.75\mathbf{c} + 0.60\mathbf{c}}{1 + (0.75\mathbf{c})(0.60\mathbf{c}) / \mathbf{c}^2} = 0.93\,\mathbf{c}$$

10. **A** We need to use the relativistic mass formula but with the relative velocity measured in problem 9 ($\mathbf{v} = 0.93\mathbf{c}$):

$$m = \frac{150}{\sqrt{1 - (0.93\mathbf{c})^2 / \mathbf{c}^2}} = 408\,\text{g}$$

Free-Response Problems

1. (a) To find the kinetic energy of a fast-moving electron, we use the kinetic energy formula of Section 27.4 and substitute known values:

$$KE = \frac{m_0\mathbf{c}^2}{\sqrt{1 - \mathbf{v}^2 / \mathbf{c}^2}} - m_0\mathbf{c}^2$$

$$= \frac{(9.1 \times 10^{-31})(9 \times 10^{16})}{\sqrt{1 - (0.9\mathbf{c})^2 / \mathbf{c}^2}} - (9.1 \times 10^{-31})(9 \times 10^{16}) = 1.06 \times 10^{-13}\,\text{J}$$

(b) To show what happens at low velocities, $\mathbf{v} \ll \mathbf{c}$, we use the binomial expansion:

$$(1 - x^2)^{-1/2} \approx 1 + \frac{x^2}{2} + \cdots \qquad (x \ll 1)$$

In our expression, $x^2 = \mathbf{v}^2 / \mathbf{c}^2$ and if $\mathbf{v} \ll \mathbf{c}$, we can write

$$\left(\frac{1 - \mathbf{v}^2}{\mathbf{c}^2}\right)^{-1/2} \approx 1 + \frac{\mathbf{v}^2}{2\mathbf{c}^2}$$

and

$$KE = m_0\mathbf{c}^2\left(1 + \frac{\mathbf{v}^2}{2\mathbf{c}^2}\right) - m_0\mathbf{c}^2 = \frac{1}{2}m_0\mathbf{v}^2$$

2. (a) The expressions for relativistic energy and momentum are as follows:

$$E = \frac{m_0\mathbf{c}^2}{\sqrt{1 - \mathbf{v}^2 / \mathbf{c}^2}}$$

$$\mathbf{p} = \frac{m_0\mathbf{v}}{\sqrt{1 - \mathbf{v}^2 / \mathbf{c}^2}}$$

Now, we need to square both of these quantities:

$$E^2 = \frac{(m_0\mathbf{c}^2)^2}{1 - \mathbf{v}^2 / \mathbf{c}^2}$$

$$\mathbf{p}^2\mathbf{c}^2 = \frac{m_0^2\mathbf{c}^2\mathbf{v}^2}{1 - \mathbf{v}^2 / \mathbf{c}^2}$$

To the second equation we add the quantity $(m_0\mathbf{c}^2)^2$:

$$\mathbf{p}^2\mathbf{c}^2 + (m_0\mathbf{c}^2)^2 = \frac{m_0^2\mathbf{c}^2\mathbf{v}^2}{1 - \mathbf{v}^2 / \mathbf{c}^2} + (m_0\mathbf{c}^2)^2$$

$$= \frac{m_0^2\mathbf{c}^2\mathbf{v}^2}{1 - \mathbf{v}^2 / \mathbf{c}^2} + \frac{(m_0\mathbf{c}^2)^2(1 - \mathbf{v}^2 / \mathbf{c}^2)}{1 - \mathbf{v}^2 / \mathbf{c}^2}$$

$$= \frac{m_0\mathbf{c}^2\mathbf{v}^2 + (m_0\mathbf{c}^2)^2(1 - \mathbf{v}^2 / \mathbf{c}^2)}{1 - \mathbf{v}^2 / \mathbf{c}^2}$$

$$= \frac{(m_0\mathbf{c}^2)^2}{1 - \mathbf{v}^2 / \mathbf{c}^2} = E^2$$

(b) If the photon has no rest mass, the expression obtained in part (a) reduces to $E = \mathbf{pc}$. For a photon, this is consistent with the expression $\mathbf{p} = h / \lambda$, since $E = hf$.

(c) Energy and momentum are relativistic quantities that depend on the frame of reference and its relative velocity. However, by verifying that the expression $E^2 = \mathbf{p}^2\mathbf{c}^2 + (m_0\mathbf{c}^2)^2$ is valid, we know that the expression $E^2 - \mathbf{p}^2\mathbf{c}^2$ depends only on the rest mass (which is the same in any frame of reference) and the square of the velocity of light (which is of course an invariant).

3. (a) To find the velocity of the proton, we need to use the relativistic kinetic energy formula and substitute known values:

$$KE = \frac{m_0\mathbf{c}^2}{\sqrt{1 - \mathbf{v}^2 / \mathbf{c}^2}} - m_0\mathbf{c}^2$$

$$3.5 \times 10^{-11} = \frac{(1.67 \times 10^{-27})(9 \times 10^{16})}{\sqrt{1 - \mathbf{v}^2 / \mathbf{c}^2}} - (1.67 \times 10^{-27})(9 \times 10^{16})$$

$$1.853 \times 10^{-10} = \frac{1.503 \times 10^{-10}}{\sqrt{1 - \mathbf{v}^2 / \mathbf{c}^2}}$$

$$\mathbf{v} = 0.958\mathbf{c}$$

(b) Now that we know the velocity, we can use the relativistic mass formula to find the ratio of mass increase:

$$m = \frac{m_0}{\sqrt{1 - \mathbf{v}^2 / \mathbf{c}^2}}$$

$$\frac{m}{m_0} = \frac{1}{\sqrt{1 - (0.958\mathbf{c})^2 / \mathbf{c}^2}} = 3.49$$

The proton's mass increases by a factor of 3.49.

Practice Examinations

The following two practice examinations were designed to simulate the actual AP Physics B Examination. As mentioned earlier, ETS copyrights its examination, so that the level of difficulty, percentage of topics covered, and wording of questions may differ from the actual examination.

Further, since these are simulated examinations, you cannot determine how many points you would be awarded for each solution; nor is it possible to determine a simulated grade on the AP 1–5 scale.

Do not use a formula sheet for Section I since you will not be provided one during the actual examination.

As of May 1996, there will be two changes in the AP Physics B Examination procedures:

1. A formula sheet will be provided for Section II.
2. Calculators will no longer be allowed for use on Section I.

Finally, doing these practice problems, even if they are different from the actual examination problems, can only help your understanding of physics and problem solving, and of course help prepare you for the real thing.

Answer Sheet: Practice Examination 1

1. Ⓐ Ⓑ Ⓒ Ⓓ Ⓔ
2. Ⓐ Ⓑ Ⓒ Ⓓ Ⓔ
3. Ⓐ Ⓑ Ⓒ Ⓓ Ⓔ
4. Ⓐ Ⓑ Ⓒ Ⓓ Ⓔ
5. Ⓐ Ⓑ Ⓒ Ⓓ Ⓔ
6. Ⓐ Ⓑ Ⓒ Ⓓ Ⓔ
7. Ⓐ Ⓑ Ⓒ Ⓓ Ⓔ
8. Ⓐ Ⓑ Ⓒ Ⓓ Ⓔ
9. Ⓐ Ⓑ Ⓒ Ⓓ Ⓔ
10. Ⓐ Ⓑ Ⓒ Ⓓ Ⓔ
11. Ⓐ Ⓑ Ⓒ Ⓓ Ⓔ
12. Ⓐ Ⓑ Ⓒ Ⓓ Ⓔ
13. Ⓐ Ⓑ Ⓒ Ⓓ Ⓔ
14. Ⓐ Ⓑ Ⓒ Ⓓ Ⓔ
15. Ⓐ Ⓑ Ⓒ Ⓓ Ⓔ
16. Ⓐ Ⓑ Ⓒ Ⓓ Ⓔ
17. Ⓐ Ⓑ Ⓒ Ⓓ Ⓔ
18. Ⓐ Ⓑ Ⓒ Ⓓ Ⓔ
19. Ⓐ Ⓑ Ⓒ Ⓓ Ⓔ
20. Ⓐ Ⓑ Ⓒ Ⓓ Ⓔ
21. Ⓐ Ⓑ Ⓒ Ⓓ Ⓔ
22. Ⓐ Ⓑ Ⓒ Ⓓ Ⓔ
23. Ⓐ Ⓑ Ⓒ Ⓓ Ⓔ
24. Ⓐ Ⓑ Ⓒ Ⓓ Ⓔ
25. Ⓐ Ⓑ Ⓒ Ⓓ Ⓔ
26. Ⓐ Ⓑ Ⓒ Ⓓ Ⓔ
27. Ⓐ Ⓑ Ⓒ Ⓓ Ⓔ
28. Ⓐ Ⓑ Ⓒ Ⓓ Ⓔ
29. Ⓐ Ⓑ Ⓒ Ⓓ Ⓔ
30. Ⓐ Ⓑ Ⓒ Ⓓ Ⓔ
31. Ⓐ Ⓑ Ⓒ Ⓓ Ⓔ
32. Ⓐ Ⓑ Ⓒ Ⓓ Ⓔ
33. Ⓐ Ⓑ Ⓒ Ⓓ Ⓔ
34. Ⓐ Ⓑ Ⓒ Ⓓ Ⓔ
35. Ⓐ Ⓑ Ⓒ Ⓓ Ⓔ
36. Ⓐ Ⓑ Ⓒ Ⓓ Ⓔ
37. Ⓐ Ⓑ Ⓒ Ⓓ Ⓔ
38. Ⓐ Ⓑ Ⓒ Ⓓ Ⓔ
39. Ⓐ Ⓑ Ⓒ Ⓓ Ⓔ
40. Ⓐ Ⓑ Ⓒ Ⓓ Ⓔ
41. Ⓐ Ⓑ Ⓒ Ⓓ Ⓔ
42. Ⓐ Ⓑ Ⓒ Ⓓ Ⓔ
43. Ⓐ Ⓑ Ⓒ Ⓓ Ⓔ
44. Ⓐ Ⓑ Ⓒ Ⓓ Ⓔ
45. Ⓐ Ⓑ Ⓒ Ⓓ Ⓔ
46. Ⓐ Ⓑ Ⓒ Ⓓ Ⓔ
47. Ⓐ Ⓑ Ⓒ Ⓓ Ⓔ
48. Ⓐ Ⓑ Ⓒ Ⓓ Ⓔ
49. Ⓐ Ⓑ Ⓒ Ⓓ Ⓔ
50. Ⓐ Ⓑ Ⓒ Ⓓ Ⓔ
51. Ⓐ Ⓑ Ⓒ Ⓓ Ⓔ
52. Ⓐ Ⓑ Ⓒ Ⓓ Ⓔ
53. Ⓐ Ⓑ Ⓒ Ⓓ Ⓔ
54. Ⓐ Ⓑ Ⓒ Ⓓ Ⓔ
55. Ⓐ Ⓑ Ⓒ Ⓓ Ⓔ
56. Ⓐ Ⓑ Ⓒ Ⓓ Ⓔ
57. Ⓐ Ⓑ Ⓒ Ⓓ Ⓔ
58. Ⓐ Ⓑ Ⓒ Ⓓ Ⓔ
59. Ⓐ Ⓑ Ⓒ Ⓓ Ⓔ
60. Ⓐ Ⓑ Ⓒ Ⓓ Ⓔ
61. Ⓐ Ⓑ Ⓒ Ⓓ Ⓔ
62. Ⓐ Ⓑ Ⓒ Ⓓ Ⓔ
63. Ⓐ Ⓑ Ⓒ Ⓓ Ⓔ
64. Ⓐ Ⓑ Ⓒ Ⓓ Ⓔ
65. Ⓐ Ⓑ Ⓒ Ⓓ Ⓔ
66. Ⓐ Ⓑ Ⓒ Ⓓ Ⓔ
67. Ⓐ Ⓑ Ⓒ Ⓓ Ⓔ
68. Ⓐ Ⓑ Ⓒ Ⓓ Ⓔ
69. Ⓐ Ⓑ Ⓒ Ⓓ Ⓔ
70. Ⓐ Ⓑ Ⓒ Ⓓ Ⓔ

Useful Constants

1 atomic mass unit	$1\ \mu = 1.66 \times 10^{-27}$ kg
Rest mass of the proton	$m_p = 1.67 \times 10^{-27}$ kg
Rest mass of the neutron	$m_n = 1.67 \times 10^{-27}$ kg
Rest mass of the electron	$m_e = 9.11 \times 10^{-31}$ kg
Magnitude of the electron charge	$e = 1.60 \times 10^{-19}$ C
Avogadro's number	$N_0 = 6.02 \times 10^{23}$ per mole
Universal gas constant	$R = 8.32$ J/(mole · K)
Boltzmann's constant	$k_B = 1.38 \times 10^{-23}$ J/K
Speed of light	$c = 3 \times 10^8$ m/s
Planck's constant	$h = 6.63 \times 10^{-34}$ J · s $= 4.14 \times 10^{-15}$ eV · s
1 electron volt	1 eV $= 1.6 \times 10^{-19}$ J
Vacuum permittivity	$\epsilon_0 = 8.85 \times 10^{-12}$ C²/Nm²
Coulomb's law constant	$k = 1/4\pi\epsilon_0 = 9 \times 10^9$ N · m²/C²
Vacuum permeability	$\mu_0 = 4\pi \times 10^{-7}$ Wb/(A · m)
Magnetic constant	$k' = k/c^2 = \mu_0/4\pi = 10^{-7}$ Wb/(A · m)
Acceleration due to gravity at Earth's surface	$g = 9.8$ m/s²
Universal gravitational constant	$G = 6.67 \times 10^{-11}$ m³/(kg · s²)
1 atmosphere pressure	1 atm $= 1.0 \times 10^5$ N/m² $= 1.0 \times 10^5$ Pa
1 nanometer	1 nm $= 1.0 \times 10^{-9}$m

PRACTICE EXAMINATION 1

Section I

Multiple-Choice Questions

70 questions
90 minutes
50 percent of total grade

Directions: For each of the questions or incomplete statements below there are five choices. In each case select the best answer or completion and fill in the corresponding oval on the answer sheet.

I. All frames of reference are assumed to be inertial.
II. Electrical current will follow the direction of a positive charge (conventional current).
III. For any isolated charge, the potential at infinity is taken to be equal to zero.

1. A particle has a position-time function given by

$$x = 2t^2 + t + 2$$

What is the average velocity of the particle from $t = 0$ to $t = 2$ seconds?
(A) 2 m/s
(B) 4 m/s
(C) 6 m/s
(D) 12 m/s
(E) 5 m/s

2. A 2-kilogram cart has a velocity of 4 meters per second to the right. It collides with a 5-kilogram cart moving to the left at 1 meter per second. After the collision, the two carts stick together. What are the magnitude and the direction of the velocity of the two carts after the collision?
(A) 0.43 m/s left
(B) 1.6 m/s right
(C) 0.43 m/s right
(D) 1.6 m/s left
(E) 8 m/s right

3. A projectile is launched at an angle θ and an initial velocity $\mathbf{v}_0$ such that its maximum height is equal to its range. Which of the following expressions will determine the correct value of angle θ?
(A) tan θ = 2
(B) tan θ = 4
(C) tan θ = 1
(D) sin θ = 1/2
(E) cos θ = 1/4

GO ON TO THE NEXT PAGE ➤

4. A rubber stopper is swung overhead in a horizontal circle with a radius of 0.25 meter, as shown below. If the stopper has a period of 0.45 seconds, what angle does the stopper sweep out in 1 second?

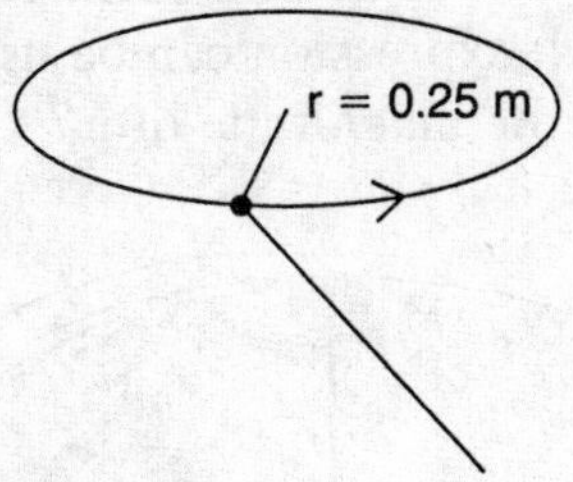

(A) 14 rad
(B) 2π rad
(C) 0.25 rad
(D) 0.45 rad
(E) 2.83 rad

5. A stone is dropped from a height of 49 meters. Two seconds later, a similar stone is thrown from the same height. If the two stones hit the ground at the same time, what was the initial velocity of the second stone?
(A) −37.62 m/s
(B) −47.92 m/s
(C) −52.35 m/s
(D) −27.83 m/s
(E) −16.25 m/s

6. A projectile is launched horizontally with an initial velocity $\mathbf{v}_0$ from a height h. If it is assumed that there is no air resistance, which of the following expressions represents the vertical trajectory of the projectile?
(A) $-\mathbf{g}\mathbf{v}_0^2/2x^2$
(B) $-\mathbf{g}\mathbf{v}_0^2 x^2$
(C) $-\mathbf{g}x/2\mathbf{v}_0^2$
(D) $-2\mathbf{g}x^2/\mathbf{v}_0^2$
(E) $-\mathbf{g}x^2/\mathbf{v}_0^2$

Questions 7 and 8 are based on the information and diagram below:

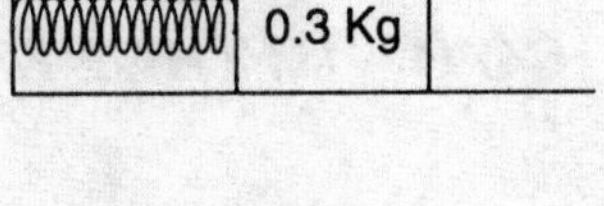

A 0.3-kilogram mass is attached to a spring that has a force constant of $k = 1000$ newtons per meter.

7. What is the maximum velocity attained by the mass if the amplitude of oscillations is 0.15 meter?
(A) 2.17 m/s
(B) 57.7 m/s
(C) 15.63 m/s
(D) 8.66 m/s
(E) 32.42 m/s

8. Which of the following statements concerning the oscillatory motion described above is correct?
(A) The maximum velocity and maximum acceleration occur at the same time.
(B) The maximum velocity occurs when the acceleration is a minimum.
(C) The velocity is always directly proportional to the displacement.
(D) The maximum velocity occurs when the displacement is a maximum.
(E) None of the preceding statements is correct.

9. A pendulum of length ℓ is swinging in an arc AB as shown below. It has a velocity $\mathbf{v}$ at point O. What is the tension T in the string at point O?

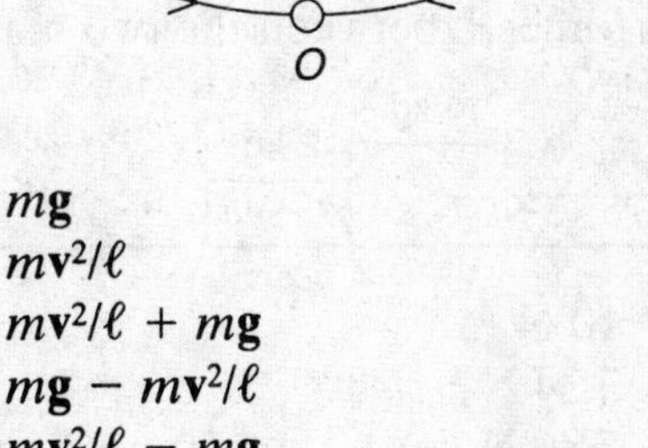

(A) mg
(B) $m\mathbf{v}^2/\ell$
(C) $m\mathbf{v}^2/\ell + mg$
(D) $mg - m\mathbf{v}^2/\ell$
(E) $m\mathbf{v}^2/\ell - mg$

GO ON TO THE NEXT PAGE ➤

10. A conical pendulum consists of a mass M attached to a light string of length ℓ. The mass swings around in a horizontal circle, making an angle θ with the vertical, as shown below. What is the tension **T** in the string?

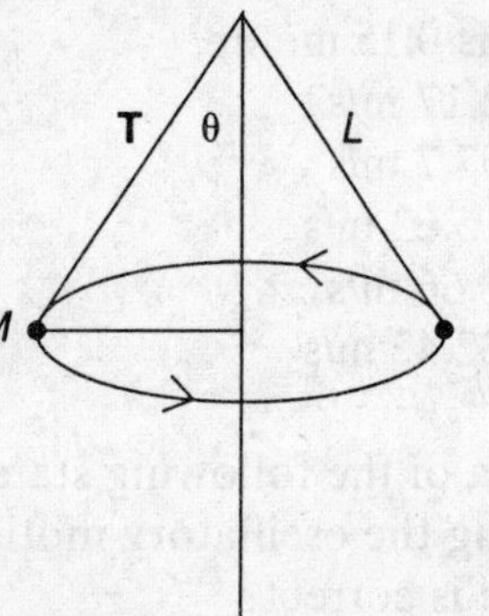

(A) $mg / \cos\theta$
(B) $mg \cos\theta$
(C) $mg / \sin\theta$
(D) $mg \sin\theta$
(E) $mg / \tan\theta$

11. Kepler's third law of planetary motion states that, for any orbiting system, the ratio $R^3/T^2 = k$ is a constant. The value of k depends on the mass of the body being orbited. Which of the following expressions is equivalent to the Newtonian representation of k?
(A) $G \rho R^3 \pi$
(B) $G \rho R/3 \pi^2$
(C) $G \rho \pi/3R^2$
(D) $G4 \pi R^3/3 \rho$
(E) $G \rho R^3/3 \pi$

12. A 10-newton force is applied to two masses, 4 kilograms and 2 kilograms, respectively, in contact as shown below. The horizontal motion is along a frictionless plane. What is the magnitude of the contact force, **P**, between the two masses?

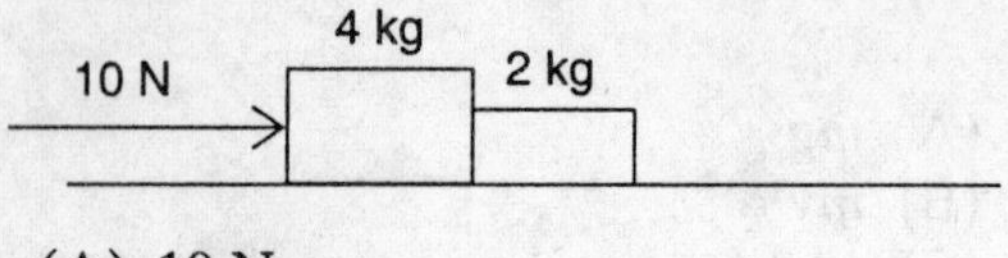

(A) 10 N
(B) 3.34 N
(C) 7.86 N
(D) 39.2 N
(E) 4 N

13. A mass M rests at the edge of a turntable that has a coefficient of static friction μ. The turntable is rotating with a constant angular frequency ω and has a radius r. If the magnitude of the angular frequency is such that the mass is just about to fly off, which expression can be used to determine the magnitude of μ?

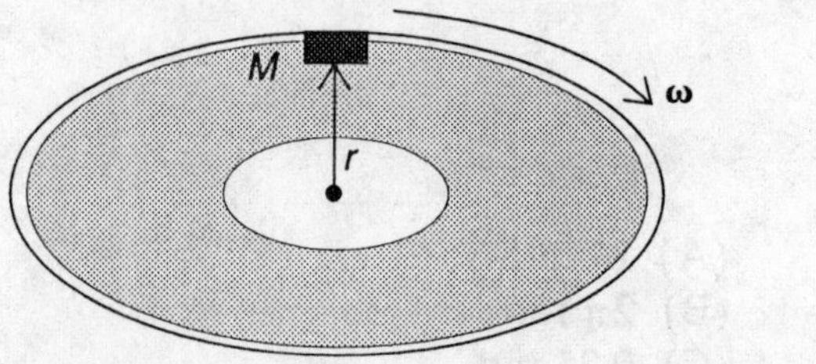

(A) $\omega^2 rg$
(B) ω^2/rg
(C) $\omega r^2/g$
(D) $\omega^2 g/r$
(E) $\omega^2 r/g$

14. A 1500-kilogram car has a velocity of 25 meters per second. If it is brought to a stop in 15 seconds, what was the magnitude of the braking force applied?
(A) 22,500 N
(B) 2500 N
(C) 14,700 N
(D) 16,000 N
(E) 1500 N

GO ON TO THE NEXT PAGE ➤

15. A block of mass M rests on a rough incline, as shown below. The angle of elevation of the incline is increased until an angle θ is reached. At that angle, the mass begins to slide down the incline. Which of the following is an expression for the coefficient of static friction μ?

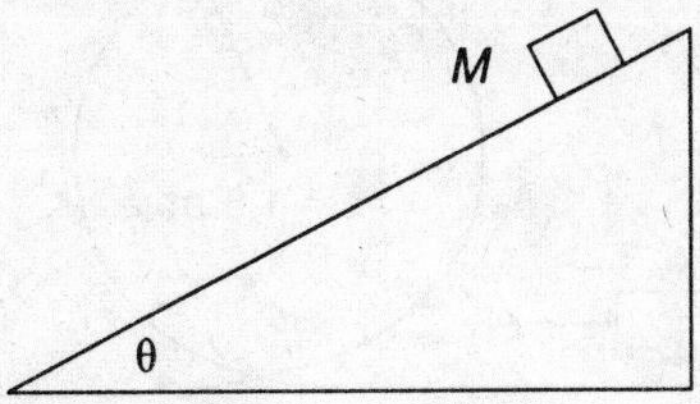

(A) $\mu = \tan\theta$
(B) $\mu = \sin\theta$
(C) $\mu = \cos\theta$
(D) $\mu = 2\sin\theta$
(E) $\mu = 1/\cos\theta$

16. Which of the following physical constants has the same units as angular momentum?
(A) Planck's constant
(B) Boltzmann's constant
(C) Kepler's constant
(D) Gravitational constant
(E) Rydberg's constant

17. A 0.2-kilogram wad of putty is moving horizontally with a velocity of 15 meters per second, as shown below. It strikes a stationary sphere of radius R at a distance above the ground equal to (4/5) R. What will be the angular momentum of the putty-sphere system after the collision has taken place?

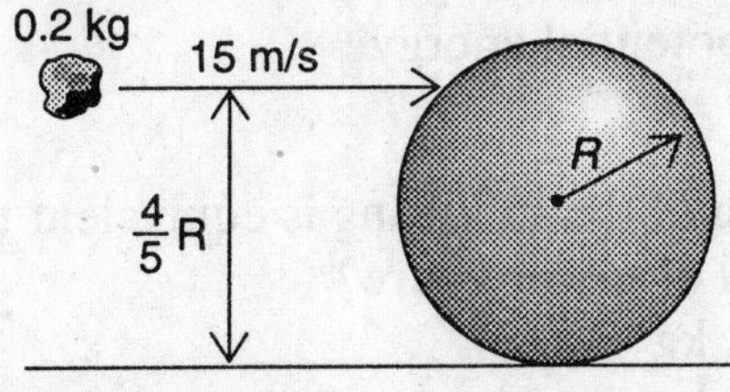

(A) (4/5) R kg · m²/s
(B) R kg · m²/s
(C) (8/5) R kg · m²/s
(D) (12/5) R kg · m²/s
(E) Not enough information is given.

18. A pendulum of length ℓ has a period T. If the period is to be doubled, the length of the pendulum should be
(A) increased by $\sqrt{2}$
(B) quartered
(C) quadrupled
(D) halved
(E) doubled

19. A skater holding two equal masses, one in each arm, is spinning vertically about an axis through her body. Her arms are outstretched fully, making a radius R. She has an angular frequency of ω_1. She now brings in her arms to a new radius r, and the angular frequency changes to ω_2. Which of the following expressions represents the ratio ω_1/ω_2?
(A) r^2/R^2
(B) R^2/r^2
(C) r/R
(D) R/r
(E) $\sqrt{r}/R$

20. A 200-kilogram cart rests on top of a frictionless hill as shown below. What will be the kinetic energy of the cart when it is at the top of the 10-meter hill?

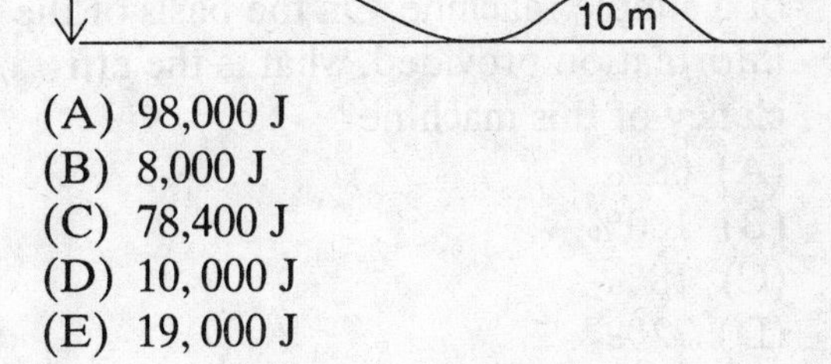

(A) 98,000 J
(B) 8,000 J
(C) 78,400 J
(D) 10,000 J
(E) 19,000 J

GO ON TO THE NEXT PAGE ➤

Questions 21 and 22 are based the following information:

The magnitude of the one-dimensional momentum of a 2-kilogram particle obeys the relationship $\mathbf{p} = 2t + 3$.

21. What was the velocity of the particle at $t = 1$ second?
(A) 5 m/s
(B) 2 m/s
(C) 4 m/s
(D) 1.5 m/s
(E) 2.5 m/s

22. What was the average force applied to the particle from $t = 1$ second to $t = 3$ seconds?
(A) 2 N
(B) 5 N
(C) 9 N
(D) 10 N
(E) 14 N

23. A 50-kilogram box is pushed up a 1.5-meter incline with an effort of 200 newtons. The top of the incline is 0.5 meter above the ground. How much work was done to overcome friction?
(A) 55 J
(B) 75 J
(C) 245 J
(D) 300 J
(E) 490 J

24. The incline in question 23 is an example of a simple machine. On the basis of the information provided, what is the efficiency of this machine?
(A) 68%
(B) 100%
(C) 18%
(D) 72%
(E) 82%

25. A cart with a mass of 1.5 kilograms needs to complete a 1.5-meter radius loop-the-loop, as shown below. What is the minumum velocity required to achieve this goal?

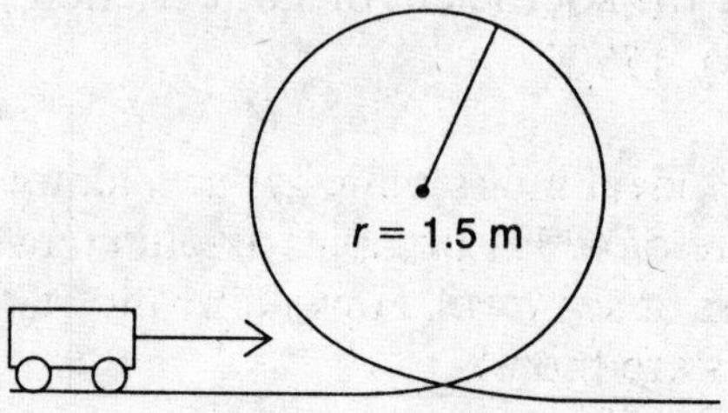

(A) 3.83 m/s
(B) 12.2 m/s
(C) 15.62 m/s
(D) 14.7 m/s
(E) 9.95 m/s

26. A 200-gram metal block absorbs 1500 joules of heat, and its temperature changes by 150 degrees Celsius. What is the specific heat capacity of this metal?
(A) 7.5 J / g · °C
(B) 0.13 J / g · °C
(C) 2.14 J / g · °C
(D) 0.05 J / g · °C
(E) 0.62 J / g · °C

27. Isobaric changes in an ideal gas imply that there is no change in
(A) volume
(B) temperature
(C) pressure
(D) internal energy
(E) potential energy

28. Which of the following is equivalent to 1 pascal of gas pressure?
(A) 1 kg · m^2/s^2
(B) 1 kg/ m · s^2
(C) 1 kg · m^3/s^2
(D) 1 kg · m/s
(E) 1 kg · m^2/s^3

GO ON TO THE NEXT PAGE ➤

29. A change in temperature of 75° Celsius is equivalent to a change in absolute temperature of
(A) 348 K
(B) 75 K
(C) 273 K
(D) 198 K
(E) 175 K

30. An ideal monatomic gas at a temperature of 400 K occupies a volume of 2.5 liters at sea level. How many moles of the gas are there?
(A) 160
(B) 0.076
(C) 2.5
(D) 12.2
(E) 0.68

31. For an ideal monatomic gas, the ratio of the molar specific heats, γ, is approximately equal to
(A) 1.4
(B) 2.5
(C) 1.7
(D) 1.5
(E) 1.0

Questions 32 and 33 are based on the following circuit:

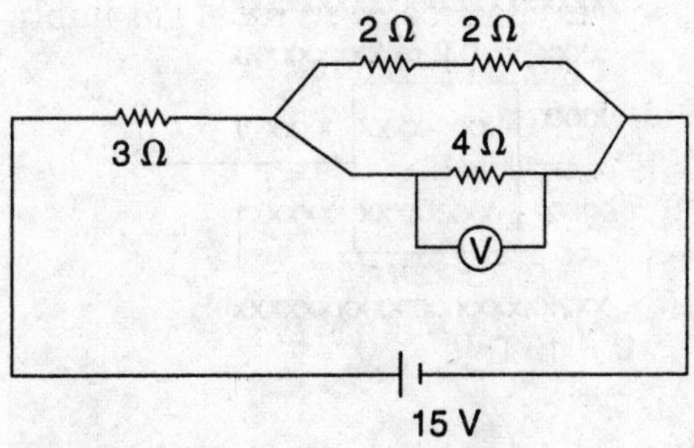

32. What is the equivalent resistance of the circuit?
(A) 6 Ω
(B) 8 Ω
(C) 5 Ω
(D) 15 Ω
(E) 3 Ω

33. What is the reading of the voltmeter across the 4-ohm resistor?
(A) 9 V
(B) 8 V
(C) 15 V
(D) 12 V
(E) 6 V

34. The diagram below shows a leaf electroscope that has been charged positively by a negatively charged rod. Which of the following statements is correct?

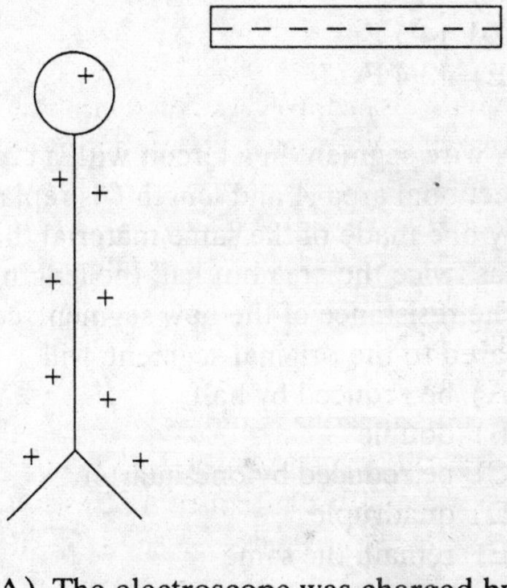

(A) The electroscope was charged by conduction.
(B) The electroscope was charged by contact.
(C) If the rod is brought closer, protons will be attracted to the top of the electroscope.
(D) If the rod is brought closer, protons will be repelled from the top of the electroscope.
(E) None of the preceding statements is correct.

GO ON TO THE NEXT PAGE ➤

35. What is the equivalent capacitance of the circuit shown below?

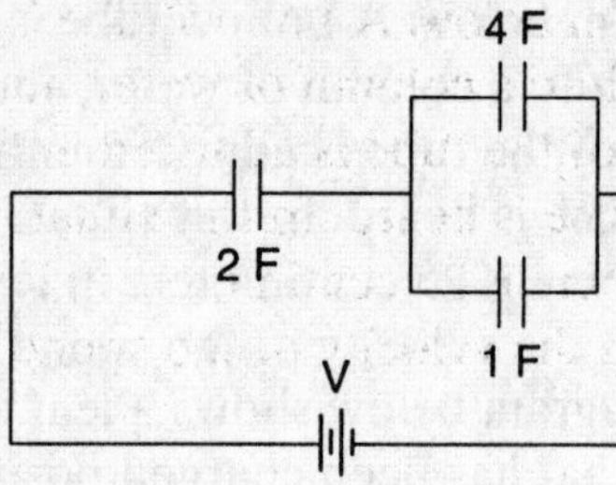

(A) 7/10 F
(B) 10/7 F
(C) 7 F
(D) 14/5 F
(E) 13/4 F

36. A wire segment in a circuit with a cross-sectional area A and length ℓ is replaced by one made of the same material that has twice the area but half the length. The resistance of the new segment, compared to the original segment, will
(A) be reduced by half
(B) double
(C) be reduced by one-quarter
(D) quadruple
(E) remain the same

Questions 37 and 38 are based on the circuit shown below:

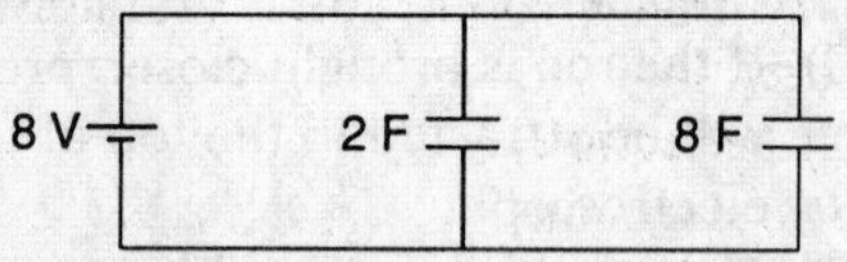

37. What is the charge stored in the 2-farad capacitor?
(A) 4 C
(B) 16 C
(C) 10 C
(D) 6 C
(E) 64 C

38. What is the energy stored in the 8-farad capacitor?
(A) 64 J
(B) 24 J
(C) 32 J
(D) 128 J
(E) 256 J

39. An electron is moving through a pair of crossed electric and magnetic fields in such a way that its path remains straight. Which of the following is an expression for the kinetic energy of the electron?
(A) $(1/2)\ M\mathbf{EB}$
(B) $M / 2\mathbf{EB}$
(C) $M\mathbf{E}^2\mathbf{B}/2$
(D) $1/2\ M\ (\mathbf{E}/\mathbf{B})$
(E) $m\mathbf{E}^2/2\mathbf{B}^2$

40. An electron is trapped in a circular path because of a uniform perpendicular magnetic field **B**. The velocity of the electron is **v** and the radius of the path is r. Which of the following expressions represents the angular velocity ω?
(A) $\mathbf{B}e/M$
(B) $\mathbf{B}eM$
(C) $\mathbf{B}M/e$
(D) $e / \mathbf{B}M$
(E) $\mathbf{B}e^2M$

Questions 41 and 42 are based on the following information and diagram:

A square wire frame is pulled to the right with a velocity of 4 meters per second across an inward magnetic field of strength 10 teslas. The length of each side of the frame is 0.2 meter.

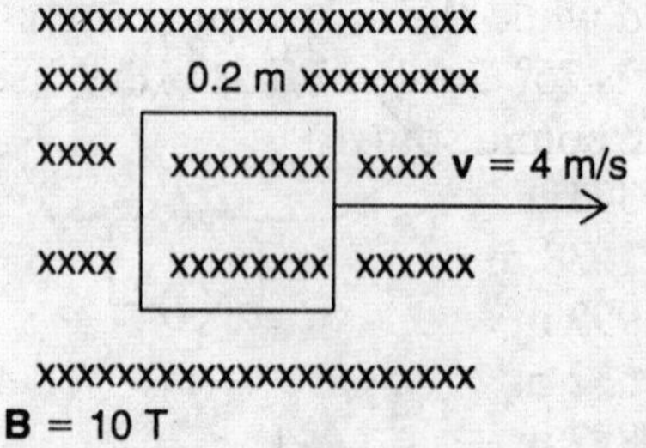

41. What is the magnitude of the induced motional electromotive force in the wire?
(A) 40 V
(B) 20 V
(C) 8 V
(D) 16 V
(E) 2 V

GO ON TO THE NEXT PAGE ➤

42. As the wire is moved to the right, a force appears to oppose it. This force is explained by
(A) Lenz's law
(B) Farady's law
(C) Ohm's law
(D) Coulomb's law
(E) Henry's law

43. If the tension in a taut string is doubled, the velocity of propagation of transverse waves in the string will change from **v** to
(A) 2 **v**
(B) **v** / 2
(C) 4 **v**
(D) **v** / 4
(E) $\sqrt{2}$**v**

44. In the standing wave shown below, what is the magnitude of one wavelength?

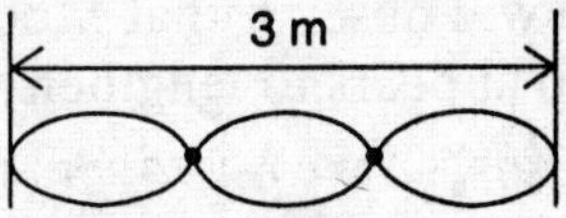

(A) 1 m
(B) 1.5 m
(C) 2.0 m
(D) 2.5 m
(E) 3.0 m

45. It takes 3 seconds to detect a sound produced while the air temperature at sea level is 25° Celsius. What is the distance to the sound source?
(A) 331 m
(B) 1038 m
(C) 993 m
(D) 632 m
(E) 852 m

46. A set of waves is coherent if the waves
(A) all have the same amplitude, frequency, and phase
(B) all have the same phase
(C) all have the same frequency
(D) are transverse in a dispersive medium
(E) None of the preceding statements is correct.

47. A 340-hertz tuning fork sets an air column vibrating in fundamental resonance as shown below. A hollow tube is inserted into a column of water, and the height of the tube is adjusted until strong resonance is heard. In this situation, the air column is 25 centimeters in length. What is the velocity of the sound?

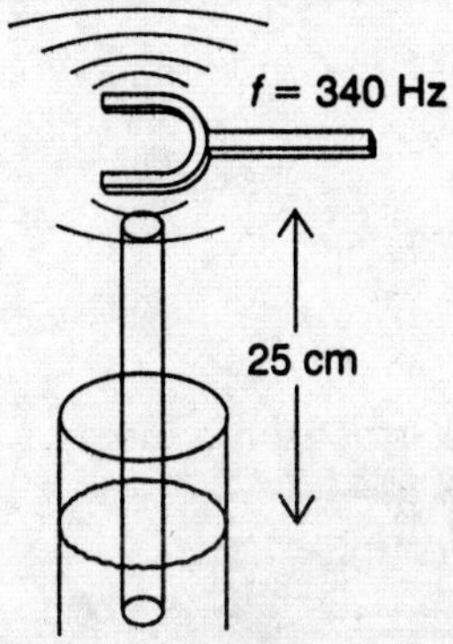

(A) 340 m/s
(B) 331 m/s
(C) 342 m/s
(D) 350 m/s
(E) 360 m/s

48. A shadow is formed by a point source of light. Upon closer inspection, the edges of the shadow seem to be diffuse and fuzzy. This phenomenon is probably caused by
(A) reflection
(B) refraction
(C) diffraction
(D) polarization
(E) dispersion

GO ON TO THE NEXT PAGE ➤

49. A light ray is incident on a glass-air interface as shown below. Which path will the light ray follow after it enters the air?

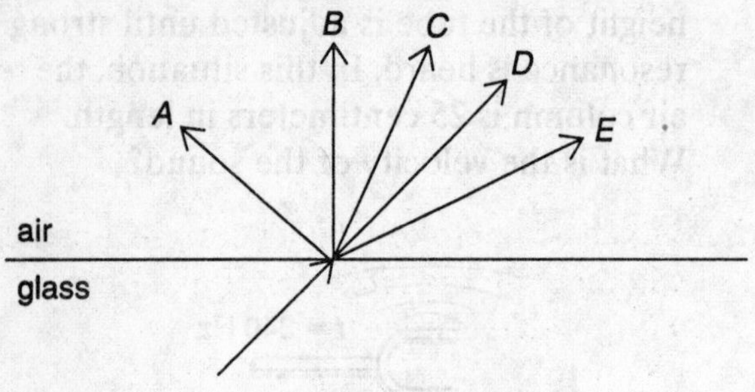

(A) *A*
(B) *B*
(C) *C*
(D) *D*
(E) *E*

50. What is the approximate critical angle of incidence for a light ray incident on a crown glass ($n = 1.51$) to water ($n = 1.33$) interface?
(A) 0°
(B) 37°
(C) 62°
(D) 77°
(E) 90°

51. A 5-centimeter-tall object is located 10 centimeters in front of a converging lens that has a 6-centimeter focal length. What is the size of the image produced?
(A) 5 cm
(B) 7.5 cm
(C) 10 cm
(D) 15 cm
(E) 30 cm

52. Which of the following statements about a diverging mirror is correct?
(A) The mirror must be concave in shape.
(B) The images are sometimes larger than the actual objects.
(C) The images are always erect.
(D) The images are sometimes real.
(E) Algebraically, the focal length is designated as $+f$.

53. Which of the following waves cannot be polarized?
(A) Sound waves
(B) X rays
(C) Infrared rays
(D) Microwaves
(E) Blue light waves

54. Moe and Joe are twins. Moe boards a spaceship and takes a round trip to Mars, traveling near the velocity of light **c**. Joe remains at home, waiting for Moe. Which of the following statements is correct?
(A) Moe will observe that time passes more slowly while in the ship.
(B) Joe will observe that time passes more quickly for Moe.
(C) Moe will observe that time passes more quickly for Joe.
(D) Joe will observe a relative velocity for Moe greater than *c*.
(E) Joe will observe that Moe's spaceship appears to lengthen while traveling.

55. Which of the following quantities is a relativistic invariant?
(A) Momentum
(B) Charge
(C) Kinetic energy
(D) Mass
(E) Velocity

56. The special theory of relativity is sometimes referred to as the "restricted" theory of relativity because
(A) nothing can exceed the velocity of light in a vacuum
(B) all inertial frames are equivalent
(C) gravity was not taken into account
(D) charge was not taken into account
(E) the two names refer to the same thing

GO ON TO THE NEXT PAGE ➤

57. In a photoelectric effect experiment, the emitted electrons could be stopped with a retarding potential of 12 volts. What was the maximum kinetic energy of these electrons?
(A) 12 eV
(B) 24 eV
(C) 36 eV
(D) 1.92×10^{-18} eV
(E) 1.6×10^{-19} eV

58. What units are associated with the quantity h/mc^2?
(A) N
(B) J / s
(C) J
(D) kg · m/s
(E) s

59. What energy is associated with a 150-nanometer photon?
(A) 9.845×10^{-32} J
(B) 4.42×10^{-27} J
(C) 1.6×10^{-19} J
(D) 1.32×10^{-18} J
(E) 2.42×10^{-16} J

Questions 60 through 62 are based on the following simulated energy level diagram for a mythical hydrogen-like atom:

60. What energy is associated with a photon emitted during a transition from level 4 to level 2?
(A) 9.2 eV
(B) 5.7 eV
(C) 3.5 eV
(D) 6.3 eV
(E) 14.9 eV

61. What is the wavelength of the photon emitted in the transition described in question 60?
(A) 250 nm
(B) 355 nm
(C) 425 nm
(D) 568 nm
(E) 770 nm

62. Which of the following level transitions will result in the emission of a photon with the largest energy?
(A) 1 to 3
(B) 5 to 2
(C) 2 to 1
(D) 5 to 3
(E) 4 to 2

63. One atomic mass unit is defined to be equal to
(A) 1/2 the mass of a hydrogen molecule
(B) 1/12 the mass of the carbon atom
(C) 1/16 the mass of the oxygen atom
(D) 1/4 the mass of the helium atom
(E) 1/56 the mass of the iron atom

64. How many neutrons are contained in the isotope ${}^{238}_{92}U$?
(A) 92
(B) 100
(C) 146
(D) 330
(E) 238

65. "K capture" is another term for
(A) alpha-particle capture
(B) electron capture
(C) proton capture
(D) neutron capture
(E) positron capture

66. In the reaction

$${}^{27}_{13}Al + {}^{4}_{2}He \rightarrow {}^{30}_{15}P + X$$

what is the mass number for particle X?
(A) 1
(B) 2
(C) 0
(D) −1
(E) 4

GO ON TO THE NEXT PAGE ➤

67. Radon gas ($^{222}_{86}Rn$) is radioactive with a half-life of 4 days. A sample is sealed in an evacuated tube for more than 1 week. At that time, the presence of a second gas is detected. This gas is most probably
(A) hydrogen
(B) helium
(C) oxygen
(D) lithium
(E) argon

68. According to the scale of binding energy per nucleon, which atom has the most stable nuclear isotope?
(A) Hydrogen
(B) Helium
(C) Iron
(D) Lithium
(E) Uranium

69. Heisenberg's uncertainty principle can be written as $\Delta \mathbf{p}\, \Delta x \geq h / 2\pi$. Which of the following is an equivalent expression of the uncertainty principle?
(A) $\Delta m\, \Delta t \geq h/2\pi$
(B) $\Delta E\, \Delta t \geq \mathrm{h}/2\pi$
(C) $\Delta \mathbf{p}\, \Delta t \geq h/2\pi$
(D) $\Delta L\, \Delta t \geq h/2\pi$
(E) $\Delta E\, \Delta \mathbf{p} \geq h/2\pi$

70. Which of the following materials can be used as a moderator in a nuclear fission reactor?
(A) Iron
(B) Graphite
(C) Cadmium
(D) Aluminum
(E) Steel

STOP

THIS IS THE END OF SECTION I.
YOU MAY USE ANY REMAINING TIME TO CHECK YOUR WORK IN THIS SECTION.

Section II

Free-Response Questions

6 questions
90 minutes
50 percent of total grade

> *Directions*: Solve the following problems. Be sure to show all work, including substitution with units, and to explain clearly.

1. A mass m is suspended by a light string attached to a ring stand as shown below. The ring stand sits on top of a rough platform that can rotate with an angular frequency ω such that the mass is pulled outward, making an angle θ with the vertical.

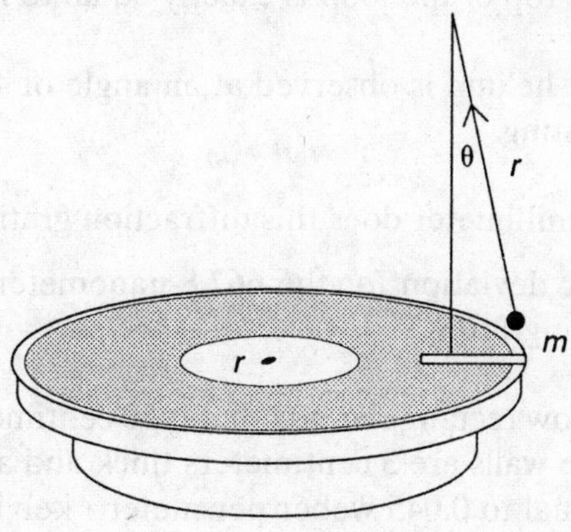

(a) Draw a free-body diagram for the forces acting on the mass. Label each force appropriately!

(b) In terms of **g**, r and ω, derive an expression for the magnitude of angle θ.

(c) If $r = 0.25$ meter, $m = 0.15$ kilogram, and the period of rotation is 0.45 second, what is the value of angle θ?

2. A mass m is resting at a height h above the ground. When released, the mass can slide down a frictionless track to a loop-the-loop of radius R, as shown below:

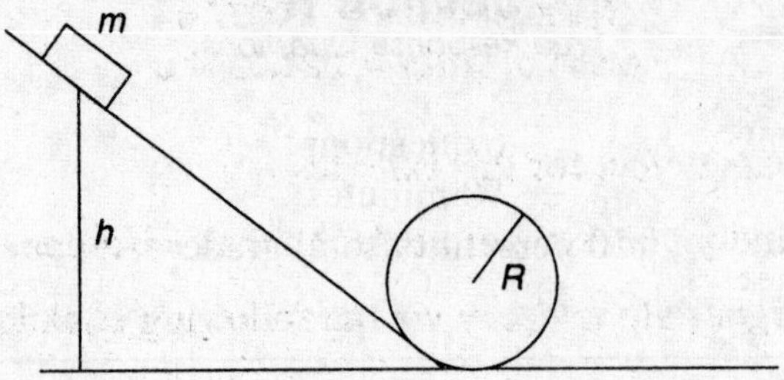

(a) Draw free-body diagrams for the mass when it is (i) at the top and (ii) at the bottom of the loop.

(b) Derive expressions for the reaction force of the track on the mass when the mass is (i) at the top and the (ii) at the bottom.

(c) At what height h must the mass be released so that the reaction force of the track on the mass when it is at the top of the loop is exactly equal to its weight?

3. The 501.5-nanometer line of helium is observed at an angle of 45 degrees in the second-order spectrum of a diffraction grating.

(a) How many lines per millimeter does this diffraction grating have?

(b) Calculate the angular deviation for the 667.8-nanometer helium line in the first-order spectrum for the same grating.

4. A cooler is made from a hollow rectangular box that is 50 centimeters long, 20 centimeters wide, and 20 centimeters high. The walls are 3 centimeters thick and are made of a thermal material that has a conductivity k equal to 0.045 weber per meter · kelvin. The internal temperature is maintained at 0 degrees Celsius, using ice, and the outside temperature is 30 degrees Celsius.

(a) Write an expression that represents the amount of heat transferred per unit time across the walls of the cooler.

(b) Show that the units on both sides of your equation reduce to joules per second.

(c) How much ice melts each hour, based on your equation and the conditions given above?

5. An electron is projected at an angle of 35 degrees above the horizontal with a velocity of 300,000 meters per second. It encounters an upward electric field of strength 600 newtons per coulomb. Neglecting all gravitational effects:

(a) Determine the time the electron takes to return to its initial height.

(b) Determine the maximum height reached by the electron.

(c) Determine the horizontal displacement when the electron has reached its maximum height.

GO ON TO THE NEXT PAGE ➤

6. Given the following information:

$$\text{Proton mass} = 1.0078 \text{ u}$$
$$\text{Neutron mass} = 1.0087 \text{ u}$$
$$\text{Mass of } {}^{226}_{88}\text{Ra} = 226.0244 \text{ u}$$

(a) Determine the mass defect for this isotope.

(b) Determine the binding energy per nucleon for this isotope.

(c) Radium-88 undergoes alpha decay via the following equation:

$${}^{226}_{88}\text{Ra} \rightarrow {}^{222}_{86}\text{Rn} + {}^{4}_{2}\text{He} + Q$$

If the mass of the radon-86 isotope is 222.0165 u and the mass of the helium-4 isotope is 4.0026 u, how much energy, in million electron volts, is associated with quantity Q?

STOP

THIS IS THE END OF SECTION II.
YOU MAY USE ANY REMAINING TIME TO CHECK YOUR WORK IN THIS SECTION.

Answer Key for Section I

1. **E**	15. **A**	29. **B**	43. **E**	57. **A**
2. **C**	16. **A**	30. **B**	44. **B**	58. **E**
3. **B**	17. **D**	31. **A**	45. **B**	59. **D**
4. **A**	18. **C**	32. **C**	46. **A**	60. **C**
5. **B**	19. **A**	33. **E**	47. **A**	61. **B**
6. **C**	20. **C**	34. **E**	48. **C**	62. **C**
7. **D**	21. **E**	35. **B**	49. **E**	63. **B**
8. **B**	22. **A**	36. **C**	50. **C**	64. **C**
9. **C**	23. **A**	37. **B**	51. **B**	65. **B**
10. **A**	24. **E**	38. **E**	52. **C**	66. **A**
11. **E**	25. **A**	39. **E**	53. **A**	67. **B**
12. **B**	26. **D**	40. **A**	54. **C**	68. **C**
13. **E**	27. **C**	41. **C**	55. **B**	69. **B**
14. **B**	28. **B**	42. **A**	56. **C**	70. **B**

Answer Explanations for Section I

1. **E** The average velocity is given by the change in distance over time. At $t = 0$ s, the particle's position, x is $x = 2$ m. At $t = 2$ s, $x = 12$ m. Thus, $\Delta x = 10$ m and $\Delta t = 2$ s. The average velocity is therefore equal to 5 m/s.

2. **C** Conservation of linear momentum implies that the total momentum before the collision of the two carts must equal the total momentum after the collision. This collision is inelastic since the two carts stick together. Thus, taking the "left" as negative, we have

$$(2 \text{ kg})(4 \text{ m/s}) - (5 \text{ kg})(1 \text{ m/s}) = (2 \text{ kg} + 5 \text{ kg})\, \mathbf{v}_f$$

and $\mathbf{v}_f = 0.43$ m/s to the right (since the answer is positive).

3. **B** The formulas for the range and the maximum height of a projectile must be set equal to each other:

$$\frac{\mathbf{v}_0^2 \sin 2\theta}{\mathbf{g}} = \frac{\mathbf{v}_0^2 \sin^2\theta}{2\mathbf{g}}$$

Recalling that $\sin 2\theta = 2 \sin\theta \cos\theta$, we get $\tan\theta = 4$.

4. **A** The angle (in radians) swept out per second by the stopper is the angular frequency, ω, which is equal to $2\pi / T$. Since the period is given as 0.45 s, then, in 1 s, $\theta = \omega t = 14$ rad.

5. **B** The first stone will take 3.16 s to fall 49 m. The second stone is thrown downward 2 s after the first one is dropped. Therefore, it will take only 1.16 s to hit the ground. The vertical displacement, y, is still -49 m. Thus,

$$y = \mathbf{v}_{0y}t - \left(\frac{1}{2}\right)\mathbf{g}t^2$$

$$-49 \text{ m} = y_{0y}(1.16 \text{ s}) - (4.9 \text{ m/s}^2)(1.16 \text{ s})^2$$

and

$$\mathbf{v}_0 = -47.92 \text{ m/s}$$

6. **C** The vertical trajectory is given by $y = -(1/2)\mathbf{g}t^2$. The horizontal velocity is constant, and so the time t is given by the initial velocity $\mathbf{v}_0$ and the horizontal displacement x: $x/\mathbf{v}_0$. Thus we get

$$y = \frac{-\mathbf{g}x^2}{2\mathbf{v}_0^2}$$

7. **D** The maximum velocity is given by the formula $\mathbf{v} = A\omega$. In this problem, $A = 0.15$ m and

$$\omega = \sqrt{\frac{k}{m}} = \sqrt{\frac{1000 \text{ N/m}}{0.3 \text{ kg}}} = 57.73 \text{ rad/s}$$

Thus $\mathbf{v}_{max} = 8.66$ m/s.

8. **B** The maximum velocity occurs when the acceleration is a minimum in simple harmonic motion.

9. **C** At the bottom of the swing

$$F = ma = \frac{m\mathbf{v}^2}{r} = \mathbf{T} - m\mathbf{g}$$

Thus,

$$\mathbf{T} = \frac{m\mathbf{v}^2}{r} + m\mathbf{g} = \frac{m\mathbf{v}^2}{\ell} + m\mathbf{g}$$

10. **A** From the diagram we can see that the upward component of the tension, in magnitude, is given by

$$\mathbf{T}\cos\theta = m\mathbf{g}$$

Thus,

$$\mathbf{T} = \frac{m\mathbf{g}}{\cos\theta}$$

11. **E** The Newtonian formulation of Kepler's third law holds that $k = GM/4\pi^2$. The density is given by $\rho = M/V$. Assuming a spherical planet, we have

$$V = \left(\frac{4}{3}\right)\pi R^3$$

Substituting for M and V gives

$$k = \frac{G\rho R^3}{3\pi}$$

12. **B** Since the two masses are in contact, force $\mathbf{F} = 10$ N gives them the same acceleration:

$$\mathbf{a} = 10 \text{ N}/6 \text{ kg} = 1.67 \text{ m/s}^2$$

If we isolate the 2-kg mass in a free-body diagram, the only force acting on it is **P** the contact force exerted by the 4-kg mass. However, in magnitude, **P** = m**a**, where m = 2kg and **a** is the acceleration of the system. Thus we find that **P** = 3.34 N.

13. **E** In the frame of reference of the mass, the centripetal force is balanced by the force of friction. The normal force, in this case, is equal to the weight, mg. Thus,

$$m\,\omega^2 r = \mu m\mathbf{g}$$

$$\mu = \frac{\omega^2 r}{\mathbf{g}}$$

14. **B** Since **F** = m**a**, we have

$$\mathbf{F} = \frac{m\Delta\mathbf{v}}{\Delta t} = 2500\text{ N}$$

upon substitution.

15. **A** On the incline, the force of friction must just balance the component of weight down the incline. The normal force on an incline is given by mg cos θ, and the force down the incline (in magnitude) is given by mg sin θ. Thus, we write

$$m\mathbf{g}\sin\theta = \mu m\mathbf{g}\cos\theta$$

and

$$\mu = \tan\theta$$

This angle θ is sometimes called the "angle of repose."

16. **A** Planck's constant has the same units as angular momentum: joule · seconds, which are equivalent to kilogram · square meters per second.

17. **D** The instantaneous angular momentum of the system is given by

$$\mathbf{L} = m\mathbf{vr} = (0.2\text{ kg})(15\text{ m/s})[(4/5)R]$$

Thus the magnitude of the angular momentum is equal to (12/5) R $kg \cdot m^2/s$.

18. **C** The period of a pendulum is proportional to the square root of its length. To double the period, the length must therefore be quadrupled.

19. **A** In conservation of angular momentum, we have

$$\mathbf{v}_1 R = \mathbf{v}_2 r$$

In general, **v** = ωR, and so

$$\frac{\omega_1}{\omega_2} = \frac{r^2}{R^2}$$

20. **C** Using the law of conservation of energy, we see that the total energy at the start is $E = mgh$ which is (200)(9.8)(50) = 98,000 J. At the top of the second (10-m) hill, the kinetic energy is equal to the difference in potential energies:

$$98{,}000 \text{ J} - 19{,}600 \text{ J} = 78{,}400 \text{ J}$$

21. **E** At $t = 1$ s, the momentum of the particle is given by $\mathbf{p} = 5$ kg m/s. With a mass of 2 kg, that implies an initial velocity of 2.5 m/s.
22. **A** The average force is given by $\mathbf{F} = \Delta\mathbf{p} / \Delta t$. In this situation, $\Delta t = 2$ s and $\Delta\mathbf{p} = 4$ kg m/s. Thus, $\mathbf{F} = 2$ N.
23. **A** The work done by friction is the difference between the work input and the work output. In this problem

$$W_{\text{input}} = (200 \text{ N})(1.5 \text{ m}) = 300 \text{ J}$$

We can take $g = 9.8$ N/kg here. Then

$$W_{\text{output}} = (50 \text{ kg})(9.8 \text{ N/kg})(0.5 \text{ m}) = 245 \text{ J}$$

Thus

$$W_{\text{friction}} = 55 \text{ J}$$

24. **E** For a simple machine the efficiency, e, is given by the ratio of the work output to the work input times 100. Thus

$$e = \frac{245 \text{ J}}{300 \text{ J}} \times 100\% = 82\%$$

25. **A** The minimum velocity is given by the formula

$$\mathbf{v} = \sqrt{\mathbf{g}r}\ \sqrt{(9.8 \text{ m/s}^2)(1.5 \text{ m})} = 3.83 \text{ m/s}$$

26. **D** The specific heat capacity is given by the formula

$$c = \frac{\Delta Q}{m\,\Delta T} = \frac{1500 \text{ J}}{(200 \text{ g})(150° \text{ C})} = 0.05 \text{ J/g} \cdot °\text{C}$$

27. **C** Isobaric changes in an ideal gas imply that the pressure in the gas remains constant.
28. **B** One pascal of gas pressure is equivalent to

$$1 \text{ N/m}^2 = 1 \text{ kg/m} \cdot \text{s}^2$$

29. **B** A change of 75° C is equal to a change in absolute temperature of 75 K. The magnitudes are the same.
30. **B** The number of moles, n, is equal to 12.2 PV/T if P is in atmospheres, V in liters, and T in kelvins. The gas is at sea level, so $P = 1$ atm and $n = 0.076$ mole after substitution.
31. **A** For an ideal monatomic gas, the ratio of the molar specific heats, $\gamma = 1.4$.
32. **C** First we reduce the series portion in the parallel branch:

$$R = 2\ \Omega + 2\ \Omega = 4\ \Omega$$

Now, this 4-Ω resistance is in parallel with the other 4-Ω resistor. Recalling that

$$\frac{1}{R} = \frac{1}{R_1} + \frac{1}{R_2}$$

we find that the next equivalent resistance is equal to 2 Ω. Finally, this resistance is in series with the 3-Ω resistance, giving a final equivalent resistance of 3 Ω + 2 Ω = 5 Ω.

33. **E** With a 5-Ω equivalent resistance, Ohm's law states that the circuit current will be equal to

$$I = \frac{15\text{V}}{5\Omega} = 3\text{ A}$$

In a series circuit, the potential drop across each resistor is given by $V = IR$. Now, the 4-Ω resistor is part of a branch that has an equivalent resistance of 2 Ω. Thus, the potential drop across that entire branch is equal to 6 V. The voltmeter recording the potential difference across the 4-Ω resistor will register 6 V also.

34. **E** None of the statements is correct about the electroscope described in the problem.

35. **B** Capacitors add up directly in parallel and add up reciprocally in series. This is the opposite of what resistors do. Thus, in the parallel branch, the equivalent capacitance is 5 F.
For the two series capacitors, we have that

$$\frac{1}{C} = \frac{1}{2} + \frac{1}{5}$$

which implies $C = 10/7$ F.

36. **C** For a resistor at constant temperature we have $R = \rho L / A$, where ρ is the resistivity. When the area is made twice as large and the length one-half as long, the result is a reduction in resistance of one-quarter.

37. **B** Both capacitors have the same potential difference, 8 V. Thus, $Q = CV = 16$ C.

38. **E** The energy stored in the 8-F capacitor is given by

$$E = \left(\frac{1}{2}\right)QV = 256\text{ J}$$

39. **E** In crossed electric and magnetic fields, the velocity of the electron is given by $\mathbf{v} = \mathbf{E}/\mathbf{B}$. Thus we have

$$KE = \left(\frac{1}{2}\right)Mv^2 = \left(\frac{1}{2}\right)\frac{ME^2}{\mathbf{B}^2} = \frac{ME^2}{2\mathbf{B}^2}$$

40. **A** In a uniform perpendicular magnetic field, the centripetal force on the electron is balanced by the magnetic force:

$$\frac{mv^2}{r} = \mathbf{B}ev$$

Thus

$$\mathbf{v} = \frac{\mathbf{B}er}{M}$$

Now, $\boldsymbol{\omega} = \mathbf{v} / r$, so $\boldsymbol{\omega} = \mathbf{B}e / M$.

41. C The motional emf = **B***l***v** in this case. Substituting yields

$$\text{emf} = (10\text{T})(0.2\text{ m})(4\text{ m/s}) = 8\text{ V}$$

42. A Lenz's law will provide an opposing force by inducing a magnetic field to oppose the initial change in *B*.

43. E In a taut string, the velocity of propagation of transverse waves is proportional to the square root of the tension. Thus, if the tension is doubled, the velocity will increase from **v** to $\sqrt{2}$ **v**.

44. B In a standing wave, the nodes occur at one-half wavelength intervals. Since the entire segment is 3 m long, each nodal segment is 1.0 m long. Thus, $\lambda = 2.0$ m.

45. B The velocity of sound increases by approximately 0.6 m/s for each 1° C rise in the temperature of the air. At 25° C, the velocity of sound in air is 346 m/s. At 3 s of travel, the distance to the source is 1038 m.

46. A A set of waves is coherent if all the waves have the same amplitude, frequency, and phase.

47. A In a closed-end tube, the standing wave resonance point occurs at a length, ℓ, equal to $\lambda/4$. Thus, $\lambda = 1.0$ m; and since $\mathbf{v} = f\lambda$, $v = 340$ m/s in this case.

48. C In the seventeenth century, the Italian scientist Grimaldi discovered that the fuzzy appearance of the edges of shadows was caused by the diffraction of light near the edges of the object.

49. E Light will bend away from the normal as it enters air from glass. This is best represented by path *E*.

50. C The critical angle of incidence is given by

$$\sin\theta = \frac{n_2}{n_1} = \frac{1.33}{1.51}$$

and $\theta = 62°$.

51. B To find the size of the image we must first locate its position:

$$\frac{1}{f} = \frac{1}{p} + \frac{1}{q}$$

$$\frac{1}{6} = \frac{1}{10} + \frac{1}{q}$$

$$q = 15\text{ cm}$$

The magnification of the image is given by the ratio $q/p = 1.5$, and so

$$S_i = 5 \times 1.5 = 7.5\text{ cm}$$

52. C Diverging mirrors always produce erect virtual images. They can be convex in shape.

53. A A sound wave is a longitudinal wave that cannot be polarized.

54. **C** According to the theory of special relativity, a moving clock runs slower. Thus, Moe will appear younger relative to Joe. While Moe and his crew are in the spaceship, time will appear to pass at its normal rate for them. Thus Moe will think time passed more quickly for Joe.
55. **B** The electric charge of matter is a relativistic invariant. This means that the magnitude of the charge will be the same to all observers.
56. **C** Einstein referred to his special theory of relativity as "restricted" because gravitational fields were not taken into account.
57. **A** The stopping potential of 12 V will imply a maximum kinetic energy of 12 eV for each electron since KE_{max} = e V, and for one electron

$$KE_{max} = 12 \text{ V} \times 1 \text{ electron}$$

which equals 12 eV.
58. **E** Planck's constant is expressed in units of joule · seconds, and the quantity mc^2 is in units of joules. Thus the ratio of these two quantities leaves seconds (s) as the units.
59. **D** $E = hf$, and for 150 nm the frequency is equal to

$$f = \frac{c}{\lambda} = \frac{3 \times 10^8 \text{m / s}}{1.5 \times 10^{-7} \text{m}} = 2 \times 10^{15} \text{s}^{-1}$$

Multiplying this by Planck's constant yields

$$E = hf = (6.63 \times 10^{-34} \text{ J} \cdot \text{s})(2 \times 10^{15} \text{ s}^{-1}) = 1.326 \times 10^{-18} \text{ J}$$

60. **C** The energy of the emitted photon is equal to the difference between energy levels 4 and 2. Thus:

$$-5.7 \text{ eV} - (-9.2 \text{ eV}) = 3.5 \text{ eV}.$$

61. **B** Using the Bohr equation, we have

$$f = \frac{E_i - E_f}{h}$$

where the energy difference is in joules.
We know from question 60 that the energy difference is equal to 3.5 eV, thus:

$$f = \frac{(3.5 \text{ eV})(1.6 \times 10^{-19} \text{ J / eV})}{6.63 \times 10^{-34} \text{ Js}} = 8.446 \times 10^{14} \text{s}^{-1}$$

and

$$\lambda = \frac{c}{f} = 3.55 \times 10^{-7} \text{ m} = 355 \text{ nm}$$

62. **C** In any hydrogen-like atom, the greatest energy emitted is a transition to the lowest energy state, level 1. In this case a transition from level 2 to level 1 emits the most energy.
63. **B** By definition, 1 u is equal to 1/12 the mass of the carbon atom.
64. **C** The number of neutrons is equal to the difference

$$A - Z = 238 - 92 = 146.$$

65. **B** "K-capture" is an alternative term for "electron capture."
66. **A** Balancing the superscripts on the two sides of the arrow, we see that the mass number for X must be 31 − 30 = 1.
67. **B** Radon decays by alpha-particle emission. Alpha particles are helium nuclei.
68. **C** Iron has the most stable nuclear isotope, based on the graph of average binding energy per nucleon.
69. **B** Planck's constant is expreseed in units of joules × seconds, which represent energy × time. Thus, the uncertainty principle can be expressed as $\Delta E \, \Delta t \geq h/2\pi$. Planck's constant, *h*, is also referred to as "the elementary quantum of action."
70. **B** Graphite is sometimes used as a moderator in a fission reactor. Water can be used also.

Solutions to Section II

1. (a) A free-body diagram for the mass *m* is shown below:

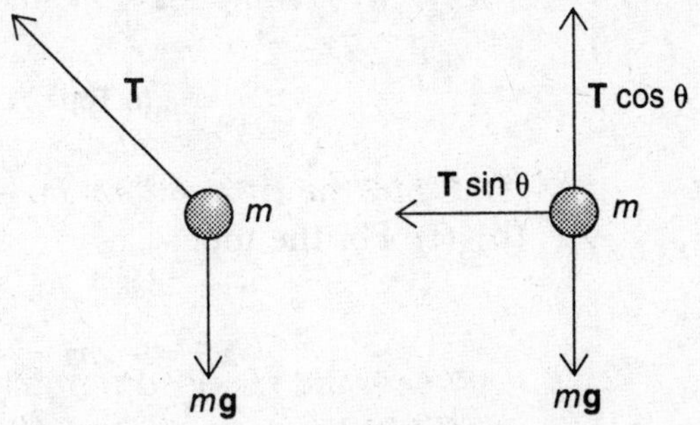

(b) In equilibrium the sum of all vector forces is equal to zero. If there is acceleration, the sum of all vector forces must equal *ma*. In the vertical direction, we have equilibrium between the weight (*mg*) and the upward component of the tension:

$$\Sigma F_y = 0 = T\cos\theta - mg$$

This establishes that

$$T = \frac{mg}{\cos\theta}$$

In the x-direction, the horizontal component of the tension is in the same line as the apparent centrifugal force acting on the mass since the ring stand is resting on the rotating platform. Thus,

$$\Sigma \mathbf{F}_x = ma = m\omega^2 r = \mathbf{T} \sin \theta$$

Substituting for the tension T, we obtain

$$\tan \theta = \frac{\omega^2 r}{\mathbf{g}}$$

(c) To find θ, we first need to know the value of the angular frequency:

$$\omega = \frac{2\pi}{T} = \frac{6.28}{0.45\text{s}} = 14 \text{ rad/s}$$

Making the other substitutions, we find that

$$\tan \theta = \frac{\omega^2 r}{\mathbf{g}} = \frac{(14 \; rad/s)^2 (0.25 \; m)}{9.8 \; m/s^2} = 5$$

Thus angle $\theta = 78.7°$.

2. (a) The free-body diagrams for the top (i) and bottom (ii) situations is given below:

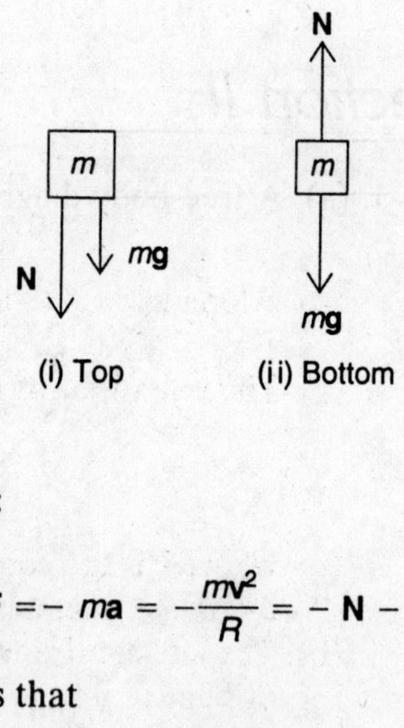

(b) (i) For the top:

$$\Sigma \mathbf{F} = -\, ma = -\frac{mv^2}{R} = -\,\mathbf{N} - \mathbf{mg}$$

This implies that

$$\mathbf{N} = \frac{mv^2}{R} - mg$$

(ii) For the bottom:

$$\Sigma \mathbf{F} = ma = \frac{mv^2}{R} = \mathbf{N} - mg$$

This implies that

$$\mathbf{N} = \frac{mv^2}{R} + mg$$

(c) We want the reaction force **N** at the top to be equal to $m\mathbf{g}$. Thus,

$$N = \frac{mv^2}{R} - mg$$

$$mg = \frac{mv^2}{R} - mg$$

$$2gR = v^2$$

We now need to find the square of the velocity, using conservation of energy:

$$mgh = mg(2R) + \left(\frac{1}{2}\right)mv^2$$

$$v^2 = 2gh - 4gR$$

Substituting, we get

$$2gR = 2gh - 4gR$$

which implies that $h = 3R$.

3. (a) For diffraction our relationship is

$$n\lambda = d \sin \theta$$

The information given is that $\lambda = 501.5$ nm, $n = 2$, and $\theta = 45°$. Solving for d, we get $d = 1.433 \times 10^{-6}$ m. The reciprocal of d is the number of lines per meter. Thus

$$\frac{1}{d} = 69{,}706.28 \text{ lines/m} = 698 \text{ lines/mm}$$

(b) Along with the value for d obtained in part (a), we use $n = 1$ and $\lambda = 667.8$ nm to solve for θ. Direct substitution yields $\theta = 27.8°$.

4. (a) The equation for heat transfer is

$$\frac{\Delta Q}{\Delta t} = \frac{kA\,\Delta T}{\Delta L}$$

where k is the conductivity in units of watts per meter · kelvin, and ΔL is the thickness in meters.

(b) The left-hand side of the equation for part (a) is the rate of change of heat in units of joules per second. We can do the dimensional analysis on the right-hand side to verify the units:

$$(\text{W/m} \cdot \text{K})(\text{m})(\text{m})(\text{K}) / \text{m} = \text{W} = \text{J/s}$$

(c) A is the total surface area. The dimensions in SI units are $\ell = 0.5$ m, $h = 0.2$ m, $w = 0.2$ m. Each square side has an area of 0.04 m². Each rectangular side has an area of 0.1 m². Thus $A = 0.48$ m². Given that $\Delta T = 30$ K, we have

$$\frac{\Delta Q}{\Delta t} = \frac{(0.045 \text{ W / m} \cdot K)(0.48 \text{ m}^2)(30 \text{ K})}{0.03 \text{ m}} = 21.6 \text{ J/s}$$

In 1 hr, we transfer 77,760 J, which is equal to 18,558.472 Cal. Now, 80 cal/g is needed to melt ice at 0° C. Thus, $m = 232$ g of ice must melt in 1 hr.

5. (a) The electron is initially projected into the field at some arbitrary position relative to the ground. We can treat this as the "zero" level and determine the total time of flight. From the theory of projectiles we know that the magnitude of the acceleration of the electron (downward) is given by $\mathbf{a} = e\mathbf{E}/m$. Substituting, we get

$$\mathbf{a} = \frac{e\mathbf{E}}{m} = \frac{(1.6 \times 10^{-19}\ \text{C})(600\ \text{N/C})}{9.1 \times 10^{-31}\ \text{kg}} = 1.05 \times 10^{14}\ \text{m/s}^2$$

Now, the initial vertical velocity is given by

$$\mathbf{v}_{0y} = \mathbf{v}_0 \sin\theta = (300{,}000\ \text{m/s}) \sin 35 = 172{,}073\ \text{m/s}$$

The total time is equal to

$$t = \frac{2\mathbf{V}_{oy}}{\mathbf{a}} = 3.28 \times 10^{-9}\text{s}$$

(b) The maximum height achieved by the electron is given by

$$y = \left(\frac{1}{2}\right)\mathbf{a}t^2 = (0.5)(1.05 \times 10^{14}\ \text{m/s}^2)(1.64 \times 10^{-9}\text{s})^2 = 1.4 \times 10^{-4}\text{m}$$

where we have used half the total time of flight and incorporated the maximum height at the equivalent free-fall distance in this uniform electric field, provided there is uniformly accelerated motion.

(c) Neglecting air resistance and gravity, the horizontal displacement, x, in the total time of flight is given by the product of the total time and the horizontal velocity, with

$$\mathbf{V}_{ox} = \mathbf{V}_o \cos\theta = 245{,}745.6\ \text{m/s}$$

Thus:

$$x = (245{,}745.6\ \text{m/s})(3.27 \times 10^{-9}\ \text{s}) = 8 \times 10^{-4}\ \text{m}$$

6. (a) To find the mass defect we first find the total constituent mass:

$$88\ \text{protons: } m = (88)(1.0078) = 88.6864\ \text{u}$$

$$138\ \text{neutrons: } m = (138)(1.0087) = 139.2006\ \text{u}$$

$$M\ (\text{total}) = 227.8870\ \text{u}$$

Then we have

$$\text{Mass defect} = 227.8870\ \text{u} - 226.0244\ \text{u} = 1.8626\ \text{u}$$

(b) The total binding energy is

$$BE = (931.5\ \text{MeV/u})(1.8626\ \text{u}) = 1735.0119\ \text{MeV}.$$

The binding energy per nucleon is

$$BE\,/\,\text{nucleon} = 1735.0119\,/\,226 = 7.677\ \text{MeV}$$

(c) The equivalent mass of quantity Q is given by

$$Q = 226.0244 - 222.0165 - 4.0026 = 0.0053\ \text{u}$$

Then the energy associated with Q is

$$E = (931.5\ \text{MeV / u})(0.0053\ \text{u}) = 4.94\ \text{MeV}$$

Answer Sheet: Practice Examination 2

1. Ⓐ Ⓑ Ⓒ Ⓓ Ⓔ
2. Ⓐ Ⓑ Ⓒ Ⓓ Ⓔ
3. Ⓐ Ⓑ Ⓒ Ⓓ Ⓔ
4. Ⓐ Ⓑ Ⓒ Ⓓ Ⓔ
5. Ⓐ Ⓑ Ⓒ Ⓓ Ⓔ
6. Ⓐ Ⓑ Ⓒ Ⓓ Ⓔ
7. Ⓐ Ⓑ Ⓒ Ⓓ Ⓔ
8. Ⓐ Ⓑ Ⓒ Ⓓ Ⓔ
9. Ⓐ Ⓑ Ⓒ Ⓓ Ⓔ
10. Ⓐ Ⓑ Ⓒ Ⓓ Ⓔ
11. Ⓐ Ⓑ Ⓒ Ⓓ Ⓔ
12. Ⓐ Ⓑ Ⓒ Ⓓ Ⓔ
13. Ⓐ Ⓑ Ⓒ Ⓓ Ⓔ
14. Ⓐ Ⓑ Ⓒ Ⓓ Ⓔ
15. Ⓐ Ⓑ Ⓒ Ⓓ Ⓔ
16. Ⓐ Ⓑ Ⓒ Ⓓ Ⓔ
17. Ⓐ Ⓑ Ⓒ Ⓓ Ⓔ
18. Ⓐ Ⓑ Ⓒ Ⓓ Ⓔ
19. Ⓐ Ⓑ Ⓒ Ⓓ Ⓔ
20. Ⓐ Ⓑ Ⓒ Ⓓ Ⓔ
21. Ⓐ Ⓑ Ⓒ Ⓓ Ⓔ
22. Ⓐ Ⓑ Ⓒ Ⓓ Ⓔ
23. Ⓐ Ⓑ Ⓒ Ⓓ Ⓔ
24. Ⓐ Ⓑ Ⓒ Ⓓ Ⓔ
25. Ⓐ Ⓑ Ⓒ Ⓓ Ⓔ
26. Ⓐ Ⓑ Ⓒ Ⓓ Ⓔ
27. Ⓐ Ⓑ Ⓒ Ⓓ Ⓔ
28. Ⓐ Ⓑ Ⓒ Ⓓ Ⓔ
29. Ⓐ Ⓑ Ⓒ Ⓓ Ⓔ
30. Ⓐ Ⓑ Ⓒ Ⓓ Ⓔ
31. Ⓐ Ⓑ Ⓒ Ⓓ Ⓔ
32. Ⓐ Ⓑ Ⓒ Ⓓ Ⓔ
33. Ⓐ Ⓑ Ⓒ Ⓓ Ⓔ
34. Ⓐ Ⓑ Ⓒ Ⓓ Ⓔ
35. Ⓐ Ⓑ Ⓒ Ⓓ Ⓔ
36. Ⓐ Ⓑ Ⓒ Ⓓ Ⓔ
37. Ⓐ Ⓑ Ⓒ Ⓓ Ⓔ
38. Ⓐ Ⓑ Ⓒ Ⓓ Ⓔ
39. Ⓐ Ⓑ Ⓒ Ⓓ Ⓔ
40. Ⓐ Ⓑ Ⓒ Ⓓ Ⓔ
41. Ⓐ Ⓑ Ⓒ Ⓓ Ⓔ
42. Ⓐ Ⓑ Ⓒ Ⓓ Ⓔ
43. Ⓐ Ⓑ Ⓒ Ⓓ Ⓔ
44. Ⓐ Ⓑ Ⓒ Ⓓ Ⓔ
45. Ⓐ Ⓑ Ⓒ Ⓓ Ⓔ
46. Ⓐ Ⓑ Ⓒ Ⓓ Ⓔ
47. Ⓐ Ⓑ Ⓒ Ⓓ Ⓔ
48. Ⓐ Ⓑ Ⓒ Ⓓ Ⓔ
49. Ⓐ Ⓑ Ⓒ Ⓓ Ⓔ
50. Ⓐ Ⓑ Ⓒ Ⓓ Ⓔ
51. Ⓐ Ⓑ Ⓒ Ⓓ Ⓔ
52. Ⓐ Ⓑ Ⓒ Ⓓ Ⓔ
53. Ⓐ Ⓑ Ⓒ Ⓓ Ⓔ
54. Ⓐ Ⓑ Ⓒ Ⓓ Ⓔ
55. Ⓐ Ⓑ Ⓒ Ⓓ Ⓔ
56. Ⓐ Ⓑ Ⓒ Ⓓ Ⓔ
57. Ⓐ Ⓑ Ⓒ Ⓓ Ⓔ
58. Ⓐ Ⓑ Ⓒ Ⓓ Ⓔ
59. Ⓐ Ⓑ Ⓒ Ⓓ Ⓔ
60. Ⓐ Ⓑ Ⓒ Ⓓ Ⓔ
61. Ⓐ Ⓑ Ⓒ Ⓓ Ⓔ
62. Ⓐ Ⓑ Ⓒ Ⓓ Ⓔ
63. Ⓐ Ⓑ Ⓒ Ⓓ Ⓔ
64. Ⓐ Ⓑ Ⓒ Ⓓ Ⓔ
65. Ⓐ Ⓑ Ⓒ Ⓓ Ⓔ
66. Ⓐ Ⓑ Ⓒ Ⓓ Ⓔ
67. Ⓐ Ⓑ Ⓒ Ⓓ Ⓔ
68. Ⓐ Ⓑ Ⓒ Ⓓ Ⓔ
69. Ⓐ Ⓑ Ⓒ Ⓓ Ⓔ
70. Ⓐ Ⓑ Ⓒ Ⓓ Ⓔ

Useful Constants

1 atomic mass unit	$1\ \mu = 1.66 \times 10^{-27}$ kg
Rest mass of the proton	$m_p = 1.67 \times 10^{-27}$ kg
Rest mass of the neutron	$m_n = 1.67 \times 10^{-27}$ kg
Rest mass of the electron	$m_e = 9.11 \times 10^{-31}$ kg
Magnitude of the electron charge	$e = 1.60 \times 10^{-19}$ C
Avogadro's number	$N_0 = 6.02 \times 10^{23}$ per mole
Universal gas constant	$R = 8.32$ J/(mole · K)
Boltzmann's constant	$k_B = 1.38 \times 10^{-23}$ J/K
Speed of light	$c = 3 \times 10^8$ m/s
Planck's constant	$h = 6.63 \times 10^{-34}$ J · s $= 4.14 \times 10^{-15}$ eV · s
1 electron volt	1 eV $= 1.6 \times 10^{-19}$ J
Vacuum permittivity	$\epsilon_0 = 8.85 \times 10^{-12}$ C^2/Nm^2
Coulomb's law constant	$k = 1/4\ \pi\epsilon_0 = 9 \times 10^9$ N · m^2/C^2
Vacuum permeability	$\mu_0 = 4\pi \times 10^{-7}$ Wb/(A · m)
Magnetic constant	$k' = k/c^2 = \mu_0/4\pi = 10^{-7}$ Wb/(A · m)
Acceleration due to gravity at Earth's surface	$g = 9.8$ m/s^2
Universal gravitational constant	$G = 6.67 \times 10^{-11}$ m^3/(kg · s^2)
1 atmosphere pressure	1 atm $= 1.0 \times 10^5$ N/m^2 $= 1.0 \times 10^5$ Pa
1 nanometer	1 nm $= 1.0 \times 10^{-9}$m

PRACTICE EXAMINATION 2

Section I

Multiple-Choice Questions

70 questions
90 minutes
50 percent of total grade

Directions: For each of the questions or incomplete statements below there are five choices. In each case select the best answer or completion and fill in the corresponding oval on the answer sheet.

I. All frames of reference are assumed to be inertial.
II. Electrical current will follow the direction of a positive charge (conventional current).
III. For any isolated charge, the potential at infinity is taken to be equal to zero.

1. A vector has the following components: $\mathbf{a}_x = 3$ units and $\mathbf{a}_y = 5$ units. What angle does this vector make with the positive x-axis?
(A) 31°
(B) 43°
(C) 51°
(D) 59°
(E) 65°

2. Two vectors, **A** and **B**, have components $\mathbf{a}_x = -2$, $\mathbf{a}_y = 3$, $\mathbf{b}_x = 1$, and $\mathbf{b}_y = 4$. What is the magnitude of the vector **A** + **B**?
(A) 3.8
(B) 6.2
(C) 8.2
(D) 5.6
(E) 7.1

3. How long will a rock, thrown from a height of 96 meters with an initial velocity of 20 meters per second, take to hit the ground?
(A) 1.7 s
(B) 2.8 s
(C) 3.3 s
(D) 4.8 s
(E) 5.6 s

4. A car with a 500-newton driver goes over a hill that has a radius of 60 meters, as shown below. The velocity of the car is 20 meters per second. What are the force and the direction that the car exerts on the driver?
(A) 840 N, up
(B) 160 N, down
(C) 160 N, up
(D) 840 N, down
(E) 500 N, up

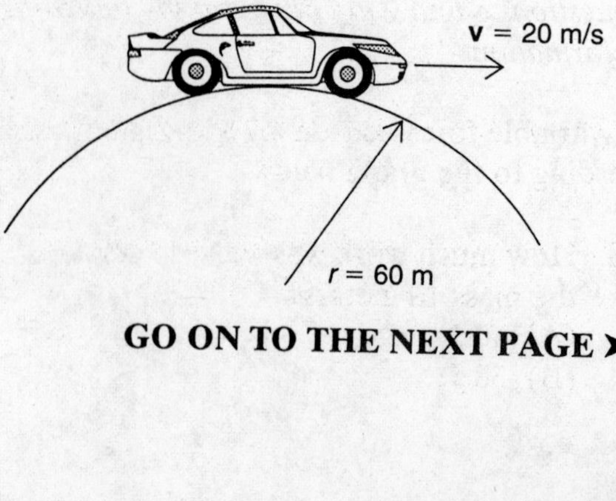

GO ON TO THE NEXT PAGE ➤

5. At what angle should a projectile be launched in order to achieve the maximum range for a given initial velocity?
(A) 0°
(B) 30°
(C) 45°
(D) 60°
(E) 90°

6. In the diagram below, two masses connected by a light string slide over frictionless surfaces. If the angle of the incline is θ, what is the acceleration of both masses?

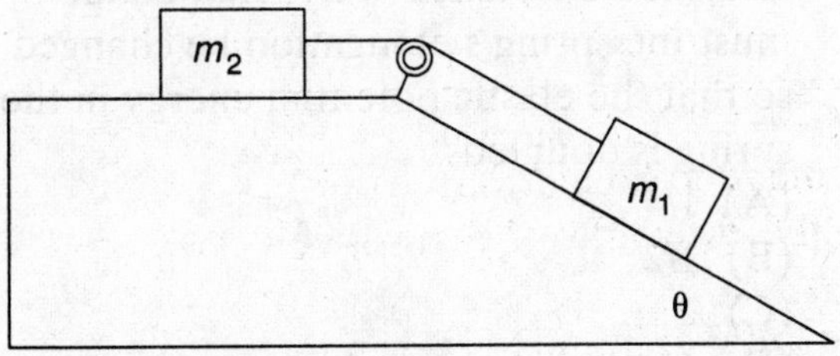

(A) $(m_1 + m_2)\mathbf{g} \sin \theta$
(B) $m_2\, \mathbf{g} / (m_1 + m_2)$
(C) $m_1\, \mathbf{g} \cos \theta / (m_1 + m_2)$
(D) $(m_1 / m_1 m_2)\, \mathbf{g} \sin \theta$
(E) $m_1\, \mathbf{g} \sin \theta / (m_1 + m_2)$

7. A boat moving due north crosses a 190-meter-wide river with a velocity of 8 meters per second relative to the water. The river flows east with a velocity of 4 meters per second. How long will the boat take to cross the river?
(A) 27 s
(B) 24 s
(C) 21 s
(D) 29 s
(E) 26 s

Questions 8 and 9 are based on the following information:

A variable force acts on a 2-kilogram mass according to the graph below.

8. How much work was done to displace the mass 10 meters?
(A) 40 J
(B) 38 J

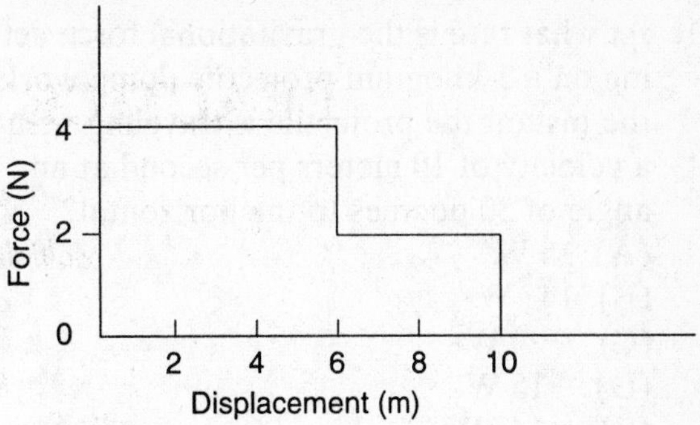

(C) 32 J
(D) 30 J
(E) 26 J

9. What was the average force supplied to the mass for the entire 10-meter displacement?
(A) 3.2 N
(B) 1.2 N
(C) 4.4 N
(D) 4 N
(E) 2.6 N

10. A block is pushed along a frictionless surface for a distance of 2.5 meters, as shown below. How much work has been done if a force of 10 newtons makes an angle of 60 degrees with the horizontal?

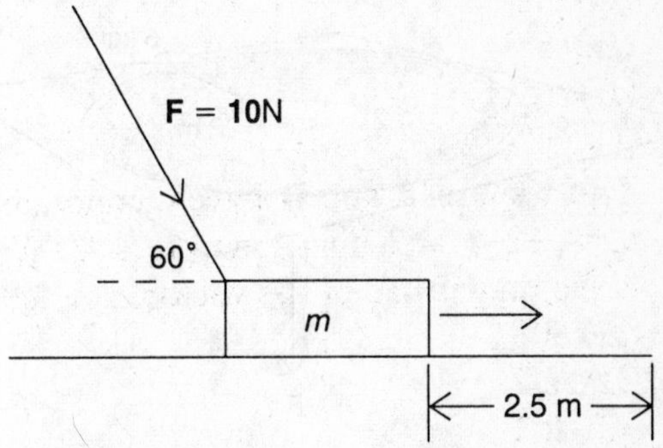

(A) 10.5 J
(B) 8.5 J
(C) 6.5 J
(D) 12.5 J
(E) 25 J

GO ON TO THE NEXT PAGE ➤

11. At what rate is the gravitational force acting on a 3-kilogram projectile doing work the instant the projectile is traveling with a velocity of 10 meters per second at an angle of 30 degrees to the horizontal?
(A) 15 W
(B) 147 W
(C) −29 W
(D) −15 W
(E) −147 W

12. A person weighing 490 newtons is standing on a bathroom scale in an elevator that is accelerating upward at a rate of 0.2 meter per second squared. What does the bathroom scale indicate the person's weight is?
(A) 480 N
(B) 490 N
(C) 588 N
(D) 500 N
(E) 392 N

13. A 5-kilogram disk is attached to a light string, as shown below. The disk is rotating in a circle of radius 2 meters with an angular velocity of 3 radians per second. What is the angular momentum of the disk?

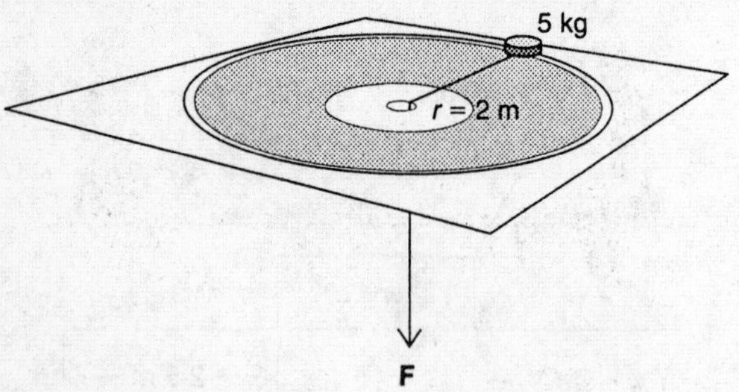

(A) 70 kg · m²/s
(B) 60 kg · m²/s
(C) 40 kg · m²/s
(D) 30 kg · m²/s
(E) 20 kg · m²/s

14. A hockey puck with a mass of 0.2 kilogram is sliding along ice that can be considered frictionless with a velocity of 10 meters per second. The puck then crosses over onto a rough floor that has a coefficient of kinetic friction equal to 0.2. How far will the puck travel before friction stops it?
(A) 17.6 m
(B) 42.7 m
(C) 25.5 m
(D) 59.6 m
(E) 62.3 m

15. A spring with a force constant k is stretched a distance x. By what factor must the spring's elongation be changed so that the elastic potential energy in the spring is doubled?
(A) 1/4
(B) 1/2
(C) 2
(D) 4
(E) $\sqrt{2}$

Questions 16 and 17 are based on the information and the diagram below:

Two masses are connected by a light string. The horizontal mass of 2 kilograms is being pulled to the right with a force of 30 newtons along a frictionless surface.

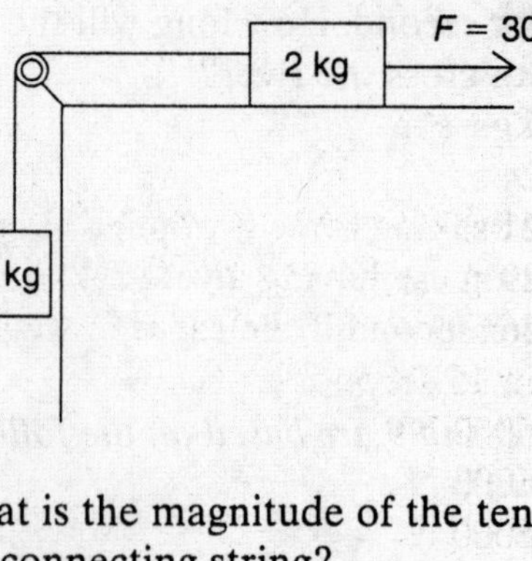

16. What is the magnitude of the tension in the connecting string?
(A) 16.5 N
(B) 18.7 N
(C) 20 N
(D) 34.6 N
(E) 44.2 N

GO ON TO THE NEXT PAGE ➤

17. What is the magnitude of the acceleration of both masses?
(A) 3.5 m/s^2
(B) 6.75 m/s^2
(C) 8.25 m/s^2
(D) 9.0 m/s^2
(E) 10.3 m/s^2

18. Which of the following is an expression for power?
(A) $\mathbf{F}t / m$
(B) $\mathbf{F}m / t$
(C) $\mathbf{F}^2 m/t$
(D) $\mathbf{F}m^2/t$
(E) $\mathbf{F}^2 t/m$

19. A 0.3 kilogram mass rests on top of a spring that has been compressed by 0.4 meter. The force constant for this spring is 20 newtons per meter. When released, how high will the mass rise?
(A) 1.24 m
(B) 0.75 m
(C) 0.54 m
(D) 1.04 m
(E) 1.34 m

20. Which of the following is an equivalent expression of the units for a spring's force constant k?
(A) kg · m^2/s^2
(B) kg · m/s
(C) kg · s^2
(D) kg/s^2
(E) kg · s/m

21. What braking force is applied to a 2500-kilogram car having a velocity of 30 meters per second if the car is brought to a stop in 15 seconds?
(A) 5000 N
(B) 6000 N
(C) 8000 N
(D) 10,000 N
(E) 12,000 N

22. A 1-kilogram object is moving to the right with a velocity of 6 meters per second. It collides with, and sticks to, a 2-kilogram mass, also moving to the right, with a velocity of 3 meters per second. How much kinetic energy was lost in this interaction?
(A) 1.5 J
(B) 2 J
(C) 3 J
(D) 3.5 J
(E) 0 J

23. A ball with a mass of 0.2 kilogram strikes a wall with a velocity of 3 meters per second. It bounces straight back with a velocity of 1 meter per second. What was the magnitude of the change in momentum for this ball?
(A) 0.1 kg · m/s
(B) 0.8 kg · m/s
(C) 0.4 kg · m/s
(D) 0.6 kg · m/s
(E) 0.7 kg · m/s

24. A 50-kilogram person is sitting on a seesaw 1.2 meters from the balance point. On the other side, a 70-kilogram person is balanced. How far from the balance point is the second person sitting?

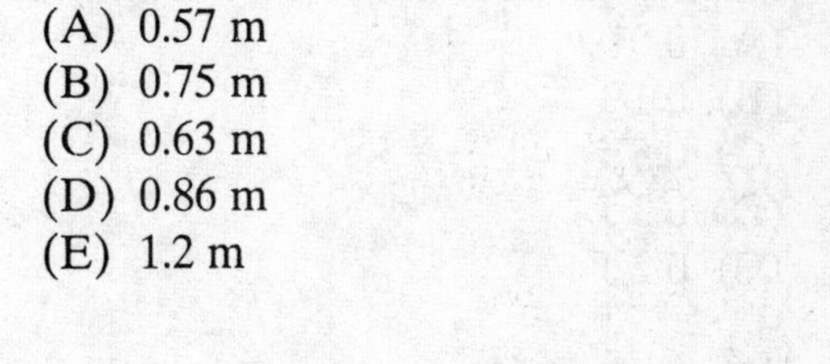

(A) 0.57 m
(B) 0.75 m
(C) 0.63 m
(D) 0.86 m
(E) 1.2 m

25. What is the net torque acting on the pivot supporting a 2-meter-long, 10-kilogram beam, as shown below?

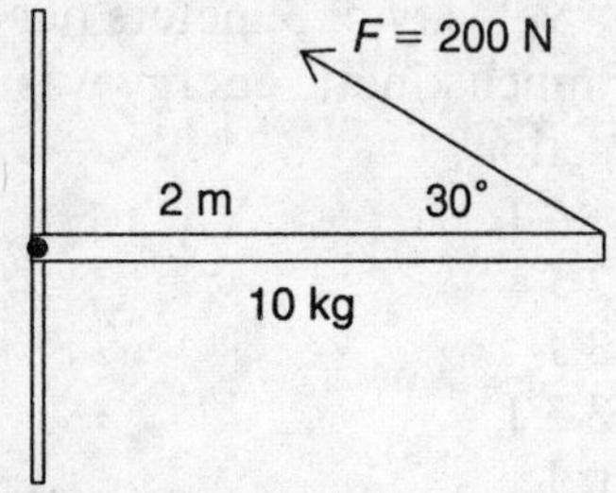

(A) 198 N · m
(B) −198 N · m
(C) −102 N · m
(D) 102 N · m
(E) −120 N · m

26. Which of the following is an equivalent expression for the maximum velocity attained by a mass oscillating horizontally along a frictionless surface? The mass is attached to a spring with a force constant *k* and has an amplitude of oscillations of *A* meters.
(A) $\sqrt{Ak/m}$
(B) $\sqrt{A^2mk}$
(C) $\sqrt{A^2m/k}$
(D) $\sqrt{A^2k/m}$
(E) Akm

27. A 0.5-kilogram mass is attached to a spring with a force constant of 50 newtons per meter. What is the total energy stored in the mass-spring system if the amplitude of oscillations is 2 centimeters?
(A) 0.01 J
(B) 0.1 J
(C) 0.5 J
(D) 0.3 J
(E) 0.2 J

28. What is the value of **g** at a position above the Earth's surface that is equal to the Earth's radius?
(A) 9.8 m/s^2
(B) 4.9 m/s^2
(C) 3.35 m/s^2
(D) 2.45 m/s^2
(E) 1.6 m/s^2

29. What is the escape velocity from the Moon, given that the mass of the Moon is 7.2×10^{22} kg and the radius of the Moon is 1.778×10^6 m?
(A) 1.64×10^3 m/s
(B) 2.32×10^3 m/s
(C) 2.69×10^6 m/s
(D) 5.38×10 m/s
(E) 3×10^8 m/s

30. What is the gravitational force of attraction between two 40,000-kilogram trucks that are separated by 0.5 meter?
(A) 0.0054 N
(B) 0.43 N
(C) 0.75 N
(D) 0.21 N
(E) 0.57 N

GO ON TO THE NEXT PAGE ➤

Questions 31–33 are based on the following information and graph.

Three-tenths kilogram of a substance begins as a solid and absorbs energy according to the graph below:

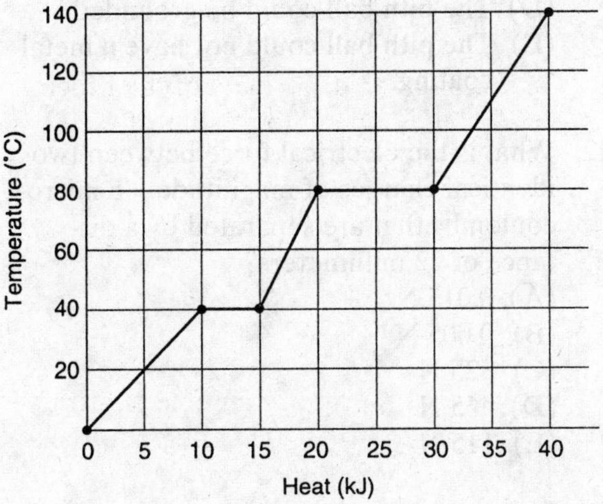

31. What is the melting point of this substance?
(A) 0°C
(B) 40°C
(C) 80°C
(D) 100°C
(E) 140°C

32. What is the latent heat of fusion of this substance?
(A) 5 kJ/kg
(B) 7.5 kJ/kg
(C) 9.5 kJ/kg
(D) 11.3 kJ/kg
(E) 16.7 kJ/kg

33. What is the specific heat capacity of this substance in the liquid phase?
(A) 0.67 kJ/kg · °C
(B) 0.38 kJ/kg · °C
(C) 0.18 kJ/kg · °C
(D) 0.42 kJ/kg · °C
(E) 0.25 kJ/kg · °C

34. An ideal gas undergoes an isochoric change. Which of the following remains constant?
(A) Phase
(B) Temperature
(C) Internal energy
(D) Pressure
(E) Volume

35. At 2 atmospheres of pressure, 100 cubic meters of an ideal gas at 50° degrees Celsius is heated until its pressure and absolute temperature are doubled. What is the new volume of the gas?
(A) 62 m^3
(B) 100 m^3
(C) 58 m^3
(D) 50 m^3
(E) 112 m^3

36. Which of the following graphs represents an isothermal expansion of an ideal gas?

(A)
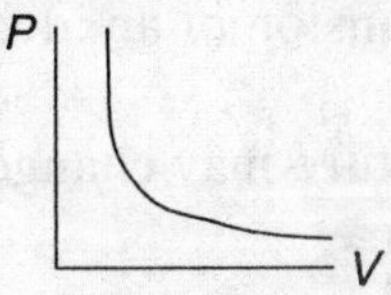

(B)
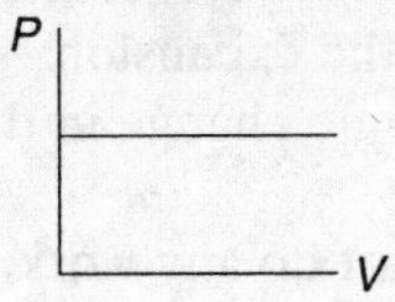

(C)
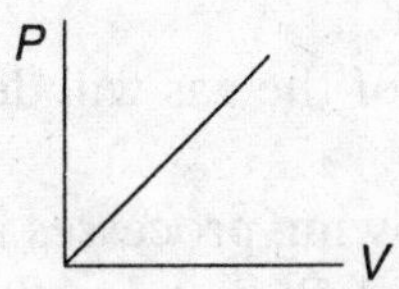

(D)
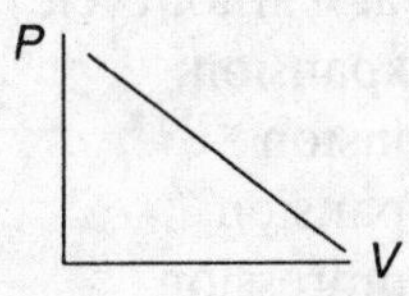

(E)
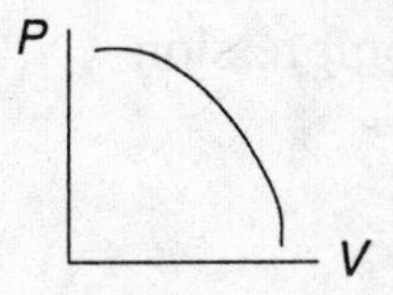

GO ON TO THE NEXT PAGE ➤

37. At a temperature of 30 degrees Celsius, 1 mole of hydrogen gas and 1 mole of nitrogen gas must have the same
(A) density
(B) number of molecules
(C) root mean square velocity
(D) volume
(E) pressure

38. A sample of helium gas is compressed isothermally until its volume is one-half the original. If the root mean square velocity of the molecules at the original volume was **v**, the new root mean square velocity will be equal to
(A) 2**v**
(B) 4**v**
(C) **v**/2
(D) **v**
(E) **v**/4

39. Which of the following statements about the adiabatic expansion of an ideal gas is correct?
(A) The temperature may change during the expansion.
(B) The temperature must remain constant during the expansion.
(C) There will be no change in the internal energy.
(D) The gas cannot do any work during the expansion.
(E) The entropy of the gas will decrease.

40. Which of the following processes is *not* involved in an ideal Carnot cycle?
(A) Isothermal expansion
(B) Isobaric expansion
(C) Adiabatic expansion
(D) Adiabatic compression
(E) Isothermal compression

41. A charged rod attracts a suspended pith ball. Which of the following statements is correct?
(A) The pith ball has the same sign charge as the rod.
(B) The rod must be negatively charged.
(C) The pith ball might be neutral.
(D) The pith ball could be grounded.
(E) The pith ball could not have a metal coating.

42. What is the electrical force between two identical charges of magnitude +5 microcoulombs that are separated by a distance of 22 millimeters?
(A) 0.015 N
(B) 0.005 N
(C) 325 N
(D) 465 N
(E) 115 N

43. The ratio of Coulomb's constant k to the magnetic constant k' is equal, where **c** is the speed of light, to
(A) $\mathbf{c}^2$
(B) $\sqrt{\mathbf{c}}$
(C) **c**
(D) 2 **c**
(E) **c** / 2

44. An electron is moving between two metal plates that are separated by 20 millimeters. The acceleration of the electron is 3 $\times 10^{12}$ meters per second squared. What is the potential difference between the two plates?
(A) 17 V
(B) 0.34 V
(C) 5.7 V
(D) 0.27 V
(E) 12.2 V

GO ON TO THE NEXT PAGE ➤

45. A circuit consists of two 10-microfarad capacitors in series, which are then connected in parallel to a 5-microfarad capacitor, as shown below. What is the equivalent capacitance of this circuit?

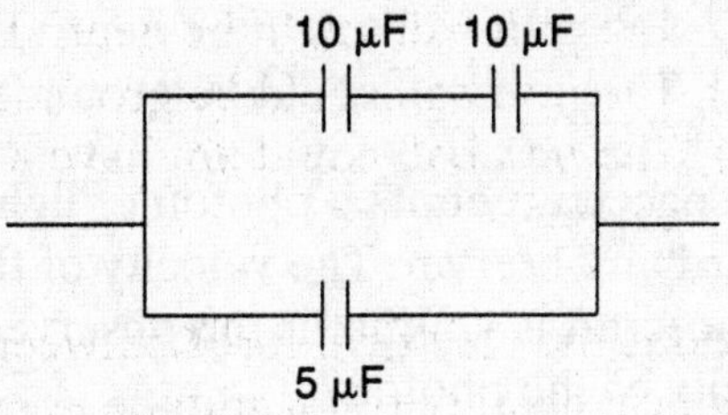

(A) 10 μF
(B) 5 μF
(C) 2 μF
(D) 4 μF
(E) 3 μF

46. Which of the following units is equivalent to 1 ohm of resistance?
(A) kg · m²/C²
(B) kg · m / C
(C) kg · m²/sC²
(D) kg · C²/m · s²
(E) kg · m · C / s

47. An electric motor operates from a 120-volt source, using 4 amperes of current. What is the power rating of this motor?
(A) 30 W
(B) 48 W
(C) 120 W
(D) 480 W
(E) 124 W

48. Which of the following correctly describes the magnetic field near a long, straight wire?
(A) The field consists of straight lines perpendicular to the wire.
(B) The field consists of straight lines parallel to the wire.
(C) The field consists of radial lines originating from the wire.
(D) The field consists of spirals wrapping around the wire.
(E) The field consists of concentric circles centered on the wire.

49. A current-carrying wire is rotating by itself in a uniform magnetic field. The rotation will continue until the plane of the loop is
(A) perpendicular to the field
(B) parallel to the field
(C) at a 45° angle to the field
(D) either perpendicular or parallel to the field, depending on the strength of the current
(E) either perpendicular or parallel to the field, depending on the strength of the field

50. On which of the following does the magnetic field inside a solenoid of *N* turns not depend?
(A) The core material
(B) The length of the solenoid
(C) The current in the solenoid
(D) The number of turns of wire
(E) The diameter of the solenoid

51. When is the back emf of an electric motor the greatest?
(A) When the motor is first switched on
(B) While the motor is speeding up
(C) When the motor is at maximum speed
(D) While the motor is slowing down
(E) None of the above

52. A steel wire is stretched between two points. The length of the wire is 2.5 meters, and its mass is 0.5 kilogram. A transverse pulse is sent down the wire and returns in 0.2 second. What is the tension in the wire?
(A) 125 N
(B) 115 N
(C) 120 N
(D) 100 N
(E) 130 N

GO ON TO THE NEXT PAGE ➤

53. Which of the following represents the units for sound wave intensity?
(A) J / s
(B) W/m²
(C) W · m²
(D) J/m²
(E) W / s

54. A ray of light is incident from air to a glass plate at an angle of 30 degrees. If the absolute index of refraction of the glass is equal to 1.6, the angle of refraction is
(A) 9°
(B) 18°
(C) 30°
(D) 42°
(E) 50°

55. The colors observed in thin films are caused by interference and
(A) reflection
(B) refraction
(C) diffraction
(D) polarization
(E) luminosity

56. Which of the following *cannot* produce polarized light?
(A) A polaroid filter
(B) Reflection
(C) Scattering
(D) Selective absorption
(E) Diffraction

57. As the number of lines on a diffraction grating are increased,
(A) the spacing between the spectral lines increases
(B) the spacing between the spectral lines decreases
(C) the intensity of the spectral lines increases
(D) the intensity of the spectral lines decreases
(E) everything about the spectral lines remains the same

58. What must be a person's velocity, relative to the speed of light **c**, such that his observed mass is 1.5 times his rest mass?
(A) 0.5**c**
(B) 0.4**c**
(C) 0.75**c**
(D) 1.5**c**
(E) **c**

59. A spacecraft emits a photon of light toward an observer. The velocity of the spacecraft is **v**. What is the observed velocity of the photon?
(A) $\mathbf{c}/\sqrt{1 - \mathbf{v}^2/\mathbf{c}^2}$
(B) $\mathbf{c}\sqrt{1 - \mathbf{v}^2/\mathbf{c}^2}$
(C) **c** − **v**
(D) **c**
(E) **c** + **v**

60. What energy is associated with a 350-nanometer photon?
(A) 350 J
(B) 3.5×10^{-9} J
(C) 5.68×10^{-19} J
(D) 2.32×10^{-14} J
(E) 1.37×10^{-19} J

61. What is the de Broglie wavelength for a 1500-kilogram car moving with a velocity of 30 meters per second?
(A) 2.7×10^{-19} m
(B) 1.5×10^{-38} m
(C) 7.2×10^{-36} m
(D) 6.63×10^{-34} m
(E) 8.7×10^{-33} m

GO ON TO THE NEXT PAGE ➤

62. In a photoelectric effect experiment, increasing the intensity of the incident electromagnetic radiation will
(A) increase only the number of emitted electrons
(B) have no effect on any aspect of the experiment
(C) increase the maximum kinetic energy of the emitted electrons
(D) increase the de Broglie wavelength of the emitted electrons
(E) increase the stopping potential of the experiment

63. What happens to the half-life of a radioactive material as it decays?
(A) It decreases.
(B) It increases.
(C) It remains the same.
(D) The answer depends on the amount of material.
(E) The answer depends on the type of material.

64. The "characteristic time" for a radioactive substance is the time required to reduce the substance to what fraction of the original amount?
(A) $1 / e$
(B) $1 / \pi$
(C) $1 / 2$
(D) $1 / 10$
(E) e / π

65. What is the magnitude of the classical electron radius in a hydrogen atom?
(A) 0.5 nm
(B) 0.05 nm
(C) 1 nm
(D) 0.01 nm
(E) 0.1 nm

66. Photons can scatter electrons, and the trajectories of the electrons will obey the law of conservation of momentum. These facts are observed in the
(A) Rutherford scattering experiment
(B) Michelson-Morley experiment
(C) Compton effect
(D) Doppler effect
(E) Lorentz-Fitzgerald effect

67. As hydrogen is fused into helium, the stability of the new nuclei, compared to that of hydrogen, will
(A) be greater
(B) be less
(C) be the same
(D) depend on how much hydrogen is used
(E) depend on which atoms are being fused

68. How many neutrons are contained in the isotope $^{211}_{84}$Po?
(A) 84
(B) 211
(C) 295
(D) 127
(E) 156

69. Silver-108 has a half-life of 2.4 minutes. If M grams are originally present, what fraction will remain after 7.2 minutes have elapsed?
(A) M
(B) $M/2$
(C) $M/4$
(D) $M/8$
(E) $M/16$

70. What is the maximum angle at which alpha particles can be scattered in Rutherford's experiment?
(A) 180°
(B) 135°
(C) 90°
(D) 60°
(E) 45°

STOP

THIS IS THE END OF SECTION I.
YOU MAY USE ANY REMAINING TIME TO CHECK YOUR WORK IN THIS SECTION.

Section II

Free-Response Questions

6 questions
90 minutes
50 percent of total grade

> *Directions*: Solve the following problems. Be sure to show all work, including substitutions with units, and to explain clearly.

1. A cannon fires a shell with an initial velocity **v** and a launch angle θ from the ground. At a height *h* above the ground, fast winds would alter the trajectory of the shell. Under these conditions:

   (a) Derive an expression for the maximum range possible such that the projectile remains on course. Your expression should be in terms of **v**, **g**, and *h* only.

   (b) If $h = 2000$ meters and $\mathbf{v} = 500$ meters per second, what is the maximum range?

   (c) Using the information given in part (b), find the value of the launch angle θ.

2. Two cars are separated by 25 meters. Both are initially at rest. Then the car in front begins to accelerate uniformly at 2 meters per second squared. The second car, behind, begins to accelerate at 3 meters per second squared.

   (a) How long does it take the faster car to catch up with the slower car?

   (b) How far does the faster car go during that time?

   (c) What is the velocity of each car at the moment the second car catches up with the first car?

3. (a) Determine the root mean square velocities of hydrogen and oxygen molecules at 0 degree Celsius.

   (b) To what is the ratio of the root mean square velocity of hydrogen to the root mean square velocity of oxygen equal?

   (c) How does this ratio of root mean square velocities compare with the ratio of the molecular masses?

   (d) Write a formula that expresses the relationship described in part (c) for any two molecules X and Y.

   (e) Use the formula written in part (d) to determine the ratio of root mean square velocities of hydrogen and carbon dioxide at 0 degree Celsius.

GO ON TO THE NEXT PAGE ➤

4. Determine the magnitude of each current in the network shown below:

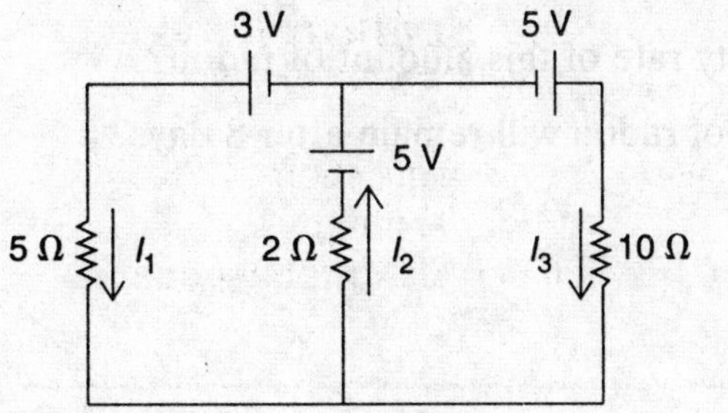

5. A person is looking at a fish in a tank of water from a nearly vertical position. The actual depth of the fish is h, and its apparent refractive depth is h'. The distance to each fish from the normal is x.

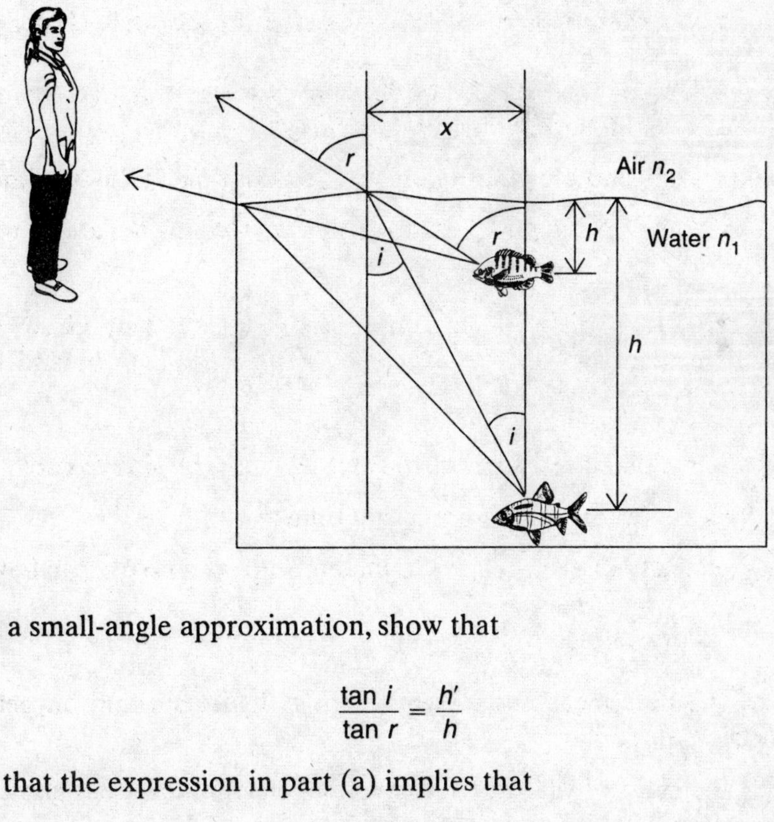

(a) Using a small-angle approximation, show that

$$\frac{\tan i}{\tan r} = \frac{h'}{h}$$

(b) Show that the expression in part (a) implies that

$$\frac{h'}{h} = \frac{n_2}{n_1}$$

where n_1 and n_2 are the absolute indices of refraction of the two media.

(c) If the absolute index of refraction for water is 1.33, and the actual depth of the fish is 1.5 meters, what is the observed depth of the fish?

6. The half-life of the isotope $^{222}_{86}Rn$ is 3.8 days.

   (a) How many atoms are contained in 5 milligrams of radon?

   (b) What is the activity rate of this amount of radon?

   (c) What percentage of radon will remain after 8 days?

STOP

THIS IS THE END OF SECTION II.
YOU MAY USE ANY REMAINING TIME TO CHECK YOUR WORK IN THIS SECTION.

Answer Key for Section I

1. **D**	15. **E**	29. **B**	43. **A**	57. **A**
2. **E**	16. **A**	30. **B**	44. **B**	58. **C**
3. **B**	17. **B**	31. **B**	45. **A**	59. **D**
4. **C**	18. **E**	32. **E**	46. **C**	60. **C**
5. **C**	19. **C**	33. **D**	47. **D**	61. **B**
6. **E**	20. **D**	34. **E**	48. **E**	62. **A**
7. **B**	21. **A**	35. **B**	49. **A**	63. **C**
8. **C**	22. **C**	36. **A**	50. **E**	64. **A**
9. **A**	23. **B**	37. **B**	51. **C**	65. **B**
10. **D**	24. **D**	38. **D**	52. **A**	66. **D**
11. **E**	25. **C**	39. **B**	53. **B**	67. **A**
12. **D**	26. **D**	40. **B**	54. **B**	68. **D**
13. **B**	27. **A**	41. **C**	55. **A**	69. **D**
14. **C**	28. **D**	42. **D**	56. **E**	70. **A**

Answer Explanations for Section I

1. **D** The angle is given by

$$\tan\theta = \frac{\mathbf{a_y}}{\mathbf{a_x}} = \frac{5}{3} = 1.67$$

Thus = $\theta = 59°$.

2. **E** The sum of two vectors can be found by adding their components:

$$\mathbf{c_x} = \mathbf{a_x} + \mathbf{b_x} = -2 + 1 = -1 \quad \text{and} \quad \mathbf{c_y} = \mathbf{a_y} + \mathbf{b_y} = 3 + 4 = 7$$

The magnitude of the sum is now given by the Pythagorean theorem:

$$|\mathbf{A}+\mathbf{B}|\sqrt{(-1)^2 + (7)^2} = \sqrt{50} = 7.1$$

3. **B** The formula for a downward displacement, *y*, is given by

$$-y = +\mathbf{v}_{0y}t + \left(\frac{1}{2}\right)\mathbf{g}t^2$$

Substituting known values gives

$$-96 = -20t - 4.9t^2$$

The time can be found by using the quadratic formula and taking the positive value:

$$t = \frac{-b \pm \sqrt{b^2-4ac}}{2a}$$

$$= \frac{-20 \pm \sqrt{400 + (4)(4.9)(96)}}{(2)(4.9)} = 2.8 \text{ s}$$

4. **C** The force that the car exerts on the driver is equal to the normal force **N**. If we write Newton's second law for the car at the top of the hill, we get

$$\Sigma \mathbf{F}_y = ma = \frac{-mv^2}{r} = \mathbf{N} - m\mathbf{g}$$

Since $\mathbf{W} = m\mathbf{g} = 500$ N, we know that the mass is approximately equal to 51 kg. Making the necessary substitutions for velocity and radius, we obtain $\mathbf{N} = +160$ N, up.

5. **C** The maximum range possible for a given initial velocity is achieved at an angle of 45°.
6. **E** From the diagram we can see that the force acting on mass m_1 is the component of its weight down the incline:

$$\mathbf{F} = m_1\mathbf{g} \sin \theta$$

However, this force must cause the two masses to accelerate together since they are coupled:

$$\mathbf{F} = (m_1 + m_2)\, \mathbf{a}$$

Equating these two expressions gives us the accleration:

$$\mathbf{a} = m_1\mathbf{g} \sin \theta \,/\, (m_1 + m_2)$$

7. **B** The two velocities are independent of each other. Thus, to find the time needed to cross the river, we consider only the velocity component involved in heading across the river:

$$t = \frac{190 \text{ m}}{8 \text{ m/s}} = 24 \text{ s (actually 23.75 s)}$$

8. **C** The work done by the variable force is equal to the total area under the graph. Using rectangles, we find this total area to be equivalent to 32 J of work.
9. **A** The average force applied is equal to the total work done, divided by the displacement:

$$\mathbf{F}_{avg} = \frac{32\ J}{10\ m} = 3.2 \text{ N}$$

10. **D** The work done is equal to the product of the magnitude of the force component parallel to the direction of motion and the displacement. In this case, the force component is equal to

$$(10 \text{ N}) \cos 60 = 5 \text{ N}$$

Thus,

$$W = \mathbf{Fd} = (5\text{ N})(2.5\text{ m}) = 12.5\text{ J}$$

11. **E** The force of gravity acting on the projectile (assuming $\mathbf{g} = -9.8$ m/s^2) is equal to -29.4 N. The rate at which work is done is equal to the power, which is found by multiplying the force and the instantaneous velocity along the same line. We need the vertical component of the velocity:

$$\mathbf{v_y} = (10\text{ m/s}) \sin 30 = 5\text{ m/s}$$

Thus, $P = -147$ W.

12. **D** The upward acceleration of the elevator will increase the force that the scale exerts on the person, who will observe an increase in his weight, determined as follows: Let **F** be the force that the scale exerts on the person (his perceived weight).

$$\mathbf{F} - mg = ma$$

The person weighs 490 N, implying a mass of 50 kg. The acceleration is 0.2 m/s^2. Making the necessary substitutions yields **F** = 500 N.

13. **B** The angular momentum is found as follows.

$$\mathbf{L} = m\mathbf{v}r = m\omega r^2 = (5\text{ kg})(3\text{ rad/s})(2\text{ m})^2 = 60\text{ kg}\cdot\text{m}^2\text{/s}$$

14. **C** The force of friction is given by $\mathbf{f} = -\mu m\mathbf{g}$ in this case. Since this is a net force acting on the puck,

$$\mathbf{f} = m\mathbf{a} = -\mu mg$$

Thus, $\mathbf{a} = -1.96$ m/s^2. We know that the puck is going to stop, so $\mathbf{v}_0^2 = 2\,\mathbf{ax}$. Given that the initial velocity is 10 m/s, and using the acceleration obtained above, we get $x = 25.5$ m.

15. **E** The elastic potential energy stored in a stretched spring is proportional to the square root of the spring's elongation. To double this quantity, the elongation must be increased by a factor equal to $\sqrt{2}$.

16. **A** Using free-body diagrams for both masses, we can set up the equations of motion for forces in the x and y directions:

In the x-direction: $30 - \mathbf{T} = m\mathbf{a} = 2\mathbf{a}$
In the y-direction: $\mathbf{T} - M\mathbf{g} = \mathbf{T} - 9.8 = M\mathbf{a} = \mathbf{a}$

We need to solve these two simultaneous equations for the tension **T**:

$$30 - \mathbf{T} = 2\mathbf{a}$$

$$\mathbf{T} - 9.8 = \mathbf{a}$$

Eliminating **a** from both equations yields **T** = 16.5 N.

17. **B** Using the tension derived for question 16, we substitute and find **a** = 6.75 m/s^2.

18. **E** We know that **P** = **Fv** where **v** = **at** (assuming we start from rest). Also, **a** = **F** / *m*; thus *P* = **F**² *t*/*m*.

19. **C** According to the law of conservation of energy, the potential energy stored in the spring will be transferred into kinetic energy as the mass rises. This energy, in turn, will be converted into gravitational potential energy. Thus the starting elastic potential energy is equal to the final gravitational potential energy:

$$\left(\frac{1}{2}\right)kx^2 = m\mathbf{g}h$$

$$\left(\frac{1}{2}\right)(20\ \text{N/m})(0.4\ \text{m})^2 = (0.3\ \text{kg})(9.8\ \text{m/s}^2)h$$

$$h = 0.54\ \text{m}$$

20. **D** The units of *k* are newtons per meter. Newtons can be expressed as kilogram · meters per second squared (kg · m/s²). Thus, the units for *k* can be expressed as kilograms per second squared (kg/s²).

21. **A** We use

$$\mathbf{F} = m\mathbf{a} = m\frac{\Delta\ \mathbf{v}}{\Delta\mathbf{t}} = \frac{(2500\ \text{kg})(30\ \text{m/s})}{15\ \text{s}} = 5000\ \text{N}$$

22. **C** We first find the velocity of the two masses after they collide and stick together. Using conservation of momentum, we know that

$$(1\ \text{kg})(6\ \text{m/s}) + (2\ \text{kg})(\ 3\ \text{m/s}) = (\ 1 + 2)\ \mathbf{v}$$

and **v** = 4 m/s. The total initial kinetic energy is equal to 27 J, and the final kinetic energy is 24 J. Thus 3 J of kinetic energy was lost.

23. **B** The change in momentum is given by $\Delta\mathbf{p} = m\ \Delta\mathbf{v}$. In this case, there is a change in direction, so

$$\Delta\mathbf{v} = \mathbf{v}_f - \mathbf{v}_i = 3\text{m/s} - (-1\ \text{m/s}) = 4\ \text{m/s}$$

Thus,

$$\Delta\mathbf{p} = (0.2\ \text{kg})(4\ \text{m/s}) = 0.8\ \text{kg} \cdot \text{m/s}$$

24. **D** We need to balance the torques on the two sides of the pivot:

$$(50\ \text{kg})(\mathbf{g})(1.2\ \text{m}) = (70\ \text{kg})(\mathbf{g})(x)$$

implies that $x = 0.86$ m.

25. **C** We take counterclockwise torques as positive. Acting on the pivot, we have two forces contributing to a net torque.

First, the component of force **F** acting at right angles to the beam contributes a torque:

$$\tau_1 = (200\ \text{N})\ (\sin 30)\ (2\ \text{m}) = 200\ \text{N} \cdot \text{m}.$$

Second, the weight of the beam acts from its center of mass (x = 1 m, since the beam is uniform). This torque will be clockwise and negative:

$$\tau_2 = -(98 \text{ N})(1\text{m}) = -98 \text{ N}$$

Thus, the net torque is −102 N · m.

26. **D** The maximum velocity attained by an oscillating mass on a spring is given by A**ω**. Now, $\omega = \sqrt{k/m}$, so

$$\mathbf{v}_{max} = \sqrt{\frac{A^2k}{m}}$$

27. **A** The total energy is given by $E = (1/2)kA^2$, where A is in meters. Here $A = -02$ m, so $E = 0.01$ J
28. **D** Since **g** varies inversely as the square of the distance from the Earth's center, if we start at the surface and go to a height equal to the Earth's radius, we have effectively doubled the radius. Thus **g** is decreased by one-fourth to 2.45 m/s^2.
29. **B** The formula for escape velocity is

$$\mathbf{v} = \sqrt{\frac{2GM}{R}} = \sqrt{\frac{(2)(6.67 \times 10^{-11} \text{ N} \cdot \text{m}^2/\text{ kg}^2)(7.2 \times 10^{22} \text{ kg})}{1.778 \times 10^6 \text{ m}}} = 2.32 \times 10^3 \text{ m/s}$$

30. **B** We use Newton's formula for universal gravitation:

$$\mathbf{F} = \frac{GM_1M_2}{d^2} = \frac{(6.67 \times 10^{11} \text{ N} \cdot \text{m}^2/\text{ kg}^2)(40{,}000 \text{ kg})(40{,}000 \text{ kg})}{(0.5 \text{ m})^2} = 0.43 \text{ N}$$

31. **B** The melting point is the temperature at which a substance changes from a solid to a liquid. Here, this change in state occurs at 40°C.
32. **E** The latent heat of fusion is the number of kilojoules per kilogram required to change a substance from a solid to a liquid. According to the graph, 5 kJ is needed to melt the 0.3 kg of substance. Thus, the heat of fusion is 16.7 kJ / kg.
33. **D** The specific heat capacity is expressed as

$$c = \frac{\Delta Q}{m\Delta T}$$

For a liquid,

$$c = \frac{5 \text{ kJ}}{(0.3 \text{ kg})(40°\text{C})} = 0.42 \text{ kJ/kg} \cdot °\text{C}$$

34. **E** In isochoric change the volume of an ideal gas remains the same.
35. **B** Using the ideal gas law, we first convert 50°C to 323 K. We know that for an ideal gas PV / T = constant. Thus, if both the pressure and the absolute tmperature are doubled, the volume of gas will remain the same (100 m^3).

36. **A** In an isothermal expansion, the temperature remains the same and the pressure varies inversely with the volume (Boyle's law). Graph A displays this case.
37. **B** At the same temperature, 1 mole of each gas contains Avogadro's number of molecules; that is, the two gases have the same number of molecules.
38. **D** If the compression happens isothermally, the temperature of the gas remains the same. Since temperature is related to the average kinetic energy of the molecules, the root mean square velocity, which is temperature dependent, will also remain the same, equal to **v**.
39. **B** "Adiabatic" means that no heat enters or leaves the system. During an adiabatic process the temperature, however, may change.
40. **B** An isobaric (constant-pressure) expansion is *not* part of the Carnot cycle.
41. **C** If the pith ball is initially attracted to the charged rod, it is either neutral or is charged with the opposite sign (not one of the choices).
42. **D** We use Coulomb's law to find the magnitude of this repulsive force:

$$\mathbf{F} = \frac{kQ_1Q_2}{d^2} = \frac{(9 \times 10^9\ \mathrm{N \cdot m^2/\,C^2})(5 \times 10^{-6}\ \mathrm{C})(5 \times 10^{-6}\ \mathrm{C})}{(0.022\ \mathrm{m})^2} = 465\ \mathrm{N}$$

43. **A** The ratio $k\,/\,k' = \mathbf{c}^2$, as can be verified from the Useful Constants.
44. **B** The force on the electron is given by

$$\mathbf{F} = ma = (9.1 \times 10^{-31}\ \mathrm{kg})(3 \times 10^{12}\ \mathrm{m/\,s^2}) = 2.73 \times 10^{-18}\ \mathrm{N}$$

For the electric field experienced by the electron, we have

$$\mathbf{E} = \frac{\mathbf{F}}{Q} = \frac{2.73 = 10^{-18}\ \mathrm{N}}{1.6 \times 10^{-19}\ \mathrm{C}} = 17\ \mathrm{N/\,C}$$

Between two parallel plates,

$$\mathbf{V} = \mathbf{E}\mathbf{d} = (17\ \mathrm{N/C})(0.02\mathrm{m}) = 0.34\ \mathrm{V}$$

45. **A** The two series capacitors add up reciprocally:

$$\frac{1}{C} = \frac{1}{C_1} + \frac{1}{C_2} = \frac{1}{10\ \mu F} + \frac{1}{10\ \mu\ \mathrm{F}}$$

implies that $C = 5\ \mu\mathrm{F}$. This capacitor is now in parallel with another 5-μF capacitor. The equivalent capacitance is equal to the sum of these two. Thus, $C_{eq} = 10\ \mu\mathrm{F}$.
46. **C** One ohm is equal to 1 V/A; 1 V is equal to 1 J/C; and 1 A is equal to 1 C/s. Thus, $1\ \Omega = 1\ \mathrm{kg \cdot m^2/s \cdot C^2}$.
47. **D** Power is equal to potential difference times current. Thus,

$$P = VI = 480\ \mathrm{W}.$$

48. **E** The magnetic field around a long, straight-current carrying wire is a set of concentric circles centered on the wire.
49. **A** The rotation will continue until the plane of the loop is perpendicular to the field. Induced force will be zero at that point. The use of commutator rings makes it possible for the rotation to continue by alternating the direction of the current.
50. **E** In calculating the strength of the magnetic field inside a solenoid, one does *not* consider the diameter of the solenoid.
51. **C** The back emf of a motor is greatest when the velocity of the motor is greatest.
52. **A** The formula for the velocity of wave propagation along a stretched wire is

$$\mathbf{v} = \sqrt{\frac{\mathbf{T}}{M/L}}$$

The tension **T** is in newtons. In this problem the velocity of the pulse is 25 m/s. Solving for the tension, we find that **T** = 125 N.
53. **B** The units for sound wave intensity are watts per square meter, which indicate the amount of energy falling on a unit area each second.
54. **B** Snell's law states that

$$\frac{\sin i}{\sin r} = \frac{n_2}{n_1}$$

In this case $n_1 = 1.0$ and $n_2 = 1.6$. Given the angle of incidence, we get

$$\frac{\sin 30}{\sin r} = 1.6$$

and r = 18°.
55. **A** The colors observed in thin films are caused by the reflection and interference of light.
56. **E** Diffraction is a process that cannot produce polarized light.
57. **A** Increasing the number of lines on a diffraction grating decreases the spacing between each two lines. This has the effect of increasing the spacing between the spectral lines. The formula $\lambda/d = x / L$, where λ is the wavelength of light, d is the spacing between the grating lines, L is the distance from the grating to the screen, and x is the spectral line separation. If λ and L remain constant, then, as d decreases, x increases.
58. **C** The formula for relativistic mass is

$$m = \frac{m_0}{\sqrt{1 - v^2/c^2}}$$

We want m to be equal to 1.5 times the rest mass. Making the substitution and solving for v, we obtain **v** = 0.75**c**.

59. **D** The speed of light remains the same for all observers. The observed velocity of the photon is *c*.

60. **C** The frequency of the 350-nm photon is equal to $8.5 \times 10^{14}\ s^{-1}$. Now,

$$E = hf = (6.63 \times 10^{-34}\ J \cdot s)(8.5 \times 10^{14}\ s^{-1}) = 5.68 \times 10^{-19}\ J$$

61. **B** The de Broglie wavelength is given by the formula $\lambda = h / m\mathbf{v}$. Using the given values, we have

$$\lambda = \frac{h}{m\mathbf{v}} = \frac{6.63 \times 10^{-34}\ J \cdot s)}{(1500\ kg)(30\ m/s)} = 1.5 \times 10^{-38}\ m$$

62. **A** Increasing the intensity of the incident electromagnetic radiation onto a photoelectric metal will increase only the number (current) of emitted electrons. No change will occur in the kinetic energy of the electrons. This was the contradiction with the wave theory of light!

63. **C** The half-life is preset by nature. It remains the same during the decay process.

64. **A** The "characteristic time" for a radioactive substance is the time required to reduce the substance to $1 / e$ of the original amount.

65. **B** The classical electron radius in a hydrogen atom is equal to 0.05 nm or 5×10^{-11} m.

66. **D** The scattering of electrons by photons and the fact that both electrons and photons obey the law of conservation of momentum are detected in the Compton effect.

67. **A** The fusion process results in a higher binding energy per nucleon. This increases the stability of the new nucleus (and releases energy).

68. **D** The number of neutrons is equal to the difference between the mass number and atomic number. For this isotope

$$211 - 84 = 127 \text{ neutrons.}$$

69. **D** For silver −108, 7.2 min equals three half-lives. Thus, one-eighth ($M/8$) of the original amount remains.

70. **A** In Rutherford's experiment, the maximum scattering angle was 180°.

Solutions to Section II

1. (a) The general equations of motion for a projectile are

$$x = (\mathbf{v} \cos \theta)\, t$$

$$y = (\mathbf{v} \sin \theta)\, t + \left(\frac{1}{2}\right) \mathbf{g} t^2$$

Now, the time to reach maximum height is related to the time that gravity takes to declerate the initial upward component of velocity:

$$t' = t_{up} = \frac{\mathbf{v} \sin \theta}{\mathbf{g}}$$

Thus y_{max} is the value of y when t' is used for the time. If we eliminate time from the equation, the formula for y_{max} is:

$$\mathbf{y}_{max} = \frac{\mathbf{v}^2 \sin^2 \theta}{2\mathbf{g}}$$

On the basis of the initial conditions, we want $\mathbf{y}_{max} = h$. We can now solve for sin θ:

$$\sin \theta = \frac{\sqrt{2\mathbf{g}h}}{\mathbf{v}}$$

The formula for the range, R, independent of the time is:

$$\mathbf{R} = \frac{2\mathbf{v}^2 \sin \theta \cos \theta}{\mathbf{g}}$$

We have solved for sin θ; now we must find cos θ. Using the definition of the sine of an angle in a right triangle, we form the arrangement shown in the figure below. From the triangle, we see that $\cos \theta = \mathbf{x} / \mathbf{v}$ and $x^2 + 2\mathbf{g}h = \mathbf{v}^2$. Thus,

$$\mathbf{x} = \sqrt{\mathbf{v}^2 - 2\mathbf{g}h} \qquad \text{and} \qquad \cos \theta = \frac{\sqrt{\mathbf{v}^2 - 2\mathbf{g}h}}{\mathbf{v}}$$

Finally, substituting for sin θ and cos θ in the range formula, we obtain

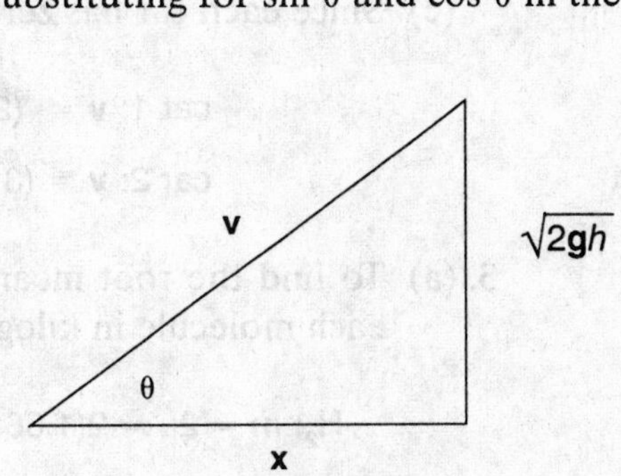

$$\mathbf{R} = \frac{2\mathbf{v}^2 \dfrac{\sqrt{2\mathbf{g}h}}{\mathbf{v}} \dfrac{\sqrt{\mathbf{v}^2 - 2\mathbf{g}h}}{\mathbf{v}}}{\mathbf{g}}$$

$$\mathbf{R} = \frac{2\sqrt{2\mathbf{g}h\,(\mathbf{v}^2 - 2\mathbf{g}h)}}{\mathbf{g}}$$

(b) To find the range, we use $h = 2000$ m and $\mathbf{v} = 500$ m/s in the equation derived in part (a)

$$\mathbf{R} = \frac{2\sqrt{2\mathbf{g}h(v^2 - 2gh)}}{\mathbf{g}} = \frac{2\sqrt{(39{,}200)(250{,}000 - 39{,}200)}}{0.8} = 18{,}551.6 \text{ m}$$

We can now find the value of θ by using the formula derived for sin θ:

$$\sin\theta = \frac{\sqrt{2\mathbf{g}h}}{\mathbf{v}} = \frac{\sqrt{39{,}200}}{500} = 0.396$$

$$\theta = 23°$$

2. (a) At the beginning, car 1 is 25 m ahead of car 2. The inital velocity of each car is zero. When they meet, the position of each car, relative to the origin, must be the same. Since each car undergoes uniformly accelerated motion from rest, we can write

$$\left(\frac{1}{2}\right)\mathbf{a}_2 t^2 = \left(\frac{1}{2}\right)\mathbf{a}_1 t^2 + 25 \text{ m}$$

$$\left(\frac{1}{2}\right)(3 \text{ m/s}^2)\, t^2 = \left(\frac{1}{2}\right)(2 \text{ m/s}^2)\, t^2 + 25 \text{ m}$$

$$t^2 = 50 \text{ s}^2$$

$$t = 7.07 \text{ s}$$

(b) Car 2, the faster car, in 7.07 s goes a distance of

$$\left(\frac{1}{2}\right)\mathbf{a}_2 t^2 = (0.5)(3 \text{ m/s}^2)(7.07 \text{ s})^2 = 75 \text{ m}$$

(c) Since each car has zero initial velocity, for any time t, $\mathbf{v} = \mathbf{at}$:

$$\text{car 1: } \mathbf{v} = (2 \text{ m/s}^2)(7.07 \text{ s}) = 14.14 \text{ m/s}$$

$$\text{car 2: } \mathbf{v} = (3 \text{ m/s}^2)(7.07 \text{ s}) = 21.21 \text{ m/s}$$

3. (a) To find the root mean square velocity, we first need the mass of each molecule in kilograms:

$$H_2\text{: } m = 2\text{u} = 2(1.66 \times 10^{-27} \text{ kg/u}) = 3.32 \times 10^{-27} \text{ kg}$$

$$O_2\text{: } m = 32\text{u} = 32(1.66 \times 10^{-27} \text{ kg/u}) = 5.312 \times 10^{-26} \text{ kg}$$

The formula for the root mean square velocity (where k is Botlzmann's constant) is

$$H_2\text{: } \mathbf{v}_{rms} = \sqrt{\frac{3kT}{m}} = \sqrt{\frac{3(1.38 \times 10^{-23} \text{ J/ K})(273 \text{ K})}{3.32 \times 10^{-27} \text{ kg}}} = 1845 \text{ m/s}$$

$$O_2\text{: } \mathbf{v}_{rms} = \sqrt{\frac{3kT}{m}} = \sqrt{\frac{3(1.38 \times 10^{-23}\text{ J/ K})(273\text{ K})}{5.312 \times 10^{-26}\text{ kg}}} = 461.23\text{ m/s}$$

(b) The ratio of root mean square velocities is equal to 4 : 1 .

(c) The ratio of the mass of oxygen to the mass of hydrogen is equal to 16 : 1. Thus, the ratio of root mean square velocities is equal to the inverse ratio of molecular masses.

(d) Thus, for any two molecules X and Y,

$$\frac{\mathbf{v}_{rms}\,(X)}{\mathbf{v}_{rms}\,(Y)} = \sqrt{\frac{M(Y)}{M(X)}}$$

(e) The molecular mass of carbon dioxide is 44 u, and the molecular mass of hydrogen is 2 u. The ratio of molecular masses is therefore equal to 44 : 2 or 22 : 1. This means that hydrogen molecules (at the same temperature) are faster than carbon dioxide molecules, by a factor equal to the square root of 22, which is about 4.7.

4. We write Kirchhoff's laws for the network:

$$I_2 = I_1 + I_3$$

If we go around each loop clockwise, we examine the potential differences we cross and the resistors that we meet:

$$-3 - 5 + 2I_2 + 5I_1 = 0$$

$$5 - 10I_3 - 2I_2 + 5 = 0$$

These two equations become:

$$5I_1 + 2I_2 = 8$$

$$2I_2 + 10I_3 = 10$$

We eliminate I_2 from these equations, using the first equation above:

$$5I_1 + 2(\,I_1 + I_3) = 8$$

$$2\,(I_1 + I_3) + 10I_3 = 10$$

These equations now become:

$$7I_1 + 2I_3 = 8$$

$$2I_1 + 12I_3 = 10$$

Solving for I_1 yields $I_1 = 0.95$ A.

Substituting for I_1 and solving for I_3 yields $I_3 = 0.675$ A.

Since $I_2 = I_1 + I_3$, then $I_2 = 1.625$ A.

5. (a) For small angles, $\sin\theta \approx \tan\theta$ (see Appendix A) . We can therefore write

$$\frac{\sin i}{\sin r} \approx \frac{\tan i}{\tan r}$$

Now, from the diagram, we can see that $\tan i = x / h$ and $\tan r = x / h'$ so

$$\frac{\tan i}{\tan r} = \frac{x/h}{x/h'} = \frac{h'}{h}$$

(b) From Snell's law, for an angle of incidence i and an angle of refraction r:

$$\frac{\sin i}{\sin r} = \frac{n_2}{n_1}$$

Therefore, using the results from part (a), we see that

$$\frac{h'}{h} = \frac{n_2}{n_1}$$

(c) If $h = 1.5$ m, the observed depth is

$$h' = 1.5\text{m}\left(\frac{1.00}{1.33}\right) = 1.13 \text{ m}$$

6. (a) To find out how many atoms are contained in 5 mg of radon, we note that the mass number, 222, of the isotope is approximately equal to the actual atomic mass of the nucleus. Therefore:

$$N_0 = \frac{5 \times 10^{-6} \text{ kg}}{(222\ u/\text{atom})(1.66 \times 10^{-27} \text{ kg/u})} = 1.36 \times 10^{19} \text{ atoms}$$

(b) The activity rate is given by the formula

$$R = \frac{\Delta N}{\Delta t} = \frac{0.693}{T} N_0 = \frac{0.693}{(3.8 \text{ days})(86{,}400 \text{ s/day})} (1.36 \times 10^{19} \text{ atoms})$$
$$= 2.86 \times 10^{13} \text{ Bq}$$

For the activity, the half-life T is in units of seconds. The units of activity are events per second or becquerels (bq).

(c) To find the percentage of radon remaining after 8 days, we use the formula

$$\frac{N}{N_0} = \frac{1}{2^{t/T}}$$

In this case, $t = 8$ days and $T = 3.8$ days (the half-life). Thus, $t / T = 2.1$, and therefore

$$\frac{N}{N_0} = \frac{1}{2^{2.1}} = 0.233$$

The percentage left is 23.3%.

Glossary

Absolute index of refraction For a transparent material, a number that represents the ratio of the speed of light in a vacuum to the speed of light in the material.

Absolute temperature A measure of the average kinetic energy of the molecules in an object; on the Kelvin scale, equal to the Celsius temperature of an object plus 273.

Absolute zero The theoretical lowest possible temperature, designated as 0 K.

Absorption spectrum A continuous spectrum crossed by dark lines representing the absorption of particular wavelengths of radiation by a cooler medium.

Acceleration A vector quantity representing the time rate of change of velocity.

Action A force applied to an object that leads to an equal but opposite reaction; the product of total energy and time in units of joules times seconds; the product of momentum and position, especially in the case of the Heisenberg uncertainty principle.

Activity The number of decays per second of a radioactive atom.

Adiabatic In thermodynamics, referring to the process that occurs when no heat is added or subtracted from the system.

Alpha decay The spontaneous emission of a helium nucleus from certain radioactive atoms.

Alpha particle A helium nucleus that is ejected from a radioactive atom.

Alternating current An electric current that changes its direction and magnitude according to a regular frequency.

Ammeter A device that, when placed in series, measures the current in an electric circuit; a galvanometer with a low-resistance coil placed across it.

Ampere (A) The SI unit of electric current, equal to 1 C / s.

Amplitude The maximum displacement of an oscillating particle, medium, or field relative to its rest position.

Angle of incidence The angle between a ray of light and the normal to a reflecting or transparent surface at the location where the ray intercepts the surface.

Angle of reflection The angle between a reflected light ray and the normal to a mirror or other reflecting surface at the location where the ray intercepts the surface.

Angle of refraction The angle between an emerging light ray in a transparent material and the normal to the surface at the location where the ray first enters the material.

Angstrom (Å) A unit of wavelength measurement equal to 1×10^{-10} m.

Angular frequency The rate, in radians per second, at which a point mass undergoing uniform circular motion sweeps out a given angle each second; the product of 2π and the frequency f; angular velocity.

Angular momentum For a point mass undergoing uniform circular motion, a vector quantity equal to the product of the mass, velocity, and radius.

Angular velocity For a point mass undergoing uniform circular motion, a vector quantity equal to the ratio, in radians per second, of the tangential velocity and the radius; angular frequency.

Antinodal lines A region of maximum displacement in a medium where waves are interacting with each other.

Aphelion The point in a planet's orbit at which the planet is farthest from the Sun.

Armature The rotating coil of wire in an electric motor.

Atomic mass unit (u) A unit of mass equal to one-twelfth the mass of a carbon-12 nucleus. Older texts use the abbreviation "amu."

Atomic number The number of protons in an atom's nucleus.

Atmosphere (atm) A unit of pressure, equal to 101 kPa at sea level.

Average speed A scalar quantity equal to the ratio of the total distance to the total elapsed time.

Avogadro's number The number of molecules in 1 mole of an ideal gas, equal to 6.02×10^{23}. Named for Italian chemist/physicist Amedeo Avogadro.

Back emf The induced potential difference in the armature of an electric motor that opposes the applied potential difference.

Balmer series In a hydrogen atom, the visible spectral emission lines that correspond to electron transitions from higher excited states to lower level 2.

Battery A combination of two or more electric cells.

Beats The interference caused by two sets of sound waves with only a slight difference in frequency.

Becquerel (Bq) A unit of radioactive decay, equal to one decay event per second.

Beta decay The spontaneous ejection of an electron from the nuclei of certain radioactive atoms.

Beta particle An electron that is spontaneously ejected by a radioactive nucleus.

Binding energy The energy required to break apart an atomic nucleus; the energy equivalent of the mass defect.

Boltzmann's constant In thermodynamics, a constant equal to the ratio of the universal gas constant, R, to Avogadro's number, N_a, equal to 1.38×10^{-23} J/K. Named for German physicist Ludwig Boltzmann.

Boyle's law At constant temperature, the pressure in an ideal gas varies inversely with the volume of the gas. Named for British physicist/chemist Robert Boyle.

Bright-line spectrum The display of brightly colored lines on a screen or photograph indicating the discrete emission of radiation by a heated gas at low pressure.

Capacitance The ratio of the total charge to the potential difference in a capacitor.

Capacitor A pair of conducting plates, with either a vacuum or an insulator between them, used in an electric circuit to store current.

Carnot cycle In thermodynamics, a sequence of four steps in an ideal gas confined in a cylinder with a movable piston (a Carnot engine). The cycle includes an isothermal expansion, an adiabatic expansion, an isothermal compression, and an adiabatic compression. Named for French physicist Sadi Carnot.

Cartesian coordinate system A set of two or three mutually perpendicular reference lines, called axes and usually designated as *x*, *y*, and *z*, that are used to define the location of an object in a frame of reference; a coordinate system named for French scientist Rene Descartes.

Cathode ray tube An evacuated gas tube into which a beam of electrons is projected. Their energy produces an image on a fluorescent screen when deflected by external electric or magnetic fields.

Celsius temperature scale A metric temperature scale in which, at sea level, water freezes at 0° C and boils at 100° C. Named for Swedish astronomer Anders Celsius.

Center of curvature A point that is equidistant from all other points on the surface of a spherical mirror; a point equal to twice the focal length of a spherical mirror.

Center of mass The weighted mean distribution point where all the mass of an object can be considered to be located; the point at which, if a single force is applied, translational motion will result.

Centripetal acceleration The acceleration of mass moving uniformly in a circle at a constant speed directed radially inward toward the center of the circular path.

Centripetal force The deflecting force, directed radially inward toward a given point, that causes an object to follow a circular path.

Chain reaction In nuclear fission, the uncontrolled reaction of neutrons splitting uranium nuclei and creating more neutrons that continue the process on a self-sustained basis.

Characteristic time In radioactive decay, the time required for the original mass to decay to a factor of $1 / e$ of that value.

Charles's law At constant pressure, the volume of an ideal gas varies directly with the absolute temperature of the gas. Named for J. A. C. Charles.

Chromatic aberration In optics, the defect in a converging lens that causes the dispersion of white light into a continuous spectrum, with the result that the lens refracts the colors to different focal points.

Coefficient of friction The ratio of the force of friction to the normal force when one surface is sliding (or attempting to slide) over another surface.

Coherent Referring to a set of waves that have the same wavelength, frequency, and phase.

Commutator A split ring in a direct current (d-c) motor whose segments are connected to opposite terminals in a battery. As the armature turns, the split in the rings helps reverse the direction of the current every half-revolution.

Component One of two mutually perpendicular vectors that lie along the principal axes in a coordinate system and can be combined to form a given resultant vector.

Concave lens A diverging lens that causes parallel rays of light to emerge in such a way that they appear to diverge away from a focal point behind the lens.

Concave mirror A converging spherical mirror that causes parallel rays of light to converge to a focal point in front of the mirror.

Concurrent forces Two or more forces that act at the same point and at the same time.

Conductor A substance, usually metallic, that allows the relatively easy flow of electric charges.

Conservation of angular momentum A principle of physics stating that, in the absence of external torques, the total angular momentum of an isolated system remains the same.

Conservation of energy A principle of physics that states that the total energy of an isolated system remains the same during all interactions within the system.

Conservation of mass-energy A principle of physics that states that, in the conversion of mass into energy or energy into mass, the total mass-energy of the system remains the same.

Conservation of momentum A principle of physics that states that, in the absence of any external forces, the total momentum of an isolated system remains the same.

Conservative force A force such that any work done by this force can be recovered without any loss; a force whose work is independent of the path taken.

Constructive interference The additive result of two or more waves interacting with the same phase relationship as they move through a medium.

Continuous spectrum A continuous band of colors, consisting of red, orange, yellow, green, blue, and violet, formed by the dispersion or diffraction of white light.

Control rod A device, usually made of cadmium, that is inserted in a nuclear reactor to control the rate of fission.

Converging lens A lens that will cause parallel rays of light incident on its surface to refract and converge to a focal point; a convex lens.

Converging mirror A spherical mirror that will cause parallel rays of light incident on its surface to reflect and converge to a focal point; a concave mirror.

Convex lens See **Converging lens.**

Convex mirror See **Diverging mirror.**

Coordinate system A set of reference lines, not necessarily perpendicular, used to locate the position of an object within a frame of reference by applying the rules of analytic geometry.

Core The interior of a solenoidal electromagnet, usually made of a ferromagnetic material; the part of a nuclear reactor where the fission reaction occurs.

Coulomb (C) The SI unit of electrical charge, defined as the amount of charge 1 A of current contains each second.

Coulomb's law The electrostatic force between two point charges is directly proportional to the product of the charges and inversely proportional to the square of the distance separating them. Named for French physicist Charles-Augustin de Coulomb.

Critical angle of incidence The angle of incidence to a transparent substance such that the angle of refraction equals 90° relative to the normal drawn to the surface.

Current A scalar quantity that measures the amount of charge passing a given point in an electric circuit each second.

Current length A relative measure of the magnetic field strength produced by a length of wire carrying current, equal to the product of the current and the length.

Cycle One complete sequence of periodic events or oscillations.

Damping The continuous decrease in the amplitude of mechanical oscillations due to a dissipative force.

Decay constant The ratio between the number of decay nuclei per second and the total number of nuclei available at a given time.

Decibel (dB) A logarithmic unit of sound intensity, defined so that 0 dB equals 1.0×10^{-12} W/m^2.

Deflecting force Any force that acts to change the direction of motion of an object.

Derived unit Any combination of fundamental physical units.

Destructive interference The result produced by the interaction of two or more waves with opposite phase relationships as they move through a medium.

Deuterium An isotope of hydrogen containing one proton and one neutron in its nucleus; heavy hydrogen (a component of heavy water).

Dielectric An electric insulator placed between the plates of a capacitor to alter its capacitance.

Diffraction The ability of waves to pass around obstacles or squeeze through small openings.

Diffraction grating A reflecting or transparent surface with many thousands of lines ruled on it, used to diffract light into a spectrum.

Direct current Electric current that is moving in one direction only around an electric circuit.

Dispersion The separation of light into its component colors or spectrum.

Dispersive medium Any medium that produces the dispersion of light; any medium in which the velocity of a wave depends on its frequency.

Displacement A vector quantity that determines the change in position of an object by measuring the straight-line distance and direction from the starting point to the ending point.

Dissipative force Any force, such as friction, that removes kinetic energy from a moving object; a nonconservative force.

Distance A scalar quantity that measures the total length of the path taken by a moving object.

Diverging lens A lens that causes parallel rays of light incident on its surface to refract and diverge away from a focal point on the other side of the lens; a concave lens.

Diverging mirror A spherical mirror that causes parallel rays of light incident on its surface to reflect and diverge away from a focal point on the other side of the mirror.

Doppler effect The apparent change in the wavelength or frequency of a wave as the source of the wave moves relative to an observer. Named for Austrian physicist Christian Doppler.

Dynamics The branch of mechanics that studies the effects of forces on objects.

Efficiency In a machine, the ratio of work output to work input; in a transformer, the ratio of the power from a secondary coil to the power from a primary coil.

Elastic collision A collision between two objects in which there is a rebounding and no loss of kinetic energy occurs.

Elastic potential energy The energy stored in a spring when work is done to stretch or compress it.

Electrical ground The passing of charges to or from the Earth to establish a potential difference between two points.

Electric cell A chemical device for generating electricity.

Electric circuit A closed conducting loop consisting of a source of potential difference, conducting wires, and other devices that operate on electricity.

Electric field The region where an electric force is exerted on a charged object.

Electric field intensity A vector quantity that measures the ratio of the magnitude of the force to the magnitude of the charge on an object.

Electric motor A coil of wire, carrying current, that is caused to rotate in an external magnetic field because of the alternation of electric current.

Electromagnet A coil of wire, wrapped around a ferromagnetic core (usually made of iron), that generates a magnetic field when current is passed through it.

Electromagnetic field The field produced by an electromagnet or moving electric charges.

Electromagnetic induction The production of a potential difference in a conductor due to the relative motion between the conductor and an external magnetic field, or due to the change in an external magnetic flux near the conductor.

Electromagnetic spectrum The range of frequencies covering the discrete emission of energy from oscillating electromagnetic fields; included are radio waves, microwaves, infrared waves, visible light, ultraviolet light, X rays, and gamma rays.

Electromagnetic wave A wave generated by the oscillation of electric charges producing interacting electric and magnetic fields that oscillate in space and travel at the speed of light in a vacuum.

Electromotive force (emf) The potential difference caused by the conversion of different forms of energy into electrical energy; the energy per unit charge.

Electron A negatively charged particle that orbits a nucleus in an atom; the fundamental carrier of negative electric charge.

Electron capture The process in which an orbiting electron is captured by a nucleus possessing too many neutrons with respect to protons; also called K-capture.

Electron cloud A theoretical probability distribution of electrons around the nucleus due to the Heisenberg uncertainty principle. The most probable location for an electron is in the densest regions of the cloud.

Electron volt (eV) A unit of energy related to the kinetic energy of a moving charge and equal to 1.6×10^{-19} J.

Electroscope A device for detecting the presence of static charges on an object.

Elementary charge The fundamental amount of charge of an electron.

Emf See **Electromotive force**.

Emission spectrum The discrete set of colored lines representing the electromagnetic energy produced when atomic compounds are excited into emitting light because of heat, sparks, or atomic collisions.

Energy A scalar quantity representing the capacity to work.

Energy level One of several regions around a nucleus where electrons are considered to reside.

Entropy The degree of randomness or disorder in a thermodynamic system.

Equilibrant The force equal in magnitude and opposite in direction to the resultant of two or more forces that brings a system into equilibrium.

Equilibrium The balancing of all external forces acting on a mass; the result of a zero vector sum of all forces acting on an object.

Escape velocity The velocity attained by an object such that, if coasting, the object would not be pulled back toward the planet from which it came.

Excitation The process by which an atom absorbs energy and causes its orbiting electrons to move to higher energy levels.

Excited state In an atom, the situation in which its orbiting electrons are residing in higher energy levels.

Farad (F) A unit of capacitance equal to 1 C / V.

Faraday's law of electromagnetic induction The magnitude of the induced emf in a conductor is equal to the rate of change of the magnetic flux. Named for British chemist/physicist Michael Faraday.

Ferromagnetic substances A metal or a compound made of iron, cobalt, or nickel that produces very strong magnetic fields.

Field A region characterized by the presence of a force on a test body like a unit mass in a gravitational field or a unit charge in an electric field.

Field intensity A measure of the force exerted on a unit test body; the force per unit mass; the force per unit charge.

First law of thermodynamics A statement of the conservation of energy as applied to thermodynamic systems: The change in energy of a system is equal to the change in the internal energy plus any work done by the system.

Fission The splitting of a uranium nucleus into two smaller, more stable nuclei by means of a slow-moving neutron, with the release of a large amount of energy.

Flux A measure, in webers, of the product of the perpendicular component of a magnetic field crossing an area and the magnitude of the area.

Flux density A measure, in webers per square meter, of the field intensity per unit area.

Focal length The distance along the principal axis from a lens or spherical mirror to the principal focus.

Focus The point of convergence of light rays caused by a converging mirror or lens; either of two fixed points in an ellipse that determines its shape.

Force A vector quantity that corresponds to any push or pull due to an interaction of matter that changes the motion of an object.

Force constant See **Spring constant**.

Forced vibration A vibration caused by the application of an external force.

Frame of reference A point of view consisting of a coordinate system in which observations are made.

Free-body diagram A diagram that illustrates all of the forces acting on a mass at any given time.

Frequency The number of completed periodic cycles per second in an oscillation or wave motion.

Friction A force that opposes the motion of an object as it slides over another surface.

Fuel rods Rods packed with fissionable material that are inserted into the core of a nuclear reactor.

Fundamental unit An arbitrary scale of measurement assigned to certain physical quantities, such as length, time, mass, and charge, that are considered to be the basis for all other measurements. In the SI system, the fundamental units used in physics are the meter, kilogram, second, ampere, kelvin, and mole.

Fusion The combination of two or more light nuclei to produce a more stable, heavier nucleus, with the release of energy.

Galvanometer A device used to detect the presence of small electric currents when connected in series in a circuit.

Gamma radiation High-energy photons emitted by certain radioactive substances.

Gravitation The mutual force of attraction between two uncharged masses.

Gravitational field strength A measure of the gravitational force per unit mass in a gravitational field.

Gravity Another name for gravitation or the gravitational force; the tendency of objects to fall to the Earth.

Ground state The lowest energy level of an atom.

Half-life The time required for a radioactive material to decay to one-half its original amount.

Heat The energy observed due to particle collisions in matter; the energy produced when matter interacts with particles that are colliding randomly with each other, as in a gas.

Heat of fusion The amount of energy per kilogram needed to change the state of matter from a solid to a liquid or from a liquid to a solid.

Heat of vaporization The amount of energy per kilogram needed to change the state of matter from a liquid to a gas or from a gas to a liquid.

Heisenberg uncertainty principle The product of the momentum and position of a subatomic particle is greater than or equal to Planck's constant. Named for German physicist Werner Heisenberg.

Hertz (Hz) The SI unit of frequency, equal to 1 s^{-1}.

Hooke's law The stress applied to an elastic material is directly proportional to the strain produced. Named for English scientist Robert Hooke.

Ideal gas A gas for which the assumptions of the kinetic theory are valid.

Image An optical reproduction of an object by means of a lens or mirror.

Impulse A vector quantity equal to the product of the average force applied to a mass and the time interval in which the force acts; the area under a force versus time graph.

Induced potential difference A potential difference created in a conductor because of its motion relative to an external magnetic field.

Induction coil A transformer in which a variable potential difference is produced in a secondary coil when a direct current, applied to the primary, is turned on and off.

Inelastic collision A collision in which two masses interact and stick together, leading to an apparent loss of kinetic energy.

Inertia The property of matter that resists the action of an applied force trying to change the motion of an object.

Inertial frame of reference A frame of reference in which the law of inertia holds; a frame of reference moving with constant velocity relative to the Earth.

Instantaneous velocity The slope of a tangent line to a point in a displacement versus time graph.

Insulator A substance that is a poor conductor of electricity because of the absence of free electrons.

Interference The interaction of two or more waves, producing an enhanced or a diminished amplitude at the point of interaction; the superposition of one wave on another.

Interference pattern The pattern produced by the constructive and destructive interference of waves generated by two point sources.

Isobaric In thermodynamics, referring to a process in which the pressure of a gas remains the same.

Isochoric In thermodynamics, referring to a process in which the volume of a gas remains the same.

Isolated system A combination of two or more interacting objects that are not being acted upon by external force.

Isotope An atom with the same number of protons as a particular element but a different number of neutrons.

Joule (J) The SI unit of work, equal to 1 N · m; the SI unit of mechanical energy, equal to 1 kg · m^2/s^2.

Junction The point in an electric circuit where a parallel connection branches off.

K-capture See **Electron capture**.

Kelvin (K) The SI unit of absolute temperature, defined in such a way that 0 K equals −273° C.

Kelvin temperature scale See **Celsius**.

Kepler's first law The orbital paths of all planets are elliptical. Named for German astronomer Johannes Kepler.

Kepler's second law A line from the Sun to a planet sweeps out equal areas in equal time.

Kepler's third law The ratio of the cube of the mean radius to the Sun to the square of the period is a constant for all planets orbiting the Sun.

Kilogram (kg) The SI unit of mass.

Kilojoule (kJ) A unit representing 1000 J.

Kilopascal (kPa) A unit representing 1000 Pa.

Kinematics In mechanics, the study of how objects move.

Kinetic energy The energy possessed by a mass because of its motion relative to a frame of reference.

Kinetic friction The friction induced by sliding one surface over another.

Kinetic theory of gases The theory that all matter consists of molecules that are in a constant state of motion.

Kirchhoff's first law The algebraic sum of all currents at a junction in a circuit equals zero. Named for German physicist Gustav Kirchhoff.

Kirchhoff's second law The algebraic sum of all potential drops around any closed loop in a circuit equals zero.

Laser A device for producing an intense coherent beam of monochromatic light; an acronym for *l*ight *a*mplification by the *s*timulated *e*mission of *r*adiation.

Law of inertia See **Newton's first law of motion**.

Lens A transparent substance, with one or two curved surfaces, used to direct rays of light by refraction.

Lenz's law An induced current in a conductor is always in a direction such that its magnetic field opposes the magnetic field that induced it. Named for German physicist Emil Lenz.

Line of force An imaginary line drawn in a gravitational, electrical, or magnetic field that indicates the direction a test particle would take while experiencing a force in that field.

Longitudinal wave A wave in which the oscillating particles vibrate in a direction parallel to the direction of propagation.

Magnet An object that exerts a force on ferrous materials.

Magnetic field A region surrounding a magnet in which ferrous materials or charged particles experience a force.

Magnetic field strength The force on a unit current length in a magnetic field.

Magnetic flux density The total magnetic flux per unit area in a magnetic field.

Magnetic pole A region on a magnet where magnetic lines of force are most concentrated.

Mass The property of matter used to represent the inertia of an object; the ratio of the net force applied to an object and its subsequent acceleration as specified by Newton's second law of motion.

Mass defect The difference between the actual mass of a nucleus and the sum of the masses of the protons and neutrons it contains.

Mass number The total number of protons and neutrons in an atomic nucleus.

Mass spectrometer A device that uses magnetic fields to cause nuclear ions to assume circular trajectories and then determines the masses of the ions based on their charges, the radius of the path, and the external field strength.

Mean radius For a planet, the average distance to the Sun.

Meter (m) The SI unit of length.

Moderator A material, such as water or graphite, that is used to slow neutrons in a fission reaction.

Mole (mol) The SI unit for the amount of substance containing Avgadro's number of molecules.

Moment arm distance A line drawn from a pivot point.

Moment of inertia A measure of the relative distribution of matter about a rotating axis; rotational inertia.

Momentum A vector quantity equal to the product of the mass and the velocity of a moving object.

Monochromatic light Light consisting of only one frequency.

Natural frequency The frequency with which an elastic body will vibrate if disturbed.

Net force The resultant force acting on a mass.

Neutron A subatomic particle, residing in the nucleus, that has a mass comparable to that of a proton but is electrically neutral.

Newton (N) The SI unit of force, equal to $1\ kg \cdot m / s^2$.

Newton's first law of motion An object at rest tends to remain at rest, and an object in motion tends to remain in motion at a constant velocity, unless acted upon by an external force; the law of inertia. Named for British mathematician/physicist Sir Isaac Newton.

Newton's second law of motion The acceleration of a body is directly proportional to the applied net force; $\mathbf{F} = m\mathbf{a}$.

Newton's third law of motion For every action, there is an equal, but opposite, reaction.

Nodal line A line of minimum displacement when two or more waves interfere.

Nonconservative force A force, such as friction, that decreases the amount of kinetic energy after work is done by or against the force.

Normal A line perpendicular to a surface.

Normal force A force that is directed perpendicularly to a surface when two objects are in contact.

Nuclear force The force between nucleons in a nucleus that opposes the Coulomb force repulsion of the protons; the strong force.

Nucleon Either a proton or a neutron as it exists in a nucleus.

Ohm (Ω) The SI unit of electrical resistance, equal to 1 V / A.

Ohm's law In a circuit at constant temperature, the ratio of the potential difference to the current is a constant (called the resistance). Named for German physicist Georg Ohm.

Optical center The geometric center of a converging or diverging lens.

Parallel circuit A circuit in which two or more devices are connected across the same potential difference and provide an alternative path for charge flow.

Pascal (Pa) The SI unit of pressure, equal to $1\ N / m^2$.

Perihelion The point in a planet's orbit at which the planet is closest to the Sun.

Period The time, in seconds, to complete one cycle of repetitive oscillations or uniform circular motion.

Permeability The property of matter that affects an external magnetic field in which the material is placed, causing it to align free electrons within the substance and hence magnetizing it; a measure of a material's ability to become magnetized.

Phase The relative position of a point on a wave with respect to another point on the same wave.

Photoelectric effect The process by which surface electrons in a metal are freed through the incidence of electromagnetic radiation above a certain minimum frequency.

Photon A single packet of electromagnetic energy.

Planck's constant A universal constant representing the ratio of the energy of a photon to its frequency; the fundamental quantum of action, having a value of 6.63×10^{-34} kg · m^2 / s. Named for German physicist Max Planck.

Polar coordinate system A coordinate system in which the location of a point is determined by a vector from the origin of a Cartesian coordinate system and the acute angle it makes with the positive horizontal axis.

Polarization The process by which the vibrations of a transverse wave are selected to lie in a preferred plane perpendicular to the direction of propagation.

Polarized light Light that has been polarized by passing it through a suitable filter.

Positron A subatomic particle having the same mass as an electron but a positive electrical charge.

Potential difference The difference in work per unit charge between any two points in an electric field.

Potential energy The energy possessed by a body because of its vertical position relative to the surface of the Earth or any other arbitrarily chosen base level.

Power The ratio of the work done to the time needed to complete the work.

Pressure The force per unit area.

Primary coil In a transformer, the coil connected to an alternating potential difference source.

Principal axis An imaginary line passing through the center of curvature of a spherical mirror or the optical center of a lens.

Prism A transparent triangular shape that disperses white light into a continuous spectrum.

Pulse A single vibratory disturbance in an elastic medium.

Quantum A discrete packet of electromagnetic energy; a photon.

Quantum theory The theory that light consists of discrete packets of energy that are absorbed or emitted in units.

Radian (rad) A unit of angle measure based on the unit circle; 360° equals 2π rad.

Radioactive decay The spontaneous disintegration of a nucleus due to its instability.

Radius of curvature The distance from the center of curvature to the surface of a spherical mirror.

Ray A straight line used to indicate the direction of travel of a light wave.

Real image An image formed by a converging mirror or lens that can be focused onto a screen.

Refraction The bending of a light ray when it passes obliquely from one transparent substance to another in which its velocity is different.

Resistance The ratio of the potential difference across a conductor to the current in the conductor.

Resistivity A property of matter that measures the ability of that substance to act as a resistor.

Resolution of forces The process by which a given force is decomposed into a pair of perpendicular forces.

Resonance The production of sympathetic vibrations in a body, at its natural vibrating frequency, caused by another vibrating body.

Rest mass The mass of an object when the object is not moving.

Rotational equilibrium The situation when the vector sum of all torques acting on a rotating mass equals zero.

Rotational inertia The ability of a substance to resist the action of a torque; moment of inertia.

Scalar A physical quantity, such as mass or speed, that is characterized by magnitude only.

Second (s) The SI unit of time.

Secondary coil In a transformer, a coil in which an alternating potential difference is induced.

Second law of thermodynamics Heat flows only from a hot body to a cold one; the entropy of the universe is always increasing.

Series circuit A circuit in which electrical devices are connected sequentially in a single conducting loop, allowing only one path for charge flow.

Shunt A low-resistance coil that is connected parallel across a galvanometer to turn it into an ammeter.

Sliding friction A force that resists the sliding motion of one surface over another; kinetic friction.

Snell's law For light passing obliquely from one transparent substance to another, the ratio of the sine of the angle of incidence to the sine of the angle of refraction is equal to the relative index of refraction for the two media. Named for Willebrord Snell.

Solenoid A coil of wire used for electromagnetic induction.

Specific heat The amount of energy, in kilojoules, needed to change the temperature of 1 kg of a substance by 1° C.

Speed A scalar quantity measuring the time rate of change of distance.

Spherical aberration In a converging spherical mirror or a converging lens, the inability to properly focus parallel rays of light because of the shape of the mirror or lens.

Spring constant The ratio of the applied force and resultant displacement of a spring.

Standard pressure At sea level, 1 atm, which is equal to 101.3 kPa.

Standing wave A stationary wave pattern formed in a medium when two sets of waves with equal wavelength and amplitude pass through each other, usually after a reflection.

Starting friction The force of friction overcome when one of two objects begins to slide over the other.

Static electricity Stationary electric charges.

Static friction The force that prevents one object from sliding over another.

Statics The study of the forces acting on an object that is at rest relative to a frame of reference.

Superposition The ability of waves to pass through each other, interfere, and then continue on their way unimpeded.

Temperature The relative measure of warmth or cold relative to a standard; see also **Absolute temperature**.

Tesla (T) The SI unit of magnetic field strength, equal to 1 W / m^2.

Test charge A small, positively charged mass used to detect the presence of a force in an electric field.

Thermionic emission The emission of electrons from a hot filament.

Thermometer An instrument that makes a quantitative measurement of temperature based on an accepted scale.

Third law of thermodynamics The temperature of any system can never be reduced to absolute zero.

Threshold frequency The minimum frequency of electromagnetic radiation necessary to induce the photoelectric effect in a metal.

Torque The application, from a pivot, of a force at right angles to a designated line that tends to produce circular motion; the product of a force and a perpendicular moment arm distance.

Total internal reflection The process by which light is incident on a medium in which its velocity would increase at an angle greater than the critical angle of incidence.

Total mechanical energy In a mechanical system, the sum of the kinetic and potential energies.

Transformer A device consisting of two coils used to change the alternating potential difference across one of them (the primary) to either a larger or smaller value.

Transmutation The process of changing one atomic nucleus into another by radioactive decay or nuclear bombardment.

Transverse wave A wave in which the vibrations of the medium or field are at right angles to the direction of propagation.

Uniform circular motion Motion around a circle at a constant speed.

Uniform motion Motion at a constant speed in a straight line.

Unit An arbitrary scale assigned to a physical quantity for measurement and comparison.

Universal law of gravitation The gravitational force between any two masses is directly proportional to the product of their masses, and inversely proportional to the square of the distance between them.

Vector A physical quantity that is characterized by both magnitude and direction; a directed arrow drawn in a Cartesian coordinate system used to represent a quantity such as force, velocity, or displacement.

Velocity A vector quantity representing the time rate of change of displacement.

Virtual focus The point at which the rays from a diverging lens would meet if they were traced back with straight lines.

Virtual image An image, formed by a mirror or lens that cannot be focused onto a screen.

Visible light The portion of the electromagnetic spectrum that can be detected by the human eye.

Volt (V) The SI unit of potential difference, equal to 1 J / C.

Voltmeter A device used to measure the potential difference between two points in a circuit when connected in parallel; a galvanometer with a high-resistance coil placed in series with it.

Volt per meter (V / m) The SI unit of electric field intensity, equal to 1 N / C.

Watt (W) The SI unit of power, equal to 1 J / s.

Wave A series of periodic disturbances in an elastic medium or field.
Wavelength The distance between any two successive points in phase on a wave.
Weber (Wb) The SI unit of magnetic flux, equal to 1 T × 1 m^2.
Weight The force of gravity exerted on a mass at the surface of a planet.
Work A scalar measure of the relative amount of change in mechanical energy; the product of the magnitude of the displacement of an object and the component of applied force in the same direction as the displacement; the area under a graph of force versus displacement.
Work function The minimum amount of energy needed to free an electron from the surface of a metal using the photoelectric effect.

APPENDIX A

Review of Mathematics

I. Algebra

Equations and Relationships

Physical relationships are often expressed as mathematical equations, and the techniques of algebra are often needed to solve these equations as part of the process of analyzing the physical world. In general, the letters u, v, w, x, y, and z are used as variable unknown quantities, with x, y, and z the most popular choices. The letters $a, b, c, d, e, \ldots$ often represent numbers or coefficients, with a, b, and c the most popular.

An equation of the form

$$y = ax + b$$

is called a **linear** equation, and its graph is a straight line. The coefficient a is called the **slope** of the line, and b is termed the ***y*-intercept**, that is, the point at which the line crosses the y-axis (using standard Cartesian coordinates). An equation of the form

$$y = ax^2 + bx + c$$

is called a **quadratic** equation, and a graph of this relationship is a parabola. The **order** of the equation is the highest power of x, which is the **independent variable**.

The variables x and y can represent any physical quantities being studied. For example, the following quadratic equation represents the displacement of a particle undergoing one-dimensional uniformly accelerated motion (see Chapter 7):

$$x = x_0 + v_0t + \left(\frac{1}{2}\right)at^2$$

In this equation x_0, v_0, and a are all constants, while x and t are the variables (x representing displacement and t, time).

While there is only one solution to a linear equation, a quadratic equation has two solutions. However, in physics, it is possible that only one solution is physically reasonable; for example, there is no "negative time" in physics.

A linear equation represents a **direct relationship** (see Figure A.1.a) between two quantities. We would say that y varies directly with x. A quadratic equation also expresses a direct relationship, but not a linear one. An **inverse relationship** (Figure A.1.b) is one in which, as the independent variable increases, the dependent variable decreases. This relationship is expressed as

$$y = \frac{a}{x}$$

and its graph is a hyperbola. It is possible that the power of x is larger than 1 (like the inverse square law of gravity; see Chapter 14) in the denominator, but the graph remains a hyperbola, although a steeper one (Figure A.1.c).

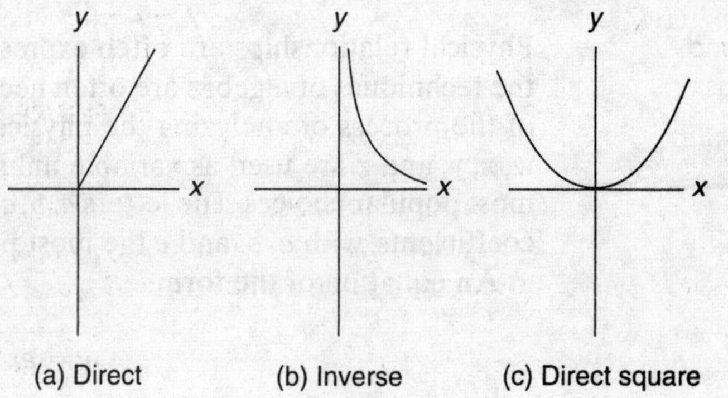

FIGURE A.1

Solutions of Algebraic Equations

A set of points (x,y) is a solution of an algebraic equation if the number of points for each variable is the same and if, for each x, there is one and only one y value (this is also the definition of a **function**) when the value of x is substituted into the equation and the subsequent arithmetical operations are performed. In other words, the equation $3x + 2 = -4$ has only one solution since there is only one variable, x (the solution being $x = -2$). The equation $y = 3x + 2$, however, requires a pair of numbers (x,y) since there are two variables. We could try an imprecise method of trial and error, but an easier way is to graph the equation using test values for the independent variable x. A table of sample numbers for x and the subsequent y values is presented below.

x	y
0	2
1	5
2	8
−1	−1
−2	−4

In Figure A.2., a graph of the equation $y = 3x + 2$ is given. The "solution" is somewhat arbitrary in the sense that the value of y for any given x can be interpolated (or extrapolated) from the graph.

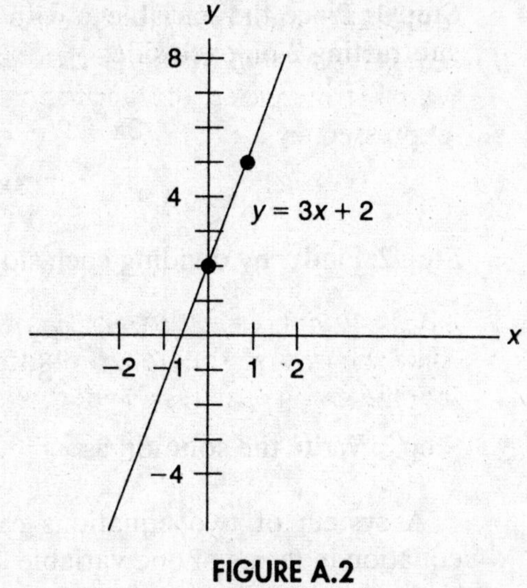

FIGURE A.2

Technically, there is no one solution to $y = 3x + 2$. Since both x and y are variables, we need another equation to make a coupled system of two equations and two unknowns. Suppose such a set consists of

$$y = 3x + 2$$

$$x - y = -1$$

The solution to this system is a unique set of numbers (x,y) that satisfies both equations. Graphically, we can solve this system by plotting both equations (with sample data) and then looking for the points of intersection (see Figure A.3.).

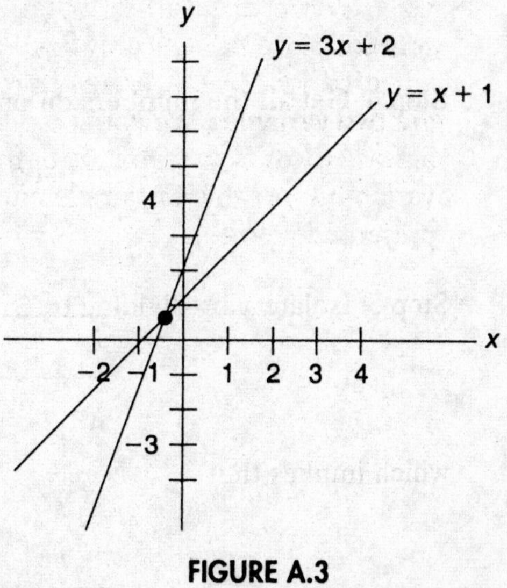

FIGURE A.3

The intersection points are $x = -0.5$ and $y = 0.5$. Substitution of these values into both equations will yield similar results.

The same results can be achieved algebraically. The equation $3x + 2 = -4$ can be solved using the rules of algebra.

Step 1: Place the variable x with its coefficient on one side, by itself, by subtracting 2 on each side:

$$3x + 2 - 2 = -4 - 2 = -6$$

$$3x = -6$$

Step 2: Find x by dividing each side by 3:

$$\frac{3x}{3} = \frac{-6}{3} = -2$$

Step 3: Write the solution as $x = -2$.

A system of two equations can be solved either by expressing one equation in terms of one variable only and substituting or by working with both equations. In our example we had the set

$$y = 3x + 2$$

$$x - y = -1$$

Step 1: Write the second equation as $y = x + 1$.

Step 2: In the first equation substitute for y: $x + 1 = 3x + 2$.

Step 3: Following the preceding example, get all the x variables on one side through addition or subtraction. In this case subtract x from both sides of the equation obtained in step 2:

$$x + 1 - x = 3x + 2 - x$$

$$1 = 2x + 2$$

Step 4: Get all the numbers on one side by subtracting 2:

$$1 - 2 = 2x + 2 - 2$$

$$-1 = 2x$$

Step 5: Isolate x by dividing by 2:

$$-\frac{1}{2} = \frac{2x}{2}$$

which implies that

$$x = \frac{1}{2}$$

Step 6: Substitute the value for x into any equation to solve for y:

$$y = -\frac{1}{2} + 1 = \frac{1}{2}$$

Step 7: Write the final solution as $x = -1/2$ and $y = 1/2$.

Quadratic equations can be solved using the **quadratic formula**. Given the quadratic equation

$$ax^2 + bx + c = 0$$

we can write

$$x = \frac{-b \pm \sqrt{b^2 - 4ac}}{2a}$$

The quantity under the radical sign, called the **discriminant**, can be positive, negative, or zero. If the discriminant is negative, the square root is an **imaginary number**, which usually has no physical meaning for our study.

For example, suppose we wish to solve $x^2 + 3x + 2 = 0$ using the quadratic formula. In this equation $a = 1$, $b = 3$, and $c = 2$. By direct substitution and taking the necessary square roots, we find that $x = -1$ or $x = -2$.

Another way to solve this quadratic equation is by **factoring**. Some quadratic equations can be written as the product of two linear factors. In this case, we can write

$$x^2 + 3x + 2 = (x + 2)(x + 1) = 0$$

The solution is found by recognizing that, for this equation to be zero, either $x + 2 = 0$ or $x + 1 = 0$. Thus, either $x = -2$ or $x = -1$ is a solution (as before).

Often, equations given in one form need to be expressed in an alternative form. The rules of algebra allow us to manipulate the form of an equation. For example, we might have this problem: Given $x = (1/2)at^2$, solve for t. First, we clear the fraction by multiplying by 2, obtaining $2x = at^2$. Now, we divide both sides by a to get $2x/a = t^2$. Finally, to solve for t, we take the square root of each side. Mathematically, there are two solutions. However, in physics, we must allow for the physical reality of a solution. Since this equation represents uniformly accelerated motion from rest, the concept of "negative time" is not realistic. Hence, we discard the negative square root solution and state simply that

$$t = \sqrt{\frac{2x}{a}}$$

Exponents and Scientific Notation

Any number, n, can be written in the form of some base number, B, raised to a power a. The number a is called the **exponent** of the base number, B. In other words, we can write

$$n = B^a$$

One common base number is 10. The use of products of numbers with powers of 10 is called **scientific notation**. Some examples of powers of 10 are $10 = 10^1$, $100 = 10 \times 10 = 10^2$, and $1000 = 10 \times 10 \times 10 = 10^3$.

By definition, any number raised to the zero power is equal to 1; that is, $10^0 = 1$.

Decimal numbers less than 1 have negative exponents, since they are fractions of the powers of 10 previously discussed. Some examples are $0.1 = 10^{-1}$, $0.01 = 10^{-2}$, and $0.001 = 10^{-3}$. The use of negative exponents for small numbers comes from the law of division of exponents, which is defined as follows:

$$\frac{10^a}{10^b} = 10^{a-b}$$

Since a reciprocal means "1 over . .," and 10 raised to the power of zero is equal to 1, then, if, in the division example above, $a = 0$ and $b =$ any number, we have negative exponents for small decimal numbers.

The law of multiplication of exponents is as follows:

$$10^a 10^b = 10^{a+b} \quad \text{and} \quad (10^a)^b = 10^{ab}$$

Scientific notation involves the use of numbers and powers of 10 as products. For example, the number 200 can be expressed in scientific notation as 2.0×10^2, and the number 3450 as 3.45×10^3. Finally, the number 0.045 is expressed in scientific notation as 4.5×10^{-2}.

On most scientific calculators, scientific notation can be activated using the "exp" button. It is not necessary to push "× 10" or "times 10" on the calculator. The "exp" button automatically implies "times 10 to the . . . " in the notation. Since the use of a scientific calculator is permitted on the AP Physics Examination, we will not spend time reviewing the addition, subtraction, multiplication, and division of numbers in scientific notation. Consult a mathematics textbook for more examples and details.

The following prefixes designating exponentiation are often used in physics:

10^{18}	*exa-*	10^{-1}	*deci-*
10^{15}	*peta-*	10^{-2}	*centi-*
10^{12}	*tera-*	10^{-3}	*milli-*
10^{9}	*giga-*	10^{-6}	*micro-*
10^{6}	*mega-*	10^{-9}	*nano-*
10^{3}	*kilo-*	10^{-12}	*pico-*
10^{2}	*hecto-*	10^{-15}	*femto-*
10^{1}	*deca-*	10^{-18}	*atto-*

Logarithms

Since any number, n, can be written as a base number, B, raised to a certain power, a, we have an inverse process to exponentiation. For our designation $n = B^a$, we can also state that a is the "logarithm" of n to the base B:

$$a = \log_B n$$

If we are using base 10, we do not usually write the base number; we simply use the designation **log** for what we call the **common logarithm**. For example, the logarithm of 100 is 2 (since 2 is the power by which 10 is raised in order to make 100); that is, $\log 100 = 2$. Since logarithms are basically exponents, the rules of multiplication and division of exponents apply to logarithms as well. Therefore:

$$\log xy = \log x + \log y$$

$$\log \frac{x}{y} = \log x - \log y$$

$$\log x^n = n \log x$$

Another common base number is the irrational number e, equal to 2.71828.... Logarithms to the base e are called **natural logarithms** and are designated an **ln**. These logarithms follow the same rules as common logarithms.

The use of scientific calculators obviates the necessity for extensive logarithm tables. Consult your own caluclator's instructions for using logarithms.

II. Geometry

Some common formulas from geometry are of use in physics. We first review some of the more common geometric shapes and their equations:

Straight line with slope m and y-intercept b: $y = mx + b$

Circle of radius R centered at the origin: $x^2 + y^2 = R^2$

Parabola whose vertex is at $y = b$: $y = ax^2 + b$

Hyperbola: $xy = \text{constant}$

Ellipse with semimajor axis a and semiminor axis b: $\frac{x^2}{a^2} + \frac{y^2}{b^2} = 1$

We now review the equations for some of the physical characteristics of selected geometric shapes.

Circle of radius R: Area $= \pi R^2$; Circumference $= 2\pi R$

Sphere of radius R: Volume $= \frac{4}{3}\pi R^3$; Surface area $= 4\pi R^2$

Cylinder of radius R and length ℓ: Volume $= \pi R^2 \ell$

Right circular cone of base radius R and height h: Volume $= \frac{1}{3}\pi R^2 h$

Ellipse with semimajor axis a and semiminor axis b: Area $= \pi ab$

Rectangle of length ℓ and width w: Area $= \ell w$

Triangle with base b and altitude h: Area $= \frac{1}{2}bh$

III. Trigonometry

Trigonometry is the branch of mathematics that deals with the algebraic relationships between angles in triangles. If we have a right triangle, with hypotenuse c and sides a and b, the relationship between these sides is given by the Pythagorean theorem:

$$a^2 + b^2 = c^2$$

The ratios of the sides of a right triangle to its hypotenuse define the **trigonometric functions** of sine, cosine, and tangent (see Figure A.4.a) and set 1 below.

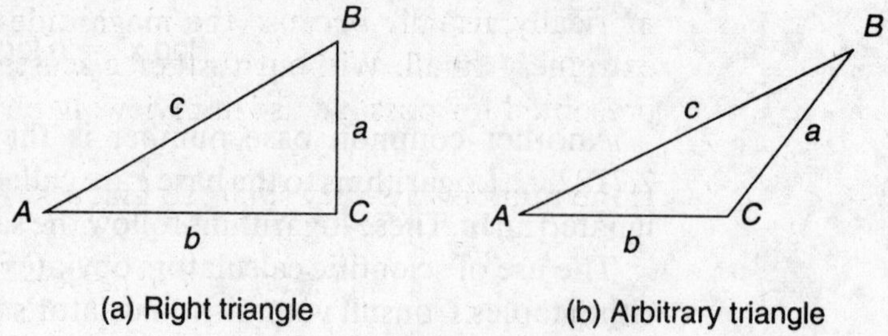

FIGURE A.4

1. $\sin A = \dfrac{a}{c}$ $\quad \cos A = \dfrac{b}{c}$ $\quad \tan A = \dfrac{a}{b}$ $\quad \tan A = \dfrac{\sin A}{\cos A}$

2. $\sec A = \dfrac{c}{a}$ $\quad \csc A = \dfrac{c}{b}$ $\quad \cot A = \dfrac{b}{a}$

The functions in set 2 are the reciprocals of set 1. A table of values for the standard trignometric functions is provided in Appendix B. For any angle θ, in a right triangle,

$$\sin \theta = \cos (90 - \theta) \quad \text{and} \quad \cos \theta = \sin (90 - \theta)$$

In the arbitrary general triangle shown in Figure A.4.b, the sides are related through the law of cosines and the law of sines. These formulas are extremely useful for the study of vectors (see Chapter 6):

$$\text{Law of cosines: } c^2 = a^2 + b^2 - 2ab \cos C$$

$$\text{Law of sines: } \frac{a}{\sin A} = \frac{b}{\sin B} = \frac{c}{\sin C}$$

For angles between 0 and 90 degrees, all of the trigonometric functions have positive values. For angles between 90 and 180 degrees, only the sine function is positive. For angles between 180 and 270 degrees, only the tangent function is positive. Finally, between 270 and 360 (0) degrees, only the cosine function is positive.

Some useful identities (relationships) between the various trigonometric functions often encountered in the the study of physics are listed below without proof:

$$\sin^2 \theta + \cos^2 \theta = 1$$
$$\sin 2\theta = 2\sin \theta \cos \theta$$
$$\cos 2\theta = \cos^2 \theta - \sin^2 \theta$$
$$\sin (\theta + \phi) = \sin \theta \cos \phi + \cos \theta \sin \phi$$
$$\sin (\theta - \phi) = \sin \theta \cos \phi - \cos \theta \sin \phi$$
$$\cos (\theta + \phi) = \cos \theta \cos \phi - \sin \theta \sin \phi$$
$$\cos (\theta - \phi) = \cos \theta \cos \phi + \sin \theta \sin \phi$$

IV. Series Expansions of Functions

Often it is useful to approximate a complicated equation or function numerically; usually because the magnitudes of the quantities involved are extremely small. Without further discussion, three **series expansions** are presented for possible use in reviewing physics.

Binomial Expansion

If the number a is very small, so that $a \ll 1$, the quantity

$$(1 + a)^n \approx 1 + na + \frac{n(n-1)}{2}a^2 + \dots$$

which can sometimes be further simplified to just $1 + na$.

Sine Function Expansion

If the angle θ is measured in radians (see Chapter 8), we can state that

$$\sin\theta \approx \theta - \frac{\theta^3}{6} + \frac{\theta^5}{120} - \dots \approx \theta - \frac{\theta^3}{3!} + \frac{\theta^5}{5!} - \dots$$

The exclamation point (!) means "factorial"; for example,

$$3! = 3 \times 2 \times 1 = 6$$

Furthermore, if $\theta \ll 1$, then $\sin\theta \approx \theta$ and $\sin\theta \approx \tan\theta$.

Cosine Function Expansion

If the angle θ is measured in radians, we can state that

$$\cos\theta \approx 1 - \frac{\theta^2}{2!} + \frac{\theta^4}{4!} - \dots$$

Furthermore, if $\theta \ll 1$, then $\cos\theta \approx 1$.

APPENDIX B

Table of Trigonometric Functions

Angle	Sine	Cosine	Tangent	Angle	Sine	Cosine	Tangent
0	0.000	1.000	0.000				
1	0.017	1.000	0.017	46	0.719	0.695	1.036
2	0.035	0.999	0.035	47	0.731	0.682	1.072
3	0.052	0.999	0.052	48	0.743	0.669	1.111
4	0.070	0.998	0.070	49	0.755	0.656	1.150
5	0.087	0.996	0.087	50	0.766	0.643	1.192
6	0.105	0.995	0.105	51	0.777	0.629	1.235
7	0.122	0.993	0.123	52	0.788	0.616	1.280
8	0.139	0.990	0.141	53	0.799	0.602	1.327
9	0.156	0.988	0.158	54	0.809	0.588	1.376
10	0.174	0.985	0.176	55	0.819	0.574	1.428
11	0.191	0.982	0.194	56	0.829	0.559	1.483
12	0.208	0.978	0.213	57	0.839	0.545	1.540
13	0.225	0.974	0.231	58	0.848	0.530	1.600
14	0.242	0.970	0.249	59	0.857	0.515	1.664
15	0.259	0.966	0.268	60	0.866	0.500	1.732
16	0.276	0.961	0.287	61	0.875	0.485	1.804
17	0.292	0.956	0.306	62	0.883	0.469	1.881
18	0.309	0.951	0.325	63	0.891	0.454	1.963
19	0.326	0.946	0.344	64	0.899	0.438	2.050
20	0.342	0.940	0.364	65	0.906	0.423	2.145
21	0.358	0.934	0.384	66	0.914	0.407	2.246
22	0.375	0.927	0.404	67	0.921	0.391	2.356
23	0.391	0.921	0.424	68	0.927	0.375	2.475
24	0.407	0.914	0.445	69	0.934	0.358	2.605
25	0.423	0.906	0.466	70	0.940	0.342	2.748
26	0.438	0.899	0.488	71	0.946	0.326	2.904
27	0.454	0.891	0.510	72	0.951	0.309	3.078
28	0.469	0.883	0.532	73	0.956	0.292	3.271
29	0.485	0.875	0.554	74	0.961	0.276	3.487
30	0.500	0.866	0.577	75	0.966	0.259	3.732
31	0.515	0.857	0.601	76	0.970	0.242	4.011
32	0.530	0.848	0.625	77	0.974	0.225	4.332
33	0.545	0.839	0.649	78	0.978	0.208	4.705
34	0.559	0.829	0.675	79	0.982	0.191	5.145
35	0.574	0.819	0.700	80	0.985	0.174	5.671
36	0.588	0.809	0.727	81	0.988	0.156	6.314
37	0.602	0.799	0.754	82	0.990	0.139	7.115
38	0.616	0.788	0.781	83	0.993	0.122	8.144
39	0.629	0.777	0.810	84	0.995	0.105	9.514
40	0.643	0.766	0.839	85	0.996	0.087	11.430
41	0.656	0.755	0.869	86	0.998	0.070	14.300
42	0.669	0.743	0.900	87	0.999	0.052	19.080
43	0.682	0.731	0.933	88	0.999	0.035	28.640
44	0.695	0.719	0.966	89	1.000	0.017	57.290
45	0.707	0.707	1.000	90	1.000	0.000	

APPENDIX C

Values of Some Fundamental Physical Constants

Quantity	Symbol	Value
Speed of light (vacuum)	c	2.99792458×10^{8} m/s
Permeablility of vacuum	μ_0	$4\pi \times 10^{-7}$ H/m
Permittivity of the vacuum	ϵ_0	$8.854187818 \times 10^{-12}$ F/m
Planck's constant	h	6.626176×10^{-34} J/Hz
Elementary charge	e	$1.6021892 \times 10^{-19}$ C
Avogadro's number	N_A	6.022045×10^{23} /mol
Atomic mass unit	u	$1.6605655 \times 10^{-27}$ kg $= 931.5016 \times 10^{6}$ eV
Gravitational constant	G	6.6720×10^{-11} kg · m²/kg²
Bohr radius	a_0	$5.2917706 \times 10^{-11}$ m
Charge-to-mass ratio of electron	e/m_e	1.7588047×10 C/kg
Compton wavelength of electron	λ_C	$2.4263089 \times 10^{-12}$ m
Rest mass of the electron	m_e	9.109534×10^{-31} kg $= 5.485803 \times 10^{-4}$ u
Rest mass of proton	m_p	$1.6726485 \times 10^{-27}$ kg $= 1.0072764$ u
Rest mass of neutron	m_n	$1.6749543 \times 10^{-27}$ kg $= 1.008665$ u
Rydberg constant	R_∞	$1.097373177 \times 10^{7}$ /m
Boltzmann's constant	k	1.380662×10^{-23} J/K
Molar gas constant	R	8.31441 J /mol · K
Coulomb constant	k	9×10^{9} Nm²/C²
Faraday constant	F	9.65×10^{4} C/mol

APPENDIX D
The Greek Alphabet

Alpha	Α	α
Beta	Β	β
Gamma	Γ	γ
Delta	Δ	δ
Epsilon	Ε	ϵ
Zeta	Ζ	ζ
Eta	Η	η
Theta	Θ	θ
Iota	Ι	ι
Kappa	Κ	κ
Lambda	Λ	λ
Mu	Μ	μ
Nu	Ν	ν
Xi	Ξ	ξ
Omicron	Ο	ο
Pi	Π	π
Rho	Ρ	ρ
Sigma	Σ	σ
Tau	Τ	τ
Upsilon	Υ	υ
Phi	Φ	φ
Chi	Χ	χ
Psi	Ψ	ψ
Omega	Ω	ω

APPENDIX E

The SI Units

Fundamental SI Units Used in Physics

Quantity	Unit Name	Abbreviation
Length	Meter	m
Mass	Kilogram	kg
Time	Second	s
Electric current	Ampere	A
Temperature	Kelvin	K
Amount of substance	Mole	mol

Some Derived SI Units Used in Physics

Quantity	Unit Name	Abbreviation	Expression in Other SI Units
Plane angle	Radian	rad	
Force	Newton	N	$kg \cdot m/s^2$
Frequency	Hertz	Hz	s^{-1}
Pressure	Pascal	Pa	$N/m^2 = kg/m \cdot s^2$
Energy (work, heat)	Joule	J	$N \cdot m = kg \cdot m^2/s^2$
Power	Watt	W	$J/s = kg \cdot m^2/s^3$
Electric charge	Coulomb	C	$A \cdot s$
Electric potential (emf)	Volt	V	$J/C = J/A \cdot s = kg \cdot m^2/A \cdot s^3$
Capacitance	Farad	F	$C/V = A^2 \cdot s^4/kg \cdot m^2$
Resistance	Ohm	Ω	$V/A = kg \cdot m^2/A^2 \cdot s^3$
Magnetic flux	Weber	Wb	$V \cdot s = kg \cdot m^2/A \cdot s^2$
Magnetic flux density	Tesla	T	$Wb/m^2 = kg/A \cdot s^2$
Inductance	Henry	H	$Wb/A = kg \cdot m^2/A^2 \cdot s^2$

APPENDIX F

Values of Some Often Used Physical Quantities

Quantity	Value
Acceleration due to gravity (*g*)	9.8 m/s^2
Density of air (20° C, 1 atm)	1.2 kg/m^3
Density of water (20° C, 1 atm)	1.00×10^3 kg/m^3
Standard atmospheric pressure (1 atm)	1.013×10^5 Pa
Mass of the Earth	5.98×10^{24} kg
Mass of the Moon	7.36×10^{22} kg
Mass of the Sun	1.99×10^{30} kg
Mean radius of the Earth	6.37×10^6 m
Mean radius of the Moon	1.74×10^6 m
Mean Earth-Moon distance	3.84×10^8 m
Mean Earth-Sun distance	1.496×10^{11} m

APPENDIX G

Table of Conversions

Length
1 in. = 2.54 cm
1 m = 100 cm = 39.37 in.
1 ft = 12 in. = 0.3048 m
1 yd = 3 ft = 0.9144 m
1 km = 1000 m = 0.621 mi
1 mi = 5280 ft = 1.609 km
1 Å = 1×10^{-10} m
1 u = 1×10^{-6} m

Area
1 m^2 = 10^4 cm^2 = 10.76 ft^2
1 ft^2 = 0.0929 m^2

Volume
1 m^3 = 10^6 cm^3 = 35.32 ft^3
1 ft^3 = 0.0283 m^3
1 L = 1000 cm^3
1 gal = 3.786 L

Mass
1000 kg = 1 metric ton
1 u = 1.66×10^{-27} kg
1 slug (English mass) = 14.59 kg

Force
1 N = 0.2248 lb
1 lb = 4.448 N

Velocity
1 mi/h = 1.47 ft/s = 0.447 m/s = 1.6 km/h
1 m/s = 100 cm/s = 3.281 ft/s

Acceleration
1 m/s^2 = 100 cm/s^2 = 3.28 ft/s^2
1 ft/s^2 = 0.3048 m/s^2 = 30.48 cm/s^2

Pressure
1 Pa = 1 N/m^2
1 atm = 1.013×10^5 Pa

Time
1 yr = 365 days = 3.16×10^7 s
1 day = 24 h = 86,400 s

Energy
1 J = 0.738 ft-lb
1 cal = 4.186 J
1 Btu = 252 Cal = 1054 J
1 eV = 1.6×10^{-19} J
931.5 MeV is equivalent to 1 u.

Power
1 W = 1 J/s
1 hp = 746 W

Index